Douglas R. McManis

LAWRENCE HENRY GIPSON

AUTHOR

JARED INGERSOLL: A STUDY OF AMERICAN LOYALISM
  IN RELATION TO BRITISH COLONIAL GOVERNMENT

STUDIES IN CONNECTICUT COLONIAL TAXATION

THE MORAVIAN INDIAN MISSION ON WHITE RIVER

LEWIS EVANS

THE COMING OF THE REVOLUTION, 1763–1775

THE BRITISH EMPIRE BEFORE THE AMERICAN REVOLUTION

THE BRITISH EMPIRE
BEFORE THE AMERICAN REVOLUTION
VOLUME XV

A GUIDE TO MANUSCRIPTS
RELATING TO THE HISTORY OF THE BRITISH EMPIRE
1748–1776

THE BRITISH EMPIRE
BEFORE THE AMERICAN REVOLUTION
VOLUME XV

A GUIDE
TO MANUSCRIPTS

RELATING TO THE HISTORY OF
THE BRITISH EMPIRE, 1748–1776

BY

LAWRENCE HENRY GIPSON

MCMLXX
ALFRED A. KNOPF
NEW YORK

THIS IS A BORZOI BOOK
PUBLISHED BY ALFRED A. KNOPF, INC.

Library of Congress Catalog Card Number: 58–9670

FIRST EDITION

This volume is dedicated to

W. DEMING LEWIS
President of Lehigh University

*in recognition of his support of
this historical project.*

Preface

No task that has faced me in the preparation of *The British Empire before the American Revolution* series has been more difficult than the selection and rounding out to my satisfaction of materials suitable for this final volume on manuscripts.

Manifestly, it is beyond the power of any individual to examine all the pertinent manuscripts, resting in the many depositories both in Great Britain and in those areas that were once a part of the Old British Empire of the eighteenth century, and even beyond those areas. It was therefore imperative that in pursuit of my objective my chief reliance should be placed upon the compilations of those scholars who have concentrated upon a description of some segment or segments of the vast array of manuscript sources. Only here and there have I supplemented or corrected their published listings of documents and annotations. These printed aids, it may be pointed out, were in turn based in most cases on earlier listings, many in typescript or in pen, laboriously prepared by others. As a result the work here presented can have little claim to originality. Nevertheless, I believe I can safely venture to state that no other historian past or present has had over so many years a more intimate and first-hand acquaintance with a greater number of the manuscript collections, both in the Old and New World, that throw light on the Empire covering the brief period 1748–1776.

In fulfillment of my plan I therefore addressed letters to those compilers who were still alive and whose guides had direct bearing upon the history of the Empire between the years 1748–1776, asking permission to quote freely from their listings. The responses to my letters were without exception most favourable and appreciative of my undertaking in seeking to bring together in a single volume a listing of the chief documents that throw light on the Empire for the brief period 1748–1776. Recognition of these guides will be indicated at the appropriate places in the text.

It would have been useful to give a comprehensive listing in this guide of the location of reproductions of the manuscripts presented. Unfortunately such a list would never be complete. Numerous institutions, such as the Library of Congress, the Public Archives of Canada and the Virginia State Library, are still in the process of reproducing documents from other depositories. Also, in 1961 there appeared the very useful *Guide to Photocopied Historical Materials in the United States and Canada* edited by Richard W. Hale, Jr. and published by the Cornell University Press for the American Historical Association. It should therefore be understood why only here and there will reference be made to the presence of copies of documents.

As this guide will doubtless be used most frequently by American students I have been urged to provide in the table of contents a fuller statement of the contents of depositories of manuscripts in the British Isles. This I have done on account of their relative importance and also because such archives as the Public Record Office contain material that could be easily overlooked in the midst of the vast numbers of other documents of less importance for my purpose. It is appropriate to turn first of all to London, the center of the Empire, and to the Public Record Office, the chief depository of official papers there.

Before concluding this prefatory statement I must not fail to acknowledge with gratitude the continued liberal support over the years of my project by Lehigh University. Nor must I fail to express my deep appreciation of the excellent quality of the services rendered by Miss Jean M. Stauffer, Mr. Jerome J. Gillen, Mr. Kenneth E. Jones, Mr. Stephen J. Hudson, and Mr. Edward J. Cody, my research assistants, and by Mrs. Evelyn J. Evans, my secretary, as well as by the always helpful staff of the Linderman Library, where for over the past twenty-five years my project has been given quarters.

In my *A Bibliographical Guide to the History of the British Empire, 1748–1776*, which appeared early in 1969, I expressed my desire for information respecting either errors that had crept into the text or omissions of data that should have been included. I repeat with emphasis my plea now with the publication of this guide to manuscripts, so that future printings of these volumes may be as useful as possible to those who turn to them for guidance.

The Linderman Library   Lawrence Henry Gipson
Lehigh University
Bethlehem, Pennsylvania
July 30, 1969

Contents

CONTENTS xiii

PART II

THE ENGLISH COUNTIES

PART III

WALES

PART IV

SCOTLAND

PART V

NORTHERN IRELAND

PART VI

REPUBLIC OF IRELAND

PART VII

FRANCE

PART VIII

SPAIN

PART IX

CANADA

PART X

ATLANTIC AND WEST INDIES ISLANDS

CONTENTS

PART XI

THE UNITED STATES

THE BRITISH EMPIRE
BEFORE THE AMERICAN REVOLUTION
VOLUME XV

A GUIDE TO MANUSCRIPTS
RELATING TO THE HISTORY OF THE BRITISH EMPIRE
1748–1776

PART I

London Depositories of Manuscripts

THE PUBLIC RECORD OFFICE

THE Public Record Office on Chancery Lane, London, is the chief depository of the official records of Great Britain, especially those no longer required for examination by officials of the various departments of the government. Here are most of the great body of eighteenth-century records relating to the history of the Old British Empire, although important collections are elsewhere, as will be indicated in the course of this volume. Within the Office various aids are at hand to lighten the work of the student. All printed guides to the records are based upon these lists, cards, calendars, etc., which were prepared with great care.

Of all the printed aids designed to orient the student who begins to work here, none is better than *The British Public Record Office: History, Description, Record Groups, Finding Aids, and Materials for American History with Special Reference to Virginia*, which was published in 1960 by the Virginia State Library, Richmond, Va. It reprints "Special Reports" 25 through 28 of the Virginia Colonial Records Project. Two other useful books, especially suited to those interested in earlier phases of English and British history, are those by Hilary Jenkinson: *Guide to the Public Records, Part I: Introductory* (London, 1949), and V. H. Galbraith: *An Introduction to the Use of the Public Records* (London, 1934; rev. edn., 1952). However, the standard guide for all the records has for many years been that by the late M. S. Giuseppi, Assistant Keeper of the Records. First published as *A Guide to the Manuscripts Preserved in the Public Record Office* (2 vols., London, 1923-4), it was after revision re-published as *Guide to the Contents of the Public Record Office* (2 vols., London, 1963), and extended so as to bring the account of the continually enlarged holdings up to 1960. Of all printed guides the one to present in greatest detail pertinent papers bearing upon all parts of the Empire in the New World for the period 1748–1776 is that by Charles M. Andrews: *Guide to the Materials for American History, to 1783, in the Public Record Office of Great Britain*, published in two volumes in 1912 and 1914 by the Carnegie Institution of Washington, D.C. Hand in hand with the Andrews *Guide* should go that part of the guide by B. R. Crick and Miriam Alman: *A Guide to Manuscripts Relating to America in Great Britain and Ireland* (London, published for the British Association for American Studies, 1961), which is concerned with the Public Record Office (pp. 257–94), supplementing and at times correcting Andrews's account.

We shall begin with the papers of the Chancery and then turn to those of the other great offices.

Records of the Chancery

The office of Lord High Chancellor was one of great eminence and responsibility in the eighteenth century. The holder of it was always a man distinguished in the practice of the law. He was sworn of the Privy Council, *ex officio* a member of the Cabinet Council, and presiding officer in the House of Lords. He was, moreover, both the keeper of the King's conscience, in which capacity he presided over the High Court of Chancery, and the custodian of the Great Seal, affixed together with his signature to letters patent for creating a trading company or a colony or for commissioning the governor of a colony. Thus his office was closely identified with the growth of the British Empire. It, therefore, is not inappropriate that among the papers in the Public Record Office we first survey the Chancery records. In doing so we shall follow the treatment of the Chancery as presented in Giuseppi: *Guide*, I, 7–44; see also the Virginia State Library: *British Public Record Office*, pp. 139–42, and Henry Churchill Maxwell Lyte: *Historical Notes on the Use of the Great Seal of England* (London, 1926).

CHANCERY ENROLMENTS

In the general category of Chancery Enrolments are copies of documents and accounts of various proceedings. The documents, chiefly letters patent, charters, and letters close, make grants and express the King's wishes. There are also special categories relating to a particular country or problem. Sometimes the copies are contemporary, as part of the legal process; in other cases, they were made later simply to have them on record. Among the accounts of proceedings are narratives of sessions of Parliament and coronations. The following classes of documents cover the years 1748–1776 although few bear specifically upon the Empire:

C. 54. Close Rolls. Include enrolment of private deeds, etc., 1603–1848 (4,884 rolls).

C. 65. Parliament Rolls. Include enrolment of all private and public Parliamentary Acts, 1603–1783 (1,037 rolls).

C. 66. Patent Rolls, 1606–1783 (2,092 rolls). These papers are the most important Chancery Records for a study of the British Empire because they include colonial grants, appointments of colonial officials, instructions to governors, trading company charters, and boundary dispute settlements. Since not all patents were enrolled, the Warrants and Docquet Books among the papers of the Chancery, Privy Seal Office and Signet Office should also be consulted.

C. 67. Patent Rolls, Supplementary. Include ships' passes, 1748–1751 (rolls 86–92).

C. 83. Warrants for the Great Seal, Series III, 1714–1783 (bundles 1 through 1,786).

C. 210. Specification and Surrender Rolls, Petty Bag Office, 1709–1848 (287 rolls). These include enrolments of specifications of inventions and surrenders of offices.

Indexes *Nos. 4209–4219.* Crown Office Docquet Books, 1603–1787. Here are commissions which were not enrolled on the Patent Rolls. Similar information may be found in the Privy Seal Office, the Signet Office, and in the Entry Books of Warrants among the Colonial Office papers.

CHANCERY JUDICIAL PROCEEDINGS (EQUITY SIDE)

Before the Supreme Court of Judicature Act of 1873, the High Court of Chancery had two functions. As a common law court it issued, as has already been indicated, all writs passing under the Great Seal and had power to hold pleas upon its writ *scire facias* for the repeal of letters patent—as was the case when in 1684 it annulled the charter granted in 1628–1629 to the Governor and Company of the Massachusetts Bay in New England. However, the most frequent activity of the High Court of Chancery was the exercise, in the name of the King and as the keeper of his conscience, of equitable jurisdiction, whereby the rigours of the common law might be mitigated by the exercise of mercy.

These records for equitable jurisdiction for the eighteenth century contain various references to the American colonies. Since the chief records, the various series of *Proceedings*, which include the plaintiff's bill initiating the suit, are listed under the names of the plaintiffs, perhaps the best means of dealing with this group for the purpose of extracting colonial material is through the *Masters' Exhibits* (*C. 103–116*) in which are listed the names of the plaintiffs, the defendants, and the places concerned. It was the practice of the Court of Chancery to refer various matters to one of the masters in ordinary, who duly reported to the Court. When the evidences produced by the parties in suits were unclaimed at the end of the hearing, the documents remained in the custody of the Court. The following records should be noted:

C. 11. Proceedings in Chancery, 1714–1758 (2,793 bundles).

C. 12. Proceedings in Chancery, 1758–1800 (2,434 bundles).

C. 33. Entry Books of Decrees and Orders in Chancery, 1603–1783 (vols. 105–462).

C. 37. Registrars' Court or Minute Books, 1639–1875 (4,776 vols.).

C. 38. Reports and Certificates, 1544–1875 (vols. 5,330), which include reports of Masters in Chancery to the Court on problems assigned to them for investigation.

C. 39. Reports: Supplementary, 1703–1793 (8 vols.).

C. 103–116. Masters' Exhibits: See especially *C. 105, ff. 33 & 44.* Grants of land in East Florida, 1765–83; *C. 107, f. 169.* Estate records from New Jersey and Philadelphia wills, 1775; and *C. 110, f. 186.* William V. Wallaby, accounts, letters of marque, and correspondence concerning the ship *Oliver,* London and North America, 1758–1767.

Signet Office

As has been indicated, unusual grants of authority and privilege came under the Great Seal. A series of checks were created, however, so that the use of that seal would not be abused. For example, a document designed to come under the Great Seal required, first of all, the King's signature, called the sign manual, countersigned by one of the great officers of state. It then moved to the Signet Office. On a transcript of it, made by a signet clerk, was placed the signet seal (at an early period by use of the King's signet ring that came into the keeping of his principal Secretary of State). This transcript now passed on to the Privy Seal Office at the head of which was, as the name implies, the Lord Privy Seal. By warrant from the Signet Office, the Lord Privy Seal affixed his seal to a transcript, made from the Signet Seal transcript, and sent it to the Lord Chancellor with his warrant for placing the Great Seal. Lesser grants of authority did not require the Great Seal, and therefore might be limited simply to the sign manual, or to the signet seal in addition, or to the privy seal added to the other two means of validation.

Two series of papers of the Signet Office are of use to students; the same is true of the Privy Seal Office:

S.O. 4. Docquet Books: Indexes *Nos. 6801–6828* for the period 1603–1789.

S.O. 7. King's Bills: 1661–1783 (264 bundles), valuable for the issue of letters patent.

See Giuseppi: *Guide,* II, 258–9, and Virginia State Library: *British Public Record Office,* p. 142.

Privy Seal Office

The following papers of the Privy Seal office bear upon the years 1748–1776:

Indexes, *Nos. 6744–6767*. Docquet Books, 1600–1785.

P.S.O. 3. Warrants for Privy Seal, Series III, 1766–1768. Valuable for letters patent.

P.S.O. 4. Miscellaneous Records, 1717–1884 (63 bundles +), including account books, journals, and letters.

See Giuseppi: *Guide*, II, 237–9, and the Virginia State Library: *British Public Record Office*, p. 143.

Privy Council Office

Responsibility for making decisions concerning the administration of the royal colonies, among other duties, rested with the Privy Council. It was concerned with such problems as the limits of power to be exercised by the colonial assemblies and the nature of commissions and instructions to be given to the royal governors. Its orders, known as orders in council, and other formal actions were of the highest importance with respect to the government of the Empire and no body of material is of more significance with respect to the administrative and judicial history of the Empire than these papers.

The Privy Council, which had evolved from the earlier *Curia Regis*, was stripped of most of the powers it had exercised under the Tudors and the Stuarts by the rise of the Cabinet Council, a body which functioned outside the constitutional framework, kept no records as such, and advised the King on the more weighty political issues. Despite its weakened position, the Privy Council remained a vital link in uniting the Empire and giving a certain uniformity to the administrative and judicial control.

The most important documents based upon the register of the Council and relating to the colonies have, under the able editorship of W. L. Grant, James Munro, and Almeric W. Fitzroy, been published with the following title: *Acts of the Privy Council of England. Colonial Series, 1613–1783* (6 vols., London, 1908–12). However, among the great number of unbound papers in the Privy Council Office certain of importance were omitted both from Volume VI of the *Acts of the Privy Council Unbound Papers* and also from C. M. Andrews and Frances G. Davenport: *Guide to the Manuscript Materials for the History of the United States to 1783, in the British Museum, in Minor London Archives, and in the Libraries of Oxford and Cambridge* (Published by the Carnegie Institution of Washington, Washington, D.C., 1908), pp. 170–87. A description of these missing papers is given by B. R. Crick and Miriam

Alman in their *Guide,* pp. 283–4. Those papers that are relevant to the period under review are as follows:

P.C. 1. Unbound Papers, 1481–1946 (4,559 bundles +). Includes petitions, letters, and appeals to the council as well as the Council's minutes and orders. The following material is of particular relevance to the Empire, 1748–1776: *No. 58,* 1701–1761; *No. 59,* 1762–1769; and *No. 60,* 1769–1778. *Nos. 58–60* contain a substantial collection of Board of Trade representations, reports, and petitions relating to such colonial affairs as appointment of officials, boundary disputes, repeal of laws, and Indian relations. *Nos. 3130–3153,* 1706–1782, contain information similar to that found above. *Nos. 3161–3163,* 1767–1784, comprise material relating to Nova Scotia; *Nos. 3164–3167,* 1763–1786, relate to Isle St. John (Prince Edward Island); *Nos. 3182–3184,* 1708–1776, contain material relating to Newfoundland.

P.C. 2. Register, 1540–1920 (445 vols.). Includes minutes, committee reports, and orders of the Council only for those problems on which the Council acted.

P.C. 4. Minutes, 1670–1928 (27 vols.). Includes at least brief reference to all matters which came before the Council and its various committees.

P.C. 5. Plantation Books, 1678–1806 (16 vols.). Copies, usually contemporaneous, of official documents: colonial acts, charters, various warrants, commissions and instructions, and surrenders of land.

From the Privy Council we must now turn to the offices of Secretary of State.

Secretaries of State

Early in English history the "secretarius" was simply the king's private clerk. During the reign of Henry VIII, however, the office became an independent one of some importance; its significance greatly increased under Elizabeth I. While Henry VIII had two secretaries, the number varied until the reign of Charles I when it became constant at two. In 1768 a third secretary was added, that of Secretary of State for the Colonies. In the early seventeenth century a division in all matters involving foreign relations took place. The Secretary of State for the Southern Department was in charge of Great Britain's relations with the southern European states beginning with France; Ireland and the English colonies also came within his particular sphere of interest. With respect to the affairs of Ireland it should be pointed out that the Lord Lieutenant assumed the chief responsibility. The Secretary of State for the Northern Department was concerned with the states of northern Europe; his office, important as it was, however, lacked the prestige of that of his colleague.

In matters relating to domestic matters in Great Britain, there was no such division of authority.

Since the duties of the Secretary of State for the Southern Department comprehended the colonies, the work of his office was intimately connected with that of the Lords Commissioners for Trade and Plantations, better known as the Board of Trade. While at periods the Board was permitted to enjoy a goodly measure of independence, as was true when the Earl of Halifax was its President, the prestige of the Secretary of State was so high that when a person of great energy, such as William Pitt, occupied this office, the Board became to a great extent a mere agency of it. The correspondence of the Secretary of State is extensive; much of it was with other departments of state; much of it with those holding office in the colonies. That which is in the Public Record Office and relates to domestic rather than foreign affairs of the Empire is described in Andrews: *Guide*, I, 18–73; Giuseppi: *Guide*, II, 1–14; and Virginia State Library: *British Public Record Office*, 155–60. Of these listings the following papers are of importance for the period 1748–1776 and will be considered under three headings: (a) State Papers, Domestic, (b) State Papers, Foreign, and (c) Colonial Office and Board of Trade Papers.

STATE PAPERS, DOMESTIC

With respect to "State Papers, Domestic," it should be kept in mind that there was continuous interchange betweeen the Secretary's Office and various other departments of the British government. The papers are classified under such headings as "Original Correspondence," including Ireland and the Colonies. In this connection there are great series of "Entry Books," including the Secretary's and the Under-Secretary's "Letter-Books." Among the papers are the "Church Books" concerning ecclesiastical matters, the "Military" and also the "Naval" series; volumes denominated "Petitions," those concerned with "Regencies" (when the Lords Justices were acting for the King while he was absent from the Kingdom), "Law Reports," including correspondence with "Law Officers." The student should note that this material has been fully re-classified in the Public Record Office so that all surviving papers pertaining to a particular topic are together. Papers of importance to a study of the Empire, 1748–1776, are as follows:

S.P. 36. George II

Nos. 1–150, 1727–1760. Letters and papers.

No. 153. A letter from Richard Partridge, Pennsylvania agent, May 1755.

No. 155, A–E. (1) James Belanger and Joseph Nunes desire a land grant to grow trees that bear cochineal; (2) Samuel Bowen of Georgia seeks encouragement to produce sago powder, vermicilli, etc.;

(3) John Bridger wants compensation as surveyor of the woods in America.

S.P. 37. George III

Letters and papers, 1761–1781, among them the following:

No. 1. (1) The Treasury desires information about troops furnished by the colonies in 1759 in order to distribute the £200,000 grant by Parliament; (2) About the Duke of Montague's right to St. Lucia; (3) Some colonial petitions, involving New York and Nova Scotia.

Nos. 2–3. Petitions, some from the colonies.

No. 4. (1) Concerning colonial trade; (2) The Earl of Halifax to the Board of Trade; (3) Regarding the Cherokee Indians; (4) Victualling Newfoundland; (5) Palatines for South Carolina.

No. 5. (1) Warrant for salary of Gov. Tryon of North Carolina out of the West Indies four and a half per cent tax; (2) Replies from masters of ships, etc., about conditions in Spanish territories.

No. 6. (1) Lord Botetourt seeks to form a copper company; (2) Opinion of Attorney General Yorke that the Test Act does not extend to the colonies.

No. 7. (1) About the relations between the Spaniards and the Creek Indians; (2) Case of Capt. Ferguson tried for murder in Virginia; (3) Concerning the "elopement" of slaves from Jamaica to Cuba.

No. 8. Opinion of Thurlow and Wedderburn that no express law forbids the conferring of the title of baronet of Great Britain on a new subject remaining in Canada, June 4, 1771.

No. 9. (1) Letters from Egerton Leigh of South Carolina, 1772; (2) Privy Council minutes regarding the *Gaspee* affair in Rhode Island, July 30, 1773; (3) Petition of Marquis D'Aubarède, 1772, who plans a revolution in Mexico.

No. 10. (1) Concerning Capt. Brereton's conduct at Manila; (2) Advocate General Marriott's report on Quebec, 1773; (3) About Major Debbieg's secret expedition to the coasts of France and Spain, 1768; (4) About quartering troops in America, 1774; (5) London protest against the Quebec Act.

No. 11. (1) Marriott's heads of a bill for better regulating law proceedings connected with the seizure of ships, 1775; (2) The London memorial opposing measures taken against the American colonies and the King's reply, 1775; (3) Advertisement of the Constitutional Society seeking relief for widows, orphans, and aged parents of American fellow-subjects "murdered" at Lexington and Concord, called a seditious libel by Thurlow and Wedderburn; (4) The Corporation of London concerning the address and petition that the King refused to receive, July 1775; (5) Minutes of Cabinet Council meetings, June 1775; (6) The Attorney and Solicitor General on the city of London's petition, Aug. 1, 1775; (7) Letter by "A True Englishman" about American affairs, Aug. 15, 1775; (8) American Committee of Correspondence circular; (9) Parliament's address to the King, Oct. 26, 1775; (10) List of Americans taken prisoner near Montreal and placed in confinement at Pendennis Castle; (11) Another city of London address, with the King's answer, March 22, 1776; (12) A letter from Major Hugh Debbieg, April 16, 1776; (13) About American vessels seized in May and June, 1776; (14) Sir Guy Carleton made K.B., July 4, and Sir William Howe in Oct. 1776; (15) A letter from the Lord Advocate of Scotland to Lord Germain on American affairs, Oct. 18, 1776; (16) The case of the British ship *Spiers* seized by Americans, which then escaped, carrying off Lieut. Hale of Rhode Island; (17) Carleton's naval battle on Lake Champlain, Oct. 1776; (18) The case of Ebenezer Platt of Georgia, Dec. 10, 1776.

No. 16. (1) Entry book relating to British trade and its improvement, 1715 to 1765; (2) Circular letter from the Earl of Halifax to British consuls with their replies.

No. 22. A bound volume of letters from the Treasury to the Secretaries of State, 1763–1775.

S.P. 41. Military

Nos. 1–48, 1702–1782, are original papers sent to the Secretary of State from the War Office and Ordnance Board. Most of these papers are for an earlier period, but some bear upon the years 1748–1776. These are as follows: *No. 20*, 1750–1752, contains many memorials and papers regarding regiments in the West Indies and Nova Scotia. However, one paper, Sept. 15, 1752, concerns the troops in Georgia which the Trustees are no longer to support. *No. 26*, 1773–1777, is concerned with North American and West Indies relief plans. A part of those plans is a paper (approved by the King, Feb. 1773) with proposals for ascertaining with greater precision the execution of his Majesty's commands concerning the transport of troops—involving the three principal Secretaries of State, the Lords of the Admiralty and the Secretary at War. *No. 38*, 1754–1764, is concerned with the following: (1) A warrant for arms for North Carolina and Virginia, Oct. 1754; (2) Respecting an expedition to North America, Nov. 22, 1754, and developments in Nova Scotia, 1754–1755; (3) Warrants for ordnance, stores and a train of artillery for Halifax, New York and Pennsylvania, 1758; (4) Regarding the 1758–1759 campaign, also matters respecting Antigua, 1759, and Grenada, 1763; (5) About brass ordnance and stores sent to New York, 1761, and for North America frontier forts, 1764. *No. 39* has a variety of papers among them the following: (1) Numerous Newfoundland papers, 1765; (2) St. Vincent papers; (3) The New York Stamp Act riots; (4) Report, 1766, on the state of forts and garrisons in his Majesty's dominions abroad; (5) About the Ceded Islands, 1766; (6) Maj. Hugh Debbieg's memoir, Aug. 10, 1774.

S.P. 42. Naval

Nos. 6–66, 1700–1782, Admiralty Board letters with enclosures to the Secretary of State. Only a few letters relate to the period 1748–1776. They are as follows: *No. 29* is made up largely of papers having to do with the Louisbourg expedition. There is also a complaint of Capt. Frankland against Gov. Glen of South Carolina. *No. 41* includes: (1) Report on West Indies vice-admiralty proceedings, April 3, 1758; (2) A collection of papers (partly in French) secured with the capture of the French frigate *Rhinoceros* by H.M.S. *Isis,* giving much information about French American affairs; *No. 42* contains: (1) An important despatch from Secretary of State Egremont to the Admiralty, Nov. 20, 1761; (2) A large number of papers of proceedings in American vice-admiralty courts with answers to queries sent by the Admiralty Board to the colonies, both in North America and the West Indies; (3) Copies of letters found on board prizes, 1761; (4) Regarding trade in the West Indies, Nov. 18, 1760.

Continuing with *S.P. Domestic 42, Naval,* we now come to the naval commanders' despatches.

S.P. 42. Naval commanders' despatches

Nos. 67–104, 1700–1772, are made up of letters with enclosures to the Secretary of State from admirals and naval commanders with drafts of the Secretary's instructions. While most of these papers are for an earlier period, some fall within the period 1748–1776 and are as follows: *No. 100* is an entry book of secret instructions from the Lords Justices to Sir Edward Hawke concerning the blockade of the Brest and Rochefort, 1755–1757. There are also plans by Pitt for expeditions against either Rochefort or Bordeaux, with minutes of councils of war. *No. 101* is concerned with Mediterranean trade and relations with Algiers, Tunis, and Tripoli.
No. 138, 1704–1782, although a part of the naval series, is made up of law reports and papers. The following are germane: (1) The case of Gov. Fleming of the Leeward Islands and pirate treasure, June 4, 1751; (2) About the King's power to impose additional in

structions on captains of private ships in time of war, May 3, 1757, with a number of papers concerned with instructions to privateers and their abuses; (3) Case of the ship *Nelly* against Horatio Herbert, deputy collector, Aug. 1, 1760.

S.P. 43. Regencies

Nos. 267–325, 1716–1760. These are entry books of letters of the Lords Justices sitting in council during the absence of the King. The last four volumes of this series throw light on the period 1748–1776. *No. 321* has: (1) A copy of a memorial and report of the Georgia trustees; (2) A letter to Commissioner Hughes about the Palatines for South Carolina. *No. 323* contains the following papers: (1) A warrant by the Lords Justices requiring the laws in force in Maryland, Connecticut, and Rhode Island to be sent to England; (2) Instructions to the governors and councils of royal colonies to consider and revise laws then in force; (3) Petition of merchants concerned with Labrador; (4) Warrants for the King's bill for the surrender of Georgia to the Crown; (5) Warrants for appointing members of Councils in America and for granting leave of absence. *No. 324* embodies the following: (1) Information about cannon to be sent to America, 1755; (2) Directions to Admiralty about vessels on Lakes Ontario and Erie; (3) Bills drawn by Gen. Braddock; (4) About North American prisoners; (5) Supplies for the King's troops in Nova Scotia; (6) Shirley's commission; (7) M. de Lamberty's complaint against Rhode Island. *No. 325* is concerned with: (1) Military supplies for America; (2) Appointment of James Dulany as chief justice of North Carolina; (3) Appointment of Thomas Pownall as governor of New Jersey; (4) Appointment of Peyton Randolph as attorney general of Virginia; (5) Appointment of Richard Dorrill as governor of Newfoundland; (6) John Henniker to be treasurer "in New England"; (7) Warrants for members of colonial councils.

Nos. 326–331, 1716–1790, are Treasury accounts in entry books of letters from the Secretary of State to the Treasury. References to American affairs chiefly concern trade, the movement of troops, and such matters.

Nos. 332–385, 1660–1784, contain the Secretary of State's warrants.

Nos. 386–413, 1697–1784, comprise chiefly ships' passes and passes to individuals.

Nos. 415–420, 1748–1800, are circular letters. For example, the letter of Dec. 1, 1768 has to do with illicit trade.

No. 421, 1706–1780, is index volumes, twenty-six in number.

S.P. 44. Entry books

Nos. 77–96, 1704–1782. Criminal. These comprise entries of commitments, reprieves, and pardons.

Nos. 97–143, 1688–1782. Domestic. Secretary's letter-books. Among these volumes the following should be noted: *No. 137* contains a letter from Shirley, July 11, 1760, about the naval force on Lake Ontario. *No. 138* is concerned with a number of matters, among them are: (1) The case of Gov. Reynolds of Georgia; (2) The Cherokee Indians; (3) Instructions to Lieut.-Col. Prevost about East Florida; (4) Maj.-Gen. Keppel's instructions to Maj. Farmer of the 34th Regiment; (5) Additional papers about the Floridas, 1763; (6) Applications for redress by French inhabitants of Grenada; (7) Papers concerning Havana and Turks Island. *No. 139* has to do with the following: (1) The transportation of German families to Florida; (2) The Clifford case in Surinam; (3) Appointment of Guy Carleton to Quebec as lieutenant-governor, 1766. *No. 142* is concerned with the Hudson's Bay Company and the decline of trade, 1768, and also with the French fisheries at Newfoundland.

Nos. 146–149, 1702–1771, embody the under-secretary's letter-books.

Nos. 150–159, 1688–1799. Church Books. These are concerned with many ecclesiastical questions, mostly domestic in nature.

Nos. 164–203, 1679–1782. Military. These volumes set forth commissions of various ranks and lists of warrants.

Nos. 204–234, 1689–1782. Naval. They contain the Secretary of State's out-letters to the Admiralty and are concerned with naval appointments, instructions, transportation of troops, convoys, etc. For example, *No. 230* contains copies of Pitt's instructions to the Admiralty from Dec. 1757 to July 1760, while *No. 231* has to do with the following topics: (1) Canadians taken to France after the fall of Quebec but who return to Canada; (2) The Newfoundland fisheries; (3) The St. Lawrence River contraband trade; (4) Grenada illicit trade; (5) French acts of violence in the West Indies; (6) The relief of troops in America by rotation; (7) The advocate general in Massachusetts; (8) The importation of bullion into America. *No. 232* is a letter from Jonathan Forward, 1768, dealing with the transportation of criminals.

H.O. 49. Law officers

Finally among the State Papers, Domestic, we come to the papers classified as Home Office Papers. Among them in *H.O. 49* are Law Officers' Letter-Books. These are chiefly entries of letters from the Secretaries to the Attorney General and Solicitor General.

No. 1. has the following entries addressed to the law officers that are pertinent to this survey: (1) Entries regarding the John Wilkes case; (2) Opinions about the cession of Cape Breton and other islands in the Gulf of St. Lawrence; (3) The question, Can the King make a Roman Catholic a baronet, 1771?

No. 2. has the following entries that come from the law officers: (1) About the demands of the Jesuits in the Ceded Islands, 1764; (2) Respecting clergymen in the Floridas, 1764; (3) With reference to Jesuits in Canada, 1765; (4) Report by the law-officers on the address of the City of London, 1775; (5) Various letters and papers, reported on by the law officers in Dec. 1774, questioning whether rebellion in New England constitutes treason.

STATE PAPERS, IRELAND

S.P. 63. Elizabeth I–George III

These State Papers, Ireland, extend from 1558 to 1782 and are in 480 volumes. Here are *Nos. 303–467, 1660–1779,* original papers relating to Ireland, which have been calendared in the State Papers, Domestic. Among them *No. 309* contains proclamations.

S.P. 67. 1681–1783

This series in 23 volumes, also relating to Ireland, has materials covering the years 1748–1776. Here are entry books and the Secretary's letter-books and warrant books, both series concerned with Ireland. Entry books are *Nos. 1–16,* 1681–1783, and warrant books are *Nos. 17–23,* 1713–1776.

STATE PAPERS, FOREIGN

General series

Turning from State Papers, Domestic, we come to the relations of Great Britain with foreign powers. They are arranged alphabetically. It should be pointed out that there are great gaps in the series in the Public Record Office. Only those series that fall within the years 1748–1776 are here included and only those states that have a definite relationship to the British Empire for this period are given more than passing mention.

S.P. 71. The Barbary States, 1577–1780, 29 vols. and other papers. The following states are included: Algiers, 1595–1780; Morocco, 1577–1774; Tripoli, 1590–1766; and Tunis, 1622–1769.

S.P. 75. Denmark, 1577–1780, 138 vols. and other unbound papers.

S.P. 77. Flanders, 1585–1780, 112 vols.

S.P. 78. France, 1577–1780, 335 vols., etc. The papers falling within the period 1748–1776 relating to France with the person or persons representing the Crown in Paris are as follows: *Nos. 256–257,* Jan.–Aug. 1763, Duke of Bedford and Richard Neville; *No. 258,* Sept.–Nov. 1763, Earl of Hertford and Richard Neville; *Nos. 259–267,* Nov. 1763 to Sept. 1765, Earl of Hertford; *Nos. 268–269,* Oct. 1765 to April 1766, Duke of Richmond; *No. 270,* May–Aug. 1766, Lord Lennox; *Nos. 271–275,* Sept. 1766 to Aug. 1768, Earl of Rockford; *No. 276,* Sept. to Dec. 1768, Robert Walpole; *No. 277,* Jan. to March, 1769, Earl Harcourt; *Nos. 278–281,* April 1769 to Dec. 1770, Earl Harcourt and Robert Walpole; *Nos. 282–283,* Jan. to Dec. 1771, Earl Harcourt and Col. Blaquiere; *No. 284,* Jan. to April 1772, Earl Harcourt; *Nos. 285–286,* April–Dec. 1772, Earl Harcourt and Lord Stormont; *Nos. 287–306,* Jan. 1773 to 1779, Lord Stormont; *No. 322,* 1761–1765, has supplementary papers; this is also true of *No. 323,* 1768–1777.

S.P. 79. Genoa, 1584–1775, 26 vols. and other unbound papers.

S.P. 80. Germany (Holy Roman Empire) and Hungary, 1578–1780, 240 vols. and other unbound papers.

S.P. 81. The German States, 1577–1780, 197 vols. and other unbound papers. Under heading "Army in Germany, 1775–1784," are the volumes that have references to securing German troops to serve in America in the British army against the colonials, that are of especial interest. Among these papers are *Nos. 154–157,* 1775–1780, under the heading "Cologne"; they cover the papers of George Cressener. Also in the so-called "Foreign Office Series," under Germany, *Nos. 1–2,* are many other papers that relate to the activities of Cressener, both at Cologne and at Cassel, as well as Ralph Heathcote and others. Returning to *S.P. 81, No. 165,* 1737–1777, has papers concerning Hesse-Cassel; *Nos. 181–196,* 1775–1784, relate to the general recruiting activities among the German princes of Col. William Faucitt, at times assisted by Charles Rainsford. Beyond the contribution of the German states to the British effort in America, *S.P. 81* also has much about the relations of Great Britain to various German states. For example, financial claims, 1748–1750, arising out of the War of the Austrian Succession; negotiations respecting the election of Archduke Joseph as King of the Romans, 1752–1754; financial claims, 1762–1772, arising out of the German Seven Years' War; and many papers relating to Hesse-Cassel, 1737–1777.

S.P. 82. Hamburg and other Hansa towns, 1577–1780, 103 vols., etc.

S.P. 84. Holland, 1585–1780, 590 vols., etc. Among these volumes the following have pertinence to the period 1748–1776: *Nos. 535, 542, 546, 547, 552 to 558,* May 1772 to Dec. 1777, with Sir Joseph Yorke representing Great Britain at the Hague. *No. 588,* 1763, has to do with the Jeronimy Clifford case in Surinam which had its basis in the seventeenth century.

S.P. 85. Italian states including Rome, 1577–1773, 16 vols., etc.

S.P. 86. Malta, 1664–1765, 4 vols.

S.P. 87. Military expeditions, 1695–1763, 48 vols., etc.

S.P. 88. Poland, 1577–1781, 118 vols., etc.

S.P. 89. Portugal, 1577–1780, 92 vols., etc. See especially *Nos. 74, 75, 79–83*, Jan. 1773 to Dec. 1776, with Robert Walpole representing Great Britain at Lisbon.

S.P. 90. Prussia, 1698–1780, 107 vols., etc.

S.P. 91. Russia, 1579–1780, 111 vols., etc. See *Nos. 98–100*, with Sir Robert Gunning representing Great Britain at St. Petersburg, followed by Richard Oakes, 1775–1776.

S.P. 92. Savoy and Sardinia, 1577–1780, 91 vols., etc.

S.P. 93. Sicily and Naples, 1584–1779, 32 vols., etc.

S.P. 94. Spain, 1577–1780, 255 vols., etc. In this series see *Nos. 195–200*, 1774–1776, with Lord Grantham representing Great Britain at Madrid.

S.P. 95. Sweden, 1577–1780, 136 vols., etc.

S.P. 96. Switzerland, 1582–1780, 52 vols., etc.

S.P. 97. Turkey, 1577–1779, 60 vols., etc.

S.P. 98. Tuscany, 1582–1780, 86 vols., etc.

S.P. 99. Venice, 1578–1778, 80 vols., etc.

S.P. 100. Foreign ministers in England, 1683–1780, 70 bundles.

S.P. 101. News Letters, 1565–1763, 135 vols., etc. These are chiefly unsigned despatches and news from foreign gazettes, etc.

S.P. 102. Royal Letters, [1569]–1780, 68 bundles. They are letters from foreign royalties and drafts of letters from British royalties and are listed by states. Among the surviving royal letters are the following, all involving German states, with material concerned with the period 1748–1776: *No. 13.* Anspach, 1727–1780, and Baden, 1690–1780; *No. 16.* Brunswick, 1759–1780; *No. 17.* Cologne, 1688–1780, and Mentz, 1689–1780; *No. 20.* Hesse-Cassel, 1741–1780; *No. 21.* Hesse Darmstadt, 1690–1780; *Nos. 28–29.* The minor German states of Waldeck, Hanau, and Anhalt-Zerbst.

S.P. 103. Treaty papers, 1577–1780, 118 bundles. Among the bundles *No. 117* may be noted. It is concerned with the negotiations between Great Britain and France over North America, 1754–1755, with twenty-two papers.

S.P. 104. Entry books, 1571–1783, 271 vols. Among these entry books the following are important for the Empire, 1748–1776: *Nos. 68–71*, 1756–1760, and *Nos. 73–75, 77–78, 80* and *86*, 1760–1775. These are entries of letters received and letters sent.

S.P. 105. Archives of British legations, 1568–1866, 343 vols., etc. These are letter-books and correspondence of British embassies and legations. Among these are also the books and papers of the Levant Company from 1606 to 1866.

S.P. 106. Cipher documents, both ciphers and deciphers. From Elizabeth I to George III, 67 vols., etc.

S.P. 107. Confidential. These are intercepted despatches, 1726–1766, 110 vols.

S.P. 108. Treaties, 1579–1780, 556 documents. These include protocols and ratification of treaties, with supporting documents. Among these treaty papers that are within the period 1748–1776 are the following listed by countries: *Nos. 1–31.* Barbary states, mostly with Algiers, many are concerned with Mediterranean trade and passes, 1662–1765; *Nos. 108, 117, 118, 123, 124,* and *127.* Negotiations with France leading up to the Treaty of Paris, 1763, and the convention of 1766 with France for the liquidation of the old French paper money in Canada; *No. 276.* Convention with Brunswick, Jan. 9, 1776; *Nos. 277, 279,* and *280.* Conventions signed with Hesse-Cassel, Jan. 15 and Feb. 5 and 24, 1776; *No. 525.* Ratification by Spain, Feb. 25, 1763, of the Treaty of Paris.

S.P. 109. Foreign Office, Various, Charles II to George III, 87 vols., etc. These are made up of précis books (that is, abstracts of letters, etc.), first drafts of letters, etc.

S.P. 110. Supplementary materials, 1616–1825, 90 vols. Here are additional archives of British legations, with some Levant Company documents, 1616–1825, and more entry books, 1669–1800.

The Board of Trade

When considering the British Empire in its internal aspects and the relation of the work of the Privy Council and of the Secretary of State to its development, the activities of the Lords Commissioners for Trade and Plantations are of especial importance.

Brought into existence under the Great Seal by William III in 1696, the Lords Commissioners, some eight in number, generally called the Board of Trade, were legally but a body of advisers who aided the Privy Council and the Secretaries of State, especially the Secretary of State for the Southern Department, and, after 1768, the Secretary of State for the Colonies, to carry on their work. In fact, after 1768 the Secretary of State for the Colonies was President of the Board. As a rule, most matters relating to trade and many matters concerning the colonies that came before the Privy Council were referred to the Board for its careful consideration and for its recommendation. The reports on these matters were called representations, and, almost without exception, the appropriate Privy Council Committee and the Privy Council acting as a body treated them with great respect and only seldom—with the consent and in the name of the King—refused to follow the Board's advice in reaching a decision which was then announced with the consent of and in the name of the King. Charles M. Andrews, in his *Guide to the Materials for American History, to 1783, in the Public Record Office of Great Britain* (Published by the Carnegie Institution of Washington, 2 vols., Washington, 1912, 1914), I, 78–112, has given a comprehensive account of the activity of the Board with the changing degrees of authority that it enjoyed. As the Board ceased to function after 1782, its papers came into the keeping of the Public Record Office, where they now rest, together with those of the appropriate secretary of state. Since Andrews prepared his important *Guide*, there has appeared the *Journal of the Commissioners for Trade and Plantations* [From April 1704 to May 1782] *Preserved in the Public Record Office* (14 vols., London, 1920–38). The *Journal*, although a storehouse of information, represents but a fraction of the Board's papers. These papers are now listed together with many of the papers of the Secretary of State under the heading, the Colonial Office Papers; they are divided into classes. For analyses of the Colonial Office Papers, see Giuseppi: *Guide*, II, 52–92; Andrews: *Guide*, I, 112–264; Crick and Alman: *Guide*, pp. 261–2; and Virginia State Library: *British Public Record Office*, pp. 160–3.

Colonial Office Papers

They are made up of papers from the office of the Secretary of State and of those in the Board of Trade which have been combined and unified under the general heading Colonial Office Papers. The following papers help to throw light on developments within the British Empire, 1748–1776:

AMERICA AND THE WEST INDIES

C.O. 5

Among all the Colonial Office papers no class is of greater importance for the purpose of this *Guide* than Class 5 which includes thousands of documents, many of them falling within the years 1748–1776. These are numbered 1 to 1450, but each number may embody numerous documents. Those that bear upon the Empire during the above period are as follows:

No. 6, 1749–1754, has papers relating to royal instructions to governors, to contraband trade, to a specific colony such as Nova Scotia or to the Hudson's Bay Company's possessions, to the Albany Plan of Union of 1754, and to instructions to General Braddock.

No. 7, 1755–1779, includes the despatches of the Secretary of State for the Southern Department from 1755 onward. It should be mentioned that the papers noted above and classified as "Plantations

General, 1689–1783" are not among those documents transcribed for the Historical Society of Pennsylvania under the heading "Plantations General."

No. 10, 1710–1752, is papers concerned with New England; while most of them are of an earlier date, some relating to New Hampshire come down to 1752 and the administration of Governor Benning Wentworth.

Nos. 13–20, 1742–1762, are made up of correspondence with the colonial governors and chiefly fall within the years 1752 and 1762 and contain Pitt's dispatches. The papers should be used in conjunction with *Nos. 48–64*, and *Nos. 211–215*.

Nos. 21–37, 1728–1822, are orders in council sent by the Privy Council to the Board of Trade. Those orders sent between 1748 and 1776 are in *Nos. 21–30*.

No. 38, 1739–1775, is made up of two groups of papers: (1) The letters of two artists, both Loyalists, Henry Pelham of Boston and his half-brother John Singleton Copley in London; (2) Intercepted letters from London, Philadelphia, and New York; among them are also the proceedings before the Board of Trade relative to the extent of illicit trade of the Thirteen Colonies with the foreign West Indies.

No. 39, 1770–1782, contains letters received by Henry Pelham from various correspondents. In connection with the Pelham correspondence the student should consult *Letters & Papers of John Singleton Copley and Henry Pelham*, Massachusetts Historical Society, *Collections*, LXXI ([Boston], 1914).

No. 40, 1774–1777, contains "Intercepted Letters," a collection of letters and documents, over forty in number, written from South Carolina, Virginia, Philadelphia, and Rhode Island.

No. 43, 1743–1783, "Miscellaneous Papers." Here again is another considerable collection of papers, some forty in number, most of them falling between the years 1765 and 1778. These deal with such matters as the British interest in Cuba, 1769; Canadian financial claims against France, 1769, 1771; the relations of the Spaniards and Southern Indians, 1768; Turks Island, 1767; a summary of governors' letters from North America, 1765; letters respecting frontier conditions in Augusta County, Va., 1765; the state of Canada, 1763; the problem facing British merchants interested in trade with Canada who were paid in Canadian paper money bills, 1771; debts due to British merchants in America, 1776.

Nos. 44–45, 1746–1750, pertain to the Louisbourg expedition, with letters from Sir William Pepperrell, Admiral Warren and Governors Hopson and Knowles.

Nos. 46–47, 1755–1756, papers relating to the early years of the Great War for the Empire with letters and enclosures from Generals

Edward Braddock, William Shirley, Sir William Johnson, Daniel Webb, James Abercromby, Lord Loudoun, and Admirals Boscawen and Holburne.

Nos. 48–64, 1756–1763, constitute another large body of military correspondence between William Pitt and Lord Egremont and generals and admirals serving in North America and the West Indies. These letters are also to be found in the British Museum in Additional Manuscripts *No. 21634.*

Nos. 65–82, 1760–1784, which carry the title "Plantations General," contain many letters from merchants trading to the North American colonies as well as from colonial agents and others, including those holding offices in the colonies. They are concerned with a variety of matters such as Indian relations, the costs of the civil establishments in South Carolina and Georgia, conditions in West Florida, the desirability of establishing a colony in the Illinois country, the courts of vice-admiralty in America, and a petition for lands on the Ohio.

Nos. 83–111, 1763–1784, comprise a large body of military correspondence, similar to that of *Nos. 48–64*, with many letters from Generals Gage, Haldimand, Howe, Clinton, and Carleton and drafts of letters to these generals from the Secretary of State.

Nos. 112–113, 1767–1768, contain estimates of annual expenses for maintaining the colonial establishments.

Nos. 114–117, 1768–1781, are made up largely of memorials addressed to the Secretary of State for the Colonies from soldiers, military officers, and British officials in North America; they concern a variety of matters, such as East Florida lands, the Labrador fishery, the transporting of Protestants from Belfast to settle in South Carolina, and the return to Great Britain of East India Company tea shipped to North America. Many of these papers are concerned with the period after 1776.

No. 118, 1768–1775, comprises letters which were in the house of patriot leader Thomas Cushing of Boston at the time the British seized them in 1775. There are thirteen from Benjamin Franklin, nine from Joseph Price of London, five from the Earl of Buchan, as well as letters from Sheriff Lee of London, Arthur Lee, John Dickinson and others.

Nos. 119–132, 1771–1781, are entry books of letters from the Secretary of State for the Colonies to the Lords of the Admiralty together with letters from the Admiralty to the Secretary of State. This correspondence, exclusively concerned with American affairs, is of great value.

No. 133, 1771–1774, is a miscellaneous collection of letters including Dartmouth's correspondence with the East India Company, Nov. 1773–April 1774.

Nos. 134–137, 1771–1780, contain the correspondence of the Secretary of State for the Colonies and the Postmasters General with many important enclosures. These concern conditions in colonial post-offices and include a number of confiscated letters to and from America from such prominent people as Benjamin Franklin and John Wesley. *Nos. 134–135* cover the period 1771–1776.

Nos. 138–144, 1771–1781, embody the correspondence over these years of the Secretary of State for the Colonies with other secretaries. They deal with such matters as English relations with Spain and France in North America, the West Indies, and South America, and colonial trade relations with Holland, Ireland, and Africa. The first two numbers are pertinent.

Nos. 145–153, 1771–1780, bring together the correspondence of the Secretaries of State for the Colonies with the Treasury and the Custom House. While most of the papers are dated beyond the year 1776, in *Nos. 145–148* there is much germane material covering the years 1771–1776. Mention is made, for example, of the seizure of 54 packets and letters in one ship from Georgia in 1776.

Nos. 154–158, 1771–1781, contain many private letters and other papers which deal with matters of a miscellaneous nature. Among other writers are Lord Dunmore, William Tryon, Robert Rogers, Robert Eden and Arthur Lee. See especially *Nos. 154–155.*

Nos. 159–160, 1772–1781, embody the correspondence of two of the Secretaries of State for the Colonies with the Attorney General and Solicitor General. As would be anticipated these letters are largely concerned with such legal questions as, for example, under what circumstances have the rebellious colonists committed acts of treason. There are a number of papers dealing with the Boston Tea Party.

Nos. 161–166, 1772–1781, contain the corespondence of the Secretary of State for the Colonies with the Ordnance Office. These letters relate particularly to the fortification of those British possessions in the New World not in revolt. See particularly the first two numbers.

Nos. 167–173, 1772–1781, bring together the correspondence of the Secretary of State for the Colonies with the Secretary at War.

Nos. 175–176, 1774–1783, contain the letters exchanged between the Secretary of State for the Colonies and the English civil officials of the rebellious colonies; most of them are post-1776.

Nos. 188–208, 1702–1784, embody the so-called "Entry Books" where are to be found copies of commissions, various types of instructions to colonial governors and others. Most of these documents are of course too early for specific reference. *No. 204,* 1770–1779, carries the title "Patents" and relates to appointments.

Nos. 211–218, 1753–1769, are also entry books of letters to governors, military and naval officers and others written chiefly by the

Secretary of State for the Southern Department; these papers also include instructions and reports and are concerned with a variety of matters such as land-grants, ecclesiastical affairs in Quebec, and the Indian trade.

Nos. 219–220, 1765–1768, include despatches to the Commander-in-Chief in North America.

No. 221, 1766–1767, carries the title "Plantations General" and is largely extracts of letters from the governors of colonies.

No. 222, 1766–1768, has letters sent by Secretary of State Shelburne to Governor Moore in New York.

No. 223, 1766–1768, embodies letters from the Secretary of State to the Board of Trade.

No. 224, 1766–1768, contains letters from the Secretary of State to the Treasury.

No. 225, 1766–1768, has the Secretary's letters relating to North American Indian affairs.

No. 226, 1766–1768, offers letters received by the Secretary of State from the Surveyors General and others.

Nos. 227–231, 1766–1782, provide a very large number of letters by the Secretary of State on North American Indian affairs from officials in the colonies. *Nos. 227–229* pertain to the period under review.

No. 232, 1768–1775, contains documents bearing upon disorders in the colonies, especially in Massachusetts Bay, the erection of fortifications in America, the establishment of Canada as a colony after 1763, and proposals for the creation of a colony to be called Pittsylvania.

Nos. 233–240, 1768–1782, are military entry books.

Nos. 241–242, 1768–1790, contain dispatches to governors.

Nos. 243–245, 1770–1783, bring together dispatches to commanding officers in America.

No. 246, 1771–1777, contains mostly private letters sent to or received from leading people both in the colonies and in Great Britain, including Lord George Germain, Earl of Dartmouth, Lord North, the Earl of Hillsborough, and Hugh Finlay.

Nos. 247–249, 1771–1782, are letters received by the Secretary of State for the Colonies.

Nos. 273–281, 1638–1776, are a series of volumes setting forth the acts passed in all the British colonies including those of the West Indies. *Nos. 273–276* give the laws passed up to 1758; *Nos. 277–281* give the laws passed from 1758 to 1776.

The *C.O.* 5 series now turns to papers relating to individual colonies which are presented in the following order:

NORTH CAROLINA

Nos. 293–304, 310–318, 1730–1777, contain the original papers, including letters, from the governors of North Carolina, while *No. 305*, 1765–1775, contains drafts of letters sent to the colony.

Nos. 319–322, 1707–1775, are concerned with patents and other grants of land in North Carolina.

Nos. 323–332, 1730–1782, are the entry books and abstracts of letters concerning North Carolina.

Nos. 333–341, 1734–1774, comprise the acts passed by the North Carolina Assembly.

Nos. 342–357, 1731–1774, present the minutes of the North Carolina Council, the Assembly, and the Council in Assembly.

SOUTH CAROLINA

Nos. 358–380, 1720–1775, bring together a variety of papers, including letters from the governors or acting governors of South Carolina, while *No. 381*, 1722–1774, contains drafts of letters sent to the colony.

Nos. 385–386, 1744–1776, are miscellaneous papers, including original correspondence.

Nos. 387–397, 1715–1751, 1762–1777, embrace collections of letters with enclosures as well as other papers from the colony.

Nos. 398–399, 1674–1765, 1768–1773, provide abstracts of South Carolina land grants.

Nos. 400–410, 1720–1781, are entry books, with abstracts of letters covering the years 1721–1756.

Nos. 411–424, 1663–1770, embrace the acts passed in the colony. It will be noted that no acts were passed after 1770 by reason of a deadlock between the Commons House of Assembly and the Council.

Nos. 425–507, 1721–1774, bring together in 80 volumes the minutes of the South Carolina Council, the Commons House of Assembly, and the Council in Assembly.

Nos. 508–511, 1716–1765, contain shipping returns for South Carolina.

No. 512, 1759–1763, presents three reports from the Treasurer of South Carolina.

CONNECTICUT

By reason of the fact that Connecticut was a corporate colony, there is little material in the Colonial Office respecting it. *No. 536*, 1693–1751, has a few relevant papers, and *No. 539* contains the acts and laws of the colony as of the year 1750.

EAST FLORIDA

Although British East Florida was not established as a British colony until 1763, the papers embodied in *Nos. 540–547* run from 1702 to 1783. Among the documents, *Nos. 542–543* are made up of post-1763 petitions for land grants; there are also many letters from Governors James Grant and Patrick Tonyn. The same applies to *Nos. 548–561*.

Nos. 563–569, 1763–1783, are entry books concerning the colony.

Nos. 570–572, 1764–1781, contain the minutes of the East Florida Council and Assembly. The Assembly did not meet until March 1781.

No. 573, 1765–1769, is East Florida shipping returns.

WEST FLORIDA

Nos. 574–598, 1763–1782, contain many original papers, including letters with enclosures from Governors George Johnstone and Peter Chester.

Nos. 599–622, 1763–1782, are entry books either of the Board of Trade or of the Secretary of State relating to West Florida matters. *Nos. 606–611,* 1767–1780, are concerned with land grants.

Nos. 623–624, 1766–1771, 1781–1783, embody acts passed by the West Florida Assembly.

Nos. 625–635, 1764–1780, contain the minutes of the Council and Assembly.

GEORGIA

Nos. 636–656, 1734–1782, contain papers and letters relating to Georgia while a trusteeship, 1734–1752, and as a colony, 1752–1782; included are letters from Governors James Oglethorpe, John Reynolds, and James Wright, with drafts of Board of Trade letters to those in control of the colony.

No. 657, 1733–1783, is made up of miscellaneous papers concerned with both civil and military issues.

Nos. 658–665, 1761–1780, are letters from Governor James Wright.

Nos. 666–671, 1732–1752, are out-letters and entry books of the Trustees, including instructions to the governor, leases, petitions, and land grants.

Nos. 672–674, 1752–1757, are entry books of the Board of Trade relating to the colony.

No. 675, 1760–1768, embodies abstracts of Georgia land grants.

No. 676, 1766–1767, is the Earl of Shelburne's entry book containing both in-letters and out-letters.

No. 677, 1768–1782, is the entry book of out-letters of the Secretary of State for the Colonies.

Nos. 678–680, 1767–1781, contain in-letters relating to Georgia received by the Secretary of State.

Nos. 681–685, 1732–1781, are acts passed either by the Trustees or after 1752 by the Georgia Assembly.

Nos. 686–691, 1732–1752, embody the journal of the Trustees as well as the minutes of the Trustees' Council.

Nos. 692–708, 1741–1780, contain minutes of the Georgia Council, the Assembly, and the Council in Assembly.

Nos. 709–710, 1752–1767, are the Georgia shipping returns.

No. 712, 1756, is devoted to a consideration of the case of that remarkable couple, the Rev. Thomas Bosomworth and his Creek Indian wife, Mary.

MARYLAND

Here again the manuscripts in the Colonial Office bearing upon Maryland, a proprietary of the Baltimore family, covering the years 1748–1776 are limited.

Nos. 729–738, 1692–1771, with a break between 1753 and 1769, are devoted to the acts of the Maryland Assembly. Maryland, together with the corporate colonies of Connecticut and Rhode Island, was not obliged by its letters patent to submit its laws to the Privy Council for acceptance or rejection.

No. 750, 1754–1765, contains shipping returns made out by naval officers stationed in the colony.

MASSACHUSETTS BAY

Among the Colonial Office papers relating to Massachusetts there is nothing about royal land grants for the period 1748–1776, which is also true for corporate Connecticut and Rhode Island and proprietary Maryland and Pennsylvania, and royal New Jersey, since the Crown had divested itself of the lands in these colonies. In contrast to the purely corporate and proprietary colonies, Massachusetts Bay, with a Crown-appointed governor and also some other officials, provides a much larger body of papers relating to the government of the colony.

No. 753, 1742–1753, has but few papers concerned with the years under consideration. Those that are pertinent have chiefly to do with the designs of the French and with the war against the Penobscot Indians in what is now the State of Maine but then a part of Massachusetts Bay.

No. 754, 1754–1776, is made up of rather miscellaneous papers, including Governor William Shirley's letters to the Board of Trade, 1754, and a very long letter also from Shirley to Lord Holderness, 1755. There are other papers relating to the expedition against the French in Nova Scotia, the problem of the disposal of the Acadians, and a long report about the disorders in Massachusetts Bay, post–1770 (56 pages).

Nos. 755–763, 1761–1774, contain letters with enclosures from Governors Francis Bernard, Thomas Hutchinson, and Gen. Gage.

Nos. 764–769, 1766–1776, are entry books of in-letters and out-letters of the Secretaries of State concerning developments in Massachusetts Bay.

Nos. 770–784, 1692–1774, contain acts passed by the Assembly of the colony.

Nos. 791–847, 1709–1774, bring together minutes of the provincial Council, the House of Representatives and the Council in Assembly; there are also here the printed journal and votes of the House of Representatives, 1721–1774.

Nos. 849–851, 1752–1765, present the Naval Office lists for Massachusetts Bay.

Nos. 852–854, 1743–1769, contain accounts of the "Treasurer and Receiver General of his Majesty's revenues within the Province of Massachusetts Bay."

NEW ENGLAND

This series in *C.O. 5* called "New England" is largely concerned with the period before 1741 when New Hampshire, as well as Maine, was under the government of Massachusetts Bay. Yet even after the separation of New Hampshire the same designation continues.

Nos. 883–895, 1741–1778, include letters relating particularly to New England problems, addressed to the Board of Trade by governors of Massachusetts Bay.

Nos. 896–897, 1687–1774, contain drafts of letters of the Board of Trade sent to Massachusetts Bay.

Nos. 918–921, 1741–1774, are Board of Trade entry books.

No. 923, 1705–1757, provides abstracts of letters having to do with New England.

NEW HAMPSHIRE

The Colonial Office papers bearing upon New Hampshire for the period under consideration are as follows:

Nos. 925–928, 930, 1741–1778, are original papers including letters of Governors Benning and John Wentworth to the Board of Trade.

Nos. 931–933, 1692–1794, are miscellaneous papers, most important of which are the New Hampshire Assembly sessional papers (*No. 933*).

Nos. 934–939, 1763–1775, contain Governor John Wentworth's letters and enclosures to the Secretary of State.

Nos. 941–943, 1741–1775, are the entry books of the Board of Trade relating to New Hampshire.

No. 944, 1705–1775, comprises an abstract of Board of Trade letters.

Nos. 945–947, 1767–1777, are the Secretary of State's entry books of both in-letters and out-letters concerning New Hampshire affairs.

Nos. 949–959, 1699–1774, contain the acts of the New Hampshire Assembly.

Nos. 960–966, 1710–1774, provide the minutes of the Council, the Assembly, and the Council in Assembly.

Nos. 967–969, 1723–1769, are concerned with New Hampshire shipping returns.

NEW JERSEY

Although New Jersey was a royal colony for the period under consideration there are no Board of Trade papers or any from the office of the Secretary of State respecting land grants as all lands within the province not granted to individuals or corporate groups belonged to the Proprietors of East Jersey and the Proprietors of West Jersey. The boundaries of the colony as well as other matters were, however, of direct concern to the Crown. The following Colonial Office papers have a bearing upon the colony for the years 1748–1776:

Nos. 970–979, 1702–1776, are original papers including letters to the Board of Trade from the governors of the province. In this connection it should be pointed out that from 1702 to 1738 the governor of the Province of New York was also commissioned governor of New Jersey.

Nos. 983–993, 1728–1779, comprise letters and papers from the governors to the Secretary of State.

Nos. 994–999, 1702–1774, are Board of Trade entry books, relating to the province.

No. 1000, 1703–1754, contains abstracts of letters made for the Board of Trade.

Nos. 1001–1002, 1766–1781, are the Secretary of State's entry books of in-letters.

No. 1003, 1768–1782, is the Secretary of State's entry book of out-letters.

Nos. 1004–1018, 1703–1774, embody the acts of the New Jersey Assembly.

Nos. 1019–1034, 1703–1774, contain the minutes of the Council, the Assembly, and the Council in Assembly.

Nos. 1035–1036, 1722–1764, provides shipping returns relating to the province.

NEW YORK

The Province of New York was a typical royal colony. The manuscripts in the Colonial Office bearing upon the years 1748–1776 are as follows:

Nos. 1037–1078, 1691–1779, consist of letters and other documents from the governors addressed to the Board of Trade or to its predecessor, the Lords of Trade.

No. 1080, 1738–1779, is Board of Trade out-letters relating to New York.

Nos. 1081–1090, 1689–1793, are made up of miscellaneous papers, among which are those concerned with the boundary dispute between New York and New Jersey.

Nos. 1091–1110, 1696–1752, 1762–1780, consist of letters to the Secretary of State from the New York governors.

Nos. 1114–1132, 1696–1779, are Board of Trade entry books.

No. 1134, 1666–1755, 1761–1764, is concerned with land grants.

Nos. 1137–1140, 1766–1781, are the Secretary of State's entry books of in-letters.

No. 1141, 1768–1782, is the Secretary of State's entry book of out-letters.

Nos. 1143–1182, 1691–1775, consist of laws passed by the Assembly.

Nos. 1184–1220, 1684–1775, contain minutes of the Council, Assembly, and Council in Assembly.

Nos. 1222–1228, 1713–1765, embody the Naval Office lists.

No. 1232, 1773, consists of a printed volume setting forth the claims of New York to all lands eastward up to the Connecticut River and also to lands on Lake Champlain. It carries the title *A State of the Right of the Colony of New York* . . . (New York, 1773). There is also a printed *Narrative of the Proceedings* . . . (New York, 1773), supporting New York land claims up to the Connecticut River.

PENNSYLVANIA

As in the case of Maryland, the Province of Pennsylvania was a proprietary colony with the land at the disposal of the Penn family and the governor appointed by the family with the approval of the Crown. Since the Penn family also claimed as a proprietary the colony of the Lower Counties on the Delaware, it is of interest to note in passing that there is no recognition of this claim among the Colonial Office papers and therefore no file of papers under title the Lower Counties on the Delaware.

Among the documents that bear upon the years 1748–1776 are the following:

No. 1233, 1690–1767, is made up of miscellaneous papers, only a few of which relate to the period under review. Among them, however, are royal instructions to Thomas and Richard Penn, the Proprietors; in this connection are to be noted orders and instructions to them under date, April 24, 1767.

Nos. 1237–1255, 1700–1775, contain acts passed by the Pennsylvania Assembly.

No. 1256, 1754–1759, has the printed votes and proceedings of the Assembly. It may be noted that in Pennsylvania the Assembly was a unitary body; the Council simply advised the Governor.

THE PROPRIETIES

Among the Board of Trade papers listed under *C.O. 5* is "The Proprieties"; it is concerned with those colonies which had proprietary governments at some time during the period 1697–1776. Among the colonies listed are the Bahamas, Connecticut, Carolina, Maryland, East and West Jersey, Pennsylvania, and Rhode Island. Two colonies, Connecticut and Rhode Island, were not, however, considered proprietary but corporate from the time of the granting of their charters in the seventeenth century.

Nos. 1257–1279, 1697–1776, contain original papers relating to the above-mentioned governments. It should be noted that all these volumes except *No. 1272* were transcribed for the Historical Society of Pennsylvania.

Nos. 1280–1286, 1762–1776, consist of miscellaneous papers mostly relating to Connecticut, Rhode Island, Pennsylvania and Maryland. Here are brought together many letters from the governors: for Connecticut, from Fitch to Trumbull, for Rhode Island, from Ward to Wanton; from the governors of Pennsylvania, and from Sharpe of Maryland.

Nos. 1287–1297, 1696–1776, are Board of Trade entry books.

No. 1298, 1706–1753, contains abstracts of letters.

Nos. 1299–1300, 1766–1776, are the in-letter entry books of the Secretary of State.

No. 1301, 1768–1776, is the out-letter entry book of the Secretary of State.

RHODE ISLAND

Rhode Island as a corporate colony, although listed among the proprieties, accumulated few papers in the Colonial Office. There is but one volume that has a direct bearing upon the period 1748–1776. This is *No. 1302*, 1698–1782, which contains miscellaneous papers but none of sufficient importance to be noted here.

VIRGINIA

Most of the papers in the Colonial Office listed under Virginia are too early for consideration. However, some of the items do fall within the period 1748–1776:

Nos. 1308–1334, 1691–1774, are made up largely of letters with enclosures from the governors of the colony to the Board of Trade.

Nos. 1335–1336, 1702–1774, are drafts of letters sent by the Board of Trade relating to the colony.

Nos. 1337–1338, 1694–1753, contain letters sent by the governor to the Secretary of State.

No. 1344, 1722–1780, 1783, is made up of miscellaneous papers. Among them are a number of letters from the Board of Trade, 1750; instructions to Gov. Dinwiddie, with a covering letter from the Earl of Holderness, 1753; and accounts by Washington and Ensign Ward of the beginning of hostilities against the French in the Ohio Valley, 1754.

Nos. 1345–1353, 1762–1777, contain letters from the governors to the Secretary of State.

Nos. 1358–1369, 1689–1774, are entry books of the Lords of Trade (before 1696) and the Board of Trade (after 1696).

No. 1370, 1704–1753, contains abstracts of letters sent by the Board of Trade.

Nos. 1372–1375, 1767–1777, are made up of entry books of the Secretary of State consisting both of in-letters and out-letters.

Nos. 1376–1404, 1661–1773, embrace the acts passed by the Virginia Assembly.

Nos. 1406–1440, 1680–1774, contain the journals of the Council, House of Burgesses, and Council in Assembly.

Nos. 1441–1450, 1699–1770, bring together with omissions the shipping returns and the Naval Office Lists.

This brings to an end the very extensive Class 5 documents. It should be noted that the subsequent classes of documents are much more restricted, with more than one class included under individual colonies or possession until one comes to the heading "Colonies General." The arrangement is alphabetical with respect to the British possessions.

ANTIGUA

C.O. 7

No. 1, 1702–1786, includes correspondence from the governors of the island to the Secretary of State.

C.O. 8

Nos. 2–20, 1684–1783, comprise acts of the Assembly.

C.O. 9

Nos. 1–43, 1704–1787, contain proceedings of the Council, Assembly, and Council in Assembly with many other papers.

THE BAHAMAS

C.O. 23

Nos. 1–10, 1717–1780, contain original correspondence with enclosures to the Board of Trade.
No. 11, 1721–1754, is composed of abstracts of letters to the Board of Trade.
No. 15, 1735–1783, is also made up of abstracts of letters.
Nos. 16–25, 1762–1786, contain letters from governors of the Bahamas.

C.O. 24

Nos. 1–5, 1717–1784, are Board of Trade entry books of the Bahamas with commissions, instructions, and other official papers.
Nos. 6–7, 1766–1781, are letters to the Secretary of State with other papers which relate not only to the Bahamas but to nearby Turks Island, valued for its salt ponds.
No. 14, 1768–1801, contains letters of the Secretary of State for the Colonies bearing on the Bahamas.

C.O. 25

Nos. 1–5, 1729–1781, are made up of acts of the Assembly of the Bahamas.

C.O. 26

Nos. 1–11, 1721–1787, embody the sessional papers of the Bahamas in the Board of Trade office.

C.O. 27

Nos. 12–13, 1721–1757, present the shipping returns of the islands.

BARBADOS

The island of Barbados (Barbadoes) was much more important as a British possession than were the Bahamas and the papers relating to it are quite extensive.

C.O. 28

Nos. 1–35, 1689–1782, constitute original correspondence of the governors with the Board of Trade.
No. 36, 1705–1753, comprises abstracts from Board of Trade letters relating to the island.
Nos. 37–60, 1689–1786, embody the governors' correspondence with the Secretary of State.

C.O. 29

Nos. 1–20, 1627–1782, are the entry books in the Board of Trade office having to do with Barbados.
Nos. 21–22, 1767–1782, are the entry books of letters sent to the Secretary of State for the Colonies.

C.O. 30

Nos. 1–16, 1643–1796, embody acts passed by the Barbados Assembly.

C.O. 31

Nos. 5–43, 1694–1785, are the Board of Trade Barbadian sessional papers involving a variety of matters.

C.O. 33

Nos. 13–17, 1678–1764, contain shipping returns from Barbados with much useful information.

THE BERMUDAS

C.O. 37

Nos. 1–21, 1692–1782, embody original correspondence, with enclosures, from the governors of these islands to the Board of Trade.

No. 24, 1714–1756, provides abstracts of letters relating to the islands.

Nos. 25–38, 1689–1751, 1762–1784, contain correspondence with the Secretary of State's office.

C.O. 38

Nos. 3–10, 1691–1782, are Board of Trade entry books.

Nos. 12–13, 1766–1781, are the Secretary of State's entry books.

C.O. 39

Nos. 1–9, 1690–1783, contain acts passed by the Assembly of the Bermudas.

C.O. 40

Nos. 2–32, 1698–1783, embody the Board of Trade sessional papers on the Bermudas.

C.O. 41

Nos. 6–7, 1715–1751, are shipping returns from the Bermudas.

CANADA

Although Canada did not become a part of the British Empire until its cession in 1763, a number of papers in the Colonial Office bear upon the colony before this date.

C.O. 42

Nos. 1–10, 1763–1781, bring together original correspondence to the Board of Trade office relating to Canada including letters of Governors James Murray and Guy Carleton.

Nos. 13–15, 1700–1783, are miscellaneous papers. In *No. 13* among the manuscripts there is a letter, Aug. 10, 1751, from La Jonquière, Governor General of New France, to Gov. Clinton of New York; one, Apr. 13, 1758, from M. Rouillé to the Duc de Mirepoix; a plan of the French in Canada to invade the British colonies, 1759; a declaration made by the inhabitants of Trois Rivières concerning Canadian paper money, Dec. 9, 1763, with "Recapitulation ou Somaire Général du Papier du Canada," and a copy of the commission given to James Murray as Governor of the Province of Quebec, Nov. 21, 1763. In *No. 14* also are several documents bearing upon the period 1748–1776. Among them are a number of papers relating to Indians in London and their return to Virginia and other colonies; a plan to raise regiments to be stationed in Canada "without any expense to Great Britain"; a return of pelts from Michilimackinac, June–Oct. 1767; a deed of cession by the Indians of lands to the Crown at Fort Stanwix, Nov. 5, 1768; a printed copy of the Quebec Act, 1774 and with it "Heads of what was done relative to Quebec previous to the Quebec Act," and "Draft of an Ordinance for establishing Courts of Justice in the Province of Canada," May 1, 1775.

No. 23, 1750, is made up of intercepted correspondence written largely by Canadian *habitants.*

Nos. 24–46, 1760–1784, contain letters sent by the British governors in Canada to the Secretary of State.

Nos. 86–87, 1764–1789, are miscellaneous papers, a number of which are of considerable importance for the period 1748–1776, among them the following: (1) Documents relating to Canadian paper money; (2) Papers regarding French claims to a monopoly of trade at Bay de Puans on Lake Michigan; (3) Papers relative to Thomas Walker of Montreal against Governor Murray, 1766; (4) The claim of M. Hoquart, former intendant of New France, to lands in Canada; (5) Papers delivered by Henry Ellis, secretary and clerk of the Council, to his deputy at Quebec, George Alsop, 1767; (6) An address in French by the Huron Indians for themselves and others that they represent, n.d.; (7) Letters from Pierre Roubaud with a dissertation (in French) on Canada; (8) Gov. Murray's report, 1762; (9) A Board of Trade representation regarding the government of Quebec, Sept. 2, 1765; (10) A printed tract on the need of an act of Parliament to settle the government of the Province of Quebec, 1766, with manuscript additions to it; (11) A copy in French of a *procès verbal* by the Superior Council of Quebec with reference to the civil code of the province, April, 1767.

C.O. 43

Nos. 1–3, 1763–1786, are Board of Trade entry books relating to Canada.

Nos. 5–6, 1764, embody declarations respecting the paper money of the province.

Nos. 7–8, 1766–1783, contain the Secretary of State's entry books of letters to Canada.

Nos. 12–15, 1766–1781, contain the Secretary of State's entry books of letters from or pertaining to Canada.

C.O. 44

Nos. 1–5, 1764–1797, are acts relating to Canada.

C.O. 45

Nos. 1–3, 1764–1780, contain the minutes of the Quebec Council.

C.O. 47

Nos. 84–108, 1764, are composed of declarations about Canadian paper money.

No. 109, 1770, carries a list of Canadian lands held in *roture*.

No. 110, 1773, is concerned with a "Code of Laws, Civil and Criminal, for the Province of Quebec" considered in five headings.

DOMINICA

C.O. 71

Dominica was one of the so-called neutralized islands of the West Indies in the contest between the British and French. By the Peace of 1763 it became a British possession.

No. 1, 1770–1778, is made up of original documents in the office of the Board of Trade, including letters from the governors concerned with the establishment of Dominica as a separate government.

No. 2, 1730–1801, is letters and other papers from Dominica to the Secretary of State. Among them is a description of the island in the 1770's with lists of proprietors of lands.

Nos. 3–7, 1770–1779, are other letters addressed to the Secretary of State.

C.O. 72

Nos. 1–3, 8, 1770–1801, are entry books, either of the Board of Trade or of the Secretary of State.

C.O. 73

Nos. 1–2, 5–8, 1768–1787, 1768–1803, 1768–1785, present acts passed for the government of Dominica.

C.O. 74

Nos. 1–5, 1767–1777, contain sessional papers of the Assembly of Dominica.

C.O. 76

No. 4, 1763–1791, is shipping returns. It had been hoped that when Parliament passed the "free ports" act of 1766 that Dominica would become a great international trading centre. This did not happen.

No. 9, 1765–1766, 1772, gives an account of the sale of lands in the island with a registration of privately-owned and Crown lands.

EAST INDIES

C.O. 77

While most of the manuscripts that relate to India are in the India Office Library, among the papers in the Colonial Office is the series called "Original Correspondence," together with entry books, etc., in 66 volumes, which covers the period from 1570 to 1856.

GIBRALTAR

C.O. 91

Here is the series "Original Correspondence" in 513 volumes, concerned with the period 1705–1940. Likewise, *C.O. 95* relates to Gibraltar under the heading "Miscellanea," in 123+ volumes, and covers the years 1704–1940+.

GOLD COAST

C.O. 96

The manuscripts in this series cover the years 1753 to 1756 and from 1843 to 1940 and are in 769 volumes. The earlier volumes are concerned with the activities of Company of Merchants Trading to Africa, which took the place of Royal African Company by act of Parliament in 1750.

GRENADA

The island of Grenada became a French possession in the seventeenth century. It was well populated by the middle of the next century and prospered by the growing of cocoa, coffee, and cotton. In the course of the Great War for the Empire it was captured by the British and retained as a possession at the Peace of 1763. The following classes of papers are important for developments respecting the island for the years 1748–1776.

C.O. 101

Nos. 1–7, 1763–1778, comprise original correspondence of the governors to the Board of Trade.

No. 8, 1743–1812, is made up of miscellaneous papers including those relating to land sales, 1764; Governor Edward Matthew's instructions; and some papers relating to the 4½ per cent export tax.

Nos. 9–24, 1762–1782, contain letters from the governors of Grenada to the Secretary of State.

C.O. 102

Nos. 1–3, 1763–1783, are the Board of Trade entry books of papers relating to Grenada.

Nos. 4–8, 1766–1781 are the entry books of letters received by the Secretary of State.

Nos. 14–15, 1767–1781, are the entry books of letters sent by the Secretary of State to Grenada.

C.O. 103

Nos. 1–6, 1766–1785, embody acts of the Grenada Assembly.

C.O. 104

Nos. 1–5, 1766–1776, bring together sessional papers of the Grenada Assembly.

C.O. 106

No. 1, 1764–1767, contains Grenada shipping returns.

Nos. 9–12, 1764–1797, are concerned with the sale of lands in the island and with the transfer of much of the land from the French inhabitants to the British.

GUADELOUPE

The island was captured by the British in the course of the Great War for the Empire but was returned to France in the Peace of 1763.

C.O. 110

Nos. 1–3, 1758–1794, are composed of letters to the Secretary of State, most of them falling within the years 1758–1763. Many of them are not only concerned with Guadeloupe but also relate to Antigua, Martinique, and St. Eustatius.

HAVANA

C.O. 117

No. 1, 1762–1763, embodies papers relating to the capture of Havana by the British in 1762 and its return the following year in the peace treaty.

HONDURAS

C.O. 123

The British had long been interested in exploiting the logwood about the Gulf of Honduras and also had developed an interest in the Mosquito Shore to the southward.

No. 1, 1744–1766, is composed of miscellaneous papers relating to the area.

HUDSON BAY

C.O. 134

No. 3, 1696–1759, has few documents concerned with the years 1748–1776. Two, however, are pertinent: one setting forth the Hudson's Bay Company's claims, 1755, under its patent, and another stating the position of the Board of Trade with respect to these claims, 1759.

JAMAICA

The island of Jamaica was the most important British possession in the West Indies during the period 1748–1776. The following classes of documents relating to it bear upon the period:

C.O. 137

Nos. 2–40, 1689–1782, contain letters with enclosures from the governors to the Board of Trade.

Nos. 41–43, 1702–1753, are abstracts of letters relating to Jamaica in the Board of Trade office.

Nos. 44–50, 1689–1821, are miscellaneous documents in the office of the Secretary of State relating to Jamaica.

Nos. 51–83, 1689–1783, are letters with enclosures from the governors to the Secretary of State of the Southern Department and later the Secretary of State for the Colonies. Most of this material falls in a period previous to or subsequent to 1748–1776.

C.O. 138

Nos. 7–25, 1690–1782, are entry books in the office of the Board of Trade concerning Jamaica.

Nos. 26–29, 1766–1782, are entry books of letters addressed to the Secretary of State relating to Jamaica.

No. 40, 1768–1785, is entry books of letters, mostly to the governors, from the Secretary of State for the Colonies.

C.O. 139

Nos. 9–38, 1695–1783, contain the acts of the Assembly of Jamaica.

C.O. 140

Nos. 1–66, 1661–1783, are Jamaica Assembly sessional papers.

C.O. 142

Nos. 13–22, 1680–1807, are shipping returns for the island.

No. 31, 1754, provides a list of landholders with the holdings of each of them.

LEEWARD ISLANDS

The Leeward Islands—Antigua, St. Christopher, Nevis, Montserrat, with smaller islands—came under English control in the seventeenth century and, as in the case of Barbados, concentrated largely on the production of sugar. During the period under consideration there was one Assembly for all the islands. The classes of documents concerned with the period 1748–1776 are as follows:

C.O. 152

Nos. 1–35, 1691–1782, are made up of original correspondence addressed to the Board of Trade relating to the Leewards.

No. 36, 1704–1752, has abstracts of letters to the Board of Trade office concerning the islands.

Nos. 40–63, 1721–1751, 1754–1784, are letters to the Secretary of State, chiefly from the governors. *No. 55* contains letters from both Gov. Sir Ralph Payne and his successor, Gov. William Burt, with contrasting views by the latter of the influence of the American revolutionary movement in 1775 upon the islands.

C.O. 153

Nos. 4–21, 1689–1781, are the Board of Trade entry books relating to the Leewards.

Nos. 22–25, 1766–1782, are entry books of letters to the Secretary of State.

C.O. 154

Nos. 1–6, 1644–1758, contain acts of the Assembly of the islands.

C.O. 155

Nos. 3–8, 1704–1775, are session papers relating to the work of the Assembly.

C.O. 157

No. 1, 1683–1787, contains shipping returns from the islands in the Board of Trade office.

MARTINIQUE

As was true of Guadeloupe, the French island of Martinique fell to the British in the course of the Great War for the Empire, only to be returned by the terms of the Peace of Paris, 1763.

C.O. 166

No. 1, 1693–1814, has miscellaneous papers relating to Martinique, two of which are of particular interest for the period 1748–1776. One is a letter, March 23, 1762, about Fort Royal from the Treasury to the Lords Justices; the other, Aug. 8, 1762, has to do with the purchase of timber for the French king.

No. 2, 1761–1763, contains correspondence respecting Martinique with the Secretary of State, chiefly relating to the conquest of the island in 1762.

C.O. 174

No. 1, 1711–1802, has original correspondence and entry books relating to the island in 21 volumes.

MONTSERRAT

As was true of Antigua, so Montserrat of the Leeward Islands is dealt with not only as one of the islands taken as a group but also separately. It was not nearly so important as were Antigua and St. Christopher, but its prosperity lay with the sugar plantations as was true of the other Leewards. During the period under consideration a large part of its population was Roman Catholic.

C.O. 175

No. 1, 1726–1787, contains miscellaneous material, little of which is of value for the years 1748–1776.

C.O. 177

Nos. 4–15, 1729–1780, are sessional papers relating to the island in the office of the Board of Trade.

NEVIS

Nevis was another small island of the Leeward group but larger than Montserrat.

C.O. 184

No. 1, 1703–1787, is made up of miscellaneous papers with little of importance for the period 1748–1776.

C.O. 185

Nos. 3–7, 1699–1799, contain acts of the Assembly.

C.O. 186

Nos. 1–8, 1721–1781, are Nevis sessional papers in the Board of Trade office.

NEWFOUNDLAND

This great island was not supposed to be a colony but rather a Crown possession, with the governor appearing late in the spring and returning to England in the fall. As such the British government dealt with it during the period under review, although it had actually become a colony. Its importance lay of course in its fisheries. The following classes of documents bearing upon it are of special interest:

C.O. 194

Nos. 1–20, 1696–1782, contain original correspondence with the Board of Trade from the part-time governor of the island and others. The letters deal with many things: the provisioning of the island, chiefly from the New England colonies; the carrying off to New England of seamen and fishermen; and the activities of the missionaries of the Moravian church on Newfoundland and elsewhere.

No. 21, 1730–1793, comprises a large number of miscellaneous papers, few of which relate to the period 1748–1776. Among those that do, a report on the state of the French cod fisheries, 1769–1774, is important. There are also printed lists indicating the state of the cod fisheries for certain years between 1699–1792. In addition to these lists, there is a document giving a comparative view of British fisheries off Newfoundland, 1763–1791.

Nos. 24–35, 1706–1752, 1762–1784, contain letters from the Newfoundland governors to the Secretary of State.

No. 41, 1771–1798, is a copy of a grant of Newfoundland land to a Mrs. Ann Williams in 1771.

C.O. 195

Nos. 2–10, 1678–1781, are Board of Trade entry books for Newfoundland.

Nos. 12–13, 1767–1782, are entry books of letters to the Secretary of State, many of them from governors of the island.

C.O. 199

No. 17, 1772–1773, is an elaborate account of the manner of carrying on the Newfoundland fisheries under royal instructions.

No. 18, 1715–1806, is largely concerned with various returns of possessions of the great fishery area in the district of Conception Bay.

NOVA SCOTIA AND CAPE BRETON ISLAND

Before 1713, Acadia—the area comprised roughly within the bounds of Nova Scotia—had been planted and governed by the French; it then passed into the hands of the British. While a British garrison was stationed on the Bay of Fundy at old French Port Royal, thereupon named Annapolis Royal, it was otherwise peopled with Acadians. Not until 1749, when Halifax was founded and made into a stronghold, did British and other European colonists make settlements along the eastern shore of the colony. There also took place a great influx of New Englanders after 1763. The following classes of documents have a bearing on Nova Scotia for the period 1748–1776:

C.O. 217

Nos. 1–29, 1711–1782, provide original correspondence by the governors and others with the Board of Trade, respecting Nova Scotia.

No. 30, 1713–1754, consists of Board of Trade abstracts of letters regarding Nova Scotian affairs.

Nos. 31–40, 1710–1752, contain many miscellaneous papers together with letters, many with enclosures, addressed to the Secretary of State for the Southern Department, mostly from the governors of the colony.

Nos. 43–57, 1762–1784, comprise additional letters with enclosures, from the governors to the Secretary of State.

No. 103, 1744–1800, is made up of documents relating to Cape Breton, located off the coast of Nova Scotia. Called by the French "Ile Royale," it was colonized by them and on it was constructed the great fortress of Louisbourg. In 1763 the island was ceded to Great Britian and became a part of Nova Scotia.

C.O. 218

Nos. 1–8, 1710–1782, are Board of Trade entry books concerning Nova Scotia.

Nos. 17–19, 1766–1782, contain entry books of letters relating to Nova Scotia received by the Secretary of State.

No. 25, 1768–1786, is the entry book of letters sent by the Secretary of State relating to Nova Scotia.

C.O. 219

Nos. 3–17, 1749–1787, are acts of the government of the province. It should be mentioned that between 1749, when Halifax was established, and 1758 all local legislation came from the Nova Scotia Council. Thereafter, with the creation of an Assembly, Nova Scotia became a typical royal province.

C.O. 221

Nos. 28–31, 1730–1765, are made up of Nova Scotia shipping returns.

No. 36, 1748–1749, is lists of emigrants, arranged alphabetically, who came to help make Nova Scotia a real British colony.

No. 37, 1755, is a printed copy of *The Memorials of the English and French*

Commissaries concerning the Limits of Nova Scotia or Acadia (London, 1755).

No. 38 contains undated papers relating to the proposed sale of Nova Scotia lands; a very interesting manuscript.

PRINCE EDWARD ISLAND (ST. JOHN)

Prince Edward Island, an island of great fertility, was colonized by the French under the name Île St. Jean. When ceded to Great Britain in 1763, it retained the name St. John and until 1769 was a part of Nova Scotia, at which time it was made a separate province. Its name was changed to Prince Edward Island in 1798 in honour of the Duke of Kent, who was commander of the British forces in North America, and also on account of the many names of St. John in the area. The classes of documents relating to the island are as follows:

C.O. 226

Nos. 1–2, 1769–1782, comprise correspondence from the governors to the Board of Trade.

No. 3, 1772–1818, contains miscellaneous documents, chiefly beyond the period 1776.

Nos. 4–8, 1769–1785, embody letters addressed to the Secretary of State for the Colonies from governors of the island and others.

C.O. 227

No. 1, 1769–1793, is the Board of Trade's entry book relating to St. John (Prince Edward Island).

No. 2, 1769–1781, contains the Secretary of State's entry books of letters received.

No. 3 is an undated entry book of instructions.

C.O. 228

No. 1, 1770–1781, is made up of acts passed by the Assembly of the island.

C.O. 229

Nos. 1–2, 1770–1781, are the St. John sessional papers.

ST. CHRISTOPHER

With respect to St. Christopher, another of the prosperous, sugar-producing Leeward Islands group of the West Indies, the following classes of documents bear upon the period 1748–1776:

C.O. 239

No. 1, 1702–1812, is made up of miscellaneous papers, none of them of particular importance for the period under examination.

C.O. 240

Nos. 1–13, 1701–1781, contain acts of the Leeward Islands Assembly relating to St. Christopher.

C.O. 241

Nos. 1–18, 1685–1786, embody sessional papers of the government of the island.

ST. LUCIA

Claimed by both the British and the French, St. Lucia was recognized in 1748 as a "neutral island." Colonized by the French in 1762 it was captured by the British but in the Peace of Paris of 1763 was restored to France. A well-populated island it was captured again by the British in 1778, but in 1783 was returned to France. It continued to seesaw in control until in 1814 it was finally ceded to Great Britain.

C.O. 253

No. 1, 1709–1798, contains miscellaneous St. Lucia papers, with only a few concerned with the period 1748–1776.

C.O. 258

No. 4, 1775, is *Memorials of the English and French Commissioners Concerning St. Lucia.*

ST. VINCENT

Before 1763 St. Vincent, one of the Windward West Indian islands, was a "neutral" island; with the Peace of Paris it became a British possession. It was the only one of these islands still populated in the middle of the eighteenth century by a large number of Caribs. The following classes of documents have relation to the period 1748–1776:

C.O. 260

Nos. 1–2, 1773–1779, contain original correspondence of the governor with the Board of Trade.

No. 3, 1668–1812, is made up of miscellaneous papers, the more important of which are much earlier or later than the period under review.

C.O. 262

Nos. 1–3, 1768–1777, contain acts of the St. Vincent Assembly, which came into existence in 1767.

C.O. 263

Nos. 1–3, 1769–1788, are made up of St. Vincent sessional papers.

SIERRA LEONE

The area of Sierra Leone was and is inhabited by various tribes or groups of Negroes. Soon after the Royal African Company was created by letters patent in 1672 it took over Bance Island at the mouth of the Sierra Leone estuary, where it built a fort and also established itself on Banana Islands. The slave trade was its chief economic activity in this region.

C.O. 267–268

In *C.O. 267* is to be found the original correspondence relating to Sierra Leone covering the years 1664–1940, which is in 677 volumes. This involves not only Sierra Leone but also Senegambia, Cape Coast Castle, Gambia, and the Gold Coast. As for the Gold Coast it has in *C.O. 96* already been dealt with for the brief period 1753–1756. *C.O. 268* contains the entry books, 1672–1872, in 57 volumes.

TOBAGO

As was true of Dominica, St. Lucia, and St. Vincent of the Windward Islands, Tobago was also before 1763 a "neutral" island in the Anglo-French contest despite its habitation by French settlers. Its development was slow. From 1763 to 1768 it was politically attached to Grenada, although a lieutenant governor was appointed for it in 1764; in 1767 a Council was created for it and in 1768, an Assembly. The following classes of documents among the Colonial Office papers have a bearing upon the island for the years 1748–1776:

C.O. 285

No. 2, 1700–1808, is made up of miscellaneous papers with few of these of importance for the period under review.

C.O. 287

No. 1, 1768–1781, contains the acts of the Tobago Assembly.

C.O. 288

Nos. 1–3, 1768–1780, are made up of sessional papers.

VIRGIN ISLANDS

In 1666 the English established themselves on the island of Tortola where they have remained.

C.O. 314

No. 1, 1711–1791, is made up of miscellaneous papers. Chiefly concerned in the rivalry of Great Britain and France for the control of the Virgin Islands, with little relevant material covering 1748–1776.

C.O. 315

No. 1, 1774–1788, contains acts relating to Tortola.

C.O. 316

No. 1, 1773–1780, contains Virgin Islands sessional papers.

WEST INDIES

Among the Colonial Office papers, many of the West Indian islands are listed separately as has been indicated. There are, however, several classes which treat the British West Indies as a whole. The following class relates to the period 1748–1776:

C.O. 318

Nos. 1–2, 1624–1808, are commonplace books with comments and statistical tables regarding trade. *No. 2* is of especial interest with much in the way of vital statistics, but is chiefly well beyond the year 1776.

Nos. 3–10, 1699–1785, are miscellaneous papers, few of which have any direct bearing upon the years 1748–1776.

PLANTATIONS GENERAL

Following the classification of documents among the Colonial Office papers there now appears a still broader classification than the British West Indies by bringing under survey all the colonies under the heading

Plantations General. The following classes have relation to the years 1748–1776:

C.O. 323

Nos. 1–29, 1689–1780. Original papers. It should be noted that this portion of the important class of documents was transcribed for the Historical Society of Pennsylvania and is available in its library. The papers listed below have relevance to the period under examination. *No. 19, 1764–1766,* is concerned with colonial currency, doubtless occasioned in connection with the passage of the Currency Act of 1764. *No. 20, 1764,* contains reports from colonial governors and the two superintendents of Indian affairs about the management of relations with the Indians. *Nos. 21–22, 1765–1766,* have to do with applications for lands in North America. *No. 23, 1764–1766,* contains reports from the superintendents of Indian affairs in North America, connected with the great Indian uprising of 1764.

No. 30, 1764–1766, brings together in an entry book letters from the Secretary of State to the Board of Trade, with copies of letters from colonial officials.

Nos. 31–33, 1756–1759, contain abstracts of letters by the Board of Trade pertaining to all the North American colonies, as well as Newfoundland, and the British West Indies during these war years.

C.O. 324

Nos. 6–19, 1696–1782, are Board of Trade entry books relating to the colonies.

No. 21, 1702–1782, embraces a number of important documents relating to the colonies and Great Britain's claims in the New World: (1) Memoirs, both English and French, on their respective rights to the island of St. Lucia, 1751; (2) Draft of the Proclamation of 1763 with additions and erasures; (3) Draft of other letters relating to Indian policy, to surveys of land, and to fees of office; (4) A letter to the Superintendent of Indian Affairs, 1764; (5) A report on Indian affairs, 1768; (6) Regrants of mines in the Lake Superior area, 1769, 1771; (7) Petition of John Stuart, Superintendent of Indian Affairs for the Southern District, to be made councillor extraordinary, 1769; (8) Reports sent by Maj. Robert Rogers, 1772, and William Gerard de Brahm, surveyor for the Southern District, 1774; (9) Many letters from John Pownall, Secretary to the Board of Trade, to Richard Jackson, the Board's legal adviser; (10) Letters sent by the Board of Trade to colonial governors, 1744–1752.

No. 38, 1749–1760, contains: (1) Instructions and letters to Governors Edward Cornwallis of Nova Scotia, Robert Dinwiddie of Virginia, Francis Bernard of New Jersey and (from 1760) of Massachusetts Bay, and Henry Ellis of Georgia; (2) An order for the exchange of Indian prisoners in America; (3) Orders determining the rank of regular officers upon serving with provincial forces in America; (4) A warrant settling the question of military rank of provincial officers in the armed forces; (5) Letters relating to the surrender of islands, etc.; (6) Letters to Governor Glen of South Carolina respecting presents to the Indians; (7) Letters having to do with the case of the Rev. Mr. Bosomworth of Georgia; (8) An order in council of March 11, 1752; (9) The case of the Spanish ship *St. Joseph and St. Helena* brought into Connecticut waters; (10) Military commissions to Generals Loudoun, Abercromby, Webb, and William Johnson.

No. 39, 1759–1763, contains instructions to Gov. Arthur Dobbs of North Carolina and to Lieut.-Gov. Francis Fauquier of Virginia.

No. 40, 1760–1764, is concerned with a variety of matters, among them the following: (1) Commissions, instructions, warrants, and letters to civilian and military officials serving in America, among them Sir Jeffrey Amherst of Virginia, William Henry Lyttelton of South Carolina, and Arthur Dobbs of North Carolina; (2) Particular instructions relating to the dispute between Pennsylvania and Connecticut over lands in the Wyoming Valley in northern Pennsylvania; (3) Particular instructions to Governor Bernard pertaining to the Acadians in Massachusetts Bay; (4) Warrants authorizing the erection of courts of vice-admiralty in Quebec, East and West Florida, and Grenada in the West Indies; (5) Particular instructions for altering the boundary of Georgia; (6) Official report on the Cardigan claims to the islands of St. Lucia and St. Vincent.

No. 41, 1764–1768, includes: (1) A warrant for the creation of a court of Vice-Admiralty for all North America; (2) Letter from the office of Postmaster General regarding postal service in America; and (3) Warrants of appointments and the additional instructions.

No. 42, 1768–1772, is concerned largely with the work of the newly-appointed Secretary of State for the Colonies, the Earl of Hillsborough, and touches on a variety of matters, such as: (1) Appointments to office in America, both civilian and military; (2) Warrants replacing the single court of vice-admiralty for all America with district courts of vice-admiralty; (3) Warrant for General Gage to succeed General Amherst as colonel-in-chief of the Royal American Regiment; (4) Warrant to John Henry to engrave a new map of Virginia; (5) Warrant for supplying bedding for companies serving in North America and Newfoundland;

(6) Warrant for the creation of a court of inquiry about the burning of the *Gaspee;* (7) Warrant appointing John Stuart of the southern Indian district as councillor extraordinary in the southern provinces of America; (8) Warrant for incorporating a company to exploit the copper mines near Lake Superior; (9) Warrants for making of various grants of land; (10) Commission to Elias Durnford to be lieutenant-governor of West Florida.

No. 43, 1773–1777, is concerned with the crisis in America and contains many War Office notifications, commissions, and orders.

No. 48, 1706–1770, comprises lists of councillors appointed for all the royal colonies.

Nos. 49–53, 1714–1782, are Board of Trade entry books of letters patent, warrants, affidavits, grants, and licenses relating to America.

No. 54, 1750–1771, is divided into seven groups all of which refer to grants of land in America: (1) Nova Scotia grants, 1750–1760, 1765–1767; (2) Copies of patents for all lands granted in the Province of Quebec between May 20 and Nov. 5, 1767; (3) North Carolina land patents granted Nov. 30, 1770; (4) South Carolina land grants between May and Oct. 1771; (5) East Florida land grants, 1765–1767; (6) The grant of townships of Massachusetts Bay in 1764 in the territory of "Sagadahoc"; (7) Three lists of patents to land made in Virginia during the years 1752–1765.

Nos. 55–56, 1740–1761, contain lists of persons "that have intituled themselves to the Benefit of the Act, 13 George II., for Naturalizing such Foreign Protestants and others as are settled or shall settle in any of His Majesty's Colonies in America." These lists, arranged by colonies, include each applicant's religion.

Nos. 57–58, 1741–1766, contain some documents that should be noted: (1) Commission to Samuel Holland to be surveyor of land in the Northern District, March 6, 1764; (2) List of colonial governors; (3) Warrant to Robert Monckton to be lieutenant governor of Annapolis Royal; (4) Warrants to the postmaster generals in England and Ireland to open letters at the London and Dublin post-offices and to have suspected and dangerous matters in them copied and sent to the Secretary of State.

No. 60, 1703–1782, is a Board of Trade entry book devoted to the appointment of agents by the colonies to represent their interests in London. The list is incomplete and names of agents appointed by New York, Pennsylvania, the Lower Counties on the Delaware, Maryland, East Florida, and the Bermudas do not appear.

C.O. 325

No. 1, 1753–1758, is made up of the following miscellaneous manuscripts, some of very considerable interest: (1) A narrative concerning events on the Ohio, 1753; (2) Papers regarding the Albany Congress, 1754; (3) An account of Gov. Shirley's two Indian conferences in Maine, 1754; (4) A copy of secret instructions given to Vice-Admiral Boscawen, 1755; (5) A journal dating from the surrender of Quebec, Sept. 18, 1759 to May 16, 1760, prepared by H. T. Cramahé; (6) Abstracts from two letters written by Montcalm to M. Berryer, Minister of Marine, April 1757 and Oct. 1758, and a third to M. de Molé, President of the Parlement of Paris, Aug. 1759; (7) The costs of administering Nova Scotia and the means of meeting them, 1768; (8) The Board of Trade on the new acquisitions in America, June 1763; (9) A paper on the Indian trade; (10) A document concerning the contract between the Royal Havannah Company and certain British subjects involving slaves and flour, 1763; (11) A Board of Trade representation regarding the appointment of colonial London agents, 1768; (12) A description of the island of Cape Breton agreeable to the orders of the Board of Trade; (13) Captain Hugh Debbieg's memorial respecting a general military survey of North America, 1766.

No. 2, 1744–1770, is also composed of miscellaneous documents. Among these are the following: (1) Extract of a letter from Gov. Hutchinson, Oct. 23, 1772, enclosing two papers relating to the claims of Massachusetts Bay to lands between the Kennebec and St. Croix rivers; (2) Two memorials respecting trade by British subjects under flags of truce with the French of Hispaniola, 1760; also a plan of the coast of Hispaniola between Cap François and Monte Christi, 1761; (3) Three papers relating to the Mosquito Shore in Central America, especially the one by Joseph Smith Speer; (4) A Board of Trade representation as to Great Britain's right to Turks Island, Aug. 15, 1764; (5) A French account of the Spanish island of Trinidad with a map of the island; (6) A statement about the defunct Royal African Company, after 1752; (7) John Pownall to the Earl of Suffolk about the African disputes, n.d.; (8) A paper, July 12, 1774, on the benefits of the island of St. Vincent; (9) Explanation for the appointment of a provost marshal in the province of New York; (10) A state of the government of Massachusetts Bay in 1757.

No. 5, 1764, comprises returns of fees of offices, collected by colonial governors and arranged by colonies.

THE BOARD OF TRADE

C.O. 326

Nos. 11–13, 1703–1759, make up a register of papers regarding trade. Nos. 16–74, 1703–1782, comprise additional and much more detailed registers of the Board of Trade papers relating to the colonies and possessions in America. The following volumes include the period 1748–1776: *No. 16*, North Carolina, 1730–1759; *Nos. 17–18*, South Carolina, 1720–1758; *No. 19*, Georgia, 1752–1758; *Nos. 22–23*, New England, 1731–1759; *No. 24*, New Hampshire, 1741–1758; *Nos. 25–26*, New Jersey, 1702–1758; *Nos. 28–29*, New York, 1737–1758; *No. 30*, Proprieties, 1704–1757; *Nos. 31–32*, Virginia, 1704–1759; *No. 33*, the Bahamas, 1717–1759; *No. 35*, Barbados, 1731–1759; *Nos. 36–37*, the Bermudas, 1703–1759; *Nos. 40–41*, Jamaica, 1734–1759; *No. 44*, the Leeward Islands, 1744–1759; *Nos. 45–46*, Newfoundland, 1703–1758; *Nos. 47–48*, Nova Scotia, 1712–1758; *Nos. 49–50*, Plantations General, 1704–1757; *No. 51*, Miscellaneous, 1696–1759; *Nos. 52–74*, 1759–1782, entitled Colonies General, bring the colonies together with a volume allotted to each year.

(B O A R D   O F   T R A D E ,   C O M M E R C I A L)

C.O. 388

No. 45, Dd, 1750–1753, embodies a computation of the Negroes required in the American plantations and other papers connected with the Company of Merchants Trading to Africa. In this volume there are also papers relating to Rhode Island, Labrador, Hudson Bay, Moravian activities, and woollen manufactures.

Nos. 46, Ee to *58, Qq*, 1754–1772. Although each volume is chiefly concerned with the African trade, other references to important matters are also included. *No. 46*, 1754–1755, also deals with customs frauds at New Castle, in the Lower Counties on the Delaware and in Pennsylvania, 1753, and gives printed instructions to colonial customs collectors; *No. 47*, 1755–1757, brings in the East India Company and illicit trade involving Ireland and the colonies; *No. 48*, 1758–1760, refers to the Levant Company and to the Hudson's Bay Company; *Nos. 49–50*, 1760–1763, deal with trade to Russia and illicit trade at Quebec; *No. 51*, 1763–1764, includes petitions from New England merchants for the free importation into England of whale fins, also hatmakers' petitions; *No. 52*, 1764–1765, throws light on the relations of Ireland with the plantations; it also deals with a Russian commercial treaty and with the East India Company and the Levant Company; there are also memorials from English weavers and others; *No. 53*, 1765–1766, while carrying forward an account of the African trade, is, in fact, largely concerned with the trade dispute with Portugal, which dispute is also continued in *No. 54;* there are likewise some papers relating to Ireland as well as reports respecting colonial trade with the continent of Europe; *No. 54*, 1766–1767, in addition, gives figures respecting the Hamburg trade and throws light on the English herring fishery and also relations with Tripoli; *No. 55, 1767–1768,* also gives information that a Dresden manufacturer of cambrics desires to establish a manufactory of this fabric in America; *No. 56, 1762–1769,* has tables relating to the West India trade and contains a letter of Henry Eustace McCulloh, 1769, regarding naval stores; *No. 57, 1769–1770,* embodies statistics with reference to the St. Petersburg trade and many memorials against reducing the bounty on American naval stores; *No. 58, 1770–1772,* is concerned with the British whale fishery, has more memorials about naval stores, and includes a letter from Copenhagen about an order issued there with reference to American trade.

Nos. 59, Rr to 74, Bbb, 1773–1782, are largely concerned with orders in council issued during the period of the crisis with the Thirteen Colonies, indicating restrictions placed on trade, with permission granted in favour of some colonies against others.

Nos. 75–84, 1696–1782, are largely concerned with the quarterly expense accounts rendered by the Board of Trade to the Treasury, but *No. 76* has papers on the German Palatines.

No. 95, 1765–1766, is made up of consular commercial reports in reply to Secretary of State Halifax's request on Jan. 18, 1765 for information. Reports are recorded from the following places: Barcelona, Copenhagen, Danzig, Hamburg, Leghorn, Lisbon, Madeira, Messina, Narva, Nice, Ostend, Port Mahon, Riga, Rotterdam, St. Petersburg, Seville, Smyrna, Tripoli and Venice. Some of these reports are extensive, such as those from Madeira and Smyrna; others are very brief, such as those from Nice with nothing to report and from Danzig with only complaints.

C.O. 389

Nos. 14–34, 1696–1782, are entry books of the Board of Trade. These provide information about conventions, treaties, patents, naval stores.

Nos. 36–39, 1696–1782, are expense accounts of the Board covering these years.

Nos. 54–58, 1714–1803, are also Board of Trade entry books concerning Gibraltar and Minorca.

C.O. 390

No. 4, 1662–1799, is concerned with excise duties and includes tables relating to them.

No. 9, 1725–1771, embodies the Custom House accounts of imports with rather full accounts of the imports of various materials particularly from North America mostly between 1760 and 1771. Here also are to be found drawbacks on the re-exportation to America from England of certain important articles, covering the years 1761–1772, the exports of goods to North America from Newfoundland, ships engaged in the whale fishery and the value of goods exported from England, 1768–1771.

No. 10, 1750–1766, is concerned with commercial relations with Spain during these years. One item is of especial interest. In 1764 there was re-exported from Great Britain to Spain 1,714,730 pounds of North American tobacco.

No. 11, 1714–1757, is an index to custom house accounts.

(BOARD OF TRADE JOURNAL)

C.O. 391

It is only necessary to point out that the journal is now in print and is an indispensable aid to the student.

The Treasury Board

We have already considered the records of the office of Lord High Chancellor, with those of the Privy Council, the Board of Trade, and the Secretaries of State—in so far as the activities of these royal officials related to the functioning of the British Empire during the period under examination. It is now necessary to turn to the agencies that were responsible for securing the revenues needed to support the state, for the disbursement of these revenues, and for auditing the accounts of all receipts and payments. Under the Tudors the earlier office of the King's Treasurer had become second in importance and trust only to that of Lord High Chancellor because of the financial control that he and those associated with him in this office exercised over public expenditures. Concerned as the Lord High Treasurer was with the larger aspects of financial affairs of the state, the detailed operation of the Exchequer fell to his subordinate, the Chancellor of the Exchequer, whose office in the course of time became a distinct one of great importance. With the coming of George I to the throne the great office of Lord High Treasurer was put "into commission," as the saying is, in 1714 and so continued. To take its place a board, known as the Lords Commissioners of the Treasury, was created, made up of the First Lord of the Treasury, the Chancellor of the Exchequer, and three other Lords of the Treasury. It may be added that the First Lord of the Treasury inherited much of the prestige of the Lord High Treasurer and usually wielded great power under the King in such matters as the disposal of the secret service money and in other ways. As a rule he was the King's chief minister. The Chancellor of the Exchequer prepared the budget which, after approval of the King's Cabinet Council, he was expected to defend when submitted to Parliament. Within the Exchequer were such divisions of accounting as the King's Remembrancer, the Lord Treasurer's Remembrancer, the Exchequer of Receipt, and the Audit Office. On the judicial side, there was a Court of Exchequer, one of the three great common law courts.

Between 1733 and 1847 the Treasury Chambers were located in an impressive building facing St. James Park and the Horse Guards Parade, and adjoining the Cockpit, which lay between it and the street leading from Charing Cross to Westminster. At the western end of Downing Street, connected with the Treasury by a passageway, was the home of the First Lord of the Treasury, occupied by Robert Walpole in 1731 and probably by his successors. This residence was remodelled about 1750 and continuous occupancy by the First Lord can be proved from Lord North's ministry in 1772 to the present time.

The Treasury papers for the period under consideration now rest in the Public Record Office. Charles M. Andrews in his *Guide,* II, 66–107, 136–269, gives a very full account of them which will be followed in so far as it is applicable to the years 1748–1776. It seems desirable, however, to vary Andrews's order while still relying upon his listing. The papers will be considered as follows: (a) Treasury records, including the Treasury Solicitor papers, (b) The Exchequer and Audit Office papers, and (c) the Customs papers. In connection with the latter by reason of uncertainty respecting the actual location of many of these papers when Andrews prepared his *Guide,* it will be desirable to follow the Crick and Alman *Guide,* pp. 192–207. See, in addition, Giuseppi: *Guide,* II, 283–300; Virginia State Library: *The British Public Record Office,* pp. 272–4; and Public Record Office List, "T. 1: Treasury Board papers, 1557–1902," typescript in two volumes.

In this survey of Treasury papers it is logical to begin with requests made upon that department by other departments or agencies of the government or by private individuals and with the grounds for these requests. We, therefore, begin by considering the In-letters received by the Treasury Board.

IN-LETTERS

Treasury Board I.

T. *1,* 1557–1920, is a very large collection of documents, etc., of some 12,625 volumes, bundles, and boxes.

As these papers are in the main arranged chronologically they will be considered in that way in so far as they relate to the years 1748–1776. The year, the number of the bundle, and its contents are as follows:

1 7 4 8

No. 329. (1) Tobacco imports and exports and duties thereon; (2) Customs disputes in Barbados; (3) Memorial concerning Rhode Island bills of credit.

No. 330. (1) Henry McCulloh's petition respecting quit-rents; (2) Letter concerning Gov. Trelawny's financial expenditures on the Mosquito Shore; (3) Gov. Shirley's affidavit in regard to the brigantine *Boston Packet;* (4) Papers relating to money granted to Massachusetts Bay by Parliament for the capture of Louisbourg; (5) Horatio Walpole's report on the memorial of John Grymes of Virginia; (6) The report of the Attorney and Solicitor General on reimbursement payments to the colonies in the expedition against Cape Breton; (7) A petition of the people of Annapolis Royal, with many papers; (8) Account of the support of New England troops by inhabitants of Nova Scotia.

No. 331. Papers regarding the sugar plantations and the duty on molasses, etc.

No. 332. (1) A memorial from the creditors of the Royal African Company; (2) Proposals for preventing tobacco frauds; (3) An opinion of the Attorney and Solicitor on the matter of reimbursement of the New England colonies (see *No. 330*).

No. 333. (1) Papers concerned with reimbursement appropriations for Massachusetts Bay and New Hampshire; (2) Rhode Island's account of expenditures; (3) Respecting the account of Hugh Whitefoord connected with Lord Cathcart's West Indies expedition; (4) Governor Shirley to Secretary Pelham, Jan. 25; (5) About regiments in America; (6) Admiral Peter Warren's memorial with an account of expenditures at Louisbourg; (7) Concerning the collection of duties on strong liquors in Canada (in French); (8) Frauds in tobacco and other goods; (9) The Rattan island garrison; (10) Thomas Marriott's memorial; (11) John Catherwood's memorial relative to the proposed expedition against Canada.

1 7 4 9

No. 334. A few tobacco papers.

No. 335. (1) Letter from John Catherwood about the planned expedition against Canada, April 11; (2) Letter from Gov. B. Wentworth of New Hampshire, June 12; (3) Letter from John Thomlinson, agent for New Hampshire, regarding Massachusetts Bay and New

Hampshire financial claims, with other papers; (4) Shirley to the Duke of Bedford about Massachusetts currency; (5) The claim of Gov. Clinton of New York; (6) Col. Joseph Dwight's oath and bond; (7) Report on Eleazer Allen's accounts as receiver in North Carolina; (8) Virginia statistics, 1748–1749; (9) Georgia and Nova Scotia papers; (10) The appointment of Capt. Hodgson as governor of the Mosquito Shore; (11) Letter from Shirley, May 10, 1749.

No. 336 Victualling of Chebucto (Halifax, N.S.).

No. 337. (1) Orders regarding droits of admiralty; (2) Statement of the case of the Connecticut regiment; (3) The memorial regarding Joshua Pierce's ship taken by the French.

No. 338. Undated memorials and petitions, 1750–1800.

1 7 5 0

No. 340. (1) Expenses involved in transporting to Nova Scotia men once in the King's sea service; (2) Proposals for a British South American colony; (3) Christopher Kilby, agent for Nova Scotia, papers; (4) Papers relating to the memorial of John Roberts, joint receiver general of Virginia; (5) Accounts of expenditures of the colonies on the intended expedition against Canada, with letters and a memorial from John Thomlinson, Gov. Wentworth, and Gov. Shirley supporting these claims; (6) Instructions to David Dunbar, surveyor of the King's Woods in North America; (7) Secretary Harrington to the Treasury about additional troops for Nova Scotia; (8) Certificates for the transportation of criminals to America; (9) Excise Office report on coffee from St. Christopher and tea from Philadelphia; (10) Gov. Cornwallis writes that no customs officer is needed at Halifax, N.S., as the officer for Canso can reside at Halifax and watch Annapolis and Canso.

No. 341. (1) Account of the amounts of tobacco seized in British ports, 1732–1748; (2) The War Office establishment, 1750; (3) Report on Col. Hopson's memorial relating to the capture of Louisbourg; (4) Tobacco frauds.

No. 342. Two reports on Henry McCulloh's memorial.

No. 343. (1) About Lieut.-Col. Heron's Georgia accounts; (2) Memorial on behalf of Gov. George Clinton of New York; (3) Gov. Shirley's memorial; (4) William Pitt regarding the financial claims of the colonies, Aug. 30; (5) Memorial from Richard Partridge, agent for Rhode Island, April 9.

1 7 5 1

No. 344. Victualling lists, Halifax, 1751–1752.

No. 345. (1) St. John's and Placentia establishments; (2) Various war estimates; (3) Board of Trade to the Treasury as to Rhode Island's financial claims; (4) Nova Scotia's victualling.

No. 346. Memorial of Lieut.-Col. John Caulfield, commander of the Rattan garrison.

No. 347. (1) South Carolina quit-rents accounts, 1746–1751; (2) Letter of President Louis Burwell of the Virginia Council on the 2 shillings a hhd. export tax and on the application of the statute of Champerty (32 Henry VIII. 69) to Virginia; (3) Mosquito Shore accounts; (4) Memorial of Edward Holland, agent of Indian affairs, New York, Dec. 21, 1751.

1 7 5 2

No. 348. (1) The case of Charles MacNaire of South Carolina; (2) Petition of Peter Wraxall, agent of Indian affairs, Albany; (3) Report of the Board of Trade on Georgia silk culture accounts, Dec. 20, 1752; (4) The grant of Cornwallis Island to his sons by Gov. Cornwallis of Nova Scotia; (5) The Harman Verelst claims against Oglethorpe; (6) Gov. Dinwiddie's account of Virginia quit-rents and the 2 shillings per hhd. export tax, Dec. 10, 1752; (7) The Connecticut Mohegan Indian case papers; (8) The case of John Roberts, joint receiver of Virginia revenues; (9) Extract of letters from Gov. Lyttelton of South Carolina, Oct. 2, 1752.

No. 349. (1) Pennsylvania act regulating fees; (2) Regarding an escheated land case with papers and a petition from Craister Greatheed, St. Christopher, Sept. 21, 1752; (3) Petition of merchants trading to Virginia relating to the Spanish prize ship, *St. Juan Baptista,* that they bought and made free; (4) Customs commissioners' report relating to ships stranded on the Irish coast with enumerated goods on board.

No. 350. (1) Report on Gov. Trelawny's petition; (2) Memorial of Charles MacNaire, employed on an expedition to the Choctaw nation, Dec. 20, 1752; (3) Warrant for paying Henry McCulloh; (4) Memorial of the widow of Gabriel Johnston, late governor of North Carolina.

1 7 5 3

No. 351. (1) Memorial of merchants and others regarding the whale fishery; (2) Report by Auditor General Horatio Walpole on the Greatheed petition about land in St. Christopher; (3) Report on the request by Cecilius Calvert that arms for 300 men raised for the Canada expedition be replaced in the Maryland magazine; (4) MacNaire's memorial for money spent in arming the Choctaws against the French; (5) Order in Council about pay of judges in Virginia.

No. 352. (1) Report on tobacco smuggling; (2) Board of Trade request for report on Pennsylvania fees and customs, and on grants of land and quit-rents in Georgia.

No. 353. (1) Ordnance for Nova Scotia; (2) Petition of Benjamin Martyn respecting the money for the Georgia civil list; (3) Extract of law of Virginia regulating the governor's fee for signing land grants; (4) Statement of Carolina merchants about loss of revenue by converting tar into pitch in England; (5) Report of Board of Trade on the memorial of Gov. Osborn of New York about Indian presents; (6) Quit-rents in Nova Scotia; (7) Gov. Dinwiddie *re* the pistole fee.

No. 354. (1) Order in council concerning the charge that Andrew Stone, secretary to the Lords Justices, had drunk the health of the Pretender; (2) The Bishop of London on an allowance to the commissary of Virginia and of the appointment of Thomas Dawson to that post.

1 7 5 4

No. 355. (1) List of ships entering or leaving Annapolis, Maryland; (2) Gov. Arthur Dobbs of North Carolina on the need of small coins and on the number of white people in the province.

No. 356. (1) Disbursements for the Mosquito Shore; (2) Concerning the pay of American regiments; (3) Regarding Abraham Bosomworth's military and other services in Georgia; (4) Quit-rents in Virginia.

No. 358. (1) Memorial of Gov. Lyttelton of South Carolina about Indian relations; (2) About experiments in the making of potash in America; (3) Embezzlement in Jamaica by Deputy Receiver Hume; (4) Dinwiddie on the fee question; (5) William Bollan on the reimbursement of Massachusetts; (6) Bosomworth papers; (7) Christopher Kilby about expense for paying troops in North America.

1 7 5 5

No. 359. (1) Annapolis naval lists, 1754–1755; (2) Petition of Thomas Stephens for encouragement of colonial potashes.

No. 360. (1) Halifax naval lists; (2) Dinwiddie's commission to Peter Randolph and William Byrd, commissioners to the Catawba and Cherokee Indians; (3) Warrants drawn by General Shirley, 1755, with explanations; (4) List of ships ready to sail, with masters' requests to ship gunpowder; (5) Harman Verelst's plan for an American revenue by means of a stamp duty; (6) The Board of Trade to Dinwiddie on fees for patented lands; (7) Letter from Gov. Knowles of Jamaica about the protection of the Mosquito Shore against the Spaniards; (8) The case of the importers of whale fins; (9) Craister Greatheed's case involving St. Christopher escheated lands; (10) Ordnance for Nova Scotia; (11) Letter regarding Lord Baltimore's petition for importing salt into Maryland; (12) Papers concerning supplies furnished by Kilby and Baker for expeditions; (13) North Carolina quit-rents act; (14) Letters to and from the West Indies; (15) Thomas Bosomworth's petition relating to his Indian wife's lands and services; (16) Subsistence for forces in America provided by Thomlinson and Hanbury, 1754–1755; (17) Prices allowed for New England masts, etc.; (18) Answer of John Rutherford, receiver general of North Carolina, to charges against him, with Gov. Dobbs's explanation of the case; (19) Case of Francis Dalby, who had planned to sail to Madeira and then South Carolina for a cargo of rice.

No. 361. (1) Continuation of Craister Greatheed's case; (2) Letters concerning the packet service to New York; (3) Memorial of James Abercromby, agent for Virginia, and an address by the Council of Virginia; (4) An account of the Virginia 2 shillings a hhd. export duty; (5) Naval office lists of vessels clearing from Savannah with enumerated commodities; (6) The same for Annapolis, Maryland; (7) Letter from Gen. Braddock on the need for money before leaving Fort Cumberland, May 10; (8) Braddock's instructions to Shirley, April 16; (9) Comparison of prices for provisions in New York in 1755, 1756, 1759, and 1760; (10) The quit-rent act of North Carolina with Sir Matthew Lamb's report on it; (11) Case of French ships seized at Jamaica before a declaration of war.

No. 362. Accounts of money available "for His Majesty's Civil Government," including Georgia and Nova Scotia.

No. 363. Document relating to payment of forces in Nova Scotia.

1 7 5 6

No. 364. Army estimates of expenses.

No. 365. (1) Savannah naval office list; (2) Papers relating to General Shirley's warrants; (3) Concerning the distribution of £150,000 voted to the colonies by Parliament; (4) Letters from Lord Loudoun; (5) A proposal by Anthony Bacon for carrying provisions to America; (6) Papers on commercial affairs in Canada; (7) Contracts for furnishing provisions for armed forces in America; (8) An act for appointing a South Carolina agent; (9) Gov.

Benning Wentworth of New Hampshire receives bounty money; (10) List of papers concerning lands in the Bermudas; (11) Papers relating to trade between Milford Haven, Wales, and the colonies.

No. 366. (1) About Indian presents; (2) Letter from Thomas Pownall concerning American currency and payments in America; (3) Military contracts and estimates.

No. 367. (1) Copy of Gen. John Winslow's commission from Connecticut; (2) Papers concerning Shirley's accounts; (3) Gen. Winslow's papers; (4) Georgia establishment payments; (5) State of claims for money of several American colonies; (6) Shirley's accounts connected with the Niagara expedition; (7) Papers concerning French prizes in the West Indies; (8) Gov. Ellis's memorial on the state of the colonies; (9) Order in council concerning Antigua barracks; (10) On the Stevens experiment with potash in Pennsylvania.

No. 368. (1) On the pay of foreign officers of the American regiment; (2) On the seizure of a ship in North Carolina waters; (3) Report on ordnance and stores supplied by various northern colonies for the Crown Point expedition in 1756; (4) The supply of gunpowder for Virginia and of carrying it out of Great Britain; (5) Letters from Loudoun and Abercromby to Gen. Winslow; (6) Gen. Winslow's petition for his pay with Shirley's instructions to him; (7) Hessian papers.

No. 369. (1) Papers relating to Gen. Shirley's warrants and the payment of troops in America; (2) Memorial of Henry McCulloh about his salary and the payment of quit-rents on his lands; (3) Halifax, N.S. naval office lists.

No. 370. (1) Account of money raised by South Carolina for the King's services, 1756–1757; (2) Account of provisions sent to America (Canada) for 10,000 men for 13 months; (3) Account of provisions furnished by Massachusetts for the Crown Point expedition and the resolution of that colony's Assembly about the pay of officers; (4) Order in council regarding the McCulloh petition, Oct. 13; (5) Dinwiddie's letters concerning the costs of the Ohio expedition, 1754–1755; (6) About the payment of salary of William Clifton, Georgia attorney general; (7) Draft of a provision contract; (8) Account of articles furnished for the Crown Point expedition by Rhode Island; (9) The 2 shillings per hhd. revenue in Virginia, with Dinwiddie's letter of June 11.

No. 371. (1) Numerous papers on ordnance and supplies for America; (2) Memorial of Commissaries Peter Van Brugh Livingston and Lewis Morris, Jr., regarding their services in the American campaigns; (3) Acount of English ships taken by the French before a declaration of war by way of reprisal for French ships taken.

Value of the English prizes taken from the French £65,000 and of the French prizes taken from the English £20,000.

1 7 5 7

No. 372. (1) War Office estimates; (2) Supply from Ireland of provisions for French settlements; (3) Virginia revenues and disbursements; (4) Virginia and North and South Carolina claims to money granted by Parliament; (5) Additional material on the Receiver General John Rutherford case in North Carolina; (6) Shirley's memorial respecting the difficulty over warrants; (7) The William Byrd and Peter Randolph memorial for compensation in the negotiations with the Indians; (8) Auditor General Robert Cholmondeley's report on North Carolina land grants; (9) Loudoun to Pitt, April 25, on the Shirley dispute; (10) Cholmondeley to Adm. Frankland claiming the right to audit all prize money cases; (11) Gov. Dobbs to the Board of Trade.

No. 374. (1) Annapolis, Md., naval office lists; (2) Nova Scotia victualling papers; (3) Numerous Hessian and Hanoverian papers.

No 375. (1) Complaints against James St. John, surveyor of South Carolina; (2) Hessian and Hanoverian supply papers.

No. 376. (1) Gen. Winlow's case; (2) Description of vessel built on Lake Ontario; (3) Letter of Samuel Waldo; (4) Affidavits relating to the Shirley case with letter of Spencer Phips; (5) James Wright, agent of South Carolina, on the colony's claim to a share of the £50,000 grant by Parliament; (6) Regarding crown lands in the Bermudas; (7) How Virginia, North Carolina, and South Carolina shared the £50,000 grant; Virginia quit-rents.

No. 377. (1) Barrington on the payment of troops in Nova Scotia; the matter referred to Parliament; (2) A memorial respecting the sale of French ships taken before a declaration of war; (3) Loudoun criticizes the claims of the colonies, May 3; (4) Shirley appeals to the Treasury in his own behalf; (5) The disposition of the £800,000 authorized by Parliament for military expenses with American claims; (6) The disposal of Connecticut's claim for victualling provincial troops; (7) A letter from Hanbury and Thomlinson relating to complaint against Sir William Johnson.

No. 378. (1) Gov. Dobb's proclamation against James Murray and John Rutherford for issuing notes to "pass current as money"; (2) An order in council on the exportation of corn from New York to St. Augustine; (3) Cholmondeley's claim to audit prize money upheld; (4) Shirley's memorial, with War Office letter.

No. 379. (1) The Admiralty and the payment of charges for transport service to the colonies; (2) Halifax, N.S., naval lists; (3) Colonial claims to money granted by Parliament; (4) Dinwiddie on the quit-rents and the 2 shillings a hhd. tax, as well as on the state of Virginia; (5) Currency rates in America and the transportation of money.

1 7 5 8

No. 380. (1) Naval supply contracts with allowances of provisions for each man; (2) Some custom house papers; (3) General James Abercromby gives James Abercromby, London agent, power of attorney for meeting the needs of the Royal America regiment; (4) New Hampshire and the Parliamentary grant; (5) The Privy Council's committee report on allowances to North Carolina councillors out of the quit-rents. (6) Pitt on the need of careening wharves at Halifax.

No. 381. (1) Barrington about the supply of rum to the Oswego garrison by Indian traders, as well as other War Office and Admiralty letters about the progress of the war; (2) Petition of Edward Dismore, postmaster general of Jamaica, 1754–1758; (3) Account of presents sent to the Mosquito Indians by Gov. Moore of Jamaica.

No. 382. (1) A letter concerning the charge that Boston collectors exact illegal fees and connive at illegal trade; (2) Many papers about Cholmondeley's right to audit prize money; (3) Hessian and other German papers; (4) Annapolis, Md., naval office lists and those of South Potomac; (5) The case of former governor of Georgia, John Reynolds, taken prisoner by the French, asking for reimbursement; (6) John Rutherford explains his conduct to Gov. Dobbs of North Carolina; (7) Memorial of Gov. Hopson of Nova Scotia; (8) Instructions to Gov. Popple of the Bermudas respecting the Crown lands there; (9) The Privy Council report on Henry McCulloh's petition; (10) Pay list of troops used to erect a fort on the Island of St. John (Prince Edward Island).

No. 387. (1) Papers concerning Lieut.-Col. Burgoyne's regiment; (2) Joseph Caruthers and the John Rutherford case; (3) Payment to Henry McCulloh authorized by order in council; (4) Memorial of Richard Cumberland, agent of Nova Scotia; (5) Halifax naval lists.

No. 388. (1) Expenses of Massachusetts connected with the King's service; (2) The claims of a number of colonies for reimbursement; (3) Regarding the collectorship at Piscataqua; (4) McCulloh's receipt for payment; (5) Memorial of Benjamin Martyn, agent of Georgia, for £1510 spent in Indian presents; (6) Abercromby's statement of the number of troops raised in each colony in 1758; (7) Gov. Reynolds on the expenses of the Georgia rangers; (8) Benjamin Franklin's memorial as agent of Pennsylvania with an account of expenses for the year 1758; (9) South Potomac naval lists; (10) Virginia's claim to a share of the £200,000 voted by Parliament to the colonies; (11) John Rutherford's petition to be restored to his post of receiver general of quit-rents in North Carolina; (12) General Winslow to Gov. Fitch of Connecticut; (13) The House of Commons resolutions, 1756–1768, regarding reimbursement of certain colonies and persons; (14) The Virginia revenue on the export of tobacco; (15) Various papers regarding the financial state of Massachusetts.

1 7 5 9

No. 389. (1) The favourable report of the Attorney General as to Cholmondeley's claim to audit prize money accounts; (2) Virginia's claim to money granted by Parliament to the colonies; (3) Many papers on the victualling and transport service connected with the American campaigns; (4) The state of the New Jersey debt; (5) Admiral Cotes regarding trading with the enemy at Monte Christi, and other papers; (6) Memorial of Brig. Forbes stating the problems that faced him in launching the expedition against Fort Duquesne, with a letter from Secretary at War Barrington; (7) Memorial from Virginia asking that the deficiencies in tobacco duties be made up out of the quit-rents; (8) Board of Trade regarding the bond given by Gov. James Hamilton of Pennsylvania.

No. 390. (1) Papers relating to the capture of Guadeloupe; (2) Memorial of the commissioners for the sale of French prizes taken before the declaration of war; (3) Treasury minutes (extract) relating to the case of Admirals Frankland and Cotes, 1759–1763.

No. 391. (1) Military estimates, including the colonies; (2) Annapolis naval lists; (3) The garrison at St. John (Prince Edward Island); (4) Cape Breton victualling lists.

No. 392. (1) Instructions for stamp distributors in England; (2) Important representation of the Commissioners of the Customs respecting abuses in the plantation trade; (3) Memorial of Thomas Chapman, receiver general and collector at Guadeloupe, with the Customs Board report, July 19.

No. 393. (1) Halifax naval office lists; (2) Georgia accounts and unpaid bills held by merchants in London covering military expenses; (3) Accounts of other colonies.

No. 394. (1) South Carolina claims for reimbursement of war expenses; (2) Papers relating to Louisbourg.

No. 395. Hessian papers.

No. 396. (1) Board of Trade representation on Indian presents; (2) Papers on victualling troops in Germany and America; (3) Board of Trade representation about illicit colonial trade with the enemy at Monte Christi; (4) De Lancey to Pitt, Aug. 10, with enclosures.

No. 397. (1) Cholmondeley on the Rutherford case; (2) Papers relating to Guadeloupe; (3) Pay lists for carpenters under Col. Meserve; (4) Agent Joseph Sherwood's memorial in behalf of Rhode Island; (5) Maryland's claim for reimbursement since 1754; (6) Massachusetts expenditures.

1 7 6 0

No. 398. Victualling and paymaster papers.

No. 400. Account of Gen. Forbes' expenses in 1758, with other papers concerned with colonial reimbursement.

1 7 6 1

No. 406. Victualling and army estimates.

No. 407. (1) Guadeloupe trade papers; (2) McCulloh on troubles in South Carolina, 1748–1760.

No. 408. (1) Gov. Boone of New Jersey on smuggling; (2) Papers relating to corruption charges against Collector Benjamin Barrons (Barons) at Boston.

No. 409. (1) Gov. Ellis of Georgia on the Creek Indians; (2) Bosomworth and the Georgia rangers; (3) Stores at Oswego.

No. 412 (1) Military expenses in New England; (2) The Boston fire.

1 7 6 2

No. 414. (1) Annapolis naval lists; (2) Officers victualled at Halifax and Quebec.

No. 415. Reimbursements to Massachusetts, Rhode Island, North Carolina, and South Carolina for expenses incurred in 1760; Boston merchants defend Barons.

No. 416. (1) Southern Indian affairs; (2) Halifax naval lists; (3) Plans for custom houses at Montreal and Martinique.

No. 418. (1) Value of exports from England to the colonies, 1740–1761; (2) The case of the salary of Chief Justice Pratt of New York.

No. 419. (1) New York provisions contracts; (2) South Carolina Indian relations; (3) Affairs in Manila.

No. 421. (1) Additional material on South Carolina Indian relations; (2) Quebec customs.

1 7 6 3

No. 423. (1) Quit-rents in the southern colonies; (2) Reimbursement of military expenses of the colonies; (3) Civil estimates for Georgia and Florida; (4) Smuggling in New York and the West Indies.

No. 424. French Protestants of South Carolina.

Nos. 425–426. Numerous papers on customs reforms in the American colonies.

1 7 6 4

No. 429. (1) The Molasses Act enforcement; (2) A projected court of vice-admiralty for all America; (3) John Temple's charges against both Collector Cockle at Salem and Gov. Bernard.

No. 430. (1) Papers on an American stamp act; (2) Customs receipts in American ports, 1764–1768.

No. 431. West Indian trade and customs.

No. 433. Tea smuggling from Holland and the Channel Islands.

No. 434. Calculations on the molasses duty.

No. 435. Annapolis naval lists.

1 7 6 5

No. 437. (1) Stamp Act riots; (2) Gov. Johnstone of West Florida discusses Spanish trade; (3) Gage correspondence from New York.

No. 439. The stamp distributors for the colonies.

No. 441. The Temple-Gov. Bernard dispute.

No. 442. (1) Letters from governors on illicit trade; (2) Canadian Indian affairs.

No. 443. On the Spanish bullion trade.

1 7 6 6

No. 445. (1) America and a tea tax; (2) Stamp distributors' reports.

No. 446. (1) Daniel Malcolm of Boston and smuggling; (2) Grey Cooper and the Stamp Act repeal debate.

No. 447. Papers in opposition to the Stamp Act.

No. 448. (1) The return of the stamped papers; (2) South Carolina Indian affairs.

Nos. 449–450. Mississippi Valley Indian affairs.

No. 452. Papers on Stamp Act riots and clearance of vessels without stamps.

No. 453. (1) On unstamped bonds, etc.; (2) Attorney General De Grey's opinion on enforcement of acts of trade; (3) The Boston Malcolm case.

No. 455. (1) The Yorke and De Grey opinion on the Spanish bullion trade; (2) Letters from stamp distributors.

1 7 6 7

No. 456. (1) Many letters from customs boards in London and Boston; (2) Major Robert Rogers and posts in the Great Lakes region; (3) West Florida papers.

No. 458. (1) More letters from stamp distributors; (2) Letters from Pensacola and Fort Cavendish.

No. 459. Plan for an American customs board.

No. 460. Papers on the Ceded Islands of Tobago, St. Vincent, Dominica, and Grenada.

No. 461. (1) About American Customs Board finances; (2) On Quebec affairs with letters from Gen. Carleton.

No. 462. (1) Proceeds from the Molasses Act during the years 1734–1764; (2) Proceeds from the Sugar Act of 1764; (3) Estimates of the War Office on the cost of maintaining the American colonies and the African posts, 1767–1768.

1 7 6 8

No. 463. (1) Enforcement of the trade acts with comments by De Grey and Dunning; (2) Victualling of troops in West Florida; (3) Roupell, searcher at Charleston, S.C., on vice-admiralty matters; (4) Canadian financial matters; (5) Memorial in behalf of Collector Lancelon Graves Berry of North Carolina; (6) John Mason's petition in behalf of the Mohegan Indians in Connecticut; (7) The case of the *Liberty* seized in Boston harbour; (8) Memorial of the Nova Scotia agent; (9) Memorial of Sir William Burnaby with reference to the entertainment of the Mortar King and other Indians at the Pensacola Indian congress; (10) Memorial of Richard Shuckburgh, New York secretary of Indian affairs; (11) Memorial regarding the expenses of the West Florida provincial sloop; (12) Letter from John Robinson, one of the Commissioners of Customs in America, enclosing a copy of a paper posted up in Rhode Island; (13) Two bundles of papers relating to the government of Quebec sent by Gov. Carleton; (14) Treasury statement of account including the American revenue, 1767; (15) Charles Garth's memorial in behalf of South Carolina; (16) Lieut.-Col. Christie's memorial.

No. 464. (1) Gen. Gage about bills of exchange; (2) The case of Grover, late chief justice of East Florida; (3) Memorial with papers regarding the impressment of the snow *Polly* at Quebec, Feb. 1767; (4) Memorial of Chief Justice William Clifton of West Florida; (5) Memorial of William Robinson, comptroller of customs in Jamaica; (6) Extracts of letters to the War Office from Generals

Gage and O'Hara; (7) The proper form of a bond for non-enumerated goods; (8) Draft of a bill to require customs officers to inform masters of ships about the requirements for entering and clearing the ships arriving at American ports.

No. 465. (1) Certificates witnessing the transportation of prisoners to America, June 8; (2) Proceedings in the South Carolina vice-admiralty court re George Roupell vs. the Anne; (3) Twenty-one papers relating to the Boston Liberty case; (4) An account of receipts, payments, and net produce at Boston of all revenue acts from Jan. 5 to Jan. 8, 1769; (5) Estimate of the establishment of Georgia, 1766–1769; (6) Letter to the American Commissioners of Customs, signed by Gov. Bernard, Lieut.-Gov. Hutchinson, Sec. Oliver, Vice-Admiralty Judge Auchmuty, and read June 1769; (7) Two other collections of papers relating to the Liberty case; (8) A survey of part of Lake Champlain with trees marked for the royal navy; (9) Report of the examination of the accounts and claims against the government of Quebec; (10) Legal opinions with reference to ships that pass from port to port in America; (11) The case of Melchisedec Kinsman charged with the murder of William Odgers, customs officer at Penzance, Cornwall; (12) Extract of a letter from a Boston "Gentleman of Character," June 14, that the radical leaders hope to bring on a general revolt in America; (13) A long commentary from the collector and comptroller of the Boston custom house giving a history of the Boston custom house administration, with table of fees, from 1716 to 1764; (14) Representation of the Speaker of the Mass. Assembly by its order, Feb. 17; (15) Memorial of Andrew Brown, searcher in South Carolina, about illicit trade in East India goods carried on in New England and New York; (16) Minutes of the Massachusetts Council regarding insults of the Commissioners of Customs and disturbances in Boston; (17) Certificate from John Temple in favour of Folger of Nantucket; (18) A letter from David Lisle expressing fear of a total revolt of Massachusetts; (19) Memorial to the Commissioners of Customs from Richard Reeve and Thomas Irving about insults from a Boston mob, June 25; (20) Charles Garth on the conduct of the South Carolina collector, Jan. 20; (21) Gov. Bernard to Sec. Hillsborough, July 11; (22) Order in council setting up four vice-admiralty court districts in North America; (23) Letters about the suspension of Collector of Customs Fisher at Salem; (24) A series of memorials from the Commissioners of Customs in America, Jan. 26, Feb. 12, May 12, July 11, Aug. 25, Sept. 15, and Oct. 4—these are very important papers involving writs of assistance.

No. 466. (1) Circular letter from the Secretary of State to ministers and consuls in European ports warning them to look out for North

American vessels engaged in illicit trade; (2) The case of the brigantine *Lydia* with Attorney General Philip Yorke's opinion.

No. 467. (1) About plantation goods granted on lease to the French inhabitants of Dominica according to the agreement of May 4, 1766; (2) Instructions to commissioners in the Ceded Islands, Feb. 2; (3) Petition of Glasgow merchants relative to duties on iron imported from America; (4) Attorney General De Grey's discussion of colonial collectors taking securities in Great Britain and the colonies from the officers of customs there; (5) The Admiralty regarding Sir William Burnaby's request for reimbursement referred to earlier; (6) Warrant for James Pott's appointment to the office of judge of vice-admiralty at Quebec; (7) Stephen Fuller's petition relating to money raised in Jamaica by the Stamp Act; (8) The American Commissioners of Customs to Gov. Wentworth of New Hampshire; (9) The case of the *Aurora* considered by the governor of North Carolina as guilty of breach of the trade acts.

No. 468. (1) Case of a schooner with 30 hhds. of uncustomed molasses on board seized and the conduct of the people of Boston following that, set forth in Gov. Bernard's letter and by the Earl of Hillsborough; (2) Opinion of the Attorney General on the question whether the East India Company should not be required to make up the deficiency caused by the drawback on export of tea to Ireland and the colonies; (3) Nuthall's report on John Mason's memorial respecting the Mohegan Indians; (4) Letter from Consul Walters of Rotterdam regarding ships destined for America; (5) Opinion of John Sewall, attorney general of Massachusetts, on the meaning of 7 Geo. III, c. 46; (6) Francis Noble Knipe's memorial about interference by Deputy Quartermaster Christie with his shipbuilding at Montreal; (7) Secretary of State Hillsborough's instructions about the collection of duties in America; (8) Letter from Collector of Customs Moore stating why he left Charleston; (9) Memorial of comptroller of customs William Russell explaining why he left his post in Georgia; (10) Charles Stewart, Surveyor General of Customs in America, asks leave of absence to go to England, June 3. Request denied.

1 7 6 9

No. 469. (1) Quebec fees; (2) West Florida accounts; (3) Memorial of the lieut.-gov. of Nova Scotia, Michael Francklin; (4) Payments made out of the West Indies 4½ per cent export tax, 1752–1760; (5) Victuals for Mobile; (6) Scottish trade to America, 1768–1775, with specified colonies and valuation of goods; (7) Quebec accounts; (8) John Temple to Lord Hillsborough, Boston, Oct. 25,

1768; (9) Letters from Dr. Moffat estimating his losses in the Newport riot in 1765 and desiring recognition; (10) Quebec accounts; (11) Affidavit of E. Davis, temporary collector at Charleston; (12) Virginia quit-rents; (13) The 4½ per cent British West Indies account; (14) Papers concerning Tortola and the Virgin Islands; (15) Memorial of Dr. John Campbell, agent for Georgia.

No. 470. (1) Memorial of John Williams, inspector general of customs in North America; (2) Memorial from John Foxcroft about the post-office in America; (3) John Michael Dwyer writes about Jamaica; (4) About a customs officer for Nantucket; (5) Memorial of William Randall, late surveyor general of the Southern District in America; (6) Papers about payments to customs officers in America; (7) The governor of East Florida writes of the Greek colonists introduced by Dr. Andrew Turnbull; (8) Copy of petition for a grant of land back of the Virginia settlements to the Grand Ohio or Walpole Co.

No. 471. (1) Letters and memorials about the Boston troubles; (2) American customs receipts, payment and produce; also account of receipts and remittances to London, 1769–1770, drawn up for Charles Stewart, paymaster; (3) Papers about the government of Rhode Island refusing to allow an appeal on customs fees; (4) About the treatment of customs officers in Philadelphia who made a seizure; (5) Account of duties from Charleston; (6) About the white pine timber on the Kennebec River; (7) Vice-Admiralty judge Auchmuty's decrees in the case of Folger *vs.* the sloop *Cornelia*; (8) Mobile port statistics; (9) About the destruction of the sloop *Liberty* in Rhode Island waters; (10) Quebec accounts; (11) Statistics from Maryland, Pennsylvania, Nova Scotia, Virginia, Massachusetts, West Florida, Lower Counties on the Delaware, and South Carolina; (12) Plan for vice-admiralty court districts in North America; (13) Commissioner Temple about the troubles with Samuel Venner; (14) The Mohegan Indian case; (15) Papers largely relating to the problems faced by the customs collectors in North America, especially in Pennsylvania, Connecticut, and Rhode Island; (16) The American Board of Customs Commissioners and its problems, with particular attention to coastal trade.

No. 472. (1) The case of Searcher Roupell at Charleston appears once again; (2) Memorial of Stephen Fuller, Jamaica agent, regarding the case of the *Lawrence*.

No. 473. Papers relating to New York, Quebec, Newfoundland, West Florida, and Grenada.

No. 474. (1) Many papers relating to the Floridas, Quebec, Grenada, St. Vincent, and Dominica; (2) On money due to Rhode Island; (3) The Mohegan Indian case; (4) The opinion of Attorney General

Sewall of Massachusetts on the coastal trade; (5) Vice-admiralty case, Quebec, Nov. 17; (6) Letter of Duncan Stewart from New London, Conn.

1 7 7 0

No. 475. (1) The case of vessels carrying wine to America; (2) About whalebone exported to New England and elsewhere from Scotland; (3) Land sales in the Bermudas; (4) A number of papers concerning America, especially West Florida, Niagara Falls, the exploration of interior Virginia; petition for western lands and the erection of a new colony.

No. 476. (1) The American Board of Customs and Commodore Hood; (2) West Florida civil establishment; (3) Account of American receipts and remittances; (4) Memorial of Thomas Walpole and his associates for lands within the late Fort Stanwix Indian cession —the Grand Ohio Company project; (5) Memorials from Receiver General Charles Stewart; (6) Receipts of customs and warrants for expenditures; (7) From Lieut.-Gov. Bull of South Carolina; (8) Quebec papers; (9) On the Greek settlement in East Florida; (10) Duties collected at the several American ports; (11) Report of American Board of Customs; (12) The situation in New Hampshire; (13) The South Carolina Bussard case; (14) The New York quit-rent act; (15) Mr. Wegg on the seizure of the *Little Bob* at Mobile in 1765; (16) Custom house accounts in America.

No. 477. Quebec accounts.

No. 478. (1) Quebec accounts again; (2) The cases of the *Recovery* and the *Sea Flower* in Nova Scotia waters; (3) From Gov. James Grant of East Florida, Sept. 18, 1769; (4) From Lieut.-Gov. William Bull of South Carolina about remitting fines from German settlers; (5) The payment of bills at Michilimackinac and Sir William Johnson; (6) The case of Major Robert Rogers; (7) Memorial of the West Florida collector of customs; (8) West Florida letters; (9) The case of the *Betsey*, Quebec; (10) Major Rogers's petition; (11) Gov. Carleton of Quebec to the Commissioners of Customs, July 4, 1770; (12) Petition of Jonathan Carver; (13) Quebec papers; (14) Again, the Major Rogers case; (15) Copies of letters from the Quebec collector; (16) John Temple to Lord North about the American Board of Customs, with Charleston enclosures; (17) Memorials of John Mein of Boston; (18) Memorials of Deputy Paymaster Thomas Barrow and John Ellis, agent of West Florida; (19) Case of the *Sea Flower.*

No. 479. (1) Report of the Attorney and Solicitor General on a Massachusetts tax act; (2) Quebec accounts; (3) West Florida papers;

(4) Petition of Surveyor General De Brahm; (5) Gen. Gage on the Maj. Rogers case; (6) "Observations on the tobacco trade in America and Scotland"; (7) Hillsborough on the suspension of fines in Virginia; (8) More victualling papers; (9) Case involving damage from confiscation of stamped paper carried to Philadelphia in 1765; (10) Both Pensacola and Quebec papers; (11) Moses Park and the Mohegan Indians; (12) Nova Scotia quit-rents; (13) Grenada papers.

No. 480. (1) About the importation of rum into Ireland; (2) Memorial of Georgia agent, John Campbell; (3) Gov. Gage on provisions; (4) Memorial concerning the late surveyor general of Barbados; (5) Memorial for Francis Lewis, commissary for Shirley's Niagara expedition of 1755; (6) About the illegal importation from America of spirits and tobacco into Great Britain; (7) Memorial of London merchants for a change in rating American rice; (8) Petition of prisoner Thomas Doten, formerly of Boston, in Lancaster gaol.

No. 481. (1) List of vessels entering the port of Hampton, Va., with the nature of their ladings, 1771; (2) List of vessels clearing from York River, 1771; (3) Gage to Hillsborough about the *Florida Pacquet*; (4) About smuggling American rum into Scotland; (5) Provost Marshall Turner's petition, Quebec; (6) From St. Christopher about smuggling; (7) Regarding surveys about Lake Champlain.

1771

No. 482. (1) Hillsborough to Gov. Tryon of North Carolina about riots, Feb. 11; (2) The Mississippi River peltry trade; (3) Newfoundland customs difficulties; (4) About outrages in Massachusetts, Pennsylvania, East Florida, and Rhode Island; (5) From Samuel Venner, also the customs establishment in America; (6) The American Customs Board reports on the *Liberty* incident, illicit trade in the West Indies, and financial matters; (7) The American Customs Board account of money received, paid out, and remitted in 1771; (8) The Halifax and Quebec accounts, also those of the Rappahannock River; (9) Naval office fees from American ports; (10) The collector of New York to the American Customs Board; (11) Arguments for establishing a West Florida custom house on the Mississippi; (12) Letters from the American surveyor of woods and the inspector of white pines; (13) Quebec and other accounts.

No. 483. (1) Papers about lands in the Ceded Islands; (2) The Bahamas, collectors accounts; (3) Estimates for Nova Scotia.

No. 484. (1) Hillsborough's action respecting outrages against officers in America, in letters to governors, etc.; (2) Letters regarding New Hampshire, New York, and East Florida fees; (3) Memorials from Robert Johnston about public roads in East Florida and from Zachary Hood, late stamp distributor for Maryland; (4) Important memorial of William Randall, late surveyor general of the Southern District; (5) Jamaica, Dominica, and West Florida papers; (6) Memorial, signed by several persons, supporting Major Rogers's proposal to find a northwest passage with several papers about the affairs of Major Rogers; (7) Letters from Gov. Tryon of New York about his difficulties.

No. 485. (1) Royal American regiment accounts; (2) Pensacola and Dominica papers; (3) Thurlow's opinion on the question whether to require supreme courts in America to issue writs of assistance; (4) The case of the *Speedwell* laden with Dutch tea seized in Philadelphia; (5) Dominica and West Florida papers.

No. 486. (1) Memorial of Hodgson, superintendent of the Mosquito Shore; (2) Reports of the Attorney and Solicitor General on the Rhode Island naval officer case, also on a Quebec case; (3) Memorial of the receiver general at Quebec; (4) The application of the money received in America from duties; (5) About the neglect of the inspector of tar in North Carolina; (6) The disallowance of a 1770 Pennsylvania act; (7) St. Vincent papers; (8) About Jamaica fees.

No. 487. (1) Martinique and Jamaica papers; (2) Accounts involving the extraordinary service of the army chiefly in 1771; (3) Account of the disposition of all money raised through duties by acts of Parliament, 1770; (4) The Mohegan Indian case; (5) Report on Collector Francis Waldo's petition.

No. 488. (1) Adolph Benzel's remarks on Lake Champlain; (2) On a Rhode Island case; (3) Letter from Collector of Customs Thomas Dicey of Jamaica.

1772

No. 489. (1) Report on the memorial of Montfort Browne, late governor of West Florida; (2) Address of the rector of King's College and New York inhabitants asking for the remission of certain quitrents; (3) About the address of the governors of the college in New York to be made a university; (4) About rum exported from America to Ireland; (5) Naval lists for Montserrat, Nevis, and St. Christopher; (6) Halifax victualling lists.

No. 490. (1) Lists of transported criminals; (2) Papers on the Bermudas and St. Vincent; (3) Another letter from Benzel; (4) On the Nova Scotia establishment; (5) About the mahogany duty; (6) Concerning clandestine trade between America and the Mediterranean; (7) Memorial from the proprietors of a Maryland iron works.

No. 491. (1) A large number of important American Board of Customs papers with accounts of outrages in America, including the Hatton and Mackay cases and the case of the *Gaspee;* (2) Quebec accounts and Mobile statistics; (3) Memorial of George Suckling, late attorney general of Quebec; (4) Warrants granted by Gage for expenses; (5) Various naval office lists, with the civil establishments of Georgia and West Florida.

No. 492. (1) Map of the Connecticut River indicating the tracts of white pine; (2) A plan for locks at the great falls of the Connecticut River; (3) Surveyor Timothy Ruggles's report; (4) Papers of the American Board of Customs about writs of assistance, Rhode Island outrages, permission for enumerated articles to go under bond to Gibraltar, Minorca, and Senegambia; also about the controversy between the Patuxent and Chester collectors and Quebec difficulties; (5) Another letter from Benzel regarding Lake Champlain.

No. 493. (1) Leeward Islands naval lists; (2) Memorial of Agent Ellis of West Florida; (3) About the deception of Collector Duncan Stewart at New London; (4) Gage papers, including warrants; (5) Dominica and Grenada papers; (6) About Admiral Gambier's extra services; (7) Copies of letters from Lieut.-Gov. Bull about the Milligan memorial, from Gov. Wentworth of New Hampshire, from the proprietary of Pennsylvania, and from the governor of Rhode Island about customs officers; (8) Receipts and payments, Sept. 1767 to April 1772; (9) Gov. Gage's estimates with plans for public works in North America, such as at Pensacola.

No. 494. (1) Virginia papers, with naval office lists; (2) Letter from one Fraser about a vessel with a cargo of tea sailing from Amsterdam to New York; (3) About a West Florida schooner; (4) Many papers from and relating to Montfort Browne of West Florida; (5) Extract from Wooten's report from New London; (6) Hillsborough relating to salaries of officers of the Bahamas; (7) About Collector Duncan Stewart; (8) Many papers concerning the Rhode Island outrages; (9) Bills and warrants from Gen. Gage; (10) Deputy Vice-Admiral A. Johnstone's memorial, Quebec; (11) A condemnation at Pensacola; (12) A memorial from De Brahm; (13) Also one from Dr. Moffatt at New London.

No. 495. (1) About the piloting of certain vessels used in aiding officers in America; (2) Another letter from Benzel; (3) More about the Duncan Stewart case; (4) Warrants, Gen. Gage; (5) Many papers regarding timber cutting conflicts in Maine.

No. 496. (1) A ship seizure off Newfoundland; (2) Quebec papers; (3)

Gov. Martin of North Carolina on quit-rents; (4) A petition from the New York Dutch Reformed Church about quit-rents; (5) From Collector Scammell of Falmouth, Casco Bay, July 20; (6) Petition of merchants for bounty on timber; (7) Memorial of the collector at Mobile; (8) Inventory of the effects lost on the *Gaspee* by Lieut. Dudingston; (9) Memorial asking satisfaction for the loss of the *Hawk,* a royal vessel with South Carolina troops.

No. 497. (1) The Admiralty on the merits of the "essence of Spruce" to protect crews of vessels from scurvy; (2) Gov. Leyborne of Grenada about lands in the Ceded Islands; (3) A group of papers from Thomas Dunn, relating to various expenditures in Quebec; (4) Victualling papers from Pensacola and Grenada; (5) The proprietary of Pennsylvania writes about Philadelphia customs troubles.

1 7 7 3

No. 498. (1) Naval office lists for Montserrat, St. Christopher, Nevis, Antigua, as well as for Virginia; (2) Returns of Nova Scotia imports, Sept. 1767–Jan. 1773; (3) Halifax victualling lists; (4) Memorial of Liverpool merchants trading to Africa and the West Indies respecting the Free Port Act.

No. 499. (1) Memorial of John Robinson of the American Board of Customs Commissioners; (2) Report on the West Indies island of Bequia; (3) Joseph Smith Speer reports on his chart of the West Indies; (4) John Robinson's proposal respecting Windward Islands inspectors; (5) Grenada and St. Vincent accounts; (6) Petitions from Dominica about lands and tenures; (7) Secretary Col. Blaquiere of Ireland on Irish illicit trade with the colonies; (8) Report of Adolph Benzel, inspector of unappropriated lands in Canada and the Lake Champlain area; (9) Charges against the Collector Henry Bennett of St. Christopher as a party to illicit trade; (10) On the enforcement of the revenue laws in the Channel Islands; (11) John Robinson on inspection in Barbados and the Leeward Islands; (12) Papers on indigo imports from America.

No. 500. (1) Report on a proposed copper currency for Virginia; (2) Papers about land difficulties in Dominica, St. Vincent, and Antigua, with other papers about the Ceded Islands; (3) Robert Jones comments on the North Carolina quit-rent act; (4) Important letters relating to emigration from Scotland to America.

No. 501. (1) A group of papers relating to colonial finances, civil establishments, surveys, etc.; (2) Concerning revenue laws and writs of assistance in Massachusetts, Pennsylvania, Maryland, and Virginia; (3) The draft of a bill to regulate American coastal trade, with comments; (4) Halifax port papers, etc.; (5) Important American Board of Customs papers.

No. 502. (1) Many American and West Indian financial papers; (2) Memorial in support of Samuel Rous, president of the Barbados Council; (3) North Carolina quit-rents; (4) Hillsborough on judges' salaries in Massachusetts; (5) Memorial of Dartmouth merchants about the Newfoundland collector's assertions; (6) Naval lists for Antigua, Montserrat, and St. Christopher; (7) Gov. Tonyn of East Florida wants allowance for a schooner.

No. 503. (1) Many financial papers; (2) Claim of Admiral George Clinton, one-time governor of New York; (3) Virginia royal revenues; (4) From Collector Patterson, Philadelphia; (5) Jacob Blackwell's memorial, Mobile; (6) Papers of the late Gov. Fitzmaurice of St. Vincent; (7) Memorial of John Campbell in charge of Canadian Indian affairs; (8) Memorial of Collector Alexander Dunn, Newfoundland; (9) Nevis and Montserrat naval office lists.

No. 504. (1) Ceded Islands contract papers; (2) A memorial of the 31st Regiment in West Florida; (3) The produce of the customs in America, 1767–1773; (4) A group of memorials; (5) Dr. Moffatt on his losses at Newport; (6) Gen. Gage on Indian matters, April 7; (7) On the value of the South Carolina office of receiver general; (8) On the seizure of a ship; (9) Memorial of Capt. Samuel Hood (later Admiral Lord Hood) on his career to 1773; (10) West Florida, Nova Scotia, and Mosquito Shore financial papers.

1 7 7 4

No. 505. (1) About the *Buchanan* of Glasgow, lost while carrying New York flour to Bordeaux; (2) The destruction of tea in Boston harbour, many enclosures, including memorials from ships' captains; (3) Gov. Martin of North Carolina writes about Fort Johnston and Capt. Collet; (4) Petition of Isaac Chorrurier of Dominica about his land dispute, with a map; (5) Gov. Legge about Nova Scotia quit-rents; (6) About the prohibition of the export from Great Britain to America of military stores, with reports from Rhode Island, Piscataqua, and Boston; (7) A group of papers relating to Boston and American affairs, together with customs statistics; (8) A petition for grant of unappropriated New York land; (9) William Gerard de Brahm's petition to be restored to his post as surveyor of East Florida, recounting his many services; (10) Customs papers; (11) Cramahé to Carleton concerning an admiralty case, Quebec; (12) Gov. Martin of North Carolina about quit-rents and the receiver general; (13) Pensacola customs duties, 1763–1764, and those at New London, May–Oct., 1774; (14)

Produce of the American customs, 1772–1773; (15) Account of tea imported in American ports with tables; (16) Collector Charles Dudley's petition and an order in council covering it.

No. 506. (1) Naval office lists covering Virginia ports of entry, 1773–1774; (2) Petition of George Suckling, former Attorney General of Quebec; (3) Petitions of Joseph Smith Speer with supporting papers; (4) Memorial from Manchester regarding Jamaica free ports.

No. 507. (1) Newfoundland ships and emigrants; (2) About absentee customs officers; (3) The case of the ship *Betsey* seized at St. John's; (4) From Plymouth, Eng. custom house, about a ship sailing to Philadelphia loaded with gunpowder; (5) St. Christopher, Montserrat, and Nevis naval office lists; (6) Halifax victualling lists.

No. 508. (1) On Joseph Sanguinet's claim for goods furnished the Canadian Indians in 1767; (2) On New York escheated estates; (3) Expenses involved in the court of inquiry over the *Gaspee* affair, Dec. 1772 to May 1773.

No. 509. (1) About the bail for Benjamin Roberts, commissary for Indian affairs at Michilimackinac, Nov.; (2) Memorial of the receiver general of Dominica about obstructions to payments; (3) Dominican planter Jacques Blancard's memorial; (4) On the state of the wool-card trade in North America; (5) Antigua, Montserrat, and Nevis naval office lists; (6) Petition of London merchants who shipped 16 chests of tea to Boston in the *Fortune*, which was boarded and the tea thrown overboard. Asks for £472. 2s 10d; (7) John Foxcroft, deputy postmaster general in America, about the case against Goddard, former postmaster at Providence; (8) Gov. Wentworth of New Hampshire about the destruction of tea; (9) The Secretary at War about payments to regiments sent to America; (10) John Gregg, secretary of the commissioners for the sale of Dominica lands; (11) Another petition of Joseph Smith Speer; (12) Memorial about British West Indies coffee plantations and the reduction of duty on coffee.

No. 510. (1) St. Christopher naval office lists; (2) Victualling for West Florida, Ceded Islands, etc.; (3) Petition of John Malcolm, Boston customs officer, for reimbursement for his experiences at the hand of a mob, and the same for Collector Alexander Dunn, Newfoundland; (4) Quebec accounts and other papers.

No. 511. (1) About the decline of the Dominica coffee industry; (2) Contract and expense papers; (3) Memorial of Thomas Irving, receiver general of quit-rents in South Carolina, London, Feb. 22; (4) Memorial of South Carolina Collector Archibald Baird; (5) Memorial of George Ball, waiter and searcher at Roseau, Dominica; (6) About the establishment of a court of exchequer in Dominica and Grenada for collection of quit-rents; (7) Representation of proprietors of St. John (Prince Edward Island) against the governor being also collector and receiver of quit-rents; (8) Memorial of John Temple of the American Customs Board, superseded in 1770; (9) Another De Brahm memorial; (10) Memorial of Alexander Grant, London merchant, who sold goods to the Nova Scotia Indian agent.

1 7 7 5

No. 512. (1) Naval office lists for the Leewards and Virginia ports; (2) Memorial of John Christopher Roberts, late office-holder, Quebec; (3) Memorial of James Grant, late governor of East Florida.

No. 513. (1) Nova Scotia customs reports; (2) Case of the *Lady Gage,* illegally importing arms to New York; (3) Memorial of Elizabeth Fitz Roy, regarding New York lands; (4) A number of important papers from the American Customs Board about occurrences.

No. 514. (1) American war correspondence, War Office; (2) From Gen. Carleton, Quebec, Dec. 20; (3) Some American financial statements; (4) Letters from Secretary John Robinson of the Treasury Board concerning New England ships about to sail for America and the seizure of ships carrying intelligence to the American rebels, Nov. 28; (5) Grenada accounts; (6) Account of money collected in America and disbursed and of duties levied by acts of Parliament, 1767–1771; (7) From Gen. Howe, Boston, Dec. 19; (8) Victualling and contract papers; (9) About Palatines going to America by way of Rotterdam; (10) On the losses of Duncan Campbell on a contract for transporting felons; (11) Three letters from Gov. Thomas Shirley, Dominica.

No. 515. (1) Gage's warrants for extraordinary military expenses in America; (2) St. Vincent quit-rents; (3) War Office papers, estimates, etc.; (4) Inventory of losses of James Dundas, master of the *Gaspee;* (5) Large numbers of victualling and ordnance papers; (6) Collector Thomas Ainslee, Quebec, to Gov. Carleton; (7) About Joseph Sanguinet's petition for compensation; (8) William Pollock's memorial in behalf of De Brahm; (9) Collector Richard A. Harrison, Boston, reviews events since 1772 and also petitions.

No. 516. (1) George Sullivan, agent for injured British subjects in the Province of New York; also a letter from Gov. Tryon about the *Hawk,* seized by the Spaniards; (2) Memorial from the wife of the late Gov. Leyborne of St. Vincent; (3) Petition of the son of Collector Grosvenor Bedford at Philadelphia; (4) Petition of William Randall, late surveyor general of the Southern District; (5) About the expedition of the East India Company to Manila, 1762; (6) Secretary for the Propagation of the Gospel writes about a Barbados plantation; (7) Papers about shipping money to America;

(8) Papers about the conduct of the surveyor general of Barbados; (9) On the bounty on indigo from America; (10) Papers relating to the American clandestine trade in arms, etc.

No. 517. (1) Hessian papers; (2) Memorial of James Glen, late governor of South Carolina; (3) Petitions from George Wilmot and Ebenezer Richardson, late of Boston, relating to their services.

No. 518. (1) Account of tonnage of vessels employed in the trade between Scotland and the colonies, 1772–1775; (2) Amount of tobacco imported at Glasgow, July 5–Oct. 11; (3) Petition to Parliament from agents of American Loyalists; (4) Memorial of Des Barres, surveyor of coast and harbours of North America; (5) Memorial of Peter Livius, judge of the Quebec court of vice-admiralty; (6) Memorial of Robert Rogers with a proposal; (7) Memorial in behalf of Capt. Samuel Holland.

1776

No. 519. (1) Treasury letters to Anthony Merry about shipping livestock to Boston, etc.; (2) Guy Johnson about Indian expenses; (3) About settling land disputes in the Ceded Islands; (4) Canadian victualling.

No. 520. (1) Petition of Francis Rotch and Aaron Lopez about whale fishing in southern waters; (2) From Samuel Porter, lawyer of Salem, Mass., on his suffering from the American Revolution; (3) From Alexander McAlister, Dominica planter, about land sold; (4) From officers of the Royal Highland Emigrants Regiment about its place in the establishment, informative; (5) From James Hume, late acting attorney general of Loyalists in Georgia; (6) Invoices of Indian presents sent to St. Augustine and Pensacola in care of John Stuart; (7) American Customs Board papers, including a list of customs officers in America; (8) Two letters from Andrew Elliot, Perth Amboy, May 22, and New York, Nov. 30, that all of the collector's and receiver general's books and papers had been burnt; (9) About losses sustained during the siege of Quebec; (10) Memorial regarding the 8th King's Regiment, stationed in the Great Lakes area.

No. 521. (1) Gen. Gage on the case of the *Charming Peggy* of Philadelphia, seized and sent to Boston and her cargo sold there; (2) Case of the *Concord* of Philadelphia at Rotterdam; (3) List of His Majesty's ships, their size, and location; (4) Petition of Owen Byran, late master of the merchant ship *Diana*; (5) James Marriott, King's advocate, about the operation of the Prohibitory Act; (6) Scottish Board papers relating to the American scene, especially about trade including cases of the *Polly*, the *Logan*, the *Christian*, and the *Betsey*, also concerning fleeing Loyalists; (7) About convicts received for transportation who were pardoned, provided they enlisted in the King's service; (8) Dominica land papers; (9) Major George Etherington's petition for permission to purchase St. Vincent Carib land; (10) St. Vincent quit-rents; (11) Thomas Shirley regarding lands in the Ceded Islands; (12) Report on a Jamaica case; (13) Case of the *Morris* of Philadelphia loaded with powder and lead; (14) The difficulty faced by the herring fishery for lack of oak staves due to North American disturbances.

No. 522. (1) A large number of papers about the supply of provisions, including rum, for the troops in America; (2) Papers chiefly concerned with Robert Gilmour's press taken from Norfolk, Va. by the governor, Lord Dunmore; (3) Memorial of the society for the relief of the widows and orphans of soldiers who died in America; (4) A quantity of bills, etc., concerned with American barracks, hospitals, etc.; (5) Memorial of the Tobago council and assembly about threatened prosecution of people for default of land payments; (6) An affidavit respecting events in Savannah harbour; (7) Memorial of George Gregory, merchant and lieutenant of the artillery company "of the British militia," whose house, barn, etc. were burned by order of Gov. Carleton; (8) Memorial of John Williams, inspector general of customs in America, about occurrences in Boston since 1768 and his unjust treatment by the American Board of Customs; (9) Memorial of James Chambers, late commander of the ship *London*, about events in New York harbour including the destruction of 18 chests of tea; (10) Petition of Charles Mackenzie, dealing in goods for the use of troops in Boston; (11) Order in council on the case of the South Carolina Loyalist, John Gordon.

No. 523. (1) London Custom House about a ship suspected of communicating with the rebels; (2) About American ships taken by the navy; (3) Vessels sailing on orders for America; (4) Vessels entering London and outports, 1775–1776; (5) Outport papers chiefly concerned with vessels arriving from America; (6) About lowering duties on British plantation coffee; (7) About the American brig *Betsey* seized at Falmouth (not the *Betsey* of *No. 521*), with a report by Dr. Marriott; (8) Relating to German auxiliaries; (9) Memorial of Capt. John Fenton, taken prisoner by Montcalm and confined in France and later served again in America; (10) Commissary orders, Canada; (11) Report by William Barr, purveyor of hospitals in North America.

No. 524. (1) Commissary accounts; (2) Letters from Gov. John Wentworth; (3) Petition of merchants, Henry Fleming and John Pew, late of Norfolk, Va.; (4) Memorial of Charles Thompson, commander of the *Boreas;* (5) Petition of Richard Sharwin, saddler of Boston; (6) Memorials of Commissary-General John Christopher Roberts, Receiver General Sir Thomas Mills, Quebec, and Gov. Tonyn of East Florida.

No. 525. (1) Many victualling and contract papers; (2) Petition of London merchant John Schoolbred engaged in trade to Canada; (3) Memorials of Deputy Paymaster-General Richard Reeve, on a southern expedition; of Col. John Wilkinson, late governor of the Illinois country; and of Francis Waldo, late collector of Falmouth, who refers to the burning of the town, including the custom house; (4) Reports of American receivers of quit-rents and other revenues, including the British West Indies; (5) John Stuart on Indian affairs; (6) Letters from Lord Germain and from John Thomas, deputy superintendent of Indian affairs, to the Treasury.

No. 526. (1) Accounts of the provisions, etc., imported from Great Britain and Ireland into the British West Indies (Jamaica excepted) with permission for the Leeward Islands, by reason of failure of supplies from North America, to import provisions from any part of Europe; (2) Petition of Gov. Des Barres of Cape Breton; (3) About the reorganization of the business of the Treasury.

No. 527. (1) Papers concerning the bringing to England deputies of the Mosquito Indians; (2) Account of acting receiver general, Quebec, May 1775–Nov. 1776; (3) Petition of Edward James, London merchant, whose transport took an American prize; (4) A final petition from Joseph Sanguinet, Canada; (5) Memorial of James Stewart, contractor, Newfoundland; (6) Still another petition for Dr. Thomas Moffatt of Newport; (7) Drugs, surgeon's instruments, and other medical supplies delivered to hospitals and armed forces in Africa and America, including Canada and East Florida, by orders of the Secretary at War; (8) Petition and other papers from the owners of the ship *Dunmore*, impressed into the King's service by Gov. Lord Dunmore, Aug. 22, 1775.

It should be noted that Treasury I Papers continues to 1785 and that there are, of course, documents from 1776 to this year that have a relation to events between 1748 and 1776.

Treasury 4. Indexes: Reference books

Many, if not most, of the Treasury In-Letters were referred to other departments of the government for report and advice. Not all of the reference books have survived. In dealing with the period 1748–1776 it is necessary to begin with the year 1758.

No. 12, 1758–1788. (1) Application from Gen. Shirley, 1758, for funds for specific needs of his regiment; (2) A large number of applications from those with contracts from the government; (3) Gov. Reynolds of Georgia wants to raise a troop of rangers; (4) Gov. Gabriel Johnson of North Carolina seeks arrears of his salary; (5) Joseph Sherwood, agent for Rhode Island, seeks reimbursement for the colony's war expenditures in 1756; (6) Proposals of London agent for Georgia, Benjamin Martyn, also of John Roberts, receiver general, about security for Virginia quit-rents; (7) From Charles Garth, agent for Georgia; (8) From George Saxby, receiver general of South Carolina quit-rents; (9) London agent Sherwood answers objections of the Secretary at War to certain payments to Rhode Island, 1765; (10) Peter de Lancey, inspector of stamps for Quebec, Nova Scotia, and New Hampshire, prays for some relief, 1766; (11) John Mason's memorial for the Mohegan Indians; (12) Jared Ingersoll, Connecticut stamp distributor, asks that his bond be cancelled, May 9, 1770; (13) From settlers in Quebec and Nova Scotia about the fishing trade, April 7, 1773; (14) English merchants seek reduction of the duty on plantation coffee, May 11, 1774.

Since the papers in the in-letters deal very fully with matters that came before the Treasury Board together with the decisions reached, it will be necessary to mention only briefly other papers classified among the Treasury papers.

OUT-LETTERS

Treasury 11. Customs

Nos. 1–33, 1667–1784, contain letters relating to the years 1748–1776, including many extracts of in-letters already surveyed. For example, in *No. 26, 1759–1762*, is found a rather complete list of customs appointments with details about each appointment, and in *No. 27, 1762–1765*, are detailed instructions to collectors by reason of changes in the revenue acts.

Treasury 27. General letters

Nos. 1–34, 1668–1783, contain letters to a great many people about a variety of topics, most of which have been well covered by Treasury Papers already noticed. For the period 1748–1776 there are letters to General Amherst regarding bills; to Messrs. Colebrooke and Hanbury about transporting gold and silver to New York; about East Florida quit-rents; numerous papers to John Pownall with references to the illicit Monte Christi trade; letters about coin in America and the payment of forces there; regarding commercial conditions in Canada; about the Rhode Island contraband trade; relating to the bill for the repeal of part of the revenue act of 1733 preparatory to the passing of the revenue act of 1764; concerning the case of the *Gaspee* and also that of the *Liberty*; finally, about writs of assistance.

Treasury 28. Various. Letters relating to America

Nos. 1–3, 1763–1823, are entry books largely devoted to setting forth fully commissions, warrants, letters patent and privy seals given by the direct action of the Crown. These books are concerned with subjects connected with the overseas possessions already dealt with in in-letters. Beyond the out-letters, attention must be called to other Treasury Board series. They are as follows:

MINUTE BOOKS

Treasury 29.

Nos. 1–54, 1667–1783, embody the minutes of the meetings of the Treasury Board. Every important matter that came before it is duly noted. It should also be mentioned that *No. 628*, 1771–1777, contains copies of minutes relating to the American war during the years 1775–1777.

ACCOUNTS GENERAL

Treasury 30. Accounts general. Yearly

Nos. 1–18, 1688–1785, largely limited to Great Britain.

Treasury 31. Accounts general. Quarterly

Nos. 1–328, 1701–1783, constitute a more important source than the Accounts General, Yearly, with accounts of the plantations duty, the cost of the colonial civil establishments, including the salaries paid to British officials in America.

Treasury 33. Accounts general. Auditors' declarations

Nos. 1–191, 1660–1788. Some of these volumes throw light on the years 1748–1776, especially Volumes 75, 150, and 151. It may be noted in passing that these declarations of receipts and expenditures are in Latin.

Treasury 34. Accounts general. Declarations, pells

Nos. 1–131, 1636–1783, are much like the above auditors' series except that these declarations are of the clerk of the Pells. This of course means clerk of the parchments, which were of two kinds, *pellis receptorum* and *pellis exituum*, that is, recorded revenues coming in and recorded revenues going out.

Treasury 38. Auditors' states of accounts

Most of these papers are either too early or too late. However, *No. 269*, 1773–1783, presents an account of English exports to and imports from the British West Indies.

No. 340, 1679–1761, is made up of abstracts of yearly receipts from the customs for the years covered.

No. 357, 1746–1780, brings together abstracts of annual receipts of customs. The figures for the years 1746–1761 here set forth agree with the figures in *No. 340*.

Nos. 362–363, 1691–1784, represent other tabulations of English customs accounts of imports and exports, almost entirely concerned with the period before 1748.

REGISTERS

Treasury 42. Establishment lists

No. 1, 1766, contains a list of customs officers, but for England only.

Treasury 46. Victualling lists

No. 21, 1765–1770, is limited to Halifax, with lists of civilians and military at the place during the years dealt with.

Treasury 47. Emigration lists

Nos. 9–11, 1773–1776, contain lists of persons leaving Great Britain for the New World with age, occupation, former residence and destination. The lists are imperfect but still very useful. Most who left were either redemptioners or indented servants.

No. 12, 1773–1776, is limited to Scots destined for many colonies. Reasons given for leaving Scotland included "high rents and oppression."

WARRANTS AND OTHER RECORDS

Treasury 52. The King's warrants

Nos. 1–68, 1667–1783, are books of letters patent, privy seals, and royal sign manuals, relating to commissions, salaries, or pensions, including payments to ambassadors, governors, etc.

Treasury 53. Warrants related to money

Nos. 1–56, 1676–1783, are entries of warrants, so-called "Money Books," from the Treasury Board to the auditor of the receipt of the Exchequer authorizing certain payments.

Treasury 54. Warrants not related to money

Nos. 1–44, 1667–1786, are warrants that authorized a person or persons to do something, usually as the result of a petition or memorial. For example, *Nos. 38–39* are warrants authorizing the transportation of money to the colonies; authorizing the distribution of parliamentary grants to the colonies in a specified manner, and recommending the extension of the 4½ per cent old British West Indies export duty to Grenada, and other West Indies islands incorporated into the British Empire in 1763.

Treasury 55. Warrants for Crown Land leases

Nos. 1–32, 1727–1819, are warrants mostly related to land and leases in England. In the first four volumes, however, reference is made to lands in St. Christopher and in New York. Most of these papers antedate 1748.

Treasury 56. Warrants various

No. 36, 1765–1832, has to do with the levy of the 4½ per cent export tax in the British West Indies.

OTHER TREASURY RECORDS

Treasury 60. Auditor's order books

Nos. 1–25, 1667–1783, contain auditor's orders on authorization of the Treasury to make certain payments such as the salaries of governors, allowances for clergymen or schoolmasters going to the colonies. These books throw light on how the revenue drawn from the colonies was distributed. For example, on March 17, 1764, an order was issued to pay to Charles Garth, London agent for Georgia, the sum of £4,031. 8s. 8d. for the civil establishment of that colony.

Treasury 61. Public deposition books

Nos. 1–43, 1679–1785, are volumes that contain letters of direction indicating from what particular fund payment was to be made.

Treasury 64. Miscellanea various: Appointments, etc.

Nos. 20–22, 1759–1763, embody Sir Jeffrey Amherst's military accounts. They include the following: (1) Accounts of transports taken up at Boston for the 1759 expedition up the St. Lawrence; (2) Accounts and disbursements in upper New York for military construction, 1760–1762; (3) Muster rolls of Georgia rangers, 1761–1763; (4) Thomas Hancock's disbursements for supplies sent to Louisbourg, St. John (Prince Edward Island), and Halifax; also much material about construction work of the army at Halifax, 1761–1762; (5) George Croghan's accounts for his Indian services, 1761; (6) Major Robert Rogers's account against the Crown, 1761; (7) Many accounts with vouchers of the military contributions made by Massachusetts, Connecticut, and Rhode Island in 1759. Since it was required that reimbursement of the expenses of the colonies should be based upon the exact nature of the contributions made to the war effort, most of these records are doubtless quite complete.

No. 44, 1750, a representation of the Board of Trade, presents in elaborate detail the part taken by each of the New England colonies in the intended expedition against Canada planned for 1748.

No. 45, 1751–1771. There were bitter disputes over customs fees. In this volume there are presented tables of fees taken by the officers of customs at various ports from Newfoundland, Quebec, and Halifax to the Bermudas and the Bahamas.

Nos. 48–49, 1772–1780, present in detail Barbados shipping returns.

No. 71, 1765, has to do with an ordinance for establishing courts of common pleas and error in the Ceded Islands of Grenada, St. Vincent, and Dominica.

No. 82, 1770, contains Newfoundland shipping returns.

No. 84, 1749–1753, contains Halifax, N.S., shipping returns.

No. 101, 1772–1776, is a commissariat supply book, listing supplies needed for carrying on public works and other services in North America with yearly returns of provisions issued to troops stationed in the colonies.

Nos. 106–107, 1774–1783, contain letters to and from commanders-in-chief in North America.

No. 150, 1756, contains representations of the Register General of Tobacco for Scotland made to the Commissioners of Customs of Edinburgh.

No. 188, 1763–1783, contains opinions of the law officers of the Crown. These concern the following matters: (1) Duties levied at Havana, 1764; (2) The government of the Province of Quebec, 1764; (3) About Auditor General Cholmondeley's patent, 1764; (4) Collecting revenues at Quebec, 1764; (5) Contractors in America, 1766;

(6) Collecting customs in America, 1766; (7) The recovery of debts from agents of American contractors, Nov. 1766 and Sept. 1777; (8) Seizure of a ship at Boston, 1768; (9) The taking of security in Great Britain for offices in America, 1768; (10) The unloading of ships in American ports, 1768; (11) What ships may engage in coastal trade in America, 1768; (12) The granting of writs of assistance in America, 1768; (13) On a tax in Massachusetts, 1770.

Nos. 215–216, 1761–1782, are entry books of patents relating to all officers who received their appointments by letters patent, including colonial governors and customs collectors in America.

No. 252, 1772–1785, presents a report on the amount of linens (British, Irish, and foreign) exported to the various colonies from Scotland.

No. 274, 1750–1779, Various: (1) Charges for maintaining Nova Scotia, 1750–1751; (2) Account of plantation duty imposed by 25 Chas. II in Jamaica for seven years to 1751; also account of specie and amounts of goods exported to North America from Jamaica in the same seven years; (3) Amount of Jamaican sugar exported to England to the year 1751; (4) Papers related to export of sugar and rum from the West Indies to England and the Northern colonies to 1751; (5) Account of British and Irish linens exported to the British colonies, 1740–1753; (6) Quantity of pig and bar iron imported from the colonies, 1749–1756, with colony and amount each year; (7) Account of all corn, malt, etc., exported from England to all places including the plantations in 1757, 1758, 1766, 1768, 1769, 1770; (8) Account of British plantations' brown sugar imported into and exported out of England for ten years before 1758; (9) Account of prices of Muscovado sugar from Barbados and the Leeward Islands sold in England between 1727–1758; (10) Account of beaver skins imported and exported, 1763; (11) Account of rice exported from North America before 1766; (12) Account of duties paid on molasses imported into the northern colonies for three years before 1766; (13) Account of merchandise imported into England from Guadeloupe, Martinique, and Havana between 1761–1764; (14) Account of duties levied by 4 Geo. III on goods imported into and exported from the colonies to Nov. 1766; (15) Account of duties payable on sugar from 1764 to 1766; (16) Account of the gross and net produce of molasses duty laid on the colonies by 6 Geo. II, from 1734 to 1764; (17) Account of gross and net produce of molasses duty laid by 4 Geo. III; (18) Account of rice, sago powder, and vermicilli imported from the colonies into England between May and November 1767; (19) Account of colonial wheat or flour imported into England from the colonies between Jan. and Oct. 1767; (20) Account of whale fins and oil imported into England from America between 1765 and 1767; (21) Account of net produce on tea for five years preceding

1767, with the produce of duties and excise upon teas between July 1768 and July 1769.

No. 275. Custom House reports mostly after 1783 but some falling within the period 1748–1776: (1) Account of British linens exported, 1773 and 1774; (2) Account of foreign linens exported, 1773 and 1774; (3) Account of West Indies products exported from England, 1773 and 1774; (4) Account of West Indies products imported, 1773 and 1774.

No. 276. Custom House reports (continued): (1) Account of British soap exported to the colonies, 1764–1769; (2) Account of all goods exported from England to East and West Florida and imports from the same colonies, 1763–1767; (3) Account of all tobacco imported into England from the colonies, 1762–1769; (4) Account of salted beef, pork and bacon imported from America, 1769–1770; (5) Account of the produce of St. Vincent, Tobago, and Grenada imported into England, 1762–1770; (6) The same for Dominica; (7) Account of cereals imported into England from the colonies in 1772; (8) Account of free port duties collected in Dominica by 6 Geo. III, c. 49; (9) Account of raw hides imported from America, 1768–1769; (10) Two large reports of exports from England to Jamaica, 1748–1755; (11) Report of the value of all articles exported from England to the America colonies, Jan. 26, 1775, £2,462,148. 15s. 10d.; (12) Papers concerned with the export of tobacco and sugar; (13) Value of exports and imports to and from the West Indies and England, 1737–1762; (14) Quantity and value of tobacco imported into England from the colonies, 1769–1773; (15) Value of silk, cotton, worsted, linen, and mixed hose exported from England to North America and the West Indies, 1772–1774; (16) Quantity of salt imported into the several colonies, 1755–1768; (17) Account of coffee exported from England, 1773–1774; (18) Account of coffee imported into England from American colonies, 1773–1774; (19) Account of bounties paid out of customs on all goods imported from the colonies, 1761–1777; (20) Account of duties paid on goods imported into England from the colonies (exclusive of tobacco) for six years ending 1776; (21) Account of plantation tobacco imported into and exported from England, 1760–1776; (22) Account of iron, hemp, and wood products imported into England, 1760–1766; (23) Account of cotton-wool growth of the colonies imported into England, 1767–1777; (24) Account of all cotton-wool imported into England, distinguishing the foreign from the colonial, 1767–1777.

No. 291. King's warrants. Among them are the following: (1) Pension to Francis Fauquier of £300, 1768; (2) Allowance to German Protestants settling in South Carolina; (3) Allowance to Peter Randolph and William Byrd for services relating to the treaty with the

Cherokee and Catawba Indians, 1761; (4) Warrant for the appointment of members of the American Board of Customs Commissioners, 1767.

No. 312, 1769. Exports from Ireland to America, drawn from papers at the Dublin Custom House, from 1769 on, with some papers on smuggling, especially American ships carrying rice to Holland and returning with tea, linen, and liquor.

PAPERS OF THE AFRICAN COMPANIES

Treasury 70. Royal African Company and the Company of Merchants Trading to Africa

In 1662, there was organized a company of "Royal Adventurers of England trading to Africa"; in 1672 a charter was granted to it under the title "Royal African Company of England." This was a joint-stock company with a monopoly of the African trade. This monopoly was greatly restricted in 1697. As a result, despite financial assistance from Parliament, the company fell into practical bankruptcy. In 1747 it was dissolved by act of Parliament. In its place there was created a regulated company, "The Company of Merchants Trading to Africa," which survived until 1821. The following series of papers bearing upon the activities of these companies fall within the years 1748–1776:

Nos. 1–67, 1678–1750. Letters received from Africa and the West Indies.

Nos. 68–74, 1750–1818. Letters sent to Africa.

Nos. 75–99, 1663–1752. Minutes of the Court of Assistance of the Royal African Company.

Nos. 102–150, 1725–1817. Minutes of various committees of the two companies.

Nos. 151–154, 1750–1818. Acts of the council at Cape Coast Castle, etc.

Nos. 155–162, 1770–1792. Reports, examinations, orders, and instructions.

Nos. 176–177, 1756–1757. Parliamentary reports, relating to the trade to Africa.

Nos. 178–215, 1674–1752. Regarding the Royal African Company stock and stock transfers.

Nos. 216–961, 1662–1821. These are the African Companies cash books, bill books, warrants books, ledgers, and invoice books.

Nos. 974–1182, 1750–1821. Day books of the African forts.

Nos. 1198–1207, 1699–1807. Books concerning customs.

Nos. 1210–1220, 1674–1816. Ships books, including ships accounts, diaries, invoices, etc.

Nos. 1250–1262, 1703–1790. Ivory and gold books.

Nos. 1263–1269, 1755–1792. Books concerning slaves.

Nos. 1273–1414, 1751–1821. Garrison ledgers, Cape Coast Castle.

Nos. 1415–1416, 1763–1765. Senegal.

Nos. 1417–1421, 1758–1759. Papers concerning a place not designated.

No. 1422, 1771–1780. Tantumquerry and elsewhere on the African coast.

Nos. 1428–1431, 1671–1751. Security books.

Nos. 1454–1456, 1750–1815. Register of company servants and officers.

Nos. 1457–1461, 1751–1816. Cape Coast Castle pay bills.

Nos. 1474–1487, 1713–1809. Letter-books of particular persons.

Nos. 1488–1498, 1769–1794. Account books of particular persons.

Nos. 1499–1504, 1718–1822. Effects of dead men and sales of these effects.

Nos. 1508–1510, 1756–1819. List of stockholders of the Company of Merchants.

Nos. 1516–1606, 1750–1820. Detached papers.

TREASURY SOLICITOR PAPERS

These papers are in bundles, eleven thousand in number. They relate to suits. Many have been destroyed and comparatively few bear upon the period 1748–1776. Those that do are as follows, listed chronologically:

No. 3888, 1756. Appeal in Privy Council by Samuel Mason, guardian of the Mohegan Indians, *vs.* the Governor and Company of Connecticut and persons intruding on the land. There are many papers connected with this interesting issue, some of them already listed.

No. 5158, 1763. Printed papers on the dispute between the Governor and Commons House of Assembly of South Carolina.

No. 1210, 1766. In the Exchequer, case of Surveyor and Auditor General Cholmondeley, plaintiff, *vs.* William Mathew Burt, late agent for Guadeloupe, defendant.

No. 825, 1767. In the Court of Common Pleas. A number of plaintiffs *vs.* Gov. James Murray of the Province of Quebec, involving duties levied by Murray.

No. 4957, 1768. Major Robert Rogers *vs.* Gen. Gage on grounds of trespass, assault, and imprisonment. Asking £20,000 damage. There are four interesting exhibits among these papers.

No. 3321, 1768. An Exchequer case. The Attorney General *vs.* the East India Company respecting duties on tea. This has to do with the exportation of tea to America and the drawbacks; an interesting case with papers relating to it.

No. 65, 1769. The King *vs.* George Robinson for publishing a libel in the *Independent Chronicle* (a Junius letter). In this connection see *No. 765,* the King *vs.* John Almon for publishing the same libel.

No. 4377, 1771. Appeal to Privy Council. Harry Smith, collector of customs, St. Vincent, *vs.* Richard Otley.

No. 62, 1775. The King *vs.* John Horne [Tooke] for publishing a libel accusing the King's troops of committing murder at Lexington and Concord. (He was fined and imprisoned for the libel.)

Custom House Papers

Until 1671 the English customs duties were farmed out; that is, by agreeing to pay a fixed sum into the Exchequer of Receipt, certain individuals were authorized to collect and then retain these duties. In that year Charles II appointed by letters patent a Board of Customs Commissioners to manage the revenues. During the period under review there were two boards in Great Britain; one for England and Wales with nine commissioners and a second with five commissioners for Scotland. Under warrant from the Treasury each board could appoint and remove inferior officers. Under authorization of 25 Chas. II, c. 7 a collector of duties on enumerated goods in the colonies was provided for, but no steps were taken at the time to implement it. However, customs officers were later assigned to ports in the colonies. They were appointed by the Lords of the Treasury on nomination of the English Customs Board which prepared the instructions for these officers. When in 1767 the American Board of Customs Commissioners was created by act of Parliament, the members of it received their commissions under the Great Seal. The new board, with its headquarters at Boston, was authorized to enforce the navigation and trade laws in North America and the more northern of the islands adjacent to its coast, excluding the British West Indies which continued under the supervision of the English Customs Commissioners.

The customs records in Great Britain that have survived are still scattered. We have already dealt with such of these records as are among the Colonial Office papers and those among the Treasury Board papers. Another customs series in the Public Record Office is among the Board of Trade papers and still another there, the Inspector-General's accounts, will be taken up. Beyond the Public Record Office there are customs records in the library of Her Majesty's Customs and Excise at King's Beam House, Mark Lane, London, E.C. 3 and the out-ports. It would be best to treat them as a whole. At this point it is necessary to lean chiefly on the M. S. Giuseppi *Guide*, II, 105–8, and also on B. R. Crick and Miriam Alman: *Guide*, pp. 192–6, for customs records that fall within the years 1748–1776. The Public Record Office lists the following volumes:

Customs 1, 1716–1829. Here in 428 volumes are the minutes of the proceedings of the Irish Revenue Commissioners. Each volume has been indexed.

Customs 3, 1697–1780. This series in 80 volumes is made up of ledgers of imports and exports at London and the out-ports. These indicate the movement not only of goods but also of bullion.

Customs 14, 1755–1827. These ledgers of imports and exports in 39 volumes are the returns of the Inspector General of Imports and Exports for Scotland.

Customs 15, 1698–1829. These ledgers in 140 volumes are arranged under the countries importing to or exporting from Ireland with the volume of the goods each year.

Customs 16, 1768–1773. This volume is concerned with North America and indicates the nature and volume of trade at each of the ports. A most informative volume.

Customs 17, 1772–1808. This series in 30 volumes is concerned with the state of navigation, commerce, and revenue for the above years.

Customs 18, 1675–1813. These 607 listed volumes (some of them missing) called Series I of the Establishment Registers, are concerned with the quarterly payment of the salaries of the customs officers. Attention is particularly called to *Nos. 310* and *312* which set forth for the latter half of 1767 the "Establishment of the Officers of His Majesty's Customs in the Plantations."

Finally, there are in the Public Record Office the Exchequer Port Books, called by Crick and Alman (p. 194) "the most important source for the study of English maritime trade" for the earlier centuries. This great series in 1,464 bundles contains over 14,000 vellum books prepared by local customs officers and sent to the Exchequer where they were received by the Inspectors-General of Imports and Exports. Although the surviving London port-books in this series are all in the seventeenth century the out-ports supply much information bearing upon the years 1748–1776. The following outports are represented:

Nos. 161–184, Berwick, 1606–1784;
Nos. 185–302, Newcastle upon Tyne, 1579–1798;
Nos. 303–386, Hull and neighbouring ports, 1654–1787;
Nos. 387–424, Boston (Lincs.), 1565–1773;
Nos. 425–470, Lynn, 1565–1794;
Nos. 471–586, Great Yarmouth and neighbouring ports, 1565–1780;
Nos. 638–736, Sandwich and Deal and neighbouring ports, 1565–1756;
Nos. 814–863, Southampton and Portsmouth, 1565–1758;
Nos. 864–924, Poole, with Lynne and Weymouth, 1565–1759;
Nos. 925–1009, Exeter with neighbouring ports, 1565–1788;
Nos. 1010–1080, Plymouth and neighbouring ports, 1565–1758;
Nos. 1081–1127, Bridgewater and Moorehead, 1566–1776;
Nos. 1128–1240, Bristol, 1565–1788;
Nos. 1241–1269, Gloucester, 1581–1776;
Nos. 1270–1297, Cardiff and neighbouring ports;
Nos. 1298–1322, Milford Haven and neighbouring ports, 1565–1784;
Nos. 1323–1447, Chester and neighbouring ports, 1565–1789.

While on the subject of the customs records, it is desirable to turn temporarily from the Public Record Office to the Customs Library at King's Beam House, in Mark Lane, London.

THE LIBRARY, HIS MAJESTY'S CUSTOMS AND EXCISE

Among the papers at Beam House Library that throw light on the period 1748–1776 are the minutes and letter-books of the Commissioners of Customs, including:

Nos. 887–896, the General Business minutes of the Board in 10 volumes, 1734–1813;

Nos. 1268–1275, the Receiver-General's minutes in 9 volumes, 1716–1784;

Nos. 1319–1332, digests of the Board's minutes in 14 volumes, 1696–1869;

Nos. 1480–1542 and *1621,* the Scottish Board's minutes in 64 volumes, 1723–1828.

In this library are to be found other important series, among them the ledgers of the inspector-general:

Nos. 1683–1735, ledgers of imports and exports in 53 volumes, 1682–1776.

Again, there is a series of volumes called "Opinions of Counsel. England" and "Opinions of Counsel. Scotland." These opinions, dealing with the application and interpretation of the laws of trade, include:

Nos. 200–206, 17796, 21618–21638, opinions in 29 volumes that relate to England, 1701–1841;

Nos. 1547–1549, opinions in 3 volumes that relate to Scotland 1760–1783.

The library also has certain plantation records. For example:

No. 760, a ledger, covering the years 1767–1775, which indicates the nature of the collections made at various ports in Virginia;

No. 767, also a single volume, outlining in detail the customs establishment in America in 1767;

Nos. 766 and *768,* two volumes concerned with the customs in the colonies from 1767 to 1776.

CUSTOMS RECORDS AND THE OUT-PORTS

While much custom house material is embodied in the papers at the Public Record Office and in the Library of Customs and Excise, the records still remaining at the outports and covering the years 1748–1776 are very numerous. We shall again rely on Crick and Alman, pp. 197–207, in noting the volumes of these records that apply to the period under survey:

Dover: The Board to the collector, from 1746, 20 vols.; other records, from 1693, 9 vols.;

Portsmouth: The Board to the collector, from 1726, 140 vols.; other records, from 1689, 8 vols.;

Southampton: The Board to the collector, from 1756, 128 vols.; the collector to the Board, from 1714, 126 vols.; other records, from 1728, 18 vols.;

Cowes: The Board to the collector, from 1703, 79 vols.; letter-books, order books, etc., from 1703, 27 vols.; the collector to the Board, from 1749, 60 vols.;

Poole: The Board to the collector, from 1760, 6 vols.; letter-books, order books, etc., from 1758, 28 vols.;

Weymouth: The Board to the collector, from 1694, 117 vols.; the collector to the Board, from 1716, 103 vols.;

Exeter: The Board to the collector from 1676, 121 vols.; the collector to the Board, from 1743, 50 vols.; other records from 1738, 12 vols.;

Dartmouth: The Board to the collector, from 1675, 112 vols.; other records, from 1687, 14 vols.;

Penzance: The Board to the collector, from 1722, 119 vols.; the collector to the Board, from 1738, 35 vols.;

Bristol (including Barnstable and other minor ports): The Board to the collector, from 1717, 90 vols.; the collector to the Board, from 1727, 56 vols.; other records, from 1760, 23 vols.;

Cardiff: The Board to the collector, from 1689, 93 vols.; the collector to the Board, from 1746, 23 vols.; other records, from 1704, 32 vols.;

Swansea: The Board to the collector, from 1709, 155 vols.; the collector to the Board, from 1730, 43 vols.; other records, from 1711, 23 vols.;

Caernarvon: The Board to the collector, from 1714, 103 vols.; the collector to the Board, from 1757, 53 vols.;

Liverpool: Registers of ships, from 1739, 152 vols. For the port letter-books see *Customs Letter Books of the Port of Liverpool, 1711–1813* (R.C. Jarvis, ed., Manchester, Eng., 1954);

Heysham (Lancaster): Letter-books, order books, etc., from 1715, 6 vols.; other records, from 1689, 1 vol.;

Whitehaven: The Board to the collector, from 1703, 19 vols.; the collector to the Board, from 1730, 32 vols.; other records from 1771, 13 vols.;

Dumfries: The Board to the collector, from 1727, 76 vols.; the collector to the Board, from 1708, 16 vols.;

Ayr: The Board to the collector, from 1740, 5 vols.; the collector to the Board, from 1729, 30 vols.;

Greenock: The Board to the collector, from 1723, 342 vols.; the collector to the Board, from 1749, 81 vols.; other letter-books, order books, etc., from 1749, 26 vols.; other records, from 1707, 39 vols.;

Glasgow: The Board to the collector, from 1773, 86 vols.;

Campbeltown: The Board to the collector, from 1738, 60 vols.; the collector to the Board, from 1749, 47 vols.; registers of British ships, from 1763, 13 vols.; other records, from 1764, 7 vols.;

Stornoway: The collector to the Board, from 1765, 26 vols.;

Inverness: Certain records, from 1707, 16 vols.;

Aberdeen: The Board to the collector, from 1733, 98 vols.; the collector to the Board, from 1721, 32 vols.; other records, from 1708, 23 vols.;

Montrose: The Board to the collector, from 1708, 52 vols.; the collector to the Board, from 1724, 29 vols.; other letter-books, order books, etc., from 1710, 59 vols.;

Dundee: The Board to the collector, from 1708, 206 vols.; the collector to the Board, from 1735, 39 vols.; other records, from 1716, 19 vols.;

Alloa: The Board to the collector, from 1744, 19 vols.; the collector to the Board, from 1736, 14 vols.; other letter-books, etc., from 1718, 106 vols.;

Leith (including Dunbar): The Board to the collector, from 1707, 309 vols.; other records, from 1707, 6 vols.;

Newcastle upon Tyne: The Board to the collector, from 1706, 27 vols.; the collector to the Board, from 1724, 120 vols.; other letter-books, etc., from 1725, 164 vols.; other records, from 1764, 19 vols.;

Sunderland: The Board to the collector, from 1740, 103 vols.; the collector to the Board, from 1732, 65 vols.;

Stockton-on-Tees: The Board to the collector, from 1675, 71 vols.; the collector to the Board, from 1736, 35 vols.; other records, from 1748, 7 vols.;

Whitby: The collector to the Board, from 1721, 10 vols.; letter-books, etc., from 1715, 16 vols.;

Hull: Letter-books, etc., from 1733, 213 vols.; other records from 1756, 18 vols.;

Boston: The Board to the collector, from 1732, 99 vols.; the collector to the Board, from 1766, 14 vols.;

King's Lynn: The Board to the collector, from 1700, 124 vols.; other letter-books, etc., from 1728, 25 vols.;

Great Yarmouth: The Board to the collector, from 1662, 114 vols.; the collector to the Board, from 1702, 110 vols.; other letter-books etc., from 1731, 99 vols.;

Harwich: The Board to the collector, from 1699, 129 vols.; the collector to the Board, from 1713, 89 vols.; other records, from 1699, 10 vols.

Returning again to the Public Record Office in dealing with the collection and disbursement of revenue for the period 1748–1776 we now come to the records of those agencies created to see that funds were spent according to order. This brings us to the Audit Office and the Pipe Office.

Audit Office and Pipe Office Papers

The careful auditing of the multitudinous accounts relating to money received into and money paid from the royal exchequer was a most important function and also sheds much light on the growth and means of support of the British Empire. This was the major responsibility, as the name implies, of the Audit Office. It was in New Palace Yard, Westminister, then at 3 Whitehall Yard before removal to Somerest House, where its papers were transferred to the Public Record Office in December 1859. These papers are divided into two classes: "Accounts, Various" and "Declared Accounts," that is, accounts that had been settled. They will be considered in this order and in doing so the description of these papers as presented in the C.M. Andrews *Guide*, II, 66–106 will be followed as far as the documents relate to the Empire during the years 1748–1776.

ACCOUNTS, VARIOUS

No. 126, 1764–1767: (1) Account of Gov. George Johnstone of West Florida for Indian presents, Oct. 1764–Jan. 1767, also his contingent account for the same years; (2) Three accounts of Commander-in-Chief Thomas Gage, 1763–1773, involving cash paid, bills of exchange drawn, and debit and credit accounts, with a part of the money payable to Brig.-Gen. Guy Carleton; (3) Account of Gov. James Murray of Quebec, 1766; (4) Drummond, Franks, and Nesbitt's accounts for victualling soldiers in America, 1766–1778; (5) Other victualling accounts, 1766–1778; (6) Two accounts of Edward Codrington, West Florida, 1767–1775; (7) Barrack-Master's accounts, 1765–1776, Gen. James Robertson, barrack-master general; (8) Account of Maj.-Gen. Christie, 1757–1777.

No. 127, 1760–1785, involves the accounts of the following persons: (1) Maj.-Gen. Ralph Burton at Three Rivers, Canada, 1760–1763; (2) Guy Johnson, Indian Department, 1774–1783; H. T. Cramahé, Quebec, 1774–1780; (3) Edward Lewis, West Florida, payment of troops, 1767–1781; (4) John Montrésor, engineer, 1768–1775; (5) John Ellis, agent of West Florida, 1772–1776; (6) S. Fludyer and John Drummond for remitting money to America, 1767–1769; (7) Gov. Peter Chester of West Florida, contingent and Indian expenses, Aug. 1770 to the surrender of the province, 1781; (8) John Moultrie, expenses of building the state house and making roads in East Florida, 1772–1774; (9) John Campbell, agent for Georgia, 1774–1775; (10) Sir James Colebrooke, for remitting money for the Louisbourg garrison, 1759–1762.

No. 128 includes: (1) Ledger of the cost of engineering works in North America, to 1774; (2) Pay account of Gen. James Murray's staff at Quebec, 1760; (3) Gen. Guy Carleton, Quebec contingencies, 1766–1770; (4) Christopher Kilby, settling emigrants in Nova Scotia, 1749–1758; (5) Nova Scotia accounts, 1750–1760, 1775–1778.

No. 396, 1764–1788. This group of papers relates to the efforts of the government of Great Britain to secure accurate surveys of North America. In 1764 the Privy Council ordered the Lords of the Treasury to carry out Capt. Samuel Holland's suggestion that a complete survey be made of British North American possessions. From 1764 to 1776 Holland worked in America and produced a number of maps, mostly involving surveys in Canada and New England. The papers appear to have been presented to the Audit Office by Holland to facilitate the auditing of his accounts.

No. 400, 1754–1835. Accounts involving Cape Breton, St. John (Prince Edward Island), Georgia, West Florida, the Bahamas, and Barbados. Two items falling within the period 1748–1776 may be mentioned: (1) Account of the Georgia agent for promoting silk culture, 1754; (2) A commission for Samuel Hannay as provost marshall, West Florida.

No. 401, 1764–1776. East Florida. General record book. This entry book provides a variety of valuable information including instructions, petitions, land grants.

No. 441, 1775–1777. Virginia. Gov. Dunmore's expenses in raising regiments and equipping them and also the purchase of three vessels for government use.

No. 500, 1751–1769. Newfoundland. These commissariat papers have to do with providing stores for the garrison on the island, with lists of soldiers.

No. 912, 1754–1780. Hospitals in North America: (1) Receipts for pay of hospital officials, 1762–1763; (2) Accounts current of His Majesty's hospitals in North America for the years 1754–1764, signed by James Napier.

Nos. 1255–1280, 1703–1783. Papers relating to British stamp duties. Among information provided are lists of British newspapers and names of publishers.

No. 1391, 1765–1772. American stamp duties. This paper book provides a great deal of information in connection with the plan to levy stamp taxes on the colonies by 5 Geo. III, with names of distributors, etc.

Nos. 1398–1399, 1689–1786. Accounts of the Treasurer Solicitor. Some of the items that fall within the period 1748–1776 are as follows: (1) The passing of a patent for the surrender of Georgia to the Crown by the Trustees, 1752; (2) Patent relating to Georgia and South Carolina, 1752; (3) Claim of the Earl and Countess of Cardigan to St. Lucia, 1763–1764; (4) The Wilkes and Almon cases, 1764–1765.

Nos. 1609–1667, 1670–1783. These are enrollment books of warrants, with copies of patents, letters of attorney, etc. Among pertinent items are: (1) Patent to Charles Stewart, paymaster of customs in America, 1767; (2) Warrant allowing Jared Ingersoll, judge of Vice-Admiralty in America, £238. 16s. 8½d., out of the sale of old naval stores, with letters of attorney to Thomas Life to receive the money.

DECLARED ACCOUNTS

The term "declared accounts" represents, as has already been stated, the final settlement of accounts with the government on the part of those entrusted with funds for disbursement. Two copies of this account were made at the Audit Office, one on paper and the other on parchment. These were then sent to the Treasury Office and signed. The paper copy was thereupon returned to the Audit Office and the parchment copy forwarded to the office of the King's Remembrancer of the Exchequer where it was enrolled in a series called "Enrolments of Public Accounts"; but the parchment itself then went to the office of the Lord Treasurer's Remembrancer where an abstract was made of it in the series called "States and Views of Public Accounts" before it was finally deposited in the office of the Clerk of the Pipe among the pipe roll series. It may be noted that in 1833, by 4 Will. IV, c. 99, Par. 41, the office of Clerk of the Pipe was abolished in England and the following year, by 4 and 5 Will. IV. 316, c. 16, Par. 1, in Scotland. Why the term "pipe" is used in this connection is not clear; it is possible that at an earlier period after being enrolled the parchments were then placed in tubes or pipes for preservation. With the abolition of the Pipe Office all parchments of date later than 1714 that duplicate the paper rolls in the Audit Office were transferred to the Bodleian Library at Oxford.

Pipe Office, declared accounts

Only two manuscripts pertaining to the period 1748–1776 that were in the Pipe Office need be mentioned:

Nos. 1264 and 1265, 1765–1770, are the declarations of accounts of W. Mellish. Between 1775 and 1786 he was receiver general and cashier for Barbados, the Leeward Islands, and the Caribbees (see *Nos. 1249–1250*).

ARMY

Audit Office, declared accounts

Nos. 66–92, 1746–1783. Here are the declared accounts of various pay-masters-general for the armed forces, including those of William Pitt, Henry Fox, Richard Rigby, Edmund Burke, and Isaac Barré.

Barracks masters (Abroad) *accounts*

No. 147, 1765–1776. Declaration of the account of Lieut.-Gen. James Robertson, barrack-master general in North America. Robertson received funds from the paymaster-general in London and disbursed this money on warrant of Maj.-Gen. Gage for barracks, etc. Bills were drawn on Robertson by officers at Fort Pitt, Pensacola, Newfoundland, Canada, and the Floridas. At the end of this account there is a statement, "Barrack expences at the several Posts: Quebec, Three Rivers, Montreal, Oswegatchie, Michilimakinac, Fort George, Halifax, Mobile, Pensacola, St. Augustine, Fort Chartres, Crown Point, Fort Frederic, Fort Pitt, New York, Boston, Boston (Castle William), Providence."

Commanders-in-chief, military governors, etc., accounts

Those accounts that fall within the years 1748–1776 are as follows:

No. 162, 1762–1765. Declaration of the account of Lieut.-Gen. Haldimand, governor of the Three Rivers.

No. 163, 1765–1770. Declaration of the accounts of the following: (1) Lieut.-Gen. Thomas Gage, commander-in-chief in North America, 1765–1767; (2) Lieut.-Gen. E. Massey, commander in the Northern District, North America, 1766–1767; (3) Lieut.-Gen. Carleton, commander in the same, 1766–1770.

No. 164, 1775–1778. Declaration of the account of Sir William Howe, commander-in-chief in North America.

Contractors, purveyors, etc. (Abroad), *accounts*

Nos. 187–196, 1720–1782. Here are the declarations of account of the following contractors and purveyors: (1) T. Missing and M. Woodford, for Placentia, Canso, and Annapolis, 1720–1768; (2) Purveyors for Nova Scotia, 1745–1752; (3) Purveyor for Halifax, N. S. and St. John's, Newfoundland, 1750–1760; (4) John Thomlinson and John Hanbury, London, providing money for Gen. Braddock's campaign, a lengthy account, Dec. 1754–May 1757; (5) Thomlinson and Hanbury for remitting money for forces in America, 1754–1765, and Fludyer and J. Drummond for the same service, 1767–1769; (6) Harley and Drummond for the same service, 1769–1778; (7) W. Baker, Kilby, and R. Baker, purveyors for North America, 1756–1760; (8) J. Colebrooke and Nesbit, contractors to remit money to Louisbourg, 1759–1767; (9) J. Kennion, for supplying provisions to forces against Havana, 1762; A. Bacon, for provisions for Tobago, St. Vincent, and Dominica, 1764–1770; Cuming and Mason, for provisions for East Florida, 1764–1776; Major and Henniker and E. Codrington, for victuals for West Florida, 1765–1775; (10) E. Lewis, for remitting money to Pensacola and Mobile garrisons, 1767–1781; (11) Stephenson and Blackburn, for forwarding victuals to West Florida, 1775–1778, and Mason and Jones, for victuals for East Florida, 1776–1778; (12) Stephenson and Blackburn, purveyors for Nova Scotia, Newfoundland, and Penobscot, 1768–1782.

EXPEDITIONS, ACCOUNTS

Of these accounts two fall within the years 1748–1776:

No. 218. The declared account of Lieut.-Col. J. Hale, Secretary to the Earl of Albemarle in connection with the expedition against Havana, 1762 and the declared account of Maj.-Gen. Dalrymple, commander-in-chief in the expedition against the Caribs on St. Vincent, 1772–1773.

QUARTERMASTERS, ACCOUNTS

Nos. 335–336. These accounts contain declarations of the following North American quartermasters: (1) Lieut.-Col. Bradstreet, 1756–1760; (2) Lieut.-Col. Robertson, 1757–1765; (3) Lieut. T. Gamble, 1765–1773; (4) Lieut.-Col. Irving, 1760–1765, at Quebec; (5) Lieut.-Col. William Shirreff, 1768–1776, two accounts; (6) Maj. J. Maxwell, Montreal, 1770–1772; (7) Maj. J. Carden, Montreal, 1775–1777; (8) Maj. T. Campbell, Canada, 1775–1779.

CLAIMS FOR COMPENSATION, ETC.

No. 458, 1756. Here is a declaration of John Thomlinson and John Hanbury of the distribution to the various colonies of money granted by Parliament for their respective contributions to the war then being waged.

COMPTROLLERS AND CASHIERS

For this very large collection of papers it is necessary not only to designate the number but also the roll. Only two accounts in this collection fall within the period, 1748–1776:

No. 843, Roll 1134, 1767–1777. Here are the declared accounts of James Porter, comptroller of the customs, containing customs and duties on goods imported into and exported from any of his Majesty's North American colonies and islands belonging thereto, including the Bermudas and the Bahamas.

No. 844, Roll 1137, 1767–1776. The declared account of Charles Stewart, cashier and paymaster of his Majesty's customs of revenue received.

GOVERNORS, AGENTS, ETC.

No. 1259, Roll 140, 1765–1772. Declared account of Gov. Melville of St. Vincent, Dominica, Grenada, and Tobago.

No. 1261, Rolls 147–151, 1772–1786. Declared accounts of Gov. John Moultrie and Lieut.-Gen. Patrick Tonyn of East Florida, and of W. Knox and J. Cowan, agents; *Rolls 152–155*, 1767–1781. Declared accounts of Gov. Grant of East Florida and Governors Johnstone and Chester of West Florida. *No 1261* offers many interesting insights into the history of both East and West Florida.

No. 1263, Rolls 162–170, 1752–1783. Declared accounts of the following agents of Georgia: B. Martyn, J. Campbell, and J. B. West.

No. 1273, Roll 242, 1762–1763. Declared account of Lieut.-Gen. Keppel, governor and commander-in-chief of Havana.

No. 1282, Roll 314, 1747–1749. Declared account of Gov. Hopson of Louisbourg.

No. 1295, Roll 432, 1775–1777. Declared account of Gov. John Wentworth of New Hampshire, an especially interesting statement of the use of money received.

Nos. 1301–1303, Rolls 482–489, 1749–1785. Declared accounts of Christopher Kilby and Richard Cumberland, agents of Nova Scotia.

No. 1324 contains the declared accounts of the following persons: *Roll 624*, 1760–1763, Gen. R. Burton of Three Rivers, Canada; *Roll 626*, 1755, Lieut.-Gov. Dinwiddie of Virginia, connected with the Ohio expedition; *Roll 627*, 1775–1777, the Earl of Dunmore of Virginia.

HOSPITALS AND INFIRMARIES

No. 1506 has the declared accounts of the following people: *Roll 213*, 1755–1763, J. Napier with the British army in North America; *Roll*

215, 1758–1760, G. Corryn with the expedition against Guadeloupe; *Roll 217*, 1758–1764, J. A. F. Hesse in the West Indies.

NORTH AMERICAN INDIANS

No. 1530 contains the declared accounts of the following people: *Roll 1*, 1755–1756, 1758, 1760–1761, 1763, Benjamin Martyn, late agent of Georgia, for Indian presents, etc.; *Roll 2*, 1755–1774, Sir John Johnson, representing Sir Wm. Johnson, who disbursed £146,545 for presents and other contingent and incidental expenses, including salaries. The report was defective in that in 1776 Sir William's house was plundered and burnt by the Americans and his papers in the home destroyed; *Roll 3*, 1756, John Pownall for expending £4000 for Indian presents sent to New York; *Roll 4*, 1758, James Wright, late agent of South Carolina, for expending £2000 for South Carolina Indian presents; *Roll 5*, 1774–1783, Col. Guy Johnson, late superintendent of Indian affairs.

SETTLERS IN NOVA SCOTIA

No. 2131, Rolls 1–2, 1751–1753. Declared accounts of those charged with settling persons in Nova Scotia, including foreign Protestants transported to the colony.

STAMP DUTIES

No. 2192, Roll 207, 1765. Declaration of the comptroller general of the several duties arising on stamped vellum, parchment, and paper in America. Amount collected £224,119. 0s. 4d.; expense £160,043. 7s. 10½d.; unaccounted-for stamps to the value of £64,155. 12s. 5½d. Much information is provided.

PUBLIC WORKS AND FORTIFICATIONS

No. 2531. Here are two declarations of army engineers: *Roll 662*, 1756–1761, 1764, 1767, by Harry Gordon, employed in building and repairing forts in North America; *Roll 663*, 1768–1778, by John Montrésor in building not only forts but batteries, barracks, magazines, etc.

Admiralty Papers

The beginnings of the modern admiralty system date from the years 1660–1673, when James, Duke of York, was Lord High Admiral, and Samuel Pepys was clerk of the accounts of the Navy Board. From 1689 to 1782, with the exception of the temporary revival of the office of Lord High Admiral early in the eighteenth century, this office was put in commission. The admiralty system consisted of an Admiralty Board—the Lords Commissioners for executing the Office of Lord High Admiral, headed by a First Lord of the Admiralty—with its secretary; a Navy Board with its four principal officers; and a series of lesser boards and offices, nearly all of which, as business increased, had been thrown off from the principal offices. The subordinate branches were: the Treasurer's Office, the Navy Pay Office, the Victualling Board, the Board of Transport Service, the Board for Sick and Wounded Seamen, the Prize Office, the Rendezvous Office, the Marine Pay Office and Chest at Chatham, the Sixpenny Receiver's Office, the Board of Longitude, the Royal Naval Academy at Portsmouth, and, finally, Greenwich Hospital.

The directive branch of the Admiralty during the period under review consisted of the Lords Commissioners of the Admiralty with their secretary. The board met daily, and in times of urgency twice daily, and carried on the routine work of directing the business of the navy. It shaped the policy of the government, generally under the direction of the king, as expressed in orders in council, or in instructions from the Secretary of State. It also controlled the movement of ships of war, determined the times of sailing, and kept a watch upon the execution of its orders. It corresponded with the admirals, vice-admirals, captains, commanders, and lieutenants of the squadrons and after 1762 kept elaborate digests of the contents of letters received from them. Having control over vice-admiralty jurisdiction, it was in very close touch with the High Court of Admiralty, issuing commissions for vice-admiralty officials and taking cognizance of all difficulties that arose in the exercise of vice-admiralty jurisdiction. It also issued warrants for letters of marque, controlled the holding of naval courts-martial, and had immediate supervision of the marines in all parts of the world. For details of the Admiralty records see C. M. Andrews: *Guide*, II, 1–63, and Crick and Alman: *Guide*, 248–54; likewise M.S. Giuseppi: *Guide*, II, 15–24.

The following pertinent papers relating to the period 1748–1776 are among those listed:

SECRETARY'S DEPARTMENT

Admiralty 1. In-letters

Nos. 230–243, 1713–1789. Despatches from Jamaica stations: *No. 234*, 1746–1758, from Admirals Knowles and Townshend; *No. 235*, 1752–1761, from Admiral Cotes; *No. 236*, 1759–1761, from Admiral Holmes; *No. 237*, 1762–1765, from Admirals Pocock and Keppel; *No. 238*, 1763–1772, from Admirals Burnaby and Parry, Commodores Forrest and Mackenzie; *No. 239*, 1771–1774, from Admiral Rodney; *No. 240*, 1774–1778, from Admiral Gayton.

Nos. 305–314. Despatches from the Leeward Islands stations: *No. 306*, 1747–1759, from Admirals Osborn and Frankland, Commodores Holburne and Pye; *No. 307*, 1757–1765, from Admirals Douglas and Rodney, and Commodore Moore; *No. 308*, 1761–1769, from Admirals Swanton, Tyrrell, and Pye; *No. 309*, 1769–1777, from Admirals Man, Parry, and Young.

Nos. 470–471, 1766–1783. Despatches from Newfoundland before 1766 are missing, but see *No. 470*, 1766–1776, which contains despatches from Admiral Duff and Commodores Palliser, Byron, and Shuldham.

Nos. 480–489, 1745–1784. Despatches from North American stations, north of Carolina: *No. 480*, 1745–1763, from Admirals Warren, Townshend, Savage, Mostyn, and Watson, Commodores Spry and Keppel; *No. 481*, 1755–1760, from Admirals Boscawen, Hardy, Holburne, Holmes, and Durell; *No. 482*, 1759–1766, from Admirals Saunders and Colville; *No. 483*, 1767–1772, from Commodores Hood and Gambier; *No. 484*, 1771–1777, from Admirals Montague and Shuldham; *No. 485*, 1774–1777, from Admiral Graves; *No. 486*, 1775–1784, from Admirals Byron and Arbuthnot, and Commodore Parker.

Nos. 1435–2733, 1698–1792. Ship Captain letters. These letters are arranged alphabetically under each captain's name and are as follows: *A. Nos. 1435–1477*, 1698–1792; *B. Nos. 1462–1504*, 1698–1785; *C. Nos. 1588–1615*, 1698–1783; *D. Nos. 1692–1710*, 1698–1784; *E. Nos. 1754–1762*, 1698–1783; *F. Nos. 1776–1791*, 1698–1783; *G. Nos. 1822–1840*, 1698–1792; *H. Nos. 1871–1907*, 1698–1783; *I* and *J. Nos. 1979–1988*, 1698–1792; *K. Nos. 2004–2015*, 1698–1792; *L. Nos. 2033–2057*, 1698–1785; *M. Nos. 2090–2124*, 1698–1785; *N. Nos. 2215–2223*, 1698–1792; *O. Nos. 2241–2250*, 1698–1792; *P. Nos. 2277–2307*, 1698–1784; *R. Nos. 2374–2394*, 1698–1787; *S. Nos. 2438–2486*, 1698–1786; *T. Nos. 2568–2593*, 1698–1783; *U.* and *V. Nos. 2624–2628*, 1698–1792; *W. Nos. 2636–2676*, 1698–1783; *Y. Nos. 2732–2733*, 1717–1792.

Nos. 3665–3681, 1680–1783. Letters received relating to the Solicitor's Department. The following are pertinent: *No. 3676*, 1747–1753: (1) Regarding the appeal of Capt. Innes of the *Aldborough*, for impressing three seamen belonging to colonial trading vessels, from the judgment of the court of common pleas, Charleston, Dec. 16, 1749. Appeal not allowed; (2) Combination of offices of judge of vice-admiralty and attorney general on one person in Barbados deemed unwise, Sept. 11, 1751; (3) Group of papers relating to a South Carolina case, June 3, 1752, with copy of vice-admiralty court proceedings; (4) Case of a New York boat flying a pennant "in contempt of the King's colors," which was fired on by H.M.S. *Greyhound* and a maid servant killed. Question: Was Lieut. How of the *Greyhound* liable to court-martial? Yes, but was finally acquitted; see Aug. 8 and Oct. 18, 1750, Aug. 28, 1751, and Feb. 25, 1752; (5) Action by Roger Passmore against Capt. Lloyd of H.M.S. *Winchester*, for impressing him in New England in 1744, Oct. 18, 1750. [Papers covering the years 1754 and 1767 not listed.] *No.* 3679, 1767–1775: (1) Certain cases of murder and other high crimes committed on board vessels voyaging between the British Isles and the plantations; (2) Case of Thomas Austin sent from Boston by Lieut.-Gov. Hutchinson on suspicion of piracy, Feb. 12, 1770; (3) Case regarding a Negro purchased in Maryland by the master of a ship, Jan. 1 and March 1, 1771; (4) Regarding commissions for trying pirates in America, Aug. 26, 1772, with a list dated Jan. 14, 1762; (5) Case of deserters from the 31st Regiment of Foot stationed in [New?] Providence, March 31, 1774; (6) Case of murder on the high seas on board a ship bound for Carolina, Aug. 17, 1775; (7) Copy of patent for the establishment in America of four courts of vice-admiralty, Aug. 11, 1768.

No. 3818, 1746–1758. Letters from Governors of Plantations and others: (1) From Gov. Glen of South Carolina on South Carolina trade, Jan. 19, 1748, and Sept. 23, 1752; (2) From Gov. Clinton of New York, Nov. 23, 1748, June 11, 1749, Dec. 30, 1750, June 20 and July 16, 1751, and Dec. 14, 1753; (3) From Gov. Popple of the Bermudas, March 7, 1750, and Sept. 7, 1756; (4) From Gov. Cornwallis of Nova Scotia about the murder of Capt. Howe, with enclosures, Dec. 2, 1750; (5) From Gov. Fleming of Tortola, Dec. 13, 1750; (6) From Gov. Dinwiddie of Virginia, Dec. 10, 1752, and Feb. 1, 1754; (7) From Gov. Hopson of Nova Scotia, April 14, 1753; (8) From Secretary Willard of Massachusetts, Sept. 13 and Nov. 6, 1754, Jan. 30, 1755; (9) From Gov. Lyttelton of South Carolina, July 19 and Nov. 20, 1756; (10) From Gov. Fauquier of Virginia, Sept. 23, 1758; (11) From Admiral Hardy, 1756 and Jan. 1757; (12) From Gov. Dobbs and the North Carolina Council, March 3, 1757; (13) From Gov. Pinfold of Barbados, July 13, 1757; (14) From Gov. Pownall of Massachusetts, Sept. 12, 1757, Jan. 12 and July 11, 1758; (15) From Andrew Oliver of Massachusetts, about passes, Jan. 10, 1758; (16) List of persons taken in captivity, 1756–1757, among them the names of 300 Massachusetts men.

No. 3819, 1759–1770: (1) From Gov. Stephen Hopkins of Rhode Island to Joseph Sherwood, Rhode Island London agent, about courts of vice-admiralty, Jan. 15, 1759; (2) From Gov. Pownall of Massachusetts, March 30, 1760; (3) From Andrew Oliver of Massachusetts, Oct. 8, 1760; (4) From Lieut.-Gov. Bull of South Carolina, June 15, 1761; (5) From Gov. Sir Henry Moore of Jamaica, Oct. 29, 1761; (6) From Gov. Lyttelton of South Carolina, Oct. 17, 1761; (7) From Gov. Pinfold of Barbados, Dec. 28, 1761; May 28 and Dec. 24, 1763; (8) From Gen. Amherst, New York, fourteen letters from May 11, 1762 to Sept. 17, 1763; (9) From Gov. Fauquier of Virginia, four letters from Dec. 26, 1761 to June 22, 1764; (10) From Gov. Popple of the Bermudas, Nov. 3, 1762 and ———, 1763, on an admiralty case and smuggling; (11) From Andrew Oliver of Massachusetts, five letters, from June 4, 1763 to Dec. 22, 1770, mostly about ship passes; (12) From Thomas Penn, proprietor of Pennsylvania, London, March 6, 1769; (13) From Gen. Gage, New York, Jan. 25, 1764; (14) From Gov. Johnstone of West Florida, March 3, 18, and 30, 1764; (15) From Charles Williams of New York, Feb. 22 and July 12, 1764 and April 19, 1768, chiefly about stamps and ship passes; (16) Gov. Wentworth of New Hampshire, Sept. 3, 1767; (17) Deputy Gov. John Penn of Pennsylvania, Nov. 4, 1768 and Jan. 3, 1770 about ship passes; (18) Gov. Hutchinson of Massachusetts, Jan. 1 and 13, Aug. 4, and Sept. 4, 1770; (19) President Nelson of Virginia, Dec. 20, 1770.

No. 3820, 1771–1790: (1) List of French, Dutch, and Spanish ships brought into Jamaica in the course of the war, also colonial ships; (2) From Gov. Hutchinson, Nov. 12 and Dec. 8, 1772, relating to the vice-admiralty court; (3) From Lieut.-Gov. Richard Penn, Oct. 17, 1772; (4) From Gov. John Wentworth, Jan. 13, 1773, about the state of the King's woods.

Nos. 3825–3838, 1719–1784. Letters from British consuls. These letters among other things throw light on the trade of the Empire, 1748–1776, with registers of Mediterranean passes, with names of vessels bound for colonial ports. However, the list is incomplete.

Nos. 3863–3867, 1694–1799. Letters from the Custom House: *No. 3865*, 1720–1756. While this bundle carries down to 1756, the documents worthy of note precede the year 1748. *No. 3866*, 1757–1780, relates chiefly to passes, convoys, smuggling and other matters in which the Custom House and the Admiralty were involved. Extracts from three letters, June 20 and Aug. 15, 1771 and May 4, 1774, relate to problems faced by the American Board of Customs Commissioners. Another letter from the customs officials of Falmouth, Oct. 5, 1771, contains comments from the British Customs Commissioners.

Nos. 3878–3887, 1740–1782. Letters from the Doctors' Commons. *No. 3882*, 1748–1757. Among the letters that fall within the years 1748–1776 are the following: (1) An interesting letter from the collector of customs in Boston, Charles H. Frankland, Feb. 5, 1749, who complained of the neglect of duty of Andrew Belcher, one of the customs officials. In a letter by Belcher, dated Aug. 13, 1750, there is a memorial signed by 53 persons, among them leading Boston merchants in support of Belcher; (2) There is also a group of letters from custom officials and others at a number of ports relating to admiralty matters. Among them is a letter from William Smith, Jr., New York, April 8, 1758 relating to the French snow *Bon Rencontre,* laden with sugar and indigo, and bound for New York. *No. 3884,* 1768–1777: (1) A bundle of papers concerning the court of vice-admiralty at Halifax, 1768; (2) About the conviction of David Ferguson for murder on board the merchant ship *Betsey* off the coast of Virginia; (3) The petition of William Story, deputy register of the court of vice-admiralty of Massachusetts, 1772, whose home was wrecked by a mob on the night of Aug. 26, 1765, and many of his records destroyed. Granted £50 by the General Court in 1772, he desires to return to his native town of Boston; (4) The case of John Andrews, judge of the Rhode Island court of vice-admiralty, involving admiralty proceedings and the jurisdiction of the superior court of the colony, with the chief justice of the latter issuing a writ of prohibition, April 1773; (5) Correspondence with a number of judges of the vice-admiralty courts in the colonies, with list of Virginia seizures and papers, from Richard Starke including a memorial with letter, March 12, 1771; (6) A group of papers regarding the seizure and condemnation of American vessels, with questions put to the King's advocate and the King's proctor; (7) Papers regarding the power of the government of Antigua to fit out vessels against the Americans; (8) Warrant authorizing West Indian governors to seize American ships.

Nos. 3930–3974, 1697–1785 and 1738–1800. Letters of intelligence in two series. These letters, mostly written in French and sent home chiefly from leading seaports in Europe, provide intelligence regarding French ships and shipping.

Nos. 3999–4013, 1703–1783. Letters from the Ordnance Office to the Admiralty, in bound volumes. These papers are concerned with ordnance for the Navy, equipment of store-ships and convoys and ordnance sent to the colonies.

Nos. 4080–4151, 1689–1785. Letters from the Secretary of State to the Admiralty. For the period 1748–1776, there is much material. To illustrate this C. M. Andrews in his *Guide,* II, 29–30, lists the contents of *No. 4121,* 1756–1757, chiefly orders and instructions from the Secretary in connection with the waging of the war with France. These are as follows: (1) To agree with the contractors

Kilby and Baker to supply beef for the troops in North America, May 3, 1756; (2) To provide a man-of-war for Lord Loudoun and to give positive orders to commanders-in-chief of the King's ships to cooperate fully with him to prevent trade between English and French subjects, May 5; (3) To provide vessels for carrying arms to North America, May 15; (4) To order transports to proceed to New York, May 31; (5) A letter from Gov. Thomas of the Leeward Islands about the capture of the *Warwick*, Antigua, June 8; (6) About the treatment of French prisoners by governors in the colonies, June 16; (7) To acquaint Messrs. Van Neck about the proper care of the Acadians, June 16; (8) To embark the German planters at Portsmouth for Nova Scotia and to release as many Protestant prisoners at Bristol as will serve under Col. Prévost, Sept. 15; (9) To send transports with troops at Cork to New York rather than Nova Scotia, Oct. 2; (10) To permit the *Seaflower* with provisions for the troops to proceed to Barbados and the Leeward Islands, Jan. 4, 1757; (11) To despatch to New York by sloop information for Loudoun and North American governors; (12) To cause 12 ships of the line with frigates to be ready for immediate service and proceed first to Cork and then to North America, Jan. 7; (13) A letter to be forwarded to Gen. Lawrence by sloop going to Halifax; (14) The Admiralty to grant the usual powers to Gov. Pownall of Massachusetts; (15) Transports to North America to be furnished with 1200 hooks, lines, etc.; (16) To provide transports to carry two Highland battalions to North America under convoy.

Nos. 4283–4289, 1698–1789. Letters from the Treasury. The following groups may be especially noted: *No. 4285, 1744–1756.* This bundle relates to convoys, smuggling, transportation of troops and provisions, general expenses, prisoners of war, and the protection of men from impressment. *No. 4286, 1757–1770.* These papers are concerned with the following: (1) Gov. Dinwiddie of Virginia asks for protection, Jan. 4, 1757; (2) Papers relating to provisioning North American troops and money involved; (3) Memorial of Customs Commissioners about Rhode Island smuggling, May 24 and Nov. 28, 1763; (4) Papers about smuggling in the West Indies and distribution of forfeitures, Dec. 17, 1764; (5) Lieut.-Gov. Colden of New York to the Earl of Halifax (extract), regarding illicit trade, Oct. 9 and Nov. 27, 1764; (6) Gov. Sharpe of Maryland to Halifax (extracts), Oct. 20, 1764 and Jan. 18, 1765; (7) Case of Capt. Brown in New York, in letters of the Customs Commissioners, Feb. 4, 1765. *No. 4287, 1771–1777:* (1) Paper concerning smuggling, Jan. 16, 1771; (2) The prosecution of Capt. Keeler in Rhode Island courts, Aug. 19, 1773; (3) Regarding expenses of Scammell and Ruggles, surveyors of white pine trees in North America, Oct. 29, 1772, July 6, 1773, and April 12, 1774; (4) The pay of troops in Boston, May 2, 1774; (5) On the prevention of illicit trade on the Mississippi, with many papers regarding trade, smuggling, military and naval matters.

Nos. 4316–4330, 1697–1794. Letters from the War Office. These letters relate to convoy of transports with troops, to the despatch of arms and accoutrements, to the conveyance of passengers, to the shipment of money, medicines, clothing, etc. In *No. 4324* and the following volumes are many orders regarding prisoners of war.

No. 4352, 1756–1800. Secret letters to the Admiralty. One paper, a memorial from George Walker, London Barbados agent, June 28, 1772, has to do with the planting of mango and breadfruit in the West Indies to prevent the denuding of the lands. He writes that to protect the Ceded Islands after occupation, it was provided that part of the land should remain wooded. In his opinion, the cultivation of the breadfruit tree in Barbados would be beneficial.

Nos. 5114–5118, 1686–1790. Miscellaneous letters, reports, etc. Among these papers is one in *No. 5116* of interest: the register of a plantation vessel with its passes, covering the years 1768–1777, showing its movements over these years. *No. 5117* has the following papers of interest: (1) Admiral Rodney papers, 1771; (2) Account of the fishery at Newfoundland, 1774; (3) A scheme of English Newfoundland fishery, sent by Commodore Shuldham, 1774; (4) Papers regarding piracy in Grenada in the West Indies, with questions about jurisdiction, 1772–1775.

Nos. 5138–5176, 1673–1783. Orders in council sent to the Admiralty. In these the King in Council lays down policies that come within the cognizance of the Admiralty. Each order is accompanied by other papers bearing upon the orders, many of which are not elsewhere to be found.

Nos. 5253–5323, 1680–1783. Reports of courts-martial. Here are to be found the minutes of courts-martial held on board ships of the Navy; in some cases these ships were in colonial waters. Here also are inquiries concerning losses in time of war in American waters.

Admiralty 2. Out-letters

Nos. 1–115, 1665–1679, 1689–1783. Orders and instructions from the Lords of the Admiralty. These entry books are bulky volumes, evidently much used; the contents are listed chronologically and not by names or places. They are concerned with such topics as convoys, North America, foreign voyages, passengers, prisoners, etc. The orders and instructions were issued to admirals and other naval officials, to the Navy Board, the Victualling Board, the officials of the High Court of Admiralty, and certain officials in the colonies.

Nos. 169–259, 1689–1783. Letters from the Admiralty Board to other great divisions of the government, such as to the Secretary of State. With respect to the last named office, correspondence to it is entered separately. These are the Board's letter-books and contain letters also to the Privy Council, Board of Trade, Trinity House. The volumes are especially important to the historian for periods of international crisis.

Nos. 502–581, 1746–1783. Secretary of the Admiralty's letters to public officers and admirals, written under orders from the Admiralty Board. They are less formal and frequently include more detail than the Board's orders and instructions, and embrace a variety of topics.

Nos. 1045–1061, 1689–1783. Letters in this series relate to the proceedings of the High Court of Admiralty, the High Court of Appeals for Prizes, and the vice-admiralty courts in America. They are addressed to officers of these courts, also to the Board of Trade, the Navy Board, and many other officials in connection with maritime matters. Here, moreover, are warrants for vice-admiralty commissions as well as warrants for letters of marque. *No. 1057, 1762–1770,* is of particular interest to the student concerned with the period under examination. It contains warrants, orders, and regulations in connection with the courts of vice-admiralty in America. They are as follows: (1) Samuel Fitch to be advocate general of Massachusetts and New England in place of Jonathan Sewall, resigned, Nov. 1769; (2) Egerton Leigh of South Carolina and Peyton Randolph of Virginia, each of whom held both the office of judge of Admiralty and attorney general, to resign one of the offices; (3) District court at Halifax to have jurisdiction in all cases within the limits of Quebec, Newfoundland and Nova Scotia, with Jonathan Sewall as judge and Alexander Chorley as register; (4) The district court at Boston to include cases within the limits of New England, with Robert Auchmuty as judge and Charles Howard as marshall; (5) The district court at Philadelphia to embrace the Middle Colonies from New Jersey up to but not including North Carolina, with Jared Ingersoll as judge, Arodi Thayer as marshall, and Richard Peters as register; (6) The district court at Charleston to include all the more southern North American British colonies, with Augustus Johnston as judge and Andrew Dummer as register.

Nos. 1147–1174, 1703–1721, 1745–1783. Letters relating to the Marines. These were regular regiments on marine service. Their orders came only from the Admiralty Board during the period under consideration. *No. 1168, 1773–1775,* may be noted. It relates to the Chatham division of marines under the command of Maj. John Pitcairn; they wore white shirts and white worsted stockings and came by the transports *Boyne* and *Somerset,* while Pitcairn came in the *Asia.* Many of the Marines died as the result of excessive drinking, while others were lost in the battles of Lexington and Concord and in the march back to Boston. In the battle of Bunker Hill, Pitcairn himself was killed, together with many of his men. Apparently the Marine corps acted with great gallantry. This information is contained in letters of July 28 and Aug. 3, 1775 in the bundle.

Nos. 1319–1323, 1730–1786. Letters relating to passes. All British and colonial ships going into the Mediterranean for trade required passes. These also served as protection from cruisers of the Barbary states. Under the system established in 1729, rules were laid down for the use of passes and colonial governors were bound by instructions to see that they were observed. These are outlined in *No. 1319. f. 2* and *No. 1321. ff. 336–339.* To care for the observation of the regulations by ship masters, instructions were sent to British consuls located at various Mediterranean ports, who placed endorsements on the passes. That these Mediterranean passes were in great demand by colonial shippers is indicated by the fact that between 1749 and 1760 some 650 passes were sent to Sec. Willard of Massachusetts.

Nos. 1331–1341, 1745–1782. Secret orders and letters. They are valuable entry books containing secret despatches. *No. 1331, 1745–1761,* is concerned with the Louisbourg expedition of 1745 and the Braddock expedition of 1755. Here also are to be found the secret instructions given to Boscawen in 1755, to Byng in 1756, to Hawke in 1756; to Hardy, Cotes, Holbourne, Frankland, Moore, Palliser, Gordon, and Wheelock in 1757; to Saunders, Holmes, and Cotes in 1759; to Colville and Swanton in 1760; to Colville, Douglas, and Rodney in 1761. Here is also to be found a list of ships stationed in North America. *No. 1332, 1762–1768,* is a continuation of *No. 1331.* Here are to be found secret instructions to Houlton, Colville, Rodney, Holmes, Pocock, Keppel, Richards, and Spry, all in 1762. Here are also instructions to Byron about making discoveries in the south seas (Falkland Islands); also to Capt. Cook, 1772; and instructions in 1768 to aid the Royal Society in its expedition to observe the transit of Venus; also instructions to Graves, Shuldham, Bellew, and Cooper, in 1775. There are also orders for the movements of the navy in North America and the West Indies, and another list of his Majesty's ships in North American waters or bound to North America. *No. 1333, 1770–1779.* This small volume continues secret instructions and is chiefly related to hostilities connected with the American War for Independence.

Admiralty 3. Minutes of the Admiralty Board

Nos. 1–98, 1689–1783. These minutes in so far as they relate to the period 1748–1776 are, as a rule, brief, giving the location and movement of ships of the navy, and other essential details. Sometimes orders are inserted but not always. After 1770 the minutes become more ample in stressing American affairs.

Admiralty 5. Original patents

Nos. 33–40, 1746–1763. *No. 33,* 1749, contains the commission issued to Rodney as governor of Newfoundland, together with his instructions. *No. 38,* 1746, has to do with the setting up of a court of vice-admiralty at Cape Breton. *No. 39,* 1763, is concerned with the creation of vice-admiralty courts in Quebec, the Floridas, and elsewhere. *No. 40,* 1763, is of special interest as it has to do with the creation of a vice-admiralty court for all North America.

Admiralty 6. Various

Nos. 3–23, 1695–1789. Commissions and warrant books.

Admiralty 7. Miscellanea

Nos. 75–103, 1683–1783, are registers of passes. In these volumes all ships whether British or colonial are arranged chronologically by years and days. The information gives the date of the certificate, the ship's name, to what place, its general type and equipment, where built.

Nos. 134–140, 1729–1784, present a register of all foreign passes. They therefore throw light on the course of colonial trade and clarify the nature of Irish trade.

Nos. 201–205, 1746–1747, 1766, 1781, are naval instructions, both sailing and fighting. These were generally printed.

Nos. 298–300, 1733–1783, embody the law officers' opinions, especially the decisions of the advocate of the Admiralty. Here is a large body of reports with reference of impressment, privateering, courts-martial, vice-admiralty cases. *No. 298,* 1733–1756, contains matters falling within the period 1748–1776. Here, for example, is a complaint from Ireland of interference by the common-law courts in maritime matters, Jan. 23, 1750. *No. 299,* 1756–1777, includes the following issues: (1) Dec. 29, 1757. Question: Have Lords of the Admiralty power to erect vice-admiralty courts in the East Indies? (2) Nov. 1, 1760. This has to do with the confiscation of a vessel carrying provisions from New York and Philadelphia to Jamaica; (3) March 1764. A murder on a King's ship at Jamaica. Should the trial be by court-martial on the ship or in a civil court of the island? (4) May 1764. Question: Can the Lords of the Admiralty appoint a vice-admiral for all America, with a court and its officers and leave the existing colonial vice-admiralty courts exercising jurisdiction? Answer: Yes, to the first part, but that such single court cannot have jurisdiction in cases where particular acts of Parliament have confined the recovery of penalties and forfeitures to local jurisdiction; (5) Dec. 29, 1768. Here is a case of seamen's wages with a letter from James Simpson of Charleston, S.C., to Capt. Robinson of the *Fowey*, Aug. 11, 1768; (6) Dec. 29, 1768. The case of the *Resolution* of Philadelphia, bound for Amsterdam but wrecked off the coast of France, with the wilful destruction of the ship; (7) April 18, 1776. Question: Can an American vessel—the snow *Dickinson* of Philadelphia—seized by its crew for his Majesty's use, be condemned as prize after the passage of the Prohibitory Act?

Nos. 333–342, 1695–1787, contain various memorials and reports.

Nos. 413–439, 1741–1784 are muster books, containing the names of ships, their stations, etc., but not including the lists of crews.

No. 592, 1768–1769. Here are tabular statements of exports and imports into and from North American colonial ports and those of the Bermudas and the Bahamas.

ACCOUNTANT GENERAL'S DEPARTMENT

Admiralty 16. Accounts

Nos. 1–116, 1681–1783. Admiralty Treasurer accounts of bills paid, etc.

Admiralty 17. Accounts various

Nos. 2–7, 1742–1795. Admiralty Officers' contingent accounts. *No. 5*, 1744–1782, has the following items bearing upon the period 1748–1776: (1) Rodney accounts on the Jamaica station, 1762–1763 and 1771–1774; (2) Colville on the St. Lawrence, 1760; (3) Cotes at Jamaica, 1757–1760; (4) Knowles in the West Indies, 1747–1749; (5) Saunders on the St. Lawrence, 1759–1763; (6) Keppel at Virginia, 1754–1755; (7) Holburne at Barbados, 1749–1752; (8) Duff at Newfoundland, 1775.

No. 150, 1757–1808, is concerned with the naval storekeeper at Halifax.

Nos. 174–176, 1747–1783, is the same for the Jamaica storekeeper.

Admiralty 49. Miscellanea. Various

These papers of the Admiralty Accountant General are concerned with a variety of accounts.

No. 1, 1756–1766, relates to expense in North America and the West Indies and is particularly concerned with the cost of maintaining ships in these waters for a ten-year period, as well as with other items respecting the maintenance of the crews, the use of transports, etc.

Admiralty 50–52. Ship journals and log books

The Public Record Office has a great collection of admirals' journals, 1702–1911, captains' logs, 1669–1852, and masters' logs, 1672–1840. The names of ships are arranged alphabetically and the dates of the journal or log are given. An index in five volumes has been prepared to aid the researcher.

GREENWICH HOSPITAL

Admiralty 65. In-letters, 1702–1869

Admiralty 66. Out-letters, 1685–1881

Admiralty 67. Hospital minutes, 1695–1871

Admiralty 68. Accounts various, 1686–1865

Nos. 89–143, 1732–1783, of this last series calls for additional comment. Here are the annual acounts of the receiver of the "sixpence." In 1696 by 7–8 Wm. III, c. 21. Par. 10, mariners in Great Britain, Ireland, and the "Dominions therewith belonging" were obliged to contribute out of their wages sixpence a month toward the maintenance of Greenwich Hospital. As the colonies were not specifically mentioned in this act or the subsequent acts of 1697 or 1711, no effort was then made to collect this sum in America. To remedy the defect, the act of 2 Geo. II, c. 7, passed in 1729, extended the duty not only to the Channel Islands and the Isle of Man but to "all and every his Majesty's Colonies." The receiver of the sixpence was authorized to call upon the collectors of customs at the colonial ports to deduct and detain this amount in sterling money from the wages of seamen. By an order in council issued in 1730 the term "seamen" included masters and commanders, servants, apprentices, and boys from whose services the master received any profit. As to the amounts raised, as Professor

Andrews points out (*Guide*, II, 61–2), of the total of £9403 received from all ports in 1754 America (including the West Indies) contributed £947 and out of a total of £10,435 in 1765 America contributed £977.

Nos. 194–204, 1725–1784. This series of volumes comprises ledgers giving the names of ships that came to the port of London and the amounts paid in sixpences. Similar ledgers were kept at the outports. As most of the Virginia trade was with Scotland, the ships going there paid in that country. The arrangements of the ledgers are strictly chronological. Much information other than the payment of the sixpence is supplied about the individual ships. The amount that a ship had to pay depended on the number of men and the length of the voyage, the payment ranging from a shilling to £150, but averaging from £2 to £5.

Admiralty 80. Miscellanea

Here are to be found a great variety of papers under the heading of Greenwich Hospital, among them a register of dead men's wages, diaries and papers, with books and warrants for payments all related to the hospital. In addition, there is *No. 121, 1749–1805*, an entry book of orders and proclamations by governors of Newfoundland, which seems to be out of place. As other volumes containing orders and proclamations in full relating to Newfoundland seem to have disappeared, this entry-book has peculiar value. The orders were issued on board the governor's ship or at some port such as St. John's or Trinity. They were given to justices of the peace, a sheriff, or individuals, and refer to such matters as riots, strong liquors, debtors, the use of gallows, Roman Catholics, churches, marriages, wrecks, the Eskimos of Labrador, fishing, the abducting of handcraftsmen, seamen and fishermen by American traders, French rights, the protection of trees, etc. It is not clear as already stated why this entry book should be with the Greenwich Hospital Miscellanea. However, *No. 131, 1768–1777*, is germane. It is a book of letters sent by H. Hulton, deputy receiver of the sixpenny Greenwich Hospital duty in America. *No. 132, 1768–1783*, is a book of letters received by Hulton with reference to his duties. These letters indicate the ports under his charge, including Newfoundland, Nova Scotia, the Bermudas, and all of North America south of the Province of Quebec. Quebec, however, is not mentioned in the listing of the ports.

MARINE OFFICE

Admiralty 96. Records

Nos. 1–4, 1690–1790, are made up of in-letters. Among these letters and papers bearing upon the years 1748–1776 is the interesting journal of Edmund Herbert, deputy paymaster of marines, 1739–1769, with a record of his activities and the frustrations in attempting to carry out his duties.

Nos. 125–154, 1739–1790, provide effective and subsistence lists of marine regiments, with muster rolls and returns, including *No. 153*, 1772–1780, which contains lists of marines stationed at Philadelphia, New York, and Halifax.

MEDICAL DEPARTMENT

Admiralty 97. In-letters

Nos. 85–87, 1709–1754, 1766–1779, are in-letters from surgeons and agents as well as from officers in command in all waters. *No. 85*, 1709–1754, comprises packets of letters from surgeons and agents for sick and wounded seamen and marines from many of the colonies. *No. 86*, 1766–1775, continues *No. 85*, reporting on hospitals, food and medicine. There are four letters from Admiral James Gambier, three of them from Boston, 1770–1771.

As for the out-letters, *Admiralty 98*, those listed as having survived, 1742–1833, are, with a few exceptions, too early or too late for the purposes of this guide.

Admiralty 99. Minutes

Nos. 1–49, 1701–1781, are the general minutes of the Board of Commissioners for sick and wounded prisoners and for the exchange of prisoners.

Admiralty 105. Miscellanea

No. 43, 1756–1764, contains legal opinions. Since the work of the Medical Department comprehended prisoners, legal questions were raised from time to time. The following, listed chronologically, fall within the period 1748–1776: (1) 1760. Two ships with cargoes for Louisbourg intending thereupon to go to Virginia for freight home were detained and impressed by the governor. Question: Is payment for four months sufficient, or should further claims be made? Answer. They are legally and justly entitled to such freight as they would have made; (2) 1761. The *Peggy* of Boston bound from Newcastle-on-Tyne for Boston was captured, Oct. 1756, by a French privateer, ransomed by the master, James Freeman, for 5000 livres and the mate left as hostage. The ship was afterwards lost and the captain died. Sitwell of London, on whom the bill of 5000 livres was drawn, received the insurance money but not the ransom, and the mate was kept prisoner. Opinion: that there was a gross breach of faith; the only way was for Sitwell to sue the owners in New England. In the opinion of Solicitor General Yorke the correct procedure was to carry the ransom bill to a proper admiralty jurisdiction in France for sentence of condemnation as lawful prize and then obtain an action in England against the owners who were bound by the act of the master; (3) 1762. The case of a French inhabitant of Guadeloupe, who signed the capitulation and had lately arrived in London with a pass. As the pass did not give him special permission to go to England, was such an inhabitant a prisoner of war? Opinion: Under the circumstances such persons may be so considered; (4) 1757. Coverdale Richardson, master of the *Prince Frederick*, merchant ship, applied in New York to the agent for taking care of prisoners of war for three men in working the ship home. On arrival one Gautier apparently aided the three men, French prisoners, to escape. The Board wishes to punish Gautier. How? Opinion: Gautier's behavior was unwarrantable but not criminal and no prosecution could be carried on.

NAVY BOARD

Admiralty 106. Records, 1658–1837

No. 274, 1741–1759, has many letters relating to American transports. Here among other items is the cash account of James Randall, transport agent for carrying troops to North America, etc., 1757–1759.

Nos. 275–280, 1746–1779, contain a variety of despatches relating to transports. These letters from both boards and individuals are official as well as personal.

Nos. 281–1299, 1673–1789, are volumes of miscellaneous correspondence, chiefly related to a great variety of routine matters connected with maintenance of the navy.

Nos. 2178–2210, 1738–1783, are the Navy Board's out-letters to the Admiralty entered chronologically.

Nos. 2544–2614, 1729–1783, constitute the minutes of the Navy Board.

Admiralty 107. Passing certificates

The Navy Board examined the qualifications of lieutenants for the Navy on directions from the Admiralty; *Nos. 1–9*, 1691–1785, are records of such examinations.

VICTUALLING DEPARTMENT

Admiralty 110. Out-letters

Nos. 1–31, 1683–1783, are letter-books of the Victualling Board of the
Navy. They were addressed to the Admiralty, the Navy Board,
contractors, transport agents, etc. The later volumes are of especial
interest with respect to American affairs.

Admiralty 111. Minutes

Nos. 1–96, 1702–1783, contain the minutes of the Victualling Board and
of its committees.

High Court of Admiralty

The Admiralty Court dates back to the fourteenth century when the
Lord High Admiral designated judges to settle disputes coming under the
jurisdiction of his office. This court determined civil and criminal maritime cases arising at sea and in ports and harbours and within navigable
rivers below the first bridge. Since 1660 the court has sat in two capacities:
as an Instance Court and as a Prize Court. As an Instance Court it had
both civil and criminal jurisdiction. In civil proceedings it met in Doctors' Commons, a stone house on St. Bennet's Hill, leased from the dean
and chapter of St. Paul's, and was concerned with such matters as seamen's wages, salvage and bottomry. In its criminal proceedings it acted
as a court of oyer and terminer and gaol delivery. As such it sat in the
Justice Hall in the Old Bailey where commissioners tried such cases as
murder at sea and piracy. Again, as a Prize Court it was concerned with
naval captures in time of war. While the surviving papers in the Admiralty Court series are very extensive there are many gaps. Only those
series are cited that have reference to the period 1748–1776. See Giuseppi: *Guide*, I, 156–62; and Andrews: *Guide*, II, 304–45.

CRIMINAL PROCEEDINGS

H.C.A. 1, 1535–1834. These are oyer and terminer records in 101 volumes
and bundles which relate to criminal cases, such as piracy and
other crimes committed on the high seas. As has been indicated,
this Court of Oyer and Terminer and Gaol Delivery was the
criminal branch of the Instance Court of the High Court of Admiralty and its sessions were held in the Old Bailey. The judges
were commissioners from Doctors' Commons although the proceedings were under the rules of the common law. *Nos. 5–27*, 1604–

1797, consist of indictments, while *No. 28,* 1537–1782, is a calendar of indictments. *Nos. 39–54,* 1601–1768, are examinations of those accused of piracy. *No. 55,* 1759–1824, contains minutes of proceedings in oyer and terminer trials. *Nos. 57–58* are such miscellaneous papers as warrants for summonses of juries, precepts for the removal of prisoners, orders for sheriffs to attend executions. These date from about 1760. *Nos. 60–72,* 1660–1800, contain the original commissions of the court.

INSTANCE AND PRIZE COURT RECORDS

H.C.A. 2, 1628–1889. Instance and Prize Courts proceedings, in 567 volumes and bundles. Here are fee books, accounts of prize commissioners and navy agents, and suitors' money. *Nos. 38–58,* 1731–1778, have material pertinent to the period under consideration. The arrangement is alphabetical in each volume and bundle.

H.C.A. 3, 1524–1786. These 290 volumes and bundles called "Acts" are really three series. They are: (1) Act Books, 1524–1749; (2) Minutes or drafts of acts, 1577–1752; and (3) Prize acts, 1643–1786. In them are recorded the proceedings of each meeting of the High Court, both in court and in Chambers, with the decisions.

H.C.A. 5–6, 1746–1810. Here are the so-called assignation books of the Instance Court. Series I, 1746–1767, is in 30 volumes, and Series II, 1767–1810, is in 58 volumes. The notes of the proceedings are brief.

H.C.A. 8, 1718–1840. These also are assignations or assignment books with the High Court sitting in its capacity as a Prize Court; they are in 161 volumes and record the decisions.

H.C.A. 13, 1536–1826. This series, in 223 volumes and bundles, is also concerned with the proceedings of the Prize Court. Here are the depositions and the examinations of witnesses.

H.C.A. 14, 1531–1768. This series, in 79 files, is labeled "Exemplifications"; it is miscellaneous in nature, largely concerned with the proceedings of both the Instance Court and the Prize Court. Exemplifications are copies of judgments or orders to carry out the judgments of the court. The order is addressed to the Marshall of the High Court and it might be to release a ship or goods wrongly seized, or to summon the owners of a ship to attend a meeting of the court, or to recover bond in case the person indicted for piracy, had fled, or to cite bailsmen to appear. In the case of an appeal from a colonial court the command was addressed to vice-admiralty, justices of the peace or others, to prevent the carrying out of the desire of the colonial court. Again, in prize cases the command was addressed to the captors of a ship or to those in possession of the ship. *Nos. 36–79, 1606–1768,* have pertinent material for the period 1748–1776.

H.C.A. 15, 1629–1778. This series is also concerned with the work of the Instance Court. It is called the "Early Series"; the papers are arranged alphabetically for each year and are in bundles, *Nos. 1–58.*

H.C.A. 16, 1772–1806. This series is also concerned with the work of the Instance Court. It is called, perhaps erroneously, the "First Series," and is also composed of bundles, *Nos. 59–106.*

H.C.A. 24, 1519–1814, contains not only libels, but allegations and other pleadings, with interrogatories, writs, etc. While the original files of the Instance Court no longer exist for the period beyond 1739, its allegations in prize cases come down to 1814.

H.C.A. 25, 1549–1815. This series lists the bonds required of vessels receiving letters of marque and reprisal with orders for the observance of instructions that went with them; they are in 229 bundles. See particularly *Nos. 11–13, 1689–1797,* bonds from commanders of privateers; *Nos. 38–52, 1756–1762,* French bails; and *Nos. 53–55, 1762,* French and Spanish bails.

H.C.A. 26, 1689–1814. In this series are the so-called letters of marque, declarations made in court by commanders of vessels after warrants had been issued to them of letters of marque and reprisal by the Lords Commissioners of the Admiralty; these declarations are in 111 volumes. The following bundles are especially pertinent to the years 1748–1776: *Nos. 1–12, 1689–1761,* connected with hostilities against France, and *Nos. 17–28, 1702–1762,* connected with hostilities against both France and Spain.

H.C.A. 30, 1531–1888. The series is made up of a wide variety of miscellaneous papers connected with the Prize Court proceedings. It consists of 803 volumes and bundles; among these are *Nos. 1–6, 1689–1786,* which are draft instruments, and *Nos. 19–26, 1690–1783,* account books of fees.

H.C.A. 31, 1664–1815. Here are monitions given by the marshal of the court of the seizure of a ship. These are warnings directed to interested persons to appear before the court within a fixed period to show cause why the ship should not be condemned as lawful prize. Monitions were also affixed to a pillar of the Royal Exchange.

H.C.A. 32, 1661–1855. This series of Prize Court papers is a large one consisting of 1,846 bundles of documents such as claims, attestations, commissions, examinations, and a variety of other exhibits. *Nos. 161–259, 1756–1763,* cover the Great War for the Empire. These papers are arranged alphabetically.

H.C.A. 34, 1643–1854. In this series are the sentences pronounced by the Prize Court; they are in 65 volumes and bundles. *Nos. 1–7, 1672–1772,* cover almost all of the period 1748–1776.

H.C.A. 38, 1541–1772. This series is made up of registers of warrants for the arrest of ships, etc.; they are in 77 volumes. Further, *H.C.A. 39,* 1515–1760, in 55 files, is also made up of warrants, monitions, decrees, etc., as returned to the Prize Court duly endorsed. *H.C.A. 40,* 1760–1853, denominated "Royal Warrants," were granted for the capture of enemy ships and property; they are in 27 parcels.

H.C.A. 41, 1689–1813, is made up of prize appeal records, both volumes and bundles. Among these volumes are 16 that cover the period 1750–1800, and are chiefly devoted to cases to be heard.

H.C.A. 42, 1698–1883, is a large series also of appeal papers in 574 bundles. The bundles are arranged under the initial letters of the ships' names and are in groups according to a particular war.

H.C.A. 43, 1689–1801. This is Series I of the so-called "Assignation Books," in 38 volumes. These books contain the preliminary proceedings in appeal cases. As has been noted *H.C.A. 5, 6,* and *8* are also assignation records.

H.C.A. 45, 1750–1818. The series is made up of 71 volumes of printed cases.

H.C.A. 47, 1689–1844. This series is the prize appeal records in 44 bundles and volumes. It is made up of miscellaneous materials, including draft instructions, minutes, fee books, etc.

H.C.A. 48, 1672–1772. Here are to be found the sentences in prize appeals; the collection is a small one in 7 bundles.

H.C.A. 49, 1636–1875. This series, concerning the vice-admiralty courts, in 106 volumes and bundles, contains both prize and instance papers, including assignment books, registers of power of attorney, precedents. These are proceedings in cases called up from vice-admiralty courts by the High Court of Admiralty or sent in on appeal from a vice-admiralty court.

H.C.A. 50, Elizabeth I to 1873, is a series of Admiralty muniment books, in 24 volumes. They are entry books of commissions, letters patent, warrants, etc., relating to appointments in the Admiralty; *H.C.A. 51,* Elizabeth I to 1955, are the indices in two volumes concerned with the above.

INTERCEPTED LETTERS

Among the papers of the High Court are the so-called "Intercepted Letters." The only bundle of these that has survived concerned with the period 1748–1776 is *No. 1066,* 1756. It would appear that these letters from Maryland and Virginia were on board vessels that were captured by a French ship which in turn was captured by British men of war. The letters throw a great deal of light upon the activities of people in these colonies. One particularly interesting letter written on Oct. 30 by Lieutenant Alexander McBean of the Royal American Regiment of Foot, who was on recruiting service in Maryland, indicates that he is in Annapolis with Gov. Sharpe who is doing all that he can to promote the service, "Tho his patience is greatly try'd by the Damn'd assembly men that will hardly do anything for their own or the publick's safety with good will, they mind nothing but contention and complaining of taxes and grievances of that kind when their all is almost at stake." Another letter, dated Oct. 16, was from Nicholas Rogers of Baltimore Town, who was planning to send his eldest son to England in about seven or eight years to be educated as a lawyer. He informs his London correspondent that at the present his boy was "at a latting [Latin] school and about 8 years old." A third letter is also of interest. It was written by Graham Frank from Virginia on Nov. 11 to the Bishop of London urging the appointment of a suffragan bishop for the colony. Among other letters that Frank wrote is one in which he says: "Tis customary with the gentlemen here to send to Scotland for tutors for their children, for the sake of cheapness." Finally, this bundle contains a packet of letters from the firm of George and John Murdoch, tobacco merchants. The firm was concluding its business and the letters are from 1750 to 1756.

War Office Papers

The War Office in 1748 was quartered in a structure near the present War Office building. In 1756, however, it moved to the building now occupied by the Horse Guards. There the Secretary at War, the Paymaster-General, the Quartermaster-General, and the Commissary-General of Musters were quartered.

The office of Secretary at War, originating in 1661, was one of great importance with respect to military affairs for the years 1748–1776 and so remained until in 1794 a Secretary of State for War was appointed and in 1795 a Commander-in-Chief, which officers thereupon took over many of the responsibilities previously exercised by the Secretary at War. It was through the latter during the period under consideration that the King communicated military arrangements; the Secretary also had the responsibility of keeping the army efficient, raising levies in order to maintain it up to strength, issuing to it marching orders, and providing proper quarters for its units. In order to perform these duties, he was in constant touch with other departments of the government. Those who filled this post during the period under consideration were Henry Fox, Lord Barrington, Charles Townshend, and Welbore Ellis. In the case of Barrington he received this office in 1755 and in 1765 was reappointed to it and continued in it until 1778.

The Secretary at War did not direct war policy. After the Cabinet Council had come to decisions respecting it, this duty rested with the Secretary of State who was responsible for implementing policy for the area of the world indicated by his office—be it the Secretary of State for the Southern Department, the Secretary of State for the Northern Department, or toward the latter part of the American colonial period, the Secretary of State for the Colonies. Nor was the Secretary at War accountable for the militia, controlled by the Secretary of State for the Southern Department, or for arms, etc., contracted by the Ordnance Board, or for the payment of the army, controlled by Paymaster General of the armed forces. Yet with such a person as Barrington occupying this office, its influence on military developments was very great.

W.O. *1, In-letters,* 1732–1868, consists of 1,138 volumes and papers. *Nos. 1–13,* 1756–1783, are letters from officers in America. Among the chief correspondents for the years 1756–1763 are Abercromby, Amherst, Loudoun, and Shirley; between the years 1764–1783, the chief correspondents are Carleton, Clinton, Gage, Haldimand, and Howe. *No. 19,* 1760–1763, contains letters from the commanders of the conquered islands of Guadeloupe and Martinique or those holding responsibilities in connection with them. *No. 49,* contains more letters from the West Indies, 1760–1764, and from West Florida, 1763–1764. *No. 50,* 1768–1777, is letters from various British West Indies islands. *No. 57,* 1772–1773, embodies letters and papers relating to the West Indian expeditions of those years for gathering information. *No. 404,* 1763–1767, is a note book containing intelligence that was brought to the attention of the plantations committee of the Privy Council; it relates to issues not only in the West Indies but also in North American colonies. *Nos. 678–684,* 1756–1784, are letters from the Secretary of State or of the Treasury, to the Secretary at War. *Nos. 823–826,* 1763–1784, also contain letters from the Treasury, while *Nos. 857–868,* 1757–1783, are letters from various departments of the government, which is also the case with *Nos. 869–877,* 1759–1783. *No. 891,* 1756–1783, contains orders of either the House of Lords or the House of Commons requiring information. *Nos. 972–1020,* 1756–1783, are miscellaneous letters arranged chronologically and alphabetically within the above years.

W.O. *2,* 1759–1858, in 107 volumes, is indexes to correspondence with brief abstracts of letters.

W.O. *3, Out-letters,* 1765–1868, is in 617 entry books. *Nos. 1–6,* 1767–1778, are letter-books of the Commander-in-Chief and Adjutant General; the same is true for *Nos. 23–26,* 1765–1786.

W.O. *4, Out-letters,* 1684–1861, is in 1,053 entry books. *Nos. 1–123,* 1684–1783, are general letters from the Secretary at War. *Nos. 273–275,* 1775–1784, are American letter-books; *No. 273,* 1775–1777, is concerned with the beginnings and early years of hostilities between Great Britain and the Thirteen Colonies. *Nos. 333–*

334, 1775–1785, are letters of the Secretary at War to governors and various officials with civil and military responsibilities, while *Nos. 981–983,* 1751–1798 are "private" letter-books having to do with confidential matters of promotions and appointments, as well as the granting of leaves of absence. *Nos. 987–988, 1763–1784,* are American letter-books, containing many despatches from the Secretary at War that are concerned with policy and directed to commanders-in-chief in the New World and governors. *No. 1044, 1763–1767,* contains chiefly miscellaneous materials, among them instructions to Gen. Gage and officers about maintaining *esprit de corps* among the forces in the West Indies.

W.O. 5, 1683–1852, in 122 volumes, is marching orders and has to do, for example, with orders for troops going to America as well as elsewhere.

W.O. 7, 1715–1862, in 130 volumes. *Nos. 24–28,* 1715–1790, are lists of the Board of General Officers for inspecting and regulating clothing for the army. *Nos. 122–125,* 1716–1787, are the papers of the Muster Master General.

W.O. 8, 1709–1823, in 12 volumes, contains the entry books of the Muster Master General of Ireland, and also letters and warrants of the Lords Justices General and of the Lords Lieutenant relating to military matters.

W.O. 9, 1679–1865, in 48 volumes, is miscellaneous military accounts.

W.O. 10, 1708–1878, in 2,876 volumes, has to do with the artillery.

W.O. 12, 1732–1878, denominated "General Series," consists of over 13,000 volumes of muster-rolls and pay lists for the various branches of the service. *Nos. 1882–11099, 1757–1783,* present lists of regiments serving during these years, many of them in America. The table reproduced in the C.M. Andrews *Guide,* II, 284–5, is most useful, listing 64 regiments and battalions with period of service.

W.O. 17, 1759–1865, in 2,812 volumes, is the monthly or general returns. *Nos. 1–254,* 1759–1782, and *Nos. 1153–1155, 1764, 1771–1775, 1776–1782,* give the forces in North America and the West Indies. Among these volumes *No. 1153* is of especial interest as it gives a 1764 return of troops for both North America and the West Indies. *No. 1373* gives the returns from the Bermudas in 1755 and 1761 as well as for a later period. *Nos. 1489–1498, 1758–1786,* are additional North American returns, while *No. 2480,* 1759–1773, gives the returns from the West Indies.

W.O. 18, 1770–1820, in 213 volumes, is made up of vouchers for disbursements by the army agents for the artillery arm of the service. Among these volumes *Nos. 1–39, 1770–1783,* refer especially to army agents' disbursements made in connection with the War for American Independence. In connection with W.O. 18, see also the warrants issued by the Board of Ordnance to its agents to be found in *W.O. 50*, 1677–1778, with Bill Books, Series I, in 21 volumes. *W.O. 51*, 1630–1806, contains Bill Books, Series II, in 313 volumes, as does *W.O. 53*, 1660–1822, Series IV, in 534 volumes.

W.O. 24, 1661–1864, in 892 volumes, is registers of military establishments. *Nos. 283–484*, 1748–1775, fall within the period under review and have direct relation to the establishment of military installations in North America and the West Indies, including estimated costs of pay and provisions.

W.O. 25, 1660–1938, in 3,992 volumes, is made up of a series of registers, notification books, succession books, etc. *Nos. 1–38*, 1660–1786, and *Nos. 89–94*, 1728–1783, are commission books in two series; likewise *Nos. 112–117*, 1760–1805, are commission books, while *Nos. 122–152*, 1708–1783, are notification books of commissions granted. *Nos. 209–212*, 1754–1788, and *Nos. 221–222*, 1773–1788, are regimental succession books in two series, listing rank and other pertinent information. *No. 1145*, 1758–1797, contains embarkation returns in connection with various expeditions. *Nos. 2979–2983*, 1712–1755, are estimates of half-pay and retired pay, while *Nos. 2990–2991* are registers of warrants for half-pay. *Nos. 3020–3036* record payments of pensions to widows of full-pay officers, and *Nos. 3180–3194*, 1704–1784, contain warrants for leaves of absence.

W.O. 28, 1746–1901, in 346 volumes, is Headquarters Records. *No. 1*, 1746–1747, is the muster roll of Connecticut troops raised for an expedition against Canada; *No. 4*, 1775–1783, throws much light upon the raising of Loyalist regiments; *No. 10*, 1775–1782, comprises returns, lists, and letters, with special reference to provincial troops serving the King in Canada.

W.O. 30, 1684–1903, in 132 volumes, is listed as miscellanea. *No. 1*, 1775–1783, is a register of letters of attorney and concerns the pay of soldiers; *No. 13*, 1754–1794, is a register relating to clothing, while *Nos. 17–35*, 1684–1785, are registers of royal warrants for the holding of courts-martial in America. *No. 54*, 1756–1793, has to do with the defence of Great Britain and Ireland during these years.

W.O. 34, 1712–1784, in 260 volumes, contains the military correspondence, order-books, reports, plans, etc., of Sir Jeffrey Amherst while commander-in-chief in America and also while governor of Virginia, and later of Guernsey, and still later as Commander-in-Chief at home. They were presented to the War Office in 1923 by Earl Amherst.

W.O. 35, 1775–1922, contains the records of the army in Ireland, with out-letter books from Dublin Castle, as well as in-letters of the Irish Office.

W.O. 36, 1773–1783 and 1798–1799, in 4 volumes, the first three of which relate to the revolt of the American colonies. Before 1927 the volumes were in the Royal Military College but in that year were transferred to the Public Record Office. The first three volumes contain orders and returns of British forces in North America.

W.O. *40*, 1753–1815, consists of selected unnumbered papers in 32 bundles. They are arranged chronologically and alphabetically, according to the individual or the office or the colony, and contain a variety of documents including petitions and applications, relating to America, to India, to Ireland, to barracks, billeting, etc. *Nos. 1–28*, 1753–1783, are especially related to the period 1748–1776; among the papers, for example, in *No. 1* are those having to do with the trial of Capt. Preston in connection with the so-called "Boston Massacre."

W.O. *42*, 1755–1908, in 73 bundles, consists of certificates of birth, baptism, marriage, wills, and death, and other papers, of officers and their families.

W.O. *44*, 1682–1873, in 732 volumes, etc., is Ordnance Office in-letters, most of them pertaining to the 19th century.

W.O. *46*, 1660–1861, in 169 volumes, consists of entry books of out-letters of the Ordnance Office. *Nos. 5–16* are concerned with the years before 1783. Like W.O. *44*, this series is largely 19th century materials.

W.O. *47*, 1644–1856, in 2,897 volumes, contains the minute-books or journals of the Board of Ordnance. The only documents in this series relating to the years 1748–1776 are *Nos. 34–102*, 1749–1792, the minutes of the surveyor general.

W.O. *48*, 1660–1847, in 357 volumes. *Nos. 1–127* are ledgers with the accounts of the treasurers and paymasters of the ordnance; *Nos. 254–262*, 1748–1783, are expense ledgers, while *Nos. 339–343*, 1752–1777, are called "Works Ledgers."

W.O. *49*, 1592–1858, in 293 volumes, etc., present a variety of accounts, including estimates of expenditures. *Nos. 284–285*, 1711–1800, are classified as miscellaneous subsidiary papers, many of which relate to American operations.

Reference has already been made to W.O. *50*, Series I, W.O. *51*, Series II, and W.O. *53*, Series IV, in the bill books series. These contain detailed accounts of the expenditures of the Ordnance Board. It may be pointed out that in Series IV, there are the accounts for Gibraltar, 1710–1822, and for Port Mahon, 1708–1782.

W.O. *54*, 1594–1871, in 947 volumes, etc., is further registers made up of the following: (1) Quarter books, 1594–1837, which are records of quarterly payments of salaries, wages, pensions, etc; (2) Establishments, 1676–1855, which are lists of civil and military establishments at home and abroad; (3) Commission books, 1740–1852, which are entry books of commissions of officers of the artillery and engineers; (4) Description books, 1755–1783, which supply information about those in the artillery battalions, having to do with discharges, transfers, and casualties, as well as salaries and pensions.

W.O. 55, 1568–1923, in 3,038 volumes, is made up of miscellaneous Ordnance Office documents; among them the following: *No. 283*, 1757–1760, North American reports; *Nos. 330–375*, 1660–1783, entry books of warrants and orders in council; *No. 450*, 1772–1857, warrants and orders in council; *Nos. 469–496*, 1670–1810, Series I, and *Nos. 497–513*, 1711–1795, Series II, entry books of warrants of the Master General and Board of Ordnance; *No. 1537*, 1773–1777, local letter-books, artillery, America; *No. 1550* (8), 1752, observation reports, etc. on defence, fortifications, etc., with respect to Antigua; *No. 1553* (4), 1770, defence observations reports with respect to Dominica; *No. 1557* (1–4), 1774, 1776, 1778, 1780, defence observations reports concerning Newfoundland; *No. 1558* (2–3), 1740, 1783, defence observations reports concerning Nova Scotia; *No. 1617* (1–6), 1770–1780, reference reports on lands, rents, buildings, etc., for Annapolis Royal, N.S., Antigua, the Bahamas, Barbados, Berbice, and the Bermudas; *No. 1618*, 1770–1780, report as above, with respect to Province of Quebec; *No. 1619* (3–4), 1770–1780, reports on Demerara (not a part yet of the British Empire) and Dominica; *No. 1620* (2, 3, 6), 1770–1780, reports on Grenada, Halifax, and Jamaica; *No. 1621* (5, 7) 1770–1780, reports on Newfoundland and Nova Scotia; *No. 1622* (1, 3, 4, 7), 1770–1780, reports on St. Christopher, St. Lucia, St. Vincent, and Tobago; *Nos. 1625–1766*, 1571–1754, accounts of surveys of military stores and arms issued; *No. 1813*, 1745–1750, entry books of letters respecting the Louisbourg expedition; *No. 1814*, 1749, the answer of Paul Wibault to Maj.-Gen. Bastide's complaints, Placentia, Newfoundland; *No. 1817*, 1753–1754, letter-books concerning Canada and other colonies, also Africa; *No. 1820*, 1758–1772, letter-books, Quebec, Halifax, America in general; *No. 1821*, 1761–1762, letter-book, Halifax; *No. 1822*, 1768–1772, returns and estimates, Quebec.

W.O. 64, 1702–1823, army lists of officers, manuscripts, 13 volumes: *Nos. 1–12*, 1702–1752, and *No. 13*, 1755–1816.

W.O. 65, 1754–1879, annual printed army lists, 168 volumes; of these see *Nos. 1–33*, 1754–1783, and also *No. 164*, 1770–1778.

W.O. 68, 1759–1925, militia records in 564 volumes. This includes both the militia of Great Britain and Ireland, with letters, entry books, pay lists, monthly returns, etc.

W.O. 71, 1668–1850, in 342 volumes, etc., and proceedings in courts martial that were in the Judge Advocate General's office. For proceedings concerned with the period 1748–1776 see in particular the following: (1) Proceedings of General Officers, 1706–1806; (2) General courts martial, 1692–1796, entry books; (3) Courts martial, 1715–1790, home and abroad; (4) Courts martial, 1757–1789, marching regiments; (5) Courts martial papers, 1668–1850, original proceedings in courts martial.

W.O. 72, 1696–1850, in 103 bundles. These papers, also from the Judge Advocate General's office, comprise miscellaneous documents in courts martial proceedings and many in-letters.

W.O. 78, 1627–1946, military maps and plans, 4,991 pieces. This great collection embodies the older W.O. 38.

W.O. 81, 1715–1900, Judge Advocate Generals' letter-books, in 133 volumes. See, for example, Nos. 8 and 9 for the court martial of Maj.-Gen. Charles Hay, 1759, North America.

Paymaster-General of the Forces

Although identified with the Treasury on account of the nature of his responsibilities, the Paymaster-General of the Forces was, nevertheless, housed in the War Office so that he with his staff could be closely connected with the activities of the Secretary at War and with other departments of the War Office. During the period under consideration the Paymaster-General was a member of the Cabinet Council. His position was one of the highest standing in the government. It may be pointed out that William Pitt between 1746 and 1755 occupied this office. Other occupants, who considered it a lucrative position, were Henry Pelham, Henry Fox, Charles Townshend, Lord North, and, for a later period, Edmund Burke. Out of various earlier offices concerned with the pay of the troops there was created in the days of George I the office of Paymaster-General of the Guards and Garrisons and Land Forces. The holder later was simply designated as Paymaster-General of the Forces. Documents connected with this office falling within the period 1748–1776 are as follows:

P.M.G. 2. Army ledgers, 1757–1840, in 227 volumes. These were annual and semi-annual reports of the credits and debts of the various military units. Nos. 1–33 of these ledgers cover the period 1757–1783.

P.M.G. 4. Army half-pay and retired pay ledgers, 1737–1921, in 277 volumes. Nos. 1–34 cover the period 1737–1782.

P.M.G. 14. Army miscellaneous books, 1721–1861, in 187 volumes. Nos. 1–5 are the accounts of the Deputy Paymaster for America and cover the period 1751–1773. Nos. 70–72 are labelled "Extraordinaries in North America," and are concerned with the extraordinary payments for the period 1753–1777. No. 70, 1755–1764, is warrants, etc., drawn for service of Braddock, Shirley, Dunbar, Abercromby, Loudoun, Webb, Hopson, Howe, Forbes, Stanwix,

Amherst, Gage, Monckton, and Murray; *No. 71*, 1765–1777, brings in Gage, Carleton, William Howe, Clinton, Pigot, Earl Percy, Prescott, Smith, and Burgoyne. *Nos. 86–102* are cash books, 1749–1780, containing the King's accounts current with the Bank of England, with records of disbursements. *Nos. 104–111* are entry books of letters and powers of attorney, 1759–1783. Among these papers are authorizations by the colonies for the Treasury to make payments to their London agents. *Nos. 142–146* are also registers of letters of attorney, 1756–1784. *No. 169* carries the title "Off-Reckonings or Clothing Accounts," 1759–1765, and concerns the business of regimental agents in Great Britain furnishing supplies for the army units.

P.M.G. 60. This series in 3 volumes carries the title "Army Services: Estimates" and covers the period, 1756–1766 and 1807–1820.

P.M.G. 67. This series in 8 volumes is concerned with exchequer bills; they are both minute and warrant books for the period 1730–1848.

Special Collections of Manuscripts

RODNEY PAPERS

In the Public Record Office among the special collections are two groups of papers that must be noted as bearing upon the years 1748–1776: The Rodney and the Chatham manuscripts. We shall first turn to the Rodney papers.

This is a collection of the papers of Admiral George Brydges Rodney (1719–1792), in 26 volumes and bundles, listed as P.R.O. 30:20. Rodney played an important role in the Empire during the years 1748–1776. The material that is pertinent follows:

Nos. 1–2, 1759–1763, are order-books.

No. 4, 1748–1752, contains journals of H.M.S. *Rainbow*.

Nos. 6 and *8*, 1749–1759, 1761–1762, are Rodney's letter-books.

No. 11, 1761–1780, contains letters from the Admiralty.

Nos. 12–14, 1749–1782, bring together various letters other than those from the Admiralty, including copies of those he wrote, and are concerned with a variety of topics.

Nos. 15–18, 1758–1781, contain miscellaneous papers, some of importance for the period under consideration. For example, in *No. 15* there are the following: (1) "An Extract of the transactions at Louisbourg, in the time of the siege," 1758, endorsed "Corrected by G. B. Rodney"; (2) About a proposed French Protestant colony at Cape Sable, Nova Scotia, 1767; (3) "Plan of attack of New Orleans," 1771, in connection with the crisis over the Falkland Islands; (4) "Plan to attack Mexico," 1771, also connected with the above crisis. *No. 16*, 1762–1763, presents Rodney's orders to officers under his command. *No. 18,* 1772–1781, has the following pertinent papers: (1) Sailing directions to Port Royal and Kingston, Jamaica, 1772; (2) A letter from David Hodges, Pensacola, Sept. 5, 1772, dealing with advantages to the Spaniards of Mexico were they to ship money via Vera Cruz and Pensacola, West Florida, to England and France; (3) Gov. Chester of West Florida, enclosing Council minutes concerning the need of vessels both to prevent illicit trade with the French on the Mississippi and for the protection of Pensacola, Feb. 19, 1773.

CHATHAM PAPERS

These papers, listed as P.R.O. 33:8 in 373 bundles in two series, are frequently called the Admiral Pringle manuscripts from their donor. The first 100 bundles present the correspondence of Lord and Lady Chatham with which we are concerned; the remaining bundles have to do with William Pitt, the younger, and John, 2nd Earl of Chatham.

Nos. 1–69, 1756–1761, are letters from colonial governors and military and naval leaders and are of great importance in this survey. Arranged alphabetically, the writers are as follows: Gen. Abercromby, Gen. Amherst, Gen. Barrington, Adm. Boscawen, Gov. Dinwiddie, Gov. Arthur Dobbs, Gov. Harry Ellis, Lieut.-Gov. Fauquier, Gen. Forbes, Gen. J. Hopson, Lord Loudoun, Gen. Monckton, Commodore Moore, Gov. R. H. Morris, Gov. Murray, Gov. Thomas Pownall, Gen. Stanwix, Gen. Townshend, Gen. John Thomas, and Adm. Saunders.

No. 70, 1758–1759, a letter-book, has letters relating to Louisbourg and Quebec.

No. 73, 1747–1767, contains correspondence mostly petitions both dated and undated, among which are the following: (1) Petition to Pitt from Gen. John Winslow respecting his services in Nova Scotia; (2) Petition from planters and merchants in the Sugar Islands; (3) Petition from the Marquis Duquesne, Northampton, Sept. 18, 1758; (4) Petition from Capt. John Stuart of the South Carolina provincial regiment, July 26, 1761; (5) Petitions to the King from "Dutiful and Loyal Subjects" praying for peace with the American colonies; (6) Petition from John Hale who served in America; (7) Petition from officers of the 78th Regiment for land grants on St. John (Prince Edward Island) and in Nova Scotia; (8) Petition from nine captains who raised companies in North America for the proposed expedition against Canada, 1748–1751; (9) Petition to the House of Commons from Jacob Fletcher of Liverpool whose brig, the *Nelly,* was burned at Savannah, Georgia, Dec. 1775; (10) Petitions to the House of Commons from London merchants trading to North America; (11) Memorial of the pay-master-general relating to the value of coins in America.

No. 75, 1739–1756, is composed of army papers, estimates and accounts.

No. 76, 1757–1774, has more army papers, including some undated.

No. 78, 1739–1759, contains Admiralty papers, including: (1) Two papers about a slave ship captured by pirates, 1752; (2) Papers concerning Louisbourg, 1758–1759; (3) Journal of a voyage to Halifax on the expedition planned by Lord Loudoun against Louisbourg, 1757; (4) About what happened from the time the man-of-war *Blandford* was taken until Gov. Lyttelton's arrival in England, 1755.

No. 79, 1759–1767, is made up of Admiralty papers about Canada.

No. 80 embodies more Admiralty papers, including prize cases and a précis of papers from Adm. Boscawen.

No. 81 contains both dated and undated papers: (1) Papers relating to exports and imports; (2) Why the Asiento contract between Spain and Great Britain should be continued; (3) Why no further duty or additional hardship should be placed on tobacco planters or the colony of Virginia; (4) Against levying any new tax on sugar or the beaver hat trade; (5) Copy of Lord Holderness to the Board of Trade, March 30, 1752, about correspondence with colonial governors and the appointment of colonial officials; (6) State of exports from Great Britain to North America in 1764; (7) State of North American fisheries; (8) Bounties paid on goods exported to North America and imported from North America, Dec. 1771–Dec. 1774; (9) Papers relating to tobacco, sugar, molasses, and the codfishery.

No. 82 comprises miscellaneous papers, among them the following: (1) Printed sermon by the Rev. Nathaniel Appelton of Cambridge, Mass., on the repeal of the Stamp Tax; (2) Letter by "Amor Patriae" about American taxation and a plan for colonial representation in Parliament, Nov. 17, 1770.

No. 95 is an exceedingly large bundle of important papers, 1742–1757, most of them bearing upon the period 1748–1776. Among them are the following: (1) A sketch of Fort Ticonderoga sent to James Abercromby in a letter, 1757; (2) On the present state of North America by a general officer in letters from New York, Albany, and Fort Edward, 1756; (3) Abercromby to Pitt, Nov. 25, 1756, on encroachments in North America made by France; (4) An undated paper on North American trade and its advantages to Great Britain; (5) Braddock's instructions to Col. Johnson relating to the Indians, April 16, 1755; (6) Two letters from Col. John Bradstreet to Sir Richard Lyttelton, Aug. 15 and Sept. 5, 1757; (7) James Buchanan and others to Pitt about Virginia and Maryland trade, London, Jan. 6, 1757; (8) Paper by Major William Corry on the North American colonies which "abound with Inhabitants," 1756; (9) George Croghan's information that sixty people had signed a paper agreeing to go to Fort Duquesne, Albany, Sept. 20, 1756; (10) Extracts of a letter from Daniel Dulany of Maryland and of one from a gentleman in Philadelphia, both Nov. 1756; (11) Gov. Fitch's brief account of Connecticut's part in the war since 1755; (12) N. Hardinge, Treasury Chambers, Oct. 16, 1755, to Pitt about instructions to Treasury deputies in North America; (13) From the Earl of Holderness to Lord Loudoun, 1757; (14) From M. G. Hopson to Loudoun, Halifax, Oct. 23, 1757; (15) Thomas Knox to James Abercromby, relating to Virginia trade, Bristol, Jan. 4, 1757; (16) Examination in Berks County, Penna., of Michel La Chauvegnère, Jr., a French prisoner, and later by the Chief Justice of Pennsylvania, 1757; (17) Commission appointing Lord Loudoun commander-in-chief of British forces in North America, endorsed March 5, 1756, together with an extract of his instructions; (18) A circular letter to North American governors on Lord Loudoun's arrival in America; (19) Statement of forces under Loudoun's command; (20) Letters from Loudoun to Gov. Pownall, Nov. and Dec., 1757; (21) Précis of Loudoun's letters with enclosures, 1756–1757, together with memoranda from Loudoun's letters, 1757; (22) Col. Lydius's declaration about Oswego and his proposal to Shirley to attack Fort Niagara, Sept. 21, 1756; (23) On the state of America by "W. M.," London, Nov. 16, 1756; (24) Two papers by Charles Pinckney about the strength of South Carolina and a scheme for its defence and security, 1756; (25) Three letters from Gov. Pownall of Massachusetts to Lord Loudoun, 1757; (26) Intelligence from Col. Peter Schuyler, a prisoner at Quebec, 1757; (27) Account of Shirley's expedition against the French posts at Niagara; (28) Extract from the journal of Maj. John Smith of the Virginia Rangers about the French forts where he was imprisoned, 1756–1757; (29) Papers proposing to raise regiments for American service from Capt. von Wreden of Hesse Darmstadt, Samuel Waldo of Boston, and Messrs. Lauchlan and others in Glasgow; (30) Copy of the lead plate buried by Céleron at the Ohio River; (31) A list of officers in the colonies whose nomination was vested in the Board of Trade by order in Council, March 11, 1752, with names, salaries, etc.; (32) "Recencement général du Pais des Ilinois, 1752"; (33) Some unsigned letters or extracts of them about military and political affairs, 1755–1756; (34) Extract of letter from a Fort Edward officer, Nov. 17, 1756; (35) Memorandum as to the supposed number of regular troops in North America, Dec. 13, 1756; (36) Unsigned paper with some thoughts on American affairs; (37) Extract of a letter from an officer in Albany, Jan. 6, 1757; (38) Papers relating to the Louisbourg and Quebec expeditions.

No. 96 is composed of a large number of miscellaneous papers relating to North America, 1758–1763, including: (1) Draft of instructions for Amherst, March 3, 1758; (2) Amherst to Wolfe (extract), Louisbourg, Aug. 15, 1758; (3) Précis of 35 papers enclosed in Amherst's letter of February 28, 1759; (4) Letters or précis of letters from Amherst, 1759–1760, to various officers in North America, as well as to victualling contractors; also a letter to Lord Barrington, Oct. 18, 1760; (5) Capt. Thomas Bell at Kilkenny Barracks writes two letters, Sept. 2 and Dec. 4, 1763, pointing out the mistakes made in the Proclamation of 1763 "in the present Limits of the Government of Quebec"; (6) Ephraim Briggs writes from Philadelphia, Aug. 2, 1759, on how to destroy the power of France in America; (7) Lieut.-Gov. Bull of South Carolina to the Board of Trade (extract) about the Spaniards at Pensacola and the French at Mobile, June 30, 1760; (8) Correspondence between Lieut.-Gov. Ellis of Georgia and the Spanish governor of St. Augustine, 1757–1758; (9) Lieut.-Gov. Colden to Pitt, New York, April 5, 1761; (10) Major William Corry's two papers, 1763, on the defense of British possessions in America; (11) From Maj. Craven of the late Pepperrell Regiment, Feb. 1, 1758; (12) From William Davis, Philadelphia, Sept. 16, 1758, enclosing the examination of an English sailor who came with a flag of truce from New Orleans; (13) An account of Col. Bradstreet's success at Cataraqui, 1758; (14) The Earl of Egremont's letter, July 9, 1763, to the governors in America; (15) Gov. Ellis of Georgia relating to the Creek Indians, July 10, 1760; (16) Maj.-Gen. Forbes, July 12, 1758, enclosing a military sketch map of Pennsylvania from Philadelphia to Fort Duquesne; (17) Particulars of Forbes's army for the Hon. Thomas Penn; (18) Paper giving the views of Benjamin Franklin and Richard Jackson on the points presented to them connected with the Fort Duquesne campaign; (19) Count de Fuentes writes about Newfoundland, Sept. 9, 1760; (20) A paper relating to Georgia, 1758; (21) Col. Jeremiah Gridley writes to Christopher Kilby, Jan. 19 and 28, 1758, about the difficulty between the Massachusetts Assembly and the governor, and the arrival of the Connecticut commissioners; (22) Halifax to the Board of Trade about the superintendent of the Mosquito Shore settlement, with the Board's reply, Nov. 12 and Dec. 2, 1764; (23) Petition of William Kelly and Samuel Stilwell, New York merchants, for a letter to the British ambassador at the Spanish court in order to reclaim a ship and cargo taken out of Santo Domingo by a French frigate, 1758; (24) Capt. Joshua Loring's journal of events at Lake George from July 5 onward, Aug. 19, 1758; (25) Another report from Loring, now at Isle Royale, Aug. 26, 1760; (26) Loudoun to Gov. Pownall, Jan. 18, 1758, and to the Duke of Argyll, New York, Feb. 14, 1758; also a précis of a letter from Loudoun, Feb. 14, 1758; (27) Gov. Lyttelton of South Carolina to Amherst, Charleston, March 16, 1759; (28) Lieut. Arch. McAulay to Capt. Horatio Gates, Oswego, Aug. 30, 1758; (29) Governor and council of North Carolina recommends appointment of Maj. Robert Rogers for superintendent of southern Indian affairs, Dec. 9, 1761; (30) Paterson to Pitt, about a future peace as it relates to Great Britain, Oct. 30, 1759; (31) Thomas Penn, to Pitt, enclosing a letter from Richard Peters about important issues to be settled with the Ohio Indians at a proposed treaty and a message from an Indian chief in behalf of several Indian nations living on the Ohio River, Feb. 3, 1759; (32) Extracts from two letters from Pitt to American governors, Dec. 6 and 9, 1758; (33) Gov. Pownall to Lord Loudoun, Boston, Jan. 9, 1758; (34) A précis of Thomas Pownall's letters [1758]; (35) Exchange of messages between the Pennsylvania Assembly and the governor, Sept. 5–14, 1758; (36) From John Robinson, speaker of the Virginia House of Burgesses, June 11, 1758; (37) Paper expressing the alarm of the South Carolina merchants that Col. Montgomery was about to leave the colony with his troops to join Gen. Amherst in New York; (38) William Vassall to Drake and Long about the illicit trade of the northern colonies with the French at Monte Christi, Boston, March 3, 1759; (39) The Virginia House of Burgesses represents to the King the colony's hardships since the beginning of the war; also the accompanying address to the King; both undated; (40) The Society of Merchants in London Trading to Virginia and Maryland congratulates Pitt on the capture of Fort Duquesne, Feb. 7, 1759; (41) A clause in the Virginia act, passed Oct. 15, 1760, relating to the forces of the province; (42) Gen. Whitmore to Maj.-Gen. Wolfe, July 1759; (43) Massachusetts, New York, and New Hampshire ask for reimbursement money for 1756 and 1758; (44) Memorandum of the number of provincials raised for campaigns of 1758, 1759 and 1760; (45) Many papers relating to Loudoun's proposed campaign against Louisbourg, 1758, and letters from Louisbourg from among Boscawen's papers, including a French officer's journal, June 1–July 27, 1758; (46) Papers relating to Boscawen's request for sailors from Pennsylvania and the action of the assembly, Sept. 1758; also letters from Louisbourg and one from Fort Amherst; (47) Account of the action on Sept. 14, 1758 near Fort Duquesne; (48) Abercromby writes about troops from Louisbourg, Oct. 30, 1758; (49) Lists of winter-quarters for troops in North America, Nov.–Dec. 1758;

(50) List of promotions in America, Dec. 1758–Jan. 1759; (51) Proposal for an expedition from the northern colonies against the French in Canada [1758]; (52) Extracts from French letters from Montreal and Quebec, 1758–1759; (53) Materials needed for a hospital, March 17, 1759; (54) Amherst to Brig.-Gen. Whitmore about Quebec, March 16, 1759; (55) Proceedings of an Indian conference at Philadelphia, April 1759; (56) List of transports taken at New York, Boston, and Philadelphia, April 1759; (57) Gov. Moore includes a Spanish letter in his own letter of March 20, 1760; (58) Papers relating to two privateers cruising in the West Indies, 1759–1760; (59) Disposition and state of his Majesty's troops in North America, 1760–1761; (60) A bill to grant commissions in America to foreign Protestants who have served abroad, 1760 (Printed); (61) An estimate for erecting barracks.

No. 97, 1764–1774, is made up of miscellaneous papers including: (1) From "An American Farmer" [1765]; (2) From "Amor Patriae," relative to the Stamp Act, Feb. 2, 1766; (3) Précis of enclosures in Amherst's letters of March 29 (no year); (4) Précis of letters from Amherst, de Lancey, Pownall, and Ellis, relative to the war with the French in North America; (5) Gov. Bernard to Shelburne, Boston, Dec. 6, 1766; (6) Comments of James Bowdoin, Samuel Pemberton, and Joseph Warren on the Boston Massacre, March 23, 1770; (7) Major William Corry about the disciplining and provisioning of the army in America; (8) Two copies of a letter from Thomas Cushing, speaker of the Mass. House of Representatives, Feb. 2, 1768; (9) Letter from John Dickinson, Philadelphia, Dec. 21, 1760, with an extract of a letter to Lord Baltimore from Daniel Dulany; (10) From Lieut. James Eidingtoun of the Royal Highland Regiment about taking possession of Fort Chartres, Oct. 17, 1765; (11) Extract from Gov. Franklin of New Jersey to Shelburne, Dec. 18, 1766; (12) Gov. Johnstone to Col. William Taylor, Pensacola, Oct. 4, 1766; (13) Proposal of London merchants to import grain from the colonies to relieve distress at home, Oct. 31, 1766; (14) From the House of Representatives to Shelburne, Boston, Dec. 4, 1766; (15) Mississippi Company papers sent to Pitt, April 2, 1774; (16) Chiefs of the Mohecaunnuck and Wappinger tribes thank Pitt for an interview, July 25, 1766; (17) Gov. Sir Henry Moore of New York to the Board of Trade, Dec. 10, 1766; (18) Gov. Moore to Shelburne about the quartering of troops, Dec. 19, 1766; (19) Gov. Moore to the New York Assembly about quartering troops, Nov. 17, 1766 (copy); (20) Petition of merchants of New York to the House of Commons about trade restrictions, Nov. 28, 1766; (21) Précis of letters from Pownall, Boston, Aug. 22 [1757] and de Lancey, New York, Aug. 24 and 25 [1757], about the surrender of Fort William Henry and Gen.

Webb; (22) Gov. Pownall's plan for quartering regular troops in America; (23) "The Case of Captain Thos. Preston," Mar. 17, 1770; (24) A remonstrance of London merchants trading to Virginia and Maryland and a petition to the King asking for protection adequate to meet the danger, n.d.; (25) Respecting the present mutiny act in America [1765]; (26) Mr. Huske's plan for extending and securing Great Britain's trade to the colonies, Nov. 1, 1765; (27) An agreement between West Indian and North American merchants relating to trade of the colonies, March 10, 1766; (28) House of Lords protests against repeal of the Stamp Act, March 11 and 17, 1766; (29) Distribution of H. M. forces in North America, March 29, 1766; (30) The question of the value of American frontier outposts, May 1766; (31) A Cabinet Council minute regarding the quartering of troops in New York; (32) American mutiny bill, 1766, showing changes made; (33) The House of Lords protest against the bill for better regulating the government of Massachusetts, May 11, 1774; (34) Address of the Continental Congress to the King, Oct. 26, 1774; (35) Representation respecting the offer made by merchants trading to Boston to compensate the East India Co. for the destroyed tea [1774]; (36) Report of a committee on colonial import duties, n.d.; (37) Thirteen proposals related to American trade and colonial import duties, n.d.; (38) Unsigned and undated papers on the molasses trade, with the statement that two million Americans owe Great Britain £4,000,000 sterling; (39) A committee report on the sugar question, n.d.; (40) A paper on the relation between the colonies and the home government, n.d.; (41) "Heads of Arguments of the Principles of *Right* and *Law* with respect to the Stamp Act," n.d.; (42) "Some facts stated that prove the French to have been the Aggressors in North America," n.d.; (43) Paper on the relations between the Five Nations and the English as dictated by Gov. Pownall when in Alexandria; (44) Abercromby's paper on four necessary military operations in North America, n.d.; (45) The disposition and annual charge of the forces in America, n.d.; (46) Invoices for medicine, n.d.; (47) About two treasonable letters from America signed "Filius Gallicae," addressed to the Duc de Mirepoix, n.d.; (48) Copy of a "Provisional Act for settling the Troubles in America and for asserting the Supreme Legislative Authority and Superintending Power of Great Britain over the Colonies," n.d.; (49) Undated observations on the Molasses Act (6 Geo. II) and the Sugar Act (4 Geo. III); (50) Stores delivered out of the *Ruby* ordnance transport by order of Maj.-Gen. Wolfe; (51) A project for Indian trade in North America, n.d.; (52) A paper about measures to be taken at home relative to the colonies, n.d.; (53) Since all attempts to remove the French encroachments in North America have failed, a plan for the invasion of Canada, n.d.; (54) Memorials concerning the Gulf and River of St. Lawrence, n.d.; (55) Minutes on proposals for harrassing the French in North America and the West Indies, n.d.; (56) Opinion of an unnamed committee in relation to financial grants by the colonial assemblies, n.d.; (57) How the English may succeed in the future attempt upon Fort Duquesne, n.d.; (58) A scheme for unifying Great Britain and the colonies by granting colonial representation in the House of Commons; (59) Henry McCulloh's plan for issuing exchequer bills of union as bills of credit for use in the American colonies, n.d.; (60) Account of expenditures on the proposed expedition against Canada.

No. 98 includes the following papers: (1) Papers relating to Canada, Newfoundland, Cape Breton, Nova Scotia, and Labrador, 1755–1761; (2) Papers relating to the West Indies and the Mosquito Shore, especially illicit trade, 1742–1768; (3) From Gen. Abercromby to James Abercromby, Aug. 9, 1758; (4) "Indian intelligence from Sir Wm. Johnson," Jan. 29, 1758; (5) A French account of Braddock's defeat in 1755.

HOUSE OF LORDS PAPERS, THE TOWER

Up to the present we have been concerned with the papers of agencies of the government of Great Britain that were the creation of the Crown rather than of Parliament. As the result of the sovereign powers assumed by Parliament in the Revolution of 1688/9 and by the Act of Settlement, this body had acquired a dominating position in the affairs of state, which, in a final analysis of the location of power, eclipsed the royal authority, potent as it still was during the period under consideration. The House of Commons, especially by means of the control that it exercised over money bills, was by the middle of the eighteenth century the most weighty of the two houses—without reference to the influence that the Crown and individual peers enjoyed in determining to a great extent the composition of the membership of the House. Nevertheless, outside its *Journals,* now in print, the surviving papers, outside also of such reports as are listed in Hansard's *Catalogue and Breviate of Parliament* after the destruction of the House of Parliament early in the nineteenth century, are of little value for the years 1748–1776.

In the technical sense the House of Commons was never a court of record, as is the House of Lords with its vast collection of papers in its well-established Record Office in Victoria Tower, Westminster. A manuscript list of documents that covers the House of Lords papers has now been brought down to 1840 and beyond and is available to the student.

This can be used to great advantage in checking these manuscripts against the printed *Journals* of both the House of Lords and the House of Commons. Miss Frances G. Davenport in the Andrews and Davenport: *Guide to the Manuscript Materials for the History of the United States to 1783, in the British Museum, in Minor London Archives, and in the Libraries of Oxford and Cambridge* (Carnegie Institution of Washington, Washington, 1908), pp. 189–272, listed those papers—contemporary attested copies—that have relation to the history of the American colonies. From this list a selection of documents that bear on the period 1748–1776 is presented. These attested copies are as follows:

No. 180, Jan. 17, 1749. Treaty of Aix la Chapelle.

No. 182, Feb. 9, 1750. Representation of the Board of Trade on African trade.

No. 183, April 3 and 5, 1750. Petitions against 23 Geo. II to encourage the importation of pig and bar iron from the American colonies.

No. 184, April 3, 1750. Reports made by officers of the Navy on the tests of American iron.

No. 185, April 5, 1750. Custom House papers on the quantity of American iron imported from 1710 to 1740; also the quantity of iron exported to the colonies from 1746 to 1749.

No. 187, Jan. 31, 1751. Treaty concluded between Great Britain and Spain, Oct. 5, 1750.

No. 188, Feb. 8, 1751. Admiralty papers relating to the Royal African Company forts. These include: (1) General observations by Capt. Pye, March 18, 1749, on the African coast; (2) Letter of Feb. 10, 1749 from chiefs of the blacks to Capt. Pye asking that Richard Stockwell be again placed in charge of Cape Coast Castle; (3) Stockwell and others to Pye, Cape Coast Castle, Jan. 18, 1749; (4) Detailed account of Cape Coast Castle.

No. 189, Jan. 13, 1752. Report of commissioners appointed to examine the claims of creditors of the Royal African Company.

No. 190, Feb. 12, 1755. Account of funds received and expended by the Company of Merchants trading to Africa to support the settlements.

No. 191, March 12, 1753. The Nova Scotia settlement papers (two large bundles) from the Secretary of State and Board of Trade covering the period 1749–1752.

No. 192, March 13, 1753. Petitions of Daniel Quare and his eldest son for a bill to permit the sale of their interest in the East New Jersey propriety for the payment of debts.

No. 193, Jan. 27, 1755. Account of proceedings to divest the Royal African Company of all of the interest in the African Trade, including land and forts.

No. 194, Feb. 20, 1756. This is a very large collection of papers (210 copies of letters with enclosures), some of which are in French, received from the office of Secretary of State for the Southern Department and concerned with the French encroachments in North America. They are as follows: (1) Copies of 144 letters, memorials, etc., from such persons as Gov. Clinton, Gov. Cornwallis, M. Desherbiers, M. Duquesne, Col. Wm. Johnson, M. de la Jonquière, Lieut. Lindesay, Abbé Le Loutre, Lieut.-Col. Mascarene, M. de Puyzieulx, Count de Raymond, M. Rouillé, Gov. Shirley, and Mr. Stoddert; (2) Journal of Maj. Charles Lawrence after entering the basin of Chignecto with a detachment; (3) Memorial concerning French ships taken by English ships off the coast of New France; (4) Decree of the Nova Scotia court of vice-admiralty against the French brigantine, *St. François*; (5) An invoice of war supplies delivered to Abbé Le Loutre for the savages and sent from Quebec; (6) Instructions sent to the master of the *London;* (7) Representations against the French proceedings in the West Indies, March 7, 1752; (8) Declarations of John Patten and Thomas Bourke, captives sent from Canada to France; (9) Remarks on a French fort built at Crown Point; (10) Extract of a minute taken between the Duc de Mirepoix and the Duke of Newcastle, Dec. 20, 1752; (11) Extracts of letters between Col. Yorke, the Duke of Bedford, and the Earl of Holderness, 1749–1751, with translation of a memorial of M. Durand relating to Nova Scotia, June 17, 1749, and an answering memorial; (12) Extracts and copies of letters between the two commissaries, Shirley and Mildmay, appointed to negotiate with the French commissaries, and the Duke of Bedford, the Earl of Holderness, the Duke of Newcastle and others; (13) Extracts of letters from Commissaries Mildmay and DeCosne to Newcastle, Sir Thomas Robinson, and Holderness; (14) Extracts of letters from DeCosne to Mr. Amyand and between DeCosne and Robinson; (15) Memorials and answers thereto exchanged by the Duc de Mirepoix and Sir Thomas Robinson, 1755; (16) Copies of projects for a preliminary convention delivered to and by the Duc de Mirepoix, 1755; (17) Extracts of letters from M. Rouillé to the Duc de Mirepoix.

No. 195, Feb. 24, 1756. Here again is a very large group of papers, sent to the House of Lords from the Board of Trade. These also relate chiefly to the French encroachments in North America, 1749–1755. Among them are copies of forty-five letters sent from the Board of Trade to the Secretary of State. They are as follows: (1) Letters from the Lieut.-Gov. of Nova Scotia, Paul Mascarene, April 28 and June 2, 1749; (2) From M. de la Galissonière of Canada to Mascarene, Jan. 15, 1749, with his reply, April 25, 1749; (3) Six letters from Gov. Shirley to the Board of Trade, 1749–

1754; (4) Shirley to de la Galissonière, May 9, 1749; (5) Articles of submission and agreement by the Indians of Nova Scotia and New England, Boston, 1725; (6) Shirley to Gov. Edward Cornwallis of Nova Scotia, July 3, 1749; (7) Seven letters and extracts of letters from Gov. George Clinton of New York to the Board of Trade, 1749–1751; (8) Extract of a letter from Capt. Marshall to Clinton, June 23, 1749; (9) Letter and ten extracts of letters from Gov. Cornwallis to the Board of Trade, 1749–1751; (10) Gov. Cornwallis to Capt. Rous of H.M.S. *Albany* with a copy of an ordinance to be delivered to the French officers commanding at St. John River, July 9, 1749; (11) Cornwallis to Gov. M. Desherbiers of Louisbourg (n.d.); (12) M. Desherbiers to Cornwallis, Oct. 15, 1749; (13) M. de la Jonquière, governor general of New France, to Cornwallis, Oct. 25, 1749; (14) Lieut.-Gov. James Hamilton of Pennsylvania to Gov. Clinton of New York, enclosing a declaration by M. Céloron with a letter (n.d.); (15) Again, Hamilton to Clinton, Sept. 20, 1750; (16) Speech by a French officer to Ohio River Indians; (17) M. Léry, engineer at the French Fort Niagara, to de la Jonquière, July 5, 1749; (18) Proclamation by three Indian chiefs at Piziquid, Nova Scotia, Dec. 1749; (19) Extracts of letters of Col. Lee, Pres. of the Virginia Council to the Board of Trade, May 11 and Nov. 6, 1750; (20) Extracts from several French letters taken on a French vessel in the Bay of Fundy; (21) Lieut. Butler to Col. Wm. Johnson, Oswego, Sept. 3, 1750; (22) Message from the Twightwees addressed to all colonial governors, delivered May 29, 1750, to Hamilton; (23) Nova Scotia vice-admiralty court decree, Nov. 1, 1750 against the French brigantine *St. François* seized by Capt. Rous; (24) Col. Wm. Johnson to Gov. Clinton, Sept. 25, 1750 and July 27, 1751; (25) Inscription on a leaden plate: the French claims on both sides of the Ohio River; (26) Speech of a Cayuga chief to Col. Johnson and Johnson's reply, Dec. 5, 1750; (27) Extract of a letter from Hamilton to the Board of Trade, Feb. 8, 1751; (28) M. Céloron to Hamilton, Fort Detroit, Aug. 6, 1749; (29) Phineas Stevens to Lieut.-Gov. Spencer Phips of Mass., April 4, 1751; (30) Letters to Col. Johnson from Lieut. Lindesay and Mr. Stoddert, a trader, both at Oswego, July 1751; (31) Gov. Clinton to M. de la Jonquière, June 12, 1751, and de la Jonquière to Clinton, Aug. 10, 1751, together with Clinton's comments on this letter; (32) Four extracts of letters from Lieut.-Gov. Dinwiddie to the Board of Trade, 1752–1754; (33) Journal of Wm. Trent who was sent to the Twightwees, June 21, 1752; (34) The Twightwees's letter to Dinwiddie, June 24, 1752, together with another letter from the Indians to him (n.d.); (35) A French deserter's account of the number and strength of the French forts (n.d.); (36) Letter and extracts of letters from Gov. Hopson of Nova Scotia to the Board of Trade, 1753; (37) Capt. Trent to Lieut.-Gov. Hamilton, April 10, 1753; (38) Col. Johnson to Gov. Clinton, April 20, 1753; (39) Lieut.-Gov. Hamilton to Clinton, May 10, 1753; (40) Capt. Benj. Stoddard to Col. Johnson, May 15, 1753; (41) Capt. Holland to Clinton, Oswego, May 15, 1753; (42) Board of Trade representations to the King in Council, Aug. 16 and Dec. 7, 1753; (43) Jesuit priest Father Germain of the River St. John to an inhabitant of the Annapolis River district (n.d.); (44) Extract of letters from Capt. Handfield to Paul Mascarene, Annapolis Royal, Sept. 2, 1753; (45) Extracts of four letters from Lieut.-Gov. de Lancey to the Board of Trade, 1753–1754; (46) New York Assembly resolution, Nov. 13, 1753; (47) Extract of letter from Lieut. Holland to de Lancey, Oswego, Nov. 8, 1753; (48) Extracts of letters from Gov. Lawrence of Nova Scotia to the Board of Trade, 1754–1755; (49) Gov. Dinwiddie's commission to George Washington, Oct. 30, 1753, together with instructions; (50) Dinwiddie to the commander of the French forces on the Ohio, Oct. 31, 1753, and M. de St. Pierre's reply to Dinwiddie; (51) Maj. Washington's journal covering his negotiations with the French, 1753; (52) Address of the Massachusetts Assembly to Gov. Shirley (n.d.); (53) Extract of a letter from Lieut.-Gov. de Lancey, May 21, 1754; (54) Washington to Lieut.-Gov. Hamilton of Pennsylvania (n.d.); (55) Summons from M. Contrecoeur to the British troops at the mouth of the Monongahela, April 16, 1754; (56) Washington to Dinwiddie, April 25, 1754; (57) Ensign Ward's deposition, May 7, 1754; (58) Letter of de Lancey to Gov.-Gen. Duquesne, Oct. 16, 1754; (59) Lieut.-Gov. Lawrence of Nova Scotia to Gov. Shirley (n.d.).

No. 196, March 1, 1756. Petition of William Bollan, Massachusetts agent, against bill 29 Geo. II to permit foreign Protestants to act as officers in the armies in America.

No. 197, 1762. Diplomatic correspondence (fifty-nine papers) regarding the disagreement with Spain; among them are four papers that follow: (1) About the restitution of prizes; (2) Liberty of Spain in the Newfoundland fisheries; (3) The Bay of Honduras and the logwood issue; (4) Account of the arrival at Cadiz of the Spanish flota from the West Indies.

No. 198, April 21, 1762. Reasons for the Commons' disagreement with the Lords' amendments about foreign Protestants serving as officers in the army in America.

No. 199, April 23, 1762. Bill 2 Geo. III, for trial in the American plantations of persons guilty of murder within the Admiral's jurisdiction.

No. 200, Nov. 29, 1762. Papers relating to the treaty of peace: (1) Copy of preliminary articles signed at Fontainebleau, Nov. 3, 1762; (2)

Declaration signed Nov. 3, 1762 by the French plenipotentiary, relating to Art. 13 of the preliminaries.

No. 201, March 18, 1763. Copies of the Treaty of Paris signed Feb. 10, 1763.

No. 202, March 25, 1763. War Office Papers: (1) Estimate of the charge of his Majesty's forces in America for 121 days; (2) Estimate of the charge of his Majesty's forces in America for 244 days; (3) Estimate of the charge of four regiments on the Irish establishment serving in America for 121 days.

No. 203, March 13, 1764. Admiralty Office papers relating to the forts of the African Company prepared pursuant to 23 Geo. II.

No. 204, Jan. 15, 1765. Papers from the Secretary of State relating to English and French prisoners of war.

No. 205, Feb. 8, 1765. Admiralty Office papers relating to the state of the African forts and settlements, including two reports.

No. 206, Feb. 22, 1765. Account of corn and meal exported, 1754–1764, with names of countries receiving it.

No. 207, March 6, 1765. Resolutions about bringing to England, without proper authority, any American Indian and making a public show of him.

No. 208, March 11, 1765. Bill 5 Geo. III, to prevent any free American Indian from being carried by sea without a license.

No. 209, Jan. 14, 1766. Large bundle of papers (190 items with enclosures) from the Secretary of State relating to the Stamp Act and later disturbances. They are as follows: (1) Mr. Brettell of the Stamp Office to Secretary Jenkinson of the Treasury with Jenkinson's answer of April 3, 1765, including a list of stamp officers; (2) Mr. Whately of the Treasury to the Commissioners of Stamps, April 20, 1765, with a plan to carry the act into effect, with a reply from Mr. Brettell, May 1, 1765; (3) Representation from the Commissioners of Stamps, with a plan, April 27, 1765; (4) Brettell to Whately, July 3, 1765; (5) The Treasury approval of the plan; (6) Whately to Morgan Vane, comptroller of stamps, approving appointment of an additional clerk, July 9, 1765; (7) Whately about vacancies of distributors of stamps, July 9, 1765; (8) Treasury minute: "A proposition for obviating the inconveniences of bringing into this kingdom the money to be raised by Stamp Duties," July 9, 1765; (9) Whately to the Commissioners of Stamps about the distributors paying their money to deputy paymasters abroad, July 10, 1765; (10) A copy of a circular letter to governors abroad about the Stamp Act, Sept. 14, 1765; (11) Representation from the Commissioners of Stamps for £6,000, Sept. 10, 1765; (12) Treasury minute, Sept. 13, 1765; (13) Lowndes to the Commissioners of Stamps about the expense already incurred, Sept. 16, 1765; (14) Treasury minute, Sept. 17,

1765; (15) Mr. Lowndes to Commissioners of Stamps to recommend a distributor for the Bahamas, Sept. 19, 1765; (16) Treasury minute, Oct. 7, 1765; (17) Mr. Cowper to the clerk of the Council, transmitting two letters from Andrew Oliver, Oct. 8, 1765; (18) Cowper to Gov. Bernard about the Boston riot, Oct. 8, 1765; (19) Cowper to Gov. Shirley of the Bahamas about distributing stamps there; (20) Brettell to Lowndes about stamps abroad, Oct. 11, 1765; (21) Treasury minutes, Oct. 11 and 14, 1765; (22) Cowper to Gov. Moore about a stamp distributor to take the place of M'Evers, Oct. 16, 1765; (23) M'Evers's letter to Barlow Trecothick, Aug. 26, 1765; (24) Cowper to Brettell about a Bahamas distributor, Oct. 17, 1765; (25) Cowper to Gov. Franklin about the New Jersey distributor, Nov. 5, 1765; (26) Brettell to Lowndes, enclosing Mr. Coxe's resignation as New Jersey distributor, Nov. 14, and reply of Lowndes, Nov. 15, 1765; (27) Treasury minutes, Nov. 25 and Dec. 23, 1765; (28) Lowndes to the clerk of the Council, transmitting Mr. Freemantle's letter, together with extracts of letters from the collector and comptroller of New York, Dec. 24, 1765; (29) Extract from Brettell's letter, transmitting letters from Messrs. Coxe, Saxby, and Lloyd, and William Whitehead, Jan. 4, 1766; (30) Collector of Customs at Rhode Island to the Commissioners of Customs, Aug. 28, 1765; (31) Mr. Johnston, Rhode Island distributor of stamps, to Stamp Commissioners, Aug. 31, 1765; (32) Rhode Island Collector of Customs to Customs Commissioners, Sept. 5, 1765; (33) Intelligence from the colonies about the Stamp Act, Sept. 6, 1765; (34) Brettell to Mr. Lloyd, South Carolina distributor of stamps, Sept. 6, 1765; (35) Boston Comptroller to Commissioners of Customs, Sept. 7, 1765; (36) Mr. John Temple, surveyor general of the northern district of America, to Commissioners of Customs, Sept. 9, 1765; (37) Mr. George Meserve to Commissioners of Stamps, Sept. 30, 1765; (38) Mr. John Hughes to Commissioners of Stamps with eight enclosures: Hughes to Lieut.-Gov. John Penn, Sept. 17, 1765; W. Dowell to Hughes (n.d.); Hughes to John Dickinson, Oct. 2, 1765; Hughes to John Penn, Oct. 3, 1765; a paper addressed to Hughes requesting that he give assurance to citizens of Philadelphia that he will not execute his office; Hughes's answer to the papers, Oct. 5, 1765; a second answer by Hughes that he will not attempt to execute the Stamp Act until it shall be put into execution in the neighbouring colonies, also Oct. 5, 1765; Hughes to John Penn, Oct. 8, 1765; (39) David Colden of New York to Commissioners of Stamps, Oct. 26, 1765; (40) Hughes to Commissioners of Stamps, with enclosures, Nov. 5, 1765; (41) Zachary Hood of Maryland to Commissioners of Stamps, Nov. 10, 1765; (42) Board of Trade representation about proceedings in the

Massachusetts and New York Assemblies respecting acts and resolutions of Parliament, Dec. 11, 1764; (43) Order in council referring the Board's representation to the consideration of the Committee of Council, Dec. 12, 1764; (44) Report of the Committee of Council on the representation and papers, that these should be laid before Parliament, Dec. 14, 1764; (45) Order in council approving the report: the Earl of Halifax to receive his Majesty's pleasure as to when this should be done, Dec. 19, 1764; (46) Board of Trade transmits the extraordinary resolution of the New York Assembly about dangers that threaten the colonies through taxation by Great Britain, Jan. 17, 1765; (47) Copy of his Majesty's order in council directing the Earl of Halifax to lay the papers before Parliament, Feb. 1, 1765; (48) Papers relating to resolutions of the Virginia House of Burgesses respecting the act of Parliament for levying taxes in America, Aug. 27, 1765; (49) Copy of his Majesty's order in council referring the paper relating to the Virginia House of Burgesses to the Committee of Council, Sept. 6, 1765; (50) Representation of the Board of Trade, relating to resolutions of the House of Representatives of Massachusetts, respecting the levying of stamp taxes in America, Oct. 1, 1765; (51) His Majesty's order in council referring this representation to the Committee of Council, Oct. 2, 1765; (52) Report of the Committee of Council upon the foregoing two resolutions, proposing they be laid before Parliament, Oct. 3, 1765; (53) Order in council approving the report and directing Sec. Conway to receive his Majesty's pleasure for the time and manner of laying the papers before Parliament, Oct. 18, 1765; (54) Representation of the Board of Trade, with papers relating to Massachusetts and the outrageous behaviour of the people, Oct. 11, 1765; (55) A second representation of the Board of Trade with papers relating to the Boston riots, Oct. 17, 1765; (56) From the Secretary of the Treasury, transmitting papers from the Massachusetts stamp distributor, Oct. 8, 1765; (57) The two representations of the Board and papers ordered to be referred to the Committee of Council, Oct. 18, 1765; (58) Report of the Committee of Council on the representation and papers, Oct. 22, 1765; (59) Order in council directing Sec. Conway to signify his Majesty's pleasure to the governors in North America to stop the riots, Oct. 23, 1765; (60) The Lords of the Admiralty directed to give orders to commanders of sea forces in North America to assist in suppressing the riots, Oct. 23, 1765; (61) The Secretary at War to give order for suppressing riots to commanders of forces in America, Oct. 23, 1765; (62) Another representation of the Board of Trade giving further account of unconstitutional proceedings of the Council and Assembly of Massachusetts, with a printed paper (108

pages) of extracts from New England newspapers, Dec. 17, 1765;
(63) Extracts from two letters from the collector and comptroller
of New York customs about their inability to discharge their duty,
Nov. 4 and 6, 1765; (64) Gov. Bernard to the Earl of Halifax,
Boston, Nov. 10, 1764, with enclosures that follow; (65) Petition
of Massachusetts Council and House of Representatives to the
House of Commons, with Gov. Bernard's speech to the Assembly
and the address of the Council and House to Bernard; (66) Gov.
Hopkins of Rhode Island to Halifax, Nov. 12, 1764; (67) Gov.
Fitch to Halifax, Norwalk, Conn., Nov. 13, 1764; (68) Lieut.-Gov.
Fauquier to Halifax, Williamsburg, Va., June 14, 1765; (69) Ber-
nard to Halifax, Aug. 15–16, 1765, enclosing his proclamation;
(70) Bernard to Halifax, Aug. 22, 1765, enclosing minutes of the
Council; (71) Collector of Customs Robinson, Rhode Island, to
Halifax, Aug. 28, 1765, enclosing copy of *The Providence Gazette
Extraordinary;* (72) Lieut.-Gov. Hutchinson to Halifax, Aug. 30,
1765; (73) Bernard to Halifax, Aug. 31, 1765, with enclosures;
(74) Deputy-Gov. Sharpe of Maryland to Halifax, Sept. 5, 1765;
(75) Bernard to Halifax, Sept. 7, 1765; (76) Maj.-Gen. Gage to
Sec. Conway, with resolutions of the New York Council and a
statement of the distribution of forces in North America, New
York, Sept. 23, 1765; (77) Lieut.-Gov. Colden to Conway, New
York, Sept. 23, 1765, enclosing letters from James M'Evers to
Colden and minutes of the New York Council; (78) Gov. Franklin
of New Jersey to Conway, Sept. 23, 1765, with copy of letter from
Franklin to Gage and Gage's reply with letters relating to Wil-
liam Coxe, stamp distributor; (79) Bernard to Conway, Sept. 28,
1765, enclosing copies of papers relating to the government of
Massachusetts; (80) Lieut.-Gov. Hutchinson to Conway, New
York, Oct. 1, 1765; (81) Gov. Wentworth of New Hampshire to
Conway, Oct. 5, 1765; (82) Gage to Conway, Oct. 12, 1765; (83)
Colden to Conway, Oct. 12, 1765, with copy of *The Constitutional
Courant;* (84) Colden again to Conway, Oct. 26, 1765, with copy
of paper posted in public places; (85) Hutchinson to Conway,
Boston, Oct. 27, 1765, with appraisement of damages caused by
the mob, etc., with copy of *The Boston Evening Post* and *Supple-
ment;* (86) Copy of *The Newport Mercury,* Dec. 13, 1765; (87)
Gage to Conway, Nov. 4, 1765, with enclosures; (88) Colden to
Conway, Nov. 5, 1765, with minute of the Council; (89) Gage to
Conway, Nov. 8, 1765, with enclosures; (90) Colden to Conway,
Nov. 9, 1765, with enclosures; (91) Copy of paper put up at the
New York Coffee House, Nov. 1 and 6, 1765; (92) Extract of
letter of Conway to Gage, Oct. 24, 1765; (93) Conway to Bernard,
Oct. 24, 1765; (94) Conway to other North American governors,
Oct. 24, 1765; (95) Conway to Gage, Dec. 15, 1765; (96) Conway

to Colden, Dec. 15, 1765; (97) Fauquier to Board of Trade, Williamsburg, June 5, 1765; (98) House of Burgesses resolutions; (99) Bernard to Board of Trade, Boston, July 8, 1765; (100) Extract of Journal of the Massachusetts House of Representatives, June 25, 1765; (101) Bernard to Board of Trade, Aug. 15 and 22, 1765; (102) Minutes of Massachusetts Council, Aug. 14, 15 and 21, 1765; (103) Bernard's proclamations, Aug. 15 and 28, 1765; (104) Bernard to Board of Trade, Aug. 31 and Sept. 7, 1765; (105) Minutes of Massachusetts Council, Aug. 27–29, 1765; (106) Bernard to John Pownall of the Board of Trade, Sept. 7, 1765; (107) Bernard to Board of Trade, Sept. 28, 1765; (108) Extracts from journal of Massachusetts House of Representatives, Sept. 25–27, 1765; (109) Gov. Franklin to Board of Trade, Oct. 10, 1765; (110) Minutes of the New Jersey Council, Sept. 13 and 24, 1765; (111) Gov. Benning Wentworth to Board of Trade, Oct. 5, 1765; (112) Gov. Bernard to John Pownall of the Board of Trade, Oct. 1, 1765; (113) Bernard to Board of Trade, Oct. 12 and 17, 1765; (114) Extracts from Bernard to John Pownall of the Board of Trade, Oct. 9 and 26, and Nov. 1, 1765; (115) Minutes of Massachusetts Council, Oct. 29–31 and Nov. 4, 1765; (116) Committee of the Massachusetts Assembly, Oct. 25, 1765; (117) Votes of a meeting of inhabitants at Cambridge, Oct. 14, 1765; (118) Extract from Fauquier to Board of Trade, Oct. 2, 1765; (119) Extract from journal of the Virginia House of Burgesses, May 29–30, 1765.

No. 210, Jan. 22, 1766. Gov. Moore of New York to Conway, Nov. 21, 1765, with enclosures.

No. 211, Jan. 27, 1766. Papers relating to Stamp Act disturbances in Virginia: (1) Conway to Lieut.-Gov. Fauquier, Sept. 14, 1765; (2) Fauquier to the Board of Trade, Nov. 3, 1765, regarding Col. Mercer, Virginia stamp distributor, with enclosures.

No. 212, Jan. 28, 1766. Fauquier to Board of Trade, Nov. 8, 1765, as to the disposal of the stamps.

No. 213, Jan. 28, 1766. Lists of military and civil officers employed in America by the Admiralty.

No. 214, Jan. 29, 1766. (1) Papers from the Secretary of State relating to the Stamp Act disturbances, with letter from the Admiralty to Conway, Jan. 27, 1766; (2) Capt. Stirling of the *Rainbow* to Sec. Philip Stephens, Virginia, Nov. 5, 1765; (3) Capt. Hawker of the *Sardoine* to Sec. Philip Stephens, Nov. 19, 1765; (4) Gov. Franklin to Capt. Hawker, Nov. 9, 1765; (5) Minutes of the New Jersey Council about the danger to the stamps if brought into the colony.

No. 215, Jan. 29, 1766. List of civil officers employed in North America.

No. 216, Jan. 31, 1766. Gov. Franklin to Board of Trade, Nov. 13, 1765, about the Stamp Act.

No. 217, Feb. 3, 1766. (1) List of civil officers in North America appointed by the Treasury, Jan. 31, 1766; (2) List of civil officers for North America, distinguishing those who are absent, Jan. 28, 1766; (3) List of all officers designated to carry the Stamp Act into execution, Jan. 28, 1766; (4) From the Philadelphia collector and comptroller of customs, Dec. 1, 1765; (5) From Mr. Hinshelwood, Nova Scotia, distributor of stamps, with enclosure, Nov. 1, 1765.

No. 218, Feb. 6, 1766. Papers from the Secretary of State: (1) Fauquier to Conway, Dec. 11, 1765; (2) Gov. Tryon of North Carolina to Conway, Nov. 5, 1765; (3) From a merchant of Charles Town (Charleston, S.C.), Oct. 29, 1765; (4) Fauquier to Conway, Nov. 24, 1765; (5) Fauquier to Board of Trade, Dec. 17, 1765.

No. 219, Feb. 10, 1766. Five resolutions reported from the Lords' committee relating to the American riots.

No. 220, Feb. 10, 1766. Papers relating to American unrest: (1) Gov. Franklin of New Jersey to Sec. Conway, Nov. 30, 1765, with enclosures; (2) Minutes of New Jersey Council, Nov. 6–7, 1765; (3) Proceedings of New Jersey General Assembly, Nov. 26–30, 1765; (4) Colden to Conway, New York, Dec. 13, 1765, with enclosures; (5) Colden to Gage, Sept. 2, 1765; (6) State of the province of New York, Dec. 6, 1765; (7) Proceedings of the New York Assembly, Nov. 12, 13 and 19, 1765; (8) Gov. Sir Henry Moore to Conway, Dec. 21, 1765; (9) Gage to Conway, Dec. 21, 1765; (10) Extract from *The New-York Gazette*, Dec. 5, 1765; (11) General Advertiser to *The New-York Gazette*, (*No. 1196*); (12) *The New-York Gazette*, Dec. 19, 1765; (13) Gage to Conway with enclosures, Dec. 21, 1765; (14) Gage to Gov. Moore, Dec. 1, 1765; (15) New York Assembly resolves, Dec. 13, 1765; (16) Gov. Bernard to Conway, Nov. 25, 1765, with enclosures; (17) Massachusetts House of Representatives *Journal*, Sept. 25, 1765; (18) Massachusetts House of Representatives resolves, Oct. 29, 1765; (19) Bernard to Conway, Boston, Dec. 18, 1765, with enclosures; (20) Andrew Oliver, stamp distributor, to Bernard, Dec. 17, 1765; (21) From a Boston newspaper, Dec. 18, 1765; (22) Oliver's second letter to Bernard, Dec. 19, 1765; (23) Bernard to Conway, Dec. 19, 1765, with enclosures; (24) The same to the same, Dec. 21, 1765, with enclosures; (25) Boston town memorial to Bernard; (26) Copy of the Massachusetts Council minutes, Dec. 19, 1765; (27) Gov. Ward of Rhode Island to Conway, Nov. 6, 1765.

No. 221, Feb. 14, 1766. Two bundles of papers relating to America. First bundle from the Secretary of State: (1) Fauquier to Board of Trade, Nov. 11, 1765; (2) To naval officers of Virginia from Fauquier, Nov. 7, 1765; (3) Gov. Fauquier's certificate relative to George Mercer's declaration as Virginia distributor of stamps;

(4) Colden of New York to Board of Trade, Dec. 6, 1765; (5) New York Council minutes, Sept. 4, 1765; (6) From the New York Assembly *Journal*, 1765; (7) Bernard to John Pownall of the Board of Trade, Boston, Nov. 26, 1765; (8) Bernard to Board of Trade, Nov. 30, 1765; (9) From the Massachusetts House of Representatives *Journal*, Nov. 6–8, 1765; (10) Bernard's speech to the General Assembly, Nov. 8, 1765, printed; (11) Gov. William Franklin to Board of Trade, Dec. 18, 1765; (12) New Jersey Assembly votes, Nov. 30, 1765; (13) New Jersey Council minutes, Nov. 30, 1765; (14) Gov. Wentworth of New Hampshire to Board of Trade, Nov. 25 and Dec. 16, 1765; (15) Lieut.-Gov. Bull of South Carolina to Board of Trade, Nov. 3, 1765 (not signed); (16) From inspector and distributor of stamps for South Carolina to Bull, Oct. 29, 1765; (17) Gov. James Wright of Georgia to Board of Trade, Nov. 9, 1765. ¶ Second bundle from the Secretary of State: (1) Archibald Hinshelwood, distributor of Stamps for Nova Scotia, to Commissioners of Stamps, Nov. 21, 1765; (2) Gov. Sir Henry Moore of New York to Lords of the Treasury about enforcement of the Stamp Act, Dec. 1765; (3) Jared Ingersoll, stamp distributor for Connecticut, to Commissioners of Stamps, Dec. 2, 1765; (4) George Meserve, stamp distributor for New Hampshire, to the Commissioners, Dec. 3, 1765; (5) Andrew Oliver, stamp distributor for Massachusetts, to the Commissioners, Dec. 13, 1765 (with more letters from Meserve, Dec. 16 and 26, 1765); (6) Andrew Eliot, collector of customs for New York and Lambert Moore, comptroller, to Gov. Moore, Nov. 18, 1765; (7) From Capt. Archibald Kennedy to the New York collector and his reply, Dec. 10, 1765; (8) From the collector of customs at Perth Amboy, New Jersey, to the Commissioners of Customs, Dec. 7, 1765; (9) From the New York collector and comptroller of customs to the same, Dec. 20, 1765; (10) Letter from Messrs. Bayard and Co. of New York, Dec. 21, 1765; (11) From Maryland custom-house officers to Commissioners of Customs, Nov. 2, 1765; (12) From Boston comptroller of customs to the same, Dec. 17, 1765; (13) From Charles Stewart, surveyor-general of customs for the middle district of North America, to both the officers in his district and the Commissioners of Customs, Dec. 7–8, 1765; (14) William Houston, North Carolina distributor of stamps, to Commissioners of Stamps, Nov. 20, 1765.

No. 222, Feb. 17, 1766. Papers about American unrest: (1) Gov. Samuel Ward of Rhode Island, to Board of Trade, Nov. 19, 1765; (2) Lieut.-Gov. Bull of South Carolina to Board of Trade, Dec. 17, 1765; (3) The same to the same, Dec. 19, 1765; (4) From the South Carolina Commons House of Assembly journal, Nov. 26–29, 1765; (5) From Gov. James Wright of Georgia to Board of Trade, Dec. 2, 1765; (6) Minutes of the Georgia Council, Oct. 31 and

Nov. 12 and 22, 1765; (7) From Gov. James Grant of East Florida to Board of Trade, Dec. 9, 1765.

No. 223, Feb. 19, 1766. From the Admiralty Office, eighteen papers, titles of which are listed in *Journals of the House of Lords*, XXXI, 278.

No. 224, Feb. 19, 1766. The following papers from the Marquess of Rockingham: (1) From Charles Stewart, surveyor general of customs of the eastern middle district of America, Dec. 8, 1765; (2) From Gov. Johnstone of West Florida with estimates of repairs on the Pensacola military works, Oct. 24, 1765; (3) From Caleb Lloyd, stamp distributor for South Carolina, Dec. 12, 1765; (4) From Thomas Grahame, stamp distributor for East Florida, Dec. 9, 1765; (5) From Gov. Ward of Rhode Island about the stamp act disturbances, Dec. 26, 1765.

No. 225, Feb. 21, 1766. Papers from the Bank of England: (1) Amount of bullion brought to the bank from North America, 1748–1765; (2) Bullion brought from the British West Indies, 1748–1765.

No. 226, Feb. 24, 1766. Admiralty papers relating to the appointment of courts of vice-admiralty in North America, 1763–1764.

No. 227, Feb. 25, 1766. Custom House papers: (1) Value of exports from England to North America, 1739–1764; (2) Value of imports into England from North America, 1739–1764.

No. 228, Feb. 25, 1766. The Board of Trade on the expense of peace-time establishments in America and the state of debts incurred by the colonies in the late war.

No. 229, Feb. 25, 1766. Papers relating to American vice-admiralty courts. Eighteen papers as listed in *Journals of the House of Lords*, XXXI, 284–5.

No. 230, [March], 1766. Paper respecting the New York mail packet.

No. 231, March 5, 1766. (1) London merchants' petition supporting Stamp Tax repeal; (2) Petition of the Society of Merchants Venturers of Bristol for Stamp Act repeal.

No. 232, March 5, 1766. Account of all ships arriving in England cleared from American ports since Nov. 1, 1765.

No. 233, March 7, 1766. Account of all ships that arrived in North Britain (Scotland) from America between Jan. 14–Feb. 14, 1766, with or without proper clearance.

No. 234, March 7, 1766. Petition of Glasgow merchants respecting the Stamp Act.

No. 235, March 7, 1766. Petition of Edward Montagu, agent for Virginia, on the bill to repeal the Stamp Act.

No. 236, March 10, 1766. Letters from Lieut.-Gov. Hutchinson and Gov. Bernard, enclosing Pomfret, Conn., resolves, Dec. 25, 1765.

No. 237, March 11, 1766. From Gov. Bernard, enclosing Massachusetts House of Representatives journal of Jan. 15–16, 1766, with letter to the governor, Jan. 17, 1766.

No. 238, March 13, 1766. A large number of letters relating to North American Stamp Act matters, Oct. 30–Dec. 17, 1765.

No. 239, Nov. 25, 1766. Account of Commissioners of Customs of all corn, etc., exported from Scotland before Aug. 26, 1766.

No. 240, Feb. 4, 1767. Twelve Admiralty papers relating to the African forts and settlements, Feb. 4, 1767.

No. 241, March 12, 1767. Includes the following copies of papers received: (1) Letters from colonial governors regarding the repeal of the Stamp Act and quartering of troops; (2) Gage to Conway, Nov. 9, 1765; (3) The same to the same, Dec. 21, 1765, with enclosures; (4) Gage to Gov. Sir Henry Moore, Dec. 1, 1765; (5) Resolves of the New York Assembly, Dec. 13, 1765; (6) Answer of Albany magistrates to Col. Bradstreet's demand for quarters, Jan. 23, 1766; (7) From Lieut.-Gov. Bull of South Carolina, May 9, 1766; (8) Sir Henry Moore to Conway, May 27, 1766; (9) Gov. Franklin to Conway, June 19, 1766; (10) Sir Henry Moore to Conway, June 20, 1766, with enclosures; (11) Gov. Moore to New York Assembly, June 13, 1766, with answer of the Assembly, June 19, 1766; (12) Moore to the Assembly, June 20, 1766, with the Assembly reply, June 23, 1766; (13) Moore's speech to the Council and Assembly, June 12, 1766; (14) Address of New York Council to the Governor, June 14, 1766, with his answer, June 16, 1766; (15) Address of the Assembly to Gov. Moore, June 16, 1766; (16) Gage to Conway, June 24, 1766; (17) Lieut.-Gov. Colden to Conway, New York, June 24, 1766; (18) Gov. Bernard to Conway, Boston, June 29, 1766; (19) Lieut.-Gov. Fauquier to Conway, June 27, 1766; (20) Gage to Conway, July 15, 1766; (21) Gov. Ward to Conway, June 25, 1766; (22) Bernard to Conway, July 19, 1766, with enclosures that follow; (23) Proceedings of the Massachusetts Governor, Council, and House of Representatives about indemnification of sufferers by the Stamp Act riots, March 31–June 28, 1766; (24) Gage to the Duke of Richmond, Aug. 25, 1766; (25) Gov. Pitkin of Connecticut to Conway, Aug. 4, 1766; (26) Gov. Grant of East Florida to Conway, Aug. 21, 1766; (27) Gov. Tryon of North Carolina to Conway, Aug. 2, 1766, with enclosures that follow; (28) Address of the borough of Wilmington, N.C., to Gov. Tryon and his reply; (29) The mayor and gentlemen of Wilmington to the Governor and his answer; (30) Deputy-Gov. Sharpe of Maryland to Conway, June 27, 1766; (31) Gage to the Earl of Shelburne, Oct. 10, 1766; (32) Bernard to Shelburne, Boston, Nov. 14, 1766, with enclosures; (33) Speech of Bernard, Oct. 29, 1766, with answer of the House of Representatives, Nov. 12, 1766; (34) Bernard's speech, Nov. 13, 1766; (35) Printed act of Massachusetts for granting compensation to sufferers in the Stamp Act riots and of free pardon to offenders; (36) Gov. Ward to Shelburne, Nov. 6, 1766; (37) Gov. Moore to Shelburne, Dec. 19, 1766, with enclosures that follow; (38) Moore's message to the New York Assembly, Nov. 17, 1766, and address of the Assembly to the governor; (39) Gov. Franklin to Shelburne, with New Jersey act for supplying the barracks with furnishings; (40) Bernard to Shelburne, Dec. 6, 1766; (41) Sharpe of Maryland to Shelburne, Dec. 9, 1766; (42) Colden to Shelburne, New York, Dec. 26, 1766; (43) Gage to Shelburne, Jan. 17, 1767, with enclosures that follow; (44) Return of regular forces quartered in provincial barracks in New York; (45) Act to furnish the New York barracks with necessaries for the troops, Oct. 6, 1766; (46) Conway's circular letter to governors in America, March 31, 1766; (47) Richmond's circular letter to governors in America, July 10, 1766; (48) Earl of Shelburne to Gov. Moore, Aug. 9, 1766; (49) Shelburne to Bernard, Sept. 13, 1766.

No. 242, April 3, 1767. Papers on quartering of troops: (1) Bernard to Shelburne, Dec. 24, 1766; (2) Gage to Shelburne, Feb. 20, 1767; (3) Gage to Gov. Pitkin of Connecticut, Jan. 8, 1767, with Pitkin to Gage, Jan. 20, 1767, Gage to Pitkin, Jan. 25, 1767, and Pitkin to Gage, Jan. 31, 1767; (4) Bernard to Shelburne, Feb. 14, 1767, enclosing two messages from the House of Representatives to the Governor with his replies.

No. 243, April 6, 1767. Journal of the New York Assembly, Nov. 10–Dec. 19, 1766.

No. 244, May 11, 1767. Proceedings of the New Jersey Assembly, June 11–28, 1766.

No. 245, May 18, 1767. (1) Report of the Committee of Council, orders in council, and representation of the Board of Trade regarding the indemnity act of Massachusetts (five papers); (2) A bundle of papers endorsed May 18, 1767, also related to the Massachusetts indemnity act. For list see *Journals of the House of Lords,* XXXI, 604–5.

No. 246, May 21, 1767. Notes on Canadian affairs.

No. 247, May 22, 1767. Copies of papers relating to declaring void acts of colonial assemblies (nine papers). List in *Journals of the House of Lords,* XXXI, 613.

No. 248, May 22, 1767. Questions to be put to judges touching the Massachusetts indemnity act.

No. 249, May 27, 1767. Nineteen papers relating to the civil and ecclesiastical state of Quebec. See *Journals of the House of Lords,* XXXI, 620–1.

No. 250, June 3, 1767. Extract of letter from the governor of Georgia, with journals of the Upper House and minutes of the Commons, Jan. 20, 1767.

No. 251, Jan. 29, 1768. Report by Capt. Lambert on the state of forts and settlements in Africa (six papers).

No. 252, Nov. 28, 1768. Here are 108 papers, including enclosures, concerning the Massachusetts disturbances: (1) Bernard to Shelburne, Jan. 21, 1768; the same to the same, Jan. 30, 1768; the same to the same, Feb. 2, 1768; (2) Hillsborough to Bernard, April 4, 1768; (3) Bernard to Shelburne, Feb. 18, 1768, with enclosure of the Massachusetts circular letter to other assemblies, Feb. 11, 1768; (4) The same to the same, March 5, 1768, with enclosures that follow; (5) Resolves of Massachusetts House of Representatives, Feb. 26, 1768; (6) Letter in *The Boston Gazette*, Feb. 28, 1768, with proceedings of council on libel in *The Boston Gazette*, Feb. 28, 1768; (7) Gov. Bernard to the Council with the Council's answer and Bernard's reply; (8) Bernard to the Assembly and the Assembly's reply; (9) Appendix to journals of the House of Representatives, Feb. 1768; (10) Hillsborough's circular letter to the colonial governors, April 21, 1768; (11) Hillsborough to Bernard, April 22, 1768; (12) Hillsborough to Gage, April 23, 1768; (13) Mr. Bradshaw to Mr. Phelps, Treasury Chambers, May 7, 1768, enclosing memorial of the American Customs Commissioners, Feb. 12, 1768; (14) Hillsborough's circular letter to American governors, May 14, 1768; (15) Bernard to Shelburne, March 12, 1768; (16) Bernard to Shelburne, March 19, 1768, enclosing resolution of the Council, March 18, 1768, relating to riots, and affidavit of William Wooton, inspector general of customs; (17) Bernard to Shelburne, March 21, 1768, with *The Boston Gazette* account of the meeting of merchants; (18) Hillsborough to Gage, June 8, 1768; (19) Hillsborough to the Admiralty, June 11, 1768; (20) Hillsborough to Bernard, June 11, 1768; (21) Bradshaw to Pownall, Treasury Chambers, July 8, 1768, with memorial from the American Customs Commissioners, March 28, 1768; (22) Hillsborough's circular letters to North American governors, July 11, 1768; (23) Hillsborough to Bernard, July 11, 1768; (24) Secretary Pownall to Mr. Bradshaw, July 11, 1768; (25) Bernard to Hillsborough, June 11, 13 and 14, 1768, the latter with enclosures; (26) Minutes of Massachusetts Council, June 11, 1768; (27) Depositions respecting the Boston riot, June 10, 1768; (28) Letters between Bernard and the Commissioners of Customs, June 1768; (29) Bernard to Hillsborough, June 16 and 18, 1768, with enclosures that follow; (30) Incendiary paper posted in Boston, June 1768; (31) Petition of Boston to Bernard, June 14, 1768, with Bernard's answer, together with instructions to Boston members of the House of Representatives; (32) Bradshaw to John Pownall, July 22, 1768, with enclosures; (33) Memorial of American Commissioners of

Customs, June 16, 1758, with papers annexed, relating chiefly to the seizure of Hancock's sloop *Liberty*; the minutes of the Commissioners on board the *Romney*, June 13–14, 1768; deposition of Boston tidesman, Thomas Kirk, June 10; deposition of collector of customs, Joseph Harrison, June 11; deposition of comptroller of customs, Benjamin Hallowell, June 11; deposition of Richard Acklom Harrison, son of Joseph Harrison, June 11; deposition of inspector of imports and exports, Thomas Irving, June 11; letters from June 11 to 14, Andrew Oliver to John Robinson; the Commissioners of Customs to Captain Corner, Gov. Bernard, Commander Hood, Gen. Gage in New York, Col. Dalrymple at Halifax, together with three anonymous letters describing the situation in Boston; (34) Mr. Hallowell's examination at the Treasury Board, July 21, 1768; (35) Mr. Bradshaw to John Pownall, Nov. 22, 1768, with corrections made in Mr. Hallowell's examination; (36) Memorial in behalf of the inhabitants of Boston, presented July 21, 1768, with thirteen depositions respecting the customs offices and the *Liberty*; (37) Bradshaw to John Pownall, Aug. 4, 1768, enclosing the attorney general's opinion on the case of the *Liberty*; (38) Hillsborough to Shelburne, July 27, 1768; (39) Hillsborough to the Admiralty, July 28, 1768; (40) Hillsborough to Gage, July 30, 1768; (41) Hillsborough to Bernard, July 30, 1768, enclosing legal opinions on the application of 6 Anne, for encouraging trade to America; (42) John Pownall to Bradshaw, July 28, 1768; (43) Bernard to Hillsborough, June 17, 1768; (44) The same to the same, June 25, 28, and July 1, 1768, enclosing messages and replies between the governor and Massachusetts House of Representatives, including the answer of the House, June 30, 1768; (45) The Speaker of the Massachusetts House of Representatives to Hillsborough, June 30, 1768; (46) Extracts from printed journals of the House of Representatives, Dec. 30, 1767–June 30, 1768; (47) Bernard to Hillsborough, July 9, 1768; (48) Bernard to Hillsborough, supplemental letter, July 9, 1768; (49) Bernard to Hillsborough, July 18 and 19, 1768, with copies of Boston papers, and a petition of the Massachusetts Council to his Majesty; (50) Hillsborough to Bernard, Sept. 14, 1768; (51) Bradshaw to Pownall, Aug. 31, 1768, enclosing the memorial of the American Commissioners of Customs, July 11, 1768, with papers annexed and letters from Gage, Hood, and Dalrymple; (52) Bernard to Hillsborough, July 30, 1768, with copies of letters between Bernard and Gage, July, 1768; also minutes of the Massachusetts Council, July 27 and 29, 1768, and observations on the Council's answer to Bernard, July 29, 1768; (53) Bernard to Hillsborough, Aug. 6 and 9, 1768; (54) Also Bernard to Hillsborough, Aug. 29, 1768, with extract from *The Boston Gazette*; (55) Hillsborough to Bernard, Oct. 12,

1768; (56) Bernard to Hillsborough, Sept. 9, 1768; (57) Bernard to Hillsborough, Sept. 16, 1768, with the following enclosures: *The Boston Gazette* (extract), Sept. 5, 1768, also Boston town meeting proceedings, Sept. 12, 1768, and circular letter from Boston selectmen to other Massachusetts towns, Sept. 14, 1768; (58) Bernard to Hillsborough, Sept. 23, 1768; (59) The same to the same, Sept. 26, 1768, with Massachusetts Council minutes, Sept. 19, 22 and 26, together with a prepared Council answer to the Governor's message; (60) The same to the same, Sept. 27, 1768, enclosing proceedings of the Massachusetts Convention, Sept. 22, 1768; (61) The same to the same, Oct. 1, 1768, with minutes of the Council, Sept. 29, 1768; (62) The same to the same, Oct. 3, 1768, with the result of the Convention proceedings (printed); (63) The same to the same, Oct. 5 and 6, 1768, with minutes of the Council, Oct. 3 and 5, 1768, and also printed answer of the town of Hatfield to the Boston selectmen, Sept. 22, 1768; (64) Hillsborough to Bernard, Nov. 15, 1768, enclosing copy of letter from Stephen Sayre to Hillsborough; (65) Treasury Board minutes, transmitted to Hillsborough, Nov. 28, 1768.

No. 253, Dec. 7, 1768. Papers relating to Boston: (1) The Admiralty to the Earl of Hillsborough, Dec. 2, 1768, with enclosures; (2) Commodore Hood to Secretary Philip Stephens, Halifax, Oct. 12, 1768; (3) Col. Dalrymple to Capt. Smith, Boston, Oct. 2, 1768; (4) Dalrymple to Hood, Boston Oct. 4, 1768; (5) Capt. Corner's diary; (6) Hood to Stephens, Halifax, Oct. 23, 1768; (7) Gage to Hood, Oct. 18, 1768; (8) Gov. Bernard to Hillsborough, Oct. 14, 1768.

No. 254, Dec. 15, 1768. Resolutions of the House of Lords upon the American papers.

No. 255, Dec. 21, 1768. Admiralty Office. Fourteen reports on the state of forts and settlements on the coast of Africa. For the listing see *Journals of the House of Lords*, XXXII, 219.

No. 256, Jan. 20, 1769. Twenty-eight papers relating chiefly to Boston and the quartering of troops: (1) Earl of Hillsborough to Gen. Gage, Dec. 10, 1768; (2) Lords of Admiralty to Hillsborough, Dec. 14, 1768, enclosing Capt. Smith's letter from Boston, Oct. 26, 1768; (3) Gage to Hillsborough, Oct. 31, 1768, with address from members of the Massachusetts Council with Gage's reply; (4) Gage to Hillsborough, Nov. 3, 1768; (5) Gov. Bernard to Hillsborough, Nov. 1, 1766, enclosing answers of the justices and Bernard's order to Joseph Goldthwaite; (6) Minutes of Massachusetts Council, Oct. 12, 17 and 26, 1768; (7) Address of members of the Massachusetts Council to Gage and Gage's reply; (8) Hillsborough to Gage, Dec. 24, 1768; (9) Hillsborough to Bernard, Dec. 24, 1768; (10) Bernard to Hillsborough, Nov. 12, 1768; (11) The same to the same, Nov. 14, 1768; (12) Hillsborough to Bernard, Jan. 4, 1769; (13) The Admiralty to Hillsborough, Jan. 7, 1769, with enclosures; (14) Commodore Hood to Secy. Stephens, Nov. 15, 1768; (15) The same to the same, Nov. 22, 1765; (16) The same to the same, Nov. 25, 1768; (17) The same to the same, Nov. 27, 1768; (18) The Admiralty to Hillsborough, Jan. 13, 1769, enclosing Hood to Stephens, Boston, Dec. 7, 1768; (19) Bernard to Hillsborough, Nov. 30, 1768; (20) The same to the same, Dec. 5, 1768; (21) The Admiralty to Hillsborough, Jan. 19, 1769, enclosing letter from Hood, Dec. 12, 1768.

No. 257, Feb. 26, 1770. Admiralty papers. Eleven reports on state of the African forts and settlements.

No. 258, May 4, 1770. Papers on the "Boston Massacre": (1) Gage to Hillsborough, New York, Feb. 21, 1770; (2) Lieut.-Gov. Colden to Hillsborough, New York, Feb. 21, 1770; (3) Lieut.-Gov. Hutchinson to Hillsborough, Boston, March 12, 1770, enclosing minutes of the Council, March 6, 1770; (4) Lieut.-Col. Dalrymple to Hillsborough, Boston, March 13, 1770, with enclosures that follow; (5) Narrative of transactions at Boston, March 2, 3, and 5, 1770; (6) The case of Capt. Thomas Preston of the 29th Regiment; (7) Twenty-four depositions, etc., respecting the Capt. Preston case; (8) Gage to Hillsborough, New York, Dec. 4, 1769, enclosing Dalrymple to Gage, Oct. 28, 1769; (9) Hillsborough to Gage, Jan. 18, 1770; (10) Hillsborough to Hutchinson, Jan. 18, 1770.

No. 259, May 8, 1770. Papers relating to disturbances at Boston and Newport: (1) Commodore Hood to Sec. Stephens, Boston harbour, July 10, 1769; (2) The same to the same, July 25, 1769; (3) American Commissioners of Customs to Hood, July 24, 1769; (4) Capt. Reid of the *Liberty* to the governor of Rhode Island, enclosed in Commissioners of Customs to Hood, July 24, 1769; (5) Capt. Reid's deposition in Commissioners of Customs to Hood, July 24, 1769; (6) Collector and comptroller of the Rhode Island Custom House to Gov. Wanton, July 21, 1769; (7) Hood to Sec. Stephens, on H.M.S. *Romney*, Halifax harbour, Nov. 23, 1769; (8) Hutchinson to Hood, Oct. 31, 1769; (9) Capt. Caldwell of H.M.S. *Rose* to Stephens, Boston, March 14, 1770.

No. 260, May 15, 1770. Hillsborough to colonial governors, May 13, 1769, together with speeches delivered with reference to this letter by Gov. Tryon, Gov. Botetourt, Lieut.-Gov. Colden, and Gov. Wright, and the answers of the assemblies.

No. 261, Dec. 11, 1770. Motion in House of Lords, respecting the defense of British possessions in the Mediterranean and West Indies. Negatived. See *Journals of the House of Lords*, XXXIII, 25.

No. 262, Feb. 27, 1771. Nine reports on African forts and settlements. See *Journals of the House of Lords*, XXXIII, 87.

No. 263, March 11, 1772. Admiralty papers. Eleven reports on African forts and settlements. See *Journals of the House of Lords*, XXXIII, 294.

No. 264, Feb. 19, 1773. Admiralty papers. Nine reports on African forts and settlements. See *Journals of the House of Lords*, XXXIII, 519–20.

No. 265, Feb. 21, 1774. Nine Admiralty papers. Reports on African forts and settlements. See *Journals of the House of Lords*, XXXIV, 30–1.

No. 266, March 7, 1774. Here are 109 papers relating to the disturbances in America. They carry separate headings and are as follows:

Massachusetts

(1) Governor Hutchinson to the Earl of Dartmouth, Boston, Nov. 4, 1773, enclosing copy of letter delivered to Thomas and Elisha Hutchinson, Nov. 2, 1773; also a printed paper posted up in Boston, Nov. 3, 1773; copies of two narratives; (2) Hutchinson to Dartmouth, Milton, Mass., Nov. 6, 1773, enclosing letters from Richard Clarke & Co. and Benjamin Faneuil & Co. to John Hancock, Nov. 4, 1773; vote of Boston town meeting, Nov. 5, 1773; and Thomas Hutchinson, Jr. to John Hancock, n.d.; (3) Hutchinson to Dartmouth, Nov. 15, 1773; (4) The same to the same, Dec. 2, 1773, enclosing petitions of Richard Clarke and Sons, Benjamin Faneuil, Thomas Hutchinson, Jr. and Elisha Hutchinson, together with the proceedings of the Massachusetts Council thereon; also *The Massachusetts Gazette* (extract), Nov. 26, 1773; and a copy of a paper printed in Boston, Dec. 1, 1773; (5) Hutchinson to Dartmouth, Dec. 15, 1773; (6) The same to the same, Dec. 17, 1773; (7) The same to the same, Dec. 20, 1773; (8) The same to the same, Dec. 24, 1773, enclosing minutes of the Council, Dec. 21, 1773; (9) The same to the same, Jan. 4, 1774.

New York

(1) Maj.-Gen. Haldimand to the Earl of Dartmouth, New York, Nov. 3 and Dec. 28, 1773 and Jan. 5, 1774; (2) Copy of paper referred to in Haldimand's letter of Jan. 5; (3) Haldimand to Dartmouth, Feb. 2, 1774; (4) Governor Tryon to Dartmouth, New York, Nov. 3, 1773, enclosing copies of *The Alarm*, New York, Oct. 6 and 9, 1773, and extract from *The Alarm*, Oct. 19, 1773; (5) The same to the same, Dec. 1, 1773, enclosing a memorial from agents of the East India Co. that the tea upon arrival should be protected; also minute of the New York Council relative to the tea; (6) The same to the same, Jan. 3, 1774; (7) The same to the same, Jan. 5, 1774, enclosing minutes (extracts) of the New York Council.

South Carolina
Lieut.-Gov. Bull to the Earl of Dartmouth, Dec. 24, 1773.

New Hampshire
Governor Wentworth to Dartmouth, New Hampshire, Dec. 17, 1773, enclosing notification of Portsmouth selectmen and resolves of Portsmouth respecting the tea.

Admiralty
(1) The Admiralty to Dartmouth, Jan. 20, 1774, enclosing letter from Rear-Adm. Montagu to Philip Stephens, Dec. 8, 1773; (2) The same to the same, Jan. 27, 1774, enclosing letter from Montagu to Stephens, Dec. 17, 1773.

War Office
(1) Viscount Barrington to the Earl of Dartmouth, Jan. 28, 1774, enclosing (2) Lieut.-Col. Alexander Leslie to Barrington, Boston, Dec. 6 and 17, 1773.

East India Company
(1) Chairman of the East India Co. to the Earl of Dartmouth, Dec. 20, 1773, enclosing account of tea exports to the North American colonies; (2) The same to the same, Dec. 23, 1773, enclosing an extract of a letter from Boston, Oct. 18, 1773; extracts of two letters from New York, Nov. 5, 1773; a letter with advices from Philadelphia, Dec. 21, 1773; a letter relating to tea exported to Boston, Dec. 21, 1773; a letter relating to tea exported to South Carolina; and a letter relating to tea exported to New York; (3) Chairman of the East India Co. to Dartmouth, Dec. 24, 1773, enclosing extracts of three letters from Philadelphia, Oct. 5 and 30, 1773; (4) The same to the same, Jan. 10, 1774, enclosing letter from the Company's New York agents to the court of directors; and a memorial of Henry White and others, merchants, to the Governor of New York; (5) The Boston agent of the Company to his London correspondents, Nov. 15, 1773, and also, simply, Nov. 1773; (6) Boston agent to the Chairman of the Company, Nov. 17, 1773; (7) Chairman of the Company to Dartmouth, Jan. 21, 1774, enclosing copy of letter signed "Anglo-Americanus" to the Company, Dec. 17, 1773; (8) Chairman and Deputy Chairman of the Company to Dartmouth, Jan. 26, 1774; (9) The same to the same, Jan. 26, 1774, enclosing a letter to the Delaware River pilots and also to Capt. Ayres, Philadelphia, Nov. 27, 1773; also a declaration made by James and Drinker, Philadelphia Company agents,

n.d.; a copy of *The Pennsylvania Gazette,* postscript, Dec. 24, 1773; James and Drinker to Company Directors, Philadelphia, Dec. 28, 1773; and Thomas and Isaac Wharton, Jonathan Browne, and Gilbert Barkley to the Company, Philadelphia, Dec. 28, 1773; (10) The same to the same, Feb. 3, 1774, enclosing a letter from Thomas and Elisha Hutchinson, Richard Clarke and sons, and Benjamin Faneuil to the Company, Dec. 2 and 17, 1773; and copies of two letters from Smith, Leger and Greenwood, Charleston, S.C., Dec. 4 and 18, 1773; (11) Chairman and Deputy Chairman of the Company to Dartmouth, Feb. 9, 1774, enclosing copies of letters from Henry White, Abraham Lott & Co., and Pigou & Booth to the Directors of the Company, and also Henry White and others to Capt. Lockyer of the *Nancy,* New York, Dec. 27, 1773; (12) The same to the same, Feb. 15, 1773, enclosing questions proposed by Francis Rotch, owner, and James Hall, master of the *Dartmouth,* with answers of consignees; questions proposed by James Bruce, master of the *Eleanor,* with answers of the consignees; Francis Rotch to Richard Clarke & Sons, etc., Boston, Jan. 6, 1774; Richard Clarke & Sons, Benjamin Faneuil, Jr., to the Company, Castle William, Jan. 7, 1770; (13) Sec. Mitchell of the Company to John Pownall, Feb. 16, 1774, enclosing copy of a memorial of the Company to Dartmouth, Feb. 16, 1774.

Treasury

Still under *No. 266* are papers sent by and to the Treasury: (1) Grey Cooper, Lords of the Treasury secretary, to John Pownall, March 7, 1774, with enclosures; (2) Mr. Mather, acting secretary to the Commissioners of Customs in America, to John Robinson, secretary of the Lords of the Treasury, Oct. 7, 1773; (3) Commissioners of Customs in America to the Lords of the Treasury, Jan. 4, 1774, with enclosures that follow; (4) Collector and comptroller of customs at Boston to the Commissioners of Customs there, Dec. 17, 1773; (5) The same to the same, Dec. 23 and 31, 1773; (6) Protest of James Bruce, James Bruce, Jr. and John Finney; (7) Protest of Hezekiah Coffin and others; (8) Protest of Francis Rotch and others; (9) Depositions of Samuel Hunt and others; (10) Deposition of Thomas Rick and others; (11) Deposition of Alexander Hodgson; (12) Deposition of James Bruce and others; (13) Report of Arthur Savage; (14) Report of Robert Parker; (15) Memorial of Francis Rotch; (16) Memorial of James Bruce; (17) Memorial of Hezekiah Coffin; (18) Deposition of William Elliot and others.

No. 267, March 11, 1774. Gov. Hutchinson to the Earl of Dartmouth, Jan. 28, 1774, enclosing extract from *The Boston Gazette,* Jan. 27, 1774.

No. 268, March 24, 1774. Eleven papers relating to the free ports of Jamaica. See *Journals of the House of Lords*, XXXIV, 78, 91.

No. 269, March 28, 1774. Petition of Stephen Sayre, William Lee, Benjamin Franklin and other Americans against the Boston Port bill.

No. 270, March 30, 1774. Petition of William Bollan, agent for the Council of Massachusetts, praying to be heard against the Boston Port bill.

No. 271, April 14, 1774. Two reports of the committee of the Lords on the Boston riots.

No. 272, April 15, 1774. Papers relating to disturbances in Massachusetts: (1) Gov. Bernard to Board of Trade, Boston, July 7, 1766; (2) Bernard to the Earl of Shelburne, Feb. 7, 1767, enclosing two messages from the Massachusetts House of Representatives to Governor Bernard and his replies, n.d.; (3) The same to the same, Feb. 21, 1767 and March 21, 1768; (4) Bernard to the Earl of Hillsborough, Boston, May 30, 1768; (5) Massachusetts House of Representatives's reply to Bernard's message of June 30, 1768; (6) Printed account of Boston associations and proceedings thereof; (7) Bernard to Hillsborough, Boston, June 1, 1769; (8) Hutchinson to Hillsborough, July 11, 1769, with extract of letter from Gov. Bernard and extracts from resolves of the colony's "Representatives," July 8, 1769; (9) Gov. Hutchinson to Hillsborough, Boston, March 27, 1770; with enclosures that follow; (10) Message from the House of Representatives to Gov. Hutchinson and his reply, March 15 and 16, 1770; (11) House of Representatives to the Council, March 17, 1770; (12) The Council to the Governor, March 20, 1770; (13) The House to the Governor, March 23, 1770; (14) Committee report of the House of Representatives, March 24, 1770; (15) Hutchinson to Hillsborough, April 27 and May 21, 1770; (16) The same to the same, July 6, 1771, with message to the House of Representatives and the answer; (17) The same to the same, Nov. 28, 1771, with enclosures that follow; (18) Commissioners of Customs to Hutchinson, Nov. 26, 1771; (19) Memorial and letter from Mr. Savage, comptroller of customs at Falmouth to Hutchinson, Nov. 19 and 27, 1771; (20) Savage to Commissioners of Customs at Boston, Nov. 19, 1771; (21) Hutchinson to Hillsborough (extract), May 29, 1772, enclosing extract from *The Massachusetts Gazette*, May 29, 1772; (22) Hutchinson to the Earl of Dartmouth, Oct. 23, 1772; (23) The same to the same, Oct. 30, 1772, with enclosures; (24) The same to the same, Nov. 3, 1772; (25) Printed copy of votes and proceedings of the freeholders and inhabitants of Boston, n.d.; (26) Hutchinson to Dartmouth, Feb. 22, 1773; (27) Printed copy of Hutchinson's speeches to the general assembly, with the answers of both houses; (28) Petition and remonstrance from the Massachusetts House of Representatives, July 14, 1772; (29) Petition to the King from the

House of Representatives, March 6, 1773; (30) Hutchinson to Dartmouth, Feb. 14, 1774, with enclosures; (31) Hutchinson's speech to the Massachusetts general assembly and answer; (32) Requisition from the House of Representatives to the Superior Court; (33) Remonstrance of the House of Representatives against the Chief Justice; (34) Vote of Council and House of Representatives for adjourning the Superior Court, not consented to by the Governor; (35) Hutchinson's answer to the House of Representatives remonstrance.

No. 273, April 20, 1774. Report from committee of the House of Lords on the Massachusetts disturbances.

No. 274, April 20, 1774. Drafts of report from the committee of the Lords appointed to consider the Massachusetts disturbances, with notes. For the report as approved, see *Journals of the House of Lords*, XXXIV, 124–136.

No. 275, May 2, 1774. Act of 14 Geo. III providing for more effective government for the Province of Quebec.

No. 276, May 6, 1774. Itemized accounts of the exports from England to Jamaica, 1748–1755, and for seven years since the establishment of the Free Port Act, 6 Geo. III, 1766–1773.

No. 277, May 6, 1774. (1) Instructions from his Majesty to Gov. Guy Carleton of Quebec, respecting land grants, Aug. 12, 1768 to July 2, 1771; (2) Instructions to the governors of Nova Scotia, New Hampshire, New York, Virginia, North Carolina, South Carolina, Georgia, East Florida, and West Florida, respecting land grants, Feb. 3, 1774.

No. 278, May 9, 1774. Thirteen papers relating to the Province of Quebec, including copies of commissions, warrants appointing officers, and ordinances.

No. 279, May 11, 1774. Petition of "several natives of America" against the bill for regulating the government of Massachusetts and also against the bill for impartial administration of justice in Massachusetts.

No. 280, May 11, 1774. Petition of Mr. Bollan, agent of Massachusetts, to delay the bill for better regulating the government of Massasetts.

No. 281, May 12, 1774. Nine papers relating to ordinances passed in Quebec, Feb. 1768 to May 1773.

No. 282, May 17, 1774. Papers relating especially to the impeachment in Boston of Chief Justice Oliver and other issues: (1) Hutchinson to Dartmouth, Boston, March 9, 1774; (2) The same to the same, March 21, 1774, with enclosures; (3) Resolution of the Massachusetts House of Representatives, concurred in by the Council; (4) House of Representatives to Hutchinson and the Governor's reply to the House.

No. 283, May 18, 1774. Petition of Mr. Bollan against the bill for the impartial administration of justice in Massachusetts.

No. 284, Jan. 20, 1775. Here are 149 papers relating to the disturbances in the colonies. These papers are listed under the following colonies:

Massachusetts

Extracts from eighteen letters exchanged between Gov. Gage and the Earl of Dartmouth between April 9 and Dec. 15, 1774, together with enclosures: (1) Minute of the Treasury Board, March 31, 1774; (2) Extract from *The Massachusetts Gazette,* May 19; (3) List of the Council and the Governor's speech to both houses; (4) The Council's address and Gage's reasons for refusing it; (5) House of Representatives resolves before proceeding to business at Salem; (6) Address of the House of Representatives; (7) Resolves of June 17 of the House; (8) Proclamations; (9) Circular letter and a paper called a League and Covenant; (10) Boston town meeting proceedings, June 27; (11) Protest of several inhabitants of Worcester, June 20, against proceedings of their town meeting; (12) Notification for town meeting; (13) List of mandamus councillors; (14) Letter from Hampshire County, May 10; (15) From the Boston committee of correspondence to the several Massachusetts counties; (16) Paper posted up at Salem; (17) Minute of the Council, Boston, Aug. 31; (18) Lieut.-Gov. Oliver to Gage, Sept. 2; (19) Letter from Hampshire County judges of inferior court; (20) Proceedings against inferior court at Springfield; (21) Mr. Paine's account of proceedings at Worcester; (22) From Josiah Edson with resignation as councillor enclosed; (23) Proceedings of delegates of the county of Suffolk; (24) Proceedings of the Worcester County committee of correspondence; (25) Proceedings at Worcester, Aug. 9; (26) Reasons of grand and petty juries declining to serve, Aug. 30; (27) Letter from Maj.-Gen. Haldimand, Sept. 15; (28) Paper posted up in New York; (29) Messages to Gage and his answer; (30) Two resolutions of the Continental Congress; (31) Proclamation issued by Gage, and resolves of a committee for Worcester County; (32) Instructions by the committee of Worcester County to Timothy Bigelow, chosen to represent the county in the general court; (33) Instructions given to those to represent them at the provincial congress at Concord; (34) Two addresses of the Worcester County committee to Gage, with the governor's answer; (35) Proceedings of a congress of committees for Hampshire County and resolves of Bristol County; (36) Resolves of a provincial congress held at Concord, Oct. 14; (37) Message of provincial congress to Gage and his reply; (38) Letters between Peyton Randolph and Gage; (39) Message of provincial congress committee to Gage; (40) Proceedings of provincial congress at Cambridge; (41) Letter from *The Boston Gazette;* (42) Rhode Island assembly votes; (43) Act passed by the Rhode Island assembly; (44) Viscount Lisburne of the Admiralty to the Earl of Dartmouth, Oct. 1, 1774, enclosing Vice-Adm. Graves to Philip Stephens, Sept. 3; (45) Letters from the Admiralty to Dartmouth, enclosing extracts of Graves to Stephens, Sept. 23 and Dec. 15, 1774; and Capt. Wallace to Graves, Newport, Dec. 12.

New Hampshire

These papers consist of extracts of eight letters from Gov. John Wentworth to the Earl of Dartmouth, June–December 1774, with the following enclosures: (1) Letter from Samuel Adams, May 12, 1774; (2) Proceedings of the New Hampshire House of Representatives, May 28; (3) Wentworth to the Assembly, June 8; (4) Mr. Parry to Wentworth, June 29 and Sept. 8; (5) Letters between Wentworth and Capt. Cochran, June 29 and 30, July 18; (6) Two letters from Mr. Parker to Wentworth, June 30; (7) Speech of Wentworth to the New Hampshire committee of correspondence; (8) Instructions for Col. Folsom and Maj. Sullivan, New Hampshire delegates; (9) From the New Hampshire committee of correspondence, with form of non-importation and non-exportation agreement sent to New Hampshire towns; (10) Portsmouth town meeting vote; (11) Proceedings of New Hampshire Council, Sept. 9 and 12; (12) Committee of Portsmouth and Rochester resolves; (13) Portsmouth and Durham committee advertisements.

New York

Extracts of eight letters from Lieut.-Gov. Colden to the Earl of Dartmouth, between May and Dec. 1774, with extract from *The New-York Gazetteer* and a hand bill.

New Jersey

Two letters from Gov. Franklin to Dartmouth, May 31 and June 28, with resolves of the Essex County freeholders, June 11, 1774.

Pennsylvania

Both copies and extracts of letters from Deputy Gov. John Penn to Dartmouth, May–Dec. 1774. Also the following enclosures: (1) Proceedings of the House of Representatives; (2) Extracts from *The Pennsylvania Gazette*, July 27; (3) Three resolutions of the Continental Congress.

Virginia

Two letters and extracts of letters from Earl of Dunmore to Dartmouth, May–Aug. 14, 1774, enclosing: (1) An order of the House of Burgesses, May 24; (2) Association signed by 89 members of the House of Burgesses; (3) Resolutions of Annapolis, Maryland, inhabitants, May 25; (4) Association resolves at a meeting of delegates from the Virginia counties; (5) Instructions for Virginia delegates to the Continental Congress.

South Carolina

Extracts of three letters from Lieut.-Gov. Bull to Dartmouth, July–Nov. 1774, enclosing: (1) Extract from *The South-Carolina Gazette*, July 11; (2) Proceedings of the Commons House of Assembly, Aug. 2.

Georgia

Extracts of four letters from Gov. Sir James Wright to Dartmouth, July–October 1774, enclosing: (1) Two hand bills, July 14 and 27; (2) Proclamation by Wright; (3) Resolutions by delegates at Savannah, Aug. 10; (4) Protests of inhabitants of several Georgia districts; (5) Petition of persons in behalf of themselves and the inhabitants of several colonies, received Dec. 21; (6) Votes and proceedings of the Continental Congress.

No. 285, Feb. 1, 1775. A provisional act for settling the troubles in America and asserting the supreme legislative authority and superintending power of Great Britain over the colonies. Rejected in the House of Lords.

No. 286, Feb. 2, 1775. Eighteen papers concerning occurrences in various colonies in 1774 and 1775: (1) Gov. Martin of North Carolina to the Earl of Dartmouth, Sept. 1, 1774, with enclosures; (2) Resolutions of inhabitants of the district of Wilmington, July 21, with an address to the inhabitants of Craven County; (3) Resolutions of various counties in North Carolina, from *The North-Carolina Gazette*, Sept. 2; (4) Lieut.-Gov. Bull of South Carolina to Dartmouth, Dec. 19, with charge given by Judge Drayton and presentments of the grand jury; (5) Gov. Sir James Wright of Georgia to Dartmouth, Dec. 13, with extract from *The Georgia Gazette*, Dec. 14; (6) Gov. Gage to Dartmouth, Boston, Dec. 14, with enclosures; (7) Gov. Wentworth to Gage, Dec. 14; (8) Capt. Cochran to Wentworth, Dec. 14; (9) Wentworth to Gage, Dec. 16; (10) Lieut.-Gov. Colden of New York to Dartmouth, Jan. 4, 1775; (11) Deputy Gov. Penn of Pennsylvania to Dartmouth,

Dec. 31, 1774, enclosing extracts of printed proceedings of the assembly; (12) Deputy Gov. Eden of Maryland to Dartmouth, Dec. 30, 1774, enclosing extract from *The Maryland Gazette*, Dec. 29, and copy of a paper handed about in Annapolis.

No. 287, Feb. 3,1775. Nine admiralty papers relating to the forts and settlements in Africa. For list see *Journals of the House of Lords*, XXXIV, 304.

No. 288, Feb. 7, 1775. Address of both Houses of Parliament to the King touching American disturbances.

No. 289, Feb. 7, 1775. Petition of London merchants and others concerned in American commerce.

No. 290, Feb. 7, 1775. Petition of sugar planters resident in Great Britain, with merchants trading to the West Indies.

No. 291, Feb. 14, 1775. Earl of Dunmore, governor of Virginia, to Dartmouth, Dec. 24, 1774, on the state of affairs in the colony.

No. 292, Feb. 20, 1775. Account of nature of English exports to and imports from Africa, 1739–1773, distinguishing each year.

No. 293, Feb. 20, 1775. (1) The quantity and value of tobacco exported from England to foreign countries, 1769–1773; (2) The quantity and value of tobacco imported into England, 1769–1773.

No. 294, Feb. 20, 1775. Proceedings of Maryland deputies at Annapolis, Dec. 8–12, 1774.

No. 295, Feb. 24, 1775. House of Lords resolutions on the book, *The Present Crisis*. Two papers to be communicated to House of Commons at a conference for their concurrence.

No. 296, Feb. 24, 1775. Papers relating to New Hampshire and Rhode Island disturbances: (1) Gov. Gage to Dartmouth, Boston, Jan. 18, 1775; (2) Gov. Wentworth to Dartmouth, Dec. 28, 1774; (3) The same to the same, Jan. 14, 1775, enclosing copy of a proclamation; (4) Lords of the Admiralty to Dartmouth, Feb. 21, with enclosures; (5) Vice-Adm. Graves to Philip Stephens of the Admiralty, Jan. 8, 1775; (6) Wentworth to Graves, Dec. 20, 1774; (7) Capt. Barkley to Graves, Dec. 20, 1774; (8) Wentworth to Graves, Dec. 30, 1774; (9) Capt. Wallace to Graves, Dec. 15, 1774; (10) Capt. Wallace to Gov. Wanton of Rhode Island, Dec. 15, 1774; (11) Graves to Philip Stephens, Jan. 15, 1775.

No. 297, Feb. 27, 1775. Resolutions and orders of the Lords on a pamphlet, *The Crisis with respect to America*, 5 papers.

No. 298, Feb. 27, 1775. Petitions of aldermen and inhabitants of Nottingham regarding American disorders.

No. 299, Feb. 28, 1775. Resolutions of both houses of Parliament on *Crisis No. 3*, with a committee report.

No. 300, March 3, 1775. The following Custom House papers: (1) Account of exports and imports to and from North America and

England, 1739–1773; (2) Account of exports and imports to and from the West Indies and England, 1739–1773.

No. 301, March 6, 1775. Eleven papers on occurrences in New York, New Jersey, and Pennsylvania: (1) Lieut.-Gov. Colden of New York to the Earl of Dartmouth, Feb. 1, 1775, with copy of Colden's speech to the general assembly and the addresses of the Council and Assembly in reply; (2) Gov. Franklin of New Jersey to Dartmouth, Feb. 1, 1775, with enclosures; (3) Franklin's speech to the general assembly with the address of the Council and the governor's reply; (4) Resolves of the New Jersey Assembly and their address; (5) Deputy Gov. Penn to Dartmouth, Jan. 30, 1775, with enclosures; (6) Proceedings of a provincial convention at Philadelphia; (7) Testimony of the people called Quakers.

No. 302, March 8, 1775. Account of the net produce of duty and customs on tobacco in England, 1769–1774.

No. 303, March 10, 1775. Gov. Gage to Dartmouth, Boston, Jan. 27, 1775, enclosing petition of Loyalists of Scituate and Marshfield praying for protection, with information that Gage has sent a detachment of troops to the towns.

No. 304, March 15, 1775. Petition of the city of London against the bill to restrain the trade of Massachusetts and other colonies.

No. 305, March 15, 1775. Petition of London merchants and others against the bill to restrain the trade of colonies in North America.

No. 306, March 15, 1775. State of exports of Great Britain to North America and account of North American fisheries in 1764.

No. 307, March 17, 1775. Account of net produce of duties and customs on tobacco in Scotland, 1769–1774.

No. 308, March 22, 1775. (1) Account of all tobacco imported into Scotland from the plantations, 1769–1774; (2) Account of all tobacco exported from Scotland to other countries, 1769–1774.

No. 309, March 30, 1775. Gov. Gage to Dartmouth, enclosing extracts from records of the provincial congress at Cambridge, 1774–1775.

No. 310, May 17, 1775. Petition of his Majesty's ancient subjects settled in Quebec to repeal the Quebec Act.

No. 311, Oct. 26, 1775. Petition of the city of London that measures will be adopted by Parliament for healing the dispute between Great Britain and the colonies.

No. 312, Oct. 26, 1775. Address, petitions, and memorial of the Nova Scotia representatives acknowledging the authority of the King and Parliament and praying redress of grievances, Halifax, June 24, 1775.

No. 313, Nov. 6, 1775. Petition to the King from the Continental Congress, presented Sept. 1775.

No. 314, Nov. 10, 1775. Examination of Richard Penn upon the Continental Congress petition.

No. 315, Nov. 20, 1775. (1) Account of amount and value of exports and imports to and from North America and Scotland, 1739–1773; (2) Account of amount and value of exports and imports to and from the West Indies and Scotland, 1739–1773.

No. 316, Feb. 16, 1776. Treaties with German princes for troops: (1) Treaty with the Duke of Brunswick, Jan. 9, 1776; (2) Treaty with the Landgrave of Hesse-Cassel, Jan. 15, 1776; (3) Treaty with the Hereditary Prince of Hesse-Cassel, Feb. 5, 1776.

No. 317, April 12, 1776. Ten admiralty papers relating to the forts and settlements of the African Company.

No. 318, April 19, 1776. List of ships with the Admiralty licenses that have entered the port of London and lists of cargoes of the *Renown* and *City of London* bound for Boston.

No. 319, April 29, 1776. Copies of all licenses granted by the Admiralty for exporting provisions to America since the passing of 16 Geo. III, prohibiting all intercourse with the thirteen colonies.

No. 320, May 1, 1776. Treaty with the Prince of Waldeck for troops, April 20, 1776.

No. 321, May 7, 1776. The ulterior convention with the Hereditary Prince of Hesse-Cassel, April 25, 1776, with translation.

THE BRITISH MUSEUM

The depository of manuscripts in Great Britain that for the purpose of this series stands next to the Public Record Office in importance is the Library of the British Museum—one of the world's greatest libraries. Established at Montagu House in 1759, it was able to accommodate such great collections as the Sloane and Harleian, as well as the Cottonian manuscripts and books, and the royal library presented by George II in 1757. With respect to mansucripts relating to the period under examination, an important accession to its holdings was made in 1823 when George IV presented to the Museum not only the great collection of books that George III had gathered but also an important body of manuscripts. In 1829 it acquired by gift of the Earl of Bridgewater the Egerton Manuscripts, which include, among other important papers, those of Governor Thomas Hutchinson of Massachusetts Bay (1711–1780) and his family. William Haldimand, Esq., in 1857 turned over to the Museum not only the papers of Gen. Sir Frederick Haldimand (1718–1791), but also those of Brigadier General Henry Bouquet (1719–1765), both of whom had distinguished careers in North America. The following year it acquired from the Rev. Lord John Thynne, the papers of John Cartaret, Earl Granville (1690–1763) and in 1860 the Countess Cowper presented the papers of Sir Thomas Robinson, Baron Grantham

(1695–1770); also, between 1886 and 1889, the Earl of Chicester, a member of the Pelham family, contributed the papers of this family which include the large body of manuscripts of Thomas Pelham-Holles, 1st Duke of Newcastle (1693–1768). Soon after this came the acquisition of the Hardwicke Papers, of almost a thousand bundles; these include the papers of Philip Yorke, 1st Earl of Hardwicke (1690–1764), as well as those of his sons, all men of national distinction. Passing over other accessions, reference may be made to the acquisition in 1947 (by means of the Egerton endowment) of the Osborne family papers which previously had reposed in the muniment room of Hornby Castle, the county seat of the Duke of Leeds; among these papers are those of Robert D'Arcy, 4th Earl of Holderness (1718–1778).

In outlining the contents of the library of the British Museum it is desirable to follow the descriptions given in the Andrews and Davenport *Guide* and the more recent *Guide* by Crick and Alman, in so far as they relate to materials falling within the period under review. However, the point must be stressed that in view of constant accessions no guide is up to date. The Andrews and Davenport *Guide* under the heading "Additional Manuscripts" ends with *No. 37,067;* the Crick and Alman *Guide* ends with *No. 49,178* and carries the accessions to 1955. As for the *Catalogue of Additions to the British Museum,* put out by the Museum in 1958, the additions listed extend only to the year 1925; however, the Crick and Alman *Guide* (p. 128) points out that in 1960 the listing of accessions had been brought up to the year 1930. For additional finding aids see Theodore Cressy Skeat: *The Catalogues of the Manuscript Collections* (rev. edn., London, 1962). We shall first turn to the listing in the Andrews and Davenport *Guide,* pp. 8–169, and then to that of Crick and Alman, pp. 128–76, to supplement the former in so far as these lists concern the years 1748–1776.

Lansdowne Papers

While the great body of personal papers and those related to the Empire accumulated by William Petty, who assumed the title of Earl of Shelburne in 1764 and that of Marquis of Lansdowne in 1784, are in the Clements Library at Ann Arbor and will be later discussed, a large body of papers (1,245 bundles) is to be found in the British Museum. However, little of this material relates to the Empire during the period under review. The following items may be noted:

No. 661. ff. 51–150. Papers from the Register General of Tobacco, of importance for study of the tobacco trade. Also several representations sent to the Commissioners of the Customs, 1752–1760.

No. 809. ff. 1–32. "Historical Account of the Revolt of the Chactaw Indians in the late war from the French to the British alliance and

their return since to that of the French. In which are contained
the public and private measures pursued on that occasion in the
province of South Carolina and wherein the respective services
of the several persons claiming the merit of effecting that revolt
are placed in their proper light and the true causes shewn of each
event." Dated London, Jan. 20, 1753, and addressed to James West
by Edmd. Atkins.

Stowe Manuscripts

The great body of the Stowe Papers are in the Huntington Library, San
Marino, California, and will be considered later in this survey. Two
manuscripts in the museum which should be considered are:

Nos. 484 and 485, June 2, 1762. Returns of his Majesty's forces, including
those in North America.

Hargrave Manuscripts

Two manuscripts in this collection should also be noted:

No. 493. f. 257. "State of the different Laws and Modes respecting the
Barring of Entails in the several American colonies," and
No. 494. ff. 46–56. "Report of case between governor and House of
Burgesses of Virginia, heard before the Privy Council, June 18,
1754." See *Catalogue of the Francis Hargrave Manuscripts in the
British Museum* (London, 1818).

King's Manuscripts

The following manuscripts fall within the period 1748–1776:

No. 201. "Original letters from Dr. Franklin to the Rev. Dr. Cooper,
written in the years 1769, 1770, 1771, 1772, 1773 and 1774, on
American politics."
No. 202. "Original letters from Gov. Pownall to the Rev. Dr. Cooper,
written in the years 1769, 1770, 1771, 1772, 1773 and 1774, on
American politics."
No. 203. "Original letters from the Rev. Dr. Cooper to Dr. Franklin
written in the years 1769, 1770, 1771, 1772, 1773, 1774 and 1775,
on American politics."
No. 204. "Letters from Doctor Franklin to the Revd Doctor Cooper,
Minister of the Gospel in the Town of Boston in New England, in
the years 1769, 1770, 1771, 1772, 1773, 1774, upon the subject of
American Politics, together with Doctor Cooper's answers and
some few letters from Governor Pownall to Doct^r Cooper upon the

same subject. Taken from the Originals. To which is added a short history of those letters or an account of the manner in which they happened to fall into the hands of the present possessor of them." These are copies of letters in *No. 201*, with some of both *Nos. 202* and *203*.

No. 205. "Report on the State of the American Colonies," containing copies of letters from governors and others in America and elsewhere, probably obtained from Board of Trade papers. These letters range in date from 1730 to 1766.

No. 206. "State of Manufactures, Mode of Granting Land, Fees of Office, etc., in America." The papers are dated either in 1766 or 1767.

No. 209. Maps and plans to accompany Lieut.-Col. Morse's *Description of Nova Scotia,* mostly of Nova Scotia, but also including a chart of the coast of Delaware and New Jersey.

Nos. 210 and *211.* Gerard de Brahm's Report, 1773, that carries the following imposing title: "Report of the General Survey in the Southern District of North America. Delivered to the Board of Trade and Plantations in three separate Returns and Sections entering with the History of South Carolina and Georgia, then proceeding to the History of East Florida; and Surveys, containing in general of said Provinces, the Climates, Beginnings, Boundaries, Figures, Contents, Cultures, Soils, Natural Products, Improvements, Navigable Streams, Rivers, Cities, Towns, Villages, Vapours, their Effect and Remedies, burning of Forests, Winds, how to preserve Health, Pathology, Materia Medica, Diet and Regimen, Ports, Bars, Number of Inhabitants and Negroes, Exportations, Riches, Number of Trading Vessels, Cattle, Governments, Forces, Fortifications, of Fort Loudoun in particular, Indians and Appalachian mountains, their Soil, Natural Produce, Air and Communications, compiled from the Surveys, Voyages, Astronomical, Philosophical, and Chymical Observations and Experiments, Sea and Land Surveys of William Gerard de Brahm, His Majesty's Surveyor General for the Southern District of North America." It should be noted that the Harvard Library has portions of this famous report. There are differences between it and the British Museum copy.

No. 212. "Journal of General Braddock's Expedition in 1755," prefaced by six colored maps: (1) Map of the country between Wills Creek and Monongahela River showing route and encampment of the English army in 1755; (2) "Line of March with the whole Baggage"; (3) "Plan of the Disposition of the Advanced Party consisting of 400 men"; (4) "Line of March of the Detachments from the Little Meadows"; (5) "Encampment of the Detachments from the Little Meadows"; (6) "A Plan of the Field of Battle and Disposition of the Troops as they were on the March at the time of the Attack, July 9, 1755."

No. 213. "Journal of an Officer [Lord Adam Gordon] who travelled over a part of the West Indies and of North America in the course of 1764 and 1765."

Egerton Manuscripts

This great collection of 2,861 volumes was left to the British Museum by Francis Henry Egerton, 8th Earl of Bridgewater (1756–1829), together with £12,000 to provide for its care and augmentation. Only a few of these manuscripts fall within the period of this survey. The original body of the Egerton papers has been supplemented by purchase from time to time. For example, the Leeds Papers were acquired in 1943, as were transcripts of the Cavendish papers in 1954, neither of which, of course, is listed in the Andrews and Davenport *Guide*. The following documents among the Egerton manuscripts, including the later accessions, should be noted:

No. 929. f. 168. Letter from Rear-Adm. Sir Peter Warren to the Duke of Newcastle, concerning troops needed in Nova Scotia, Louisbourg, and Placentia, recommending civil government in Nova Scotia and land grants without quit-rent, and suggesting Gov. Shirley's fitness for the post, n.d.; *f. 173.* Copy of letter to Gov. R. H. Morris from William Trent, Benjamin Franklin's trading partner in western Pennsylvania and Washington's lieutenant on expedition against Pittsburgh, dated "Mouth of Conicocheg," July 16, 1755, saying, "we are informed that our army is beat and the Artillery taken, but that the general and the rest of the army are making a good retreat"; *f. 176.* Draft of letter from the Earl of Halifax to Pitt, relative to reduction of the Neutral West Indian Islands, St. Lucia, St. Vincent, Dominica and Tobago, Nov. 5, 1758.

No. 1717. f. 117. Extract of letter respecting discoveries of the Russians on northwest coast of America, Sept. 23, 1764.

No. 1720. Documents relating to Demerara and Berbice. Correspondence of Gedney Clarke, Sr., and Gedney Clarke, his son, on affairs of these colonies, July 1762–Aug. 1766.

No. 1747. f. 362. Letter from Gen. Bouquet to Count Bentinck, 1752. (In French.)

No. 1756. f. 183. Memoir by Sir Joseph Yorke, British minister at Paris, on right of England to the island of Tobago, April 12, 1749. Reply of the French government. (In French.)

No. 2135. f. 1. Capitulation of Martinique, February 7, 1762; *f. 5.* Letter from "A Real Churchman" to "Dear Vardell," New York, May 2, 1775, about the situation in New York and the country generally. Vardell was a tutor at King's College, later Columbia College; *f. 7.* Journal of the operations of the American army under Gen.

Sir William Howe, from the evacuation of Boston to the end of the campaign of 1776, March 7, 1776 to Dec. 26, 1776; ff. 9–18. Two papers concerning military operations in America: (1) Without heading or endorsement, June 11 to July 31, but no year, with a page showing "Distribution of the Part of the Army not moving with the main Body," written by someone in Cornwallis's army, and (2) "A Plan of Military Operations in America," n.d.

No. 2423. "Journal by a Lady (of Quality)" of a Voyage from Scotland to the West Indies and North Carolina, with an account of personal experiences in America during the year 1775 and a visit to Lisbon on her return. Oct. 25, 1774-Dec. 1775. This interesting manuscript was edited by Professor and Mrs. Charles M. Andrews under title *Journal of a Lady of Quality* and was published in 1921.

Nos. 2659–2675. The Hutchinson Papers contain family papers and correspondence, 1741 to 1880, including the letter-book, diary, memoranda, will, and general correspondence of Thomas Hutchinson, governor of Massachusetts Bay, 1769–1774; also letters of his sons, Thomas and Elisha, and of his daughter Margaret or Peggy. In addition to the Hutchinson letters these volumes also contain the letters, diaries, 1776, 1741–1821, and other papers of Chief Justice Peter Oliver, and his brother Andrew, who were Hutchinson's brothers-in-law, and of Gage, Clarke and others. Needless to say, these papers are of the highest importance. Attention should be called especially to No. 2659, which has many comments pertaining to the Boston Tea Party.

No. 2694. ff. 98, 168, 192. Papers relating to French encroachments in America, 1750–1760.

No. 2697. f. 9. Memorial to the Secretary of State in behalf of Alexander McDougall, New York merchant, 1768.

No. 2698. ff. 231, 232. Letters from the governor of the Danish islands in America, 1769.

No. 3324–3508. The Leeds Papers embody the correspondence and papers of the Osborne family, Dukes of Leeds, including the papers of Robert D'Arcy, 4th Earl of Holderness (1718–1778). Acquired in 1947, the 185 volumes supplement Add. MSS. *Nos. 28040–28095*. While formerly at Hornby Castle, the documents were examined by the Historical Manuscripts Commission in *Report*, XI (vii), which failed to cover the entire deposited collection. Since the Leeds Papers had not yet been listed when Crick and Alman made their survey, they drew their examples from the Historical Manuscripts Commission's *Report*. Two items are relevant for our period: (1) "Narrative of hostilities committed by the French on the Ohio in 1754, with papers relative to the negotiations in 1755 relating to these," and (2) A letter from Captain

Peter D'Arcy, July 27, 1759, recounting the capture of the French fort at Ticonderoga.

No. 3711. Cavendish Papers. Transcripts of forty-nine quarto volumes, *Nos. 215–263,* of shorthand notes taken by Sir Henry Cavendish of debates in the House of Commons while he was a member of the House, May 10, 1768 to June 13, 1774. John Wright edited a part of them, published in 1839, as *Debates of the House of Commons in the year 1774 on the Bill for making More Affectual Provision for the Government of the Province of Quebec;* further, in 1841–3 there came from the press also edited by Wright, in two volumes *Sir Henry Cavendish's Debates of the House of Commons during the thirteenth Parliament of Great Britain, commonly called the Unreported Parliament.* Unhappily, Volume II ends with March 27, 1771.

Additional Manuscripts

This is a vast collection of papers that is being constantly expanded. Among those that bear upon the years 1748–1776 are the following:

No. 4164. f. 32. Extract of letter from Lieut. Wm. Jacobs to ――――― Spellman, Sept. 30, 1755, giving an account of America. Sailed from Woolwich, June 3, 1754, for Halifax, then to Bay of Fundy, then to Boston, where he arrived April 17, 1755.

No. 8133B. f. 7. Account of total amount of the old subsidy retained upon foreign goods exported from England to North America, 1773–1774; *f. 141.* Account of amount of bounties paid on hemp, flax, and wood imported from America, 1771–1775; *ff. 160–165.* Indigo statistics, 1771–1775; *ff. 177–719.* Naval stores statistics, 1771–1775; *ff. 194–195.* Plantation rum statistics, 1770–1779; *ff. 283–302.* Sugar statistics, 1770–1779; *f. 309ff.* Tea statistics (see also *ff. 316, 326, 341*); *f. 350ff.* Tobacco statistics (see also *ff. 355, 363, 364*).

No. 8133C. (Contains material that is similar to that found in *No. 8133B*). *ff. 1–4.* Small printed book containing lists of the "commissions of the customs and successors of the commissioners" from 1672 to 1785, with dates of letters patent, number of commissioners and their salaries, names of new commissioners with dates when they died or were superseded, names of commissioners who had died or were superseded with dates of their first appointments; *f. 85.* Report of Sept. 16, 1763, concerning what further checks and restraints may be necessary to be imposed by Parliament for preventing frauds in the colonies by the Commissioners of Customs, with "list of seizures to be sued for in any court of record, [though if] made by admirals or commanders at sea to be delivered into the court of admiralty there to be proceded against"; *ff. 89–94.* Agreement of the West Indian and North American merchants, March 10, 1766, regarding opening the island of Dominica and proposals for indemnifying purchasers at Dominica; *f. 96.* Live stock and Negro population statistics for Jamaica in 1768; *f. 97.* Regarding St. Lucia and Dominica, with their present state, products, and commercial advantages, by Jno. Geo. Felton; *f. 140.* Annual amount of salaries paid to officers in the plantations out of the revenue of customs, 1766–1778; *ff. 163–168.* In accounts of bounties paid at London and the outports are figures for "American raw silk," 1770–1775, and the "Newfoundland fishery"; *f. 179.* Account of the value of exports from England to North American colonies, 1763–1767, distinguishing each colony; *ff. 204–217.* Memorial of merchants and planters, interested in and trading to Barbados and the Leeward Islands, to Lords of the Treasury, with objections and observations upon it, n.d.; *f. 218.* Account of gross and net produce of such part of the four and a half per cent as has passed through the hands of the husband and comptroller of that duty, 1770–1777; *f. 233.* Account of enumerated and new duties received in the ports on the continent of America since Sept. 29, 1764, so far as the accounts have been received and also of the remittances made on account of said duties, distinguishing ports; *f. 234.* Annual amount of the enumerated duties, 1761–1765.

No. 8949. Journal of the travels of Jonathan Carver in 1766 and 1767: (1) Survey journal from Detroit to Michilimackinac; (2) Journal, beginning May 20, 1766; (3) Dictionary of the Naudouwessie language; (4) Map of the Great Lakes from middle of Lake Huron westward with colored plots of various Indian "kingdoms"; (5) Map of the Great Lakes, not colored; (6) same as (5), colored to correspond to original map (4).

No. 8950 is a fair copy of the Carver survey and journal.

No. 9828. f. 122. Gov. Pownall on "whether lands granted in America can be resumed and regranted upon bare suggestion that the Conditions have not been complied with and without any legal inquest," July 22, 1773; *f. 169.* Letter from Benjamin Franklin to W.F., London, Feb. 2, 1774, speaking of the office of deputy postmaster as taken from him; *f. 169ff.* Letters from Benjamin Franklin to his son, London, Feb. 2 and 18, and Aug. 1, 1774.

No. 11287. Map of cantonment of British forces in North America, Oct. 11, 1765.

No. 11288. "Cantonment of his Majesty's Forces in North America . . . ," March 29, 1766.

No. 11514. Essay on Trade in America. To the Right Honorable Earl of Halifax. Signed Henry McCulloh, dated London, Dec. 10, 1756.

No. 11813. f. 82. Capt. Parry's account of the expedition against Louisbourg, 1758.

No. 12099. f. 22. Letter from Benjamin Franklin to Gov. Bernard, Philadelphia, Jan. 11, 1764, regarding a son of Gov. Bernard.

Nos. 12402–12440. Papers collected by Edward Long (1734–1813), judge
of admiralty in, and historian of, Jamaica. Of these volumes, *Nos.
12402–12436* deal with the history and condition of Jamaica. *No.
12440* is the correspondence of Ministers with Gov. Moore of New
York, 1766. To the same general collection belong *Nos. 18269–
18275, 18959–18963, 21931, 22639, 22676–22678, 27968.*

No. 13974. f. 474. Report relating to payment of tithes by the Jesuits in
America, 1765; *f. 502.* Tables of exports and imports with America,
1748–1815.

No. 13976. f. 268. Commerce of Spain with America, 1750.

No. 14034. ff. 143–174. Papers regarding Barbados, the Bermudas, and
the Leeward Islands; *f. 178.* Extract of letter from William West to
the governor of Pennsylvania, regarding the Indians and lands on
the Ohio, May 7, 1753; *f. 202.* King's warrant to Matthew Woodford
for £413. 18s. 7d. for provisions delivered at Annapolis to New
England recruits sent there, June 5, 1754; *f. 213.* Concerns the
cultivation of St. John Island (later Prince Edward Island); *f. 221.*
Relates to Quebec; *f. 227.* Proceedings of a congress held in East
Florida, Nov. 21, 1767; *f. 245.* About the activities of Gov. Legge of
Nova Scotia; *ff. 288 and 337.* Abstracts of acts pertaining to taxes,
duties, imposts, etc., passed in America and the West Indies, 1683–
1774; *f. 382.* Memoranda relating to the colony of West Florida, by
Capt. Johnstone.

No. 14036. Maps: (1) Plan of York Harbour on the Labrador coast, 52°
15′ north latitude, August, 1760; (2) New Hampshire, showing the
Merrimac River in order to settle the question of the boundary,
n.d.; (3) Small map of the sea-coast of New England, with outlines of several of the provinces lying therein, 1738; (4) Map of
the southern Indian district, 1764; (5) Map of the Cherokee country, by John Stuart; (6) Map of Georgia, by the surveyor general,
De Brahm; (7) Map of Georgia, by the same, 1763.

No. 15317. Copy of proceedings in the general court of Virginia between
John Hite, *et al.,* plaintiffs, and Thomas, Lord Fairfax, defendant,
relative to certain lands there; with various other papers relating
to the same suit, 1771.

No. 15484. Ports, districts, and towns of America. About 1770.

No. 15485. Account of shipping, imports, exports, their value and character of articles carried, 1768–1769.

No. 15487. Papers relating to New England boundary disputes. *f. 4.* Petition of William Bollan, agent for Massachusetts Bay, concerning

boundary dispute between Massachusetts and Connecticut. Undated, but after 1749; *f. 18.* Certificate from Governor Wolcott of Connecticut, bearing witness to the authority and trustworthiness of Erastus Wolcott and Daniel Bissell, appointed to survey the line, Feb. 28, 1750/1; *f. 19.* Evidence given by Wolcott and Bissell who surveyed the line; *f. 20.* Evidence of Daniel and Ebenezer Hayden; *ff. 22–23.* Map-plan of the boundary controversy; *f. 24.* Map of country adjacent to north boundary line of Rhode Island "as the same was run by commissioners appointed for that purpose by the General Assembly of the said colony in the year 1750"; *f. 28.* Letter from Gov. Wolcott regarding the boundary difficulty, and giving Connecticut's side of the case, Windsor, June 10, 1752; *f. 69.* State of the case in controversy between Massachusetts and Connecticut about the dividing line between the two governments. Summing up by London agent Partridge upon evidence furnished by Connecticut; *f. 75b.* State of the case in controversy, a slightly fuller statement than that above; *f. 82b.* Statement by William Murray, attorney general, Nov. 5, 1754. Unfavorable to reopening of dispute and thinks that the rearrangement of 1713 should stand; *ff. 96–103.* Plans and explanations of plans of Massachusetts and New Hampshire touching the boundary question and the bounds of certain towns such as Rumford, Suncook, Bow.

No. 15488. f. 32. "Remarks on the plan and extracts of deeds lately published by the proprietors of the Township of Brunswick (as they term themselves) agreeable to their vote of January 4, 1753." (Printed quarto, 8 pp. and 4 pp.); *f. 38.* "An Answer to the Remarks printed 'Boston in New England, Printed in the year MDCCLIII.'" Printed pamphlet, 33 pp.; *f. 55.* "A Defence of the Remarks of the Plymouth Company of September 5, 1753." Printed pamphlet, 50 pp.; *ff. 81–98.* First and second drafts of the Kennebec case, drawn up probably by Partridge. Second draft dated Aug. 27, 1755. (With plan. At bottom is signature, Jos. Sharpe.); *f. 99.* Attorney General Murray's opinion on the case of the Kennebec Company; *f. 100.* Another opinion, dated Sept. 9, 1755. Endorsed, "Case of the Kennebeck Company"; *f. 130.* Printed brief of the case: Thos. Dudley, appellant—Sam¹ Scarborough and his wife and others, respondent; *f. 131.* List of twenty-four papers also on the Kennebec affair. (See also *ff. 139, 140, 151, 153, 155* and *156*); *f. 162.* "A List of the Gentlemen of the Council of Massachusetts Bay who have been Turned out of the Council since the repeal of the Stamp Act," n.d.; *ff. 163–164.* Extracts of letters from Gov. Bernard of Massachusetts (Thirteen volumes of the Bernard correspondence are in the Houghton Library at Harvard); *ff. 165–174.* Extracts of letters from the Earl of Shelburne and others to

Gov. Bernard of Massachusetts; *f. 175*. Extracts of the journals of the House of Assembly, Massachusetts, 1761–1764.

No. 15489. f. 1. Petition from the town of Rumford, New Hampshire, saying that the colony has denied them the privilege of incorporation, with 7 supporting documents; *f. 29*. Account of voyage of the *Jupiter* from Newport to Hispaniola, and her seizure at Jamaica, Sept. 1750 to April 1752; *f. 57*. Extract of letters from Joseph Reed to Joseph Sharpe, of Lincoln's Inn, Philadelphia, Feb. 13, 1775; *f. 70*. Papers relating to laws for preventing growth of popery. The laws, all copies, date from 1751. Maryland, 1755.

No. 15491. Papers relating to Montreal, Quebec, and Newfoundland, 1771.

No. 15493. "Some facts collected and observations made on the fisheries and government of Newfoundland, showing the many advantages which will arise to this kingdom in colonizing that island, to which is added a plan for a speedy settling it." Undated, but probably written after 1784, by Dr. Gardner, formerly of Boston. Late but pertinent.

No. 15494. Maps of various Canadian and West Indian ports.

No. 15495. Draft of the Mississippi River from its mouth to the Iberville River; also charts of eastern half of Newfoundland, 1770.

No. 15535. Various plans of military operations in America, 1755, 1759, 1782, including Bowles's engraved map of the United States, 1783, with continuation of boundary line in manuscript.

No. 15563. a and *b.* Two maps showing the country between Fort Cumberland and Lake Erie.

No. 15874. f. 208. Narrative of what passed upon the river Ohio, Aug. 1753 to July 1754.

Nos. 16259–16271. Original correspondence, letters, and court papers of Sir Elijah Impey, chief justice of the supreme court of judicature, Calcutta, India, 1774–1783.

No. 17566. f. 11b. Papers relating to Spanish missionary settlements in Texas, 1715–1767.

No. 17569. f. 126. Report of Francisco Honibrados on the climate and commercial advantages of Louisiana, 1763. (In Spanish.)

No. 17570. f. 178. Description of Campeche and Yucatan, 1766. (In Spanish.) See also *No. 17654 B.*

No. 17583. f. 175. Medios que Don Alonso de Arcos Moreno propuso para recuperar la Ysla de Jamaica, 1747; *f. 283*. Various routes, among them one from Acapulco to Manila.

No. 17648A. "Descripcion geographica de la parte que los Españoles poseen actualmente en el continente de la Florida; del dominio en que estan los Yngleses" by Fernando Martinez, 1768.

No. 17693. A–D. Four charts of coast of Newfoundland, as surveyed by James Cook, 1764–1767.

No. 19038. f. 48. Letters from F. Gastry to Adm. Charles Knowles, governor of Jamaica, 1753.

No. 19071. f. 88ff. Copies of seven important letters concerning the Acadians from the collection of Dr. Belknap.

No. 19073. f. 2. Commission to Hon. Edward Cornwallis, governor of Nova Scotia, 1749.

No. 21384. ff. 1–27. Journal of explorations by M. d. Kerasoret, July 1753, among the Bahama islands.

Nos. 21631–21660. Bouquet Papers. Henry Bouquet (1719–1765) was appointed lieutenant-colonel of the Royal American regiment in 1754; in 1763 he rescued Fort Pitt from siege by the Ohio Valley Indians and the following year forced them to make peace. Shortly thereafter, he was made brigadier-general and commandant of all troops in the southern colonies. He died during an epidemic at Pensacola, Florida. ¶ His papers contain letter-books, general and regimental orders, disbursement accounts, and warrants. Correspondents include Amherst, Gage, Stanwix, Monckton, St. Clair, Loudoun, Forbes, Washington, also a large number of commissioned and non-commissioned officers, several colonial governors, agents, paymasters, and civilians in Philadelphia, New York, Charleston, etc. Nineteen volumes of these papers were published in mimeographed form by the Pennsylvania Historical and Museum Commission; and Volume II, relating to the Forbes expedition against Fort Duquense, has appeared in regularly published form to be followed by other volumes. Complete copies of the entire collection are in the archives of the Canadian government at Ottawa, constituting vols. A1–A30 of the government series. As the very full printed calendar prepared by Douglas Brymner and published in the *Report on the Canadian Archives* in 1889, is readily accessible, no attempt has been made here to list any of the documents of this collection.

Nos. 21661–21892. Haldimand Papers. Sir Frederick Haldimand (1718–1791) was appointed lieutenant-colonel of the 62nd Royal Americans in 1756 under Lord Loudoun, and rose steadily in rank, serving in northern New York and Canada till 1766 when he took command at Pensacola, Florida; later while Gage was in England, he was in command of the British forces in North America. Before his death he had become lieutenant-general in the British army. ¶ His papers contain account books, regimental returns, reports on Indian relations, orders and instructions from Gage, Amherst, Carleton, and others, journals, diaries, commissions, maps and plans, letters and warrants. For a calendar of these papers see Brymner: *Report on the Canadian Archives, 1884–1889, passim.*

Nos. 22676–22678. Papers relating to Jamaica, 1662–1791. Letters of

Jamaican planters and merchants, including those of James Knight and C. Long, 1725–1789, in *No. 22677*.

No. 22679. f. 1. "Objections offered by the Magistrates of the City of New York to his Honor the Lieutenant Governor in Council, against a Commission of the Peace being issued for the city and county of New York." (Read in council, Dec. 20, 1764); *f. 4.* Petition to Gov. Moore of New York from a number of Indians of the Mohheekunnuck tribe residing on the Housatonic River, regarding claim to lands on the Hudson River, Stockbridge, April 1, 1765; *f. 7.* Dr. John Gordon, on account of Sir Henry Moore, for orders of council, 1763–1766; *f. 8.* Letter from Jared Ingersoll to Gov. Moore, New Haven, Jan. 3, 1766, requesting Moore to receive his consignment of stamp papers into the fort at New York; *f. 9.* Letter from Gov. Bernard to Gov. Moore, Boston, February 23, 1766, telling about the rioting at New London because of the stamps; *f. 11.* An unsigned, undated statement in Bernard's handwriting telling of the same; *f. 12.* Letter from Lieut. Colville to Gov. Moore, Halifax, April 17, 1766, promising aid in case of need; *f. 14.* Letter from Gov. Bernard to Gov. Moore, Boston, May 29, 1766, regarding Gov. Colden's letter about Bernard communicated to the newspapers, and adding, "The popular madness has not abated here so much as I could wish"; *f. 16.* Formal communication from Gov. Wm. Pitkin of Connecticut, Hartford, June 4, 1766, regarding selling liquor to the Schaticook Indians; *f. 17.* Protest addressed to Follerker Dow, mayor of Albany, against the late unwarranted proceedings of a number of people under the influence of Col. John Van Ransler at a place called Noble Town. Signed by Indians of Stockbridge, June 30, 1766. Similar communication, dated July 1, 1766, follows; *f. 21.* Letter from Jared Ingersoll to Gov. Moore, New Haven, July 14, 1766, asking that he and Lieut.-Gov. Colden will see that the stamps, which are to be taken back to England, be put safely on board ship bound for London; *f. 25.* Letter from Wm. Gilliland to Col. Bird, Willsborough, Sept. 19, 1766, regarding his title to lands on Lake Champlain; *f. 29.* "Some sensible remarks on Canada boundaries," in the handwriting of Edward Long; *f. 31.* State of the paper currency at New York, dated Nov. 14, 1766, contained in a letter from Abraham Lott, merchant of New York, to Gov. Moore; *f. 33.* Address of the general assembly of New York to Gov. Moore, Dec. 15, 1766, in reply to the governor's message of Nov. 17, 1766. (*f. 35* is a duplicate); *f. 36.* Letter from Gov. Bernard to Gov. Moore, Dec. 18, 1766, regarding his own claim to lands in New York; *f. 38.* Letter from Peter Hasenclever to Gov. Moore, New York, May 11, 1768, regarding money and business matters; *f. 42.* Letter from Sir William Johnson to

Gov. Moore, Johnson Hall, July 20, 1768, also regarding money matters; *f. 44.* Johnson to Moore, Johnson Hall, Aug. 5, 1768; *f. 46.* Johnson to Moore, Fort Stanwix, Sept. 20, 1768; *f. 50.* Letter from Capt. Sam. Holland to Gov. Moore, Quebec, Oct. 9, 1768; *f. 52.* Copy of proclamation regarding religion; *f. 56.* Communication from Gov. Moore, addressed to "My Lord," regarding the state of the chancery court at New York, n.d. Unfinished.

No. 23618. In this group the following maps are pertinent: (1) Plan of siege of Havana, 1762; (2) Sketch of part of the island of St. Lucia, with the operations between the Dutch and French, 1768.

No. 23678. Narrative and remarks on the siege of Havana, 1761–1762, by Adm. Sir Charles Knowles.

Nos. 24131–24138. "Abstracts of English State Papers in the collection formed by William, Earl of Shelburne, 1st Marquis of Lansdowne. . . ." Included are papers concerning the customs and trade, the navy, the treaty of 1763, the War for Independence, and the general pacification in 1783.

No. 24323. Letters from Sir William Johnson, Sir. J. Johnson, and Col. Guy Johnson to John Blackburn, merchant, Cannon St., London, chiefly relating to Canada, 1770–1780.

No. 27578. Correspondence of Rev. W. Butler. Vol. II., 1763–1771: *ff. 109, 114, 116* are letters from the Rev. Thos. John Claggett, Maryland, 1768–1769.

No. 27916. ff. 5–11. "A Short Hint to both sides of the Atlantic," by Francis Godolphin Osborne, Secretary of State, n.d. but before the Declaration of Independence.

No. 27969. Extracts from parish and other public records in Jamaica and Barbados with copies of the inscriptions on all monuments and tombstones in the latter from 1643–1750 as well as on some up to 1800, compiled by Capt. J. H. Lawrence-Archer.

No. 28605. Journal of John Lees of Quebec from London in 1768.

No. 28727. ff. 118–123. Letters from John Bartram to Peter Collinson, 1768–1772.

No. 28973–29236. Official and private correspondence and papers of Warren Hastings.

Nos. 29256A–29259L. "Returns of his Majesty's forces at home and abroad." Monthly tables extending from Nov. 1768 to Sept. 1775. Forty-three volumes in four. Series is imperfect.

No. 29600. Papers relating to America, 1725–1776, chiefly about the iron industry in Maryland: *f. 16.* Principio Company's Quarterly Accounts to Dec. 31, 1769. Gives many names; mentions Mr. Osgood Gee, the late Col. A. Washington (younger brother of Geo. Washington), etc. Shows value of pig and bar iron exported by this company to London, Bristol, and Liverpool; *f. 20.* Letters enclosed in Mr. Thos. Russell's letter of June 22, 1772: (1) Letter from Anne Washington regarding her husband's share in the iron-works, May 28, 1772; (2) Answer from Thos. Russell, North East Forge, June 15, 1772, to Mrs. Washington at Wakefield near Leed's Town, Virginia, the old Washington plantation on the Potomac. (Principio and North East are near Port Deposit, Md.; Leed's Town is on the Rappahanock, Va.); *f. 22.* Letter from Thos. Russell to Messrs., the Widow Wightwick, Wm. Pillas, Wm. Russell and Co., regarding the company and the business, June 22, 1772; *f. 25.* Letter from the same to Michail Harris, agent at No. 16 Cullum St., London, dated New York, July 4, 1772; *f. 27.* Letter from the same to same, regarding the condemnation of one of the company's sloops before the court of admiralty, Williamsburg, Aug. 4, 1772; *f. 29.* Letter from the same to the same, regarding the same business, Norfolk, Aug. 14, 1772; *f. 31.* From same to the Widow Wightwick, Wm. Pillas, Wm. Russell and Co., about the business, giving list of bills of exchange drawn on the company for the use of the works in 1772; *f. 39.* Short note from Russell to Harris referring to enclosures that are missing, Philadelphia, Feb. 24, 1773; *f. 40.* Letter from Geo. Randell to Thos. Russell regarding some difficulties, Lancaster Furnace, May 22, 1773. Possibly this is the enclosure referred to in *f. 39; f. 42.* Letter from Russell to Harris, on business. North East, May 26, 1773; *f. 44.* Letter from Nath. Martin to Harris, Back River, Maryland, June 8, 1773; *f. 46.* Balance Sheet. June 30, 1776. This collection supplements the papers on the Principio works used in the article by Henry Whitely: "The Principio Company: A Historical Sketch of the First Iron Works in Maryland," *Pennsylvania Magazine of History and Biography,* XI (1887), 63, 190, 288.

No. 29613. Register of Customs Officials for 1768. (Relating solely to England and probably duplicate of register for that year in P.R.O., *Custom House, Registers, Series I, Establishments.*)

No. 29973. "A Short Description of the Province of South Carolina, by Surgeon General George Milligan Johnston, M.D. 1763." A printed work with the author's notes and corrections.

No. 30089. f. 70. Spanish ships taken in the West Indies, 1762.

No. 30094. f. 149. Letter from Benjamin Franklin to Capt. Dawson, Craven St., London, May 29, 1772; *f. 238.* The Royal Society and Franklin's electrical conductors.

No. 30163. "An Inquiry into the causes of the present scarcity of money and the bad consequences of it" to the island of Jamaica, "with a remedy," 1750.

Nos. 30868–30875. A collection of 25 volumes of the John Wilkes papers. Letters to Wilkes from the following people, chiefly in *Nos.* 30870 and 30871: (1) John Almon, 1764–1769; (2) John Adams,

1768–1769; (3) Benjamin Church, 1769; (4) Samuel Adams, 1770; (5) Joseph Warren, 1769–1770.

No. 32420. f. 147. Observations on present state of the Germans in Pennsylvania, by Benjamin Franklin, 1753.

No. 32450Y. Town of Porto Rico, West Indies, with soundings of the harbour. 18th century.

Nos. 32686–33057. Newcastle Papers. Official correspondence of Thomas Pelham-Holles, Duke of Newcastle, 1697–1768, arranged chronologically in 307 volumes. To the end of the year 1723 it is contained in one series; from 1724 to 1754 it is divided in two series: Home Correspondence and Diplomatic Correspondence; from 1755 to 1768, it is again contained in one series. The volumes are indexed very fully. *Nos. 33028–33030,* of the Newcastle Papers, relate wholly to the affairs of the American and West Indian colonies, 1701–1802. Papers other than letters are listed below under the volume number. Letters are arranged alphabetically under the name of the writer, as follows: (1) Maj.-Gen. Abercromby: to W. Pitt, 1758, *No. 32881, f. 279;* to J. Abercromby, 1758, *No. 32884, f. 360;* (2) Maj.-Gen. Amherst: to Newcastle, 1756, 1757, *Nos. 32863, f. 234; 32876, f. 449;* to W. Pitt, 1760, *No. 32906, f. 143;* (3) Goldsborow Banyar, deputy clerk of council of New York: to Marchand de Ligneris, 1749, *No. 32818, ff. 49, 55;* (4) Jonathan Belcher: to Newcastle, 1753, *No. 32731, f. 503;* (5) William Bollan: to Newcastle, 1751–1766, *Nos. 32725, f. 182; 32861, f. 98; 32974, f. 364;* to Col. Amyand, 1751, *No. 32725, f. 75;* to the Board of Trade, 1759, *No. 32890, f. 496;* (6) Choiseul, French minister of Foreign Affairs: to Pitt, Newcastle, and others. See *B.M. Cat. Add. MSS.,* 1882–1887. Index; (7) Geo. Clinton, governor of New York: to Gen. Shirley, *No. 32818, ff. 82, 84, 86, 90;* (8) Sir Henry Clinton: to Newcastle, 1749, *No. 32719, f. 61;* (9) Cadwallader Colden: *No. 32698, f. 383;* (10) J. Dawes, member of assembly in Jamaica: memorandum regarding, 1755, *No. 32852, f. 250;* (11) James de Lancey, governor of New York: *Nos. 32735, f. 147; 32858, f. 22;* (12) Gov. Dinwiddie: to the Board of Trade, 1753, *No. 32732, f. 452;* to Lord Holderness, 1754, *Nos. 32735, f. 186; 32850, f. 221;* to Sir T. Robinson, 1754–1755, *Nos. 32736, f. 85; 32850, f. 227; 32853, f. 321;* to Messrs. J. and C. Hanbury, 1754, *No. 32850, f. 229;* to Newcastle, 1755, *No. 32853, f. 325;* to J. Hanbury, 1755, *No. 32854, f. 378;* (13) Dobbs, afterwards governor of North Carolina: to A. Stone, 1749, *No. 32718, f. 51;* to Newcastle, 1752, *No. 32730, f. 301;* (14) Marquis Duquesne: to Newcastle, 1758, *No. 32884, f. 55;* (15) Rich. Earnshaw, late receiver general, Guadeloupe: to Newcastle, 1766, *Nos. 32974, f. 429; 32975, f. 470;* (16) Stephen Fuller, agent for Jamaica: chiefly to Newcastle, 1760–1766, *Nos. 32912, f. 487; 32917, ff. 61, 106;*

32921, *ff.* 88, 146; 32923, *f.* 292; 32925, *f.* 107; 32926, *f.* 386; 32927, *ff.* 224, 265; 32948, *f.* 79; 32975, *f.* 400; (17) Marquis de la Galissonnière, governor-general of New France: to Gov. Geo. Clinton of New York 1749, *No.* 32818, *ff.* 21, 30, 37, 41, 61; commission of, *No.* 32819, *f.* 236; (18) Gen. Gage: to Newcastle, 1755, *No.* 32857, *f.* 342; to Lord ——, 1755, *No.* 32857, *f.* 338; to Lord Gage, 1757, *Nos.* 32870, *ff.* 345, 393; 32871, *f.* 125; petition of, to George II, 1755, *No.* 32857, *f.* 340; (19) Gov. Grenville, Barbados: See *B.M. Cat. Add. MSS.,* 1882–1887. Index; (20) John Hammerton, secretary and treasurer of South Carolina, 1744–1760: See *B.M. Cat. Add. MSS.,* 1882–1887. Index; (21) Gov. Hardy, New York: to Newcastle, 1756, *No.* 32868, *f.* 606; to the Board of Trade, 1759, *No.* 32890, *f.* 507; (22) Capt. Hitchin Holland, Fort Oswego: to governor of Virginia, 1755, *No.* 32853, *f.* 359; (23) Adm. Howe: 1758, *Nos.* 32880, *f.* 369; 32881, *ff.* 145, 147; (24) John Hunter, Virginia: to J. and C. Hanbury, 1755, *No.* 32853, *f.* 29; (25) Col. Wm. Johnson: to Gov. Clinton, 1749, 1752, *Nos.* 32818, *ff.* 75, 79, 91; 32833, *f.* 404; (26) Gov. La Jonquière, Canada: to E. Cornwallis, 1750, *No.* 32822, *ff.* 5, 8; (27) Gov. Lawrence, Nova Scotia: *No.* 32861, *f.* 140; (28) Egerton Leigh, South Carolina: to Newcastle, *No.* 32894, *ff.* 436, 438; (29) Gov. Lyttelton, South Carolina: *Nos.* 32859, *f.* 18; 32866, *f.* 227; (30) Beeston Long, chairman of West Indian merchants: correspondence with Newcastle, 1760, 1766, *Nos.* 32902, *f.* 458; 32975, *ff.* 416, 430; (31) Lord Loudoun, later commander-in-chief in North America: to Newcastle, 1742–1754, *Nos.* 32699, *f.* 525; 32700, *f.* 268; 32703, *f.* 186; 32712, *ff.* 51, 133; 32727, *f.* 140; 32735, *f.* 262; (32) Henry McCulloh: to Newcastle, 1753, 1756, 1757, *Nos.* 32731, *ff.* 177, 338, 410; 32732, *f.* 86; 32862, *f.* 394; 32863, *f.* 316; 32864, *f.* 536; 32866, *ff.* 156, 357; 32874, *f.* 308; (33) Gen. Wm. Mathew, governor of Leeward Islands: correspondence, 1735–1750. See *B.M. Cat. Add. MSS.,* 1882–1887. Index; (34) Gov. Moore, New York: to Newcastle, 1758, *No.* 32880, *f.* 497; (35) Geo. Munro, late comptroller of customs, Antigua: corespondence, 1756–1759. See *B.M. Cat. Add. MSS.,* 1882–1887. Index; (36) Gov. Murray, Quebec: correspondence, 1758–1767, including instructions, memorial to Sir John Ligonier, and letters and memorandum to Gen. Amherst. See *B.M. Cat. Add. MSS.,* 1882–1887. Index; (37) Sir James Oglethorpe: to Newcastle, 1738–1755, *Nos.* 32702, *f.* 347; 32797, *ff.* 52, 292; 32859, *f.* 185; (38) Thomas Penn, 1747–1756: *Nos.* 32710, *f.* 511; 32737, *f.* 236; 32862, *f.* 159; 32868, *f.* 7; (39) Gov. Pinfold, Barbados: to Newcastle, 1756, *No.* 32867, *f.* 446; (40) Wm. Pitt: correspondence of, with Newcastle, Hardwicke, Holderness, Choiseul, etc. See *B.M. Cat. Add. MSS.,* 1882–1887. Index; (41) William Popple, governor of Bermuda: to Newcastle, 1747–1761,

Nos. 32710, f. 138; 32861, f. 251; 32864, f. 401; 32919, f. 497; 32926, f. 173; (42) John Pownall, secretary to Board of Trade, 1758–1765: *Nos. 32881, f. 170; 32884, f. 96; 33087, ff. 366, 374–376;* (43) Thos. Pownall, 1761–1765: *Nos. 32927, f. 301; 32928, ff. 274, 278, 286, 294; 32968, f. 258;* (44) John Robinson: to Newcastle, 1756, *No. 32864, ff. 237, 257, 259, 462;* (45) Thos. Robinson, governor of Barbados: letter and papers of, 1744–1756. See *B.M. Cat. Add. MSS.,* 1882–1887. Index; (46) Lord John Russell, Secretary of State: to the governor of Leeward Islands, 1750, *No. 32822, f. 15;* (47) Robt. Sawco, Jamaica: to Newcastle, 1758, *No. 32489, f. 340;* (48) H. Sharpe, governor of Maryland: *No. 32858, f. 110;* (49) Gen. Wm. Shirley, governor of Mass. Bay: correspondence of, with Newcastle, Bedford, Holderness, Sir T. Robinson, Lincoln, etc. See *B.M. Cat. Add. MSS.,* 1882–1887. Index; (50) Sir Geo. Thomas, one-time deputy governor of Pennsylvania: to Newcastle, 1752–1767, *Nos. 32730, ff. 275, 289; 32979, f. 359; 32980, f. 22; 32984, ff. 102, 281;* (51) Ed. Trelawney, governor of Jamaica: to Newcastle and others, 1738–1751. See *B.M. Cat. Add. MSS.,* 1882–1887. Index; (52) Marquis de Caylus Tubières-Grimoard, French governor of Windward Islands: correspondence, 1749–1750. See *B.M. Cat. Add. MSS.,* 1882–1887. Index; (53) Harman Verelst: to Newcastle, 1756, *Nos. 32866, f. 363; 32868, f. 588; 32881, f. 102; 32884, f. 240.*

Among other Newcastle papers the following should be noted:

No. 32715. f. 107. Complaints against Gov. Gabriel Johnston of North Carolina, 1748; *f. 172.* Observations on the colony of North Carolina, 1748.

No. 32718. f. 43. Letter from the inhabitants of Barbados to J. Sharpe, 1749.

No. 32720. f. 5. John Russell, *Falcon* at Spithead, Jan. 2, 1749/50, upon arrival from Jamaica, asks to be continued in command of the sloop; *f. 15.* John Eadie (his mark) requests £2000, South Carolina, Jan. 5; *f. 74.* Lord Colvill of the *Success* to Capt. Holbourne (copy), reports being fired at by the French, Carlisle Bay, Feb. 5, 1749/50; *f. 84.* Ab. Cayley, Feb. 8, includes "thoughts" on trade to Spanish West Indies; *f. 85.* Paper in same hand; *f. 151.* Thomas Graham (enclosure) complains of having been "divested by the Assembly of Jamaica from the office of Receiver" and reports death of his deputy, n.d.; *f. 156.* Bishop of London, March 23, sends representation of the Church of England in America, etc. (missing); *f. 160.* Newcastle's answer, March 25; *f. 311.* H. Pelham to his brother, the Duke of Newcastle, May 11, sending for H.M.'s signature warrants, one for Sir T. Robinson, mentioning his (Robinson's) residence in Barbados and honesty in his conduct; rest of letter about English affairs; *f. 405.* Lord Hardwicke, May 25, 1750, with one paragraph regarding the S.P.G.'s consideration of bishoprics in America; *f. 409.* Proceedings of the S.P.G.

No. 32721. f. 39. H. Pelham, June 5, 1750; *f. 42b.* is a mere mention of letters from Nova Scotia, expressing dislike of them; *f. 47.* Hardwicke writes, June 6; *f. 49.* contains a paragraph referring to the S.P.G. and the Bishop of London, perhaps concerning America; *f. 58.* H. Walpole, Cockpit, June 7, about the following paper; *ff. 60–68.* Long letter to Bishop of London about bishoprics in America, May 29; *f. 79.* Newcastle to Pelham, Hanover, June 9/20; *ff. 81b–82,* and *85, 87.* Concern the Duke of Bedford and affairs in Nova Scotia; *ff. 91–93b.* Dupplin, Bath, June 9; *ff. 92b* and *93b.* Concern letters received from Gov. Cornwallis regarding Nova Scotia and the French; *f. 109.* Bishop of Salisbury, June 14/25, includes a paragraph on an S.P.G. meeting, perhaps concerning its American business; *f. 113.* Pelham to his brother, June 15, expressing dissatisfaction with affairs in the West Indies; *f. 119.* Newcastle to Pelham, Hanover, June 17/23, containing one or two references to Nova Scotia; *f. 145.* Hardwicke, June 22; *f. 145b.* Paragraph on Nova Scotia; *f. 153.* Newcastle to Pelham, June 23/July 4, a long letter; *f. 157b.* Also about Nova Scotia; *f. 167.* Newcastle to Horatio Walpole, June 24/July 5, in answer to *f. 58; f. 185.* H. Pelham, June 26, with mention of Nova Scotia; *f. 192.* Newcastle to Pitt, June 26/July 7, and *ff. 248, 251,* July 4/15, partly on the same business; *f. 254.* H. Pelham, July 2; *f. 256.* is still about Nova Scotia; *f. 283.* W. Pitt, July 6, has some words about the same; *f. 341.* Newcastle to Pelham, July 11/22, including postscript with the following sentence: "I think the king is for bishops in the W. Indies"; *f. 369.* H. Walpole, July 14, the first few lines are about episcopacy in the West Indies; *f. 386.* Newcastle to Pelham, July 18/29; *ff. 390b–391.* About Nova Scotia; *f. 394.* is a duplicate; *f. 406.* Lord Halifax about Nova Scotia, July 20; *f. 449.* Wm. Mathew, from the Leeward Islands, asks continuance of support, July 26.

No. 32732. f. 663. Letter from the Board of Trade to the governor of New York, 1753; *f. 668.* Minutes of Gov. Clinton's meeting with the Mohawk Indians at New York, June, 1753.

No. 32735. ff. 119, 123, 129. Papers relating to the province of Massachusetts Bay, 1754.

No. 32736. f. 515. Plans for defence of the colony of Virginia, 1754.

No. 32737. f. 16. Thoughts on a supporting military force in America, 1754.

No 32816. f. 374. Memoir of the pretensions of the French to the island of Tobago, 1749. (In French). For description of the island in 1752, see *No. 32840, f. 367.*

No. 32818. ff. 53, 67. Copies of minutes of council held at Ft. George in New York City, Feb. 23, 1748, March 9, 22, 23, 1748, March 27, 1749 (with duplicate), April 4, 1749; *f. 73.* Extract of letter from Gov. Shirley to the Marquis de la Galissonière, governor-general of New France, Albany, July 29, 1748; *ff. 75–93.* Copies of documents relating to the French and Indians.

No. 32819. ff. 25, 106, 135. Orders to Gov. Grenville of Barbados for evacuating St. Lucia, St. Vincent, Dominica and Tobago, 1749; *ff. 147–181.* Papers relating to the Asiento of Negroes, 1749; *f. 188.* Consideration on British trade to the Spanish West Indies, 1749; *ff. 258, 271.* Orders for the exchange of Indian prisoners, with remarks, 1749.

No. 32821. f. 52. Commission to Lieut. Patrick Drummond for evacuation of the island of Tobago, 1750; *f. 54.* Letter from the same to Gov. Grenville, 1750; *f. 305.* Memoir (in French) protesting insult to the French flag at Nevis, 1750; *f. 345.* Journal of detachment under command of Maj. Charles Lawrence, governor of Nova Scotia, in the basin of the Chignecto, 1750.

No. 32826. f. 182. Decree of Benjamin Greene, judge of the vice-admiralty court in Nova Scotia, concerning a French vessel seized by an English ship, 1751.

No. 32828. f. 142. Means of conciliation between France and England in America, 1751.

No. 32831. ff. 231, 233. Correspondence of Comte Raymond, governor of Louisbourg, with Gov. Cornwallis, 1751.

No. 32837. f. 223. French commander's summons to Lieut. Ward, April 16, 1754, enclosed in letter from Gov. Dinwiddie.

No. 32850. f. 231. Extract from the *Gazette* relative to action with the French, Virginia, 1754.

No. 32851. f. 108. Intelligence of French troops being sent to the Mississippi, 1754; *f. 309.* News-letter from New York, 1754.

No. 32852. f. 108. Address of the Assembly of Pennsylvania to George III, 1755; *ff. 200–258.* Miscellaneous papers relating to Jamaica, 1775.

No. 32853. f. 13. Instructions to missionaries in North America agreed on at a special meeting of the S.P.G. Undated, but as document was transmitted in a letter from the Archbishop of York to the Duke of Newcastle dated March 1, 1755/6, it probably was drawn up in 1755 or 1756.

No. 32854. f. 252. Proposals concerning French ships trading to the West Indies, 1755; *f. 379.* News of Virginia from John Hanbury, 1755.

No. 32856. ff. 195–203. Papers relating to the capitulation of the forts in Nova Scotia in 1755.

No. 32857. f. 218. Copy of letter from Col. George Washington to Gov. Dinwiddie, 1755.

No. 32864. f. 68. On opening French West India trade, 1756; *ff. 107, 109.* Papers concerning Royal American regiment, 1756. (See also *No. 33055, f. 143.*)

No. 32868. f. 11. Information regarding state of Fort Niagara, 1756.

No. 32874. ff. 280–286. Petitions from Gov. Wm. Shirley to George II, 1757–1758.

No. 32882. ff. 149–177. Material concerning Newfoundland, 1758; *f. 245.* Resolution on conduct of the war, 1758.

No. 32888. f. 252. Proposals for American stamp duties, 1759.

No. 32895. ff. 89–94. Papers from Gen. Wolfe, regarding the town of Quebec, 1759; *ff. 449–457.* Account of battle outside Quebec, 1759.

No. 32900. f. 86. List of troops at Quebec, 1759.

No. 32901. f. 219. Petition from Mosquito Coast inhabitants to the governor of Jamaica, 1760; *f. 417.* Account of free schools in Pennsylvania, 1760.

No. 32902. f. 458. Letter from Beeston Long, Sr., chairman of the West Indian merchants of London to the Duke of Newcastle, Feb. 28, 1760. The communication is the earliest known document connected with this commercial organization, whose extant minute books date from only 1769; *f. 460.* Memorial to the Duke of Newcastle about the sugar trade, 1760.

No. 32906. f. 96. Notes of events at Quebec, 1759–1760.

No. 32933. f. 430. British investment of Martinique, 1762.

No. 32934. f. 283. List of those holding money for the German emigrants, 1762. Printed paper.

No. 32938. f. 356. A Barbados planter's reflections on British interests in the Caribbee Islands, 1762.

No. 32941. ff. 289, 293. News-letters from Havana, 1762.

No. 32942. f. 215. Notice of naval attack on Cuba in 1762.

No. 32969. f. 380. Circular letter from Charles Lowndes of the Treasury to governors in America and the West Indies, 1765.

No. 32971. f. 18. Added restrictions to be placed on foreign nations importing to or exporting from the British West Indies; *f. 64.* "An Acc^t of Bullion imported and brought to the Bank from the several colonies in North America from 1748 to 1764 inclusive"; *f. 93.* Copy of letter from the British government to Gov. Bernard, reprimanding him for not suppressing tumults in Massachusetts. Also included are similar letters to other colonial governors (to *f. 128*), Oct. 24, 1765, and copies of documents regarding colonial unrest resulting from the Stamp Act.

No. 32973. *ff. 246, 332.* Resolutions on American affairs, 1766. (*f. 332* also includes a letter from the Archbishop of Canterbury).

No. 32975. *f. 250.* Resolution of the House of Commons concerning imports into America, 1766; *f. 477.* Vote of thanks to the Duke of Newcastle from the House of Representatives of Massachusetts Bay, 1766.

No. 32980. *f. 116.* Protest of House of Representatives of Massachusetts Bay against the Stamp Act, 1767.

No. 32981. *ff. 48, 51.* Extracts from Journals of the Upper House of Assembly of Georgia, 1767.

No. 32982, *ff. 16, 21, 29, 79, 225.* Documents relating to the province of Quebec, 1764, 1767; *f. 25.* Copy of law officers' report on Canada's Roman Catholic inhabitants, 1765; *ff. 62, 64, 66, 68, 71, 73, 97, 121, 134, 198.* Papers relating to the province of Massachusetts Bay, 1767.

No. 33028. *f. 376.* "Reasons Humbly Offered in Support of a Proposal lately made to extend the Duties on Stampt Paper and Parchment all over the British Plantations," by Sir William Keith, Dec. 14, 1742. Early but important.

No. 33029. *f. 1.* Order in council regarding defence of Newfoundland, July 19, 1744; *f. 50.* Copy of letter from Grey Cooper to Gov. Francis Bernard, concerning attitude of Lords of the Treasury toward stamp problems in Boston, Oct., Nov. 1765; *f. 53.* "An Acc^t Stated which if pursued proves the Ruin and Destruction of the Massachusetts," referring to bills of credit; *f. 54.* "An Account Stated proving the Method to secure and safeguard New England," n.d.; *ff. 57–62.* Extract of Act of Parliament regarding allowance of sixpence per every pound weight of indigo of the growth of the British plantations in America imported into England from and after March 25, 1749; *f. 63.* "The State of the Ecclesiastical Jurisdiction in the Plantations in America," n.d.; *f. 65.* For the Ecclesiastical Jurisdiction in the Plantations; *f. 67.* Extract of papers relating to releasing prisoners of war at New York and Canada, 1748/9; *f. 71.* Regarding expiration of Trusteeship in Georgia, 1751; *f. 72.* Copy of Memorial of Trustees for Establishing the Colony of Georgia in America; *f. 83.* Memorial of Peter Schuyler sent to Gov. G. Clinton of New York, July 19, 1751, with Clinton's reply; *f. 85.* Schuyler's commission as colonel "upon the intended expedition against Canada" (attested copy); *ff. 88–90.* Board of Trade papers sent by Lord Holderness to "my Lord President," Jan. 22, 1752; *f. 92.* "Memorandum of the State of the Naval Offices in America that are not filled up from home, most humbly submitted to the consideration of his Grace the Duke of Newcastle," n.d.; *f. 94.* Abstract of a letter from Gov. Knowles of Jamaica to the Earl of Holderness, March 26, 1753, *re* Mosquito

Shore. A list of the papers enclosed is noted on the back; *ff. 96–103*. "The Proceedings of the French in America of which Great Britain has cause of complaint"; *f. 104*. "Considerations with respect to the manner of appointing a secretary of state for Plantation affairs"; *f. 106*. Abstract of letter from Gov. Dinwiddie, Virginia, March 12, 1754; *f. 109*. Proposal for strengthening defences upon the Ohio and other rivers to stop French encroachments; *f. 113*. Proceedings of the French in America, delivered by the Earl of Halifax to Sir Thomas Robinson, April 1754; *f. 119*. "Heads of Gov. Shirley's despatches. April 19, and May 1." [1754]; *f. 122*. "An Estimate of the Charges of the Civil Establishment of his Majesty's colony of Georgia and other incidental expenses attending the same from June 24, 1754, to June 21, 1755"; *f. 124*. Minute of a [Council] meeting at Newcastle House concerning the French in North America, June 26, 1754; *f. 126*. Draft of the king's warrant authorizing application of £3544. 10s. 5d. of Virginia's revenue to defence of the frontiers; *f. 128*. Draft of a similar warrant; *f. 130*. Extract of letter to Messrs. John and Capel Hanbury, Virginia, July 23, 1754; *f. 136*. Schedule of papers relating to North America in letter from Lord Halifax, Aug. 15, 1754; *f. 138*. "Methods of disappointing the French encroachments in North America." Delivered by Lord Halifax, Nov. 7, 1754; *f. 144*. "Sketch for the Operations in North America," Nov. 16, 1754; *f. 152*. Extract of letter from Bristol containing information given by certain persons from New York regarding Spanish attacks on the Mosquito Shore, Dec. 16, 1754; *f. 156*. Copy of representation of state of the colonies in North America, 1754; *f. 165*. Estimate of charges of supporting and maintaining settlement of his Majesty's colony of Nova Scotia for the year, 1755; *f. 167*. "Lord Halifax' observations on Thomas Robinson's paper of Points" [Feb. 1755]; *f. 172*. "Extract of private letter, dated New York, March 19, 1755"; *f. 174*. "At a council held at the Camp at Alexandria in Virginia, April 14, 1755," included in Gen. Braddock's letter of April 19, 1755; *f. 182–196*. Extracts of letters and papers pertaining to Jamaica; *f. 198*. (1) Account of Braddock's defeat; (2) Maj.-Gen. Shirley's plan of operations for destroying the French settlements on the Lakes; *f. 202*. "Plan for the Reduction of Canada," from Maj.-Gen. Shirley, Oneida, Aug. 15 [1755]; *f. 204*. Extracts of letters: from Pres. Phips, Massachusetts, Aug. 30; Mr. Fitch, Connecticut, Aug. 1; Gov. Dobbs, North Carolina, Aug. 25, and Rhode Island, April 17, 1755, and agent's petition, July 1755; *f. 206*. "A Representation of the Case of his Maj. province of Massachusetts Bay, contained in a letter from the General Assembly to their agent, dated Boston, Sept. 25, 1755"; *f. 210*. Letters from Gov. Dinwiddie of Virginia, Aug.

17, 20, Sept. 6; *f. 212.* Concerning disputes between Gov. Shirley and Gen. Johnson, Sept. 3; *f. 219.* From Gov. Lawrence of Nova Scotia, relating to forts and French inhabitants; *f. 223.* From Maj.-Gen. Shirley, Oswego, Sept. 19; *f. 227.* From Deputy Governor Morris, Oct. 28; *f. 229.* From Gov. Fitch of Connecticut, Oct. 30; *f. 232.* From Gov. Lawrence, Nova Scotia, Nov. 10; *f. 234.* From Gov. Dinwiddie, Nov. 15; *f. 238.* From Sir C. Hardy, New York, Nov. 27; *f. 242.* Mr. Hanbury's paper containing proposal regarding employment of Indians and formation of men; *f. 243.* "Information préalable, pour servir d'Introduction au Narré." The narration begins with *f. 255:* "Narré des Hostilités commises sur l'Ohio en Amérique, par les François, et de la Négociation que s'en est suivie entres couronnes de la Grand Bretagne et de France," April 1754, to 1755. Translation of the narration begins in *f. 272; f. 289.* "Upon the Four Points to be discussed relating to America," the only important being point 3, "The Course and Territory of the Ohio," *(ff. 300–309); f. 313.* Memorandum regarding French project; *f. 315.* Project for proper separation of the British and French dominions in North America, endorsed "from Alderman Baker, North America"; *f. 318.* "Draft of a preamble to an order granting general reprisals against France"; *f. 322.* Extract of letter from New England, regarding illegal trade with Canada, undated and unsigned; *f. 324.* State of New England and French forts, garrisons and militia in Nova Scotia; *f. 330.* Advertisement to be prefixed to English and French memorials; *f. 332.* State of Actual Possessions of the Crown of Great Britain; inquiry into state of the actual possessions of the Crown of Great Britain in North America at time of the treaty of Utrecht in order to discover "whether all the encroachments or most of them complained of to have been made by the French in North America have been since the conclusion of the treaty or contrary to the conditions of the cessions made thereby"; *f. 337.* Paper (imperfect) on recruits for established regiments; *f. 343.* Paper given to Lord Barrington, Secretary at War, by Lieut.-Col. Bouquet relating to the raising of militia in Pennsylvania; *f. 345.* "Reflections on the Present State of America"; *f. 349.* Scheme for the taking of part of the island of Dominique, etc., by Thos. Cole; *f. 354.* "Members of the House of Assembly in Philadelphia as they stood October 14, 1756"; *f. 355.* Extract of letter from Christopher Wilson and John Hunt, dated Philadelphia 4 of 11mo 1756; *f. 357.* "Plea for protection of Carolina and Georgia and for conquest of Louisiana," 1756; *f. 372.* "Instructions for Dan. Webb, Esq., General and Commander of all our forces in North America," March 11, 1756; *f. 378.* "To his Grace the Duke of Newcastle. Some thoughts on the French scheme and the importance of the country on the river Ohio to Great Britain" by Peter Collinson, Feb. 25, 1757; *f. 385*. Memorial of William Bollan, agent for Massachusetts Bay, to Lords of the Admiralty.

No. 33030. f. 1. Speculation regarding division of territory after the war between England and France, April 13, 1761; *f. 3*. Complaints of colonels of battalions in the Royal American regiment, their widows and executors upon accounts with the agent; *f. 5*. Regarding French fishing rights off Newfoundland. The next several folios contain extracts from similar documents, endorsed as "collection relating to fishing"; *f. 15*. State of duties on rum, etc., imported into America, 1763; *f. 47*. Query regarding the importation of coin into the plantations in foreign bottoms. Favorable answer from Yorke and de Grey, attorney and solicitor generals, dated Nov. 11, 1765. (See also *f. 69*); *f. 54*. "Précis of the American Correspondence from August 31 to November 9, 1765"; *f. 74*. Various papers belonging to or coming from a committee, either of the House of Commons or of the Privy Council, on American Papers, Jan. 31, Feb. 11, 12, 13, 17, 1766. Copy among these papers of "resolution proposed" by the committee, Jan. 31, 1766, regarding the "tumults and insurrections" in America; *f. 78*. Dr. Moffatt's account of riots at his house in Rhode Island, given at a hearing on Jan. 31; *f. 84* and *f. 86b*. Long accounts of riots in New York and Virginia, respectively; *f. 88*. Petition of the Merchants of London with Trecothick's comments; *f. 206*. Agreement reached at a meeting of committees of West Indian and North American merchants at the Kings Arms tavern, March 10, 1766; *f. 208*. Petition of merchants trading to North America to Parliament; *f. 210*. Petition of London merchants; *f. 214*. Allegations in petition of London merchants with Mr. Trecothick's proofs and observations; *f. 318*. "Observations on the Trade of Great Britain to her American colonies and on their trade to Foreign Plantations with plan for retrieving, extending and securing thereof." Endorsed "Mr. Huske's scheme for free ports in America." Undated, but probably between 1764 and 1766; *f. 334*. Plan for raising a fund in America to be applied in defraying necessary expenses attending the defence and protection of the British possessions in America, by means of a stamp act. Unsigned and undated; *f. 339*. Albany Plan of Union, 1754. The document is important for its marginal notes; immediately following is a paper by Lord Dupplin on the same subject; *f. 345*. Testimony before committee of the Whole House of Commons on Debates over Stamp Act; *f. 346*. Regarding governorship of South Carolina, salary of which was to be made up to £2400; *f. 351*. Extract of act for establishing agreement with seven of the Lords Proprietors of Carolina, for surrender of their title and interest in that province to his Majesty, early but important; *f. 353.* "Observations on a petition to the King now lying before the Lords of his Majesty's Privy Council, from some merchants and others trading to and interested in the province of So. Carolina"; *f. 355.* Note from Lord Lyttelton to the Duke of Newcastle, regarding demand for cannon from Gov. Lyttelton of South Carolina, n.d.; *f. 357.* Statement, apparently by the Earl of Lincoln, of what is to be written to Gov. Clinton of New York by the Council or by the Duke of Newcastle, n.d.; *f. 372.* State of the Crown's title to Nova Scotia; *f. 384.* Description of "the Havana"; *f. 392.* "Consideration on the laws made for the increase of navigation and for the regulation of the plantation trade so far as they relate to the Bullion trade"; *f. 394.* Draft of letter to New England concerning the violations of the plantation laws; *f. 401.* "State of an illegal and clandestine trade carried on by the British Northern Colonies in America with the French and other foreign nations both in Europe and America destructive to our own sugar settlements and greatly detrimental to the Navigation, Trade, and Manufacturers of Great Britain." No signature or date.

Nos. 33046–33048. These volumes contain a great deal of information and many statistics regarding the army and navy arrangements of the years 1755–1756.

No. 33046. f. 361. List of his Majesty's ships on commission, including those in American waters, 1755, 1756.

No. 33047. f. 22. Data concerning Shirley and Pepperrell's regiments; *ff. 45, 47, 61, 101.* Lists of ships in American waters; *f. 65.* Account of the French and English army and fleet, dated 1756; *ff. 108–109.* Lists of troops destined for Louisbourg and remaining with Lord Loudoun, sent by Ligonier; *f. 127.* Augmentation of plantation forces; *ff. 205–207.* Regarding forces in America, 1757, 1758. See also *ff. 239–304.*

No. 33048. Of character similar to preceding volume; *f. 14* contains list of expenses of the fleet, including ships in American waters.

No. 33055. ff. 27, 286, 310. Various memorials from John Hammerton, secretary and treasurer of South Carolina, asking for reinstatement in the council; *f. 33.* Memorandum on state of naval offices of Virginia, before being filled by the Crown, c. 1752; *f. 143.* Document regarding the Royal American regiment, 1756; *f. 240.* Memorial from Gov. Shirley of Massachusetts Bay for repayment of expenses, c. 1759; *f. 294.* Memorial from Lieut. Robert Hodgson to succeed his late father as superintendent of the Mosquito Shore, c. 1760; *f. 340.* Memorandum by Capt. Prescott, aide-de-camp to Gen. Amherst, of his expenses in the public service, c. 1761.

No. 33056. ff. 54, 202. William Tryon's appointment as governor of North

Carolina, 1765, 1766; *f. 56*. Henry Moore's appointment as governor of New York, 1765.

No. 33231. G.G. Canada: plan of Wolfe's attack on Quebec, 1759, and thirteen other unidentified plans; *N.N. 2*. Plan of the city of Albany shewing the several works and buildings made there in the year 1756–1757; *N.N. 3*. Detailed map of Crown Point showing woods, roads, lookouts, etc.; *N.N. 4*. Detailed map of Ft. Ticonderoga, 1759; *N.N. 5*. Detailed map of Ft. George, Lake George, with barracks, etc., erected in 1759; also road to Fort Edward through the woods southward; *N.N. 6*. Detailed map of new fort at Pittsburg, 1759; *N.N. 7*. Detailed map of Fort Ligonier (Loyalhanna Creek, Pa.); *N.N. 9*. Fort Bedford on Juniata Creek, Pennsylvania; *O.O. 2–5*. Plans of forts in Carlisle Bay, Barbados.

Nos. 33316, 33317. Brief diary, 1758–1794, and account-book, 1758–1810, of James Pinnock, a Jamaica barrister.

No. 33923. ff. 510–521. Wolfe-Amherst Correspondence, June-Aug. 1758, comprises a series of copies apparently made in connection with a monument to be erected to Wolfe in the parish of Westerham, Kent, April 5, 1760, with letters addressed to the Rev. Mr. Streatfield, Charts Edge, Westerham, Sevenoaks, including some valuable notes pertaining to Wolfe's life, the monument and epitaph, from *f. 522* to *f. 526*.

No. 33929. ff. 60–62. Extracts from Gen. Wolfe's letters to his parents, 1749–1759.

No. 34207. Letters from Col. William Burrard to his brother, Sir Harry Burrard, written mostly from the West Indies, 1740–1766, including: *f. 28*. Description of the taking of Fort Louis, March 8, 1748; *f. 39b*. Plan of Santiago de Cuba, 1748, and numerous documents regarding Burrard's case, 1748–1776.

No. 34287. Clavering-Francis correspondence relating to India, letters, 1774–1777. Letters of Clavering refer to measures concerted between himself, Francis, and Col. George Monson against Warren Hastings in India.

Nos. 34412–34471. The Auckland Papers. Correspondence and papers, political and private, of William Eden, 1st Baron Auckland, together with a few earlier diplomatic papers collected by him. William Eden was under secretary of state for the Northern Department, 1772–1778, and one of the Peace Commissioners sent to America in 1778. *No. 34412. f. 29ff*. Copies of Pitt's correspondence with Dr. Benjamin Keene, concerning Gibraltar, 1757; *f. 269b*. Statistics showing duty on tobacco imported into Holland; *f. 320*. Printed list of goods prohibited to be imported into or exported from Great Britain, Jan. 1, 1775; *ff. 321, 322*. Same list, with references to the Acts of Prohibition; *f. 345*. Draft of proclamation suppressing "rebellion and sedition," 1771, with marginal notes;

f. 366–368. Notes of a speech to be delivered by Eden against the American Revolution, entitled "Minutes," Oct. 26, 1775.

No. 35155. ff. 13–20. Various papers relating to the West Indies, particularly Grenada, Dominica, St. Vincent, 1764–1774.

No. 35192. ff. 1–18, 49. Letters from the Earl of Chatham to Adm. Hood, 1773–1777. For additional Pitt letters, consult the index to the Hardwicke papers.

Nos. 35349–36278. Hardwicke Papers. Correspondence and collections of the first four earls of Hardwicke and other members of the Yorke family in the eighteenth and nineteenth centuries. The material is divided into two parts: *Nos. 35349–35813,* correspondence, and *Nos. 35814–36278,* papers. The Hardwicke documents that follow relate to developments within the period under examination:

Nos. 35374–35375. Letters from Hon. Joseph Yorke to Lord Hardwicke, 1747–1787. Yorke was British minister and later ambassador at the Hague.

No. 35376. f. 127. Letter from Elizabeth Yorke, Lady Anson, to her brother Philip Yorke, Lord Hardwicke, giving long account of Braddock's defeat, July 9, 1755.

No. 35414. f. 155. "Plan for a concert of the colonies," 1754. Albany Plan.

No. 35415. f. 55. "Considerations of what may be necessary to be done in consequence of the late defeat in North America, upon same discourse with my Lord Anson, Sir Thomas Robinson, and Sir John Ligonier," Claremount, Aug. 25, 1755.

No. 35427. Letters to Philip Yorke, second earl of Hardwicke, from Thomas Hutchinson, 1774–1778, supplementing the letters from Lord Hardwicke in the Hutchinson papers, which are often the answers to the letters in this volume. It is said that "Lord Hardwicke honored Gov. Hutchinson with his entire confidence on American affairs." The letters, sent from St. James St., New Bond St., and Sackville St., contain a number of enclosures. At the end is a letter from John Hutchinson, Blunton Parsonage, Saturday, Oct. 15, 1825, speaking of his intended publication of his grandfather's manuscripts.

No. 35444. ff. 163, 168, 334, 336. Papers on the Dutch trade to Essequibo in Demarara, 1772.

No. 35478. ff. 241–266. Dispute between England and France concerning Nova Scotia, 1755.

No. 35504. f. 111. Letter from Sir Basil Keith, governor of Jamaica, to his brother Sir R. M. Keith, 1772.

No. 35588. ff. 33, 224. Letters from Jonathan Belcher, Jr., chief justice of Nova Scotia, to Lord Hardwicke, 1742–1755.

No. 35590. ff. 251, 273, 407. Letters from Count Zinzendorf, founder and bishop of Herrnhut sect of Moravian brethren, to the first Lord Hardwicke, 1749.

No. 35591. f. 258. Letter of Richard Rigby, paymaster of the Forces, to W. Sharpe, 1757.

No. 35593. f. 234. Narrative of Braddock's defeat, 1755.

No. 35597. f. 153. News-letter from Havana, 1762. See also *No. 35898. f. 276.*

No. 35606. f. 150. Letter from Gov. Benning Wentworth of New Hampshire to Sir. T. Robinson, 1755.

No. 35609. f. 36b. Letter from Thomas Yorke of Philadelphia to the second Lord Hardwicke, 1771.

No. 35639. f. 202. Memorial from Edward Dismore, postmaster-general of Jamaica, to Lord Leicester, postmaster-general, 1758–1759.

No. 35640. ff. 211, 301. Letters from Dr. Samuel Cooper to Charles Yorke, Lord Hardwicke, 1767, 1768.

No. 35870. f. 222. Minutes by Lord Hardwicke of a cabinet council, on "sending a further sea-force to Nova Scotia," March 28, 1751; *ff. 280, 284.* Minutes of cabinet relating to the war, Sept. 5, Oct. 7, 1757.

Nos. 35872, 35873, 35874. Warrants addressed to Philip Yorke, as Lord High Chancellor, regarding passes prepared by the Secretary of State for ships exporting American tobacco from England to France, 1745–1748, 1756.

No. 35877. f. 38. Bill relating to bequests of real estate in America, 1752.

No. 35893. ff. 232–237. Copies of correspondence of Gen. Wolfe with his brigadiers relating to plan for the attack on Quebec, Aug.–Sept. 1759. Also letter from Capt. Alexander Schomberg to Adm. Forbes, Boston, Sept. 5, 1759; *f. 245.* Lists of troops serving in America, 1759.

No. 35894. f. 28. Minutes of court martial of Lieut. Charles Lord Hay for mutinous speeches in North America in 1757, dated 1760.

No. 35898. f. 264. Extract of a letter from Adm. Rodney, Martinique, Feb. 10, 1762. (For other Rodney letters, see *ff. 27, 28, 32, 33, 35*); *f. 276.* Intelligence from Havana, endorsed in Lord Halifax's letter, Aug. 18, 1762; *f. 278.* Letter from Adm. Cornish to Lord Anson on operations in Manila, Nov. 1, 1762; *f. 291.* Account of the number of merchant ships, with special mention of the fisheries, n.d.; *f. 292.* Letter from the collector of customs, Rhode Island, regarding burning of the *Gaspee*, July 23, 1772.

No. 35909. f. 119. Papers relating to dispute between Lord Baltimore and the Penns together with Hardwicke's autograph notes, printed papers, and maps, 1750; *f. 137.* Resolutions of the S.P.G. concerning bishops in America, 1750; *f. 156.* Abstract of negotiations at Paris about limits of Nova Scotia, 1752; *ff. 168, 169.* Statements of annual expense, c. 1765, and debts, c. 1772, of the British American colonies; *ff. 176–278.* Various papers relating to defence of the colonies, 1754–1756.

No. 35910. Hardwicke Papers relating to America, 1759–1764. *ff. 1, 3, 32, 34, 110.* Correspondence of Philip Yorke, Lord Hardwicke, with Capt. John Reynolds and Capt. Edward Smith, 1760; *f. 5.* Memorial relating to bounties on linen; *f. 9.* Memorial against Hudson's Bay Company; *f. 14.* Memorial about naturalizing foreigners preparatory to their holding military commissions in the colonies; *f. 16.* Earl of Morton's plan for settling dispute with France in North America, Jan. 15, 1760; *f. 36.* Draft reports by solicitor general, Charles Yorke, to the committee of the Privy Council, on report of Board of Trade, concerning nineteen acts passed in Pennsylvania, Aug. 19, 1760; *f. 108.* Copy of letter from Lieut.-Gov. Bull of South Carolina to Board of Trade, Sept. 9, 1760; *f. 116.* Notes "of the Pretence set up by France of a Ball[ance] of power in America," n.d.; *f. 118.* "State of the case relating to importation of American iron," n.d.; *ff. 130, 229, 231, 292.* Copies of letters from Sir William Johnson, to Board of Trade, 1763, 1764; *f. 134.* Order in council relating to alteration of boundaries of Georgia, Oct. 5, 1763; *ff. 136–205, 310–323.* Papers relating to Stamp Act, particularly the proposals by Henry McCulloh, Oct. 10, Nov. 8, 1763; and Mr. Whately's plan of a stamp act (*f. 311.*); *f. 164.* Act for erecting stamp office in New York, 1757; *ff. 166–203.* List of stamp duties intended to be used in America and the West Indies; *ff. 206–215.* Extracts from colonial laws which show the fees imposed; *f. 218.* Papers regarding Lord Hardwicke's appointment as chancellor of William and Mary College, 1764; *ff. 224, 225.* Papers relating to establishment of an admiralty court for all America, May 18, 1763, June 18, 1764; *ff. 229, 231.* Treaties with Indians in America, 1764; *f. 233.* Papers relating to disputes between Gov. Boone and the assembly of South Carolina, 1763–1764; *f. 292.* Copies of various letters including extracts of letters from Gen. Gage to the Earl of Halifax, 1764; *f. 302.* Letter of the House of Representatives of Massachusetts Bay to I. Mauduit, their agent in England, 1764.

No. 35911. Hardwicke Papers relating to America, 1765. The papers in this volume concern admiralty court jurisdiction and the Stamp Act, with copies of letters from various colonies describing the unrest caused by the act. Included is a large printed folio, entitled, "Copies and extracts of several newspapers printed in New England in the months of September, October, and November, 1765, and referred to in the letters transmitted from Francis Bernard, Esq., governor of Massachusetts, to the Lords Commissioners for Trade and Plantations." *f. 60.* is a copy of a letter from Benjamin Franklin to William Shirley, Boston, Dec. 4, 1754, regarding the Albany convention and colonial taxation.

No. 35912. Hardwicke Papers relating to America, 1766–1783. Here are numerous letters and papers, manuscript and printed, concerning the Stamp Act and its repeal: *f. 158*. Printed copy of William Bollan's "An Appeal to the World or a Vindication of the Town of Boston," 1769; *f. 221*. Lord Camden's speech in the House of Lords, May 11, 1774; *ff. 76, 108, 112, 151, 221*. Other proceedings in the House of Lords concerning America; *f. 223*. Papers relating to the War for American Independence.

Nos. 35913–35915. Hardwicke Papers relating to Canada and Newfoundland, 1712–1773. Three volumes. Well catalogued.

No. 35913. f. 67. Intelligence on French forces in Canada from Col. Peter Schuyler of the New Jersey regiment, a French prisoner at Quebec, obtained by Joseph Morse, Oct. 4, 1757; *f. 69*. Paper by Baron Lyttelton on the war in America [1758]; *f. 73*. Considerations regarding the colonies in view of approaching peace between France and Great Britain, April 19, 1761.

No. 35914. f. 1. Appointment of Fowler Walker as agent for Quebec; *f. 47*. Papers relating to Isle St. John (later called Prince Edward Island), 1765.

No. 35916. Hardwicke Papers relating to the West Indies, 1734–1803. Well catalogued.

No. 36054. f. 1. Notes in Chancery relating to Maryland, 1743–1755.

No. 36063, ff. 89, 91. Suit, Attorney General *vs.* Jonathan Belcher.

Nos. 36125–36133. Hardwicke Papers, containing warrants to the attorney or solicitor general for patents for public officials, etc., with accompanying papers, 1756–1766. These were signed by the King or Lords Justices and countersigned by the Secretaries of State. The documents that concern colonial officials, etc., follow: *No. 36131. f. 50*. Maj.-Gen. Abercromby, commander-in-chief, North America, 1757; *f. 61*. Henry Ellis, governor of Georgia, 1758; *f. 82*. Francis Bernard, governor of Massachusetts, 1759; *f. 94*. Thomas Boone, governor of South Carolina, 1759; *f. 118*. Lord Amherst, commander-in-chief, North America, 1760; *f. 237*. James Webb, governor of Newfoundland, 1761. *No. 36132. f. 125*. William Franklin, governor of New Jersey, 1762; *f. 259*. Thomas Graves, governor of Newfoundland, 1763; *ff. 313, 315*. Percy Charles Wyndham, secretary of Barbados and register of Jamaica in reversion, 1763. *No. 36133. f. 21*. Edward Bishop, clerk of naval office in Canada, 1763; *f. 25*. Edward Horn, attorney general of Grenada, 1763; *f. 51*. James Murray, governor of Quebec, 1763; *f. 61*. James Grant, governor of East Florida, 1763; *f. 71*. George Johnstone, governor of West Florida, 1763; *f. 151*. Lord Charles Greville Montagu, governor of South Carolina, 1766; *f. 241*. John Wentworth, governor of New Hampshire, 1766.

No. 36194. f. 93. Lawsuit of Francis Tench of Philadelphia, 1767. See also *No. 36225, f. 309*.

Nos. 36217–36220. Printed statements of cases on appeal from the plantations to the Privy Council, first of plaintiff or appellant and then
of defendant or respondent. The cases were heard before the
Council Committee on Appeals from the Plantation. These printed
documents, probably not readily accessible elsewhere, are full of
valuable information; on many of them are difficult-to-read marginal notes by Attorney General Yorke. Those cases falling within
the period 1748–1776 follow:

No. 36217. f. 1. James MacSparran, of St. Paul's Church in Petequamscut,
Rhode Island, 1752. (On this famous case see *Talcott Papers*,
Conn. Hist. Soc., *Collections*, V(1896), 462; *ff. 25, 27, 30*. Bon-
tien, naval officer, case of ship seized, Jamaica, 1753; *ff. 34, 38*.
Antigua case, John Dunbar *vs.* attorney general of Leeward Islands, Feb. 6, 1753; *f. 46*. William Vassall, case of defamation of
character, New England, Jan. 22, 1754; *f. 70*. Vassell's petition
with notes by Yorke on the back of last folio, manuscript; *f. 103*.
St. Christopher case, Jan. 11, 1757; *f. 123*. Jamaica case, March
22, 1757; *f. 139*. Jamaica case, n.d.; *f. 152*. St. Christopher case,
May 19, 1757; *f. 161*. Charles Dunbar of Antigua *vs.* Daniel Parke
Custis, Virginia, June 24, 1757; *f. 172*. Barbados case, July 8, 1757;
f. 185. Jamaica case, n.d.; *f. 199*. Lidderdale and Harmer, merchants of Bristol, *vs.* John Chiswell of Virginia, planter, Virginia,
Feb. 27, 1758; *f. 208*. Jamaica case, March 6, 1758.

No. 36218. f. 1. Daniel Stanton of Philadelphia *vs.* Elias Thompson, a
case of land ownership in Misquamacuck, Rhode Island, March
2, 1759; *f. 11*. Jamaica case, Rev. Poole *vs.* Bayley, March 8, 1759;
f. 38. Important series of notes by Yorke on various colonial acts
declared null by the king; *f. 40*. Jamaica case, July 7, 1760; *f. 44*.
Thomas Dering *vs.* Thomas Packer, New Hampshire case, New
England, July 10, 1760; *f. 66*. Jamaica case, n.d.; *f. 78*. Nevis case,
n.d.; *f. 86*. Jamaica case, Jan. 30, 1761; *f. 90*. Barbados case, July
5, 1760; *f. 101*. Larkin case, Rhode Island, June 26, 1761; *f. 133*.
Nevis smuggling case, Chollett of St. Eustatius *vs.* Mackay, March
16, 1762; *f. 138*. Lewis Burwell estate *vs.* Philip Johnson, *et al.*,
Virginia, March 16, 1762; *f. 144*. Jamaica case, March 16, 1762;
f. 147. John Sherburne *vs.* Samuel Sherburne, a will case, New
Hampshire, March 16, 1762; *f. 151*. Trecothick of London, mer-
chant, *vs.* Wentworth of New Hampshire, New Hampshire, March
16, 1762; *f. 154*. Jamaica case, April 6, 1762; *f. 181*. Rolfe case,
New Hampshire, Dec. 17, 1762; *f. 199*. Samuel Rickards, Archibald
Maclane and others, merchants and factors, *vs.* John Hudson and
Anne, his wife, Virginia [1763], with Yorke's notes; *f. 218*. Richard
Crosse, planter in Jamaica, *vs.* Atkins, 1763; *f. 223*. John Camm,
clerk, *vs.* the Rector, Visitors, and Governors of William and Mary
College, Virginia, March 12, 1763, concerning Camm's removal as

professor of divinity "without any reasonable cause"; *f. 225*. Case of Richard Graham, professor of natural philosophy, Virginia, 1763, similar to Camm case; *f. 236*. Case of illegal importation of Irish goods into Newfoundland from Ireland, 1763; *f. 240*. John Potter of South Kingston *vs.* George Hazard of Newport, land case, Rhode Island, 1763; *f. 248*. William Tabb *vs.* Thomas and John Edmundson, Virginia, Dec. 17, 1763.

No. 36219. *f. 11*. Petition of the Earl of Cardigan and others regarding the islands of St. Lucia and St. Vincent; *f. 75*. John Freebody and brothers *vs.* Jahleel Brenton, Rhode Island, 1764; *f. 85*. Richard Cleeve and John Huide *vs.* James Mills, William Bird, *et al.*, Virginia, July 27, 1764; *ff. 94–114, 140–226*. Jamaica and Barbados cases, 1764; *f. 227*. David McMurterie and William McMurterie, merchants and insurers of the brigantine *Providence, vs.* John Brown of Providence, Rhode Island, surviving owner of the *Providence,* Pennsylvania, 1765; the case contains much information about the commerce of colonial Philadelphia; *f. 269*. John Parsons *vs.* William Parsons, Virginia, 1764; *f. 273*. Thomas Howlett *vs.* Thomas Osburn, Virginia, 1765.

No. 36220. *ff. 1–50*. Crown brief relating to the establishment of customs officers for the Channel Islands (Guernsey, Jersey and Alderney). The case was to be heard before the committee of the Council, Thursday, June 19, 1766, but was postponed until Nov. 29, 1766. Included among the manuscripts is the report of a commission appointed Sept. 4, 1764, to inquire into illicit trade carried on by the Channel Islands. In its report, July 4, 1765, it recommended the appointment of customs officers; *f. 52*. John Camm, clerk, *vs.* Charles Hansford, Virginia, 1765, 1766, "parson's cause" appeal; *f. 59*. Extract of order in council, dated March 7, 1753, approving report made by the Committee of the Council, dated March 1, 1753, which stated that it was not advisable for the king to authorize a colony (in this case Virginia), to repeal, alter and amend laws after they had received the royal approbation, without inserting a suspending clause therein; *f. 73*. Pennsylvania Land Co. *vs.* Christian Stover, Pennsylvania, July 8, 1766, with numerous marginal notes by Yorke, a plot of the survey and other charts; *f. 80*. Dominique case, four London merchants *vs.* Thomas Knowles, commander of the *Milford,* July 8, 1766. This famous case first tried in the vice-admiralty court in Antigua involved violation of the Act of 1763; judgment of forfeiture was affirmed on Dec. 11, 1766; *f. 105*. John Long and William Plumstead, of Philadelphia, merchant freighters, *vs.* Thomas Harper, John Nixon and Co., owners of the ship *Molly,* Pennsylvania, July 1766, with many informative printed papers; *f. 115*. Thomas Shearman of Portsmouth *vs.* Gideon Cornell of Newport, Rhode Island, July

8, 1766; *f. 117*. Gawin Corbin *vs.* Lunsford Lomax, Virginia, July 8, 1766; *f. 127*. Robert Lewis and Ellis Lewis of Philadelphia, merchants, *vs.* Benjamin Wilkinson, land-mortgage case, Rhode Island, 1766; *f. 135*. Barbados case, June 10, 1767. When Rear Adm. Tyrrell, of H.M.S. *Greyhound*, deputy customs officer, seized a vessel, he was tried in the Barbadian vice-admiralty court for violation of the Act of 1763; the court's decision against the seizure was reversed by the Privy Council; *f. 142*. Antigua case, June 10, 1767; *f. 148*. Grenada case, 1767; *f. 155*. Lieut.-Gen. Christie *vs.* Knipe, 1768; *ff. 156-217*. Jamaica, Barbados, and St. Christopher, cases of local interest; *f. 218*. Freebody and brothers *vs.* Jahleel Brenton, Rhode Island, March 15, 1769, second appeal with judgment upheld; see *No. 36219, f. 75*.

No. 36223. f. 60. Letter from Thomas Penn to Charles Yorke, 1759.

No. 36225. f. 179. Materials regarding court martial in Martinique, 1763.

No. 36226. f. 132. "Copy of a paper containing the opinion of a gentleman of the law in New York"; *f. 353*. "Mr. Curuy's [possibly Thomas Augustus Cruwys] scheme for an American stamp bill, presented to the Commissioners of Stamps," Sept. 30, 1763. (Compared with proposals of Keith and of McCulloh, *Nos. 33028, f. 376; 33030, f. 334; 35910, f. 137*); *f. 357*. "Draft of conference with Mr. M'Culloh, 12th Oct. 1763. Copy for the Board [of Stamps]."

No. 36593. f. 53. Letter from Benjamin Franklin, Philadelphia, Dec. 9, 1762, refers to his son's marriage and the capture of Havana.

No. 36807. Volume entitled "Negotiations with Spain, 1672-1762"; *f. 18*. Copy of draft of letter from William Pitt to the Earl of Bristol, Aug. 1, 1758, summarizing England's relations with Spain, particularly in Honduras and the West Indies; *f. 30*. A similar despatch in French, Dec. 13, 1759; *f. 46*. Letter from the Earl of Bristol to William Pitt, Dec. 19, 1759, regarding the King of Spain as mediator, and other papers about Honduras and the right of Biscayans to fish at Newfoundland. Notice Pitt's despatch of Sept. 26, 1760; *f. 225*. Summary of disputes: (1) British right of cutting logwood and having settlements at Honduras; (2) Spanish right of fishing at Newfoundland; (3) Offences supposedly committed by the English men of war and privateers in violation of Spain's neutrality. The disputes arose at different times: the first, after the treaty of 1670; the second after the treaty of Utrecht; and the third, from the renewed hostilities.

No. 36995. Documents pertaining to Gen. Studholme Hodgson's secret expedition for the capture of Belleisle, 1761.

No. 37021. f. 27. Letter from Benjamin Franklin to Peter Collinson, Philadelphia, April 30, 1764.

No. 38161. Notes of Speeches and Debates in Parliament, taken by

Philip Yorke, 1st Earl of Hardwicke, his son Philip, the 2nd Earl, and others.

Nos. 38190–38489. Liverpool Papers. Includes the papers of Charles Jenkinson, 1st Earl of Liverpool (1727–1808), who was very active in affairs of state in the 1760's and 1770's. See Ninetta S. Jucker, *The Jenkinson Papers: 1760–1766* (London, 1949). Among these papers are the following which relate to the period 1748–1776: *No. 38202. f. 342.* Refusal by the Assembly of Massachusetts of the offered alternative to the Stamp duty, 1764; *No. 38207. f. 285.* Copy of minute of Governors of King's College at New York, 1773.

No. 38334. ff. 68, 250. Troop returns for all the colonies except Delaware and Georgia, 1760–1762. (See also *No. 38332, f. 227*); *f. 134.* "Charges for carrying on the Indian Service . . . in North America," by E. Atkins, Superintendent for Indian Affairs, Southern District, 1756–1760. (Incomplete); *f. 223.* State of the North American Customs offices, with suggested improvements, written after Dec. 25, 1762; *f. 229.* Note on New York quit-rents, 1762; *f. 273.* Lists of twelve customs officers, including those at St. Augustine, East Florida, and Mobile, West Florida, 1762–1763.

No. 38335. ff. 1, 14–36, 68–77. Reflections on the settlement and government of British North America, 1763, regarding the colonies as sources of raw materials. (See also *No. 38334, f. 297*); *ff. 37, 90.* Lists of officers in North America absent from duty, 1763; *ff. 40, 82, 148–153, 237, 241.* Papers relating to quit-rents in Virginia, 1761–1763. (See also *Nos. 38201, f. 33; 38337, ff. 50, 60; 38373, ff. 80–84b, 111b–122*); *ff. 81, 95b–98, 240.* Accounts of Virginia tobacco duty, 1763; *f. 87.* Drawbacks on foreign goods re-exported from England to North America, 1761; *ff. 103, 144, 154, 327–331.* Reports, Treasury minutes, etc., on British North American customs revenue, 1763. (See also *No. 38339, f. 250*); *f. 209b.* Number of ships annually cleared from American colonies, 1760–1762, showing number going to or coming from British and foreign ports with total tonnage; *f. 233.* Copy of report of the Board of Trade on the colonization of Florida, 1763; *f. 243.* Estimate of tea, sugar, and molasses illegally imported into British North America [1764].

No. 38336. f. 155. Account of Spanish Florida by Dr. Campbell, c. 1763.

No. 38337. f. 1. Abstract of a bill for encouraging the trade of British North America [1763]; *f. 60.* Quit-rents of Virginia, the Carolinas, Georgia, and New York, 1764; *ff. 162–173b.* Extracts from report on whale fishing, fur trade, and bounty on hemp in the American colonies, 1764; *f. 234.* Note on the trade of North America, especially imports of Carolinian rice, 1764; *f. 245.* Report of seizures of uncustomed and prohibited goods at Philadelphia, Boston,

Quebec, and in Virginia, 1763–1764; *f. 314.* Auditor-General's report on the New York Quit-Rent Act, 1764.

No. 38338. f. 39. Address from the New York Assembly to Lieut.-Gov. Cadwallader Colden, stating loyalty but emphasizing that it will pay no taxes to which it did not consent, and asking Colden to inform the Ministry of its dissatisfaction with the Sugar Act, 1764.

No. 38339. ff. 131, 182–189, 306. Notes on the right to tax the colonies, c. 1765; *f. 180.* Change of military establishment in American colonies, 1750, 1765; *f. 235.* Agreement of West Indian and North American merchants, 1766; *f. 302.* Decrease of British exports to North America since the repeal of the Stamp Act, 1766.

No. 38340. ff. 163–165. Estimates of British North American military expenses, 1767; *f. 192.* Petition, c. 1767, from London merchants trading with North America, asking Parliament for relief from the Townshend Duties, which have been damaging their trade; *ff. 201–378b, passim.* Papers relating to the collection of customs in British North America, 1767–1771, including legal opinion of Jonathan Sewall, Attorney-General of Massachusetts, 1768.

No. 38341. ff. 29, 69, 163, 329. Papers relating to the collection of customs in British North America, 1767–1771; *ff. 104, 135.* Proposals for amending the taxation of the North American colonies, c. 1769; *f. 125.* Ships entered outwards from London for British North America, 1765–1770; *f. 324.* Quantities of wheat exported from British North America, 1678–1772.

No. 38342. f. 32. Protest of Massachusetts against the claims of Parliament to authority over the colony, 1773; *f. 34.* Paper on the state of unrest in Massachusetts, c. 1773; *f. 39.* Paper on the Virginia tobacco trade, giving a brief history of the trade during the eighteenth century, written after 1773; *f. 82.* Note on the New England exchange rate [1774]; *f. 153.* Paper on North American land grants, c. 1775–1776; *f. 157.* Paper urging the creation of a special fund for the American colonies, n.d., but probably late 1760's. Although the document does not state the purpose of the fund, the author also suggests that an orderly system of colonial government be established to prevent the colonies from uniting and becoming "untractable"; *ff. 161–221, 281.* Letters and papers pertaining to the American rebellion, 1774–1777, including various declarations and petitions of the colonists and proposals of parliamentary bills affecting America.

No. 38343. ff. 1–22b. Account of what the Treasury has done in freighting provision ships for America, with lists of ships, etc., 1775–1777. (See also *No. 38342, f. 302*).

No. 38374. f. 107. Reflections on the rebellious state of New York, 1775.

No. 38375. f. 136. Memorial of Duncan Campbell, chairman of the Committee of Merchants of London, Bristol, Liverpool, Whitehaven, and Glasgow, trading to Virginia, Maryland, and North Carolina, "previous to the year 1776," to the Secretary of State, complaining of inability to recover debts.

No. 38465. f. 210. "Account of the number of seamen employed in the merchants' service at the several ports in America, 1763–1772," dated Receiver's Office for Greenwich Hospital on Tower Hill, Jan. 21, 1778, among the William Draper papers.

No. 38497. Townshend Papers. Includes valuable information on the activities of George Viscount Townshend while acting Lord Lieutenant of Ireland, 1767–1772.

No. 38577. f. 1. Grievances of the several provinces of North America, 1769.

No. 38650. Miscellaneous Papers: *ff. 1–34.* Letters relating to North America, 1775, 1780; *f. 1.* William Tryon, governor of New York, to the Earl of Dartmouth, urging a change of policy towards the American colonies, New York, Aug. 7, 1775 (copy); *f. 3.* Maj.-Gen. Richard Montgomery to Gen. Sir Guy Carleton at Quebec, requesting him to surrender the city, Dec. 1775.

No. 39168. Miscellaneous Papers: *f. 128.* William Fraser, under secretary of state, to the Earl of Holderness, Feb. 1 [1774], regarding Massachusetts' petition for the removal of Gov. Hutchinson and Lieut.-Gov. Oliver, which was presented by Franklin to the Council and rejected.

No. 39190. Mackenzie Papers, vol. iv: *ff. 204–211.* Include letters of Maj. John Pitcairn of the Marines (killed at Bunker Hill, 1775) to Lieut.-Col. John Mackenzie of the Marines, recounting his difficulties in America, Boston, Dec. 10 and 28, 1774, Feb. 16, 1775.

Nos. 39304–39316. Berkeley Papers. Papers of George Berkeley (1685–1753), Bishop of Cloyne, and his family. The papers include: *No. 39311. ff. 158–159.* Copy of a letter, London, May 4, 1764, from Sir Alexander Cuming, called chief of the Cherokees, to the Earl of Bute, asking for alleviation of his poverty, enclosed in a letter from Cuming to George Berkeley, son of Bishop Berkeley, May 8, 1764.

No. 40760. Francis Papers, vol. v. Letters and papers of, and relating to, Rev. Philip Francis (1708?–1773) and his son, Sir Philip Francis (1740–1818): *ff. 220–270.* Copies of letters from Nov. 9, 1755 to Sept. 5, 1756, including Maj.-Gen. William Shirley, with Henry Fox, William Wildman Barrington, Maj.-Gen. Sir William Johnson, Horatio Sharpe, Maj.-Gen. James Abercromby, Commander-in-Chief in North America, 1758, and John Campbell, 4th Earl of Loudoun, Nov. 9, 1755–Sept. 5, 1756. Many of these letters are printed in *Correspondence of William Shirley . . . 1731–1760* (Charles Henry Lincoln, ed., 2 vols., New York, 1912).

No. 41361. Martin Papers. Correspondence of Josiah Martin (nephew of

Josiah, the elder), governor of North Carolina, 1771–1776, largely with his brother, Samuel Martin, Jr., Dec. 21, 1752–Nov. 19, 1785. The letters, mostly from the 1770's, concern Josiah's financial difficulties from which his brother extricated him, but also report on political developments in America.

Nos. 42083–42088. Grenville Papers. Approximately 500 original letters of the Grenville family, 1767–1777, chiefly of Richard Temple Grenville, afterwards Grenville-Temple, Earl Temple (1711–1799), but also some of his brother George (1712–1770). Although the letters are mostly on other topics, there are passing references to American problems. The diary and most of the other materials were published in *The Grenville Papers* (W. J. Smith, ed., 4 vols., London, 1852–3). Among these papers the following may be noted: *No. 42083.* George Grenville's political diary, 1761–1768, including a few brief references to Parliamentary debates on American issues, 1765–1767. *Nos. 42084–42087:* (1) The Earl of Suffolk to George Grenville on the Duke of Bedford's motion in the House of Lords asking for all correspondence of the several governors in America, Feb. 28, 1767; (2) George Grenville to Pownall, on the possibility of seating American members in the House of Commons; also the general situation in America, July 17, 1768; (3) Commodore Hood to George Grenville, on the extension of his American command, and his probable dispositions in view of the threatening state of affairs in America; also the landing of Gage's troops at Boston, Oct. 15, 1768; (4) Thomas Whately to Grenville, on prospects of revolution at Boston, Oct. 27, 1768; see also Whately to Grenville, Oct. 28, 1768; (5) William Knox to Grenville, contending "the revolt of New England is now unquestionable," Nov. 1, 1768; (6) John Temple, Commissioner of Customs at Boston, to Grenville, on his disagreeable position, Nov. 7, 1768; (7) Knox to Grenville, on negotiations with the colonies over the Townshend duties, Dec. 15, 1768; (8) Whately to Grenville, on the spread of disaffection to Virginia and South Carolina, Jan. 3, 1769; (9) Adm. Hood to Grenville, on the former's forbearance in order not to exacerbate American feeling, April 15, 1769; (10) Whately to Grenville, on a report that the troops are retiring from Boston, Aug. 5, 1769; (11) Hood to Earl Temple, on the worsening situation at Boston over the duties, Sept. 2, 1769; (12) Knox to Grenville, refers to American duties, Sept. 19, 1769; (13) Whately to Grenville, on a report by ex-Governor Bernard on the situation in Massachusetts, Sept. 22, 1769; (14) Whately to Grenville, on a plan for an American parliament and on American non-importation, Dec. 3, 1769; (15) Chatham to Temple, in which he says, whatever the result of the conflict with the colonists, "poor England will have fallen upon her own sword," Sept. 24, 1777.

No. 45728–45730. Auckland Papers. Papers of William Eden, 1st Baron Auckland (1744–1814), one of the Peace Commissioners sent to America in 1778.

No. 46840. Miscellaneous Papers, including J. Danford's diary of the American siege of Quebec under Montgomery and Arnold, Nov. 10, 1775–May 6, 1776.

No. 47053. Documents regarding Nova Scotia estates, 1764.

Before turning to other collections of manuscripts, the point must be stressed again that the Library of the British Museum is constantly receiving accessions of papers. Students should therefore consult the more recent accessions lists.

THE UNITED EAST INDIA COMPANY

The East India Company was incorporated by Queen Elizabeth, by letters patent, dated Dec. 31, 1600, under the title of The Governor and Merchants of London Trading into the East Indies. A fresh charter was granted by her successor nine years later; a third was obtained in 1657 from Oliver Cromwell, and a fourth in 1661 from Charles II. These were followed by other royal grants and by acts of Parliament confirming the Company's privileges. In 1698, under the sanction of an Act of Parliament, a charter was granted to a rival body, styled The English Company Trading to the East Indies (sometimes referred to as the New Company in contradistinction to the older body). This association was governed by 24 "Directors," who elected two of their number as Chairman and Deputy Chairman. In 1702 the competition between the two bodies was terminated by an agreement to amalgamate in seven years time, the trade being meanwhile controlled by a Court of Managers consisting of an equal number of delegates from each body. The union was effected in 1709, the first meeting of the Court of Directors for the United Company was held on March 23 in that year; and from that time the official style was for a century and a quarter The United Company of Merchants of England Trading to the East Indies. The shorter title of The East India Company, though used colloquially from an early date, was not legalised until the Act of 1833.

When the writer of this series first worked among the East India Company papers they were located in a building off Whitehall known as the India Office. In front of it stands in heroic size the monument to Lord Clive. Since then the building has been given the name Commonwealth Relations Building, but the vast archives of the old Company and those of the British government that succeeded it are still in their accustomed places. It should, however, be pointed out that certain important collections of papers relating to the East India Company are in the Public Record Office. They can be found by consulting: Colonial Office, Class 77, which lists 13 volumes of the correspondence of the Secretary of State concerning the Company affairs in the eighteenth century. For a list of these papers see: (a) "Public Record Office List No. 36, with indexes" and (b) Treas. 49. "Papers of Lord North relating to India." Likewise, in the British Museum there are many papers bearing upon East India Company affairs; for these consult Additional Manuscripts *Nos. 16259–71, 28973–29236, and 34287.*

A most convenient guide to the vast collection of papers in the old India Office Library is that by Sir William Foster: *A Guide to the India Office Records, 1600–1858* (London, 1919); a still more comprehensive one is a *Catalogue of Manuscripts in European Languages belonging to the Library of the India Office* (2 vols. in 3+, London, 1916–37+). This catalogue describes at length some special manuscript collections in the library. Among these S. C. Hill has excellently catalogued "The [Robert] Orme collection" (Vol. II, pt. 1); while George Rusby Kaye and Edward Hamilton Johnston, in dealing with "Minor Collections and Miscellaneous Manuscripts" (Vol. II, pt. 2), provide information on the Sir Philip Francis manuscripts. Francis, as is well known, was the bitter opponent of Warren Hastings.

Also among the guides to the East India Company papers not in London should be mentioned *Catalogue of the English Records, 1758–1858, preserved in the Historical Record Room of the Government of Bengal* (3 pts. Calcutta, 1922–5), and *Select Index to General Letters to and from the Court of Directors . . . Preserved in the Bengal Secretarial Record Room . . . Calcutta* (Calcutta, 1926). We have also descriptions of two other important eighteenth-century manuscript collections in India. These are the volumes by Arthur Fasker Kindersley: *A Handbook of the Bombay Government Records* (Bombay, 1921), and that by Henry Herbert Dodwell: *Report on the Madras Records* (Madras [1916]), and also his *Calendar of Madras Despatches, 1744–1755* (2 vols., Madras, 1920). Lord Clive's papers are in the All Souls College Library at Oxford.

In his Introduction to his *Guide of the India Office Records*, Sir William Foster quotes with approval the statement by James Grant Duff in the latter's *History of the Mahrattas* (ed. 1826, vol. II, 185): "The records of the East India Company's governments in India are probably the best historical materials in the world." Foster points out why Duff was justified in making so sweeping an assertion: "The distance separating the Company from its servants in the East, and the jealous care with which it supervised their actions, necessitated full explanations by correspondence; while the system of administration in the Company's settlements and territories, which from the first took the form of a Council, also favoured a full disclosure of the motives underlying every decision of importance. In its final development, proposals were largely made in written minutes, which often, in controverted questions, provoked equally argumentative minutes of dissent; and these were entered at full length upon the records of the Council meetings (termed 'Consultations' or 'Proceedings'), transcripts of which were regularly sent home. In early days these were accompanied by separate volumes containing copies of all letters received or sent; in later times such correspondence was either entered on the Consultations, or, in cases of special importance, transmitted as enclosures to dispatches. Since equally careful, though more concise, records were kept at home of the proceedings of the Court of Directors and of the various Committees into which it divided itself, it is obvious that, had the archives of the East India House survived in their entirety, we should now be in possession of full information regarding the transactions both at home and abroad. But during the greater part of the Company's existence little heed was paid to the value of its records for historical purposes, and the preservation of any particular series depended chiefly on its practical utility in relation to current work. Fortunately, in most cases this was sufficiently great to ensure the retention of those on which the student is likely to set chief store." The student interested in the more significant relations of India to Great Britain covering the years 1748–1776 may therefore rest assured that his needs will largely be met at the India Office Library.

The following list of papers falling within the period 1748–1776 that have survived is based upon Foster's *Guide*, pp. 1–118. Where he is simply following statements in the printed "Lists" I shall not use "Quotes" but otherwise I shall—except where for purposes of clarification for the beginning student and also for economy of space—seek to simplify this splendid *Guide* by eliminating details that do not pertain to the period under review. Many years ago while working in the India Office I came to know Sir William and to value highly his deep knowledge of its contents.

Court Records

COURT MINUTES

The "minutes" for the eighteenth and nineteenth centuries are embodied in Vols. 44–191 and cover most of the period of the life of the United East India Company from April 18, 1710 to Sept. 1, 1858; these minutes include the proceedings of the General Courts. Another series, entitled *Appendix to Court Minutes*, embodies copies of "Dissents" from resolutions of the Court of Directors. Among them is a volume containing a list of Dissents, 1764–1858, with an index; the original Dissents were destroyed in 1860. The student should note that much material, such as the *Appendix to*

Court Minutes, was printed for the use of those connected with the governing of India but was not published.

The proceedings at the "General Courts" (i.e. the assemblies of the whole body of members or holders of stock of the United East India Company) are recorded in the same series as the Court Minutes down to April 1833. There is, however, a separate record under the title of *General Court Minutes*—a series which begins in 1702 and is continuous to 1858. The first twelve volumes (to Sept. 1818) include indexes to their contents. Likewise there is a separate index (in two volumes) to the whole series, and another index to the election of Directors, 1702–1846. In addition to the manuscripts, printed accounts of some of the debates at General Courts will be found in the India Office Library.

COURT COMMITTEE OF SECRECY MINUTES

Much of the work of the Court of Directors was done by committees. Among these was the Committee of Secrecy, a very powerful committee that was apparently set up about the year 1748 and continued to function at least from time to time as need arose. Accounts of the proceedings of the Committee of Secrecy are to be found in the early Court Minutes, volumes 44–191, reference to which has already been made. It is true that beginning with 1778 and extending to 1858 there is a series of 6 volumes devoted to the work of the Committee of Secrecy. This series, however, is beyond the period under examination; the student interested in the period 1748–1776 must therefore rely on the General Court minutes.

COURT COMMITTEE OF CORRESPONDENCE

With respect to the Committee of Correspondence, there is a series of 13 volumes covering the years 1704–1793, but with gaps; these gaps, unfortunately, cover the years 1749–1754 and 1757–1783, leaving only the volumes for 1755 and 1756 that are concerned with the period 1748–1776.

COURT REPORTS

These reports, respecting the general activities of the Company, cover the years 1719–1834; this series is in 67 volumes. Most of the volumes have indexes.

COURT MEMORANDA

The memoranda series include draft of minutes and other papers relating to matters considered by the Committee of Correspondence. These cover the years 1700–1858 and are in 55 volumes.

Correspondence

HOME LETTERS RECEIVED

Miscellaneous letters

This collection brings together two earlier distinct series, viz., "Correspondence Papers," and "Court Miscellanies." It covers the years 1701–1858. The series, indexed to the year 1827, is in 195 volumes.

Auditor's references

These letters refer almost exclusively to demands upon the Home Treasury. The collection apparently belonged to the department of the Auditor of Home Accounts: hence its title. This series covers the years 1740–1835, in 106 volumes.

HOME LETTERS SENT

Copies of some early "Home Letters Out" will be found in the series of "Letter Books." Among these is the series called *Miscellanies*. This series consists of copies of letters sent out. It covers the period 1703 to 1858. In 112 volumes it is listed as A. 1–112.

LETTERS RECEIVED FROM INDIA, &C.

These letters are classified under such headings as "Shipping," "Investments," "Servants." In 1772, the Bengal government started another series, "Revenues." These letters are classified as coming either from Bengal or later from Madras, or Bombay.

Letters received from Bengal

This series of volumes embodies the original signed letters in all departments of the Bengal service. Besides the formal communications there are a number of letters from the Governor-General (with the establishment of that office in 1773) or from members of the Fort William Council, etc. The dates given are those of the letters, not that of their receipt. They cover the years 1746–1834 and the series is listed 1A–126.

Abstracts of letters received from the Coromandel Coast and Bay of Bengal

In addition to the above letters from Bengal there is a series of abstracts of letters covering the years 1703–1760 in 6 volumes that has particular relation to the Coromandel Coast. This is followed by *Abstracts of Letters Received from Bengal*. Volumes 1–9 of these abstracts cover the years 1760–1822. All departments of the Company activities in Bengal are comprehended in them. It may be well for the student to turn to these abstracts before attempting to use the fuller original correspondence. This also applies to other series of abstracts in the Library.

Letters received from Madras

The letters from Madras that have survived and that relate to the years 1748–1776 are listed as 1A–145 and cover the years 1760 to 1858. It should be noted that for the period 1746–1752, when Fort St. David was the seat of government (owing to the capture of Madras by the French), reference should be made to the *Fort St. David* series in the *Factory Records*.

Abstracts of letters received from Madras

In addition to the letters received from Madras as listed above, there are the abstracts of letters for the years 1760–1816, in ten volumes.

Letters received from Bombay

The first three Bombay series, 1709–1758, are very incomplete. The entire collection covers the years 1709–1858 in 152 volumes. In addition there are the *Abstracts of Letters Received from Bombay*, 1703–1733, 1751–1816, in ten volumes.

DESPATCHES TO INDIA

The letter books

Series 14–28 cover the period from Oct. 1710 to April 1753. These volumes contain copies of letters written by the Company to the various settlements in the East (including St. Helena), also to their agents in Europe, and in the Levant. There is also some home correspondence.

Despatches to all presidencies

The series with this heading among the surviving manuscript volumes covers the period from Jan. 18, 1703, to April 4, 1753, in ten volumes. Beyond this there are a series of despatches to the individual presidencies.

Despatches to Bengal

Again with reference to the correspondence that is pertinent there is a series of despatches to Bengal, covering the years 1753–1833, in 124 volumes. This series comprises despatches to all departments of the Bengal governments except "Secret." There are corrections in red ink, hardly legible, made by the Board of Control. It is supplied with an index in 13 volumes.

Abstracts of despatches to Bengal

These abstracts cover the years 1753–1816 in four volumes.

Despatches to Madras

This series covers the years 1753–1858 in 131 volumes.

Abstracts of despatches to Madras

These abstracts cover the years 1743–1829 in 4 volumes.

Despatches to Bombay

This series begins in 1753 and extends to 1851 in 117 volumes.

Abstracts of despatches to Bombay

The abstracts cover the years 1743–1816 in 4 volumes.

Charters

This series in twenty-three volumes is concerned not only with charters granted to the Company but statutes relating to it; it also includes negotiations for the renewal of privileges. About half of the volumes are printed.

Home Miscellaneous

Here is another very large and heterogeneous series. The volumes concerned with the period 1748–1776 are as follows:

No. 628. A collection of farmans and treaties compiled by Thomas Wilks, 1602–1789.

No. 629. Here are also treaties and grants, with correspondence, 1643–1800.

No. 631. This volume contains translations of treaties, etc., made at Fort St. David, 1690–1751.

No. 633. Treaties concluded by the Bengal Presidency, 1773–1780.

No. 642. Treaties and agreements entered into with the Nawabs of Arcot, 1763–1801.

No. 739. Transcripts of papers belonging to Mr. Verelst, consisting chiefly of correspondence with Lord Clive, 1759–1785.

No. 764. Chronological lists of holders of various appointments in India and at home, 1600–1884. Here are lists of governors, deputy governors, directors and others serving the Company.

No. 765. Letters of Major Reynell, the cartographer, to the Rev. Gilbert Burrington and others, 1758–1785.

Nos. 766–772. Here are papers compiled by Thomas Wilks, covering the period 1756–1775. Each volume is lettered. They are as follows: *No. 766.* A. Debts of the Nawab of Arcot, proposed bank in Bengal, the case of Sir Robert Fletcher, etc., 1772–1774; *No. 767.* B. Also the debts of the Nawab of Arcot, 1769–1773; *No. 768.* C. Affairs in Madras, including the war with Hyder Ali, 1769–1774; *No. 769.* D. Trade and revenue in Bengal with other matters, 1764–1773; *No. 770.* E. The French in Bengal and disputes in the Bengal council, 1764–1774; *No. 771.* F. Concerning Balambangan and Sulu, 1762–1774; *No. 772.* G. Affairs in Tanjor, also at Fort St. George, and the case of Col. Wood, 1762–1775.

No. 773. Transcripts from English and French records relating to Bengal, 1756–1758.

No. 774. Other transcripts regarding Bengal (including some from Dutch sources); also about the siege of Madura, 1756–1764.

Accounts

Among the records in the Accountant-General's department bearing upon the period 1748–1776 are the following series: *General Journals and Ledgers*, from 1644; *Private Trade and other Journals and Ledgers*, from 1671; and *Registers of Payments of Salaries, Pensions, etc.*, from 1743.

Administration of India

BENGAL PRESIDENCY

In his *Guide* Sir William Foster points out (p. 36) the many changes that took place in the connotation of the name "Bengal," especially in relation to the Bengal Presidency. It not only included Bengal itself but also the provinces of Bihar and Orissa, all three generally governed by the same Nawab. However, in the case of Orissa it was not until 1803 that it became fully administered by the East India Company, although revenues had been earlier drawn from it. After the battle of Plassey in 1757, the revenues of the so-called Twenty-Four Parganas were administered by the Bengal Presidency; again, after 1760 the districts of Bardwan, Midnapur, and Chittagong were added; further, in 1775 the frontiers of the Presidency were advanced northwestward to include the present Benares area ceded by the Nawab of Oudh; later, most of Oudh was ceded and the process continued.

Factories

Much of the activity of the Company in India as a business concern was concentrated in its "factories" where goods were purchased and, when necessary, were processed. For the period under consideration the records of but two Bengal factories have survived: (a) The Kasimbazar Factory, with diary and consultations for the period 1748–1759 and (b) The Dacca Factory, the diary of which, together with the consultations cover not only the earlier period as was true of Kasimbazar, but the years 1736–1757 and 1762–1763. The surviving factory records of Calcutta are mostly for the seventeenth century.

Consultations

From early in the eighteenth century the proceedings of the President and Council at Calcutta, listed as "Bengal Public Consultations," were duly recorded, at least before June 1756 when Calcutta was captured. At this juncture the Directors of the Company decided to appoint a Select Committee in Bengal to deal with matters of special importance. With the recapture of Calcutta by the Company's forces in Jan. 1757, the servants of the Company resumed their activities in this city. Sir William Foster in his *Guide* (pp. 40–1) has some very illuminating comments to make with reference to proceedings in Bengal that embrace the years 1748–1776. These comments follow:

"The India Office has a set of the consultations of the Fort William Select Committee (and of its predecessor, the Secret Committee), beginning 22 Aug. 1756, and ending 28 Dec. 1762 (Range A, vols. 1–4). There is, however, a gap between 10 Dec. 1756 and 21 Feb. 1757, and another between 4 July 1758 and the end of that year; while apparently no meetings were held between 2 Nov. 1759 and 28 July 1760." Still quoting Foster, "Mr. S. C. Hill printed at Calcutta in 1901 an *Abstract of the Early Records of the Foreign Department, 1756–62*, which shows that the same deficiencies exist in the old Imperial Record Department set. The earlier gap may be made good from the *Orme MSS.* in the India Office, which include (O. V. 170, and *India*, vol. vii, pp. 1146–1255) a record of the proceedings of the Committee from 15 Dec. 1756 to 8 Dec. 1757; while, as regards the later gap, the Bengal Secretariat possesses a volume of the Committee's consultations from Jan. to 7 Nov. 1758, and this was printed *in extenso* by Archdeacon Firminger in 1914. Its contents have also been abstracted in the *Calendar of Records of the Secret Committee* [1758, 1766–1767, 1770] issued by the Bengal Government in 1915.

"Reference may here be made to three volumes (Range 168, vols. 16–18) which are classed in the press list as *Miscellaneous Proceedings*. These record the examination by the Governor and Council of charges brought against Nandkumar (Jan. and Feb. 1761) of intriguing with the Bardwan Raja and (July–Oct. 1762) of correspondence with the Shahzada and the French. They are really Separate Public Consultations, excluded from the regular departmental series on account of their secrecy. Vol. 18 is a duplicate of vol. 17. A similar separate volume, dealing with Ram Charan's treacherous correspondence with Kamgar Khan (April–Sept. 1761), referred to in the Public Consultations of 27 April 1761, is missing from the India Office files, but is available at the Imperial Record Office, Calcutta, where it is classified as Secret and Separate Proceedings, vol. i."

Further significant steps are noted by Foster (pp. 41–5) in developing at Fort William means for the control of the Company's activities in Bengal. In 1763 the President and Council determined to divide their business into two distinct departments, of which the "Public Department" should deal with all matters relating to shipping, revenues, fortifications, accounts, appointments, &c., while the "Secret Department" should care for all military plans and operations and all transactions with the "Country Government." Separate records were kept for each department. This arrangement held good until the arrival in 1765 of Lord Clive as President and Governor. Then, in obedience to orders he brought from the Company, the proceedings in the Secret Department were discontinued and a Select Committee of five members was constituted instead. In 1766 the Select Committee defined its special sphere as including "all political and military matters and the collection of the revenues arising from the grant of the *Diwani,* leaving to the Board as a whole matters of trade and the management of the Company's own lands, together with the revenues of the assigned districts of Bardwan, Midnapur, and Chittagong."

Again following Foster, in 1768, the Company sent out fresh orders, by which local treaties and financial transactions were vested in the Council as a whole. Accordingly, in 1768, a Secret Department was again constituted, consisting of the full Board, with a separate record of its secret proceedings. The Select Committee continued its meetings until October 1774, when the arrival of the new members of Council appointed under the India Act of the previous year concentrated all power in the hands of the Governor-General and his colleagues with political matters being henceforward considered by the Board in its Secret Department.

The following surviving papers among the India Office Records have to do with the Fort William Secret Committee or Select Committee activities covering the years 1756–1774:

Range A, vols. 1–4. Secret Committee and then Select Committee's Consultations. 1756–1762.

Range A, vols. 5–14. Secret Department Consultations, Dec. 1763–April 1765; then Select Committee's Consultations to Oct. 1774.

Range A, vol. 15. Duplicate of part of vol. 5.

Range A, vols. 16 onwards. Secret Consultations of Council from Aug. 1768.

It may be added that the old Imperial Record Office at Calcutta published press lists of the consultations of 1756–1762 and May 1765–Dec. 1773 (Select Committee) mentioned above, and also of the Secret Department Consultations of 1763–1765 and 1768–1775. The proceedings of the Select Committee in 1766 and 1770 (with letters for 1767) have also been calendared in the Bengal Government publication *Calendar of the Records of the Secret Committee* [covering the years 1758, 1766–1767, and 1770] (Calcutta, 1915). In 1890, Sir George Forrest published three volumes of *Selections from the Letters, Despatches and other State Papers preserved in the Foreign Department of the Government of India.* These consist chiefly of selections from the Secret Department Consultations, though they are described as the "Proceedings of the Secret Select Committee."

Besides the fore-mentioned series of Consultations that include the years 1748–1776, there are other Consultation series devoted to revenue matters covering the same period. In obedience to orders from home, a Committee of Lands was formed towards the end of 1760 for the purpose of administering the revenues of the Twenty-Four Parganas. This body appears to have come to an end in Nov. 1765, when a Mr. Sumner was appointed Collector-General for that district. The India Office Library possesses in Range 98, vols. 3–12, revenue papers of the Committee including correspondence covering the period from December 1759 to September 1762 including "Calcutta Sea Customs" and "Calcutta Land Customs."

Foster's comments respecting the company's revenues from the land are of special interest and importance to the student concerned with the relations of the United East India Company with India itself. He writes (pp. 44–45) that the collection of the general land revenues of Bengal and Bihar for some time after the grant to the Company of the *Diwani* in 1765, remained in the hands of the former Indian officials as agents for the Company. The abuses that ensued led to the appointment in

1769 of English "Supravisors" in each district to watch over the local officials. But this had little practical effect. In September 1770, by the direction of the Company, two Provincial Councils were formed for revenue business, viz., one at Murshidabad for Bengal, and the other at Patna for Bihar. The Councils, however, had still to act, like the "Supravisors," through native agents, and the results were unsatisfactory. In April 1771 a special Controlling Committee of Revenue was formed at Calcutta, under orders from home, and the two Provincial Councils, as well as the officers in charge of the Twenty-Four Parganas and the assigned districts of Bardwan, Midnapur, and Chittagong, were directed to correspond with and obey the orders of the new body. Then came an important change. In August 1771 the Directors wrote the Bengal Presidency that they had decided that the Company should "stand forth as Dewan" and by the agency of its own servants take upon itself "the entire care and management of the revenues." Thereupon the new Governor, Warren Hastings (later to become Governor General of India) formed a committee of the board, consisting of himself and four members, to settle on the spot the land revenue in the various districts; while the local "Supravisors" were henceforward denominated "Collectors." This "Committee of Circuit" lasted from May 1772 to Feb. 1773. Meanwhile in Sept. 1772 the *khalsa*, or chief revenue office, was removed from Murshidabad to Calcutta (a step which put an end, for the time being, to the activities of the Council of Revenue at the former place); and it was decided that the Board (i.e., the President and Council) should form itself into a Council of Revenue. This Council commenced its sittings on October 13, 1772; thereupon the Controlling Committee of Revenue came to an end.

However, the arrangements made for collecting the land revenue failed to secure the approval of the Court of Directors, and consequently in 1773 the Bengal Government adopted a new plan. A fresh Committee of Revenue was formed at Calcutta, consisting of five members, of whom two were to belong to the Council. This body was to supervise the districts round Calcutta itself. The rest of the Presidency (except the districts of Chittagong and Tipperah, which were to remain under the management of a chief) was divided into five "Grand Divisions," centering at Bardwan, Murshidabad, Dinajpur, Dacca, and Patna, each managed by a Provincial Council of Revenue. At Calcutta the Government continued to sit as a Council of Revenue, or in other words to transact business in a separate Revenue Department, an arrangement destined to become a permanent feature of the administration of India even after the Company's downfall. For a study concerned with this aspect of the Company's rule in India see D. N. Banerjee: *Early Land Revenue System in Bengal and Bihar. Vol. I, 1765–1772* (Calcutta and London, 1936).

In the India Office certain other series have survived covering the years 1770–1780 that are also classified under the heading "Consultations." The *Factory Records, Murshidabad*, Vols. 1–7 and 17 for the years 1770–1772, and the *Factory Records, Patna*, Vols. 3–4, for the years 1772–1773, illustrate the consultation work of the first Provincial Councils. For the work of the Controlling Committee of Revenue for the years 1772–1773, see Range 68, Vols. 54–55. For the Second Committee of Revenue for the years 1774–1780, see Range 67, Vols. 58–76, and Range 68, Vols. 1–5. For the later Provincial Council covering the years 1773–1780, see the printed factory records of the following: Bardwan *Records*, 1774–1779, Vols. 1–14; Dacca *Records*, 1773–1779, Vols. 6–21; Dinajpur *Records*, 1774–1778, Vols. 1–5; Murshidabad *Records*, 1773–1779, Vols. 8–16; and Patna *Records*, 1774–1780, Vols. 5–16. Under the heading Revenue Consultations of Government at Calcutta, covering the years 1772–1785, see Range 49, Vols. 38–72, Range 50, Vols. 1–62, Range 67, Vols. 55–57.

It should be noted that in 1773 Warren Hastings appointed a special Board of Customs to manage the customs dues on inland and foreign trade. Also, with the passing by Parliament of the India Act of 1773 the Directors of the Company sent orders for the establishment of a Bengal Board of Trade which operated from 1774 to 1786. For extracts from Board of Trade meetings see *Home Miscellaneous*, Vol. 224. Again, in 1771, under orders from home there was formed at Calcutta a Controlling Military Committee to supervise all military and naval expenditures. There have survived three volumes of the Military Committee which cover the years 1771–1774. See Range 18, Vols. 41–43.

Bengal Persian correspondence

As the correspondence of Indian princes and those attached to the native courts with the local officials of the Company was in Persian, this correspondence was customarily translated into English. Three calendars of surviving in-letters falling within the period 1748–1776 have been printed and are as follows: (1) *Calendar of the Persian Correspondence* (*Receipts and Issues*), 1766–1777 (Calcutta, 1907); (2) *Calendar of the Persian Correspondence, Vol. I, 1759–1767* (Calcutta, 1911); and (3) *Calendar of the Persian Correspondence, Vol. II, 1767–1769.* (Calcutta, 1914). In the *Home Miscellaneous* series, Vols. 193–4, 201–3 and 252–3, are to be found a large number of letters to and from the Indian princes in the days of Lord Clive and Warren Hastings as well as to and from Lord Cornwallis.

Bengal accounts

Under the heading "Accounts," which were sent regularly to London from Fort William at Calcutta, are "Bengal General Journals and Ledgers," covering the years 1704–1859; they are in 464 volumes.

Calcutta Mayor's Court

The Calcutta Mayor's Court came into existence in 1727 and was reorganized in 1753. In 1776 it was superseded by the Supreme Court, which had been created by royal charter in 1774. The work of the Mayor's Court was confined to Europeans unless all members involved in suits who were natives of India agreed to accept its findings. Copies of its records for the period under consideration have survived, outside of a gap between December 1769 and December 1770. The record of its activities for the years 1748–1776 are as follows: "Proceedings against Wadham Brooke," 1744–1751, in Range 155, Vol. 23; "Court's Proceedings and copies of wills," 1744–1750, in Range 154, Vols. 44–49; "Courts Proceedings," 1750–1755, in Range 155, Vols. 24–25, 27–29; "Proceedings against Jonathan Ranson," 1751–1754, in Range 155, Vol. 26; "Court's Proceedings," 1757–1774 (with the year 1770 missing), in Range 155, Vols. 30–39, 41, 43, 45–49; "Copies of Wills proved," 1750–1774, in Range 154, Vols. 50–55; "Lord Clive's covenant and oath as Governor," Oct. 1, 1766, in Range 155, Vol. 40; "Mr. Verelst's covenant and oath," Feb. 17, 1767, in Range 155, Vol. 42; "Proceedings against Thomas Forbes," 1768–1772, in Range 155, Vol. 44; "Petitions, replications, etc.," 1757–1758, in Range 155, Vols. 69–70; "Copies of instruments, protests, etc., registered in the office of the Notary Public," 1760–1774, in Range 155, Vols. 61–68; "Copies of Decrees," 1766–1767, in Range 155, Vols. 50–51; "Probates and administrations," 1766–1774," with gaps, in Range 155, Vol. 53–59; "Inventories of estates," 1758–1776, in Range 154, Vols. 61–70, and Range 155, Vols. 1–4.

Calcutta Zamindari Court

In addition to the Calcutta Mayor's Court, designed for British subjects, there was a Calcutta Zamindari Court for natives of India which administered both civil and criminal law, based upon the custom of the land. From the end of the seventeenth century one of the members of Council acted as Zamindar for Calcutta and neighbourhood, collecting the revenues of the district and administering civil and criminal justice among the inhabitants. The only two volumes at the India Office relating to this court are: (1) a register, civil and criminal, of trials by the Zamindar during 1766 (in Range 155, Vol. 71), and (2) a record of Faujdari (criminal) trials by his native assistants during 1774 (in Range 154, Vol. 38).

For more detailed information about the Madras Records, the reader may be referred to Henry Dodwell's excellent *Report on the Madras Records* (Madras [1916]).

The actual British possessions in this part of India were long restricted to Fort St. David and the district round Madras. The Northern Circars were ceded as the result of Col. Forde's capture of Masulipatam in 1759, and the grant was confirmed by the Mughal Emperor six years later.

Consultations

As was true of the Fort William Presidency at Calcutta, the records of business transacted by the Fort St. George Presidency at Madras carried the title "Consultations." The following surviving consultations records fall within the period 1748–1776: "Diary and Consultations of the President and Council at Fort St. David," 1750–1751, *Factory Records, Fort St. David*, Vol. 7; "Diary and Consultations of the Deputy-Governor (later the Governor) and Council at Fort St. George," Jan. 1, 1750 to Dec. 31, 1751, in Range 240, Vol. 8; "Diary and (Public) Consultations of the President and Council," at Fort St. David, in 1752, and at Fort St. George, also in 1752, in Range 240, Vol. 10; the same for 1753 in Range 240, Vol. 11; "Secret Military and Political Consultations of the President and Council," at Fort St. David, 1750–1752, and at Fort St. George, 1752–1753, in Range 240, Vol. 9. (Note. These consultatons were printed by the Madras Record Office under title, *Diary and Consultation Book, Military Department*). From 1753 the ordinary (public) Consultations are continued to the end of the Company's rule, though, from the India Office files the volumes for the second halves of the years 1767 and 1769 are missing.

Beyond the "Consultations" that have been noticed, there exist the records of another series of Madras Consultations, the "Secret Consultations," that carries the title, in 1754 of "Extraordinary Occurrences and Consultations." Later in that year there arrived orders from the Directors in London that a special committee of four members of the Council together with the Governor of Fort St. George should carry on all transactions with the "Country Powers." Political and military matters requiring secrecy were therefore dealt with by this "Select Committee for Transacting Country Affairs." For consultations covering the years 1754–1756 see the *Diary and Consultation Book, Military Department*, as well as the manuscript copies of the report in the India Office covering the years 1755–1758, in Range C, Vols. 48–53.

Late in 1758 Lally besieged Madras and the siege was continued until it was raised in February of the following year. From this time on the entire Council seems to have participated in the secret consultations that carry the title "Military Affairs and Transactions with the Country Government." This series continues past the terminal date 1776 of this survey and is available at the India Office. Also among the materials relating to Madras in the Office is a series called "Miscellaneous Correspondence," covering the years 1692–1816. This is embodied in the printed *Home Miscellaneous*, Vols. 257–258. There is another series in the Office concerned with the Madras Presidency that carries the title "Miscellaneous Correspondence and Proceedings relative to Tanjore and the Company Jagir," covering the years 1771–1803 in 17 volumes. The fiscal and general business activities of the Madras Presidency are set forth in the "Madras General Journals and Ledgers," covering the years 1702–1859 in 308 volumes. Closely related to this series are the Madras "Treasury Journals and Ledgers," 1755–1814, 1833–1858, in 116 volumes.

Mayor's Court

In the administration of justice at the Madras Presidency, there was also a Mayor's Court. Its proceedings from 1727 to 1778 with some gaps, are in 63 volumes, and include probate proceedings. Another series in 25 volumes is also concerned with the Mayor's Court for the years 1753–1778; it carries the title "Minutes Only." Another series in 16 volumes and covering the years 1771–1778 is denominated "Petty Causes and Minutes"; still another series in 25 volumes, covering with some breaks the years 1753–1791, is called "Correspondence, Bonds, etc." and yet another, entitled "Wills," covers the years 1753–1779 in 5 volumes.

WESTERN PRESIDENCY

The area of the Bombay or the "Western Presidency" was the first part of India to draw the attention of the English to direct trade possibilities. Early in the seventeenth century the first centre of the early East India Company commerce was Surat. From there factories spread to such places as Agra and Ahmadabad. In 1661 the English Crown received from Portugal the island of Bombay, as a marriage dowry to Charles II; in 1687 it became the Presidency centre in place of Surat. Unlike the Madras Presidency, throughout the eighteenth century the Bombay Presidency's factories were confined to coastal cities. While there are few factory records of this Presidency in the India Office concerned with the years 1748–1776, there has survived the Surat Consultations, 1724–1800, with gaps. There is also a volume of Surat "Miscellaneous" that has to do with the years 1759 and 1775 as well as 1800.

Bombay consultations

With respect to the consultations of the Bombay Governor and Council, they appear as "Public Consultations," and cover, with gaps, 1704–1822. See the printed *List of Proceedings, etc.: Bombay, 1702–1900* (p. 122). In addition to the above there was established in 1755 out of the Bombay Council a "Committee of Secrecy." Its proceedings, together with those of the "Select Committee," created by the Directors later in that year are recorded for the years 1755–1764 in Range D, Vols. 48–51. The committee was abolished in 1764 but was recreated in 1767; from 1764 to 1767 all proceedings are recorded in the series that carries the title "Public Department." Then in 1767 a new series began for secret proceedings and continued to 1769. For these see Range D, Vols. 52–54. In April 1769 a "Select Committee" was once again constituted and continued action throughout the period under examination. The proceedings of this committee of the council are also recorded in Range D, in Vol. 54 and succeeding volumes.

Bombay correspondence and Mayor's Court

With respect to correspondence, "letters sent" from Bombay are contained in 16 volumes covering the period 1747 to 1786 with some gaps. Few "letters received" have survived for the period 1748–1776. Those that are in the India Office cover the years 1775–1786 in 12 volumes. The purely business side of the Bombay records in the India Office are vastly more complete for the period under review. They extend from 1702 to 1858 in 313 volumes. There is also a volume devoted to the journals and ledgers of the Mayor's Court covering the years 1749–1766. Likewise in the India Office the proceedings of the Mayor's Court are to be found and extend from 1729 to 1797 in 122 volumes. The records of wills, probates and letters of administration registered in the Mayor's Court cover the years 1728–1783 in 22 volumes. For a number of papers having to do with the judicial activities of the Mayor's court for the years 1728–1810 see the printed series *Home Miscellaneous*, No. 432.

East India Company Activities Outside of India

From time to time the Company sought to establish factories on the island of Borneo. In 1763 an attempt was made to establish a factory on Balambangan, a small island off the coast of Borneo. Among the printed *Factory Records* there is a volume concerned with these efforts covering the years 1648–1814. Again, in 1762 John Pybus sought to get a commercial foothold for the Company in Ceylon. However, the close connection had to await the conquest of the island in 1795–1796.

With respect to China and Japan, the East India Company depended in the early part of the eighteenth century upon the activities of the factories at Surat and Madras. The tea trade was the great lure with the sale of tea by the middle of this century amounting to over a million and a quarter pounds sterling. In fact tea became one of the chief commodities brought by the Company to England. There is a series in the India Office of 291 volumes covering the years 1518–1835 concerned with China and the area to the east of it. In *Nos. 11–12* there is "Memoir on intercourse with China, 1518–1832"; *No. 14* contains "Attempts to Trade at Chusan," 1699–1759; *No. 18* carries the title "China and Cochin China: Miscellaneous Papers," 1753–1778; *No. 19* is "Miscellaneous Correspondence," 1768–1797; *Nos. 21–55* is "China Supercargoes Ship Diaries" and includes the years 1749–1751, as well as earlier periods; *Nos. 56–89*, carry the title "Canton Diaries and Consultations," 1751, 1753, 1775–1788; finally for the period 1748–1776 there is *No. 195*, "China and Japan: Miscellaneous," 1710–1814.

SUMATRA

If the efforts by the Company to establish a permanent commercial foothold in Java failed, it was more successful on the island of Sumatra. In 1684 a factory called York Fort was established at Bencoolen (modern Benkulen); in 1714 it was moved to a more healthy site but near the earlier factory and took the name Fort Marlborough. Meanwhile, in 1703 it became a Presidency with a governor and council and so remained until 1785. The documents in the India Office Library that throw light on the Company during the years 1748–1776 are the following: (a) "Letters, etc., from Fort Marlborough, 1740–1772," in six volumes; (b) "Fort St. George Proceedings relative to a settlement at Achin, 1772–1773," in one volume; (c) "Letters, etc., from Fort Marlborough, 1773–1781," in two volumes.

PERSIA AND THE PERSIAN GULF

Direct commercial relations were established with Persia early in the seventeenth century. In 1616 a factory was erected by the Company at Gombroon (modern Bandar Abbas) and somewhat later at Shiraz and Ispahan (modern Ishahan) both well inland. In 1622 a factory appeared on the island of Ormus (modern Hormuz) and in 1640 another well up the Gulf at Basra, thus opening up trade with Turkish Arabia. When Gombroon was given up in 1763 a factory higher up the Gulf was created as Bushire. The following groups of documents have relation to Persia and the period 1748–1776: (a) "Gombroon Diary," 1726–1763, with gaps, in 12 volumes; (b) "Letters, etc., from Gombroon, Basra, etc.," 1703–

1811, with gaps, in 7 volumes; (c) "Home Correspondence on Persian affairs," 1764–1769, including also letters from Sir John Lindsay, 1770.

ST. HELENA

This island providing a port of call for the East India Company ships to and from India was occupied by its servants in 1659 and remained in the possession of the Company until in 1836 when by reason of the India Act of 1833 it was turned over to the Crown. In the India Office there is a series of 81 volumes concerned with St. Helena, carrying the title, *St. Helena Consultations*. The records of these run from 1676 to 1817, with gaps.

SHIPPING

In the early years of the East India Company the ships in its service were built at its dockyard at Blackwall. Then the experiment was begun of hiring ships to meet the Company's needs for the long voyage and by 1652 the building of ships was discontinued and the freighting of other ships became the general practice. But all ships' officers were appointed by the Company and it also made regulations regarding pay and private trade. However, in the waters of India the Company had its own ships for defence and such tasks as surveys.

Each of the principal officers of a ship kept an account of the voyage and in addition there was the official log kept in a special book. By 1818 there was such a vast accumulation of ship papers that it was decided to destroy the records of the lesser officers before the year 1800; then in 1860 there took place the destruction of all ship records except the official logs. The logs now extant in the India Office are fairly continuous from 1702 to 1833. See *List of Marine Records* (1906). Reference has been made to the *St. Helena Consultation* series, which contain a muster roll of every company vessel from 1741 to 1808, and also *A Register of Ships Employed in the Service of the Honourable the United East India Company, 1707–1760*, by Charles Hardy (1800), and the supplementary volume (1811) by his son, Horatio C. Hardy, that carries the record down to 1810. There are also in the *List of Marine Records* in some 900 volumes, Sect. III under the heading "Miscellaneous," the following pertinent records: *No. 1*. "Historical Sketch of the Company's shipping concerns and other papers, 1600–1796"; *No. 505*, "Lists of Company's own ships sent out, 1772–1810"; *Nos. 506–508*, "Lists of Ships in the service, etc., 1773–1832"; *No. 651*, "Register of Commanders, 1737–1832"; *Nos. 652–666*, "Commanders and mates: Descriptions, etc., 1771–1833"; *Nos. 680–690*, "Bombay Marine and Indian Navy establishment, 1737–1837"; and *No. 901*, "Miscellaneous papers, 1683–1813."

Englishmen Residing in India

The earliest surviving list in the India Office Library of both Company servants and other residents in India is a printed series extending from 1768 to 1799, with gaps. Also among the papers of the Accountant-General are returns carrying the title, "Baptisms, Marriages, and Burials of Europeans in the Indies." For Bengal the records extend from 1713; for Madras they begin in 1698; for Bombay they are from 1709; for Fort Marlborough on Sumatra the returns are from 1760 to 1825; and for St. Helena, they begin in 1767 and end in 1835. There is also a series of 41 volumes that carries the title "Bengal Civil Servants," which covers the years 1706–1860 and is limited before 1826 to "covenanted" servants. There is a similar list in two volumes of Madras convenanted servants, 1702–1801; the earliest Bombay records of covenanted servants in the India Office start with 1786. With respect to the army in India, there is an *Alphabetical List of the Officers of the Indian Army, with the dates of . . . promotion, resignation, or death,* 1760–1834, prepared by Edward Dodwell and J. S. Miles in 1838; the same authors also prepared a "List of Indian Medical Officers, 1764–1838."

Finally, there is the series, "Europeans not in the Company's Service." In this connection it should be noted that (based upon the Company's charters and then by various acts by Parliament relating to India) no British subject could go to India, during the period under examination, without the Company's permission or reside there without a licence. While the surviving lists of such Europeans in the Bengal Presidency does not begin until 1794, for Madras it covers the years 1702–1780 in 2 volumes and for Bombay from 1719 to 1787 in 2 volumes.

The French in India

Returning to India there is a special series in 17 volumes that carries the title *The French in India.* The parts of it concerned with the years 1748–1776 are as follows: *Nos. 1–4,* "Miscellaneous correspondence, 1664–1810"; *No. 5,* "Proceedings of the Madras Government, 1771–1775," concerned with French complaints of interruption to their commerce; *No. 6,* "Claims of the French, Dutch, and Danes, 1772–1797"; *Nos. 7–10,* "Disputes with the French, 1773–1776, 1783–1786"; *No. 16, Mémoire pour le Sieur Dupleix* in translation; and finally, *No. 17,* "Miscellaneous, 1772–1820."

The Dutch in India and the Far East

The Dutch as well as the French were rivals of the English in the area to the east of India and in India itself. The following groups of papers in the India Office relate to the Dutch activities in the Far East during the period 1748–1776: (a) "A treatise on the connexions of the Dutch in the Eastern Seas, 1596–1795"; (b) "Copies of treaties, farmans, etc., 1596–1864," in four volumes; (c) "Miscellaneous Documents," 1617–1824, with some gaps, in 8 volumes; (d) "Disputes with the Dutch," 1750–1764, in 7 volumes. Closely related to the Dutch are the series of documents on Java. In the seventeenth century the commercial relations of the Company with the island were so important as to lead to the creation of the Java Presidency before 1682 when the English were expelled from the island. Two volumes of manuscripts are, nevertheless, pertinent: (a) "The Relations between the Dutch and various states in the Eastern Seas, 1595–1795," compiled in 1818 from records at Batavia; and (b) "Letters, etc., from Bantam, 1707–1818."

HUDSON'S BAY COMPANY

Chartered in 1670 by Charles II, the Governor and Company of Adventurers of England Trading into Hudson's Bay, or simply the Hudson's Bay Company, is the only one of the great English chartered joint-stock companies that has survived. For the period with which this series is concerned, 1748–1776, the Company at the beginning of it had to face the attacks of rivals at home and competition of the French traders of Canada; and toward the end of it—in face of the penetration of the Montreal "pedlars" into the area of the Saskatchewan River—to establish well inland from the Bay such a post as Cumberland House.

The Company still continues in business at Beaver House. Although its records are voluminous, they are not always complete for a particular year or post. These holdings are divided into the following categories, for each of which there is a catalogue: (1) London records: minute books, correspondence inward and outward, correspondence with the British government, order books, etc.; (2) Post records, including correspondence, accounts, journals, etc.; (3) Ships' records, chiefly logs; (4) Governors-in-Chief of Rupert's Land, correspondence and journals; (5) Miscellaneous records, including diaries and journals.

Microfilms of most of these records are held in the Public Archives of Canada. It should also be noted that since 1938 the Hudson's Bay Record Society (until 1949 in conjunction with the Champlain Society of Toronto) has published an annual volume of source material from the archives. These volumes also contain very full introductions and biographical material.

See Andrews and Davenport: *Guide,* pp. 369–71, and Crick and Alman: *Guide,* pp. 236–7.

GENERAL POST OFFICE

The role played by the British Post Office in the eighteenth century British Empire has been described by Herbert Joyce in his *History of the Post Office from its Establishment down to 1836* (London, 1893). Among the surviving records of the General Post-Office that bear on the colonies are the 623+ volumes in the series that carries the title "Treasury Letter Books," beginning with the year 1686. These letters, reports, and memorials from the Treasury concern such matters as improvement of the post-office service, post-roads surveys in North America, and the establishment of additional routes and packet service. While Vol. 7, 1725–1760, is missing, Vols. 8 and 9, 1760–1778, are available. The following items are among those in Vol. 8 falling within the period 1748–1776: (1) "Memorandum relating to some Improvements suggested to be made in the Management of the Post Office in North America," Jan. 28, 1764 (pp. 95–105), which is concerned with the survey of post-roads undertaken by the Deputy Postmasters for North America, Benjamin Franklin and John Foxcroft, the establishment of packet boats to the southern colonies, the modification of the existing laws regarding the delivery of ship letters, and the creation of a regular post between New York and Quebec; (2) The Earl of Hillsborough to the Postmasters General, May 27, 1768, on improving the packet service to the West Indies and the southern parts of the continent of North America (p. 258); (3) The secretary of the Post-Office to Thomas Bradshaw, June 4, 1768, that Benjamin Franklin, a Deputy Postmaster General for North America, was returning to the colonies (p. 258); (4) A representation from the Post-Office to the Lords of the Treasury (n.d.), about packet boats employed "in its Foreign Correspondence," and a further representation regarding the four North American packet boats (pp. 57–74); (5) Postmasters General to the Lords of the Treasury, June 6, 1768, recommending the establishment of four packet boats between Falmouth and Charleston, South Carolina; also relating to the land post in the southern part of the continent, to the post in the West Indies, and to the victualling expenses of the New York packets (pp. 260–3); (6) The Lords of the Treasury to the Postmasters General, July 5, 1768, authorizing them to contract for four packet boats to operate between Falmouth and Charleston and to increase the allowance for victuals for the packet boats to New York (p. 264); (7) Memorials, etc., concerning packet boats between Pensacola and Jamaica, 1768–1770 (pp. 273–7; 283–5; 293–300); (8) Letters concerned with the establishment of a fifth packet boat between Falmouth and New York, June 6, 1770 (pp. 301–2).

Two items from Vol. 9 should be included: (1) Postmasters General to Lords of the Treasury, Sept. 23, 1771, suggesting increased estimate for New York and Carolina packet service (pp. 4–7); (2) Postmasters General to the Lords of the Treasury, Feb. 14, 1776, concerning the estimated cost of arming American packet boats, and a warrant, March 5, 1776, authorizing such expenditures, to be sent to Halifax by packet boat (pp. 129–34).

In addition to the "Treasury Letter Books" there is the series "Orders of the Board, 1737–1771," in three volumes, with orders appointing deputy postmasters general and other officers in North America. Here are among other orders those appointing: Benjamin Franklin and William Hunter (I, 180); Benjamin Barons for the southern department (II, 126); and Hugh Finlay and John Foxcroft (III, 25). There is also the appointment of Hugh Finlay as a riding surveyor for the continent of North America (III, 10–11); and for establishing at New York a regular central post office (III, 10). Another volume, called "Instructions," 1763–1811, lists the following instructions: (1) To Benjamin Barons, deputy postmaster general for the southern department, Jan. 5, 1765 (pp. 53–6); (2) To Capt. Arthur Clark, of the *Diligence* packet boat running between Jamaica, Pensacola, and Charleston, March 24, 1769 (pp. 82–3); (3) To Capt. Terence MacDonagh of the packet boat *Comet* running between the same places, July 30, 1770 (pp. 93–5).

Finally, there is the volume "American Letter Book, 1773–1783," which contains among other items of interest an account of cash paid by Deputy Postmasters General in North America, Benjamin Franklin and John Foxcroft, to the receiver general of the Post-Office (p. 50), and the dismissal of Franklin from his post, Jan. 31, 1774 (p. 15). See Andrews and Davenport: *Guide*, pp. 273–6; and Crick and Alman: *Guide*, pp. 219–20.

THE CORPORATION OF LONDON

The archives of the Corporation of the City of London are preserved in the Corporation of London Records Office, Guildhall, London, E.C. 2. There are among these papers two particularly relevant groups of records: (1) The Journal of the Common Council, and (2) The Common Hall Minute Books, selections from both of which have been published in *Addresses, Remonstrances, and Petitions to the Throne, Presented by the Court of Aldermen, the Court of Common Council, and the Livery in Common Hall Assembled, Commencing the 28th October, 1760, with Answers Thereto* (privately printed, London, 1865). Papers concerned with the period 1748–1776 in these two groups are as follows:

Journals of the Common Council. No. 61. ff. 113–115. Instructions to representatives in Parliament on the state of the nation, referring to losses in North America, Oct. 28, 1756; *No. 62. ff.*

36–38, 139–140, 158. Congratulatory addresses on military successes in America, Oct. 18, 1759, Oct. 14, 1760; *ff. 237–238.* Address upon the conquest of Belle Isle, June 16, 1761; *ff. 330b–334b.* Address on capture of Martinique, April 6, 1762; *No. 63. ff. 14–15.* Address to king upon the conquest of Havana, Oct. 1, 1762; *No. 66. ff. 104–105.* Petition to Parliament against the Quebec Bill, June 3, 1774; *ff. 105–106.* Petition to king against the Quebec Bill, June 18, 1774; *ff. 170–172.* Letter to Alderman Bull from Francis Masères, agent to the Protestant settlers in Quebec, etc., Jan. 31, 1775; *ff. 177–179.* Answer to Baron Masères's letter, Feb. 10, 1775; *ff. 179, 181, 182, 185.* Various resolutions in behalf of American colonies, Feb. 10, 13 and 21, 1775; *ff. 188–190.* Petition to House of Commons against "Bill to restrain the Trade and Commerce of Massachusetts Bay," Feb. 23, 1775; *ff. 191–192.* Petition to House of Lords against Massachusetts Bay Bill, March 14, 1775; *ff. 236–238.* Letter from the general committee of the association for the city and county of New York, May 5, 1775, praying that the city of London will exert itself to restore union, June 23, 1775; *ff. 239–240.* Address to the king for cessation of hostilities, July 7, 1775; *f. 241.* Motion to send a reply to a letter from New York. Lost in Common Council, July 21, 1775; *ff. 259–260.* Petitions to Lords and Commons for reconciliation with colonies, Oct. 25, 1775; *ff. 296–297, 299.* City address on war in America and king's reply, March 14, 22, 1776; *ff. 296, 354.* Thanks and freedom of the city to Dr. Richard Price for his publication of *Observations on the Nature of Civil Liberty,* March 14, 1776 and July 23, 1776.

Common Hall Minute Books, 1642–1660, 1718 to date (12 vols.+). Contain petitions, remonstrances, resolutions, and records of election, including a number of communications from the American colonies in relation to the war with the Mother Country, such as a letter from the Continental Congress, July 8, 1775, thanking the City for its mediation attempts, read in Common Hall, Sept. 29, 1775. Among the minute-books attention must be particularly called to certain documents in *No. 8.* They are as follows: *ff. 186b–188.* Address to king against the measures adopted with respect to America and proceedings upon the same, April 5, 1775; *ff. 191–192.* New address to king on American war and Proceedings, June 24, 1775; *f. 193.* Letter of thanks from Continental Congress [July 8, 1775], Sept. 29, 1775; *ff. 194–195.* Address to the electors of Great Britain on the American war, Sept. 29, 1775.

See Philip E. Jones and Raymond Smith: *A Guide to the Records in the Corporation of London Records Office and the Guildhall Library Muniment Room* (London, 1951); Andrews and Davenport: *Guide,* pp. 280–3; and Crick and Alman: *Guide,* pp. 185–7.

THE GUILDHALL LIBRARY

In the Guildhall Library, Basinghall Street, London, E.C. 2, are deposited the nonofficial papers relating to the City of London. These records do not pertain directly to the Corporation itself. The following should be noted:

Parochial Records. Include lists of members, baptisms, titles, account books, and inventories of the Church of England as well as dissenting congregations, such as Congregationalists, Baptists, Scottish Presbyterians, and French Protestants, in the city of London.

New England Company Papers. A large miscellaneous collection of papers dating from 1649 when the company was originally created by ordinance as the Society for the Propagation of the Gospel in New England. In 1662 it was chartered by Charles II as the "Company for Propagation of the Gospell in New England and the parts adjacent in America." Generally referred to as the New England Company, it is "the oldest functioning Protestant missionary society." In the pre-Revolutionary War period, it expended most of its funds on the salaries of missionaries to the New England Indians. After the war these appropriations were directed to Canada. The following records should be noted: (1) Treasurers' general and estate account books, 1660–1764 (3 vols.); treasurers' ledgers, 1726–1765 and 1764–1801 (2 vols.); treasurers' journals, 1764–1801 (1 vol.); (2) General court and committee minute-books, 1770–1816 (1 vol.), and index volume, 1770–1830; loose court minutes with some committee minutes, 1655–1816 (1 box); (3) General correspondence, 1668–1818, principally in-letters, with some drafts of letters sent (1 box); letter-book, 1762–1772, largely copies of out-letters; (4) Correspondence from Boston, chiefly concerned with Indian relations, 1677–1761 (2 files); (5) Official copy of the minutes of the Commissioners of Indian Affairs at Boston, 1699–1784 (1 file). In connection with these papers, see William Kellaway: "The Archives of the New England Company," *Archives*, II (1954), 175–82; and also by Kellaway: *New England Company, 1649–1776: Missionary Society to the Indians* (London, c. 1961).

Records of the City Companies. Include records of most of the guilds, such as carpenters, fishmongers, grocers, masons, paint-stainers, etc. These documents are potentially valuable for a study of the Empire, 1748–1776, because of the strong sympathy shown by many of the guilds for the colonists in the crisis which arose.

East India Company. Miscellaneous correspondence, bills, and receipts, 1618–1816.

Davison, Newman & Co. Business records, 1753–1897. The company, founded in 1650, imported produce from the West Indies. There are a few papers concerning the company's agents in Boston and Charleston, S.C.

See the second part of Philip E. Jones and Raymond Smith: *A Guide to the Records in the Corporation of London Records Office and the Guildhall Library Muniment Room* (London, 1951); and Crick and Alman: *Guide*, pp. 221–4.

THE LAMBETH PALACE LIBRARY

No manuscript records in Great Britain are so important for a study of eighteenth-century colonial social life as those now concentrated at Lambeth Palace, the London residence of the Archbishop of Canterbury. In fact, no student of eighteenth-century British colonial history can wisely neglect them. For this reason they are presented with a good deal of fullness. The manuscripts are in two groups: the Lambeth manuscripts, those pertaining to the office of Archbishop of Canterbury, and the Fulham manuscripts, those pertaining to the office of Bishop of London which until recent years reposed at Fulham Palace, Fulham Road, S.W. A considerable number of both Lambeth and Fulham manuscripts, as well as many of those preserved in the archives of the Society for the Propagation of the Gospel in Foreign Parts, all of which have a bearing on colonial America, were transcribed by Francis L. Hawks for the Protestant Episcopal Church in eighteen folio volumes and used to be preserved in its archives in Church Mission House, 281 Fourth Ave., New York City. These documents have since been relocated in the Church Historical Society, Theological Seminary of the Southwest, Austin, Texas, and in the New-York Historical Society, New York City. Many documents embodied in these transcripts are printed either in Francis L. Hawks and W. S. Perry, eds.: *Documentary History of the Protestant Episcopal Church in the United States of America, containing numerous unpublished Documents concerning the Church in Connecticut* (2 vols., New York, 1863–4), or W. S. Perry, ed.: *Historical Collections relating to the American Colonial Church* (5 vols. in 4, Hartford [Conn.], 1870–8). The Hawks transcripts, at least most of them, are now among the Hawks papers (about one hundred boxes) at the New-York Historical Society.

Lambeth Manuscripts

With respect to the Lambeth manuscripts in some 2500 volumes, a list of those preserved and published in 1812 by Henry John Todd carries the title, *A Catalogue of the Archiepiscopal Manuscripts in the Library at Lambeth Palace: With an Account of the Archiepiscopal Registers and other Records there preserved* (London, 1812). Miss Davenport selected for the Charles M. Andrews and Frances Davenport *Guide*, pp. 286–301, those documents bearing on the colonies. We shall follow this listing in so far as the items fall within the period 1748–1776.

1123 (3 vols.) Papers relating to the American colonies, *Vol. I: No. 35.* From Samuel Johnson, Stratford, Conn., July 25, 1745, dealing with training of missionaries in colonial colleges, and the need of bishops in America (early but important); *No. 36.* Copy of letter from Bishop of Oxford to Samuel Johnson, Westminster, March 8, 1745/6, on same subjects; *No. 38.* From the Church of England clergy in New England and New York, dated June 1, 1748. Congratulation on accession to the archbishopric, with 18 signatures; *No. 39.* From H. Frankland to his uncle, London, Dec. 13, 1748, describing state of religion in New England from Church of England standpoint; *No. 40.* From Samuel Johnson, criticizing New England government, n.d.: "Liberty is here Licentiousness; a Junto rule," and it would be advisable for the Crown to resume the government; *No. 41.* From William Gibbs, Simsburg, Oct. 9, and Hartford gaol, Dec. 28, 1749, complaining of injustice that Episcopalians should be forced to contribute to support of a Dissenting minister, and enclosing copy of the warrant for his commitment for non-payment of church rates; *No. 42.* From Samuel Johnson, March 5, 1749/50, dealing with subject of bishops for New England; *No. 43.* Minutes of meeting of Society for the Propagation of the Gospel in Foreign Parts, April 20, 1750, containing reports from missionaries in Newport, Narragansett, Newbury, Providence, etc.; *No. 44.* From Henry Barclay, New York, April 9, 1750. A plea for bishops; *No. 45.* Paper beginning "To the Kings Most Excellent Majesty, The Humble Petition of Hans Jacob Reimsperger, Late of Tuggenburgh in Switzerland, now of Saxe Gotha in South Carolina, relating to Swiss and German settlers in South Carolina," n.d.; *No. 47.* Minutes of meeting of Society for the Propagation of the Gospel in Foreign Parts, July 20, 1750. Reports of troubles on the question of church rates; *No. 48.* Paper by Philip Bearcroft beginning "The Charter of the Colony of Connecticut," relating to Presbyterian assumption of position of the established church, n.d.; *Nos. 49–50.* Papers relating to finances of the Society for the Propagation of the Gospel in Foreign Parts, 1750; *No. 51.* From H. Walpole, London, Jan. 2, 1750/1, relating to the establishment of bishops in West Indies; *No. 52.* From George Cadogan, *et al.*, Augusta, Aug. 31, 1751, on church affairs in Georgia; *Nos. 53–56.* Papers relating to collection of funds for the Society for the Propagation of the Gospel in

Foreign Parts, 1751/2; *No. 60.* Copy of a letter from Jonathan Edwards to Joseph Paice, Stockbridge, Feb. 24, 1752, relating to education of Indians, and contrasting French and English policies in this matter; *No. 61.* From Joseph Paice referring to Edwards's letter, London, July 18, 1752; *No. 62.* Minutes of the Society for the Pennsylvania Germans, London, March 23, 1753; *No. 63.* From Samuel Johnson, Stratford, June 25, 1753, introducing William Smith of Philadelphia and commending his defence of the proposed college in New York against newspaper and other opposition; *No. 64.* Letter by the same, June 25, 1753, mentioning the *Independent Whig* and *Independent Reflector; Nos. 65–68.* Letters recommending William Smith, from Samuel Seabury, *et al.*, John Ogilvie, Henry Barclay, James de Lancey, and Thomas Penn, June 25, 1753; *No. 69.* From Timothy Cutler, Boston, Aug. 30, 1753, on controversial pamphlets published in New England on the state of the church; *No. 70.* From Benjamin Avery, Guy's Hospital, Nov. 9, 1753, dealing with the case of John Pitts; *No. 71.* From David Thomson, Amsterdam, Nov. 16, 1753, referring to English assistance in his labors; *No. 72.* Extract from letter of Thomas Prince, Boston, Dec. 31, 1753, dwelling upon liberality of treatment accorded to Episcopalians in Boston; *No. 73.* From Samuel Chandler, London, Feb. 5, 1754, dealing with German emigrants to Pennsylvania; *No. 74.* Copy of letter from the Archbishop to Samuel Chandler, Croydon House, Feb. 7, 1754, on same subject; *Nos. 75–76.* From Samuel Chandler, London, Feb. 26 and March 17, 1754 on same subject; *Nos. 77–78.* From Samuel Johnson, New York, both on July 10, 1754, mentioning proposed college in New York; *No. 81.* From Timothy Cutler, Boston, Aug. 28, 1754, on controversial publications in the colonies and giving opinion of Jonathan Edwards, as "A New Light"; No. 82. Dr. MacSparran's narrative of the lawsuit concerning the glebe land at Narragansett in New England, c. 1752; *No. 83.* From William Smith, Philadelphia, Oct. 17, 1754, pleading for more missionaries on the frontiers; *No. 84. The Charter of the College of New York, in America,* 1754; *No. 85.* From Samuel Johnson, Stratford, Oct. 25, 1754, dealing with troubles with Dissenters; *No. 88.* From Timothy Cutler, Boston, Jan. 1, 1775, giving information concerning William Macclenachan.

1123 (3 vols.) Papers relating to the American colonies, *Vol. II: No. 89.* From Philip Bearcroft, Charterhouse, Jan. 18, 1755, on church affairs in New England; *No. 91.* Paper entitled "Some Hints humbly offer'd. With a View to the preserving, supporting and propagating, the great Interests of Christianity and the Protestant Religion, amongst the numerous Body of German and Swiss Emigrants, settled in the Backparts of the Province of Pennsylvania &c., and for encouraging them and their Children to learn the English Langauge . . . ," n.d.; *No. 92.* From Samuel Chandler, London, Feb. 3, 1755, on education of German settlers in Pennsylvania; *No. 93.* From Chandler, Feb. 24, 1755, on same subject; *No. 94.* From the Archbishop to the Bishop of Oxford, Croydon House, Feb. 27, 1755, on same subject; *No. 95.* From the Bishop of Oxford to the Archbishop, London, March 1, 1755, on same subject; *No. 96.* Address of churchwardens of St. Paul's Church, Narragansett, South Kingston, March 17, 1755, concerning difficulties with the Dissenters; *No. 97.* Extract from a letter to Dr. MacSparran from one of his parishioners "unless all the Colonys be reduced to some uniformity in Government and are by Some Means reduced to a single Direction *we are all undone,* and shall sooner or later, be reduced to Colonys of France," Narragansett, March 27, 1755; *No. 105.* From William Smith, Philadelphia, Nov. 1, 1756, beginning "The Misery and distress of this unhappy Province, bleeding under the murderous Knives of a Savage Enemy, instigated and led on by Popish Cruelty . . . and the Confusion arising from a Quaker Government." Deals with the missionaries, and criticizes the government; *No. 106.* From Thomas Coram, suggesting founding of a college at Cambridge, Massachusetts, to be called King's College, n.d.; *No. 109.* From Thomas Barton, York, Pennsylvania, March 12, 1757, dealing with conditions since Braddock's defeat; *No. 110.* Supplement to the *Pennsylvania Journal,* No. 782, dated Philadelphia, Oct. 29, 1757, containing letter of William Moore to Gov. Denny, defending his conduct; *No. 111.* From Samuel Johnson, New York, Dec. 5, 1757, dealing with need of bishops, and vacancies in the ministry; *No. 112.* From William Smith, dated Philadelphia County Gaol, Feb. 7, 1758, criticizing Quaker policy; *No. 113.* Paper entitled "A Brief Narrative of the Case of the Rev. Mr. Smith," giving an account of his imprisonment for publication of the Moore letter; *No. 114.* From Robert McKean to Dr. Bearcroft, New Brunswick, New Jersey, Feb. 5, 1758, about the case of William Smith; *No. 115.* Extract from a letter of William Allen to Dr. Chandler, Philadelphia, Feb. 4, 1758, criticizing the government of the colony; *No. 116.* Paper entitled "The Humble Address of the Governors of the College of the Province of New York," New York, May 27, 1758; *No. 117.* Copy of the *Public Advertiser,* London, June 9, 1758, containing letter of Gov. Denny to the Pennsylvania Assembly, dated April 27, 1758; *No. 118.* "The humble Address of the Clergy of the Provinces of New York and New Jersey in America," New York, June 22, 1758. A request for bishops, and announcement of the first commencement of King's College; *No. 121.* Copy of letter from the Archbishop to Samuel Johnson, Lambeth, Sept. 27, 1758, with brief notes on colonial affairs; *No. 122.* From the Church of England clergy in Connecticut, Oct. 5, 1758. Congratulations on accession to the archbishopric; *No. 123.* From Samuel Johnson, New York, Oct. 25, 1758, about candidates for the ministry; *No. 124.* From Robert Jenney, Philadelphia, Nov. 27, 1758, criticizing William Smith; *No. 125.* From William Allen and Richard Peters, Philadelphia, Nov. 2, 1758, on the education of German settlers, and the case of William Smith; *No. 130.* From Samuel Johnson, New York, March 20, 1759, mentioning the *Independent Reflector* and other colonial publications; *No. 132.* From Henry Caner, Boston, April 7, 1759, on the subject of a mission in Cambridge: "Socinianism, Deism, and other bad Principles find too much Countenance among us"; *No. 133.* From Samuel Johnson, New York, April 15, 1759, on same subject; *No. 136.* Minutes of a council at Philadelphia on the bill against lotteries and plays, Philadelphia, June 2, 1750; *No. 139.* Copy of report of the attorney and solicitor-general in the case of Rev. Dr. Smith, London, June 2, 1759; *No. 140.* From William Smith, Philadelphia, June 25, 1759, about his case; *No. 141.* Copy of the minutes of the Committee of Council in Dr. Smith's case, London, June 26, 1759; *No. 143.* Copy of letter from the Archbishop to Dr. Jenney, Lambeth, July 18, 1759, about Smith's case; *No. 144.* To Henry Caner, Lambeth, July 19, 1759, about the proposed Cambridge mission; *No. 145.* To Samuel Johnson, Lambeth, July 19, 1759, on same subject; *No. 146.* From Samuel Johnson, New York, July 25, 1759, giving an account of church and missions; *No. 147.* From the churchwardens of Christ Church, Philadelphia, Oct. 3, 1759, about William Macclenachan and other clergymen; *No. 149.* From William Spurgeon, Philadelphia, Nov. 29, 1758, pleading for bishops and giving an account of William Smith's case; *No. 150.* Paper docketed "Case of Rev. William Smith of Philadelphia," London, Jan. 27, 1759; *No. 151.* From J. Wetmore to Dr. Johnson, Rye, Oct. 12, 1759, about the case of Dr. Beach; *No. 152.* From Samuel Johnson, New York, Oct. 20, 1759, about the Cambridge mission, college and church affairs; *No. 153.* Paper docketed: "Remonstrance of the Clergy of Pennsylvania against Mr. Macclenachan," Philadelphia, Oct. 21, 1759; *No. 154.* From William Smith, Philadelphia, Oct. 21, 1759, chiefly about William Macclenachan, also with references to events of the war; *No. 155.* From Samuel Johnson, Stratford, Oct. 29, 1759, dealing with relations toward Dissenters; *No. 156.* From William Smith, Philadelphia, Nov. 27, 1759, giving an account of religious affairs in the colony, with estimate of numbers belonging to various denominations, and details of grievances in Christ's Church; *No. 158.* Copy of letter from William Smith to Thomas Penn, Nov. 1759, in defence of lotteries; *No. 159.* From Henry Caner, Jan. 1760, on the Macclenachan affair; *No. 162.* "Observations and Questions concerning the Barbados Estate," Jan. 26, 1760; *No. 163.* From Abraham Immer to the

Society for the Propagation of the Gospel in Foreign Parts, Feb. 14, 1760, appealing for assistance. (In Latin); *No. 164.* From Immer, London, Feb. 15, 1760, expressing thanks, and hope for continued protection of his church in Carolina. (In French); *No. 165.* From Samuel Johnson, Stratford, Connecticut, Feb. 15, 1760, dealing with affairs of King's College; *No. 166.* From Henry Barclay in behalf of the Committee of Governors of King's College, New York, Feb. 17, 1760, on same subject; *No. 167.* Extract from the last will of Gov. Christopher Codrington (1668–1710), bequeathing estates in Barbados to the Society for the Propagation of the Gospel in Foreign Parts; *No. 168.* From Bishop Drummond, London, Feb. 29, 1760, dealing with the Barbados plantations; *No. 169.* From the Archbishop to Bishop Drummond, Lambeth, March 3, 1760, on same subject; *No. 170.* "Memorandum for Mr. Trecothie of some Covenants proper for a Lease of the Society's Plantations," Barbados, March 11, 1760; *No. 171.* From Bishop Drummond, London, March 15, 1760; *No. 172.* Draft of a letter from the Society for the Propagation of the Gospel in Foreign Parts to their attornies in Barbados, March 15, 1760; *No. 174.* Copy of letter from Samuel Nicolls to Dr. Jenner, *et al.*, London, March 25, 1760, about William Macclenachan; *No. 175.* Paper entitled "Mr. Norton abt Philadelphia College," April 12, 1760. Note on the support of Pennsylvania College by lotteries; *No. 176.* From Thomas Penn, Philadelphia, April 12, 1760, on same subject; *No. 177.* Paper entitled "The humble Petition of a poor negro Woman, commonly called by the name of Esther Smith," July 19, 1760. Appeal of a slave born in New York and brought to England; *No. 178.* From Lord Hardwicke, London, July 19, 1760, delivering opinion that a slave brought to England is still a slave, and that baptism does not alter this status; *Nos. 179–180.* From Dr. Squire, Greenwich, July 20, 21, 1760, concerning Esther Smith; *No. 181.* From Silas Told on same subject, n.d., but received Aug. 20, 1760; *No. 182.* From churchwardens and vestrymen, Westchester, Aug. 1, 1760, requesting appointment of a missionary; *No. 183.* "Minutes of a Convention or voluntary Meeting of the Episcopal Clergy of Pennsylvania," Philadelphia, April 30, 1760; *No. 184.* "Some Account of the Missions in Pennsylvania, etc., delivered in at a Convention of the Clergy of that Province," Philadelphia, May 2, 1760; *No. 186.* From Presbyterian ministers of Pennsylvania, May 24, 1760, in behalf of William Macclenachan, with 18 signatures; *No. 187.* "The humble Address of the Missionaries and other Clergy of the Church of England residing in and near the Province of Pennsylvania," 1760, setting forth difficulties facing the churches; *No. 188.* From Thomas Penn, Spring Garden, June 13, 1760, enclosing copy of minutes of assembly on subject of lotteries; *No. 189.* From

William Smith, July 1, 1760, on church affairs in Pennsylvania; *Nos. 190–191.* From Samuel Johnson, New York, July 13–30, 1760, dealing with affairs of church and colony. Postscript mentions death of Gov. de Lancey, and importance that his successor be "not only a good Statesman, but a Friend to Religion and the Church"; *No. 193.* Copy of letter from the Archbishop to Lord Barrington, Lambeth, Aug. 22, 1760, referring to Ogilvie and the Mohawk Indians; *No. 194.* Letter from several members of the Church of England at Philadelphia, on behalf of William Macclenachan, n.d., but received Aug. 23, 1760; *No. 195.* From William Macclenachan, giving an account of himself, n.d., but received Aug. 23, 1760; *No. 196.* From William Smith, Philadelphia, Aug. 26, 1760, stating his position; *No. 197.* From Lord Barrington, War Office, Aug. 28, 1760, dealing with question of places of worship and chaplains for the army in America; *No. 198.* Minutes of Committee of Council about bills from Pennsylvania, Aug. 27, 28, 1760; *No. 199.* From Bishop Drummond, Brodsworth, Sept. 24, 1760, about Barbados; *No. 200.* An extract from the books of the Society for the Propagation of the Gospel, dated 1760, relating to Mr. Macclenachan; *No. 201.* From Samuel Nicolls, Northall, Middlesex, Oct. 3, 1760, also about William Macclenachan; *No. 205.* From Henry Caner, Boston, Oct. 6, 1760; *No. 206.* Copy of letter from the Archbishop to Macclenachan, Lambeth, Oct. 9, 1760, reviewing his case; *No. 207.* Copy of letter to William Smith, Lambeth, Oct. 12, 1760, about the Philadelphia convention of clergymen; *No. 208.* Copy of letter to same, Lambeth, Oct. 20, 1760, containing reference to Free-Masons; *No. 213.* Copy of letter to Samuel Johnson, Lambeth, Nov. 4, 1760, chiefly about King's College; *No. 214.* Draft of proxy for the Archbishop's representative on board of governors of King's College, dated 1760.

1123 (3 vols.) Papers relating to the American Colonies, *Vol. III: No. 216.* From Samuel Johnson, New York, Nov. 24, 1760, on colonial publications and affairs of King's College; *No. 217.* Copy of letter from the Archbishop to Samuel Johnson, Lambeth, Jan. 20, 1761, dealing with affairs of King's College and attitude of the king toward the American churches; *No. 218.* From Episcopal clergymen of Boston and vicinity, Boston, Jan. 26, 1761, enclosing *No. 219,* with 16 signatures; *No. 219.* Address from ministers in and about Boston to George III, 1761. A note states that it was not presented, because it asked for bishops; *No. 224.* From Samuel Johnson, New York, May 2, 1761, concerning candidates for the ministry and the question of bishops; *Nos. 225–226.* Address of the Governors of the College in the Province of New York to George III, May 12, 1761, 2 copies; *No. 227.* From Samuel Johnson, New York, May 20, 1761, chiefly on college affairs; *No. 228.* Draft of projected address enclosed in *No. 224; No. 229.* From Jean Moore to Bourdillon, London, May 21, 1761, in relation to Abraham Immer. (In French); *No. 230.* From Bourdillon to Jean Moore, May 22, 1761, dealing with Immer's position in Carolina; *No. 231.* From Episcopal clergy of Philadelphia, May 28, 1761, dealing with William Macclenachan; *No. 233.* From Samuel Johnson, New York, June 14, 1761, on church affairs; *No. 234.* From Charles Inglis, Dover, Del., June 21, 1761, containing references to Dunkards; *Nos. 235–236.* From William Smith, Philadelphia, July 20, Aug. 20, 1761, about church matters; *No. 238.* Copy of letter from the Archbishop to William Smith, Lambeth, Oct. 10, 1761, about church matters; *No. 242.* Memoranda of letter from the Archbishop to Samuel Johnson, Dec. 10, 1761; *No. 244.* From George Harrison, New York, Jan. 2, 1762, about church affairs on Long Island; *No. 245.* From Samuel Johnson, New York, Jan. 9, 1762, on King's College affairs; *No. 246.* From Henry Barclay, New York, Jan. 11, 1762, in behalf of committee of governors of King's College; *No. 247.* From Archbishop of York to Dr. Burton, London, Jan. 23, 1762, about estate in Barbados; *No. 251.* From Samuel Johnson, New York, Feb. 27, 1762, on church matters; *No. 252.* From Dr. Bentham, Christ Church, Oxford, March 11, 1762, referring to Mr. Cooper's leaving Oxford for the New York College, and the Archbishop's patronage of the college; *No. 254.* From Myles Cooper, Queen's College, Oxford, March 15, 1762, relative to his appointment in the College of New York; *No. 255.* Archbishop's reply to Mr. Cooper, approving of his having reasonable time to prepare for his voyage, unsigned copy; *No. 256.* From Cooper, Queen's College, Oxford, March 24, 1762, stating that he is ready to sail for New York; *No. 257.* From William Smith, London, March 29, 1762, about college affairs, and need of more missionaries; *No. 258. An Humble Representation. By William Smith, D.D., Provost of the College, Academy, and Charitable School of Philadelphia; in Behalf of the said Seminary, and by Appointment of the Trustees thereof, 1762; No. 259.* From Samuel Johnson, New York, April 10, 1762, on church and college affairs; *No. 262.* "An humble Address of the governors of the College of the province of New York on the need of funds," May 14, 1762; *No. 263.* From George Harrison, New York, July 5, 1762, asking for recommendation as judge of vice-admiralty court; *No. 264.* From James Jay, July 10, 21, 1762, on the plan for raising funds for King's College; *No. 268.* From William Smith and James Jay, London, Aug. 9, 1762, on funds for the colleges; *No. 269.* From Henry Caner, Boston, Aug. 9, 1762, on a rival society for converting the Indians; *No. 270.* Printed paper headed "Colleges of Philadelphia and New York, in America," Aug. 19, 1762, a grant from the king to collect money in Great Britain and Ireland; *No. 271. An Act to incorporate certain Persons by the Name of the Society for propagating Christian Knowledge among the Indians of North America* [1762]; *No. 273.* From William Smith, London, Sept. 27, 1762, about Harison; *No. 275.* From James Jay, Sept. 30, 1762, on collections for the colleges; *No. 276.* Copy of letter from the Archbishop to the Bishop of London, Lambeth, Oct. 5, 1762, on a "Society for propagating Christian Knowledge among the Indians in North America"; *No. 277.* To Henry Caner, Oct. 6, 1762, on same subject; *No. 278.* To Samuel Johnson, Lambeth, Oct. 6, 1762, on controversial publications and the rival society; *No. 279.* From the Bishop of London, Bath, Oct. 11, 1762, on the rival society; *No. 281.* From William Smith, London, Nov. 22, 1762, on the rival society; *No. 282.* Paper entitled: "Remarks on an Act lately passed in the Massachusetts Government erecting and incorporating a New Society 'for propagating Christian Knowledge among the Indians in America,'" by William Smith; *No. 283.* From Francis Alison, Philadelphia, Dec. 2, 1762, about funds for freeing captives from among the Indians; *No 284.* From Myles Cooper, New York, Dec. 2, 1762, about King's College; *No. 285.* From Anthony Benezet, Philadelphia, Dec. 4, 1762, against the slave trade; *No. 286.* From Samuel Johnson, New York, Dec. 5, 1762, about King's College; *No. 287.* From the Bishop of York, London, Dec. 11, 1762, about the new society; *No. 288.* From Henry Caner, Boston, Dec. 23, 1762, on same subject; *No. 289.* From Samuel Johnson, New York, Jan. 6, 1763, on same subject; *No. 290.* From Henry Caner, Boston, Jan. 7, 1763, about controversial literature published by Dissenters; *No. 291.* "The Address of the Trustees of the College, Academy and Charity School in the City of Philadelphia," Philadelphia, Jan. 11, 1763, a letter of thanks; *No. 292.* From Richard Peters, Philadelphia, Jan. 15, 1763, on church and college affairs; *No. 294.* From Edward Chester, London, Feb. 1, 1763, on the new society; *No. 295.* From Jacob Duché, Philadelphia, Feb. 4, 1763, on church affairs; *No. 296.* A letter of thanks on behalf of the college from governors of King's College, New York, Feb. 6, 1763; *No. 297.* From John Burton, Eton College, Feb. 25, 1763, about Barbados; *No. 298.* From members of St. Andrew's Church in Simsbury, Connecticut, appealing for aid for the church, n.d., but received March 1763, with 29 signatures; *No. 300.* Copy of letter from the Archbishop to Samuel Johnson, Lambeth, March 30, 1763, on church affairs; *No. 301.* To Henry Caner, Lambeth, March 30, 1763, dealing with the troubles with Dissenters; *No. 305.* To Richard Peters, Lambeth, April 18, 1763, on the same subject; *No. 306.* From Anthony Benezet, Philadelphia, April 24, 1763, against the slave trade; *No. 309.* From Henry Caner, Boston,

June 8, 1763, on troubles with the Dissenters; *No. 311.* From Myles Cooper, New York, June 23, 1763, on King's College affairs; *No. 316.* From Samuel Johnson, Stratford, Aug. 10, 1763, concerning bishops and missions; *No. 317.* From Henry Caner, Boston, Aug. 16, 1763, on the "Established Church" of New England; *No. 319.* Copy of letter from the Archbishop to Henry Caner, Lambeth, Sept. 15, 1763, chiefly about the rival society; *No. 320.* To Jacob Duché, Lambeth, Sept. 15, 1763, stating that there is danger of the college of Philadelphia becoming "a mere Presbyterian faction"; *No. 321.* From the Archbishop of York, Sept. 15, 1763, dealing with Barbados; *No. 322.* Copy of letter from the Archbishop to H. Barclay, Sept. 19, 1763, on King's College affairs; *No. 323.* To Myles Cooper, Lambeth, Sept. 19, 1763, on same subject; *No. 324.* From Myles Cooper, New York, Sept. 23, 1763, on same subject; *No. 325.* Copy of letter from the Archbishop to Samuel Johnson, Sept. 28, 1763, referring to Cooper and to missions in New England and New York; *No. 327.* From Thomas Barnard to William Hooper, Salem, Oct. 15, 1763, on the character of William Walter (copy); *No. 328.* From Richard Peters, Philadelphia, Oct. 17, 1763, on the college, George Whitefield, the great number of Presbyterians, and the question of bishops; *No. 329.* From Samuel Johnson, Stratford, Oct. 20, 1763, on church affairs in Connecticut; *No. 330.* From Myles Cooper, New York, Nov. 2, 1763, about his salary as president of King's College; *No. 331.* From Henry Caner, Boston, Nov. 16, 1763, on Dr. Mayhew's publications; *No. 332.* From William Hooper, Boston, Nov. 23, 1763, on a bequest to the church; *No. 335.* From the Archbishop of York, London, Dec. 16, 1763, dealing with Barbados; *No. 336.* From Samuel Johnson, Stratford, Dec. 20, 1763. "Is there then nothing more that can be done, either for obtaining Bishops, or demolishing these pernicious Charter Governments, and reducing them all to one form, in immediate dependance on the King?"

1124. (3 vols.) Journals of the S.P.G., 1758–1766, containing full abstracts of letters from the Society's missionaries in America and elsewhere.

Fulham Manuscripts, General Correspondence

Since the Bishop of London was considered to be the diocesan head of the Church of England in America in the eighteenth century, whether or not canonically this was true, the papers relating to his office are of particular interest and importance. Among the American papers there are over two thousand letters and documents, which are now brought together and classified in forty volumes, mostly manuscripts. When Miss Davenport examined them early in the present century in preparing the Andrews and

Davenport *Guide* the papers were uncatalogued and lying loose in boxes. Since that time they have been organized by Professor William W. Manross of the Philadelphia Divinity School and also the School's Librarian, acting under the supervision of the General Theological Seminary. From his labours have come *The Fulham Papers in the Lambeth Library, American Colonial Section: Calendars and Indexes* (Oxford, Eng., 1965). From this calendar items have been selected pertaining to the years 1748–1776, especially those that throw light on the colonial scene. To avoid errors the text of the calendar will be closely followed except when necessary to make alterations.

It should be noted that the arrangement of the Fulham papers differs from that of the Lambeth papers in that the material in each volume is organized both geographically and alphabetically as well as chronologically. The presentation of this material will therefore be by volume and within it by number or numbers rather than page or pages to conform to the general arrangement of this *Guide*. The Manross calendar is to be especially commended for its fullness.

VOLUME I

NEWFOUNDLAND

Nos. 60–61. Jos. Gorham, lieutenant-governor of Placentia, to Bishop Terrick, Nov. 12, 1771, asking for a clergyman. Town and garrison have been without a regular minister for twelve years.

NOVA SCOTIA

Nos. 88–89. Statement of Dumesnil de St. Pierre, July 1, 1767 (in French), that he has set apart 40,000 acres for the establishment of the Anglican Church in his colony of French Protestants at Cap de Sable, and proposes to appoint Jaques Adam de Martel as chaplain;

Nos. 90–91. John Eagleson to Rev. Dr. Burton, Secretary of S.P.G., Halifax, Jan. 3, 1769. He was sent by the lieutenant-governor to newly settled island of St. John (later Prince Edward Island), where he officiated five months and recommends appointment of permanent missionary. Has been assigned to Cornwallis for the winter;

Nos. 92–95. Peter de la Roche to Bishop Terrick, Lunenburg, Nov. 22, 1771. Deplores lack of bishops in colonies. Lack of confirmation gives scandal to continental Protestants, as in their home churches no one is admitted to communion without a renewal of baptismal vows. Would it be lawful for a priest to perform the ceremony, omitting the laying on of hands? Plans a series of catechical lectures, based on Osterval's catechism. On communion days, of which they have but few a year, it is necessary to hold three services between ten and two. Would it be permissible to speak the words of administration just once to each rail? In some parts of North America the priest murmurs them continuously while distributing the elements, but he feels that this practice lacks dignity. Speaks of two colleagues, Mr. Bailly, French, and Mr. Bryzelius, German;

Nos. 96–101. Peter de la Roche to ('Rev'd Sir'), Lunenburg, Aug. 4, 1772. A long complaint against Bryzelius. De la Roche was appointed on application for a French missionary, but found that what was really wanted was one who could read the English service properly. Bryzelius claims to have had a university education, but was apparently bred as a watchmaker. Was an itinerant Moravian preacher in New Jersey and Pennsylvania. Recommended for Anglican orders by Rev. Richard Peters; has the '*American Spirit* . . . of Separation, dispute, animosity to good order and discipline, and fondness for independency'; he does not understand the English service, is lax in discipline and neglects his ministerial duties for his farm. Dominated by his wife, he connived at closing the school, splitting the salary with the schoolmaster.

QUEBEC

Nos. 106–109. Petition, undated but identified (see *No. 111*) as presented in 1764, signed by civil officers, merchants, and other Protestant residents of Quebec, asking an S.P.G. allowance for J. Brooke, who has served the civil population while deputy chaplain (later chaplain) of the garrison. Also ask a missionary who can officiate in French;

Nos. 110–111. J. Brooke to Bishop Terrick, undated, but referring to 1764 petition. Living in retirement, on official leave, while retaining his chaplaincy; Brooke answers plea of deputy chaplain, Montmoulin, for compensation from him by saying that his absence does not increase deputy's duties, and by citing his own past services to garrison and civil population;

Nos. 114–115. Report of subcommittee to committee of Privy Council for plantation affairs, Whitehall, May 30, 1765 (copy). Asked to report on proposals for a Roman Catholic bishopric in Quebec from the Chapter of Quebec and from Gov. James Murray; they say they append several propositions designed to grant freedom of worship to Roman Catholics while providing for a Protestant Establishment, but cannot pass on the legality of their own proposals. Appended propositions not included in this copy;

Nos. 116–119. Jean-Baptiste Noël Veyssière to Bishop Terrick (in French), undated, but including copy of a certificate from Protestants of Quebec dated Aug. 29, 1767. Veyssière, a former Récollet priest, educated in seminaries in France and Quebec, who served for a time as missionary to Iroquois, has been converted to Protestantism and offers his services as a Protestant minister in Quebec. Copies of documents in Latin and French bearing on his career. Certificate dated as above, in English, asks his appointment to minister to French-speaking Protestants in Quebec;

Nos. 120–160. Francis Masters [Francis Masères?] to Rev. Majordie, May 28, 1768. Glad to learn that Veyssière has been appointed to Trois Rivières and DeLisle to Quebec, presuming that latter appointment is as minister to French Protestants. If to English congregation, he would prefer Mr. Montgomery. Regrets admission of Roman Catholic bishop, as without one it might have been possible to win over the priests to Protestantism by allowing them to marry and encouraging use of Anglican liturgy in French. Proposes some measures to this end under existing conditions. Bishop could be forbidden to exercise any power save that of ordination. Then the two measures proposed above could still be adopted. Monastic property could be acquired by Crown, either through sequestration or by forbidding orders to admit new members so that property would escheat on death of present members. Governor should be given power of arbitrary arrest over priests. Protestant grammar schools should be established and Catholic seminaries reduced to one. That at Montreal, the richest, should be turned into a Protestant university;

Nos. 161–162. Extract from a letter of Gov. Carleton to the Earl of Hillsborough, Quebec, July 21, 1768, objecting because Veyssière and Montmillon [Montmollin] returned with mandamus requiring him to appoint them to parishes of Trois Rivières and Quebec respectively. Criticizes Veyssière, for levity. Montmollin wants him to seize the Jesuits' church which they have repaired at some expense after it was used as a storehouse during early English occupation;

Nos. 163–166. Sir Guy Carleton to Bishop Terrick, Quebec, Aug. 13, 1768, explaining need for toleration. Inhabitants almost all Roman Catholic, and are a hardy people, inured to arms and with powerful Indian allies. Few Protestants outside of English garrison, and number diminishing. He will protect Protestant ministers, if they behave prudently, but has warned Montmollin and Veyssière against disputation. Hints at doubts as to the sincerity of Veyssière's conversion. Letter to be delivered by Dr. Brooke, of whom he speaks favourably;

Nos. 167–168. Lord Barrington to Bishop Terrick, June 8, 1769. He will appoint Montmollin, recommended by bishop, as chaplain at Quebec in succession to Dr. Brooke unless something unexpected prevents. Asks bishop to make sure that there is no monetary transaction between the two. Makes residence a condition of appointment. Indicates that Chabiand DeLisle is chaplain at Montreal;

Nos. 169–170. D. F. de Montmollin to Bishop Terrick, Quebec, Oct. 6, 1773. Thanks him for past favours and asks help in education of eleven-year-old son;

Nos. 173–183. Copy of ecclesiastical clauses in draft of instructions to Gov. Carleton, undated. They are as follows: (a) Toleration of freedom of worship does not include extending to Church of Rome the privileges of an established church; (b) All appeals to any foreign ecclesiastical authority prohibited; (c) Only such episcopal or vicarial powers to be exercised as are essential to the free exercise of religion, and those only on license from the governor; (d) No Roman Catholic, except present incumbents, allowed to hold any ecclesiastical benefice unless he is a native of province; (e) Protestant minister to be appointed to any parish where a majority of the inhabitants desire it; (f) Tithes paid by Protestants in a parish with a Roman Catholic incumbent to go to a general fund for the support of Protestant ministers; (g) All Roman Catholic holders of benefices to take oath of allegiance and incumbents to hold benefices during good behaviour; (h) Priests who marry not to suffer any penalty; (i) Burial in churchyards to be permitted to all Christians; (j) Prayers for the King required; (k) Seminaries of Quebec and Montreal to be continued, but subject to visitation by the governor; (l) Other religious orders, except Jesuits, to be continued tentatively, but forbidden (except those for women) to receive new members; (m) Jesuits to be suppressed; (n) Missionaries to Indians to be replaced with Protestants; (o) Roman Catholic clergy forbidden to proselytize or influence persons making wills; (p) Protestant clergy to be protected; they, as well as schoolmasters, to be licensed by Bishop of London, and his colonial jurisdiction to be supported, except for collating to benefices, probating of wills, and granting marriage licenses, which powers are reserved to the governor; (q) Laws against vice and immorality to be enforced;

Nos. 184–189. List of parishes, religious communities, and Indian missions, with estimated incomes, undated and in French;

Nos. 190–194. A similar, but not identical, list in English, undated;

Nos. 195–196. Undated. An estimate of ecclesiastical incomes together with proposals from an unknown correspondent for curbing Roman Catholicism and promoting Protestantism. Proposals include: establishing a Protestant ecclesiastical court; introducing a Protestant bishop, with dean and chapter, and suppressing the Roman Catholic bishops (plural used); requiring candidates to seek ordination from licensed Roman Catholic bishops in England or Ireland;

Nos. 197–202. Undated. "Heads of a plan for the Ecclesiastical Affairs in the Province of Quebec." These may be the "propositions" referred to in *Nos. 114–115,* but as they are in a different hand and on different size sheets, the identification is not thought certain enough to justify joining the two documents. The plan includes the following proposals: (a) To introduce as full a Protestant establishment as is possible while allowing freedom of worship to Roman Catholics; (b) The person "licensed to superintend the affairs of the Romish Church" (term "bishop" avoided throughout) to be limited to functions essential to freedom of worship; (c) Jesuits to be suppressed and their property transferred to S.P.G.; (d) Indian missionaries to be replaced with Protestants; (e) The Chapter of Quebec to be abolished; (f) Récollet order to be continued but forbidden to receive new members. Its property to go to S.P.G. when it dies out; (g) Seminaries of Quebec and Montreal consolidated and surplus funds to be used for Protestant purposes; (h) Religious communities of women to be continued with prohibition of new professions; (i) Dependence of all ecclesiastical organizations on any authority in France to be abolished; (j) Public processions to be prohibited; (k) Churches to be shared with Anglicans; (l) Protestants to be exempted from tithes; (m) Protestant clergy to be introduced in such numbers as may be recommended by Bishop of London and S.P.G.

CONNECTICUT

No. 288. Matthew Graves to Bishop Sherlock, New London, July 20, 1750. Introduces Mr. Copp, son of "Presbyterian" parents and former schoolmaster at New London, who is seeking orders. Having heard reports that the bishop intends to appoint a native commissary for the region, suggests that as an American is commissary for "western" part of continent, a European might be named to the "eastern" part. Too modest to propose himself, he suggests MacSparran. Church people still subjected to some persecution. Praises bishop's sermon on the earthquake;

Nos. 289–290. Samuel Johnson to Bishop Sherlock, Stratford, Sept. 17, 1750. Acknowledges what appears to be appointment as commissary, though language is vague. Pleads for a bishop, subject to London. Finds it strange that the "true protestant English church" should not be supplied with bishops, when France and Spain provide for theirs, and even the "little whimsical Sect of Moravians" have them;

No. 291. Samuel Johnson to Bishop Sherlock, Stratford, March 26, 1751. Sent by Thomas Bradbury Chandler, who is coming for orders. Expresses gratitude for the bishop's efforts on behalf of an American episcopate. Encloses paper sent by Connecticut clergy to a member of S.P.G. commenting on pamphlet sent from England with proposals for American Bishops (*No. 292*). Unable to give much account of work of former commissaries, as he had little contact with them;

No. 292. Address of Connecticut clergy to member of the S.P.G. Undated, but attached to *No. 291*. They would like an episcopate with full power, as in England, but will accept a limited one as better than none. Think that a bishop might "quieten" disputes among dissenters that have followed the Great Awakening. Can see no objections except such as proceed from hostility to the Church. Believe an American bishop necessary to cause of Christianity under infidel attacks. Think that dissenters would become reconciled to it in a little time. Bishop needed to settle disputes and maintain discipline among Church clergy;

Nos. 293–294. Samuel Johnson to Bishop Sherlock, Stratford, Sept. 25, 1755. Desire for episcopate heightened by fact that he hopes to see his son become a minister, but is shocked by thought of his having to cross the Atlantic for orders. Five of twenty-five clergy within his knowledge who have made the voyage have died before return. If a resident bishop cannot be obtained, he suggests that one of the youngest and ablest of the bishops of the small dioceses be licensed to visit the colonies for a year or two;

No. 295. Ebenezer Punderson to Bishop Sherlock, New Haven, Dec. 27, 1756. Acknowledges receipt of bishop's sermons, which he has ordered to be read in his several churches. He has four "good timber" churches and two other congregations under his care. Asks gift of Bibles and Prayer Books from S.P.G.;

Nos. 296–297. Clergy of Connecticut to Bishop Terrick, New Haven, Sept. 14, 1764 (signed by Samuel Johnson on behalf of whole group). Congratulate bishop on his translation and express hope for appointment of an American bishop;

Nos. 298–299. Clergy of Connecticut to the King, Hebron, June 5, 1765. Petition for the appointment of a bishop;

Nos. 300–301. Clergy of Connecticut to Bishop Terrick, Hebron, June 6, 1765. Enclose *Nos. 298–299* and leave presentation to the bishop's judgement;

Nos. 302–303. Samuel Johnson to Bishop Terrick, Stratford, July 15, 1765. Answering request for information about religious situation in America. Writes with difficulty, because of trembling hand (noticeable difference in handwriting). Independents, "or Congregationalists, as they call themselves," established by law in

New England, especially Massachusetts and Connecticut, but torn by "Arminian, Calvinistical, Antinomian & Enthusiastical controversies." Presbyterians strongest in the "Southwestern colonies," especially New York, New Jersey, and Pennsylvania, where they have flourishing presbyteries. Renews plea for a bishop. Dissenters claim that civil government in England is on their side, and that episcopacy may eventually be abolished there;

Nos. 304–305. Jeremiah Leaming to Bishop Terrick, Norwalk, July 20, 1765. Asks advice on case of woman who married in belief her first husband was dead. He returned after some years, but refused to live with her, as she had children by second husband, but not by him. He left again and has not been heard from for eight years. Woman and second husband desire admission to communion;

Nos. 308–309. Clergy of Connecticut to Bishop Terrick, Stratford, Oct. 8, 1766. Renew plea for a bishop, though they admit that turbulence of times makes measure temporarily inexpedient;

Nos. 310–314. Rough notes of meeting held in Brookline, town of Pomfret, Conn., Feb. 6, 1770, and protest against action of meeting. Ostensible issue was the rebuilding of the meeting-house, but real issue appears to have been whether churchmen, who were building their own church, should be taxed for it. Meeting held that they should be;

No. 317. Clergy of Connecticut to Bishop Terrick, May 19, 1771 (signed by Jeremiah Leaming as secretary). Petition for a bishop;

Nos. 318–319. Churchwardens and parishioners of Wallingford to Bishop ———. Undated. Speak of themselves as a newly organized church, served once a quarter by Theodore Morris. Some of them have been imprisoned for non-payment of ecclesiastical taxes.

VOLUME II

FLORIDA

Nos. 18–19. Nathaniel Cotton to Bishop Terrick, Pensacola, Dec. 15, 1768. Congregation includes many Presbyterians, who have no teacher of their own. They have asked him to supply them with Bibles and Prayer Books. Having exhausted those he has, he asks bishop's aid in obtaining more from the government (through Lord Hillsborough) or the S.P.G. People have sent home a petition asking government to build them a church;

Nos. 20–21. Nathaniel Cotton to Bishop Terrick, Pensacola, June 10, 1770. Acknowledges gift of Bibles, Prayer Books, and tracts and would like to have shipment repeated every year. Urges appointment of a schoolmaster.

GEORGIA

No. 25. Certificate of table companions of William Duncanson, Charlestown, S.C., Oct. 20, 1761. They saw no evidence of hard drinking, swearing, or quarreling during his stay in Charlestown, and believe that reports of misconduct are unfounded;

Nos. 26–27. E. Vanderhoof to William Duncanson, Charlestown, Dec. 30, 1761. Attests to Duncanson's good character on behalf of himself and Lt. Nun;

Nos. 28–29. William Duncanson to Bishop Osbaldeston, Savannah, March 26, 1762. Refers him to "Mr. Pearson the treasurer" for letter stating his situation and defending his character (*Nos. 30–31*). Asks to be appointed to St. Johns, S.C.;

Nos. 30–31. William Duncanson to Edward Pearson, Savannah, March 30, 1762. He was first appointed to the Bahamas to replace Robert Carter, who was ill, but Carter recovered and refused to yield. He was transferred to Savannah, but was rejected there, because of unfavourable reports received from Charleston, where he had stopped on his way to the Bahamas, though he says it was really because Bartholomew Zouberbuhler, the missionary there, did not want to retire. He went to Augusta and was well received for about six months. Then he got into a brawl with his host, named Paris, over an affront he had given to a young woman of the household. Mentions two other enemies, Williams and Barnard, both justices;

Nos. 32–33. John Moore to Bishop Osbaldeston, Charterhouse Square, Sept. 17, 1762. At the request of Mr. Pearson, he has searched S.P.G. records and finds that Duncanson was dismissed for drunkenness, swearing, and other offences before he had reached Savannah;

Nos. 34–35. Executors of Bartholomew Zouberbuhler to Bishop Terrick, Savannah, Nov. 29, 1770. Zouberbuhler left the bulk of his estate to be devoted to pious uses and especially to the religious instruction of Negroes on his plantation. They have been employing Cornelius Winter in this work and now recommend him for orders so that he can better fulfill the intent of the trust;

Nos. 36–39. Zouberbuhler's executors to Gov. Wright, Savannah, Nov. 22, 1770, asking him to recommend Winter to the bishop for orders; they also ask Samuel Frink, rector at Savannah, to support their application;

Nos. 40–41. Extract from will of Bartholomew Zouberbuhler. Copy dated Sept. 23, 1770, attested by Thomas Moody. Residue of estate, including plantation of Beth Abram, to be held by trustees, who are to employ a suitable person to instruct the slaves there. If a slave, after being instructed, shows a desire to instruct others of his race in the faith, and the trustees are convinced of his sincerity, he shall be manumitted for the purpose. Any surplus income is to be used to employ a catechist for the Negroes in Savannah;

Nos. 42–43. Samuel Frink to Bishop Terrick, Savannah, Dec. 7, 1770, recommending Winter;

Nos. 44–45. Haddon Smith to Bishop Terrick, Liverpool, April 4, 1776. Having been inducted by Gov. James Wright into the living at Savannah, worth about £300 sterling a year, he looked forward to a comfortable future, but he has had to flee to avoid being tarred and feathered by the rebels, whom he offended by writing Loyalist tracts under the name of Mercurius, by preaching on a fast day appointed by the Governor, and refusing to preach on one appointed by the provincial congress. They appointed Edward Langworthy, a layman, to officiate in his church, and would have tarred him (Smith) on the same day that they did John Hopkins, but he happened to be away from home that evening and fled next day.

VOLUME III

MARYLAND

Nos. 193–194. A. Spencer to Bishop Sherlock, Annapolis, Sept. 25, 1750. He went first to Virginia but came to Maryland, where he has been promised a parish. Glad to inform the bishop that Dr. Conyers Middleton's arguments on the miracles are repudiated by all men of sense in this part of the world, and that the bishop's letter on the earthquake is much admired. Note. Conyers Middleton (1683–1750) was a fellow of Trinity College, Cambridge, of latitudinarian views;

No. 195. Alexander Adams to Bishop Sherlock, Oct. 5, 1751. Asking Mr. Onslow, Lord Baltimore's guardian, to disallow act deducting one-fourth of 40 lb. per poll tax and allowing balance to be paid in currency. Encloses some thoughts on bishops in America (*No. 196*);

No. 196. Thoughts on the American episcopate enclosed with *No. 195.* Recommends providing support by making bishop commissary for the probate of wills;

Nos. 197–198. Hugh Jones and Henry Addison to Bishop Sherlock, Aug. 27, 1753. Urges him to take advantage of the present proprietor's expressed zeal for the Protestant establishment to restore some ecclesiastical jurisdiction in Maryland. Former commissary was prevented by government from exercising effective jurisdiction as result of dispute between former Lord Baltimore and Bishop Gibson over need for bishop's license by Maryland clergy. This also led to the preferment of unqualified clerymen;

Nos. 199–200. Alexander Adams to Bishop Sherlock, Sept. 29, 1752. Urges appointment of commissaries, one for Eastern and one for Western Shore. Recommends James Magill for Eastern and Thomas Airey for Western. Complains that some of the younger clergy omit reading the Athanasian Creed;

Nos. 201–202. Alexander Adams to Bishop Sherlock, Stepney Parish, Oct. 18, 1752. Urges bishop to have Lord Baltimore's guardians instruct the governor not to permit any undermining of the establishment, for he understands that an attack is to be made on it at the next meeting of the legislature;

Nos. 203–204. H. Addison to Bishop Terrick, Potowmack River, Oct. 29, 1776. Man known in Maryland as Congreve, but lately ordained by bishop as James Colgrave or Colgreve served for a time as schoolmaster in Addison's county. He was a notorious drunkard and ran away after running heavily in debt. After ordination, he officiated in parish where he had been schoolmaster and got drunk immediately after service. A large part of the congregation withdrew in disgust when he officiated in Annapolis. He has now gone to North Carolina, where he has a parish and a small stipend from S.P.G.;

Nos. 205–206. List of parishes in Maryland and their annual value, 1767. Gives last names only of clergy;

Nos. 207–208. Hugh Neill to Bishop Terrick, Sept. 20, 1768. Assembly passed a bill to set up a commission of the governor, three clergy, and three laymen to regulate the clergy. It was approved by the council, but governor refused to sign it pending instructions. Need for regulation admitted, but pattern of government set up is so clearly Presbyterian that clergy are obliged to oppose it;

Nos. 209–210. Thomas John Claggett to Bishop Terrick, Sept. 20, 1769. In opposition to the above measure (*Nos. 207–208*);

Nos. 211–212. Henry Addison to Daniel Burton, Queen Anne's Parish, Sept. 29, 1769. Asks to be enrolled as member of S.P.G. Pledges contribution of £2 per annum;

Nos. 213–214. Henry Addison to Bishop Terrick, Oct. 24, 1769. Recommending a young man named Hindman for orders. Does not know him personally, but he comes of a leading Maryland family, is recommended by mutual friends and has had the best education that can be obtained in America;

No. 215. Hugh Neill to Daniel Burton, Queen Anne's County, July 18, 1771. Having enrolled several of the Maryland clergy in the S.P.G., he now asks S.P.G. to intervene to secure disallowance of law making clerical stipend payable in currency. Enrollment of clergy was transmitted by Myles Cooper, president of King's College, New York, after a visit to Maryland;

Nos. 216–217. Counties and Parishes of Maryland. *Notation:* "List of clergy and livings in Maryland, 1775, given me by Mr. Boucher." The Rev. Jonathan Boucher (1737–1804) was Rector of Queen Anne's Parish;

No. 218. Conjectural estimate of value of Maryland livings before and after passage of late laws, 1775.

V O L U M E V

MASSACHUSETTS

Nos. 320–321. Charles Brockwell to Bishop Gibson, Boston, Oct. 5, 1748. Written in answer to a letter from him and in evident ignorance of his death. Concerned with complications that have arisen in the payment of Brockwell's salary;

Nos. 322–323. Petition of James Maynard to Bishop Sherlock, Westborough. Undated, but accompanied by a certificate of payment of taxes by Roger Price and wardens of Hopkinton dated, March 11, 1749. Contains copy of act of 1735 providing that taxes of Church of England members should be paid to Church ministers, if the payers regularly attended their services. Petition complains that, in spite of this, Churchmen are often prosecuted for nonpayment of taxes;

Nos. 324–325. Henry Caner and the building committee of King's Chapel to Bishop Sherlock, Boston, Oct. 25, 1749. With the aid and advice of the bishop and Henry Frankland they prepared a memorial to the King for aid in rebuilding the chapel, but it has not been presented by the minister to whom it was entrusted (Pelham). With the support of the governor, they are seeking to revive it, and ask the bishop's support;

Nos. 326–327. Timothy Cutler to Bishop Sherlock, Boston, Dec. 12, 1749. Acknowledges a letter from the bishop and expresses gratitude for his concern for the colonial Church;

Nos. 328–329. Charles Brockwell to Bishop Sherlock, Boston, Jan. 18, 1749/50. Concerning some of the difficulties he has in collecting his salary;

Nos. 330–331. Henry Caner to Bishop Sherlock, Boston, Jan. 31, 1750. Acknowledges letter from the bishop and expresses gratitude for his effort to promote a colonial episcopate;

Nos. 332–333. Charles Brockwell to Bishop Sherlock, Boston, April 13, 1750. Encloses a pamphlet (not in present collection) which he says is an attack on all the English bishops and on Laud in particular. It was occasioned by a sermon of his on the centennial of Laud's execution. He thinks it should be prosecuted;

Nos. 334–335. Charles Brockwell to Bishop Sherlock, Boston, June 23, 1750. More about his salary difficulties. Identifies the author of the offending pamphlet (*Nos.* 332–333) as Capt. Philips.

VOLUME VI

MASSACHUSETTS

Nos. 1–2. Charles Brockwell to Bishop Sherlock, Boston, Feb. 15, 1750/1. He has been reassured by the bishop that his salary will be paid more regularly in the future and that he will not lose the arrears, but nothing has been paid yet;

Nos. 3–4. Roger Price to Bishop Sherlock, Hopkinton, April 19, 1751. As Price had lost his health through service in Africa and the West Indies, Bishop Gibson gave him the living of Leigh, England. When his health did not return, the bishop approved his going to New England, while retaining his English living. Bishop Sherlock is now demanding that he return or resign that living. If the bishop insists, he will have to return. He is responsible for the support of a wife and six children of his own, besides three Negro children. Hopes for success of Sherlock's efforts to obtain American bishops;

Nos. 5–6. Timothy Cutler to Bishop Sherlock, Boston, April 14, 1751. Unable to tell the bishop much about functioning of commissary under his predecessor. Commissary in New England started to investigate cases of Theodore Morris in New London and Stephen Roe in Boston, but both terminated proceedings by leaving. Roe was also under charges in South Carolina. Main objection of dissenters to colonial episcopate is that it will strengthen the Church. He thinks it would be especially useful to have bishops in colonies where dissenters control the government;

Nos. 7–8. Henry Caner to Bishop Sherlock, Boston, May 6, 1751. He is under the impression that the former commissary (Roger Price) never qualified himself properly by exhibiting his commission to the governor and taking the required oaths. If commissarial authority is renewed, he offers some suggestions for strengthening it. Thanks bishop for his efforts for colonial bishops. Dissents from concession that no bishops would be sent to colonies with dissenting government. Thinks that that is where they would be needed most;

Nos. 9–10. Charles Brockwell to Bishop Sherlock, Boston, June 8, 1751. Sorry that plan for colonial episcopate has been defeated. Recommends restoring and strengthening of commissarial jurisdiction.

Roger Price could not be very strict because he was guilty of irregularities himself, such as deviating from some of the canons regulating the performance of marriages;

Nos. 11–12. Charles Brockwell to Bishop Sherlock, Boston, Oct. 2, 1751. Asks the bishop to help him in collecting his still unpaid first year's stipend and to appoint him as commissary to succeed Price, who is reported returning to England to occupy his living there;

Nos. 13–14. Timothy Cutler to Bishop Sherlock, Boston, Oct. 16, 1751. Introduces ———— Colton, a candidate for orders, and praises the bishop's zeal for the colonial Church;

Nos. 15–16. Roger Price to Bishop Sherlock, Boston, ———— 16, 1751. Apologizes for delay in obeying the bishop's order to return to England. He had had difficulty in selling his effects. Money is scarce;

Nos. 17–18. Charles Brockwell to Bishop Sherlock, Boston, Jan. 21, 1752. The Church in Newbury has chosen Edward Bass, "late a dissenting teacher" to be ordained as assistant to Mathias [Matthias] Plant, now largely incapacitated by age and infirmity. In spite of opposition by Brockwell and Cutler, Bass has been officiating as lay reader before going to England for orders. Brockwell now begs for a living in England, as he and his wife, who is crippled with rheumatism, both dread facing old age in New England. He has lost two Negroes within twelve months. They cost him £70 sterling;

Nos. 19–20. Charles Brockwell to Bishop Sherlock, Boston, March 21, 1752. Boston is suffering from a smallpox epidemic, the first in twenty years. Some are fleeing the city, other resorting to the "profane practice of Inoculation." Caner, who has not had the disease, is exchanging with McGilchrist of Salem, who has. Brockwell is officiating at Marblehead, vacant since Malcolm moved to Maryland;

Nos. 21–22. Roger Price to Bishop Sherlock, Boston, May 14, 1752. He has been unable to sail during the spring because he could not obtain a suitable conveyance;

Nos. 23–24. Timothy Cutler to Bishop Sherlock, Boston, July 1, 1752. Colton (see *Nos. 13–14*) died of smallpox on his return voyage;

Nos. 25–26. Charles Brockwell to Bishop Sherlock, Boston, July 2, 1752. After reflection, he decided that it was his duty to remain at his post instead of going to Marblehead during the epidemic (*Nos. 19–20*). Urges appointment of a missionary there;

Nos. 27–28. Charles Brockwell to Bishop Sherlock, Boston, Sept. 15, 1752. He is giving up pretensions to post of commissary, and again begs for a living in England;

Nos. 29–30. Charles Brockwell to Bishop Sherlock, Boston, May 3, 1753 (written April 4, but not sent until the later date). Work of tearing down the old chapel has begun. Arrangements were made to hold services in Trinity Church, but some person without authority arranged to have the weekday services in a New Light meeting house. Caner consented but Brockwell refused. Now Caner is sick and Brockwell is carrying the full duty;

Nos. 31–32. Timothy Cutler to Bishop Sherlock, Boston, June 21, 1754. Introduces McSparran, who is visiting in England for his health and who has lost the suit of his parish to recover certain lands. Cutler, who is just recovering from a serious illness, besides officiating regularly in Christ Church, had held occasional services in Woburn;

Nos. 33–34. Charles Brockwell to Bishop Sherlock, Boston, Dec. 16, 1754. He is seeking to start a Church in Cambridge and has had some success, but is at present hampered by ill health. Whitefield has again preached in Boston, his services were well attended, but produced no conspicuous effects;

No. 35. Henry Caner to Bishop Sherlock, Boston, Feb. 25, 1755. Encloses a recent act of the assembly which is described somewhat vaguely but apparently affects the corporate status of local churches;

Nos. 36–37. Wardens and vestry of King's Chapel to Bishop Sherlock, Boston, Aug. 26, 1755. Report death of Brockwell and recommend appointment of John Troutbeck as successor;

Nos. 38–39. John Troutbeck to Bishop Sherlock, Boston, Aug. 27, 1755. Applying for the post of assistant at King's Chapel. He is an S.P.G. missionary, in the country a little more than a year, and, at present settled in a "woody" part, which is bad for his health;

Nos. 40–41. Henry Caner to Bishop Sherlock, Boston, Aug. 27, 1755. Brockwell died Aug. 20. Caner seconds application for appointment of Troutbeck, who is missionary at Hopkinton. Asks permission to draw the assistant's salary during the vacancy, as has been customary;

Nos. 42–43. Caner and wardens and vestry of King's Chapel to Bishop Sherlock, Boston, June 22, 1756. Urge the bishop to appoint an assistant without further delay. Dr. Cutler has suffered a paralytic stroke and Christ Church has only the temporary services of an unnamed itinerant;

Nos. 44–45. Clergy of New England to Bishop Sherlock, Boston, Jan. 26, 1761. Enclosing an address to George III on his accession. It includes a plea for bishops;

Nos. 46–47. Henry Caner to Bishop Osbaldeston, Boston, Nov. 6, 1762. Congratulates him on his translation, urges appointment of a commissary, and introduces John Wingate Weeks, a candidate for orders, who is applying to the S.P.G. for the mission at Marblehead, vacated by the death of the incumbent;

Nos. 48–49. Remarks on an act lately passed in Massachusetts incorporating a New Society for Propagating Christian Knowledge among the Indians. *Notation*: "Recd. from the Abp. of Canterbury, 1763." The act encroaches on the rights of other American provinces, as the activities of the proposed corporation are not restricted to Massachusetts. It does not make the missionaries subject to the newly appointed Indian agents. An example of the evils that may result is shown in Pennsylvania, where a Friendly Association of Quakers has arrogated to itself the right to represent the Indians in treaty negotiations, though Sir William Johnson refuses to recognize it. The act does not even subject the corporation itself to any supervision by civil authority;

Nos. 50–51. Henry Caner to Bishop Terrick, Boston, Sept. 1, 1764. Congratulates him on his translation and introduces Samuel Wentworth, a youth educated by Caner "as my own," who is going to England to prepare for the university;

Nos. 52–53. W. Walter to Bishop Terrick, Boston, Sept. 10, 1764. Ordained by Bishop Osbaldeston, he reports his arrival in Boston, where he is assistant in Trinity Church;

Nos. 54–55. Henry Caner to Bishop Terrick, Boston, Sept. 10, 1765. The clergy of the province, assembled for Dr. Cutler's funeral, agreed, subject to the bishop's approval, to hold annual conventions voluntarily until a bishop or commissary is appointed;

Nos. 56–57. Henry Caner to Bishop Terrick, Boston, Feb. 3, 1766. Grateful for bishop's approval of the plan for voluntary conventions. In answer to a question from the bishop, he expresses the opinion that the people of Christ Church would support it if the S.P.G. aid were withdrawn, but he is not sure that they could provide sufficient support for a minister to attract a man of talent;

Nos. 58–59. William Agar to Bishop Terrick, Cambridge, Mass., April 20, 1766. A former military chaplain induced to go to America by some family crisis, he is temporarily supplying the mission in Cambridge, but plans to travel further before accepting a permanent appointment. He was kindly received by Gov. Bernard. He found New England society more cultured than he expected, but the people are mostly Congregationalist and are stirred to insurrection by their pastors. If a bishop is appointed, he must be content to confine himself to ordination and confirmation;

Nos. 60–61. Henry Caner to Bishop Terrick, Boston, May 15, 1766. Thanks him for his part in obtaining degree of D.D. from Oxford for Caner and some other American clergy;

Nos. 62–63. Clergy of Massachusetts and Rhode Island to Bishop Terrick, Boston, June 17, 1767. In their efforts to combat the present disorders and preach obedience to civil authority, they feel greatly handicapped by the want of a bishop. They introduce Willard

Wheeler and [William] Clark, candidates for orders. Wheeler is designed for a mission at Georgetown on the Kennebec. Clark, the son of a dissenting minister, is highly qualified in every way, except that he is deaf. His father, with the same defect, has served his congregation acceptably;

Nos. 64–65. Henry Caner to Bishop Terrick, Boston, July 28, 1767. Introduces Willard Wheeler and expresses gratitude for the Bishop of Landaff's sermon before the S.P.G. in support of a colonial episcopate;

Nos. 66–67. Joseph Harrison to Bishop Terrick, Boston, May 12, 1768. He has been ill a good deal of the time since his arrival as Collector of Customs. Introduces Mather Byles, a former Congregationalist minister, seeking orders. Byles was one of the few dissenting ministers who rebuked the disorders following the Stamp Act;

Nos. 68–69. Clergy of Massachusetts and Rhode Island to Bishop Terrick, Boston, Sept. 22, 1768. Wheeler has been ordained and is now settled in his mission. They are much concerned by the political disorders. Clark has been reading prayers in Dedham and Stoughton, and they are now requesting his ordination, having pledged £30 sterling for his salary;

Nos. 70–71. Clergy of Massachusetts and Rhode Island to Bishop Terrick, Sept. 21, 1769. They recommend Daniel Fogg, who is preparing for orders but is visiting the South before going to England for ordination;

Nos. 72–73. Henry Barnes to Bishop Terrick, Marlborough, Mass., Sept. 25, 1769, urges reopening of mission at Hopkinton;

Nos. 74–75. Mather Byles to Bishop Terrick, Boston, Sept. 24, 1770. Acknowledges conferring of an unspecified degree by Oxford at request of the bishop;

Nos. 76–77. Henry Caner to Bishop Terrick, Boston, Dec. 3, 1770. Daniel Fogg has been ordained and returned as Caner's assistant. The political situation seems more quiet. Introduces Capt. William Martin, an artillery officer.

NEW HAMPSHIRE

Nos. 106–107. Extract of a letter from Gov. John Wentworth to Joseph Harrison, Wentworth House, Sept. 24, 1769. Outlines a plan to promote the Church in the colony by appointment of a chaplain to the governor, who will become the centre of a system of itinerants. Province at present is ill-supplied with ministers of any sort and rent by many controversies;

Nos. 108–109. Declaration of Eleazer Wheelock and other trustees of Dartmouth College, Dec. 4, 1769. Express approval of plan to

add Bishop Terrick to the board. Copy attested by Gov. Wentworth with notes showing positions held by the various trustees;

Nos. 112–113. Gov. Wentworth to the English trustees, Portsmouth,
April 28, 1770. Encloses *Nos. 108–111* and expresses conviction that
college will help to promote civilization of the Indians;

Nos. 114–119. Gov. Wentworth to Bishop Terrick, Portsmouth, April 28,
1770. Gives an account of the growth of Wheelock's work, of which
he heartily approves, though it has been opposed by some of the
Congregationalist clergy, including Dr. Chauncey. As the colony
is growing rapidly, he believes that it can be won for the Church
if the S.P.G. will promptly supply missionaries to the new settlements. He proposes a plan by which the S.P.G. contributions will
be gradually decreased as the settlements grow in strength;

Nos. 120–121. Extract of a letter from the English trustees to Dr.
Wheelock, April 25, 1771. As the money which they raised was
contributed expressly for the conversion and education of Indian
youths, they object to the fact that the college charter authorizes
the education of English youths as well;

Nos. 122–123. English trustees to Gov. Wentworth, London, July 1, 1771
(copy). Repeat the above objection (*Nos. 120–121*).

NEW JERSEY

Nos. 150–151. Josiah Hardy to Bishop Osbaldeston, Perth Amboy, July 30,
1762. On arriving in this town as governor of New Jersey, he was
surprised to learn that, though the seat of government, it had been
without a Church minister for many years. He at once wrote the
S.P.G., urging the appointment of a missionary, but now believes
that Dr. Bearcroft was probably dead before the letter arrived,
so he [Hardy] appeals to the bishop;

Nos. 152–153. Richard Peters to Bishop Terrick, Liverpool, Nov. 30, 1764.
Asked for advice on a petition of the clergy of New Jersey seeking
an instruction to the governor to issue marriage licences only
to Protestant clergy; he thinks that this is required by the provincial law, but sees no objection to an instruction. As Mr. Penn
and he have had to review all the laws of New Jersey, he thinks it
would be wise for the bishop to confer with them before acting,
and will arrange such a conference when he returns to London;

Nos. 154–155. Anonymous letter to Bishop Terrick, New Jersey, Dec. 10,
1764, complaining that too many of the clergy practice medicine;

Nos. 156–157. Clergy of New Jersey and New York to Bishop Terrick,
Perth Amboy, Oct. 2, 1765. They petition him, as they have the
King and the archbishops, for the appointment of colonial bishops.
They are willing to accept a plan which deprives the bishops of

any civil jurisdiction, though they think that this is less than might be reasonably expected in a Christian country;

Nos. 158–159. Clergy of New York and New Jersey to Bishop Terrick, Perth Amboy, Oct. 4, 1765. Since framing the above address (*Nos. 156–157*), they have received the bishop's acknowledgement of an earlier address congratulating him on his translation. They warn him of two ex-dissenting ministers, named Potter and Murray, who have left the area under grave suspicion of immorality and may seek ordination with false testimonials;

Nos. 160–161. Nathaniel Evans to Bishop Terrick, Haddonfield, Feb. 24, 1766. Reports safe arrival at his station, where he is the first Church of England clergyman. Prospects seem favourable. One church building has been completed and another is under construction;

Nos. 162–163. Thomas Bradbury Chandler to Bishop Terrick, Elizabeth, July 10, 1766. Thanks the bishop for his part in obtaining an Oxford D.D. for him. Regrets to learn from the bishop's reply to the clergy that the authorities at home believe that the political disturbances in America make it inexpedient to press for colonial bishops at this time;

Nos. 164–167. Thomas Bradbury Chandler to Bishop Terrick, Elizabeth, Oct. 21, 1767. Is sending a copy of his pamphlet in support of the colonial episcopate. Having recently spent a fortnight on the Eastern Shore in Maryland, he reports that he found the laity remarkably sober and religious, but that the clergy there are, with some exceptions, men of poor character. P.S., Dec. 3, 1767. Letter was delayed for want of conveyance. It is now being carried by Kempt [John Tabor Kempe] attorney-general of New York;

Nos. 168–173. Thomas Bradbury Chandler and Myles Cooper to Bishop Terrick, Elizabeth, Dec. 5, 1767. They have been made a committee by the convention to defend and explain a former address. The bishop's reply showed that he felt that the address reflected on his zeal for the colonial church and that he feared that the regular voluntary conventions might assume jurisdictional functions that would give them a presbyteral character. They seek to reassure him on both points. Note: This address, probably drawn up after receiving the bishop's reply to their earlier address (See *Nos. 162–163*), does not appear in the present papers.

NEW YORK

Nos. 203–204. James Wetmore to Bishop Sherlock, Rye, Aug. 17, 1752. In a pamphlet controversy started by Noah Hobart between the Churchmen and Independents in New England, the Churchmen, on arguing that the establishment of the Church of England ought

legally to extend to the colonies, were met with a declaration from
the Lords Justices to Lieut.-Gov. William Dummer in 1725 that
there was no religious establishment in New England and a letter
from Bishop Gibson to Benjamin Coleman, holding that all Protestants should have equal freedom in New England. Wetmore
tries to show that these do not apply to present argument.

NORTH CAROLINA

Nos. 270–275. Bishop Sherlock to the Board of Trade, Feb. 13, 1759.
Asked to comment on a recent ecclesiastical act of North Carolina
with reference to its effect on his jurisdiction and the Crown's
right of patronage; he says that it certainly infringes the latter, since
the vestries have the right of presentation. It also denies the prin-
ciple of episcopal government by making the clergy subject to
direction and trial by their vestries. Whether it infringes his jurisdiction depends on whether or not he has any. When he came to
the see in 1748 he waited on the King and presented the need for
colonial bishops. He was graciously received and referred to the
ministers, but could not get an interview with them. He had another audience and asked permission to say that it was His
Majesty's will that they should consider the matter. This was
granted, and he had a conference with the ministers, but nothing
came of it. He then obtained permission to present the case to
the King in Council, but nothing came of that, either. Had the
colonial jurisdiction come to him on a traditional basis, he would
have accepted it, but Bishop Gibson's application for a royal
commission led to comments by the attorney-general which indicated that issues of prerogative were involved;

Nos. 282–283. Copy of article in instructions to Gov. Arthur Dobbs, 1761.
He is not to prefer any clergyman without a licence from the Bishop
of London and is to use "the proper and usual means" to remove
any clergymen who live scandalously;

Nos. 284–285. John Pownall, Secretary to the Lords Commissioners for
Trade and Plantations to Bishop Hayter, Whitehall, Nov. 27,
1761. Asks him to comment on latest North Carolina vestry acts;

Nos. 286–287. John Pownall to Bishop Hayter, Plantation Office, Dec. 3,
1761. Encloses Bishop Sherlock's comment on previous act (*Nos.*
276–281);

Nos. 288–289. John Pownall to Bishop Osbaldeston, Whitehall, March
22, 1762. Refers the same acts to him, as Bishop Hayter died before he could comment on them;

Nos. 290–293. Bishop Osbaldeston to the Board of Trade, Frith Street,
May 3, 1762. Commenting on the two acts, one for establishing
vestries and one for maintaining orthodox ministers, he objects

that the vestrymen are merely required, in addition to subscribing to the test and taking the oath of abjuration, to say that they will not oppose the Church of England. He thinks that they should at least be required to pledge conformity to the liturgy. The second act provides salaries of £100 currency and requires provision of glebes and rectories, but makes no provision for its own enforcement, or for the collection of fees. It subjects the clergy to trial by civil courts for ecclesiastical offenses;

Nos. 294–295. Meeting of the King in Council, June 3, 1762. Both of the above acts disallowed;

Nos. 296–297. Gov. Arthur Dobbs to Bishop Osbaldeston, Brunswick, Aug. 9, 1762. Congratulates him on his translation and introduces an unnamed candidate for orders;

Nos. 298–299. Extract from a letter of Gov. Dobbs to the Board of Trade, March 1764. There are over 24,000 white taxables (males over sixteen). He holds that these represent 100,000 white persons and 10,000 Negroes. Only six orthodox clergymen, four of whom are faithful and two "very indifferent and of suspicious morals." Salaries are £100 per annum plus £20 until a glebe is provided and vestries have power to enforce collection of 10s. tax;

Nos. 300–301. Extract from a letter of Gov. Dobbs to the Lords Commissioners for Trade and Plantations, March 29, 1764. Notes that he was able to get the new ecclesiastical laws passed because of the absence of the northern members of the assembly. Act also provides for a schoolmaster in each parish. Makes the rector a member of the vestry. Because of lack of clergy, "we abound with Sectaries, and turn Profligates and Deists";

Nos. 302–303. Extract from a letter from [James] Reed, Newbern, July 10, 1765. New act does not raise stipends, but removes some difficulties. Presentation is restored to the Crown and collection of salary is made easier. Salary is £133. 6s. 8d. currency, with glebe house and land, or £20 pounds more in lieu thereof, but the whole is only worth about £76. 13s. sterling;

Nos. 304–305. Gov. William Tryon to the S.P.G., Brunswick, July 31, 1765 (copy). Every Protestant sect abounds in North Carolina, but he thinks that the Presbyterians and New Lights are most numerous. The Presbyterians are in the western counties. The New Lights are in the maritime counties. They are not followers of Whitefield, but of "superior Lights from New England." Only five Church of England ministers, four of whom, Reed, Stewart, Earl, and Moir, are S.P.G. missionaries. He does not name the fifth. Moir is employed as an itinerant, but it would be better if he were fixed in a parish, as it is reported that he seldom preaches anywhere. Latest vestry act will create thirty-two parishes. Asks donation of Bibles and Prayer Books. Whitefield preached a sermon in Wilmington last March which would have done him credit in St. James;

Nos. 306–307. Extract from letter of Gov. Tryon to Lords Commissioners for Trade and Plantations, Aug. 12, 1765. He recommends confirmation of vestry act, though he would have preferred payment of the ministers' salaries from the general treasury;

Nos. 308–311. Printed copy of the act, and some other laws, extracted from the *Laws of North-Carolina, 1765.* Fixes salary at £133. 6s. 8d. per annum, provides for collection and payment, and regulates fees. Immoral clergy to be suspended by governor and council pending decision by the Bishop of London. Glebes and parsonages to be provided;

Nos. 312–313. John Barnett to ———— Waring, Castle Tryon, Feb. 1, 1766. His vestry have promised to pay him the legal salary, but he has only their word for it, as no legal contract can be drawn without a stamp. Widespread public disturbances. Gov. Tryon has sent a contribution to S.P.G. and wants to become a member. Stevens, a Presbyterian minister, is coming home for orders. He has offended the governor and council and is alleged to have boasted that he could obtain episcopal orders for the price of a good beaver hat;

Nos. 314–319. Bishop Terrick to the Board of Trade, March 1, 1766. Commenting on the above act (*Nos. 308–311*), he favours accepting it, in spite of some defects. As no mention is made of the right of presentation, it automatically rests in the Crown and, therefore, in the governor. This makes the absence of any requirement that the clergy be licensed by the Bishop of London less serious, since it can be covered by an instruction. He recommends issuing a fresh instruction to that effect. Because of the importance of removing immoral clergy, he is willing to accept the governor and council's having the right of suspension pending action by the bishop. He takes occasion to point out how defective his colonial jurisdiction is, and to urge the need of colonial bishops;

Nos. 320–321. Gov. Tryon to Bishop Terrick, Brunswick, Oct. 6, 1766. He is told that Stevens (see *Nos. 312–313*) presented the bishop with a document purporting to be a promise of appointment from the vestry of Wilmington. Tryon thinks this must be a forgery, as the vestry do not have the right of presentation and no one will admit signing the document. [James] Cosgreve, though denied the governor's recommendation, because of insufficient testimonials, has come back ordained. Tryon has appointed him to a parish in Pitt County, on three months probation, which he thinks is a good plan with all newcomers. He has sent [George] Micklejohn to the back settlements for the time being, but has not fixed him definitely yet;

Nos. 322–323. Gov. Tryon to Bishop Terrick, Brunswick, April 30, 1767. Concerning the placement of several clergymen;

Nos. 324–325. List of counties and parishes, 1767, with estimate of taxables and some comments. Names incumbents when there are any. Notes predominance of Presbyterians in several parishes;

Nos. 326–327. Certificate of sundry inhabitants of New Hanover County, June 6, 1768. Signers, mostly identified as justices of the peace or members of the council, attest to good character of their minister, John Wills, and recommend him to S.P.G. for a stipend;

Nos. 328–329. Gov. Tryon to Bishop Terrick, Brunswick, June 10, 1768. Wills, who arrived without the bishop's licence, and who is in poor health, is returning to England, but has agreed to come back if he receives an appointment from the S.P.G.;

Nos. 330–331. Gov. Tryon to Bishop Terrick, Brunswick, March 20, 1769. John Cramp, just arrived, is officiating in Brunswick temporarily, Barnett having been transferred to Northampton County. Cosgrove has gone south, and Tryon hopes that he does not return, as his character is bad. It is rumoured that Stevens (see *Nos. 312–313*) has been ordained and is a naval chaplain. Governor encloses a sermon of Micklejohn's and an address from the Presbyterian clergy, both in favour of the government;

Nos. 332–333. Theodorus Swaine Drage to Bishop Terrick, Newbern, Nov. 23, 1769. He has been presented by Governor Tryon to a parish in Rowan County. By a construction of the law now under litigation, the vestries claim the right to approve the governor's presentation. Poor health may force the governor to retire;

Nos. 334–335. Gov. Tryon to Bishop Terrick, New Bern, July 22, 1770. Refers to difficulties of Wills and Drage with their parishes which have been reported more fully to the S.P.G.;

Nos. 336–337. Extract from a report of the Board of Trade, on an act passed in North Carolina in 1771 authorizing Presbyterian ministers to marry without paying a fee to the orthodox clergyman. They hold that it deprives the orthodox clergyman of his legal perquisites;

Nos. 338–339. Gov. Jo. Martin to Bishop Terrick, New Bern, June 20, 1772. Trustees of the school in New Bern have dismissed the schoolmaster, Thomas Thomlinson. The governor thinks the dismissal unjust, but has no legal power to intervene. He thinks that the bishop should secure the disallowance of the act governing the school, and hints that S.P.G. aid be withdrawn;

Nos. 340–343. Petition of Theodorus Swaine Drage to Gov. Josiah Martin, Jan. 10, 1773. Though presented to St. Luke's Parish, Rowan County, by Gov. Tryon in 1770, he has never received any salary, because there has never been a qualified vestry to collect it. In one year the election was postponed. In the other years, vestries were elected but refused to qualify. Petition referred to assembly by the governor. Assembly replied that existing laws provided a sufficient remedy for the grievance of which the petitioner complained;

Nos. 344–357. Vestry Act of ———. Undated, but signed by Gov. Arthur Dobbs. From its content, it appears to belong between the act criticized by Bishop Osbaldeston (*Nos. 290–293*) and that described by Reed (*Nos. 302–303*). It incorporates the bishop's suggestion that vestrymen be required to swear conformity to the liturgy, but leaves the right of presentation in the vestry. Note: This is "An Act Concerning Vestries" passed in 1764. See *The State Records of North Carolina*, XXIII, Laws, *1715–1776*, pp. 601–7;

Nos. 358–359. An act to amend the Act concerning Marriages. Undated. Permits Presbyterian ministers, on licence, to perform marriages, but provides that the fee shall go to the Church of England minister.

VOLUME VII

PENNSYLVANIA

Nos. 314–315. Robert Jenney to Bishop Sherlock, Philadelphia, May 23, 1751. In answer to bishop's query how commissarial jurisdiction was exercised, he says that he was able to do little with it, as no one respected it. Some maintain that as the Church only exists in Pennsylvania because tolerated by the proprietor, its canons are not in force there. Some of the clergy, who come there from warmer climates for their health, misbehave;

Nos. 316–317. Testimony of Susanna, wife of Frederick Maus, stocking weaver, and others before Judge Henry Harrison, June 28, 1762. After William Sturgeon, catechist and assistant at Christ Church, had married Charlotte Maus and William Deadman without a licence, it was discovered that Deadman had another wife. The Maus family and friends testify that Sturgeon performed the ceremony, under considerable pressure from them, late in the evening, when the clerk who issued the licences could not be located, because Deadman had got Charlotte with child and they were afraid he would skip town if the ceremony was not performed immediately. Deadman swore a solemn oath before Sturgeon that he was not previously married;

Nos. 318–319. Wardens and vestry of the united congregations of Christ Church and St. Peter's to Bishop Osbaldeston, June 8, 1762. Ask him to license Sturgeon as one of the ministers of the united congregations. He has been acting as assistant for fifteen years, presumably under a licence as catechist or schoolmaster, though that is not explicitly stated;

Nos. 320–321. Wardens and vestry of St. Paul's Church to Bishop Osbaldeston, Philadelphia, June 22, 1762. Congratulate him on his translation and ask him to license William Macclenachan as their minister. Macclenachan, a former S.P.G. missionary, visited Christ Church and so pleased the congregation with his preaching that he was invited to remain as assistant. After a year, Jenney forbade him further use of the pulpit. Considering this unjust, the present members of St. Paul's withdrew and organized a new church. Note: Though it is not stated here, the dispute arose because Macclenachan was a follower of Whitefield;

Nos. 324–325. Copy of original agreement among the subscribers to St. Paul's, June 4, 1760. Copy attested by John Ross and Thomas Charlton, wardens, June 22, 1762;

Nos. 328–329. Francis Alison to Samuel Chandler, Philadelphia, June 24, 1762. Sturgeon and Jacob Duché are both going home to seek licences as ministers of the united parishes. As the Quakers have complained to the Archbishop of Canterbury about Sturgeon's action in the Maus-Deadman affair, it is thought that Chandler's intervention might have a countervailing effect. Alison gives a similar account of the affair as in *Nos. 316–317* and testifies to Sturgeon's good character and devotion as a minister;

Nos. 330–331. William Sturgeon to Bishop Osbaldeston, Philadelphia, June 29, 1762. He was ordained by Bishop Gibson and appointed catechist to the Negroes and assistant in Christ Church by the S.P.G. in 1747. After Jenney became paralysed, Sturgeon carried on the whole work of the parish for about three years, until Jacob Duché, a native of Philadelphia, returned in deacon's orders. Now the vestry propose to make both him and Duché their ministers;

Nos. 332–333. William Sturgeon to Rev. John Waring, Philadelphia, July 1, 1762. Because of complaints arising out of the Maus incident *(Nos. 316–317)*, he asks the S.P.G. to intercede with Bishop Osbaldeston on his behalf, as he needs the bishop's licence to accept the post at Christ Church;

Nos. 334–335. Testimonial of the clergy of the area to Richard Peters, Dec. 20, 1762. Approve of his becoming rector of Christ Church;

Nos. 336–337. Printed copy of patent of George III, 1762, authorizing William Smith and James Jay to raise money for the College of Philadelphia and King's College, New York;

Nos. 338–339. Printed certificate of Smith and Jay appointing collectors for the County of Stafford. Undated, but refers to the above patent *(Nos. 336–337)*;

Nos. 340–341. Printed appeal for contributions to the College of Philadelphia by William Smith, 1762. Gives names of trustees and faculty.

VOLUME VIII

PENNSYLVANIA

Nos. 1–2. Richard Peters to Bishop Osbaldeston, Philadelphia, Jan. 15, 1763. Announces his election as rector of Christ Church and asks for the bishop's licence;

Nos. 3–4. Wardens and vestry of Christ Church to Bishop Osbaldeston, Philadelphia, Jan. 21, 1763. Duché has returned with the bishop's licence and they have received him and made provision for his support. They will do the same for Sturgeon when they know that he has the bishop's approval. They have, however, decided that having two equal ministers will lead to jealousies and that the parish needs a head. So they have elected Peters rector;

Nos. 5–6. Some of the clergy of the Philadelphia area to Bishop Osbaldeston, Feb. 3, 1763. Recommend appointment of William Smith as commissary;

Nos. 7–8. Sturgeon and Duché to Bishop Osbaldeston, Philadelphia, Feb. 4, 1763. Express approval of election of Peters as rector;

No. 9. Draft of letter from Bishop Osbaldeston to the wardens and vestry of Christ Church, Fulham, May 24, 1763. He approves the election of Peters as rector and hopes he will, as soon as convenient, come to England to receive formal licence. Is willing to overlook Sturgeon's indiscretion (see Vol. VII, *Nos. 316–317*) on assurance that he will be careful to avoid giving offence in the future;

Nos. 10–11. Clergy of New York, New Jersey, and Pennsylvania to Bishop Terrick, Perth Amboy, Sept. 20, 1764. Congratulate him on his translation and express the hope that he will provide the colonies with some sort of ecclesiastical discipline;

Nos. 12–13. William Smith to Bishop Terrick, Philadelphia, Sept. 26, 1764. At the foregoing meeting (*Nos. 10–11*) he presented his plan of having agents and corresponding societies of the S.P.G. in America. The clergy approved and recommended him as agent for New Jersey and Pennsylvania. He hopes that Bishop Terrick will share the zeal of the archbishops in behalf of a colonial episcopate;

Nos. 14–15. Petition of representatives of the High German church (St. George's) in Philadelphia, Oct. 21, 1764, to the Archbishops of Canterbury and York and the Bishop of London. Finding it inconvenient to be under a foreign jurisdiction, they wish to place themselves under the English bishops. They have adopted articles providing that henceforth their ministers shall be episcopally ordained and licenced and that the Book of Common Prayer shall be used in their services;

No. 16. H. Hughes to Bishop Terrick, Philadelphia, Feb. 19, 1765. Encloses an unspecified act of the assembly which he says is in favour of the Church to refute charges which he thinks the clergy have made that it is anti-Church. He has a low opinion of the character of a majority of the clergy;

Nos. 17–18. Address of Pennsylvania clergy to Bishop Terrick, Philadelphia, May 31, 1765. Signed by William Smith as president. Congratulate him on his translation and complain of the headless plight of the American Church;

Nos. 19–20. William Smith to Bishop Terrick, Philadelphia, June 25, 1765. Encloses *Nos. 17–18* and introduces Nathaniel Evans, a candidate for orders. Whitefield has told him that, if he, Whitefield, can obtain a Crown grant for his proposed college in Georgia, he is willing that a Church clergyman should be its head. If this is done, and the governor and chief officials of Georgia and the bishop's commissary, if there is one, are made visitors, Smith approves of the project. He has sent the bishop a tract of his own on Indian affairs;

Nos. 21–22. Richard Peters to Bishop Terrick, Philadelphia, March 1, 1766. He makes a number of suggestions for combining and supplying various missions in the area;

Nos. 23–24. Wardens of St. Paul's Church to Bishop Terrick, Philadelphia, Nov. 11, 1766. Having been given to understand that they are under the bishop's disapprobation, they endeavour to reassure him as to their orthodoxy and regularity. Hugh Neil [Neill], now gone to Maryland, supplied them for a time, and was criticized for so doing;

Nos. 25–26. William Smith to Bishop Terrick, Philadelphia, Nov. 13, 1766. Introduces Samuel Magaw and John Andrews, candidates for orders and graduates of the College of Philadelphia. Though the members of St. Paul's profess loyalty to the Church, they look to Whitefield to send them a minister. He believes that they favour an "independent Church of England" and that a similar spirit pervaded the most recent convention of clergy in New York, New Jersey, and Pennsylvania which, despairing of bishops, advocated some form of conventional government. Smith was unable to attend, and has this information from Peters. Hugh Neill, he says, was a leader in the measures (see Vol. VI, *Nos. 168–173*);

Nos. 27–28. Richard Peters to Bishop Terrick, Philadelphia, Nov. 14, 1766. He criticizes the convention referred to in *Nos. 25–26* for being too zealous in its demands for bishops and unwilling to accept commissaries. St. Paul's proposed to call ———— Hagar (also spelled Agar in this letter [John Frederick Haeger?]), but he was discouraged by Peter's account of the history of the parish;

Nos. 29–30. Richard Peters to Bishop Terrick, Philadelphia, Dec. 12, 1766.

St. Paul's has now been told that Whitefield is sending it a minister, ——— Chapman, rector of Bradley and prebendary of Bristol. Paul Brizelius [Bryzelius], pastor of a church in Raritan, is going home for orders. Peters recommends him for Nova Scotia (see Vol. I, *Nos. 92–101*). Sturgeon has resigned, because of difficulties in his personal affairs;

Nos. 31–33. William Smith to Bishop Terrick, Philadelphia, Dec. 18, 1766. Introduces Bryzelius, who has been a pastor among the German Lutherans. Lutheran clergy in the area are willing to conform to the Church and Smith wonders if there is not some precedent for receiving them without reordination. William Dunlap, a printer of Philadelphia, was refused testimonials by the local clergy, when he sought ordination, because of insufficient education. He obtained testimonials from clergy in Barbados, was ordained by Bishop Terrick and is now preaching in St. Paul's while continuing his printing business. This lowers the prestige of the Church in a place where "Presbyterian preachers have all some learning" as well as some of the laity. It is also remembered that Dunlap was once in trouble over a lottery;

Nos. 34–35. Richard Peters to Bishop Terrick, Philadelphia, May 17, 1768. He has been in poor health through the winter. St. Paul's is still negotiating with Chapman but he has not come yet;

Nos. 36–39. Richard Peters to Bishop Terrick, Philadelphia, Aug. 30, 1768. Introduces Dr. Wrangel, principal minister of the Swedish churches, and domestic chaplain of the King of Sweden, who is trying to unite the German and Swedish Lutherans with the Church of England, taking advantage of hostility that the Presbyterians have excited against themselves by their attacks on Dr. Chandler. As an instrument to this end, Peters and Smith propose a German-English academy, with a theological professorship. St. Paul's is now being supplied by [William] Stringer, who was recommended by Lord Dartmouth. He is in Greek orders. Great harmony prevails in Christ Church. Mentions death of Nathaniel Evans, a missionary;

Nos. 40–41. William Smith to Bishop Terrick, Philadelphia, Oct. 22, 1768. Glad his warnings concerning Joseph Chambers's sexual immoralities arrived in time. Thomas Coombe, though only 22, is going to England to study until he is old enough to be ordained priest, but will be grateful if he can be ordained deacon and appointed to a curacy to help pay his expenses. Stringer, ordained by a Greek bishop in England, officiates at St. Paul's. His preaching is said to be Whitefieldian. Smith is sending some of his contributions to the episcopal controversy. He wishes that Dr. Chandler had not started it, but feels obliged to support him. Active opposition comes only from the Presbyterians. The Lutherans and Quakers concede that the Church is only seeking its "natural rights" in asking for bishops;

Nos. 42–43. William Smith to Bishop Terrick, Philadelphia, Nov. 8, 1769. Introduces John Mongomery [Montgomery] previously recommended, who is now of age for ordination and has a title in Maryland. Society for the relief of widows and orphans of clergy has been chartered in New York, New Jersey, and Pennsylvania. He encloses the sermon that he preached at its organization;

Nos. 44–45. Richard Peters to Bishop Terrick, Philadelphia, Oct. 22, 1770. Refers to a previous recommendation of Thomas Hopkinson and William White. Hopkinson is a relative of the Bishop of Worcester (James Johnson). They had a fairly successful meeting of the widows' fund in New York, though its opening was delayed by a storm which prevented crossing the bay. They have decided to seek a royal charter, if it can be obtained without the usual fees, which are beyond their means;

Nos. 46–47. William Smith to Bishop Terrick, Philadelphia, May, 3, 1771. Dr. Peters is too ill to officiate. Smith is now regularly serving the mission at Oxford (where he has a summer home) on a part-time basis and asks that the arrangement be continued. Hopkinson has been proposed for there, but he has an impediment in his speech which makes him unacceptable to the people. The mission is flourishing and a number of Swedish families have united with it. —— Aiken, a former Presbyterian minister, who was in trouble with the presbytery because he delayed marrying until his wife was several months pregnant, has obtained testimonials in Maryland, and is seeking orders;

Nos. 48–51. Wardens of St. Paul's to Bishop Terrick, Philadelphia, Dec. 3 and 5, 1772. Ask him to ordain and license William Stringer, convinced that the members of St. Paul's now sincerely desire conformity and that Stringer himself has worked to that end. They have consulted their brethren in New York, who agree with their view;

Nos. 52–53. Traugott Frederick Illing to Bishop Terrick, Middleton, Pa., Oct. 6, 1773. Describes his work in Juniata, Etherton, Pennsboro, and adjoining communities. He has found some families professing allegiance to the Church though ignorant of the liturgy. His principal support is derived from German Lutherans. Some of these are willing to use the Book of Common Prayer. Among others he officiates in "their own way," though he thinks that they may be brought to conform in time. He has no stipend from the S.P.G.;

Nos. 54–55. Wardens of St. Paul's to Bishop Terrick, Philadelphia, Oct. 29, 1773. Acknowledge a letter from him. Express gratitude to him and to the clergy of Philadelphia, who supplied the parish in Stringer's absence;

Nos. 58–59. Richard Peters and William Smith to Bishop Terrick, Philadelphia, Oct. 29, 1773. Peters's illness has prevented their writing before. They commend Illing's work (*Nos. 52–53*) but say that [Bernard] Page, ordained at the same time, has never gone to the place for which he was licenced, but is trying to raise a congregation in New York. Gov. Martin of North Carolina has warned them that John Beard, a graduate of the College of Philadelphia, who was ordained among the dissenters and dismissed for drunkenness, is seeking orders in the Church;

Nos. 60–61. William Smith to Bishop Terrick, Philadelphia, Oct. 30, 1773. Repeats information in *Nos. 58–59* with some additions. Page applied to Father Harding, "a worthy Jesuit of this town," for a recommendation to the Bishop of Canada. Father Harding, "who was always in good terms with us," refused to have anything to do with him. He then obtained pledges of support from people on the frontier who thought he was a Presbyterian. Beard imposed on Gov. Martin by pretending to have Smith's approval, but he had been dismissed by the Presbyterians in Pennsylvania for drunkenness;

Nos. 62–63. William Smith to Bishop Terrick, Philadelphia, July 8, 1775. Encloses an address from the Philadelphia clergy (not in present collection) and a printed sermon of his own dealing with the issues of the day. He has been an advocate of moderation throughout the revolutionary crisis, but cannot turn his back on the interests of America and thinks that great damage will be done to the Church if the clergy are thought of as tools of power;

Nos. 64–65. Resignation of Richard Peters as rector of Christ Church, Philadelphia, Sept. 23, 1775. (Copy). Gives ill health as principal reason. Acceptance by vestry, same date. Both copies certified by John Morgan and Jonathan Browne, wardens;

Nos. 66–69. Address of several clergy assembled in Philadelphia for a meeting of the widows' fund, Oct. 6, 1775. They endorse the view of the Philadelphia clergy in the address referred to in *Nos. 62–63* that prudence dictated yielding to their congregations and observing the public fast-day recommended by the Continental Congress;

Nos. 70–71. Wardens and vestry of Christ Church to Bishop Terrick, Philadelphia, Oct. 30, 1775. Announce Peters's resignation and their choice of Jacob Duché as rector;

Nos. 72–73. Clergy of Philadelphia (other than Duché) to Bishop Terrick, Philadelphia, Oct. 30, 1775. Enclose *Nos. 66–69* and approve election of Duché;

Nos. 74–75. Jacob Duché to Bishop Terrick, Philadelphia, Oct. 31, 1775. Asks bishop to give a letter of approbation to his election, as it is not convenient to come to England for a licence. He says that this was done in the case of previous rectors, but see *No. 9.*

RHODE ISLAND

Nos. 309–310. James McSparran to Bishop Sherlock, Narragansett, Jan. 3, 1749. Congratulates him on his translation. McSparran is now the oldest missionary, next to Honeyman, who is incapacitated. He has seen great growth in the Church, but regrets that he has not seen a corresponding growth in vital piety. His suit is still pending. The nature of the case is indicated by documents to follow. There has been a new outbreak of Whitefieldian enthusiasm among the Baptists;

Nos. 311–312. James McSparran to Bishop Sherlock, Narragansett, March 15, 1749. He traces the bishop's jurisdiction back to Laud. He encloses pamphlets by Nehemiah Hobart and [Jonathan] Mayhew to show the sort of opposition with which the Church is confronted;

Nos. 313–314. James Honeyman to Bishop Sherlock, Newport, March 28, 1750. He is the oldest missionary, but is not able to be very active. He would have written the bishop before, but was not sure that he was going to take jurisdiction over the colonies;

Nos. 317–318. James McSparran to Bishop Sherlock, Narragansett, July 6, 1750. Usher, whom he met at the funeral of Honeyman, told him that, in a letter from Dr. Benjamin Avery and Col. Elisha Williams [1694–1755] read before a meeting of Independent ministers in Boston, those two claimed credit for defeating the plan to send bishops to America. Dr. Avery is a dissenting minister in London. Col. Williams is an Independent minister, who served as president of Yale, ran for governor, with New Light support, and served as chaplain of the expedition against Cape Breton. The bearer of this letter is Jonathan Copp, a candidate for orders. McSparran has hopes that his suit will soon be decided;

Nos. 319–322. James McSparran to Bishop Sherlock, Narragansett, March 26, 1751. In answer to Nehemiah Hobart's criticism of the employment of missionaries in New England as a misapplication of S.P.G. funds, he says that the Independents have a fund of their own which employs missionaries in opposition to the Church and also draw on a fund in London. He gives the bishop some information about New England history and some arguments in favour of colonial bishops;

Nos. 323–324. James McSparran to Bishop Sherlock, Narragansett, Nov. 1, 1751. He is unwilling to move to Newport. He thinks that the people there have deceived the S.P.G. and could well support their own minister. If a missionary is sent, he recommends that he be a European;

No. 325. Thomas Sandford to James McSparran, March 20, 1752, and

June 2, 1752; Philip Bearcroft to McSparran, May 8, 1752 (copies). Sandford's letters say that a decision on his case is at last about to be made. Bearcroft's says that it went against him;

Nos. 326–327. James McSparren to Bishop Sherlock, Narragansett, Nov. 10, 1752. Encloses *No. 325.* His first news of his defeat in behalf of his parish came from the Boston newspapers;

Nos. 328–329. Petition of Joseph Torrey to the General Assembly, Feb. 25, 1754. In the complexities of the case, the English decision awarded him 280 acres of the original tract, but not the 20 acres for which the action was originally started. He now sues for those. He says he was able to produce proof that the original donors were Presbyterians;

Nos. 330–331. Wardens of St. Paul's Church, Narragansett, to the secretary of the S.P.G., May 11, 1754. The Presbyterians are now trying to make McSparran pay their legal fees under a law passed after the suit was commenced. As a result of all these afflictions he is going to England for his health;

No. 332. Wardens of St. Paul's to Bishop Sherlock, May 11, 1754. Enclosing *Nos. 330–331.*

VOLUME X

SOUTH CAROLINA

Nos. 120–121. Gov. James Glen to Bishop Sherlock, May 15, 1749. After expressing his sorrow on the death of Bishop Gibson, he introduces [John] Gisendeiner [Gisendanner] "a foreigner" from Orangeburg, a settlement peopled entirely by his own countrymen. Though bred a Calvinist, he is, at their desire, going to England for orders;

Nos. 122–123. Petition of the inhabitants of Orangeburg to Gov. Glen, May 27, 1749. Ask him to assist in securing the ordination of John Gisendanner. Bartholomew Zouberbuhler, previously sent home for this purpose, went to Savannah instead of returning to them;

Nos. 124–125. Wardens and vestry of St. John's, Colleton County, to Bishop Sherlock, June 12, 1749. Ask for a minister;

Nos. 128–129. Alexander Garden to Bishop Sherlock, Charleston, Oct. 2, 1749. Introducing ———— St. John, rector of St. Helen's, who is returning to England in hopes of recovering his voice. Garden's assistant left him in July. Note: The Rev. Alexander Garden (1685–1756), an opponent of the Rev. George Whitefield, was Rector of St. Philip's church in Charleston and commissary for the Bishop of London for South Carolina; his son was the famous botanist;

Nos. 130–131. Alexander Garden to Bishop Sherlock, Charleston, Oct.

23, 1749. Urges the prompt appointment of an assistant, as his health will oblige him to leave the parish next summer;

Nos. 132–133. Alexander Garden and wardens and vestry of Charleston to Bishop Sherlock, Dec. 5, 1749. Report that they have employed Alexander Keith as an assistant. He has recently resigned a distant parish in the country for "just reasons";

Nos. 134–135. Alexander Garden to Bishop Sherlock, Charleston, Feb. 1, 1750. In answer to an inquiry from the bishop, he says that he did not find a serious defect in his commission under Bishop Gibson, but he was troubled by some points of law. He proceeded against four clergymen: Winteley, Morritt, Fulton, and Whitefield. The first two resigned rather than face proceedings. The latter two he suspended. The points of law arose chiefly in Whitefield's case. Whitefield objected to Garden as judge on the ground of personal hostility. He named three arbitrators, proposing that Garden name three others. As Whitefield's three, two Independents and a French Calvinist, were his known supporters, Garden thought that he might reject them as not indifferent, but found the law unclear. If he appointed three and they divided equally, as they probably would, the law was not clear as to further proceedings, nor was it clear who would be the judge if the arbitrators rejected Garden. Because of these legal uncertainties, Garden rejected Whitefield's objection. Whitefield appealed to the commissioners appointed by the King for hearing such appeals, but failed to prosecute his appeal within the statutory twelve months. Garden then suspended him. There were no further proceedings on either side. Since the suspension did not reform Whitefield, Garden would have proceeded to a writ of excommunication, but the Elizabethan act providing for such a writ was not in force in South Carolina. Unless these legal difficulties are cleared up, the power of the commissary will never be very effective. The issue of dilapidations does not arise in South Carolina, for the law expressly relieves the clergy of them;

Nos. 136–137. William Orr to Bishop Sherlock, St. John's Parish, Colleton County, July 12, 1750. Since St. Paul's Parish would not meet the directions of the S.P.G. in contributing to his support, he was obliged to leave it. He is now settled in St. John's and asks the bishop to appoint him its minister;

No. 138. Wardens and vestry of Prince Frederick Parish to Bishop Sherlock, Oct 23, 1751. Report death of their rector, [Francis] Fordyce. Three neighbouring parishes are also vacant;

Nos. 139–140. Michael Smith to Bishop Sherlock, Prince Frederick Parish, May 13, 1753. Because of illness in his large family and inability to obtain servants, he has been obliged to move to a small town outside his parish. There are five dissenting teachers in the

parish and most of the people are dissenters. He thinks that the
Church in the province has suffered from having too many Scotch
clergymen. As Garden has resigned his parish, because of ill
health, Smith applies for that position and the post of commissary;

Nos. 141–142. Wardens and vestry of Prince Frederick Parish to Bishop
Sherlock, Black River, May 1, 1756. As the parish is again vacant,
they ask the appointment of a minister;

Nos. 143–144. Wardens and vestry of Prince Frederick Parish to Bishop
Osbaldeston, Feb. 25, 1762. Ask him to appoint a minister to
succeed James Dormer who is resigning;

Nos. 145–146. James Dormer to Bishop Osbaldeston, Prince Frederick,
Feb. 25, 1762. Says that he is separating from his parishioners in
amity as the result of a desire to return to his native country.
Clergy of South Carolina now receive £100 sterling, plus house,
glebe and various fees;

Nos. 147–148. List of parishes in South Carolina with some comments.
Attributed in *notation* to Charles Martyn, March 30, 1762. Four
of the nineteen parishes are listed as missions. Salary in the others
is said to be £110 sterling, plus house and glebe. Rectors are
elected by members of the parish who adhere to the Church of
England, and are usually elected after a year's probation. Usual
method of obtaining a rector is to apply to a merchant in Charleston, who writes to his correspondent in England. As a result,
many unworthy clergymen have come in. The appointment of a
commissary would be desirable;

Nos. 149–150. Robert Parkington to F. W. Osbaldeston, Sedgwick Inn,
April 3, 1762. Introduces Martyn as a worthy clergyman, about to
return to South Carolina after visiting England for his health,
who can supply the bishop with information about the province;

Nos. 151–152. Gov. James Glen to a brother of Bishop Osbaldeston,
Poland St., London, April 10, 1762, introducing Martyn and
recommending his appointment as commissary;

Nos. 153–154. Further notes attributed to Charles Martyn, April 11,
1762. Extent of glebes varies from 100 to 500 acres. Surplice
fees are regulated by custom, not law. They are: Marriages
with banns, 15s., with license, £1. 10s., burials in churchyard,
9s., in plantations, 15s. Fees for baptisms depend on the generosity
of the families, which is generally "diffusive." Public register
kept in every parish. Parochial business is conducted by a select
vestry of seven. A duly elected rector is entitled to preside at
vestry meetings. A probationer merely has the right to attend.
White population about 20,000 of whom 5,000 are "sectaries"
and the rest adhere to the Church of England. There are 46,000
Negroes of whom about 500 are Christians. "Some few Indians";

No. 155. Wardens and vestry of Prince Frederick Parish, to Bishop Osbaldeston, June 23, 1762. They have elected George Skene as rector. He came well recommended, with an "open mission";

Nos. 158–159. Charles Martyn to Bishop Osbaldeston, St. Andrew's, Feb. 1, 1763. St. John's, Colleton County, which has a reputation for ill-treating the clergy, has sent to England for a clergyman, but resolved to keep him on permanent probation. Martyn suggests that such abuses can be prevented if the bishop refuses to license a clergyman unless he has commitment from the parish to elect him after a year's probation unless immoralities are proven against him. A young clergyman, recently arrived and only in deacon's orders, insists on officiating as a priest and there is no authority that can stop him. Most of the present clergy are men of good character and the Church is growing, but an ecclesiastical authority is needed;

Nos. 160–161. Charles Martyn to Bishop Terrick, Oct. 20, 1765. Two bills, one to erect a college and another to raise the salaries of the clergy to £150, had been approved by the legislature, and would have been sent to the governor, but news of the Stamp Act has driven everything else from the public mind. To evade the law which allows a clergyman to sue for election after a year's probation, many parishes will only hire a minister who agrees not to sue. A number of missionaries recently sent to Florida have accepted parishes in South Carolina;

Nos. 162–163. Charles Woodmason to Bishop Terrick, Charleston, Oct. 19, 1766. He arrived Aug. 12 and has made a tour of the frontier region for which he was ordained. An unusually hot spring and summer have produced more than the usual illness. He lists eight Church clergymen who have died during the summer and early fall, besides a Dutch minister and a Presbyterian minister from Ireland. Five other clergy are seriously ill and he doubts of their recovery. The frontier region is filling rapidly, but the legislature refuses to divide it into parishes. The province is still torn by the Stamp Act controversy. Town clergy receive twice as much as the country clergy but do less work. A bill to rectify this just failed of passage;

Nos. 164–165. Alexander Keith to Bishop Terrick, St. Stephen's Parish, Dec. 30, 1766. Forwards a request from Prince Frederick Parish for a minister to succeed [Alexander] Skene, deceased. Salaries of country clergy are £760 currency, worth £100–110 sterling. Perquisites bring the amount to about £120. Parish, which reaches to the border of North Carolina, has two Presbyterian meetings, whose members sometimes attend the services of the Church of England when without a minister of their own. There are a few Anabaptists;

No. 166. Wardens and vestry of St. Mark's Parish to Bishop Terrick, April 20, 1767. (Copy, without signatures.) Ask a minister to replace ——— Evans, who has gone to St. Paul's. Theirs is the largest parish in the province, but it is not a laborious one, as much of the work is done by an itinerant;

No. 167. Half-page cut from a newspaper not clearly identified, but probably the *South-Carolina Gazette.* The entry for which it was presumably clipped is a grand jury presentment listing a long series of grievances, most relating to administrative affairs, but including the lack of free schools and the neglect of the Lord's Day;

Nos. 168–185. Copy of remonstrance presented by inhabitants of the back country to Gov. Charles Greville Montagu and the legislature, 1767. Because of the centralization of government in Charleston, the laws are very unevenly enforced in the back country. The criminals whom they want punished escape and they themselves are harrassed by prosecutions which they consider illegitimate. Because of these conditions, they have resorted to defending themselves by lynch law;

Nos. 186–191. Notes on this remonstrance framed by Woodmason, as indicated in his *The Carolina Backcountry on the Eve of the Revolution* . . . (R. I. Hooker, ed., Chapel Hill, N.C., 1953), p. 241, Woodmason warmly supports the remonstrance and pictures a general state of disorder in the region;

Nos. 192–197. Charles Woodmason to ———, undated, but enclosing *Nos. 168–191.* Protesters have obtained one of their aims, the creation of circuit courts, but they still have a good many grievances, and some of them have been prosecuted for their actions;

No. 198. Gov. G. Montagu to Bishop Terrick, Charleston, May 8, 1768. Introducing Charles Martyn;

Nos. 199–200. Printed proclamation of Lieut.-Gov. William Bull, Aug. 6, 1768. Orders suppression of lynch mobs, but recognizing that they were organized in defence against dangerous bands of criminals, he grants an amnesty for all offences committed prior to this proclamation, except to those who whipped George Thomson, a constable engaged in the lawful performance of his duty. Gideon Gibson is named as the chief offender in that crime;

No. 201. Testimonial of wardens and vestry of St. Mark's Parish to Charles Woodmason, who has occasionally officiated among them, June 6, 1769;

Nos. 204–205. J. Adam de Martel to Bishop Terrick, Purrysburg, July 13, 1769. Of the colony with which he came over, half died on shipboard and most of the others since landing. The few remaining have had to become slaves (indentured servants?) to obtain any support in the new country. He has become minister in Purrysburg. The leader of his expedition, unnamed, cheated him out of all the money he had with him. Provisions are scarce and the climate is so hot that a man of 40 is as old as one of 60 in Europe;

No. 206. Wardens and vestry of Prince Frederick Parish to Bishop Terrick, Black River, July 26, 1769. Report death of their rector, George Spencer, who has been ill ever since he came, and ask for another minister;

Nos. 207–208. Charles Woodmason to ———, undated, but enclosing copies of published pieces relating to the back country insurrection, some of which are dated in 1769 (See *Nos. 209–222*). Says that its former lieutenant-governor, now dead, endeavoured to redress their grievances, but was prevented by the lowland legislators, who were all preoccupied with resistance to Britain. Though the South Carolina insurrectionists take the name of Regulators, he denies that they are related to the North Carolina Regulators, but the grievances complained of seem to be about the same;

Nos. 209–222. The following pieces enclosed in *Nos. 207–208:* (1) Extract from a letter in defence of the Regulators, written to Henry Laurens, undated. (Each piece is followed by extensive notes by Woodmason, who is probably also the author of the pieces.) (2) An advertisement, ironic in tone, offering the Carolina highlands as a summer resort in competition with those in New York and Rhode Island favoured by the lowland planters. (3) A mock advertisement representing the inhabitants of the back country as being sold as slaves. (4) A letter, probably written to the *South Carolina Gazette,* comparing the grievances of the back country against the lowland with those of the colonies against Great Britain. (5) A reply to Mr. Gadsden's answer to no. 4. "Not suffd to be printed." (6) A letter sent to "I. R., Esq." by the Regulators, evidently in answer to an attack by him on them;

No. 223. Small clipping from newspaper, probably the *South-Carolina Gazette,* April 13–20, 1770. Contains a list of bills pending when the legislature was prorogued. These include a bill to erect public schools and a college and a bill to establish several parishes in the interior;

Nos. 224–229. Charles Woodmason to ———, St. Mark's Parish, March 26, 1771. Defending himself against criticism by Mr. Smith, the rector in Charleston, he reviews the grievances of the back country and some of his own. He lists thirty clergymen who have died since his last letter (*Nos. 207–208?*);

Nos. 230–231. Wardens and vestry of Prince Frederick's Parish to Bishop Terrick, Feb. 10, 1775. Beg for a minister, having been without one since [Charles Louis de] Villette left for England three years ago.

VOLUME XIII

VIRGINIA

Nos. 9–10. Acts of Council, April 14, 1747, and Nov. 1, 1748, permitting Samuel Davies, a dissenting (Presbyterian) minister who has qualified by taking the oaths and subscribing to the test, to officiate in certain meeting houses identified by naming the persons on whose lands they are erected, or to be erected;

Nos. 11–12. A portion of the vestry and some members of Lunenburg Parish to the vestry of the southernmost parish in Amelia County, Dec. 26, 1748. Attesting to character of William Kay, who is removing from one parish to the other and expressing disbelief in charges of lying, swearing, drunkenness, and uncleanness that have been made against him. *Notation:* "A Letter I requested at my Departure signed by five of my Vestry and Some others";

No. 13. William Mackay to the vestry and other inhabitants of the southernmost parish of Amelia County, Richmond County, Dec. 31, 1748. Says that Kay was well esteemed in the parish until he fell into a dispute with some of the influential members of his vestry, largely, in Mackay's judgment, through the imprudence of his wife. *Notation:* "A Character from a Neighbouring Clergyman when I left my first parish";

Nos. 14–15. H. Dunbar to the gentlemen of the southernmost parish in Amelia, Jan. 14, 1748/9. Expresses confidence in Kay's character and ability and attributes row to "a barbarous, bad wife" and "a certain Colonel who wants to subvert the King's Supremacy";

No. 16. John Andrews to Bishop Sherlock, Feb. 23, 1749. Reports his arrival and settlement in Cameron Parish, Fairfax County, under the patronage of Lord Fairfax. Has presented his credentials to Commissary William Dawson;

Nos. 17–18. Gov. William Gooch to Bishop Sherlock, April 20, 1749. Congratulates him on his translation, informs him of his election as chancellor of William and Mary, and introduces an unnamed candidate for holy orders. Alludes to the Bishop's having previously declined both archbishoprics;

Nos. 19–20. Latin certificate of Bishop Sherlock's election as chancellor of William and Mary, May 5, 1749;

Nos. 23–24. Act which passed the House of Burgesses, April 28, 1749, and the Council, May 6, 1749. Continues salaries of clergy at 16,000 lb. tobacco, with cask and allowance of 4 per cent for shrinkage. Requires a glebe to be set up in parishes that do not yet have one. Makes the clergy responsible for repairs, formerly provided by the parish. Provides that right of presentation shall remain with the vestry for twelve months after commencement of a vacancy. Does not say what will happen in event of its lapsing;

Nos. 25–26. William Gooch to ———, May 10, 1749. Says that Kay is leaving his former parish for the sake of peace and for no other reason. *Notation:* "From Governor Gooch to my last Parish";

Nos. 27–28. William Dawson to Vestry of Cumberland Parish in Lunenburg, William and Mary College, May 10, 1749. Recommends Kay as successor to Brunskill, who has removed to Amelia. Says that he has, "as far as appears, undeservedly incurred the Displeasure of some Gentlemen in Richmond." *Notation:* "A Letter from the Commissary to my last parish";

Nos. 29–30. William Dawson to Bishop Sherlock, William and Mary College, July 11, 1749. Introduces Adam Menzies, a candidate for orders. Surprised that young Blacknall, who was designed for his father's [John Blacknall's] parish, has misbehaved and given up all thought of the ministry. Another parish has been vacated by the death of ——— Hindman and two other parishes have been divided. Is assured of the genuineness of William Douglass's title from Nathaniel Morrell in Maryland. "Northern gentlemen," having been bred Presbyterians, do not have as high a regard for the Church as they should. Oxford and Cambridge men are preferred. William and Mary has trained some clergy who are as good as any from home;

Nos. 31–32. William Dawson to Bishop Sherlock, William and Mary, Aug. 5, 1749. ——— Jackson presented forged letters of orders to Dawson and disappeared when Dawson required him to leave the letters with him. Gov. Gooch inserted a warning advertisement in the *Virginia Gazette.* Dawson recommends that persons coming from the colonies for orders be required to exhibit a valid title to the commissary before being recommended. He fears that college and Church will suffer a great loss in the departure of Gov. Gooch;

Nos. 33–34. William Dawson to Bishop Sherlock, William and Mary, Oct. 16, 1749. Eleazar Robertson, ordained deacon and priest by the Bishop of Chester, came to Virginia to teach a school, but those who had contracted with him were unable to meet their commitments. He has applied for a parish and has been advised that he must have the bishop's license;

Nos. 35–36. Thomas Lee to Bishop Sherlock, Williamsburg, May 11, 1750. Asks the bishop's advice concerning Samuel Davies, who, since Gov. Gooch's departure, has obtained additional licences to preach from some county courts. In stressing his desire to protect the Church, Lee says that his own father was instructed in its principles by Isaac Barrow in Cambridge;

Nos. 37–38. William Dawson to Bishop Sherlock, William and Mary, July

27, 1750. Acknowledges Bishop Sherlock's acceptance of the chancellorship. Notes that Archbishop Wake left the college £50 and that Archbishop Potter presented it with the works of St. Chrysostom and Clement of Alexandria, the latter in his own edition. He relates his own experience to illustrate procedure in regard to licensing. He waited on Bishop Gibson before he sailed, but, having been recommended to his professorship by Archbishop Potter, did not think it necessary to apply for a licence. When he found that he could not officiate in Virginia without one, he obtained one through the intercession of his uncle, Dr. Troughear. He recommends a similar concession to Robertson (See *Nos. 33–34*). The licence granted to Davies by a county court has been rescinded by the general court as exceeding the authority of the county court. Dawson regrets the spread of schism in a colony heretofore distinguished for uniformity in religion. Some improper persons have been sent to the colony as clergymen by others than the bishop. One bishop actually ordained a man who was ignorant of Latin. Acknowledges continuance as commissary. The bishop's letter on the earthquake has been reprinted here;

Nos. 39–40. Extract from a letter of Samuel Davies to Philip Doddridge, Oct. 2, 1750. Copy attested by Doddridge. Little dissent in the colony until about six years ago when Sam Morice, by independent reading, arrived at substantially orthodox Calvinism and collected a small group around him. After being served briefly by ——— Robinson, they applied to the Synod of New York and Philadelphia, which was only able to send temporary supplies until two years ago, when Davies was appointed. Since his coming, he has organized seven meetings and would have an eighth, but the licence, granted by a county court, was rescinded by the general court. He complains that, though the Presbyterians have conformed to the requirements of the Toleration Act, the authorities try, in various ways, to restrict the freedom which it grants them. He has baptized about forty Negroes;

Nos. 41–42. Bishop Sherlock to Dr. Doddridge, London, May 11, 1751 (draft, initialed by the bishop). He holds that the Toleration Act, being designed to ease the consciences of those who could not conform, does not justify Davies in travelling about Virginia making proselytes. He uses some general strictures of Davies on the character of the clergy and laity in Virginia to point to the need for colonial bishops, mentioning his own efforts to secure them, and the opposition that came from New England;

Nos. 43–44. P. Doddridge to Bishop Sherlock, Northampton, May 14, 1751. While he cannot be sure of what special circumstances there may be in Virginia, he believes that Davies's practice conforms to that followed in England. Dissenting places of worship are licensed

on the application of three or more persons, including the occupant.
Ministers ordained by the presbytery are licensed on conforming
to the requirements of the act. If a licensed minister officiates in
a licensed meeting-place, the legal requirements are held to be
met. He agrees that it is unfair to deprive the Church of England
of bishops in America. He holds that the New England opposition
is the result of a fear of episcopacy inherited from their persecuted
ancestors. As to the taxing of members of the Church of England
in New England, he is not sure how far the status of the Con-
gregational churches there is that of a genuine establishment, as
of the Church of England and the Church of Scotland, but he has
always acquiesed in the propriety of requiring dissenters to pay
ecclesiastical taxes in England;

Nos. 45–46. William Dawson to Bishop Sherlock, William and Mary College, July 15, 1751. He has received a letter from the bishop by
Mr. [Adam] Menzies, but has failed to receive some others. Douglass told him that the bishop intended to send a letter by an
elderly clergyman. He assumes that this is Dr. Spencer, who has
gone to Maryland and who may have suppressed the letter because Dawson refused to recommend him for orders. He has held
one commissarial court, but has doubts about the procedure. Under
his predecessor (Blair) complaints against the clergy were heard
by the governor and council sitting as a council of state. Question,
who has the right of patronage, is still undetermined. Fees listed;

Nos. 47–48. William Dawson to Bishop Sherlock, William and Mary College, Aug. 6, 1751. Though the Council has received a Delphic
pronouncement from the Board of Trade on the Davies case, addressed to the late president, Col. Lee, the issue is still undecided.
He quotes the act of 1642 which forbids officiating by anyone but
a clergyman of the Church of England. Introduces Miles Selden,
a candidate trained at the college, and renews his suggestion
that candidates be required to present a valid title;

Nos. 49–50. William Dawson to Bishop Sherlock, William and Mary College, Feb. 10, 1752. Davies has shown him extracts of letters exchanged between Dawson and the bishop which Davies received
from a friend in England. The governor is resolved to do everything in his power to support the Church;

Nos. 51–60. Case of William Kay, clerk, *vs.* William Degge, George Russell, and Thomas Russell from its inception, April 10, 1747, to the
appeal of the defendants to the King in Council. Transcript of the
record certified by Gov. Robert Dinwiddie and Benjamin Waller,
Secretary, May 20, 1752. Kay prosecuted the defendants for trespass in intruding upon his glebe. The jury found them guilty,
reserving the point of law whether or not a minister, received by
a vestry, had the right to institute such an action. This was re-

ferred to the general court (governor and council) which decided for the plaintiff. In a statement accompanying the appeal
they say that their decision was based on the established custom
whereby a qualified and licensed clergyman was held to become
the minister of the parish when received by the vestry on recommendation of the governor, and on the provision in the act of
1749 (*Nos. 23–24*), which made the minister responsible for
delapidations. This, they hold, would be an intolerable burden
unless the minister is presumed to have *de facto* induction;

Nos. 61–62. John Camm to Bishop Sherlock, York, June 4, 1752. Defends
character of Kay, whom he has known since they were both at
Trinity College, Cambridge, though Kay later transferred to Emmanuel. Decision in favour of Kay is reported to have been reversed in England. If true, this may have a disastrous effect on the
clergy. The power of the vestries to appoint leads to a competition
for desirable vacancies which results in some unworthy practices,
such as canvassing for votes and disparagement of rivals. If the
vestries gain the power to turn the clergy out, the clergy will
become altogether subservient;

Nos. 63–64. Gov. Robert Dinwiddie to Bishop Sherlock, June 5, 1752. Surprised to discover, on coming into the government, that the clergy
of Virginia were not inducted as in other colonies of which he has
had experience. He holds that this situation, and in particular
the provision of the act of 1749 (*Nos. 23–24*) which provides a
twelve-month right of presentation without specifying any qualifications for the minister, violate the royal prerogative, the bishop's
jurisdiction, and the governor's instructions. When Davies applied
to him to license another church, the governor replied that no
minister could properly care for seven churches (his present
number) and that he could only be regarded as an itinerant.
Davies countered by asking the governor to license ———— Todd
as an assistant, which he did. As Davies professed to regard himself as belonging to the Church of Scotland, Dinwiddie reminded
him that the Church did not allow pluralism. A final paragraph,
dated July 21, reports the sudden death of Commissary William
Dawson of a violent fever and recommends the appointment of his
brother Thomas;

Nos. 65–66. William Robinson to William Dawson, June 11, 1750. Encloses
£10 to aid Kay in pursuing his case but fears that enough cannot
be raised by subscription and suggests a convention of the clergy;

Nos. 67–70. William Kay to Bishop Sherlock, Williamsburg, June 14, 1752.
Gives an account of his case. After being received in the parish
of Lunenburg, Richmond County, he was dismissed when a hostile faction, led by Col. Landon Carter, gained control of the vestry. He was locked out of both his churches. His followers broke

into one, but he officiated in the open fields by the other for two years. The glebe was granted rent free to the defendants in his suit. As the damages were only £30 an appeal to England would not normally have been allowed, but Col. Carter secured a special order permitting it;

Nos. 71–76. William Dawson to Bishop Sherlock, William and Mary College, June 17, 1752. Argues at length, with reference to the Davies case, that a dissenting teacher should be licensed for one church only;

Nos. 77–78. John Blair to Bishop Sherlock, Williamsburg, July 25, 1752. After reviewing, by way of introduction, his uncle's career and noting that he was his adopted son, he recommends the appointment of Thomas Dawson as commissary, to succeed his brother. It is hoped that he will also be made president of the college, but he has a strong rival in William Stith, formerly master of the grammar school. As Blair's recollections of the régimes of Nicholson and Spotswood show, it is important for the commissary to enjoy friendly relations with the governor, and he thinks that Dawson is more likely to do this than Stith. William Dawson had brought a widowed sister and her children to the colony shortly before his death;

Nos. 79–80. Gov. Robert Dinwiddie, to Bishop Sherlock, Williamsburg, July 28, 1752, attached to another of Aug. 5, both urging the appointment of Dawson as commissary. The second letter notes that Stith won the election as president of the college by the casting vote of the rector. Robinson was also a candidate. Stith was supported by his former pupils in the grammar school but was accused by his opponents of being unorthodox and turbulent;

Nos. 83–84. Thomas Dawson to Bishop Sherlock, William and Mary College, July 30, 1753. Encloses some papers of his brother's relating to the Davies affair. Is aware of the application made on his behalf and will be honoured to serve as commissary if the bishop desires;

Nos. 85–86. John Blair to Bishop Sherlock, Williamsburg, Aug. 15, 1752. Opposing appointment of William Stith as commissary. Stith is charged with being anti-Trinitarian because he omits the Athanasian Creed from his services;

Nos. 88–89. William Stith to Bishop Sherlock, William and Mary College, Aug. 15, 1752. Announces his election as president, offers himself as commissary, and defends his Trinitarianism;

Nos. 92–93. John Sharpe to Bishop Sherlock, Lincoln's Inn, Nov. 24, 1752. He has secured a postponement of the hearing of the appeal in the Kay case in case the bishop wants to retain him to support Kay;

Nos. 94–95. Thomas Dawson to Bishop Sherlock, William and Mary College, Nov. 24, 1752. The bishop has declared his intention of appointing him commissary, but desires an explanation of his declining an appointment to the council as reported in a letter from the governor to ———— Le Heupe. The bishop, in common with former governor Gooch, holds that the commissary should be on the council. Dawson says he will be glad to serve on the council as commissary, but declined the previous appointment to make way for Col. Carter Burwell whose support he was seeking in the contest for the presidency;

Nos. 96–98. Bishop Sherlock to (John Sharpe), Fulham, Nov. 25, 1752. (Draft.) Thanks him for acting in the Kay case and encloses papers relating to it. Notes that the vestry is seeking to take advantage of its own negligence in not presenting Kay for induction. Thinks it hard that the appeal was allowed in the case at all. If it becomes a precedent, it will make it difficult for any but the wealthy to obtain justice in Virginia;

Nos. 99–100. Gov. Robert Dinwiddie to Bishop Sherlock, Williamsburg, Dec. 10, 1752. Thanks the bishop for appointing Dawson as commissary. He still thinks that the law allowing vestries the right of presentation invades the Crown's right of patronage. He proposes some changes in the procedure of qualifying ministers;

Nos. 101–102. John Sharpe to Bishop Sherlock, Dec. 14, 1752. He thinks the Kay case turns on the interpretation of the act of 1727 which, though since repealed, was in force when his action was started. He thinks that they can sustain the verdict if they are permitted to present the explanation of the governor and council concerning the local usage (*Nos. 51–60*). Unfortunately this was not made a part of the record and the defence will oppose its admission;

Nos. 103–105. Bishop Sherlock to (John Sharpe), March 7, 1753. (Draught.) Offers some arguments relating to the Kay case;

Nos. 106–107. William Stith to Bishop Sherlock, April 21, 1753. Answering some admonitions from the bishop who apparently had been informed that he was campaigning against Gov. Dinwiddie for opposing his appointment as commissary, he says that his opposition to the governor antedated the late commissary's death and was occasioned solely by the governor's exacting a fee of one pistole on every patent for new land that passed the seal. Holding this to be an illegal tax, Stith spoke against it, and started a toast which became popular, "Liberty and Property and no Pistole." He is sending two of his printed sermons and would send his history of Virginia, but he understands that Dr. Dawson formerly sent the bishop a copy of that;

Nos. 108–109. John Sharpe to Bishop Sherlock, May 10, 1753. He encloses some printed copies of the case which he, the solicitor-general (William Murray), and [Robert] Henley have prepared in the Kay case. He is surprised, in view of the great names attached to it, to find that the opposition case contains more personal abuse than argument;

Nos. 110–111. John Sharpe to Bishop Sherlock, May 16, 1753. Reports that the Lords of the Committee have decided in Kay's favour and reported to the Crown, recommending that the judgement of the Virginia General Court (*Nos. 51–60*) be sustained. Sharpe led for Kay, on behalf of the bishop, and was supported by the solicitor-general and Henley and [Ferdinand] Paris. All served without fee. Sharpe writes in haste as he is busy preparing for the morrow when Dr. [Archibald] Cameron is to be brought from the Tower for arraignment. (Cameron was a Jacobite executed for treason);

Nos. 116–117. Thomas Dawson to Bishop Sherlock, William and Mary College, July 23, 1753. He has not yet received the royal order to pay his stipend as commissary. He denied a letter of recommendation to ——— Chisholm because of unfavourable reports respecting his character, but gave one to [John] Andrew, though he thinks that the Scotch, bred Presbyterians, do not have a sufficient regard for the Church. Mentions the placement of several clergymen. The council has again refused to license an eighth church for Davies and Todd. Dawson would like to obtain a law to restrain dissent and another to regulate presentation and induction. He has hopes of getting the first, but the second will depend on pressure from home;

Nos. 118–119. John Blair to Bishop Sherlock, Williamsburg, Jan. 25, 1754. Asks the bishop to support the appointment of Carter Burwell to the council, succeeding John Lewis, deceased, as Burwell lost the previous appointment because of the bishop's intervention on behalf of his commissary. Stith has become chaplain of the House of Burgesses and induced them to address the King against the pistole fee (See *Nos. 106–107*). Blair defends the fee, which he considers reasonable;

Nos. 120–121. Gov. Robert Dinwiddie to Bishop Sherlock, Williamsburg, Jan. 29, 1753/4. Acknowledges report of outcome of Kay case and complains of Stith's opposition to the pistole fee;

Nos. 122–123. Anonymous letter to Bishop Sherlock, Feb. 1, 1754. Writer, though professing to be a Churchman, commends Davies and Todd and attacks the learning and morals of the Church clergy. He names Mungo Marshal, George Purdie, Robert McLaurin, and John Andrew (a candidate) as being conspicuously ignorant. Purdie he also accuses of being immoral. Mentions settlement of dissenters from the northern colonies on the frontier and the growth of Deism;

Nos. 124–127. Speech of Gov. Robert Dinwiddie to the assembly, Feb. 16, 1754. Printed by William Hunter, Williamsburg, 1754. Having received reports from Major Washington that the French are fortifying the Ohio, Dinwiddie has summoned the assembly into special session to vote supplies. He has already assembled part of the militia and sent them to build a fort on the Forks of Monongahela and applied to other colonies for aid;

Nos. 128–129. Thomas Dawson to Bishop Sherlock, William and Mary College, March 11, 1754. Thanks the bishop for his support of Kay. Kay's suit for his salary has been decided in his favour in the colonial courts. Though Dawson has the bishop's letter of appointment, he fears that he cannot exercise any jurisdiction or even convene the clergy without a formal commission. Only two or three conventions were held in Blair's time and only one, on occasion of the rebellion of 1746, under William Dawson, but writer thinks more frequent conventions would be desirable;

Nos. 130–131. Thomas Dawson to Bishop Sherlock, William and Mary College, July 28, 1754. Introduces Rev. Mr. Hotchkiss, returning, for reasons of health, after two years in Virginia. Refers to defeat of English forces by French and Indians;

Nos. 132–161. Proceedings of a convention of the clergy held at the College of William and Mary, Oct. 30–31, 1754. They heard a speech by Commissary Dawson and, on his recommendation, adopted addresses to the King, the bishop, and the governor, and formulated a plan for the relief of widows and orphans of clergymen. They also petitioned the governor against an order in council excluding the clergy from commissions of the peace. Records of meetings of the trustees of the relief fund extending through 1757 are appended to the journal of the convention;

Nos. 184–185. Thomas Dawson to Bishop Sherlock, William and Mary College, Nov. 15, 1754. Notes meeting records in *Nos. 132–161.* Paris sent the clergy a bill for £40 for his services in the Kay case. It has been paid. The general assembly has voted the governor a supply of £20,000. Dawson applauds the bishop's recently published discourses. Bishop has refused to ordain James Garden because he had no title from the governor. Dawson assures the bishop that the governor had promised to recommend Garden to a parish, but, having agreed to leave all ecclesiastical affairs to the commissary, had not thought it necessary to write the bishop directly. Jacob Townshend, a clergyman, has recently arrived with a recommendation from Sir Thomas Robinson, Secretary of State, but without the bishop's license. Placement of some other clergy noted;

Nos. 186–187. Thomas Dawson to Bishop Sherlock, William and Mary College, June 10, 1755. Encloses *Nos. 162–183* and recommends Joseph Davenport, a native of Virginia and graduate of the college, for orders. Notes a preference of the people for native clergy. Mentions death of [Roscow] Cole;

No. 188. Robert Orme to Gov. Dinwiddie, Fort Cumberland, July 18, 1755. (Copy.) Gives an account of Braddock's defeat, which he attributes to panic in the ranks, though the officers made heroic attempts to rally the men. Report delayed, because all the leading officers were killed or wounded. Orme proposes to withdraw to Philadelphia and winter there as soon as his wound is healed enough for him to move;

No. 189. George Washington to Gov. Dinwiddie, Fort Cumberland, July 18, 1755. (Copy.) Attributes the defeat to cowardly behaviour of the British regulars. "Our poor Virginians behaved like Men and died like Soldiers." He estimates that two-thirds of the 300 dead and 300 wounded were hit by balls from their own forces. He himself was unwounded, though he had four bullets through his coat and two horses shot from under him;

Nos. 190–191. Gov. Dinwiddie to (Col. Dunbar), Williamsburg, July 26, 1760. (Copy.) Urges him, as commander of the remaining forces, to attempt to retrieve the defeat. Promises to raise some additional militia, and thinks that the northern campaigns of Gen. Shirley and Col. Johnson will weaken the French on the Ohio;

Nos. 192–193. Gov. Dinwiddie to Gen. Shirley, Williamsburg, July 27, 1753. (Copy.) Urges the proposal of *Nos. 190–191* for a new advance. If Shirley does not approve of this, the governor hopes that he will at least order Col. Dunbar to remain to defend the Virginia frontier;

Nos. 194–195. Thomas Dunbar to Gov. Dinwiddie, Fort Cumberland, Aug. 1, 1755. (Copy.) He held a council of war with the surviving officers on the governor's proposal (*Nos. 190–191*), and it was held to be impracticable. He is retiring on Philadelphia, leaving the Virginia and Maryland militia to hold Fort Cumberland. He will leave one of the independent companies at Winchester to await the governor's orders;

Nos. 196–197. Gov. Robert Dinwiddie to Bishop Sherlock, Williamsburg, Aug. 11, 1755. His dispute with the burgesses (over the pistole fee?; see *Nos. 106–107*) has been settled by the King, and all is harmony internally, but the army met with a serious defeat from the French and their Indian allies. Introduces James Marye, a candidate for orders. He fears that the law concerning presentation could only be repealed by a royal mandate;

Nos. 198–201. Thomas Dawson to Bishop Sherlock, William and Mary College, Aug. 13, 1755. He has received a letter from the bishop by the hand of Thomas Davis, who arrived after a protracted voyage. It spoke of the bishop's ill health and contained instructions concerning the recommendation of candidates for orders. Introduces James Marye, Jr., a graduate of the college and former tutor in the family of Col. Byrd, who has a title as curate to his father. Davenport was recommended just before the bishop's instructions were received. Dawson has received the order for his salary. He praises Dinwiddie's action in the crisis but criticizes Col. Dunbar for going into winter quarters in summer and leaving the frontier unguarded. The New Lights seemed to be declining, but have revived since Davies's return;

Nos. 202–209. Some of the clergy of Virginia to Bishop Sherlock, Nov. 29, 1755. Complain of an act recently passed permitting the payment of tobacco debts in currency at a rate below its current market value, which has the effect of reducing their salaries. Occasioned by a poor tobacco crop as the result of a drouth the bill is also defended by those who believe that indigo is about to become a profitable crop, partly replacing tobacco;

Nos. 210–211. Copies of the former act regulating clerical salaries and of the new law;

Nos. 212–219. Another protest against the same law signed by a number of other clergymen, Feb. 26, 1756;

Nos. 220–221. Thomas Dawson to Bishop Sherlock, William and Mary College, Feb. 25, 1756. He has been elected president of the college on the death of Stith. He opposed the new law in council and the governor was reluctant to sign it, but was told that his rejection of it would inflame the whole colony against the clergy and him. The bill really aids the rich more than the poor. The poor usually pay their dues early, in tobacco of their own raising, but the rich wait until the last minute and then purchase inferior tobacco to make their payments. The currency equivalent is higher than the clergy formally received, but Dawson thinks it a dangerous precedent to break in on the existing establishment. Many of the clergy wanted him to call a convention but, as a lover of peace, he prefers this private communication;

Nos. 222–223. Action of governor and council at meetings held April 21, May 19, and May 20, 1757. Hearing complaints of the vestry of Hamilton Parish, Prince William County, against their rector, John Brunskill, for drunkenness, swearing, "immoral practices" and neglect of duty, and finding him guilty, they held that the governor's 81st instruction gave him power to remove an unworthy clergyman;

Nos. 226. Gov. Dinwiddie to the vestry of Hamilton Parish, Williamsburg, May 20, 1757. Orders them no longer to receive Brunskill as their minister;

No. 227. Minute of a meeting of the visitors and governors of the College of William and Mary, May 20, 1757. They vote to discharge Thomas Robinson from his post as master of the grammar school, on the ground of physical incapacity, and to petition the bishop to recommend a successor;

Nos. 228–235. Thomas Robinson to Bishop Sherlock, William and Mary College, June 30, 1757. Protests at his dismissal. His alleged incapacity was a temporary illness from which he had recovered at the time of the meeting. He believes that their professed objection to having a clergyman as master arises from a belief that a layman would be more completely under their domination as having less resource in the event of dismissal. He says that the dispute really started in a controversy over the disciplining of an usher with important family connections. Four professors, William Preston, Richard Graham, John Camm, and Emmanuel Jones, sign a statement saying that they believe Robinson's statement to be correct;

Nos. 236–237. Thomas Dawson to Bishop Sherlock, William and Mary College, July 9, 1757. The proceeding against Brunskill (See *Nos. 222–226*) was instituted after Dawson had informed the governor that, lacking a commission, he could not exercise any jurisdiction. The clergy were alarmed by this establishment of a lay authority over them, though there were precedents in Blair's time, and wanted Dawson to call a convention, which he would have done but for the threat of war, the fear of controversy, the heat of the season, and doubt of his authority. A commission from the bishop would end the difficulty;

Nos. 238–239. Thomas Dawson to Bishop Sherlock, William and Mary College, July 9, 1757. Since he wrote (*Nos. 236–237*) he has been sent a copy of a notice in Brunskill's handwriting, several copies of which he, Brunskill, has posted, citing canon 122 and declaring his belief that the governor's order was a forgery. The governor and Dawson think that he must have been put up to the action by others as he himself is almost constantly drunk. The vestry of St. Andrew's, Brunswick, have made complaints against their minister, George Purdie;

Nos. 240–241. Gov. Dinwiddie to Bishop Sherlock, Williamsburg, Sept. 12, 1757. He recounts the proceedings against Brunskill and justified them in the absence of a commission to the commissary. He accuses Robinson (See *Nos. 228–235*) and the professor of philosophy, unnamed, who has resigned, of drunkenness and irregularity. They married and kept their families at the college, contrary to the rules. When this was stopped, they moved into the town and spent more time at home than at the college. Some of the clergy held an unofficial convention, but only nine attended, including the college professors. These have become hostile to Dawson. They refused to supply his pulpit when he was sick and have ceased from attending church in Williamsburg. Many people, in disgust with conditions in the college, are sending their sons to Philadelphia;

Nos. 242–243. Minutes of meetings of Visitors and Governors of the College of William and Mary, Nov. 1, Nov. 4, Nov. 11, and Dec. 14, 1757. They dismissed the three remaining professors, Camm, Graham, and Jones, for refusing to explain why they had discharged James Hubbard, an usher in the grammar school. Their refusal was based on the contention that the direction of the grammar school rested solely with the president and masters of the college;

Nos. 244–245. A list of all counties, parishes, and present ministers of Virginia, Jan. 4, 1758;

Nos. 246–247. Address of the clergy of Virginia to the King, signed by John Camm as agent for the convention. Undated, but enclosed with *Nos. 248–249.* Protest against a law lately passed permitting the payment of their salaries in currency;

Nos. 248–249. John Pownall, Secretary to the Lords Commissioners for Trade and Plantations, to Bishop Sherlock, Whitehall, May 24, 1759. Transmitting *Nos. 246–247* and a copy of the law in question to him for comment;

Nos. 250–251. Bishop Sherlock to the Lords Commissioners for Trade and Plantations, Fulham, June 14, 1759. He holds that the act (Act of 1758) by curtailing the operation of an act approved by the King (in 1749), without formally repealing it, is treasonable. Virginia, until recently distinguished for loyalty to Church and Crown, has become increasingly refractory in recent years;

Nos. 258–263. Lords Commissioners for Trade and Plantations to the King, Whitehall, July 4, 1759. They recommend the disallowance of the act of 1758. They refer to the earlier act (See *Nos. 23–24*) as passed in 1749. [Ferdinand] Paris represented Camm, as agent for the clergy, and [James] Abercrombie [Abercromby] appeared as agent for the colony in their hearings;

Nos. 266–271. Lords Commissioners for Trade and Plantations to the King, July 31, 1759. Since submitting their representations (See *Nos. 258–263*) they have received a petition from the merchants of London trading with Virginia, a copy of which is attached, complaining of the same act as violating contracts on which payment in tobacco had been specified;

Nos. 272–273. Record of the meeting of the Lords Commissioners for Trade and Plantations, Council Chamber, Whitehall, Aug. 3, 1759. Recommend the disallowance of the act of 1758 and three earlier acts (the acts of 1755 and an earlier act of 1758) designed to secure the same object—the substitution of currency for tobacco in payments;

Nos. 274–275. Court at Kensington, Aug. 10, 1759. The foregoing acts are disallowed;

Nos. 276–277. Additional instruction to Francis Fauquier, Governor of Virginia, given at Court at Kensington, Sept. 21, 1759. He is instructed, under pain of royal displeasure and recall from his government, to observe strictly previous instructions not to approve any act in force for less than two years, or any act repealing a former law, unless it contains a suspensory clause withholding its operation until the royal pleasure is known;

Nos. 278–279. Petition of the clergy, signed by John Camm as agent, to the Lords Commissioners for Trade and Plantations, Aug. 3, 1760. They request that the disallowance of the foregoing acts (See *Nos. 272–273*) be made retroactive to the date of their passage. Otherwise the assembly can achieve its objective by the passage of laws of temporary operation;

Nos. 284–287. Proceedings of Visitors and Governors of William and Mary College at meetings March 31, April 25, 26, and 30, May 2, and Aug. 14, 1760. Signed by Francis Fauquier, rector. ———— Rowe, professor of philosophy, on confession of drunkenness and swearing, was admonished but retained on promise of reform. When he subsequently led the students in a riot with the apprentices, and presented a pistol to John Campbell and Peyton Randolph, magistrates seeking to maintain the peace, he was dismissed;

Nos. 288–293. William Robinson to Bishop Sherlock, York River, Nov. 20, 1760. Camm was grossly insulted by the governor when he returned with the disallowance and the additional instruction (*Nos. 274–277*). Robinson encloses some pamphlets attacking the clergy and the council and endeavours to answer some of their arguments.

VOLUME XIV

VIRGINIA

Nos. 1–2. Gov. Francis Fauquier to Bishop Sherlock, Williamsburg, July 29, 1761. Complains of the appointment of William Robinson as commissary, succeeding Thomas Dawson. Robinson's great offence is that he is a friend of Camm's;

Nos. 3–4. John Camm to (Bishop Egerton?), Williamsburg, Oct. 23, 1761. Having learned of Bishop Sherlock's death, and anticipating that Gov. Fauquier will try to have someone else appointed commissary, Camm urges his correspondent to use his influence to have Robinson retained;

Nos. 5–6. William Robinson to ———— ("My Lord"), King and Queen County, Nov. 3, 1761. Having just learned of Bishop Sherlock's death, he seeks the influence of this correspondent with the new bishop of London on his behalf. Says Fauquier requested the rector at Williamsburg to omit the Athanasian Creed;

Nos. 7–8. John Camm to Bishop Egerton of Bangor, Hampton, Jan. 1, 1762. Refers to a previous letter. Death of Philip Grymes has created a vacancy in the council which Camm thinks should go to Robinson as commissary;

Nos. 9–10. William Robinson to Bishop Hayter, King and Queen County, Jan. 18, 1762. Asks to be continued as commissary. Says he was born in Virginia and educated at Oriel College, Oxford, where he spent seven years. He has an estate of £300 a year besides his parish, Stratton Major, of which he has been rector eighteen years;

Nos. 11–12. William Robinson to Bishop Osbaldeston, King and Queen County, June 8, 1762. Says he was appointed commissary by Bishop Sherlock, April 18, 1761, and by Bishop Hayter, Nov. 28, 1761. As instructed, he submitted an account of the state of the Church in Sept. 1761. Introduces Devereux Jarratt, a candidate for orders;

Nos. 13–24. William Robinson to Bishop Osbaldeston, undated, but *notation* says "rec'd in Jan'ry 1763." Reviews his and Camm's dispute with Gov. Fauquier following the disallowance of the currency act. Camm and Alexander White have both sued to recover what they claim was underpayment under the act. The governor and most of the colonial leaders hold that the act was in force until disallowed. Jury in court of first instance has decided against White. His case and Camm's will probably have to be carried to the Privy Council. Discipline at the college is poor because the visitors have restricted the authority of the faculty;

Nos. 25–26. Francis Fauquier to Bishop Osbaldeston, Williamsburg, Feb. 20, 1764. Describes the placement of several clergymen recently arrived. Says his dispute with Robinson is subsiding, but still speaks bitterly;

Nos. 27–40. William Robinson to Bishop Terrick, York River, Aug. 17, 1764. He will continue to act as commissary until the bishop's wishes are known. He has refused to co-sign testimonials with the governor, as Dawson did, because he fears it would prevent his exerting independent judgment. He required candidates to produce testimonials from a parish where they have been resident three years. Principal aim of the letter is to ask the bishop's support for Camm's appeal. White lost his right to appeal through the failure of his lawyer to make the right exceptions. [Thomas] Warrington, who sued first, got some damages. Murray [James Maury] got a court to rule that the act was no law, but a jury only awarded him a penny damages. This was the result of pleading of a young lawyer who later admitted that he was bidding for popularity. He told the jury that the use of the clergy consisted solely in promoting civil obedience, that they should be punished for opposing a law passed by the governor and assembly, and that the King in disallowing said law had forfeited his claim to the allegiance of Virginians. None of the juries in these cases was composed of the best people and that in the Murray [Maury] case had been deliberately packed with New Lights;

Nos. 41–42. J. Williams Giberne to Bishop Terrick, Lunenburgh Parish, Richmond County, Aug. 31, 1764. Seeks appointment as commissary. He came to the colony on the invitation of Gov. Fauquier and has the recommendation of the Earl of Dartmouth. He reports that vestries are careless in giving testimonials and will give false titles, requiring the candidate to sign a bond not actually to claim the title. As a result unworthy persons, notably Scots who come to the colony as indentured schoolmasters, get into the ministry. These have caused some disgust with the clergy among the people, but worthy clergymen, like the writer, get along very nicely;

Nos. 43–46. Certificate of the election of Bishop Terrick as Chancellor of William and Mary, Nov. 21, 1764. Signed by James Horrocks, President, and Richard Graham, Emmanuel Jones, and John Camm, masters;

Nos. 47–48. James Horrocks to Bishop Terrick, William and Mary, Nov. 22, 1764. Accompanying *Nos. 43–46.* Asks bishop to recommend a grammar-school master, the post formerly held by Horrocks;

Nos. 49–50. Gov. Francis Fauquier to Bishop Terrick, Williamsburg, Nov. 24, 1764. Congratulates him on his translation. Refers to previous acquaintance and speaks of Mrs. Fauquier as an old friend of Mrs. Terrick. He supports Giberne's statement (See *Nos. 41–42*) that many of those who apply for orders are Scots who come as private tutors and apply for ordination after three or four years' residence. Parishes afford a "comfortable tho by no means an affluent Subsistance." There are now twelve vacancies;

Nos. 51–72. William Robinson to Bishop Terrick, King and Queen County, Aug. 12, 1765. Thanks him for promising to attend hearing of Camm's appeal and reviews the whole controversy from 1753. Identifies the lawyer in the Murray [Maury's] case as (Patrick) Henry. He has since been elected to the House of Burgesses where he made a number of inflammatory speeches, on occasion of the Stamp Act. In one of these he compared George III to Tarquin, Caesar, and Charles I and expressed a wish to see a Cromwell arise. He proposed a resolution, which was rejected, that anyone who should write or speak in favour of the Stamp Act should be deemed an enemy of the colony. Though some of his resolutions were rejected, he succeeded in stirring up the assembly sufficiently so that the governor had to dissolve it. Thomas Dawson, in his closing years, was accused of habitual drunkenness and admitted it before the visitors of the college. The governor urged in his extenuation that he was depressed as a result of the disputes with which he was surrounded. Horrocks obtained the presidency over his seniors, Graham and Camm, by swearing to obey a statute allowing the visitors to dismiss the masters at will. This was passed after Graham and Camm had secured an order from the Privy Council overruling their previous dismissal. The masters were seeking legal opinion concerning its validity;

Nos. 73–74. Francis Fauquier to Bishop Terrick, Williamsburg, Sept. 9, 1765. Introduces [Christopher] McCrae, a candidate for orders. Is still awaiting arrival of Samuel Quincy, to whom he will assign a parish, and Edward Hawtry, recommended by the bishop as master of the grammar school;

Nos. 77–78. Edward Hawtry to Bishop Terrick, William and Mary College, Oct. 2, 1765. The grammar school has sixty-four pupils and there are two ushers under the master [Hawtry]. He gets £100 plus board and lodging;

Nos. 79–80. James Horrocks to Bishop Terrick, William and Mary, Oct. 3, 1765. In answer to a query of the bishop's he says that he does not know of any gifts to the library by previous chancellors (See Vol. XIV, *Nos.* 37–38). Offers himself as commissary;

Nos. 81–82. Francis Fauquier to Bishop Terrick, Williamsburg, Nov. 6, 1765. Townsend Dade, who has just been ordained by the bishop, presented the governor with a testimonial from Col. Washington, but none from the clergy. As he said that, though a native of Virginia, he had resided in Maryland and was known to the clergy there, Fauquier advised him to obtain a recommendation from the governor of Maryland. Fauquier complains of Robinson's refusal to sign joint testimonials;

Nos. 83–84. James Horrocks to Bishop Terrick, Williamsburg, Dec. 27, 1765. There are two vacancies in the college: Moral Philosophy, lately held by William Small, and Humanity, which Hawtry resigned on being offered a better preferment in England. A statute of the college (See *Nos.* 89–90) recently sent to the bishop is being revised (See *Nos.* 91–92);

Nos. 85–86. Bishop Terrick to James Horrocks, Jan. 7, 1766 (rough copy). He objects to claim of visitors to have power to alter statutes and dismiss professors at will, and has doubts about a planned revision of the charter. If it is undertaken, every step should be carefully considered;

Nos. 87–88. James Horrocks to Bishop Terrick, Feb. 10, 1766. He thinks a revision of the charter may be necessary to clear up ambiguities concerning the authority of the visitors;

Nos. 89–90. "A Statute for the better Government of the College." Undated, but inserted here for comparison with revised statute. Declaring that aims of the college will be frustrated without due subordination of president and masters to the visitors, the statute provides that matters usually directed by the faculty shall be taken under the control of the visitors and that masters may be dismissed at will by a majority of the visitors. President and masters required to take an oath to uphold the statutes. Parochial employment forbidden;

Nos. 91–92. Revised statute, adopted May 1, 1766. Ordinary discipline of the college is restored to the faculty, but subject to direction by visitors. There is no specific reference to the power of dismissal. Oath to uphold the statutes and prohibition of parochial work continued. Copy signed by Matthew Davenport, Clerk of Visitors;

Nos. 95–102. William Robinson to Bishop Terrick, King and Queen County, June 6, 1766. Thanks the bishop for obtaining payment of arrears of his stipend as commissary. Having been warned that the clergy may lose the appeal of their suits for arrears (as the result of the Two-penny Act), he repeats the arguments for holding the disallowance retroactively effective, under pretext of quoting what the clergy are saying. Says he is reconciled to the governor, but is still critical of him. He say that Giberne is the son of a milliner in the city of Westminster, not bred to the cloth, but employed for a time as clerk in some office on Tower-hill. He was brought over by the governor and has endeavoured to persuade the clergy to accept the currency act. He has changed parishes several times. He resigned from the relief fund because of disagreement with its policies. He is too fond of cards and gaming. Camm was summoned before the visitors and asked if he would observe the statute against holding a parish (See Nos. 89–90). He insisted that the question was a charge and was at length allowed to read a long defence which was an attack on the statute. The meeting adjourned without dismissing him. Before the next meeting, some of the visitors who had opposed him asked him to teach their sons who were not making satisfactory progress under Horrocks. At the next meeting the statute was revised (See Nos. 91–92). The prohibition of parochial employment, though retained, was held not to be retroactive and Camm retains his parish. The governor attempted to revive the old statute, but a letter from the bishop prevented it. Richard Graham is returning to England where he is fellow of the Queen's College, Oxford. Robinson joined with the governor in recommending Lee Massey and Benjamin Sebastian, though Massey has no Greek;

Nos. 103–104. James Horrocks to Bishop Terrick, Sept. 20, 1766. Indicates continuing tension between faculty and visitors. Faculty have embarked upon some project to improve their status which may cause loss of revenue to the college and, if it fails, will probably end in their dismissal;

Nos. 105–106. Gov. Francis Fauquier to Bishop Terrick, Williamsburg, Jan. 14, 1767. [John] Lyth, who recently came to the colony, after being ordained by the bishop, is suspected of being insane. In any case, he returned to England after preaching once in the parish to which the governor sent him. Lloyd has been unable to get accepted by any parish. Other assignments are mentioned;

Nos. 107–108. William Agar to Bishop Terrick, Williamsburg, Jan. 26, 1767. He has accepted a parish near enough to enable him to continue his duties at the college. He asks the bishop to recommend his appointment as professor of mathematics;

Nos. 109–110. Francis Fauquier to Bishop Terrick, Williamsburg, April 27, 1767. The parish of Albemarle has brought charges against [John] Ramsey before the general court, which is preparing to try the case. Lloyd has gone to North Carolina. Dr. Halliburton has just arrived;

Nos. 111–112. James Horrocks to Bishop Terrick, William and Mary, June 4, 1767. Reports the arrival of Dr. Halliburton, recommended by the bishop to a professorship in the college;

Nos. 113–114. Minutes of meetings of the visitors of William and Mary, June 11 and June 12. They refused to accept William Halliburton as professor of moral philosophy, the post to which he has been recommended by Bishop Terrick, chiefly because he had delayed too long in New York on his way to Virginia. The bishop's letter, dated June 4, 1766, contained some strictures on the precariousness of tenure in the college. Transcript attested by John Blair, bursar;

Nos. 115–118. James Horrocks to Bishop Terrick, William and Mary, June 22, 1767. There are now two vacancies. The visitors have applied to Dr. Porteus to recommend candidates to Bishop Terrick, though some were in favour of applying to the London merchants with whom they correspond. The college is in a bad state. As Camm is not pressing the business he is supposed to be doing for the college (probably the revision of the charter, but the wording is vague), Horrocks may come to England himself;

Nos. 119–126. Dudley Digges to Bishop Terrick, William and Mary College, July 15, 1767. Digges, rector of the college, writes on behalf of the visitors. After explaining their rejection of Halliburton, he reviews the whole conflict with the faculty, which he traces to the contest between William Stith and Thomas Dawson for the presidency following the death in 1752 of William Dawson, under whom all was harmony. In addition to reviewing some controversies covered in other letters, he goes into detail concerning the case of William Small, who came in 1758 as professor of mathematics. He went to England on leave of absence and did not return, being now established as a physician in Birmingham, but he has written letters critical of the visitors;

Nos. 127–134. William Robinson to Bishop Terrick, King and Queen County, Oct. 16, 1767. Camm's appeal [to the King in Council] has been rejected, through the influence of Lord N[orthington], on the ground that it was improperly presented, though Camm was represented by Paris, considered the lawyer most experienced in colonial cases. As the case was not decided on its merits, they are planning to press Thomas Warrington's case, which is still pending, though he seemed to imply that it was decided (See *Nos. 27–40*). [Edward] Montague, the colonial agent, claims much credit for defeating the appeal. Robert Carter Nicholas, a wealthy planter, is spoken of as one of the leading opponents of the claims of the clergy;

Nos. 135–136. James Horrocks to Bishop Terrick, William and Mary, Jan. 11, 1768. He again applies for post as commissary now made vacant by Robinson's death;

Nos. 137–140. James Horrocks to Bishop Terrick, William and Mary, March 29, 1768. The faculty are preparing a detailed statement of their case, and Horrocks expects to go to England to present it to the bishop early in the fall. He says that the visitors are ignorant and intemperate. As proof of the latter charge he says that they find it necessary to hold their meetings before dinner. They are also fickle, as shown by the fact that they have forgotten their own resolution to apply to Dr. Porteus and applied to the bishop to fill their vacancies. Horrocks did not know of Agar's application for the professorship of mathematics, but does not oppose it. Gov. Fauquier has died;

Nos. 141–142. Jonathan Watson to Bishop Terrick, Williamsburg, May 16, 1768. A recent arrival in Virginia, where he plans to settle, he recommends Thomas Baker for orders. Formerly an usher to Mr. Wade at Boxford, Baker has served Watson as tutor and land surveyor, but lacks Latin and Greek. Pending appointment of a colonial bishop, which he urges, Watson suggests that each new English bishop be required to make one tour of the colonies. Grenville and Lord Bute are being much abused in the colony. Watson has been told by the innkeeper next door that all the faculty of the College of New Jersey are Presbyterians and that students are fined for attending Church of England services;

Nos. 143–146. James Horrocks to Bishop Terrick, William and Mary, June 27, 1768. Acknowledges appointment as commissary. He suggests an instruction that candidates should be examined by the commissary before presenting their credentials to the governor. He thinks he should be a member of the council, as was every commissary except Robinson. Charges against several clergy are pending before it and it claims ecclesiastical jurisdiction. Visitors, on receiving a letter from the bishop, have invited the faculty to present their grievances;

Nos. 147–152. James M. Fontaine to Bishop Terrick, July 1, 1768. Writing for the visitors, as rector, he says, that since receiving the bishop's letter, they have conceded some points to the faculty, though he lists a number which they refused to grant. He earnestly disavows an inference the bishop drew that their former letter (See *Nos. 119–126*) was critical of him;

Nos. 153–156. Statement of the faculty with minutes of meetings of the visitors, April 28–July 1, 1768, certified by Emmanuel Jones as clerk, July 22, 1768. The faculty, James Horrocks, John Camm, Emmanuel Jones, and Josiah Johnson, object to a claim of the visitors that the power of the faculty is delegated, holding that it rests on the charter. They acknowledge the power of the visitors to make statutes, but deny their right to interfere in the administration of the college otherwise. They claim the right to award scholarships, and to decide for themselves what preferment they should accept outside. The minutes do not indicate the action of the visitors on many of these points, but in *Nos. 147–152* it is said that they conceded the granting of scholarships, except where other procedure was specified, but denied the right to accept outside preferment without their permission;

Nos. 161–192. John Camm to Bishop Terrick, William and Mary College, Sept. 8, 1768. He has been told by William Nelson that the bishop decided not to appoint him commissary because of a report that he had refused, when requested, to visit Gov. Fauquier in his last illness to be reconciled. His answer is that he never received any such message, and that he had been forbidden to enter the governor's house. He reviews the whole history of his disputes with the governor and the college visitors;

Nos. 193–194. James Horrocks to Bishop Terrick, William and Mary College, Nov. 1, 1768. Reports the arrival of a new governor, Horrocks's appointment as commissary has led to a certain coolness between him and Camm;

Nos. 195–196. James Horrocks to Bishop Terrick, William and Mary, Jan. 12, 1769. He is still seeking a post on the council, but the governor, Lord Botecourt, will not commit himself until there is a vacancy and then his instructions require him to send home the names of three men. The plan of seeking a revised charter for the college has been given up as inexpedient in the present atmosphere of political agitation;

Nos. 197–198. W. Dunlap to Bishop Terrick, Stratton Major Parsonage,

June 2, 1769. He has been elected rector of this parish, succeeding Robinson. He tried to be forgiving to Dr. (William) Smith for seeking to discredit him to the bishop (See Vol. VIII, *Nos. 31–33*);

Nos. 199–202. James Horrocks to Bishop Terrick, William and Mary College, July 6, 1769. At a convention of the clergy which Horrocks called to welcome Lord Botecourt as governor, Camm proposed petitioning for *mandamus* to bring Warrington's case before the Privy Council, it having been held by the colonial courts to be decided by the rejection of Camm's appeal. A committee was appointed, including Camm, Warrington, and Horrocks, to consider the matter. Horrocks took the view that the appeal would almost certainly be lost and that it was inadvisable to make it in the present agitated state of public affairs. The committee decided to petition the governor to permit an appeal. As Horrocks refused to present the petition it was entrusted to Arthur Hamilton, the governor's chaplain, a member of the committee. Subsequent meetings were held in a tavern within the jail, where one of the members was held for debt. As Horrocks considered this an unsuitable place, he does not know what happened, but he understands that no appeal has been sent. A postscript, July 7, says that Camm refuses to let him see the minutes of the meetings he missed without the consent of the whole committee;

Nos. 203–204. James Horrocks to Bishop Terrick, William and Mary College, Dec. 15, 1769. A vacancy having occurred on the council, Gov. Botecourt has included Horrocks's name among the three recommended. The bishop has approved Horrocks views concerning the Warrington appeal. Reference is made to some unspecified difficulties relating to the ordination of Thomas Baker (See *Nos. 141–142*). Politics are quiet at present. The assembly now sitting seems friendly to the governor;

Nos. 205–206. James Horrocks to Bishop Terrick, William and Mary, May 1, 1770. Instructed by the visitors to thank the bishop for recommending [Samuel] Henley and [Thomas] Gwatkin to professorships in the college, to which they have been elected;

Nos. 207–208. James Horrocks to Bishop Terrick, William and Mary, May 15, 1770. He has been appointed to the council. [Alexander] Lunan, who, the bishop said, was coming, has not arrived, but as several parishes have been divided, there will be no difficulty in placing him when he does;

Nos. 209–210. James Horrocks to "The Rev., The Committee, etc.," William and Mary, Feb. 12, 1771. Acknowledges the receipt of pamphlets and letters relating to an unspecified project which he will present to a convention of the clergy which he proposes to call in connection with a meeting of the relief society. From references in *Nos. 213–214* it would appear that this was addressed to the committee of a convention in New York concerned with seeking a colonial episcopate;

Nos. 211–212. Extracts from letters of President Nelson of the Virginia council to Lord Hillsborough, Nov. 15, 1770, and April 17, 1771. As there is at present no means in Virginia for the removal of unworthy clergymen, as required in the instructions to the governor, Nelson proposes the issuance of a royal commission to the Bishop of London similar to that held by Bishop Gibson;

Nos. 213–214. James Horrocks to Bishop Terrick, Oct. 8, 1771. Though the place of writing is not given, Horrocks is evidently in England, for he speaks of making arrangements to wait on Lord Hillsborough and of receiving papers from Virginia, which he is forwarding to the bishop. He refers to the application for bishops as having been unsuccessful and expresses surprise that many of the clergy opposed it. Some of the objectors asserted that it was an effort to rob the Bishop of London of his jurisdiction. Writes that Camm answered this charge effectively;

Nos. 215–216. Charles Woodmason to Bishop Terrick, Wells, Sept. 16, 1776. Because of ill health, he resigned his frontier cure in South Carolina to accept rectorship of Bromfield Parish, Culpeper County, Virginia, but waited so long for a successor in South Carolina that he lost the appointment. He tried unsuccessfully to obtain other parishes in Virginia and Maryland, was attacked by the dissenters for writing in support of episcopacy, and finally driven out for opposing revolutionary measures;

Nos. 269–270. Petition, undated, of five clergymen, David Mossom, Patrick Henry, John Brunskill, John Robertson, and Robert Barret, to the general assembly. Protest licensing of Samuel Davies and other Presbyterian ministers and ask the enforcement of earlier acts forbidding officiating by clergymen not of the Church of England. Assert that the "ringleaders" of Presbyterianism in Virginia were expelled for heresy by the Synod of Philadelphia;

Nos. 273–274. Clergy of Virginia to Bishop Sherlock. Undated. Signed only by Thomas Dawson as commissary. Thank him for aiding Kay in his appeal and for securing the appointment of Dawson to the council, undated, as are the following Virginia items:

Nos. 275–276. A memorandum of some points concerning presentation and induction in Virginia. Possibly made by Bishop Sherlock in connection with the Kay appeal, for it refers to a brief;

Nos. 277–280. Some undated notes of the Virginia laws substituting currency for tobacco payments and the suits of the clergy following their disallowance;

Nos. 281–298. William Robinson to (Bishop Sherlock), undated, but probably written in 1761. Thanks the bishop for appointing him commissary. When he waited on the governor (Fauquier), the governor told him that he could not expect his countenance unless he broke with Camm. He describes widespread resentment against the clergy as the result of the disallowance of the currency-for-tobacco laws. He gives a long account of the disputes in the college, having been a member of the board of visitors throughout, though opposed to the majority on most issues. After the dismissal of Camm (this seems to have been written before his restoration), no professor of divinity was appointed, though the charter calls for two. The visitors elected a layman to their board to succeed Thomas Dawson and are seeking to secure lay professors. They have supplanted the masters in the routine direction of the school. Gov. Fauquier has asked the rector at Williamsburg to omit the Athanasian Creed in reading the service;

Nos. 299–300. Wardens and vestry of St. Ann's, Albemarle County, *vs.* their rector, John Ramsey, before John Blair, President, and the council. Undated. They accuse Ramsey of neglect of duty, drunkenness, and endeavouring to seduce Joanna Collins. No indication of disposition of case;

Nos. 301–302. Wardens and vestry of Upper Parish, Nansemond County *vs.* Patrick Lunan, the minister, before John Blair, President, and the council. Undated. Charge Lunan with habitual drunkenness, endeavouring to officiate when drunk, neglect of duty, fighting and swearing. No indication of disposition of case;

Nos. 303–304. Wardens and vestry of Fairfax Parish *vs.* Townsend Dade, their minister, before Gov. Norborne, Baron de Botecourt and council. Undated. Accuse him of seducing and committing adultery with the wife of John Hunter. No indication of disposition of case.

VOLUME XVI

BARBADOS

Nos. 81–82. Thomas Barnard to Bishop Sherlock, Feb. 14, 1748/9. Having served as commissary under Bishop Gibson, he reports to Bishop Sherlock that Church affairs in the island are in good order. Two rectors (of St. James' and St. Lucia's) are absent, but the first parish is supplied by a curate and the second by the other clergy. The college begins to flourish. The grammar school of St. Michael's is without a master, as the former one, Ewing, has gone to England to seek orders. The clergy of the island refused to sign his [Ewing's] testimonials because of previous misconduct, though he behaved well when in charge of the school;

Nos. 83–84. R. Temple to Bishop Sherlock, St. Philip's, June 24, 1750. He came to Barbados three years ago with Gov. Henry Grenville, nephew to Lord Cobham. He was chaplain of H.M.S. *Dragon,* but being also related to Lord Cobham he persuaded Grenville to appoint him to this parish. When he returned to England for his family, Bishop Gibson was dead and Bishop Sherlock not yet appointed, so he did not obtain a licence. If one is required, he will take the necessary oaths before the governor. He served for ten years in Suffolk County in the Diocese of Norwich and was the first clergyman instituted by the present Bishop of Ely, Bishop Sherlock's brother-in-law, when he became Bishop of Norwich. This letter is brought by John Edwards, a candidate for orders;

Nos. 85–86. Gov. Charles Pinfold to Bishop Osbaldeston, July 20, 1762. Complains that Thomas Barnard has made arrangements to farm his parish (St. Michael's, Bridgetown) to curates and live in England. Barnard's brother is a canon of Windsor and Headmaster of Eton;

No. 91. Bishop Osbaldeston to Gov. Pinfold, Fulham, Nov. 20, 1762. Condemns Barnard's action and says that Lord Egremont at the colonial office has assured him that Barnard will not be granted any extension of his present year's leave of absence, which was granted by Pinfold on assurances that Barnard intended to bring his family out;

Nos. 92–93. Advocate-General James Marriott to Bishop Terrick, Southampton St., Bloomsbury, Dec. 24, 1764. Having been instructed by His Majesty's Council to find out what can be done about a clergyman in Barbados who has deserted his living in defiance of the governor, he desires a sight of Bishop Gibson's commission so he can ascertain what the bishop's powers are. A postscript notes that a reply from a previous bishop seemed to indicate that the commission was personal to Bishop Gibson;

Nos. 94–95. James Marriott to Bishop Terrick, Southampton St., 'Wednesday.' (Dec. 26, 1764. *Notation*). Names Barnard as the clergyman concerned and doubts that there is any legal remedy. Proceedings could be started under a statute of Henry VIII, but Barnard could probably escape the penalty by pleading ill health and the fact that his cure was supplied. Since the act does carry a penalty, he holds that it precludes any other proceeding;

No. 96. Memorandum by James Marriott, Henry Norton, and William De Grey, March 11, 1765. Give the opinion that His Majesty by proper powers under the Great Seal can authorize the governor of Barbados to make an inquiry, after citation, fixed upon the church door, and either sequester the income of the living or declare it vacant and collate a new incumbent;

Nos. 97–98. Record of indictment and conviction of Thomas Harris, rector of St. Lucy's, of assault with intent to ravish his sister-in-law, Frances Bennett, June 12 and 13, 1765. Petition of the vestry to Gov. Charles Pinfold, June 27, 1765, asking him either to suspend Harris or declare the living vacant;

Nos. 103–108. Reference of Nos. 97–98 by Gov. Pinfold to the attorney-general (J. Blenman) and solicitor-general (J. Stone), July 2–6, 1765. Blenman thinks that the governor has power to declare the living vacant. Stone thinks he had better refer the matter to the Bishop of London and the Lords Commissioners for Trade and Plantations. Blenman recalls two previous cases. In that of Charles Porter in 1721 he does not recollect that there were any formal proceedings. In that of Brian Hunt (in South Carolina), Commissary Johnson proceeded against and censured a clergyman for some, unspecified offence;

Nos. 113–121. Thomas Harris's answer to the vestry's petition (See Nos. 97–98) received by the governor, July 11, 1765. He holds that the vestry met illegally, since he was not present, that deprivation would be an additional penalty to the sentence already imposed on him, and that the governor has no jurisdiction;

Nos. 131–138. Replication of the vestry to Harris's answer (See Nos. 113–121) received Aug. 15, 1765. They answer Harris's objections at some length, but do not give any positive reasons for holding that the governor has the power to deprive or suspend;

Nos. 147–155. Harris's second answer to the vestry, received Aug. 26, 1765. Goes over the same ground without adding any new arguments;

Nos. 164–165. Gov. Charles Pinfold to Bishop Terrick, Sept. 3, 1765. He agrees with the solicitor-general that he does not have power to act and is referring the matter to the bishop and, in a separate letter, to the Lords Commissioners for Trade and Plantations. Thomas Barnard, rector of St. Michael's and reputed to be the bishop's commissary, has not been on the island for nine years, except for a visit of one month;

Nos. 168–169. W. Dunlap to William Dicks, secretary to Bishop Terrick, June 7, 1766. Returning to Barbados after his ordination, he had a quiet voyage, with a stop at Madeira, where he officiated for the British subjects residing there. He reached Barbados to find Bridgetown ravaged by a fire which, on May 14 had destroyed 400 houses. Gov. Pinfold had returned before he arrived, so he asks a recommendation to his successor;

Nos. 170–171. A list of the parishes and rectors in Barbados, Dec. 1772. Thomas Harris is listed as rector of St. Lucy's. Sheet is headed with a small map of the island showing location of the parishes;

Nos. 172–173. Clearances of the Coddrington estate from 1750–1783. Certified by Conrade Pile, accountant to S.P.G.

VOLUME XVII

THE BERMUDAS

Nos. 27–28. Alexander Richardson to Bishop Terrick, St. George's, June 23, 1766. He came out with Gov. Popple in 1755, having been promised a prosperous living, but finds his support inadequate. One of the two clergymen serving the country parishes (both of North American origin) has left because of insufficient support. Richardson is a graduate of St. Peter's, Cambridge. Living in Bermuda is dear;

Nos. 29–30. Gov. George James La Bruere to Bishop Terrick, Dec. 4, 1766. [John] Feveryear went to Georgia in hope of obtaining a better living, but died shortly after his arrival. Gov. Bruere recommends his widow to the bishop's charity, and asks that a clergyman be sent to replace him. He estimates the income of the country clergy at about £80;

Nos. 31–32. Alex. Richardson to Bishop Terrick, March 10, 1768. He has been disappointed in a chaplaincy which he sought from Lord Barrington, with the bishop's support. Gov. Popple tried to get an allowance from the S.P.G. for him, without success. He is sending the bishop a gift of a tortoise by the present governor's son, who is going home to seek the post of secretary, formerly held by George Browne, who died shortly after his arrival;

No. 33. Thomas Lyttleton to Gov. Bruere, Oct. 8, 1771. As Richardson persists in marrying his parishioners and as the governor refuses to charter a college that he projects, he plans to return home (Copy);

No. 34. Gov. Bruere to Thomas Lyttleton, St. George's, Oct. 9, 1771. He will seek to restrain Richardson from intrusion, but the question of a college charter must be maturely considered by the legislature. The islanders are so poor now that most debts, including the salaries of the clergy and public officials, are unpaid (Copy);

No. 35. Alexander Richardson to Gov. Bruere, St. George's, Jan. 16, 1772. Complains because the governor now restricts marriage licences to the clergyman of the parish in which the couple live (Copy);

No. 36. Gov. Bruere to Alexander Richardson, Jan. 16, 1772. He was just endeavouring to maintain harmony, and will call a court of ordinary if Richardson has any just reason to complain (Copy); also Richardson to Bruere, St. George's, Jan. 16, 1772. Unwilling to submit to the governor as ordinary, he is appealing to the bishop (Copy);

Nos. 37–38. Gov. Bruere to Bishop Terrick, Jan. 24, 1772. Encloses *Nos.* 33–36. Dispute began because Lyttleton insisted on performing marriages only in church and at the canonical hours. The governor's daughter, married about two years ago, walked to the church with him at the proper time, but "in these small Governments the Inhabitants do not choose to be under any good Regulations, or Restraint whatsoever";

Nos. 39–40. Thomas Lyttleton to Bishop Terrick, June 27, 1775. He is opposed to a law recently passed providing for the sale of pews in the churches, as the buildings are inadequate to seat all the people. He fears that the measure will drive some to the Presbyterian Church, which has a large meeting house, but has lately been declining. He has received only one year's salary in eight years. The Associates of Dr. Bray maintain three schools for Negroes in the island under Lyttleton's supervision. As the island is dependent on North America for supplies, it will suffer if the ports there are closed;

Nos. 41–42. Petition of Thomas Lyttleton to George III, June 1775, against the pew law.

VOLUME XVIII

JAMAICA

Nos. 23–26. An act of 1748 for the regulating and settling the livings of the clergy and ascertaining the same and giving the Bishop of London ecclesiastical jurisdiction over them. Passed assembly, May 17, council, July 13, approved by Gov. Edward Trelawney, Aug. 13, 1748. Preamble states that the Bishop of London, "hath never been admitted to the Exercise of any Spiritual Jurisdiction whatever but stands excluded therefrom by the law of this Island." Present act raises the salaries of the clergy, provides for the rental or building of rectories, and allows the bishop to exercise jurisdiction to the extent of maintaining discipline among the clergy only;

Nos. 37–38. William May to Bishop Sherlock, Kingston, Jan. 23, 1748/9. Congratulates him on his translation. Hopes he will name someone else as commissary, as May is frequently afflicted with gout and asthma and unable to fulfill the duties of his office. Asks for a curate;

Nos. 39–40. Opinion of Mathew Lamb, Lincoln's Inn, Jan. 28, 1749, concerning the act of 1748. He recommends its disallowance on the ground that it really curtails the bishop's jurisdiction while professing to authorize it;

Nos. 41–42. Samuel Gellibrand to Dr. Bearcroft, Whitehall, Feb. 21, 1749. Encloses *Nos. 23–26* and *39–40* for the bishop's attention;

Nos. 43–44. Thomas Hill to Bishop Sherlock, Whitehall, May 15, 1751. Encloses another copy of *Nos. 23–26*, on behalf of the Lords Commissioners for Trade and Plantations;

Nos. 45–52. John Venn to Bishop Sherlock, June 15, 1751. Told by Castlefrane that the bishop desires some information concerning the island, he undertakes to supply it on the basis of eleven years' residence. Jamaica is more civilized and less unhealthy than most English people suppose, though some physiques cannot stand the climate. Since white people cannot work in the climate, slavery is necessary, if its products are to be available to Europeans. On well-run plantations, discipline is administered evenly and moderately, but some masters are guilty of shocking cruelties which the law cannot touch. Respectable white people never marry Negroes, but concubinage is frequent. The offspring of unions are usually, though not always, freed and taught a trade. A law of the colony excludes persons of African descent, even though free, from full civil rights until the fourth generation from their African ancestor. The law allows slaves free time on Saturday afternoon and Sunday, but as they have to use it to cultivate their own gardens, he does not think that it provides time for religious instruction. Most masters are opposed to such instruction and the Negroes generally reluctant to give up their own rites, especially those for the dead. Most free Negroes and mulattoes are Christian. The island is divided into nineteen parishes, which are also counties. A list of parishes, with minister, salaries, and some other information is given. Salaries are based on the act of 1748 (See *Nos.* 23–26), though there are reports of its disallowance, which will be a hardship for the clergy. He holds that the restriction on the bishop's jurisdiction was required by the act of 1681 prohibiting penal ecclesiastical jurisdiction. Having royal assent, this law could only be repealed by another with the same assent. Spanish Town, formerly St. Jago de la Vega, is the capital. Port Royal is on the peninsula at the entrance to Kingston Harbour. Except in wartime, it is very very poor. The quality of the clergy would be improved, if the governors would wait for a recommendation from the bishop before presenting to benefices. Venn disapproves of Edward Lewis, a former merchant captain, who is seeking orders;

Nos. 53–54. William May to Bishop Sherlock, Kingston, June 21, 1751. At the bishop's request, he tells how he proceeded as commissary. He held annual visitations at which the clergy assembled at his own house. After they had attended church, he heard complaints, made a short speech, and treated them to dinner. He never had any formal complaints against the clergy from the laity, but they frequently complained of acts of intrusion by one another. In such cases, and when informed of other offences, he admonished the offenders;

Nos. 55–56. Gov. Charles Knowles to Bishop Sherlock, Nov. 9, 1752.

Encloses a list of livings and stipends (See *Nos.* 57–58). Six parishes are vacant. Not all of the clergy have as good a character
as he would wish, but he makes no specific charges;

Nos. 57–58. List of livings and their values, 1752;

Nos. 59–60. Samuel Griffith to Dr. Torton, Spanish Town, Feb. 27, 1762.
Griffith is domestic chaplain to Gov. Lyttelton. As the see of
London was vacant when he sailed, he could not ask for instructions for promoting Christianity in the island, but will be glad
to receive any now. He would also like to receive the King's
bounty;

Nos. 61–62. Henry Penlington to Bishop Terrick, Kingston, July 23, 1769.
Complains of poor morals of many of the clergy, but names only
one, James Cosgreve, a recent arrival from North America, who
is a habitual drunkard. A fund has been raised to send him back
to Ireland. Penlington is rector of Portland Parish in Jamaica.

VOLUME XIX

LEEWARD ISLANDS

Nos. 278–279. Francis Byam to Bishop Gibson, St. John's, Antigua, Oct.
12, 1748. He was unable to wait on the bishop before returning
from England, as he received a letter which made an immediate
return imperative. He refers to an act against Roman Catholics,
passed in the islands, but not presented for confirmation before
he left England. They are growing in numbers and wealth. He
encloses a list of clergy, but is not sure that it is altogether correct for Montserrat or Nevis. There are some clergy without the
bishop's licence and he asks advice concerning them;

No. 280. Francis Byam to Bishop Sherlock, St. John's, Antigua, June 14,
1749. Asks to be continued as commissary, or, if the rumour is
correct that suffragans are to be appointed for America, to be
considered for that post. He had started proceedings against an
unnamed clergyman for performing clandestine marriages, but
has discontinued them on the assumption that his authority ex-
pired with Bishop Gibson's death;

Nos. 281–282. Robert Robertson to Bishop Sherlock, Nevis, May 3, 1749.
Refers to some writings of the bishop's and recommends some of
his own;

Nos. 283–284. Charles Rose to Bishop Sherlock, Antigua, July 20, 1749.
He has been rector of St. Peter's Church, Antigua, since 1732 and
is a graduate of King's College, Aberdeen, from which he has a
degree of LL.D. He says that he alone stemmed the tide of Deism
in the island and that he would have become commissary if Bishop
Gibson had survived. He lists the clergy of the island and mentions

the recent arrival of Alexander Grant and Robert Moncrief. Grant was a dissenting teacher in the island whom Rose persuaded to seek Anglican orders. He has gone to Tortola until there is a vacancy in the Leewards;

Nos. 285–286. Charles Rose to Bishop Sherlock, Antigua, Nov. 24, 1749. Opposes the ordination of John King, who may be recommended by former Gov. George Thomas of Pennsylvania and others who are his relatives. Rose accuses him of being a deist in his views and dissolute in his manners.

VOLUME XX

LEEWARD ISLANDS

No. 1. Clipping from unidentified Antigua papers, May 4, 1750. Contains address from the clergy to Gov. William Mathew on his departure. Signed by Charles Rose;

Nos. 2–3. Charles Rose to Bishop Sherlock, St. Peter's, Antigua, May 11, 1750. Approves of the bishop's plan for colonial bishops, but fears it may meet with opposition in the islands, as many of the legislators are deists. He favours an act of Parliament providing that the bishops shall receive the ordinary fees for marriage licences and probate of wills which now go to the governor. He lately visited St. Croix, in the Danish West Indies, where the English minister, serving an English congregation, told him that he had submitted his letters of order to the Danish government for approval. Since the death of the Rev. Mr. Grant, there is no clergyman in the English portion of the Virgin Islands. Rose is disturbed by proposals, in some recently published "Disquisitions" on the revision of the Prayer Book, for the omission of the Athanasian Creed and the wedding ring;

No. 4. Charles Rose to Bishop Sherlock, Antigua, May 12, 1750. Encloses some unidentified document which he says enforces his argument for the need of a bishop, or some supervising clergyman, if no bishop can be had. Quakers are strong in Tortola. Rose plans another visit to the Virgin Islands;

Nos. 5–6. Francis Byam to Bishop Sherlock, Antigua, July 23, 1750. He also favours supporting a bishop by the ordinary fees;

Nos. 7–8. Gilbert Fleming to Bishop Sherlock, Antigua, April 1751. Reports that the leading persons "of Religious principles, and best understanding" approve Sherlock's plan for suffragan bishops. Recommends Byam for the post. Has appointed William Blair and John Douglas, just arrived with the bishop's recommendation, to benefices. He intended to send Douglas to Tortola, "lately become rich and prosperous," but as the people there showed no readiness to build a church or support a minister, he sent Douglas to Nevis;

Nos. 9–10. Francis Byam to Bishop Sherlock, Antigua, Aug. 20, 1751. In answer to a query from the bishop as to what he thought were the principal defects in the powers of the commissary, he says that he never thought that he had any power. He was supposed to have power to suspend pending final decision by the bishop, but this could be only a suspension *ab officio*, as the laws of the islands made no provision for the deprivation of a suspended clergyman, and he could not have enforced even that if any minister had chosen to defy it. He kept these thoughts to himself, and the supposition that he might have power may have had some good effect. Naval chaplains stationed in the islands were entirely outside his jurisdiction. Bishop Gibson was blocked by the Admiralty in all efforts to obtain any effective control of them. He fears that reported death of the Prince of Wales may distract the authorities from the bishop's proposals;

Nos. 11–12. Francis Byam to Bishop Sherlock, Antigua, June 23, 1753. Having received a delayed letter from the bishop inquiring about colonial opposition to bishops, he says that he does not find the people opposed, provided they are not charged with the bishop's support and provided that no spiritual courts are set up with jurisdiction over the laity. He warns the bishop that some unnamed persons whom he considers unworthy may apply for orders with testimonials from some of the clergy;

Nos. 13–14. Proceedings before Court of King's Bench, Nevis, May 1 and 15, 1764. William Tuckett and others were indicted for a riot in which they invaded the home of Edwin Thomas, rector of St. Paul's, and created a disturbance. Defendants pleaded guilty and were fined;

Nos. 15–16. Anonymous letter to Bishop Terrick, Antigua, April 13, 1769. Protests ordination of [John] Crook, whom the writer accuses of being ignorant and of scandalous character. Also complains of earlier ordination of John Symes;

No. 17. Page from *The Carribbean and General Gazette or the Saint Christopher Chronicle,* July 1, 1769. Contains memorial of Edwin Thomas to the court of King's Bench, June 29, 1769, complaining that he was abused by William Cary, John Stanley, and John Gardiner at a previous session of the court. Thomas was required to ask the court's pardon for submitting a memorial reflecting on its order and dignity;

Nos. 18–19. Edwin Thomas to William Carr, St. Christopher, July 26, 1769. Encloses *No. 17* and some papers which he had published under the name of "Eusebius" which started the dispute. He accuses John Stanley of having tried to secure the appointment of his father, lately released from jail, to the bench;

Nos. 20–21. Queries addressed to Edwin Thomas by the Court of King's Bench, St. Christopher, Aug. 26, 1769. Ask him if he was author of an article signed "Ireneus" published in the *Saint Christopher Gazette or the Historical Chronicle* which defended his memorial (*No. 17*) and attacked Gardiner and Stanley;

Nos. 24–27. Thomas's answers, presented Oct. 9, 1769. Admits authorship of article but defends it as unexceptionable. A *notation* by Thomas says that the court held him in contempt, but that his fine was remitted by Gov. Woodley;

Nos. 31–34. The *Carribbean and General Gazette,* Oct. 31 and Nov. 24, 1770. Contain "Philippics" signed by "Publicola," dealing with island politics. *Notations* in Thomas's hand indicate his authorship;

Nos. 35–36. The *Carribbean Gazette or the Saint Christopher Chronicle,* Dec. 8, 1770. Contains an article dealing with island politics signed "Publicola";

Nos. 37–38. Memorial of James Ramsay, Rector of St. John's Capisterre, St. Christopher, to Gov. Richard Hawkshaw Losack, Dec. 10, 1770. Charges that John Stanley, during an election in which he was a candidate and which was held in the church, sat in the chancel, with his feet on the communion table, ordered punch, which he drank there, swearing that he would never drink anything else there. Edward Gillard, another candidate, is also accused of standing within the chancel and using abusive language while there;

Nos. 39–42. The *Carribbean Gazette or the Saint Christopher Chronicle,* Dec. 12, 13, 19, 20, 1770. Contains political essays by "Publicola";

Nos. 43–44. Edwin Thomas to Bishop Terrick, St. Christopher, Dec. 20, 1770. Thomas Smith, whose ordination Thomas has opposed, after unsuccessful efforts to break into the English or Irish stage, is renewing his efforts to obtain ordination. One clergyman who signed testimonials for Smith, Clarkson of Nevis, is a former fisherman who got ordained by a previous bishop through the device of pretending to the bishop's chaplain that the then Gov. George Thomas had promised to send testimonials for him. The other clergymen on Nevis are Thomas Powell and William Scot. Powell was a poor lime burner whom some parishioners proposed as rector in a drunken frolic. When he took them seriously, they kept their word, provided him with testimonials, and received him as rector. Scot was a former dissenting preacher whose motives for conforming Thomas suspects of being worldly. The clergy on St. Christopher are all worthy men, though Jones, recently deceased, was subject to scandal. Thomas asks permission to return to England for a year and refers to Ramsay's petition, (*Nos. 37–38*);

Nos. 45–46. The Carribbean and General Gazette or the St. Christopher Chronicle, Jan. 5, 1771. Another political article by "Publicola";

Nos. 47–50. Affidavit of John Gardiner, June 25, 1771, St. Christopher. Testifies that John Stanley behaved as stated in Ramsay's memorial (*Nos. 37–38*) and that Edward Gillard used abusive language to Gardiner while standing within the chancel;

Nos. 51–54. Clergy of St. Christopher, Edwin Thomas, James Ramsay, and B. W. Hutchinson, to Gov. Richard Hawkshaw Losack, June 25, 1771. In support of Ramsay's complaint;

Nos. 55–58. James Ramsay to Bishop Terrick, St. Christopher, June 29, 1771. Gives an account of the case, showing some of its political ramifications. Stanley was a protégé of former governor Woodley;

Nos. 59–60. Thomas, Ramsay, and Hutchinson, to Bishop Terrick, St. Christopher, July 3, 1771. Support Ramsay's complaint. There are two other clergy in the island, Thomas Paget and John Baldrick. Paget opposes their proceedings and Baldrick has not been present at their meetings;

Nos. 61–62. Affidavit of Benjamin Clifton, St. Christopher, July 6, 1771. Confirms statements of Ramsay (*Nos. 37–38*) and Gardiner (*Nos. 47–50*) to the extent that he saw Stanley sitting in the chancel with his feet on the communion table and heard him order punch. As Clifton was walking about, he did not see Stanley actually drinking the punch or hear him say that he would not drink anything else there;

Nos. 65–66. Copy of *Nos. 43–44* with addition, dated July 20, 1771. As the clergy usually met at Thomas's house, Ramsay asked him to call a meeting to address the governor on the Stanley incident. Paget belongs to a whist club of which Gov. Losack and Stanley are both members and the meeting was fully discussed there. Though predisposed in favour of Stanley, Paget admitted that his conduct was wrong and voted for an address to the governor which Thomas and Hutchinson were appointed to draft. Before the next meeting, Stanley received word from ex-governor Woodley that the appointment as solicitor-general which Woodley had obtained for him had been stopped because of Ramsey's complaint. A great effort was then made to obtain counter-affidavits, and Paget was induced to oppose the address. Thomas delivered a speech in support of the address, a copy of which he encloses;

Nos. 67–68. The Thomas Speech;

Nos. 69–70. Bishop Terrick to Edwin Thomas, Fulham, Oct. 8, 1771. (Copy). He is always glad to do what he can to assist the clergy, "whether in my Diocese at home, or in the more distant parts, which by long usage have been considered, as having a more particular relation to the Bishop of London than to any other Bishop." He has been at pains to make himself familiar with the Stanley case, but, as Stanley's appointment has already been confirmed, all that the bishop can do is to commend the protection of the clergy to the new governor, Sir Ralph Payne;

Nos. 71–74. Summary of the Stanley case, probably made by the bishop or his secretary sometime in 1771, as it assumes the possibility of blocking Stanley's appointment. Notes that Baldrick and Paget do not have the bishop's licence;

Nos. 75–78. List of clergy in the Leeward Islands with record of ordination and dates of induction extending through 1773. Notes that Thomas Paget was unlicensed because his post as fellow of King's College, Cambridge, provided a sufficient title.

VOLUME XXXVI

COLONIES GENERAL

Nos. 134–135. A[rchibald] Spencer to Bishop Sherlock, June 12, 1749. At the bishop's request, he has inquired concerning the attitude of gentlemen in New York and Philadelphia towards the project of suffragan bishops and finds them disposed to fear that such bishops might interfere with the rights of the people and the proprietors;

Nos. 136–149. Representation of Bishop Sherlock to George II, April 11, 1750. After reviewing the history of ecclesiastical jurisdiction in the colonies, he urges the appointment of suffragan bishops;

Nos. 150–151. Draft of letter from Bishop Sherlock, apparently designed to be sent to all the commissaries, Sept. 20, 1750. Notes that his proposals for bishops have been buried in the council and asks for an account of how the commissarial jurisdiction was exercised under Bishop Gibson;

Nos. 152–153. Extracts from the proceedings of the deputies representing the English dissenters, 1749 and 1750, recording their opposition to the plan for colonial bishops;

Nos. 154–155. Philip Bearcroft to Bishop Sherlock, Feb. 29, 1752. Introducing Joseph Bewsher, formerly an usher in Coddrington College, who returned to England for his health and now desires a licence for Virginia;

Nos. 156–157. I. West to Bishop Sherlock, Treasury Chambers, June 25, 1755. Treasury approves of payment to Alexander Richardson, licensed for Bermuda, of bounty recovered from John Heyborne Chester, who was licensed for South Carolina but did not go there;

Nos. 158–159. Estimate of population of the American colonies in 1761.

Gives religious distribution among three groups: Church people; Presbyterians and Independents; all others;

Nos. 160–169. A general account of the colonies by Dr. (William?) Smith, 1762;

Nos. 170–177. Thoughts upon the present state of the Church of England in America, 1764. An argument for colonial bishops, possibly by Bishop Terrick;

Nos. 178–183. Account of the Church in the Carolinas, Georgia, and Florida by Charles Woodmason, 1766.

SOCIETY FOR PROMOTING CHRISTIAN KNOWLEDGE

Established in 1698, the Society functioned as an active missionary organization prior to 1701 when the Society for the Propagation of the Gospel in Foreign Parts was founded. Subsequently, it provided books, funds for establishing church libraries and schools, and other forms of financial aid.

The manuscripts relating to the period 1748–1776 pertain chiefly to the Salzburg emigrants, Protestant exiles who were resettled in Georgia beginning in 1731. These papers comprise 8 volumes and some unbound letters, 1731–1771. See Crick and Alman: *Guide,* p. 312; Andrews and Davenport: *Guide,* p. 331; and William Osborn Bird Allen and Edmund McClure: *Two Hundred Years: The History of the Society for Promoting Christian Knowledge, 1698–1898* (London, 1898).

SOCIETY FOR THE PROPAGATION OF THE GOSPEL IN FOREIGN PARTS

As the name implies, the Society for the Propagation of the Gospel in Foreign Parts was established in order to carry Christian knowledge to remote areas of the Empire. Founded in 1701, its chief centres of activity in the eighteenth century were in the American colonies. The manuscripts relating to America covering the years 1748–1776 are as follows:

(1) 'B' MSS. Letters received, 1702–1799 (25 vols., bound under the respective colonies) and 1701–1800 (16+ boxes of unbound papers). Transcripts and microfilms of the 25 volumes are in the Library of Congress. These letters from missionaries as well as civil officials in the colonies describe missionary activities among the Negroes and the Indians and report the difficulties faced by the missionaries before, during and after the Revolutionary War. Among the "B" volumes in vol. 1 is a memorial, *No. 268,* relating to "certain lands [in New York] to the amount of sev-

eral thousand acres . . . purchased [by Joseph Totten, Ebenezer Jessup, and others] of the native Indians on the 29 and 31 days of July 1772" intended to be granted for the benefit of the Society; in vol. 5 North Carolina and South Carolina are dealt with, 1756–1781; (2) "C" MSS. Miscellaneous manuscripts relating to the American colonies, 1630–1811 (16 boxes, unbound). The boxes, generally arranged according to colony, contain large quantities of correspondence to and from missionaries, certificates, petitions, testimonials, and accounts. The contents of the boxes are as follows: Box 1: New York, 1708–1785. Box 2: North and South Carolina, 1712–1784; it also contains "Short remarks on Indian trade, Virginia." Box 3: Connecticut, 1635–1796. Box 4: New England, 1630–1780; also New Hampshire, 1760–1811. Box 5: New Jersey, 1709–1791; Maine, 1762–1789; Maryland, 1760–1762. Box 6: Massachussetts, 1711–1798. Box 7: Pennsylvania, 1712–1784. Box 8: (i) Rhode Island, 1712–1785; (ii) Rhode Island, 1760–1800. Box 9: Georgia, 1758–1782; Vermont, 1763. Two boxes contain legal deeds. Three boxes of "Unbound American papers." One box bills of exchange and receipts. One box "American papers—New York." A box labelled "S.P.G. and Government—North America, 1715–1830" contains only two papers relating to what is now the United States. (3) *Reports* of the Society (printed), 1704+; (4) Anniversary Sermons, 1702+; (5) Journals and Minutes of the Society and its Committees, 1701+; (6) Accounts and Account Books, 1701+.

See Andrews and Davenport: *Guide,* pp. 332–3; Crick and Alman: *Guide,* pp. 313–16; Grace G. Griffin: *A Guide to Manuscripts Relating to American History in British Depositories* . . . , pp. 196–8; John W. Lydekker: *The Archives of the S.P.G., S.P.G. World Wide Series,* No. 2 (London [1936]); and Charles Frederick Pascoe: *Two Hundred Years of the S.P.G.: An Historical Account of the Society for the Propagation of the Gospel in Foreign Parts, 1701–1900* (London, 1901).

DR. BRAY'S ASSOCIATES

Dr. Thomas Bray (1656–1730), an Anglican divine, devoted his efforts over the years to spreading enlightenment among the membership of the Church both in England and the colonies. He was largely responsible for the establishment of the Society for Promoting Christian Knowledge in 1698 and the Society for the Propagation of the Gospel three years later. When in 1723 a serious illness threatened to terminate his work, Dr. Bray nominated certain people to continue his benevolent activities. These men aided him during the remainder of his life and continued afterwards as a corporate body called Dr. Bray's Associates for Founding Clerical Libraries and Supporting Negro Schools.

This Association, together with the two other societies he founded, is still in existence. It was given legal standing by a decree in chancery. Its papers are housed with those of the Society for the Propagation of the Gospel. The manuscripts relating to the period 1748–1776 are listed in the Andrews and Davenport *Guide*, p. 335: (1) Minute Books, 2 vols. (I: 1735–1768; II: 1768–1808); (2) "Catalogues of Books for Home and Foreign Libraries, 1753–1817," including titles of books sent to the American Colonies; (3) Untitled volume of parochial library catalogues.

ROMAN CATHOLIC DIOCESE OF WESTMINSTER

Prior to 1784, the Archives of the Diocese, now in the keeping of the Archbishop of Westminster, were in the custody of the London Vicar Apostolic, Westminster. Apparently, they contain most of the documents in England relating to the Roman Catholic Church in America. Even so, they are limited in nature for the period 1748–1776.

In *A. Series*, the main collection of manuscripts in 76 volumes, *A. 31, No. 208*, contains a reference to the suppression of the Jesuit order, with a list of Jesuits in Maryland and Pennsylvania enclosed in a letter of submission by Thomas Sanders, 1773. Most of the material in *B. Series*, a miscellaneous collection with a thousand letters in 14 volumes, 1701–1784, lies outside the scope of this survey. In *B. 33*, however, there is a notebook with copies of letters written by Bishop James Talbot; one, dated March 29, 1763, to the Acadians at Southhampton; another is addressed June 9, 1770, to the Bishop of Quebec. *B. 46, No. 73* contains a letter from Bishop Richard Challoner to Christopher Stoner, the Bishop's agent in Rome, dated March 15, 1764, which deals with the state of the Catholic religion in the American colonies. See Crick and Alman: *Guide*, pp. 344–6.

Other items of interest, listed in the *Guide* by Andrews and Davenport, pp. 339–41, without reference to the specific series, may also be mentioned: (1) An account (in Italian) by Abbé Nicolini of the English mission, covering the years 1756–1758, in which reference is made to Maryland and the Lords Baltimore; (2) A grant of authority for six years by the Propaganda of the Faith to the Vicar Apostolic, dated March 31, 1759, "*super coloniis et insulis Americanis Anglorum dominio subjectis*," which in translation reads: "over the American colonies and islands under English dominion"; (3) Ledger account, Jan. 1762, "Funds belonging to the L. District" with the added comment "Sir J. J. [John James] left 4000 ll in my hands principally for missionaries of the Society of Pensilvania." Thomas A. Hughes in *The History of the Society of Jesus in North America, Colonial and Federal* (4 vols., New York & London, 1907–17), II, 262, explains that this was a fund created by Sir

John James for Pennsylvania missionaries, which was kept on the ledger books in the Westminster Archives; (4) A letter from the Propaganda of the Faith to the Vicar Apostolic, July 9, 1763, respecting the "Mission of the ceded provinces in America"; (5) The same to the same, Dec. 24, 1764, about the ecclesiastical jurisdiction over the ceded provinces; (6) A pastoral letter addressed to Catholics living in the British West Indies, Dec. 19, 1770.

SOCIETY OF JESUS, ENGLISH PROVINCE

These Archives of the Society of Jesus possess a large collection of documents both bound and unbound; some of them throw light about the activities of the Jesuit Fathers in America and the movement of young Catholics from the colonies especially between 1747 and 1769 to secure an education in Catholic colleges and convents in Belgium or France. In a portfolio marked *No. 6, Maryland* are to be found letters, 1772–1815, of the Jesuit Father John Carroll, who later was appointed bishop, as well as correspondence addressed to him. For the contents of these archives see Thomas A. Hughes: *The History of the Society of Jesus in North America* (3 vols. in 4, London and New York, 1907–17), I, 14; see also Andrews and Davenport: *Guide*, p. 342.

CONGREGATIONAL CHURCH LIBRARY

The major collection relevant to the period under examination is the Sprague Papers, 1638–1863, including letters and sermons of colonial clergymen. These papers were collected by William B. Sprague. Pertinent items, as listed in the Andrews and Davenport *Guide*, pp. 347–9, are the following in chronological order:

(1) Sir William Pepperrell to Rev. Stephen Williams, Boston, May 31, 1748, on personal matters; (2) Joseph Sewall and Thomas Prince, pastors of the South Church in Boston, to the congregations at Dover Town and Duck Creek in Kent County on Delaware, Boston, April 27, 1749, recommending Rev. John Miller; (3) Andrew Oliver to Rev. Stephen Williams, Boston, May 26, 1750, on "his service at Stockbridge" for which the Commissioners are grateful; says that the Commissioners desire to know the character of a certain candidate for Stockbridge; (4) Thomas Clap, President of Yale College, to Rev. Dr. Doddridge, New Haven, May 6, 1751; (5) Gen. Thomas Gage to Col. Bradstreet, New York, Dec. 4, 1763, on sending artificers to Capt. Loring for fitting out vessels, "as affairs can't be too far advanced against the spring"; (6) President Clap,

New Haven, Dec. 5, 1763, on various matters relating to Yale College and on the prevailing hard times; (7) Mr. Nathan Strong, Yale College, June 2, 1768, writes: "College is under very good circumstances at present. The Broils we had about the time of Vacancy are mostly subsided"; (8) Rev. Dr. John Rodgers, New York, Aug. 11, 1773, relating particularly to Elizabethtown, New Jersey, and discussing the character and orthodoxy of certain persons; (9) Rev. Dr. Macclintock to Rev. David Macclure at Portsmouth, dated Greenland, N.H., Dec. 25, 1773 . . . ; (10) Susanna Anthony to Rev. Samuel Hopkins, "Nd," Aug. 9, 1775, about personal matters but also the appearance of "ten sail—coming as was thought into Nd."; (11) From J. Dana to Rev. Mr. Macclure, Boston, July 22, 1776, referring to supplying of New South pulpit, to the arrival of a "fine prize boat" and to two more carried into Salem; (12) Personal letters from various members of the Williams family: Warham Williams to his father Stephen Williams of Long Meadow, Northford, July 9, 1772; to Rev. Stephen Williams, Boston, May 31, 1748; Stephen Williams to his son Lieut. Davenport Williams, in Capt. Burt's company of Col. Wm. Williams's regiment, June 24, 1758; Rev. Dr. Williams to his sister Mrs. Elizabeth Smith in New York, July 27, 1765; also same to same, Aug. 9, 1755.

Among the Library's manuscripts are also several letters relating to George Whitefield. One, dated Oct. 30, 1754, was written to Mrs. Whitefield by the revivalist James Davenport, discussing Whitefield's religious activities in New Jersey. There are two letters, Jan. 25 and May 4, 1752, to Whitefield from John Edwards, Charleston, S.C., the first of a personal nature and the second describing religious activities in Charleston.

LIBRARY OF THE SOCIETY OF FRIENDS

Friends House is the major Quaker depository in existence. Here is concentrated a wealth of material relating to the Society of Friends in England and the American colonies.

Manuscripts of the London Yearly Meeting

(1) Minutes, 1668–(in progress); (2) London Meeting for Sufferings, 1673–(in progress); (3) Epistles Sent, 1683–1934 (10 vols. of transcripts); (4) Epistles Received, 1683–1916 (11 vols. of transcripts); (5) Testimonies concerning ministers, 1728–1872 (7 vols.); (6) London Yearly Meeting of Ministers and Elders, Minutes, 1757–1857 (2 vols. of transcripts), containing correspondence between the London and Philadelphia Meetings for Sufferings; (7) Minutes of various Quarterly and Monthly Meetings, 1668/9–(in progress).

Collections

(1) Gibson Manuscripts, 1660–1861 (10 vols. and portfolios), including many letters from Quakers in the American colonies; (2) W. C. Braithwaite Manuscripts, 1661–late 18th century, containing transcripts used by William Charles Braithwaite, a Quaker historian; (3) Southwark Manuscripts, 1667–1777 (6 vols.), mostly pertaining to London Quakers with only a small portion relating to America; (4) Penn Family Manuscripts, 1682–1779 (2 vols.). Volume 2 contains materials relevant to our period, including treaties and deeds negotiated between Thomas and Richard Penn and various Indian nations. Among the most important documents concerned with Indian treaties during the years 1748–1776 are the following: (a) Treaty of 1748 with the Twightwee nation; (b) Deed to the Penns of land by the Six Nations at Albany in 1754; (c) Appointment of Richard Peters and Conrad Weiser in 1757 to meet with the Six Nations in order to surrender the lands deeded to the Penns in 1754; (d) Lands in Lancaster County and an island in the Juniata deeded by the Conoy Indians to the Penns in 1762; (e) The Shawnee deed of lands to the Penns, also in 1762.

Journals

(1) Mary Weston (1712–1766). Travel journal (transcript made by her son-in-law, John Eliot), 1735–1752, 138 folio pp. See "Mary Weston's Journal," Friends Historical Society, *Journal,* IV (1907), 130; (2) Rachel Wilson (1720–1775). Journal of a visit to America (manuscript and typescript copies; original in private collection, 1768–1769).

Miscellaneous Letters and Documents

(1) From Dr. John Fothergill to William Logan and James Pemberton, 1766–1776 (copies; originals in the Historical Society of Pennsylvania); (2) From Patrick Henry to Anthony Benezet, January 18, 1773, on the evils of slavery.

See Crick and Alman: *Guide,* pp. 211–19 for a comprehensive survey of the above collections.

MORAVIAN CHURCH IN
GREAT BRITAIN AND IRELAND

As indicated in Crick and Alman, p. 246, the archives of the Moravian Church in Great Britain and Ireland contain a number of papers pertaining to America in the period 1748–1776. Included are bound volumes of the London Church minutes, most of which for the period under consideration are in German; extracts from and translations ot minutes; and various miscellaneous collections. These materials shed light on the Moravians' missionary activities among the Indians in the New World. It should be noted that the chief archives of the Moravian Church are located in Bethlehem, Pennsylvania.

NATIONAL MARITIME MUSEUM

The Museum contains various Admiralty records pertaining to the period 1748–1776, including orders from the Admiralty to the Navy Board, 1688–1815, with replies from the Navy Board, 1738–1831 (1,492 vols.). There is much information concerning naval stores, timber, and shipbuilding in the American colonies.

Certain personal papers are also relevant, such as those of Adm. Augustus Keppel (order books, 1754–1755); Samuel, 1st Viscount Hood (log books, 1760–1795; letter- and order-books, 1767–1795; letters received, 1771–1815); Adm. Thomas Graves (log book, papers, drafts of letters to the Admiralty, 1764–1782); and Adm. Sir William Cornwallis (letters received, order- and letter-books, and journals, 1770–1779). The latter collection was previously owned by Maj. R. J. Wykeham-Martin; see the report in Historical Manuscripts Commission, *Various Collections,* VI [55], pp. 297–434.

Another source of valuable information is the large collection of ships' logs, including records of both warships and merchant ships.

For more details see Crick and Alman: *Guide,* pp. 247–53.

ROYAL ARTILLERY INSTITUTION

One document in the library pertinent to the series should be mentioned: "A Journal Containing the Manner, Method and Execution of the Demolition of the Fortifications at Louisbourg, N.S." See Crick and Alman: *Guide,* pp. 295–6.

ROYAL SOCIETY OF ARTS

The Royal Society of Arts was founded in 1754 as the Society for the Encouragement of Arts, Manufactures, and Commerce. See D. Hudson and K. W. Luckhurst, *The Royal Society of Arts, 1754–1954* (London,

1954), and D. G. C. Allan, "The Origin and Growth of the Society's Archives, 1754–1847," *Journal of the Royal Society of Arts*, CVI (1958), 623–9. Among its major early overseas objectives were the development in the American colonies of potash and pearl-ash manufacture, mulberry tree growing and silk manufacture, etc. Premiums were awarded for such activities or for importing such commodities into England. The following manuscripts of the Society relate to the years 1748–1776:

Guard Books, 1754–1770

These "Guard Books" contain what were considered to be the most important communications relating to the objectives of the Society. They are fourteen in number. The arrangement of the correspondence is alphabetical according to the author. It is as follows: (1) An Englishman, Nov. 7, 1758, on the growth of tea in America; (2) Anon., n. d., on producing opium in Georgia, n. d., also on the culture of spices, tea, and silk in the colonies; (3) Anon., n. d., giving an account of the expenses of the filature in Georgia in 1757; (4) Edward Anthill, New Brunswick, N.J., May 9 and Aug. 28, 1766, concerning vineyards; and also two letters, one of Feb. 28, 1769 and the other without date, both relating to his agricultural improvements; (5) N. Appleton, March 31 and July 28, 1766, Boston, about silk-worms and silk; (6) H. Baker, Feb. 17, 1762, concerning Matapany tea sent by Dr. Brooke of Maryland; (7) H. Barnes, Boston, Jan. 4, 1766, relating to sarsaparilla from Massachusetts; (8) Francis Bernard, Boston, Aug. 13, 1763, recommending Mr. Willard, a maker of potash; also Aug. 28, 1767, two letters concerning potash produced by William Frobisher; (9) Samuel Blodget, Boston, Jan. 20, 1766, having to do with pearl-ash; (10) Edward Bridgen, London, Oct. 23, 1765, urging premium for importing hemp from America; (11) E. Broadfield, Philadelphia, Dec. 10, 1763, indicating that he is sending sturgeon; (12) William Bull, Charleston, S.C., Aug. 6, 1765, certifying that Jean Louis Gibert has produced thirty-five pounds of silk, and Jan. 20, 1770, concerning vines planted in South Carolina by Christopher Sherb; see under Garth; (13) C. F. C., n. d., respecting bees and wool in Virginia; (14) E. Caiger, Charleston, S.C., Sept. 15, 1766, about silk in Georgia; (15) Archibald Campbell, 3rd Duke of Argyll, n. d., two letters concerning the New England five-leaved pine; (16) Charles Carter, Virginia, seven letters, two of them in 1762 and five undated, on a variety of subjects. See Robert Levy Hilldrup: "A Campaign to Promote the Prosperity of Colonial Virginia," *Virginia Magazine of History and Biography*, LXVI (1959), 410–28; (17) Thomas Clap (and Jared Eliot), New Haven, Conn., June 2, 1760, concerning silk in Connecticut; (18) Cadwallader Colden, New York, Feb. 6, 1761, about winter food for cattle; (19) Peter Collinson, Nov. 10, 1763, relating to a garden in West Florida; (20) Committee for Promoting Arts, Williamsburg, Va., Feb. 14

and Nov. 16, 1759, minutes; (21) John Crevet, Philadelphia, n. d., papers concerning rewards for encouraging industry in Pennsylvania; (22) Thomas Cushing, Boston, Sept. 6, 1766, requesting advice about potash manufacture; and copy of a letter, July 1767, acknowledging receipt of pamphlets on this; (23) J. A. Daux, London, 1760, concerning a sawmill for clearing lands in America; (24) J. Delemare, *et al.*, London, March 29, 1755, their certificate concerning the quality of some Georgia silk; (25) Charles Dick, Virginia, June 22, 1762, and n. d., on pearl-ash, and another undated letter on the "polite arts"; (26) James Duane, *et al.*, New York, March 30, 1765, about the creation in New York of a Society for Encouraging Arts. For extracts see K. W. Luckhurst: "The Society's Early Days: New Light from its Correspondence," *Journal of the Royal Society of Arts*, CII (1954), 292–313; (27) Jared Eliot, seven letters, Killingworth, Conn., 1761 and 1762, mainly on black iron sand; also an undated extract from his essays on field husbandry in America, and an extract from a letter, March 26, 1760, on grapes and wine-making; see also under Clap and Ruggles; (28) Henry Ellis, Georgia, June 27, 1758, relating to silk, olives, and madder; (29) John Ellis, Georgia, Dec. 16, 1761, about rhubarb; (30) John and Henry Ellis, Georgia, n. d., providing a list of plants for manufacturers that would grow in Georgia, Carolina, and the Bahamas; (31) J. English, South Carolina, Nov. 15, 1760, on premiums offered for the colonies; (32) Lewis Evans, Philadelphia, Nov. 1, 1754, on settling plantations in America; (33) Francis Fauquier, Williamsburg, Va., an undated letter about Zant grapes and, with others, a certificate, Aug. 6, 1763, concerning William Carter's vineyards; (34) Benson Fearon, Oct. 9, 1764, certifying that he has received two planks, which have been laid at Mill Creek on the James River, Virginia, as part of the Society's tests concerning destruction of ships' bottoms by worms; (35) James Ferguson, Belfast, May 7, 1767, relating to American potash; (36) Benjamin Franklin, May 14, 1755, on the establishment of a society in America; June 15, 1756, a copy of letter of Nov. 27, 1755, concerning membership in the Society of Arts; Aug. 12, 1763, about Mr. Willard's methods of potash production; Sept. 2, 1764, noting the sending of sturgeon; Oct. 29, 1766, enclosing a letter from William Alexander (Earl of Stirling), New Jersey, July 31, 1765, about Aaron Miller's compass; (37) William Frobisher, Boston, Aug. 21 and 25, 1767 and May 13, 1768, on potash; (38) Benjamin Gale, five letters, Killingworth, Conn., 1763–1768, on black grass, his drill plough, and other subjects; (39) Alexander Garden, letters, extracts, and copies, South Carolina, 1757–1760 and undated, on various subjects; (40) Charles Garth, three letters, 1770, concerning Christopher Sherb's vine-planting (one includes an extract from a letter of William Bull on this subject); (41) Jean Louis Gibert, Silk Hope, S.C., n.d., relating to the production of cocoons; (42) F. Gilpin, Philadelphia, May 16, 1769, a letter to Franklin about windmills for pumping in mines or ships; (43) James Stanley

Goddard, n. d., respecting American isinglass; (44) James Habersham and J. Otolonghe, Georgia, May 20, 1756, on premiums for silk in Georgia; (45) G. Harrison, June 18, 1766, concerning black grass and sand sent by Dr. Benjamin Gale; (46) Joel Harvey, Connecticut, Aug. 20, 1764, a description of his corn-threshing machine; (47) William Homes, London, Jan. 16, 1764, proposing various premiums for America; (48) Thomas Hyam, London, Sept. 12, 1760, having to do with the import of hemp from Philadelphia; (49) Jared Ingersoll, London, Dec. 24, 1760, on the cultivation of maize in North America (8 pages); March 13, 1765, concerning Joel Harvey's threshing machine; (50) James Johnston, Berkeley County, S.C., Oct. 22, 1770, about Christopher Sherb's vine-planting; (51) John Leadly, London, 1765, a certificate of sale of New York potash, and an affidavit, 1766, of the quality of pearl-ash imported by Sir W. Baker; (52) William Lewis, Jan. 27, 1767, concerning American potash, and an undated paper containing experiments on Virginia saltpetre; (53) Philip Livingston and Peter Remsen, New York, May 3, 1765, about the establishment of a potash works; (54) Philip Ludwell, Virginia, April 21, 1760, a list of articles to be produced in America; (55) David Maine, London, March 26, 1760, about seeds for Carolina and Georgia; (56) J. Mascarene, Cambridge, Mass., Feb. 10, 1766, relating to potash; (57) A. Mason, n. d., proposing to write a description of North America; (58) The Rev. Jonathan Mayhew, Boston, Jan. 20, 1766, concerning pearl-ash, and an extract from another 1766 letter; (59) Thomas Moffat, Newport, R.I., Jan. 26 and June 26, 1761, having to do with New England climate; (60) Samuel More, July 16, 1763, rough draft of experiments on Virginia saltpetre; (61) Messrs. E. Neave, London, Nov. 7, 1760, relating to New England potash; (62) James Neilson and William Oake, New Jersey, Aug. 28, 1765, a certificate concerning Edward Anthill's vineyards; (63) Joseph Otolonghe, Georgia, May 3, 1756, on silk; see also under Habersham and Otolonghe; (64) Nat. Pattison, et al., London, Dec. 18, 1765, their certificate of the quality of J. L. Gibert's South Carolina silk; (65) J. Perrie, London, March 21, 1766, about New England sarsaparilla; (66) M. Peters, Dublin, Aug. 24, 1766, concerning Ohio grass seed; (67) "Phylopatria," April 10, 1760, on the import of hemp, iron, etc., from America; (68) Thomas Pinckney, April 1, 1766, relating to mulberry trees in the Carolinas and Georgia; (69) Robert Pringle, South Carolina, Aug. 24, 1759, respecting South Carolina logwood; (70) Edward Quincy, Boston, Oct. 17, 1766, his certificate concerning pearl-ash made by Samuel Blodget; June 30, 1765, on various matters; and an undated certificate concerning pearl-ash; (71) Peter Remsen: see under Livingston and Remsen; (72) Thomas Ruggles, n.d., describing a method for marking sheep, originally sent from Jared Eliot to Mr. Collinson; (73) William Rutherford, New York, March 29, 1766, on trade with the colonies; (74) William Rutherford and William Smith, n. d., a list of articles to be encouraged in the colonies; (75) Philip Schuyler, New York, Jan. 24, 1765, a letter to P. Skeene concerning the erection of a hemp mill; (76) Cary Selden, Virginia, Aug. 27, 1765, a certificate of John Bennet, pilot, that two planks delivered to him have been sunk in Mill Creek, Virginia, and then taken to London as part of the Society's tests concerning destruction of ships' bottoms by worms; (77) John Shakespear, Nov. 30, 1765, a letter sent with some American hemp; (78) William Shipley, July 15, 1755, on the importance of vines, hemp, etc., to South Carolina and to England; (79) Thomas Shubrick, London, Feb. 4, 1765, on the possibilities for use in making red dye of a root from the Indian country in America; (80) P. Skeene, New York, Feb. 14, 1765, about Indian dye and potash; (81) William Smith: see under Rutherford and Smith; (82) V. Stoker, et al., n. d., a certificate that silk imported by J. L. Gibert is of his own growth; (83) William Tryon, North Carolina, extract from letter, July 1767, to Edward Bridgen, concerning Mr. Stansfield's sawmill; (84) John Wentworth, New Hampshire, July 20, 1767, an extract from a letter acknowledging receipt of pamphlets on potash; (85) Sir Charles Whitworth, July 31 and Aug. 24, 1755, concerning letters from Alexander Garden; (86) Thomas Willis, n. d., experiments on American isinglass; (87) Thomas Woodin, South Carolina, Oct. 28, 1766, on various matters, and a copy of a letter of the same date on lucerne; (88) The Rev. Charles Woodmason, Carolina, May 23, 1763, on various matters; (89) Jermyn and Charles Wright, Georgia, Oct. 27, 1766, concerning vineyards and May 30, 1768, about balsam found in Georgia; (90) Henry Young, Georgia, Dec. 23, 1766, on leek taw or Chinese vetch introduced into Georgia by S. Bowen.

The guard books also contain customs' records and other documents dealing with the importation of silk, hemp, and other products from America; a printed list of premiums offered in New York, 1765, and descriptions of timber sent by the Society to North America, n. d.

Loose Archives, 1755–1840

Among the unbound papers, some 5000 in number, are the following: (1) George Box, London [1759], draft of a letter to Alexander Garden thanking him for observations on the soil and climate of Carolina; (2) Bromwich & Co., London, March 15, 1775, letter concerning a 'Carolina stain'; (3) Robert Dossie, 1767, manuscript of his "Observations on the Pot-Ash brought from America . . . to which is subjoined Processes for Making Pot-Ash and Barilla, in North America," published in London, 1767, and related papers and minutes; (4) James Habersham, Savannah, Ga., May 20, 1756, relating to mulberry trees in Georgia; (5) James Habersham and Joseph Otolonghe, Savannah, Ga., Oct. 23, 1758, reporting payment for cocoons; (6) Lane & Booth, London, Jan. 15 and 30, 1765, on potash; (7) Joseph Otolonghe, Savannah, Ga., May 20 and 24, 1756, about mulberry trees in Georgia; 1759, listing persons receiving premiums for cocoons; see also under Habersham and Otolonghe; (8) James Stewart, London, Aug. 23, 1774, on "American productions"; (9) John Watson, June 3, 1755, a receipt for £18 to be used for rewarding the planting of white mulberry trees in Georgia.

In addition to the above, there are a large number of certificates relating to the export from America and import into England of potash and sturgeon; letters on behalf of various American bodies acknowledging receipt of the Society's *Transactions;* letters from the Society to Alexander Garden about cork trees sent to Carolina, Feb. 6, 1760, and to Thomas Hyam about his hemp imports, Oct. 6, 1760; and a petition sent during the 1750's to the parish of St. Peters, Purisburgh, S.C., about the encouragement of the cultivation of silk.

Transactions

Dr. Templeman's Transactions. Peter Templeman (1711–1769), who became the secretary of the Society in 1760, compiled an "Historical Register of the Transactions of the Society . . ." in two volumes, covering the early years of the Society, 1754–1758, containing extracts from letters received, reports of matters discussed, lists of members, etc. An author and subject card index, combined with that for the Society's later manuscript transactions, is available. There is some material of American relevance similar to that listed above.

Manuscript Transactions. The early transactions of the Society, 1770/1–1783/4, are in manuscript form. A card index to these shows a small amount of American material, again similar to the above.

Minutes

Manuscript minutes of the Society begin in 1754, while minutes for standing committees, including "Colonies and Trade," date from 1758. The minutes indicate the Society's response to letters received and include debates on various premiums to be given. There are also in the archives four volumes of contemporary copies of letters or of extracts from letters received by the Society, 1767–1778. For a comprehensive listing of the materials of the Society see the Crick and Alman *Guide,* pp. 302–8.

UNIVERSITY OF LONDON LIBRARY

Among the library's mansucripts are two of relevance to this survey. One carries the title, "Value of Trade of Great Britain and Ireland" and contains statistical tables for the period, 1696–1765, listing imports and exports for each country; in addition, for the years 1747–1762 there are separate figures for each colony under the heading of "Plantations." The second document consists of the answers of Gov. James Glen of South Carolina, 1749, to queries put to him by the Board of Trade.

See Crick and Alman: *Guide*, pp. 317–21; *Catalogue of the Manuscripts and Autograph Letters in the University [of London] Library* . . . (Reginald Arthur Rye, comp.; London, 1921); *Supplement, 1921–1930* (London, 1930); also typescript catalogue with additions since 1930 available at the library.

BRITISH LIBRARY OF POLITICAL AND ECONOMIC SCIENCE, LONDON SCHOOL OF ECONOMICS

In a collection of 400 letters bearing the title "Letters of Emigrants to America, 1745–1911," there are three relating to the Empire, 1748–1776, that may be noted: (1) Lieut.-Col. Arthur Noble, Louisbourg, N.S., to Edward Noble, discussing the capture of that fort, June 29, 1745; (2) J. W. Noble, Boston, to an unknown correspondent, Feb. 3, 1752, offering butter in return for Irish linen and woollen goods; (3) James Aitken, Wilmington, N.C., to his father, the Rev. John Aitken, Glasgow, June 5, 1775, concerning his plans to purchase a plantation and reporting the military activities of the people of Wilmington.

See Crick and Alman: *Guide*, pp. 322–34.

THE LIBRARY, INNER TEMPLE

The library has a collection of Masères manuscripts. Francis Masères was very active in the affairs of the Province of Quebec for a period of years, holding the office of Attorney General. Among these papers is a document (77 pages) relating to Georgia, not Quebec. It carries the title "Instructions for Georgia" and is a report sent to the Board of Trade respecting the nature of additional instructions that should be given to Henry Ellis, appointed governor of Georgia in 1758. It includes copies of the following documents: Extract of Sir William Gooch's answer to the queries of the Board of Trade in 1749; instructions to Henry Ellis, Capt.-Gen. and Gov. of Georgia in 1758; orders and instructions to Ellis "in pursuance of several laws relating to the trade and navigation of . . . Great Britain, and our colonies and plantations in America," July 1758; and a list of ships which have entered ports in Georgia "with the particular quantity and quality of the loading of each vessel." See Historical Manuscripts Commission, *Report*, XI (vii), 304, and Crick and Alman: *Guide*, p. 238.

BANK OF ENGLAND

The manuscripts of the Bank of England, which begin in 1694 and continue to the present, are divided into the following categories: (1) The General Court of Proprietors, Minute Books (G.C.B.); (2) Court of Directors, Minute Books (C.B.); (3) Committee of Treasury, Minute Books (C.T.); (4) Letter Books (L.B.); (5) General Ledgers (G.L.); and (6) Drawing Office Ledgers (D.O.). The Archives of the Bank are essentially working records, which for earlier periods, such as the years 1748–1776, may be examined for scholarly purposes.

In this connection see Sir John Clapham's first volume, 1694–1797, of his *The Bank of England: A History* (2 vols., Cambridge, Eng. & New York, 1945). Although this work is not a guide or catalogue as such, Clapham's footnotes provide a survey of the Bank's important holdings. See also Crick and Alman: *Guide*, pp. 122–3.

COUTTS & CO. BUSINESS PAPERS

Among the Coutts & Co. papers are the papers of the London merchant James Russell of 2 Hylords Court, Crutched Friars; there are some two hundred letters, mostly covering the years 1773–1775. In this correspondence it is interesting to note the names of Richard Henry Lee of Virginia and Thomas Pownall, one-time Governor of Massachusetts Bay and a member of the House of Commons. Among additional correspondents are members of the Fendell, Galloway, Jenifer, Johns, and Warfield families of Maryland, and the Washington family of Virginia. Also of interest are some bonds and legal papers pertaining to New York, including four bonds, 1775–1776, to the Rev. Charles Inglis, a Loyalist, who was then assisting the rector of Trinity Church, New York. See Crick and Alman: *Guide*, pp. 187–8.

PART II

The English Counties

THE following section will include only papers of importance to the history of the British Empire for the period 1748–1776 which are found in English depositories outside of the political, economic, and cultural centre of the Empire, London. The depositories will be presented alphabetically by county.

BEDFORDSHIRE

The Bedfordshire Record Office in Bedford contains the Stuart Papers which include a substantial number of papers relating to Pennsylvania, 1673–1787 (approx. 200 documents, 2 vols., & 2 maps). Some of those for the period under review are documents relating to boundary disputes with Maryland, 1732–1780, and Connecticut, 1754–1774. See *Guide to the Bedfordshire Record Office* (Bedford, 1957).

At Woburn Abbey, the country seat of the Duke of Bedford, there are various papers left by John Russell, 4th Duke of Bedford. Among these manuscripts one collection in two volumes relates to the Peace of Paris of 1763 in which Bedford played a leading role; another collection, covering the years 1764–1765, deals with developments in the North American colonies. There are also a number of papers concerning the civil and military establishments in Ireland. See Historical Manuscripts Commission, *Report*, II, 2–3.

For depositories in Bedfordshire see B. R. Crick and Miriam Alman: *Guide*, pp. 3–5.

BERKSHIRE

The Berkshire Record Office in Reading contains two pertinent groups of manuscripts, the Downshire Papers and the Hartley Russell Papers. The Downshire Papers, 1609–1773, include those of Wills Hill (1718–1793), 2nd Viscount Hillsborough and 1st Marquis of Downshire. Attention should be called to one large manuscript volume with the title, "Present State of the British Colonies in America, 1773." In the Hartley Russell Papers are a number of papers of the Quaker, David Hartley, Jr. (1732–1813), who between 1774 and 1782 was active in the efforts for peace between Great Britain and the colonies. See Felix Hull: *Guide to the Berkshire Record Office* (Reading, Eng., 1952).

At the A. Godsal Estate Office, Haines Hill, Twyford, are copies of the Charles Garth (c. 1734–1784) letter-books covering the years 1762–1774, during which Garth served as London colonial agent, as well as a member of Parliament. Aspects of Garth's public career have been dealt with by the late Sir Lewis Namier, who has two articles in the *English Historical Review*, LIV (1939), 443–70, and 632–52, which also make clear the contents of the letter-books.

Mention must also be made of the extensive Royal Archives in Round Tower, Windsor Castle, Windsor, although they are not open to public inspection. Most of the material concerning the Empire and especially North America for the period 1748–1776 has been printed in the following volumes of source material: S. M. Pargellis, ed.: *Military Affairs in North America, 1748–1765* . . . (London & New York, 1936), utilizing the Duke of Cumberland papers; Sir John Fortescue, ed.: *The Correspondence of King George the Third from 1760 to December 1783* . . . (6 vols., London, 1927–8); and Sir Lewis Namier: *Additions and Corrections to Sir John Fortescue's Edition* . . . (Manchester, Eng., 1937). Two secondary works also based upon the papers in the Royal Archives and concerned with the period 1748–1776 are Sir Evan E. Charteris: *William Augustus, Duke of Cumberland, and the Seven Years War* (London, 1925), and M. S. Guttmacher: *America's Last King: An Interpretation of the Madness of George III* (New York, 1941).

For Berkshire depositories see Crick and Alman: *Guide*, pp. 5–9.

BUCKINGHAMSHIRE

The Buckinghamshire Record Office, County Hall, Aylesbury, has on deposit the Howard-Vyse papers covering the years 1775–1777. Among these are nine letters written by Richard Reeve, Boston Loyalist, to Sir George Howard, M.P., relating the opening events in the War for American Independence.

A large but unsorted collection of papers is held by Dr. J. Spencer Bernard at Nether Winchendon. It is the Bernard family papers, which may contain some letters of Sir Francis Bernard (1711?–1779), governor of Massachusetts Bay. It should be mentioned that the great body of the Governor's papers are in the Houghton Library at Harvard.

For Buckinghamshire depositories see Crick and Alman: *Guide*, pp. 9–13.

DERBYSHIRE

The next county with papers of importance for the Empire, 1748–1776, is Derbyshire. In the County Record Office at the market town of Matlock are the records of the Court of Quarter Sessions. Among these are papers concerned with the transportation of felons to America, 1720–1772.

At Chatsworth, Bakewell, there are the largely unlisted papers of the Dukes of Devonshire, among which are those of William Cavendish, 4th Duke of Devonshire (1720–1764), who was the King's chief minister, 1756–1757. See Historical Manuscripts Commission, *Report*, III, 36–45.

Melbourne Hall, Derby, residence of the Marquess of Lothian, is the depository for the Earl of Buckinghamshire papers, 1770–1782, among them the correspondence of John Hobart, 2nd Earl (1723–1793), Viceroy of Ireland, 1777–1780. Among these manuscripts are papers concerning the Stamp Act crisis; a copy of minutes of the Lords of the Committee of the Privy Council for Plantation Affairs, dated June 26, 1770, relating to disorders in Massachusetts Bay; and a paper entitled, "Commencement of the American Rebellion" in the Earl's handwriting. See Historical Manuscripts Commission, *Report, Lothian Manuscripts* [62], 260–1, 289, 291–2.

For Derbyshire despositories see Crick and Alman: *Guide*, pp. 33–6.

DEVONSHIRE

At the City Library, Exeter, are to be found the Palk Papers, among them those of Sir Robert Palk (1717–1798), who was governor of Madras, 1763–1767 and a member of Parliament, 1767–1768 and 1774–1787. Also, at Sandridge, Stoke Gabriel, the seat of Earl Cathcart, are the Cathcart Papers, 1759–1853. Since the Cathcarts were loyal servants of the King throughout the 18th century, the collection contains many documents relevant to the Empire in this period, including letters sent and received, journals, and various other papers, such as (1) An account by "P. M.," an engineer in Wolfe's expedition against Quebec in 1759; (2) "Journal de l'expédition contre Quebec, 1759" (35 pages); (3) A report on the defences of Canada and Quebec, c. 1763; (4) The answer of Francis

Bernard, governor of Massachusetts Bay, to the Board of Trade, Sept. 5, 1763; (5) Copies of letters, 1766, on American affairs from Col. Robert Clerk to the Earl of Shelburne; (6) A copy of Lord Chatham's plan, 1775, for settling American affairs. See Historical Manuscripts Commission, *Report*, II, 24–30.

For Devonshire depositories see Crick and Alman: *Guide*, pp. 36–42.

DORSET

Among the papers in the Dorset Record Office, County Hall, Dorchester, are the Cutler-Rackett-Caillouel Papers, including the letters of Dr. John Cutler of Boston to his relations in England, covering the year 1744–1761, with reference to military, naval, and Indian affairs.

Another collection of much greater importance, at Mapperton, Beaminister, the seat of Viscount Hinchingbrooke, includes a volume of treaties and letters belonging to John Montagu, 4th Earl of Sandwich (1718–1792), First Lord of the Admiralty, 1763–1765 and 1771–1782. Some of of this material has been published in *The Private Papers of John, Earl of Sandwich, First Lord of the Admiralty, 1771–1782*, Navy Records Society, *Publications*, LXIX, LXXI, LXXV, LXXVIII (G. R. Barnes and J. H. Owen, eds., 4 vols., London, 1932–8).

For Dorset depositories see Crick and Alman: *Guide*, pp. 42–4.

ESSEX

At the Essex Record Office, County Hall, Chelmsford, are six groups of papers which provide information for the period 1748–1776. First of all there are the Round Papers, covering the years 1585–1776; they contain the business records, 1743–1757, of Thomas Stebbing & Son, linen drapers of Cornhill, London, including: (1) Sixteen letters, 1746–1765, from John Guerard of Charleston, S.C., to Robert Stebbing; (2) Bills of exchange drawn in Maryland on London merchants, 1748–1751; and (3) Five letters, 1750–1757, from Charles and Alex Stedman, Philadelphia merchants. Other items from the Round Papers are a letter from Gov. Belcher of New Jersey, Nov. 14, 1748, to an unidentified correspondent, concerning the founding of Princeton and describing the crops raised in New Jersey; and eight letters (transcripts) from Thomas Falconer to Charles Gray from April 5, 1757 to April 13, 1776, about Lord Loudoun's proposed expedition against Louisbourg and American affairs in general.

The Audley End Papers, 1673–1779, in the Record Office contain the following: (1) A report of Gov. George Clinton of New York, 1749, on the state of affairs in the colony, with copies of his letters; (2) A letter, Feb. 15, 1749, from Corbyn Morris to the Earl of Halifax, on Great

Britain's balance of trade with her American colonies and the suppression of colonial paper currency.

In the Mildmay Papers is a memorandum by Shirley on the economic and strategic relationship of the American colonies to Great Britain. William Mildmay and William Shirley were British members of the Anglo-French commission to settle all disputes after the Peace of Aix-la-Chapelle, 1748.

A fourth collection is the Russell Papers, 1759–1774, including the papers of William and Samuel Braund, London merchants. As an underwriter at Lloyds and a director both of the East India Co. and of the Sun Fire Office, William Braund (1695–1774) was a man of importance in the business world. See Lucy S. Sutherland: *A London Merchant, 1695–1774* (London, 1933).

Slavery release documents, 1760–1761, about the liberation of Fortin Vrelinghuyson, a New York slave, who went on a cruise on board one of H.M. ships, are also here.

The Rigby Papers, 1772–1782, contain documents relating to the clearing of the public accounts of Richard Rigby (1722–1788), Paymaster-General of the British armed forces, 1768–1782.

A second manuscript collection in the county of Essex deserves attention, that at the Maltings, Aldham, Colchester, the estate of W. Weston Underwood, Esq. Here may be found the Weston Papers, 1757–1768, of which certain items should be noted: (1) A dispatch from Sir Benjamin Keene at Madrid to William Pitt, Sept. 26, 1757, about charges of British encroachments in America; (2) A dispatch from the Duke of Bedford to Lord Egremont from Paris, Sept. 24, 1762, about the issue of the navigation of the Mississippi (copy); (3) Sir William Johnson's preliminary peace treaty with the Seneca Indians, April 13, 1764 (copy); (4) A portion of General Gage's letter of Sept. 21, 1764, having to do with the conference with Indian tribes at Niagara (copy); (5) Nine letters (transcripts) from Edward Sedgwick to Edward Weston, 1765–1770, concerning the growing American disaffection; (6) A letter, Aug. 12, 1768, from Sir James Porter to Edward Weston about American disorders and his view that the great difficulty at Boston is due to "two or three degenerate wretches who occasion the bustle and when it comes to the push I dare say they will fear the rod." See Historical Manuscripts Commission, *Report*, X (1), 217, *passim* to page 422.

For Essex depositories see Crick and Alman: *Guide*, pp. 48–54.

GLOUCESTERSHIRE

Among the papers in the Gloucestershire Records Office in Shire Hall, Gloucester, is the Treasurer's Book, 1726–1773, of the Court of Quarter Sessions, including some sixty documents regarding conditions under which convicts were ordered for transportation to America. See *Glou-cestershire Quarter Sessions Archives, 1660–1889, and Other Official Records: A Descriptive Catalogue* (Gloucester, Eng., 1958). The Records Office also has Gloucestershire and Wiltshire records of the Quarterly Meetings of the Society of Friends, 1670–1866.

In the Public Libraries, Brunswick Road, Gloucester, is a large collection of pamphlets relating to George Whitefield (1714–1770), most of them by him. See *Catalogue of Gloucestershire Collection: Books, Pamphlets and Documents in the Gloucester Public Library Relating to the County, Cities, Towns, and Villages of Gloucestershire* (Roland Austin, comp., Gloucester, Eng., 1928).

Bristol, however, has by far the most important bodies of manuscripts possessed by the shire and bearing upon the period under consideration. In the Archives of the Moravian Church on Maudlin Street are the records of Moravian missionaries labouring in North America, including Labrador, for the period 1751–1777. In the Bristol Public Libraries on College Green are three collections of manuscripts: (1) The Jefferies Papers, 1722–1736. Although before our period, this collection is extremely relevant to a study of eighteenth-century Bristol slaving; many of these papers are embodied in W. E. Minchinton, ed.: *Trade of Bristol in the Eighteenth Century*, Bristol Records Society, *Publications*, XX (Bristol, Eng., 1957), and also by the same scholar: "The Virginia Letters of Isaac Hobhouse, Merchant of Bristol," *Virginia Magazine of History and Biography*, LXVI (1958), 278–301; (2) The Southwell Papers, 10 volumes, relating to the activities of the Southwell family, Bristol merchants, in the seventeenth and eighteenth centuries; (3) The Caleb Dickinson copybook of letters, 1757–1758, including material on trade with Virginia and Pennsylvania.

In the possession of W. E. Salt, Esq., Director of Adult Education, University of Bristol, is the letter-book, 1728–1778, of Henry Caner (1700?–1792), an Anglican minister who served in New England. Caner, a Loyalist, returned to England after the beginning of the Revolutionary War.

The greatest collection of manuscripts in Bristol relating to the expanding eighteenth-century British Empire is in the Library of the Society of Merchant Venturers, Merchants' Hall, Clifton Downs. These records throw much light on American trade and colonization and also on African slaving. The manuscript calendar of the records of the Society prepared by John Latimer in the late 1890's will be useful; see also his *The History of the Society of Merchant Venturers of the City of Bristol . . .* (Bristol, Eng., 1903). It may be mentioned that while the author of this Guide was able to use these materials other scholars in the past experienced great difficulty in securing access to them. The regulations, I understand, about their use have been modified.

For Gloucestershire depositories see Crick and Alman: *Guide*, pp. 54–65.

HAMPSHIRE

There appears to be little important manuscript material in this county relating to the Empire, 1748–1776. However, in the Hampshire Record Office, the Castle, Winchester, are to be found two account books of Henry Wyndham (1709–1788), Salisbury and Dinton merchant, covering the years 1725–1753 and concerning the Virginia tobacco trade. Further, in the Southampton Record Office, Civic Centre, Southampton, are deposited the Southampton Corporation Assembly books and journals bearing upon American trade, particularly in 1754 when the question of relieving their trade of the so-called "petty customs" arose. The Record Office also has 192 volumes of petty customs books, 1426–1803.

For Hampshire depositories see Crick and Alman: *Guide,* pp. 66–76.

HERTFORDSHIRE

In the Hertfordshire Record Office, County Hall, Hertford, there are three groups of papers: (1) The Dacarette Papers, 1745–1787, in the Gorhambury Collection, relating largely to Cape Breton Island and to the disposition of lands on the part of the French-speaking inhabitants when the island came into the possession of the British; (2) The Hertfordshire Court of Quarter Sessions records, 1589–1843, in ten volumes, with convictions involving transportation to America; (3) A contract entered into on Feb. 3, 1757, by the Commissioners of His Majesty's Treasury with John Stewart, London merchant, to transport to America prisoners from the county jails of Hertford, Buckingham, Essex, Kent and Sussex.

In the possession of the Earl of Verulam at Gorhambury, St. Albans, are the Verulam Papers, 1768–1793. Among these is the journal of a tour through the Midlands into Wales, apparently by the 3rd Viscount Grimston in 1768, with remarks about trade with America. For the Verulam papers see Historical Manuscripts Commission: *Verulam Manuscripts Report* [64].

For Hertfordshire depositories see Crick and Alman: *Guide,* pp. 76–9.

KENT

There are two collections of papers in the Kent County Archives Office, County Hall, Maidstone, that bear upon the years 1748–1776: (1) The Sandwich Borough Records, 1611–1773, include contracts, bonds, etc., for the transportation of convicts, 1721–1773; (2) Among the Wykeham-Martin Papers, 1672–1820, is the correspondence of the Fairfax and Martin families, with particular relation to their estates in Virginia, including many letters from Bryan Martin (1731–1798) who settled in America. See Felix Hull: *Guide to the Kent County Archives Office* (Maidstone, Eng., 1958).

For Kent depositories see Crick and Alman: *Guide*, pp. 80–2.

LANCASHIRE

Among the relevant papers in the Lancashire Record Office, Sessions House, Preston, are the Barcroft Papers (part of the Parker of Alkincoats and Browsholme Muniments), covering the period 1682–1780. Members of the Barcroft family of Lancashire settled in both Virginia and Pennsylvania. There are ten Barcroft letters from America, 1752–1780, dealing with financial and family affairs. See R. Sharpe France: *Guide to the Lancashire Record Office* (Preston, Eng., 1948; 2nd edn., 1962).

In Liverpool the Public Libraries, William Brown Street, have five collections of manuscripts which should be noted: (1) The Liverpool Town Books, with various documents bearing upon America, 1748–1776; (2) The Tarleton Papers, 1754–1780, chiefly the business papers of John Tarleton, Sr. (1719–1773), Liverpool, merchant and father of the famous General Sir Banastre Tarleton, with materials concerning West Indian lands, slavery, privateering, the importation of cotton, and sugar refining, 1754–1780. See W. R. Serjeant: "The Tarleton Papers: A Merchant's Accounts," Liverpool Libraries, Museums and Arts Committee, *Bulletin,* VI (1956), 28–31; (3) Case & Southworth, Jamaica merchants and ship-brokers, a sales ledger and account books, 1754–1755; (4) The Parker Family Papers, 1760–1795, some 600 items in 16 bundles. These papers largely concern James Parker (1729–1815) who settled as a merchant in Norfolk, Va., and who with the outbreak of the Revolutionary War became an officer in the British army. See J. M. Hemphill, II: "Virginia and the Parker Family Papers," *ibid.*, VI, 25–7; (5) David Samwell (1751–1798), surgeon, a collection of letters, 1774–1795, some written on board ship while in American waters. See H. A. Taylor: "David Samwell," *ibid.*, VI, 32–46.

In the eighteenth century Liverpool became the chief port for slaving, surpassing Bristol in this respect. Two notebooks in the possession of C. E. Turner, Esq., of the firm of E. W. Turner & Sons, Cunard Buildings, Water Street, Liverpool, are concerned with this trade. Some of this material has been utilized in *Sea Breezes*, n.s., XXIII (1957), 322–7.

The John Rylands Library in Manchester contains a large autograph collection of letters and manuscripts. Among these is an interesting letter written by Benjamin Franklin to George Whitefield from New York on July 2, 1756: "I sometimes wish, that you and I were jointly employ'd by the Crown, to settle a colony on the Ohio," with comments on the proposed venture. See *The Papers of Benjamin Franklin* (L. W. Labaree, *et al.*, eds., 12 vols.+, New Haven, Conn., 1959–68+), VI, 468–9. Another letter in this collection is from Lieut.-Gov. John Penn, Sept. 3, 1768, asking the recipient to secure lodgings for him on his trip to the Indian congress to be held at Fort Stanwix in upper New York. The library also contains an extensive collection of Moravian Church diaries, letters, etc., concerned with American missionary activities, and an interesting document, 1749–1787 *(Eng. Ms. 517),* listing ships engaged in the slave trade during those years.

The McLachlan Library of Unitarian College, also in Manchester, has two small collections of manuscripts bearing upon the period 1748–1776: (1) Three letters, 1751–1761, written by the famous Boston minister, Jonathan Mayhew (1720–1766) to Dr. George Benson of London, having to do with New England affairs, including Harvard College; (2) Copies of some 16 letters from Henry Hulton (1731?–1791), a member of the Board of American Customs Commissioners. Copies of these letters are also in the Manchester College Library at Oxford.

At Stonyhurst College, Whalley, Blackburn, in Lancashire, among the papers of this Jesuit college is a document respecting the disposition of Maryland estates, signed on March 8, 1758, by the Rev. Richard Molyneaux.

Finally, in the Public Library of Wigan, in the Edward Hall Ms. Diary Collection is the diary, 1765–1766, kept by the New York merchant George Folliott while in England.

For Lancashire depositories see Crick and Alman: *Guide,* pp. 83–113.

LEICESTERSHIRE

Among the manuscripts in this county mention should be made of the Leicestershire Court of Quarter Sessions Records, with particular reference to the transport of criminals to America, chiefly to Virginia and Maryland, covering the years 1720–1783. These are in the Leicestershire Record Office in Leicester.

Another Leicestershire manuscript collection, the Rutland Papers, 1611–1780, is held by the Duke of Rutland at Belvoir Castle, Grantham. Most of the papers relating to America are letters. The following fall within the years 1748–1776: (1) A number of letters, 1763–1765, concerning the Indians, West Florida, and the Sons of Liberty; (2) A letter from Gen. Thomas Gage to Lord Granby, New York, Dec. 20, 1766, with respect to military matters; (3) A letter from Lieut.-Col. Edward Maxwell, June 9, 1769, to Granby about a conflict of jurisdiction involving a court martial in the "southern district of America"; (4) A long report of Nov. 28, 1769, by John Thomas to Gen. Sir Adam Williamson, on West Florida and part of French Louisiana; (5) A description of the Battle of Bunker Hill, June 25, 1775. For these groups of papers see Historical Manuscripts

Commission, *Report, Rutland (Belvoir)*, IV [24], 231–5; *Report*, XII (V), 30, 32, 249, 289, 300–1; and *Report*, XIV (I), 2–3.

For Leicestershire depositories see Crick and Alman: *Guide*, pp. 114–16.

LINCOLNSHIRE

At the Lincolnshire Archives Office, Exchequer Gate, Lincoln, there are two bodies of manuscripts concerned with the years 1748–1776: the Monson Family Papers and the Aswarby Muniments. Among the Monson Family Papers, c. 1737–1833, are letters, 1754–1756, from Thomas Pownall (1722–1805), while governor of New Jersey, to Baron Monson. Photostats of these letters are in the Library of Congress. The Aswarby Muniments (Whichcote Family Papers), 1742–1773, contain the following pertinent material: (1) The business papers, 1742–1764, of the Cornishman, Nathaniel Tregagle while living in Georgetown and Charleston, South Carolina, respecting his estate and his import business; (2) Letters, 1742–1784, from A. Johnson of South Carolina relating to developments in that colony; (3) A letter, 1761, from George Appleby of South Carolina about the difficulties faced by the colony; (4) A bill of exchange, 1763, drawn by Alexander Rose of South Carolina on Berwicke & Co. of London; (5) A letter, 1773, from William and Mary College, Virginia, reporting the death of Josiah Johnson with a copy of his will.

For Lincolnshire depositories see Crick and Alman: *Guide*, pp. 116–19.

MIDDLESEX

Although rather extended consideration has been given to the various collections of papers in the City of London, the Middlesex County Papers in the Record Office, 1 Queen Anne's Gate Buildings, Dartmouth Street, London, S.W. 1, are still to be considered. Two important groups of papers relate to the period 1748–1776: (1) Transportation bonds, 1682–1837, including the names of the convicts sent to America, their destination, and the names of the ships and ships' owners; (2) Papers of the sessions of gaol delivery at Newgate of the Middlesex Court of Quarter Sessions held at the Old Bailey, 1755–1796.

For Middlesex County depositories see Crick and Alman: *Guide*, pp. 346–9.

NORFOLK

The only important collections in Norfolk bearing upon the Empire, 1748–1776, are in the possession of Col. G. E. Gurney, Bawdeswell Hall, Bawdeswell. These are the Gurney and Barclay Family Papers. The two Quaker families were united by the marriage of the daughter of David

Barclay, banker and merchant, to a member of the Gurney family. Among the papers relating to America are: (1) Commercial letters, 1769–1772, and banking letters, 1769–1770, of David and John Barclay; (2) Copy of a letter from Benjamin Franklin to the distinguished London Quaker physician, Dr. John Fothergill (1712–1780), dated March 14, 1764, about the hostility displayed in Philadelphia to the Quakers seeking to protect the christianized Indians; (3) A letter from Anthony Benezet of Philadelphia to David Barclay, dated April 29, 1767, about his fears of a slave rebellion in America; he also encloses one of his antislavery pamphlets; (4) An important group of papers, 1774–1777, having to do with the efforts at peace negotiations on the part of Dr. Fothergill, David Barclay, Benjamin Franklin, and Lord Hyde. Most of these papers are to be found in R. Hingston Fox: *Dr. John Fothergill and His Friends: Chapters in Eighteenth Century Life* (London, 1919), Appendix A, pp. 393–408; see also J. C. Lettsom, ed.: *Some Accounts of the Late J. Fothergill, M.D.* (London, 1783).

For Norfolk depositories see Crick and Alman: *Guide,* pp. 349–58.

NORTHAMPTONSHIRE

The Northamptonshire Record Office, Delapre Abbey, London Road, Northampton, houses the Fitzwilliam Papers, including letters and draft speeches of Edmund Burke, previously at Milton and supplementary to the Edmund Burke papers, most of which are now in the Sheffield City Libraries. These papers in the Northamptonshire Record Office relate chiefly to American affairs. Among them are: (1) Accounts of quit-rents paid in America, 1753–1763; (2) Petitions against and correspondence relating to the Stamp Act; (3) The distribution of the British Army in America, 1765; (4) An account of bullion received in England from Philadelphia and New York, 1765; (5) The resolutions of the Pennsylvania Assembly, 1766, about grants of aid to the King; (6) Reports on the validity of acts passed by the New York Assembly, 1773; (7) Records of exports and imports of New York, 1774; (8) Resolutions of the freeholders of Cork, Ireland, against any extreme proceedings against the American colonies, 1776, with other papers from elsewhere.

One further collection of Northamptonshire papers are those of Earl Spencer, Althorpe, Northampton. There are in the papers of George John Spencer, 2nd Earl Spencer (1758–1834), six letters, 1774–1783, written by Sir William Jones, who had been a tutor at Althorpe, pertaining to the Parliamentary debates regarding America. In them, Jones advocates granting the colonists their independence and then establishing "a family compact with the United States."

For Northamptonshire depositories see Crick and Alman: *Guide,* pp. 358–62.

NORTHUMBERLAND

Two groups of papers, both in private hands, elucidate the period under consideration. Among the manuscripts of the Duke of Northumberland, Alnwick Castle, Alnwick, are the letter-book and other papers of Earl Percy (1742–1817), covering the War for American Independence. See Historical Manuscripts Commission, *Report*, III, 108, transcripts.

The second group, in the possession of R. H. Carr-Ellison, Esq., Hedgeley Hall, Alnwick, includes the papers, 1737–1783, of Ralph Carr, merchant of Newcastle-upon-Tyne; among these are 60 or 70 letter-books, two volumes of which embody much of Carr's American correspondence, including a letter from Thomas Hutchinson, 1774. For the Carr Papers, see Historical Manuscripts Commission, *Report*, XV (X), 92, 94–9.

For Northumberland depositories see Crick and Alman: *Guide*, pp 362–4.

NOTTINGHAMSHIRE

In the Library of the University of Nottingham are three groups of manuscripts bearing upon the Empire 1748–1776; (1) The papers, 44 bundles of letters, documents, etc., of Henry Fiennes Pelham-Clinton, 9th Earl of Lincoln and 2nd Duke of Newcastle-under-Lyme (1720–1794). Among these are over 100 letters and documents, 1775–1782, from the papers of Sir Henry Clinton (1738?–1795). Although many of the Clinton letters are addressed to the Duke of Newcastle, who was his political patron, there are also copies of other letters sent by Clinton to Sir William Howe, Lord George Germain, Lord Cornwallis and others; (2) The Mellish Manuscripts, 1772–1784, papers belonging to Charles Mellish (1737?–1796), M.P. for Pontefract from 1774 to 1780. Among these is a bundle of 54 letters written to Mellish covering the years 1772–1782 and relating to American affairs; (3) The Portland Manuscripts, among which is the correspondence of William Henry Cavendish Bentinck, 3rd Duke of Portland (1738–1809), a member of the Rockingham group, and of his friends.

For Nottinghamshire depositories see Crick and Alman: *Guide*, pp. 364–6.

OXFORDSHIRE

The Bodleian Library, Oxford, has various pertinent manuscripts of which the most important for the period 1748–1776 are the North family papers, 1702–1778, containing several documents worthy of note: (1) Petition to the King, c. 1756, from Glasgow merchants trading to Maryland and Virginia, asking for protection for these colonies from the French and Indians; (2) Comparison of military expenditures in the American colonies and Gibraltar, 1758 and 1759; (3) Unsigned letter from London, apparently to the Duke of Newcastle, Jan. 15, 1760, recommending boundaries necessary for the defence of North America and other terms to be discussed in the negotiations with France (copy); (4) Observations of Capt. J. Innis of the Royal American Regiment on the American colonies during his residence there, 1756–1760, including remarks on Louisiana; (5) Another unsigned letter (copy) from Edinburgh, June 15, 1761, urging the exclusion of the French from North America (copy); (6) List of ships involved in the American trade between Jan. 1772 and Jan. 1773, with type, tonnage, imports, exports and other details; (7) Letter from Peter Collinson to the Earl of Bute, 1762, urging the British to take possession of St. Augustine, Florida, and thereby end its function as a Spanish base and a refuge for runaway slaves and criminals; (8) Memorial from William Franklin to the Earl of Bute, July 3, 1762, asking to be appointed to the office of secretary to South Carolina (while failing to secure this office he was appointed governor of New Jersey the following year); (9) Petition to the King, Nov. 1762, of Henry Woodward, former captain of H.M. Provincial Regiment of Virginia, asking to be appointed "Commander of Lakes Erie, Huron, etc." (10) Excerpt of a letter from Gov. Horatio Sharpe of Maryland, Dec. 9, 1762, to his brother William about an office in the colony; (11) "Short observations upon North America and the Sugar Islands." Written in 1762, it comments on the disposition of Canada and Louisiana at the upcoming peace negotiations; (12) Note on Georgia quit-rents; (13) Request of Nathaniel Ware, comptroller of customs in New England [Massachusetts Bay] to the Earl of Bute, n.d., to be given a better office; (14) Memorial from Benjamin Barons (Barrons), former collector of customs at the port of Boston, to the Earl of Bute, n.d., complaining of his suspension from office in 1761; (15) Board of Trade's representation to the King in Council, June 8, 1763, concerning the future administrative machinery for recent territorial acquisitions in North America and the West Indies; (16) "Explanation of the several branches of H.M. revenues arising in the plantations at the King's free disposal," c. 1762; (17) Lieut. Timberlake's petition for reimbursement for money spent in transporting three Cherokee chiefs to London between 1762 and 1763; (18) Statement of account by Lieut.-Col. James Robertson, Deputy Quartermaster-General of H.M. forces in North America, 1757–1765; (19) Extract of a letter from Thomas Bishop of Boston to "J. T.," indicating that the Bostonians wanted peace, not war and discord, Jan. 13, 1771; (20) Copies of the entry at the port of London and other English ports of all goods and merchandise destined for North America from Dec. 22, 1775 to May 13, 1776. In all cases, it was noted, the ships leaving English ports were bound for Canada or Florida, except those with licences granted by the Lords Commissioners of the Admiralty; (21) Rated and unrated East India goods, with the exception of tea, which were exported to Africa, foreign parts, the West Indian islands, and North America, between Christmas 1760 and Christmas 1776; (22) Alphabetical list of domestic and foreign goods imported into North America from Great Britain and Ireland between Jan. 5, 1769 and Jan. 5, 1770. It should be noted that many of the North papers listed above are in typescript in the Library at Rhodes House, Oxford.

Another interesting collection in the Bodleian Library is the Dashwood Papers. These are papers of Sir Francis Dashwood, Baron le Despencer (1708–1781), who was Chancellor of the Exchequer, 1762–1763, and later, 1770–1778, became Joint Postmaster-General. In this connection see Betty Kemp: "Some letters of Sir Francis Dashwood, Baron le Despencer, as joint Postmaster-General, 1766–1781," John Rylands Library, *Bulletin,* XXXVII (1954), 204–48.

Among the "Miscellaneous Collections" in the Bodleian are the following with their listing: (1) Ms. Top. Oxon. d. 224. Record of the campaign of the Oxford Light Infantry, 1755–1822; (2) MS. Montagu d. 18 (S.C. 25448) f. 132. A letter from George Washington, Sept. 30, 1762, about a shipment to England of tobacco; (3) MS. Gough Surrey 8 (S.C. 18247). Calendars of Lambeth Library papers, including papers relating to the American colonies and the work there of the S.P.G., 1641–1762; (4) MS. Gough Gen. Top. 40, f. 66. The Rev. W. Bush to R. Gough, Enfield, Dec. 31, 1756, that reports from America are depressing with the Indians supporting the French; the opinion expressed in New England is that if the mouth of the St. Lawrence is closed the French will surrender in three months; (5) *Ibid.,* f. 134. Again Bush to Gough, Jan. 5, 1768, asking his advice about supporting an appeal by Mr. Edwards, a Rhode Island Baptist minister, for funds to enlarge the school there; also Gough's reply, Jan. 11, 1768, f. 135; (6) MS. Eng. hist. a. 5 (S.C. 32934). George Washington to Robert Cary & Co., Mount Vernon, Oct. 6, 1773, ordering goods for himself and books for "Mr. Custis"; (7) MS. Eng. hist. c. 306, f. 5. Le Fleming Papers. Sir Michael Le Fleming to ——— Moore, Dec. 17, 1774, on the American rebellion and Lord North's attitude to it.

The library at All Souls College, Oxford, has also on deposit the Lord Clive Papers, known as the Powis Collection, turned over to the library by the Earl of Powis, a direct descendant of Clive.

In the library at Manchester College, also in Oxford, are the Rev. William Shepherd Manuscripts, Vol. XVIII of which contains copies of a number of very revealing letters written between 1760 and 1776 by Henry Hulton, one of the members of the American Board of Customs Commissioners established at Boston.

For Oxfordshire depositories see Crick and Alman: *Guide,* pp. 367–401.

SOMERSETSHIRE

In the Somerset Record Office, Obridge Road, Taunton, there is one collection of manuscripts falling within the period 1748–1776 and related to the Empire: the Prankard and Dickinson Papers. Graffin Prankard, a Quaker Bristol merchant, and Caleb Dickinson, his son-in-law, traded in many things to North America and the West Indies; but their business was largely in iron. According to the papers at the Record Office, covering chiefly the period 1730–1794 in sixty-eight boxes, their affairs involved trade to South Carolina, Virginia, and Boston. With reference to these papers it may be mentioned that in 1750 an effort was made to secure in Virginia wild turkeys, also grey and flying squirrels, which, with a hogshead of tobacco, could be carried to Bristol. See W. E. Minchinton, ed.: *The Trade of Bristol in the Eighteenth Century,* Bristol Records Society, *Publications,* XX (Bristol, 1957), pp. 101–22.

Another large body of manuscripts are the Strachie Papers, 1774–1782, at Sutton Court, the residence of Lord Strachie. These are the Sir Henry Strachey (1736–1810) papers. Among them are letters of Gov. Tryon of New York to the Earl of Dartmouth, 1774–1776. See Historical Manuscripts Commission, *Report,* VI (xiv-xv), 399–404.

For Somerset depositories see Crick and Alman: *Guide,* pp. 404–7.

STAFFORDSHIRE

Of the manuscripts in Staffordshire mention must be made, first of all, of the Nathaniel Ryder Parliamentary notes preserved at the Earl of Harrowby Estate, Sandon Hall, Stafford. Ryder (who later became Baron Harrowby), a member of the House of Commons and son of Sir Dudley Ryder, Lord Chief Justice of the Court of King's Bench, took down shorthand notes in "cypher" of the proceedings of the House between 1764 and 1766, involving the passing of the Sugar Act of 1764 and the passing and repeal of the American Stamp Act. After the cypher had been broken, the author of this series secured transcriptions of the pertinent materials, which were made by Dr. K. L. Perrin, Librarian at the Hall. A copy of these transcriptions was later secured by the Library of Congress and is now in the Manuscript Division. See in this connection L. H. Gipson: "The Great Debate in the Committee of the Whole House of Commons on the Stamp Act, 1766, as Reported by Nathaniel Ryder," *Pennsylvania Magazine of History and Biography,* LXXXVI (1962), 10–41.

A particularly important collection of manuscripts is held by the Staffordshire County Record Office at Stafford. These are the Dartmouth

Papers, 1676–1802, recently transferred from the William Salt Library, Stafford. William Legge, 2nd Earl of Dartmouth was between 1765 and 1782 President of the Lords Commissioners for Trade and Plantations, better known as the Board of Trade, and later Secretary of State for the Colonies, and in this capacity also at the head of the Board of Trade. It should be noted at this point that the Dartmouth papers relating to Canada have gone to the Public Archives of Canada at Ottawa. The following manuscripts in the Record Office throw light on American affairs: (1) A four-page letter, 1765, from Chief Justice William Smith of New York to the Rev. Mr. Whitefield about the discontents in America; (2) The Earl of Hillsborough to Dartmouth, Sept. 1765, stating that Dartmouth's powers as President of the Board of Trade should be increased; (3) Samuel Garbett of Birmingham to Dartmouth, Dec. 16, 1765, on American complaints on the quality of English nails imported; (4) The Earl of Chesterfield to Dartmouth, May 24, 1766, about Dartmouth's appointment as Secretary of State for the Colonies and with Dartmouth's reply the following day; (5) Richard Stockton, New Jersey lawyer, to Samuel Smith, March 21, 1767, on American affairs with a plan for pacification; (6) Commodore Gambier's comments, Oct. 4, 1771, on navigation, etc., involving Nova Scotia and New England; (7) Letters of George III to Dartmouth, 1773–1776, on American affairs and particularly on the need of reducing Massachusetts Bay to obedience, and of the King's disapproval of Gen. Gage as Commander-in-Chief of British forces in America; (8) Letters from Joseph Reed, Philadelphia lawyer, to Dartmouth, from July 23, 1773 to Feb. 14, 1775, involving various American affairs, including the meeting of the Continental Congress; (9) A group of letters for the years 1773–1774, from Gov. Hutchinson of Massachusetts Bay, describing the growing seriousness of the situation in that colony; (10) Various papers about the riots against the Tea Act of 1773; (11) Letters from Thomas Pownall, former governor of Massachusetts Bay, 1773, about the recall of Gov. Hutchinson and also about "The French plot for stealing away our gum trade"; (12) A report of the Board of Trade, Jan. 22, 1773, "upon a proposed formation of a colony on the banks of the River Mississippi"; (13) Gov. Hutchinson to Pownall, Boston, April 19, 1773, about disaffection in New England and the need for Parliament to deal with all the colonies together, not singly; (14) John Gray to Dartmouth, April 21, enclosing a pamphlet refuting the reply of the Bostonians to Gov. Hutchinson's address; (15) Gov. Tryon of New York to Dartmouth, May 5 and June 2, 1773, in which he points out that His Majesty's instructions to him and His Majesty's interests "are not at all times one and the same thing." He also refers to the purchase of lands from the Indians; (16) Copy of a letter from Benjamin Franklin to an unknown person or group, July 7, 1773, about the political situation in England and advising how the colonists can best obtain a redress of grievances; (17) Report on debates held by the Massachusetts Bay

Council, Nov. 23–29, 1773, indicating strong opposition to the governor; (18) Maj.-Gen. Frederick Haldimand to Dartmouth, Dec. 28, 1773, about the reaction of New York and Philadelphia to the Boston Tea Party; (19) Unsigned paper outlining "the advantages and disadvantages of the proposal for a new colony on the banks of the Ohio"; (20) Haldimand to Dartmouth, Feb. 2, 1774, that New York is quiet but that "little matters . . . might give new vigour to the spirit of opposition"; (21) Copy of a message from the Commons House of Assembly of South Carolina to Lieut.-Gov. William Bull, March 15, 1774, protesting the rejection by the Council of bills passed by the Commons House, together with Bull's answer and the subsequent resolutions of the House; (22) Hutchinson to Dartmouth, March 30, 1774, enclosing a copy of a letter from Arthur Lee, London agent of the Massachusetts House of Representatives; (23) A number of letters from Dartmouth to Gage in 1774, respecting his appointment as governor of Massachusetts Bay; (24) Dartmouth to Gage, April 9, 1774, about putting into effect the closing of the port of Boston and the removal of the seat of government to Salem; also that ringleaders in the riots are to be prosecuted at Gage's discretion and the election of members to the Council to be vetoed if not suitable to serve; (25) Notification, April 11, 1774, to Gage of the general pardon of the rioters; (26) Gage requested by Dartmouth, June 3, 1774, to procure copies of two supposedly treasonable letters written by Franklin and Lee; Dartmouth in two other letters of the same date about the abolition in Massachusetts Bay of the elective Council; (27) Dartmouth to Gage, July 6, 1774, advising him that the Boston Port Bill will be rescinded when compensation is made for the tea destroyed; (28) Gage to Dartmouth, Sept. 2, 1774 (copy) about violence offered to members of the nominated Council and the spread of disaffection to other colonies; (29) Dartmouth to Gage, Sept. 8, 1774, regrets the summoning of a Congress of Deputies from the several colonies; (30) The same to the same, Oct. 17, 1774, on the dangerous state of affairs in Massachusetts Bay, more troops are being sent; (31) Extracts of a letter from Maj. McDonald of the Virginia militia to Dr. John Connolly at Pittsburgh, Aug. 9, 1774, dealing with the Indian War of that year in the Ohio Valley; (32) Col. George Croghan to Dartmouth, Pittsburgh, Aug. 10, 1774, writes that he is trying to keep the Six Nations and the Delawares at peace with the whites but must have supplies and the Virginians must stop attacking the Shawnee Indians; (33) William Brattle to Gov. Hutchinson, Cambridge, Aug. 13, 1774, "mentioning alterations in the constitution of the province which he should rejoice to see effected"; (34) Nathaniel Colver to Dartmouth, Aug. 31, 1774, enclosing a petition from the New York Indians about ill usage; (35) Letters to Dartmouth from Mr. Fraser, Sept. 27, 1774, about disaffection and the spirit of rebellion in the colonies; (36) John Temple to Dartmouth and to Thomas Pownall, Oct. 13, 1774, "expressing his mortification at being superseded in the Lieut.-Governorship of New

Hampshire"; (37) Hon. Thomas Walpole to Dartmouth, Oct. 27, 1774, enclosing papers about the rupture with the Ohio River Indians; (38) Secretary at War Barrington to Dartmouth, Nov. 12, 1774, on the means for reducing rebellion in Massachusetts Bay; (39) The Earl of Suffolk to Dartmouth, Nov. 22, 1774, recommending the supersession of Gage; (40) Minutes of the Cabinet Council meetings of Dec. 1, 1774, and Jan. 21, 1775, to consider measures to be taken to restore order in the colonies and particularly in Massachusetts Bay. An agreement that Great Britain should desist in taxing the colonies if they would provide adequate means for their own defence and contribute extraordinary supplies in war-time; (41) Note, Dec. 20, 1774, endorsed "Mr. Pownall," about the American petition received by Franklin; (42) Two drafts of an address, 1775, from the House of Commons to the King respecting the late riots in New England; (43) "Thoughts on the State of the Colonies" [1775] by the Rev. John Vardill of King's College, New York; (44) Digest of letters between Dartmouth and the two superintendents for Indian Affairs in America, 1775; (45) A bundle of digests of correspondence between Dartmouth and mostly governors or deputy governors in the North American colonies, 1775; (46) From James Meyrick to Gov. Legge of Nova Scotia, Feb. 16, 1775, about plans for the movement of troops to Massachusetts Bay; (47) The Rev. John Rodgers to "J. T. Esq.," New York, Feb. 17, 1775, stresses the loyalty of Americans to the Crown but opposition to the claims of Parliament; (48) A long letter, Feb. 18, 1775, unsigned and unaddressed, entitled, "Thoughts upon American commerce and resistance"; (49) Two letters from Dartmouth to the deputy governor of Maryland, March 3, 1775, enclosing a resolution of the Commons about an indulgence to any colony that may return to its allegiance; (50) A group of letters from Gen. Gage to Gov. Legge, April 23–Oct. 3, 1775, about threats to Nova Scotia, the progress of the rebellion and Gage's impending departure to England; (51) Copy of letter from Joseph Warren to the Boston selectmen, Cambridge, Mass., May 13, 1775, defending the taking up of arms by the colonists; (52) A long paper "upon the rise and progress of the disputes between Great Britain and America, with suggestions for an accommodation," marked on the back "Ld D———d" [Lord Drummond]; (53) The Rev. John Wesley to Dartmouth, June 14, 1775, opposing the coercion of the colonies; (54) Two letters, June 14, 1775, from British soldiers about the Battle of Bunker Hill; (55) William Strahan to Franklin, London, July 5, 1775, urging him to help settle the dispute; (56) Henry Cruger to John Harris Cruger, Bristol, July 5, 1775, on the impending ruin of America; (57) Descriptions of Boston as a beleaguered town in letters, July 25, 26 and 27, 1775; (58) Copy of Thomas Wharton to Samuel Wharton, Philadelphia, Aug. 4, 1775, about the refusal of Canadians and Indians to fight against the colonists and rumour that Gen. Schuyler will invade Canada; (59) A paper by a Mr. Morris, Aug. 21, 1775, entitled, "The present state and condition of the colonies with respect to their governors and government"; (60) A group of letters written between Sept. 1775 and Jan. 1778 by Gen. Sir William Howe to Gov. Legge of Nova Scotia, chiefly on military matters; (61) Lord Lewisham to his father, the Earl of Dartmouth, Sept. 29, 1775, about French support of the Americans; (62) A paper, Dec. 13, 1775, on American plans to attack Nova Scotia; (63) Gen. Howe to Gov. Legge, March 17, 1776, that the army has evacuated Boston and is proceeding to Halifax. For synopses, extracts, and transcripts of these letters, see Historical Manuscripts Commission, *Reports*, II, XI (I) and (V), XIII (IV), and XIV (X).

In the Wedgwood Museum, Barlaston, Stoke-on-Trent, are the business and personal papers of the Wedgwood family, 1765+. These include letters, 1762–1795, of the famous pottery expert, Josiah Wedgwood (1730–1795), which discuss not only potter's clay in America but also political events. See in this connection Katherine E. Farrer, ed.: *Letters of Josiah Wedgwood, 1762–80* (2 vols., London, 1903).

The Raymond Richards Collection in the Library of the University College of North Staffordshire at Keele contain the business records, 1746–1782, of William Davenport & Co., Liverpool merchants. Although the records pertain largely to the West Indian trade, there are also some materials concerning North America, including the ship's book of the brig *William*, with instructions to the captain to purchase 120 Negroes in Africa for the Carolina market, to negotiate their sale in Charleston, S.C., and to secure a load of rice for the return cargo.

For Staffordshire depositories see Crick and Alman: *Guide*, pp. 407–19.

SUFFOLK

In the Bury St. Edmunds and West Suffolk Record Office in Bury St. Edmunds are the papers of Augustus Henry Fitzroy, 3rd Duke of Grafton, 1735–1881. Among them are five letters from Sir Jeffrey Amherst, July–Aug. 1768, involving the giving up the post of governor of Virginia held as a sinecure; a copy of the Earl of Hillsborough's circular letter to American governors, May 13, 1769; and a bundle of papers relating to Pitt, Thomas Walpole, and American affairs.

The Ipswich and East Suffolk Record Office, County Hall, Ipswich, has the Albemarle Papers, 1754–1766. Among these is the naval letter-book of Admiral Viscount Keppel, 1754–1761; there are other papers involving naval and military matters, 1757–1758, including a letter, April 22, 1766, from Gen. Amherst to Secretary at War, Viscount Barrington, discussing military plans for North America. The Record Office also contains the day-book, 1765–1789, of John Henniker (1724–1803), later knighted, a London merchant concerned in provisioning H. M. ships in American waters.

For Suffolk depositories see Crick and Alman: *Guide*, pp. 419–24.

SURREY

The Hammond Family Papers, 1763–1877, are in the possession of Col. A. C. Barnes, Foxholm, Redhill Road, Cobham. The documents chiefly concern two prominent, interrelated American Loyalist families, the de Lanceys of New York and the Allens of Pennsylvania, and include business papers relating to the properties of these families and their claims against the Crown for their loyalty.

In the possession of C. S. Marris, Esq., of the Fairway, New Malden, are the Crowther Family Papers, 1769–1825, which are largely business papers. In this connection see Herbert Heaton: "Yorkshire Cloth Traders in the United States, 1770–1840," *The Thoresby Miscellany*, XI (1945), 225–87, in the Thoresby Society, *Publications*, XXXVII.

For Surrey depositories see Crick and Alman: *Guide*, pp. 424–9.

SUSSEX

Sussex Archaeological Society, Barbican House, Lewes, contains the papers, 1740–1874, of Maj.-Gen. Henry Gage, son of Thomas Gage. (The Thomas Gage Papers are in the Clements Library at Ann Arbor, Mich.) Through marriage into the Warren family, Gage became involved in the American properties of Vice-Admiral Sir Peter Warren (1703–1790), located in South Carolina, New York, and New England. In the collection is Sir Peter Warren's letter-book of private letters, 1746–1747, written while he was governor of the fortress of Louisbourg; there are also letters, 1753–1772, received by Lady Susannah Warren whose brother was the New Yorker Oliver de Lancey, and the correspondence, 1768–1799, of de Lancey (1718–1785) with the heirs of the Warren properties in America.

There is also in Sussex County a body of Amherst Papers in the possession of Maj. John Wyndham, Petworth House, Petworth. The collection includes 289 manuscript pages of letters, Dec. 1761–July 1762, to and from Sir Jeffrey Amherst (1717–1797) while he served as Commander-in-Chief of the British Forces in North America, particularly from governors of colonies.

Finally, mention must be made of the papers of Maj. John Andre (1751–1780), which are the property of Brigadier J. R. A. Andre, Church House, Sidlesham, Chicester. The letters, 1775–1780, were written in

America prior to Andre's execution as a British spy. Additional papers include excellent maps and sketches.

For Sussex depositories see Crick and Alman: *Guide,* pp. 429–35.

WARWICKSHIRE

In Warwickshire there are six collections of manuscripts that should be noted, including the papers in the Record Office, Shire Hall, Warwick, which contain the Boughton-Leigh Collection of Papers. The Leigh family played an important role in South Carolina history in the latter part of the eighteenth century. Peter Leigh was appointed chief justice of South Carolina in 1753; in 1762 Egerton Leigh, his son, was given the office of judge of the South Carolina Court of Vice-Admiralty, and three years later also that of Attorney General of the province. Unfortunately, the papers are unsorted and uncatalogued and the contents unknown.

In the Birmingham Public Libraries are the Lyttelton Papers (Hagley Hall Collection) containing among other documents the appointment by letters patent in 1755 of William Henry Lyttelton, Captain-General and Governor-in-Chief of the Province of South Carolina, and also Lyttelton's commission as Vice-Admiral Commissary and Deputy in the office of Vice-Admiralty in South Carolina.

At Woodbrooke College, Bristol Road, Birmingham, there is the Bevan-Naish collection of Quaker manuscripts in twenty bound volumes and three boxes. Among these papers are lists of those Quakers who visited America from Great Britain, 1656–1775, and those from Pennsylvania and New Jersey who came to Great Britain to visit, 1693–1773. There is also a manuscript concerning the early career of Elizabeth Ashridge, 1713–1755, describing her conversion to the Quaker faith in America, her travels in New England, and her experiences as a bonded servant and a teacher.

Mention must also be made of the Matthew Boulton Collection, 1750–1810, contained in about 100 boxes in the Birmingham Assay Office. Boulton, an engineer and inventor, was closely connected with James Watt. Among his correspondents were such men as Sir Francis Baring, Lord Dartmouth, Benjamin Franklin, Joseph Priestly, and David Rittenhouse. The letters are filed alphabetically and other documents are filed according to topics, such as the box labelled "America" concerned with the critical year, 1775.

In the Coventry City Record Office, Council Offices, Earl Street, among other papers, are transportation records, 1741–1766, involving the sending of convicts to America. In this connection see Frederick Smith: *Coventry: Six Hundred Years of Municipal Life* (Coventry, Eng., 1945), pp. 103–4.

The Denbigh Papers are at the estate of the Earl of Denbigh, Pailton

House, Rugby. Among these are two interesting letters: (1) From the Earl of Sandwich to the 6th Earl of Denbigh, Oct. 6, 1774, urging him to come to Parliament to support the measures against America; (2) Draft of a letter from the Earl of Denbigh to Dr. Rochford, Oct. 19, 1775, informing him that few addresses have been delivered in support of the government. See Historical Manuscripts Commission, *Report on the Manuscripts of the Earl of Denbigh* [68], 297–8.

For Warwickshire depositories see Crick and Alman: *Guide*, pp. 436–43.

WILTSHIRE

The library of the Wiltshire Archaeological and Natural History Society, The Museum, Devizes, contains the drafts of some twenty-five letters, 1765–1767, written by Henry Wyndham (1709–1788) to his son Henry Penruddocke Wyndham (1736–1819) while the latter was travelling on the continent. The letters contain, among other news, the proceedings of Parliament during this critical period.

For Wiltshire despositories see Crick and Alman: *Guide,* pp. 445–6.

WORCESTERSHIRE

At Hagley Hall, Stourbridge, the seat of Charles John Lyttelton, Viscount Cobham, there is a large collection of manuscripts, including letters and other papers of Gov. William Henry Lyttelton of South Carolina, 1755–1762. See Historical Manuscripts Commission, *Report*, II, 36–8.

For Worcestershire depositories see Crick and Alman: *Guide*, p. 447.

YORKSHIRE

No depository of manuscripts in Yorkshire has a greater collection bearing upon the Empire, 1748–1776, than the Sheffield City Libraries. Here are five collections which merit special attention.

The Bagshawe Collection contains John Barker's letter-book, 1753–1760, which is largely concerned with the potash business in Pennsylvania.

The Fitzwilliam (Wentworth Woodhouse) Muniments contain a huge collection of relevant documents, including the papers of Charles Watson-Wentworth, 2nd Marquess of Rockingham (1730–1782). The following groups are significant for the period 1748–1776: R 1: This body of correspondence, the largest of the collections with over 2000 letters, many from America and mostly written between 1759 and 1782, has been fully listed by the Royal Commissions on Historical Manuscripts in its National Register of Archives, No. 1083; *R 19–32*: Papers relating to the taxation of the American colonists, 1763–1766, with many letters from leading colonial officials; *R 33–50*: Papers largely concerned with colonial trade and other matters of interest to the colonies, 1761–1766, including letters from Capt. Robert Rogers and Col. George Mercer of Virginia to Rockingham; *R 51–55*: Another collection of manuscripts concerned with the Stamp Tax, particularly with its repeal; *R 62*: Papers relating to the Province of Quebec with letters, Nov. 1766–Jan. 1767, from both Francis Masères and William Hey; *R 63*: A group of miscellaneous letters from America, 1767–1775, most revealing in indicating the rising revolutionary temper of colonials and described as "perhaps the most important American correspondence" among the Rockingham papers. Correspondents include Thomas Cushing, Joseph Warren, and Joseph Harrison; *R 64*: A paper dealing largely with the dispute between Gov. John Wentworth of New Hampshire and Peter Livius over New Hampshire lands; *R 65*: Various writings on American affairs including Gov. John Wentworth's long letter of Sept. 1, 1765; *R 127*: A small packet of letters from America, 1767–1769; *R 150*: Another collection of letters written in 1775 by parties in both England and America including leading colonial officials, including Sir Francis Bernard, Thomas Boone, Thomas Fitch, Stephen Hopkins, Sir Henry Moore, and Samuel Ward.

In addition to the Rockingham papers the Fitzwilliam Muniments also contain the very important Edmund Burke correspondence embodying a large number of letters from America. For a comprehensive list of this correspondence see T. W. Copeland and M. S. Smith: *A Check List of the Correspondence of Edmund Burke, Arranged in Chronological Order and Indexed Under the Names of 1,200 Correspondents* (Cambridge, Eng., 1955, distributed in America for the Index Society by the Columbia University Press, New York). See also *The Correspondence of Edmund Burke* (Thomas W. Copeland, Lucy S. Sutherland, and George H. Guttridge, *et al.*, eds., 7 vols.+, Cambridge, Eng., and Chicago, 1958–1968+).

The three remaining manuscript collections in the Sheffield Libraries while of lesser importance do throw light on aspects of the history of the Empire, 1748–1776: (1) The Cannon Hall muniments (the collection of Spencer Stanhope of Cannon Hall) contain the papers of Benjamin Spencer, London merchant, who traded to various American ports, including Charleston, S.C., 1750–1759; (2) William Vassell, two letterbooks, 1769–1799, including correspondence with the supervisors of his Jamaica plantations and requests for goods to be sent from London to his Boston residence. Vassall, a Loyalist, moved to London in 1775; (3) The Wharncliffe Muniments, 1749–1893, a large collection mostly concerned with the nineteenth century but including the family papers of

Edward Wortley Montagu (1678–1761), a member of Parliament who was concerned in the Wortley Wire Works and strongly opposed granting concessions to iron imported from America.

For the Sheffield City Libraries see *Guide to the Manuscript Collections in the Sheffield City Libraries* (Sheffield, Eng., 1956).

Another manuscript depository in Yorkshire is the East Riding County Record Office, County Hall, Beverley, where is to be found the Hotham Collection. The papers that are of interest in this survey belonged to Adjutant-General Sir Charles Hotham Thompson (1738–1792); among them are some one hundred letters from America, 1771–1779.

In the possession of Major George Howard, Castle Howard, Malton, are the Carlisle Papers. During the period under consideration, Castle Howard, a massive structure, was the seat of Frederick Howard, 5th Earl of Carlisle (1748–1825). As a friend of Charles James Fox, he was very active in public life and headed the peace commission that went to America in 1778. The manuscripts bearing upon the period 1748–1776 are chiefly in the form of letters relating to the colonies and date from Dec. 1754 to Dec. 1775.

At Shibden Hall, Folk Museum of West Yorkshire, Halifax, are the Lister Family Papers, 1733–1775. Members of the Lister family settled in Virginia and North Carolina, while others remained in England. See "John Lister, Master of Bury Grammar School, and his Correspondents," Lancashire and Cheshire Antiquarian Society, *Transactions*, XXVIII (1911), 153–4.

For Yorkshire depositories see Crick and Alman: *Guide*, pp. 448–72.

PART III

Wales

CARDIGANSHIRE

NATIONAL LIBRARY OF WALES, ABERYSTWYTH

ALTHOUGH the National Library has many papers relating to America, most of the manuscripts are of a later period. One pertinent collection, however, consists of letters written in Welsh from America by the Welsh poet Goronwy Owen (1723–1769?) who emigrated to Virginia in Dec. 1757. Another collection of greater importance is the Cyfarthfa Papers, concerned with the great Crawshay ironworks, Cyfarthfa, Merthyr Tydfil, founded by Anthony Bacon, who returned from Maryland in 1745. Two studies are based upon these papers: (1) Lewis B. Namier: "Anthony Bacon, M.P., an Eighteenth Century Merchant," *Journal of Economic and Business History,* II (1929), 20–70, and (2) John P. Addis: *The Crawshay Dynasty: A Study in Industrial Organisation and Development, 1765–1867* (Cardiff, 1957).

See Crick and Alman: *Guide,* pp. 475–84.

GLAMORGAN

CENTRAL LIBRARY, THE HAYES, CARDIFF

The Central Library possesses one very important collection of manuscripts concerned with the Empire, 1748–1776: the correspondence, 1752–1790, of John Stuart, 3rd Earl of Bute, chiefly letters written to the Earl, with some written by him. They are as follows: (1) Some 400 letters and notes from George III, among them the King's "Thoughts on the British Constitution," c. 1760; (2) A plan of military affairs in North America after the siege of Louisbourg, drawn up on Aug. 8, 1758 by Gen. Jeffrey Amherst and Adm. Boscawen; (3) Boscawen's unsigned statement from Louisbourg, 1758, on the disposition of his fleet; (4) Memorial of Sir Robert Davers, March 3, 1763, praying for a land grant at the mouth of the Detroit River; (5) A loyal address of the trustees of the College Academy and Charitable Trust of Philadelphia, May 27, 1763; (6) A letter from Edward Wortley Montague, June 27, 1763, including a map of the mouth of the Mississippi River; (7) Letters from Gov. George Johnstone of West Florida, Pensacola, June 12, July 25, and Sept. 18, 1765.

MERIONETHSHIRE

BOB OWEN, ESQ., AEL Y BRYN, CROESOR, LLANFROTHEN

The scholar and antiquarian, Mr. Bob Owen (whom the author of this series came to know in person and with whom he has corresponded) has at Ael y Bryn a large collection of Welsh emigrant letters, some as early as 1654. His articles, largely concerned with Welsh emigration to the New World, appeared in the Welsh language in the Caernarvonshire Historical Society, *Transactions*, XIII–XV (1952–4), and in *Ceredigion*, the Cardiganshire Antiquarian Society journal, II, No. 3 (1954), and No. 4 (1955); also in *Lleufer*, XIII (1957), and XIV (1958).

For Glamorgan and Merionethshire see Crick and Alman: *Guide*, pp. 485–8.

PART IV

Scotland

MIDLOTHIAN

SCOTTISH RECORD OFFICE,
H. M. GENERAL REGISTER HOUSE, EDINBURGH

IN the Scottish Record Office some four collections bear upon the Empire, 1748–1776: (1) The Barclay-Allardice Papers, with relation especially to the Barclay family, 1659–1774, some members of which were in America. When the Historical Manuscripts Commission, *Report*, V, 632, listed these manuscripts, they were in the possession of Mrs. Barclay-Allardice, Loyal House, Perthshire; (2) The Abercairny Collection of Letters, 1685–1797, among which are twenty-three letters written by Thomas Stirling to his brother Sir William Stirling, 1760–1797, while Thomas was in military service in America. In this collecton there are also twelve letters or copies of letters written by Benjamin Franklin to Lord Kames, 1760–1775; (3) In the Cuninghame of Thornton Papers, 1746–1782, is a note book containing garrison orders at Louisbourg, 1746–1749; (4) The papers of the Society in Scotland for Propagating Christian Knowledge, in eighty-five boxes, include an undated account of the Society's attempts to Christianize the North American Indians, a commission from the Society in Edinburgh to New England correspondents, 1760, and finally, a letter dated Dec. 1, 1760, from the Rev. Eleazar Wheelock of Connecticut, who was giving his efforts to educate and Christianize the Mohegan Indians and who later founded Dartmouth College.

NATIONAL LIBRARY OF SCOTLAND,
EDINBURGH

In this library there are seven distinct collections with material pertinent to our period: (1) The Yester Papers, 1662–1815. Box VII (*Acc.*

1611) contains 31 letters, 1757–1759, written by Maj.-Gen. Lord Charles Hay, a bitter critic of his superior, Lord Loudoun, and 20 letters, 1757–1781, from John McColme and others, most of which relate to the Great War for the Empire. Box VIII (*Acc. 1611*) contains the journals of Hay from April to the end of July, 1758. In this box there is also the journal of Maj. Rodolphe, 1757, while stationed in Nova Scotia, as well as a narrative account, 1756, left by Lieut. Shomberg of Maj.-Gen. Hopson's regiment stationed in Nova Scotia; (2) There are the microfilmed memoirs of the Scot Jacobite James Johnstone, better known as Chevalier de Johnstone (1719–1800?), a lieutenant in the French marines, who was an aide-de-camp of Lévis and later of Montcalm in Canada. In this connection see Johnstone's *Memoirs of the Rebellion in 1745 and 1746 . . .* (London, 1820; 3rd edn., 1822) and *Memoirs of the Chevalier de Johnstone* (C. Winchester, trans., 3 vols., Aberdeen, 1870–1); (3) A manual of religious instruction for the Micmac Indians of Canada both in French and in the Micmac language prepared by the French Catholic Father Antoine Simon Maillard who died in 1768. The Micmacs inhabited part of what is now Nova Scotia, including Cape Breton Island; (4) The Charles Steuart Papers including letter-books (on microfilm), correspondence, etc., 1751–1797. The manuscripts deal with Steuart, both as the Receiver-General of the American Board of Customs and as a merchant at Norfolk, Va.; (5) The letter-book, 1763–1770, of Charles Strahan, an Indian trader at Mobile, British West Florida; (6) The Robertson-MacDonald Papers, among which are the papers of the historian William Robertson (1721–1793), who among other historical works wrote his incomplete *History of America* and who for many years was Principal of Edinburgh University; (7) The letter-books, 1767–1774, of William Cuninghame & Co., leading Glasgow merchants who with its agents were deeply concerned with American trade.

UNIVERSITY OF EDINBURGH LIBRARY

Among the manuscript collections to be found at this library that have pertinent documents are the papers gathered by David Laing, antiquary and librarian, and called the Laing Manuscripts, 1635–1832. The following should be noted: (1) Suggestions by Duncan Forbes (1685–1747), President of the Court of Sessions, after the Battle of Culloden, that some of the defeated Highlanders be sent to America (*La. II: 123*); (2) Report, Aug. 10, 1748, on Arthur Dobbs's petition to the Privy Council respecting the Northwest Passage (*La. II: 641/24*); (3) Statement, c. 1762, about the number of members of the Church of England and number of Dissenters in Nova Scotia (*La. II: 678*); (4) Royal instructions to Gov. George Johnstone of West Florida, Dec. 7, 1763 (*La. II: 76*); (5) Correspondence, 1775–1776, about Gen. Simon Fraser's raising the 71st Regiment in Scotland to serve in America (*La. II: 506*); (6) The Earl of Rockford to the Lords Commissioners of the Treasury, Aug. 21, 1775, about the plan of Major Roche to raise recruits in Ireland to serve in America (*La. II: 640/40*). See Historical Manuscripts Commission, *Report, Laing Manuscripts*, II [72], 382, 395–9, 434–7, 440, 470–1, 486–7.

Another manuscript in the University Library contains materials for a new edition of *The Principles of Action in Matter* . . . (London, 1751), by Cadwallader Colden (1688–1776), New York scientist and later lieutenant-governor of the province (*Dc. I: 25–6*). In addition there is a printed supplement to *The Principles of Action in Matter*, prepared by Colden's son, David, with manuscript notes and corrections (*Dc. I: 26*). One final item in the library should be mentioned, the journal, 1745–1746, kept by David Brainerd (1718–1747), a missionary to the American Indians (*Dc. 7:68*). It seems to be the same journal that appeared in Jonathan Edwards: *An Account of the Life . . . of David Brainerd . . .* (Edinburgh, 1749 and 1765), pp. 375–437.

CARBERRY TOWER, MUSSELBURGH, LADY ELPHINSTONE

Outside of Edinburgh in Midlothian there are two collections to be noted: The Elphinstone Papers, owned by Lady Elphinstone, Carberry Tower, Musselburgh, which contain a copy of a letter, April 5, 1756, from the papers of Field-Marshall James Keith of the Prussian army to Frederick II, in which the writer, apparently Baron Knyphausen, informs the King that the French have begun trade to the French islands in neutral ships and would prefer to use the Prussian flag.

DALKEITH HOUSE, DALKEITH, DUKE OF BUCCLEUCH

The next collection is the Buccleuch and Queensberry Muniments at the estate of the Duke of Buccleuch, Dalkeith House, Dalkeith. The most pertinent manuscripts are the Townshend Papers which are still in boxes and bundles. Box VIII contains numbered bundles of the papers of Charles Townshend (1725–1767), as well as other papers largely devoted to American affairs, 1751–1785. In *Bundle No. 2* are War Office papers, largely relating to Indian affairs in the Northern Department, 1766. *Bundle No. 4* contains many papers in Townshend's handwriting relating to military and political matters in America covering the years

1745–1766, among them the state of the Newfoundland fisheries, May 12, 1761. In *Bundle No. 17* are papers dealing with the regulation of American trade, 1766–1767. In *Bundle Nos. 22* and *25* are surveys of American agriculture and manufactures, American exports and imports, American armed forces, together with papers relating to disturbances in America, 1691–1767. In *Bundle No. 27* are papers from the Board of Trade, including a draft bill for recruiting in North America, 1766. In *Bundle No. 28* are estimates of the expense of the army in North America, as well as other papers. *Bundle Nos. 31, 34,* and *39* also consist of American papers, 1765–1767. *Bundle No. 45* is made up of miscellaneous papers, 1759–1764, including General Wolfe's papers regarding the attack on Quebec, 1759. A complete list of the Townshend Papers is in the National Register of Archives in London.

For Midlothian see Crick and Alman: *Guide*, pp. 502–18.

ABERDEENSHIRE

In the Aberdeen Town House are the Council Registers. Volume LXIV contains various items relating to the War for American Independence. For example, for the year 1775 there is the loyal address by the Aberdeen Town Council to George III offering to raise a regiment to aid in suppressing the rebellion and also an order to the citizens of Aberdeen to be armed in case of an invasion.

The Library of the University of Aberdeen houses temporarily the Atholl Papers deposited by the Duke of Atholl. The following papers fall within the period 1748–1776: (1) Letter from Lieut. Thomas Campbell of H. M. S. *Dragon* at Portsmouth, to Lord Adam Gordon, comprising "a faithful narrative by everything remarkable he [Campbell] observed among the Creek Nations from November 1764 to June 1765," while on a mission under orders by Gov. Johnstone to interview the Creek Indians (*49 (6) 99*); (2) Letters, 1767, concerning a plan by the Duke of Atholl and others to send a number of Lincolnshire people to a New York estate owned by Lord Adam Gordon, a relative of the Duke (*49 (6) 96–98*). In this connection see *Chronicles of the Atholl and Tullibardine Families* (John J. H. H. S. Murray, 7th Duke of Atholl, ed., 5 vols., Edinburgh, priv. print., 1908); (3) Two letters from Gov. James Grant of East Florida, St. Augustine, 1768 (*49 (7) 15* and *157*).

For Aberdeenshire see Crick and Alman: *Guide*, pp. 491–4.

KIRKCUDBRIGHTSHIRE

At Cavens, Kirkbean, the estate of Maj. Richard Alexander Oswald, are the papers of the merchant and public figure Richard Oswald (1705–

1784), of Auchencruive, Ayreshire. Oswald, with estates in America and the West Indies, was sympathetic toward the rebelling colonists and played a leading role in 1782 in establishing the peace treaty of 1783. His correspondence with Lord Shelburne is to be found in the Historical Manuscripts Commission, *Report, Marquis of Lansdowne Manuscripts*, V, vols. LXX–LXXI. The papers at Cavens consist of three letter-books, 1764–1784: Book I, 1761–1763, Oswald's correspondence with his wife; Book II, 1764–1784, miscellaneous letters to Oswald, some relating to military affairs in North America, 1776–1778; Book III, 1765–1784, business letters to Oswald from John Maxwell.

For Kirkcudbrightshire see Crick and Alman: *Guide*, p. 500.

LANARKSHIRE

One collection of papers in the Mitchell Library, Public Libraries, Glasgow, are the Bogle Papers of the mercantile firm of Bogle & Scott. A letter-book contains some 100 letters, 1725–1731, and 1759–1761, many of which were written from Holland while others came from Glasgow, London, and Virginia. Among other activities, the firm was involved in the tobacco trade.

For Lanarkshire see Crick and Alman: *Guide*, pp. 500–2.

SELKIRKSHIRE

At Selkirk in Bowhill House, residence of the Duke of Buccleuch, is another body of the Buccleuch and Queensberry Muniments, (beyond those at Dalkeith House, Dalkeith, already mentioned) among which is a bundle of Townshend Papers, 1751–1785, mainly correspondence relating to American affairs. The contents of them have been listed in the National Register of Archives (Scotland).

For Selkirkshire see Crick and Alman: *Guide*, p. 520.

PART V

Northern Ireland

A N T R I M

THE Public Record Office of Northern Ireland, located in the Law Courts Building in Belfast, contains five collections pertaining to the Empire, 1748–1776. They are as follows:

The Dobbs Papers, 1683–1775. Arthur Dobbs (1689–1765) was not only deeply interested in the Hudson Bay area and in finding the Northwest Passage but also acted as Governor of North Carolina during the years 1754–1765. Among his papers are the following: (a) A group of letters, 1749–1752, either originals or copies, relating particularly to settlement in North Carolina; (b) Letter from the naturalist Peter Collinson (1699–1768) about trees and shrubs imported from America, March 10, 1750; (c) Statement about the high price and scarcity of beaver skins in the London market [1759]; (d) Paper attacking the Hudson's Bay Company for mismanagement [1752]; (e) Letter from Dobbs to Alexander McAulay, March 17, 1755, about his own efforts to direct trade from North Carolina to Ireland; (f) Anonymous diary, June 27 to Sept. 19, 1759, concerning Wolfe's campaign against Quebec; (g) Papers, 1764–1775, relating to the disposal of Dobb's North Carolina estates after his death there in 1765.

Papers, 1770–1789, of George Macartney (1737–1806), later 1st Earl Macartney, who became Chief Secretary for Ireland in 1769. Among these papers (most of them written by Thomas Allan, a member of the Irish Parliament) several relate to the debates that resulted in Parliament from Edmund Burke's motion in the House of Commons in 1770 on America and to the question of the repeal of acts bearing upon the American colonies, including Lord North's position. Among these Macartney papers see especially Vol. 3: *Nos. 39, 40, 43,* and *67.*

The Perceval-Maxwell Papers, transcripts and photostats, 1774–1778. The American papers concern the campaign against Quebec in 1775 which involved Richard Montgomery (1736–1775). Montgomery, an Irishman, who served in the British army during the Quebec campaign in 1759, settled in the Province of New York in 1772 and as a brigadier-general in the Continental Army lost his life in 1775 in the assault upon Quebec. The following documents should be considered: (a) *No. 112.* Loyal address of French-speaking citizens of Quebec, Sept. 1774, to George III; (b) *No. 113.* Letter from Boston Committee of Correspondence to "friends of liberty" in Quebec, Feb. 21, 1775; (c) *No. 114.* Draft reply to this letter by English-speaking citizens of Quebec, April 12, 1775, who criticize the proceedings of Congress respecting Quebec, emphasize both the authority of the priests over the French-speaking people and the expectation that Parliament will soon redress their grievances; (d) *No. 115.* Ethan Allen's letter, May 18, 1775, to James Morrison and "merchants that are friendly to the cause of liberty in Montreal," demanding provisions for the Continental Army; (e) *No. 116.* "Resolution of His Majesty's Loyal subjects and inhabitants of Quebec," July 20, 1775, signed chiefly by officers in the British army there; (f) *Nos. 117–121.* A group of letters from Oct. 22, 1775 to Jan. 19, 1776, most of them written by Montgomery.

The Massereene-Foster Papers, 1625–1845, a very large collection relating chiefly to the Foster family, many of which throw light on eighteenth-century Irish history and Irish-American trade; see particularly *Bundle 108.* Besides interest in trade John Foster, Baron Oriel (1740–1828), was Chief Baron of the Exchequer, 1766–1777, and he and Anthony Foster were connected with the Irish Linen Board. For details on this collection see the *Report, 1949–50* of the Deputy Keeper of the Public Record Office of Northern Ireland.

Emigrant letters and records, among which are the Blair family letters, 1774–1796, written from New York to relatives in Newry, County Down.

For Northern Ireland see Crick and Alman: *Guide,* pp. 523–30.

PART VI

Republic of Ireland

LEINSTER

THE Public Record Office of Ireland in Dublin was constructed to preserve the once-scattered Irish manuscripts laboriously collected over the years from various parts of the island. It met a sad fate in 1922 when much of that imposing structure, the Four Courts, with its Treasury Room where rested most of the precious manuscripts, was blown up in the Irish Civil War. Today the reconstructed building houses the surviving documents.

Among the most interesting of the collections bearing upon the years 1748–1776 which I found when working in the Record Office in 1929 were the so-called "Convert Rolls and Certificates." These rolls cover the period from the beginning of 1703 to September 4, 1775 and list chronologically in brief detail the passing of hundreds of Catholics into the ranks of adherents to the Church of Ireland (the Anglican communion). When I sought to use the same rolls in 1952, they were no longer available. What has happened to them I cannot say. In this depository, however, there are four volumes of "Abstracts of Exports and Imports of Ireland" covering three periods, the first from 1764 to 1773; the rest are later. These abstracts are valuable because they list the ports, the volume of commodities exchanged, and the British colonies involved in this trade, including the Carolinas, Virginia, Pennsylvania, New England, Quebec, and the West Indies. (See *M. 2482*).

The National Library of Ireland, also in Dublin, while rich in manuscripts likewise has little that bears upon the years 1748–1776, outside of newspapers. There is a very interesting document (*Ms. 246*) giving a detailed account of Isle St. John (now Prince Edward Island), Canada, for about the year 1770, listing the proprietors with their land holdings and a copy of the "Articles of Agreement between proprietors and settlers." Among the so-called Balfour Papers are three letters, 1764–1765, written by James Pillson of New York to the merchant Harry Brabazon of Drogheda, County Louth, having to do with the marketing of flax-seed and butter.

The Royal Irish Academy, Dublin, contains the papers of James Caul-field, 1st Earl of Charlemont (1728–1799). These papers are exceedingly valuable in dealing with conditions in Ireland for the period under re-view. For excerpts from these papers and especially from the Charlemont "Memoirs," see the Historical Manuscripts Commission, *Report*, XII (X).

ROSCOMMON

Irish depositories outside of Dublin contain little material for the years 1748–1776. In County Roscommon at Clonalis, Castlerea, the estate of the Rev. Charles O'Conor, S.J., are the O'Conor Papers, among which are those of Charles O'Conor (1710–1791), Irish antiquary, historian, politi-cal writer. These papers have much to say about conditions in Ireland and reflect on the more extended liberty of conscience in the American colonies than in Ireland. For a calendar of the Charles O'Conor papers see the Historical Manuscripts Commission, *Report*, VIII (I, Sec. 2), 441–92.

TIPPERARY

Among the Donoughmore Papers in County Tipperary at Knocklofty, Clonmel, the seat of the Earl of Donoughmore, there is a considerable amount of correspondence of the lawyer and statesman, John Hely Hutchinson, generally written Hely-Hutchinson (1724–1794), with such men of importance as Edmund Burke and Lord Townshend, Viceroy of Ireland. As to the latter there is a letter from him, March 16, 1774, re-lating to the beginning of the revolt of the American colonies and in the support of this revolt given by the Earl of Chatham and the Marquess of Rockingham. See the Historical Manuscripts Commission, *Report*, XII (ix), 227–333.

For the Republic of Ireland see Crick and Alman: *Guide*, pp. 533–53.

PART VII

France

Within the permissible limits of this guide it is impossible to include all French documents that have at least some bearing upon the history of the British Empire during the brief period 1748–1776. Moreover, the history of the activities of the French in Canada, the Mississippi Valley and the islands of the Caribbean Sea before these years obviously must be passed over. There is, nevertheless, abundant material in the vast collections of manuscripts in Paris archives to meet the needs of the student engaged in a study of British overseas expansion during this brief period.

Without reference to earlier publications concerned with manuscripts in Paris that throw light on France's interest in the New World there is available the pioneering work by J. Edmond Roy: *Rapport sur les Archives de France Relatives à l'Histoire du Canada*, which appeared in Ottawa in 1911 as No. 6 of the *Publications* of the Public Archives of Canada. This was followed in 1914 by David W. Parker in his *A Guide to the Documents in the Manuscript Room at the Public Archives of Canada*, the latter part of which lists the transactions of documents drawn from the Archives Nationales in Paris. This is No. 10 of the *Publications* of the Public Archives of Canada. In 1932 came the guide by Waldo G. Leland: *Guide to Materials for American History in the Libraries and Archives of Paris*, as a *Publication*, 392, No. 1, of the Carnegie Institution in Washington, and in 1943, the second volume, also under the general editorship of Leland, that carries the subtitle, *Archives of the Ministry of Foreign Affairs*, also as a *Publication*, 392, No. 2, of the Carnegie Institution.

It should be pointed out that up to 1927 the contents of manuscripts were painstakingly transcribed for such American depositories as the

Library of Congress, the Public Archives of Canada, the Archives de Québec, the state of New York, and other libraries. However, a change was initiated in that year as the result of a special grant to the Library of Congress by John D. Rockefeller, Jr. that instituted photographic copying of materials abroad. This led to its general use and then to the publication in 1961 by the American Historical Association, under the editorship of Richard W. Hale, Jr., of *Guide to Photocopied Historical Materials in the United States and Canada.*

On account of the extent to which the Public Archives of Canada has drawn upon the manuscripts in France relating to the New World, especially French Canada and French Louisiana, its new series of pamphlets begun in 1952, under title *Public Archives of Canada. Manuscript Division, Preliminary Inventory,* is most useful, especially with respect to manuscripts in Paris. Under the subtitles, Fonds des Manuscrits or Manuscript Group, the following have appeared that have a bearing upon the French in the New World for the period under consideration: *Archives des Colonies* (1952); *Archives de la Marine* (1952); *Archives Nationales* (1953); *Archives de la Guerre* (1953); and *Ministère des Affaires Étrangères* (1955).

ARCHIVES NATIONALES

All the great collections of manuscripts referred to above, outside of the Archives of the Ministère des Affaires Étrangères, rest in that great depository of public documents, the Archives Nationales. This structure erected in 1706 as the Hôtel Soubise was nationalized, as was true of many other great structures in Paris with the coming of the Revolution of 1789, and became a national depository of manuscripts.

We shall now deal with each collection in the order presented above in the inventories, in so far as the items bear upon the British Empire, 1748–1776, beginning with the Archives des Colonies.

Archives des Colonies

A selection of papers in this great collection resting in the Archives Nationales in Paris, that have a bearing upon the British Empire for the years 1748–1776, is as follows: (1) Série A. Actes du Pouvoir Souverain, 1712–1763. Here are royal edicts, ordinances, and letters patent for the French New World colonies; (2) Série B. Lettres Envoyées, 1663–1789, a very extensive series in the form of registers of copies of despatches of the ministers and memoranda from the king sent to officials in the colonies before the transfer of power in the 1760's and, after that, papers concerning the problems facing the French-speaking inhabitants in North America; (3) Série C¹¹A. Correspondance Générale, Canada, 1540–1784. Correspondence, reports, and other documents sent to the king and the ministers of marine, that is, of naval affairs, by the governors, intendants, and other Canadian officials; there are also despatches, instructions and minutes of the Council sent from France for the guidance of these colonial officials; (4) Série C¹¹B. Correspondance Générale, Île Royale, 1712–1762. Material similar to the previous series, but relating to Cape Breton Island; (5) Série C¹¹C. Amérique du Nord. These papers are concerned with Newfoundland and other islands in the North Atlantic where France had an interest; (6) Série C¹¹D. Correspondance Générale. Papers relating to Acadie, 1603–1788; (7) Série C¹¹E. Des Limites et des Postes, 1685–1787. Papers on boundaries and trading posts; (8) Série C¹¹F. Terre-Neuve et les Pêcheries. Papiers de la Commission des Pêcheries de 1876. The documents concerned with the fisheries and other Newfoundland matters cover the eighteenth-century; (9) Série C¹¹G. Correspondance Générale, especially relating to Île Royale, 1714–1758; (10) Séries C¹²A and C¹²B. Correspondance Générale, Saint Pierre et Miquelon, 1763–1802. These two series discuss mainly friction with the British over the cod fisheries by the French resorting to these two islands; (11) Série C¹³. Correspondance Générale. Louisiane, 1694–1803; (12) Série D¹. Correspondance Militaire, 1773–1780, Précis de décisions; (13) Série D². French Colonial Troops, 1656–1789. Troop lists and lists of officers and their ranks. The material deals mostly with Canada. There are also comments on the capabilities and advancement of the various officers; (14) Série E. Dossiers Personnels, 1638–1791. Dossiers on important officials and other persons, containing their correspondence with the ministers on personal matters; (15) Série F¹. Fonds des Colonies, 1670–1766. This series is largely concerned with finances to support the French Empire. The documents relate not only to Canada, but also to Louisiana, St. Domingue, Martinique, other islands of the Antilles, also to Madagascar; (16) Séries F²A and F²B. Papers largely devoted to commercial affairs, 1623–1790, of the French Empire; (17) Série F²C. Décisions de la Marine, respecting the civil administration of the various French colonies, 1704–1788; (18) Série F³. Collection made by Moreau St.-Méry, containing many official documents concerning Canada, 1540–1763, Louisiana, 1775–1778, and Île Royale, 1714–1750; (19) Série F⁵A. Missions et Cultes Religieux, 1658–1782. Papers on religious affairs especially in Canada, but with documents also relating to Louisiana (Parker lists this as F²); (20) Série G¹. Registres de l'État Civil, Recensements et Divers Documents. The documents relate to Louisbourg, 1722–1758; Île Royale, 1715–1758; Ile Saint-Jean et Port le Joye, 1752–1758, and Acadie, 1671–1752; (21) Série G². Clerk's register of the Conseil Supérieur of Louisbourg, 1711–1758; (22) Série G³. Notariat, 1637–1784. Notarial documents concerning Île Royale, Canada, Acadia, Saint Pierre and Miquelon and Terrebonne;

(23) Dépôt des Fortifications des Colonies, 1680–1880. Papers concerned not only with fortifications in the colonies but also with military actions, trade and the fisheries; (24) Dépôt des Papiers Publiques des Colonies, 1748–1760. A register of the Hôpital de Québec.

Archives de la Marine

In 1953 the Public Archives of Canada published its provisional inventory No. 2, copies of manuscripts from the Archives de la Marine in Paris, resting in the Archives Nationales. The importance of these papers lies in the special role that the French ministry of sea-affairs played in the building up of the eighteenth-century French Empire. The following collections of papers from this depository throw light on the French Empire and the interest of the French government displayed in overseas activities, especially trade, for the period 1748–1776; (1) Série A^1. A summary of "ordonnances, édits, arrêts, lettres patentes," 1610–1777; (2) Série B^1. Délibérations du Conseil de Marine, 1715–1786; (3) Série B^2. Orders and despatches, 1662–1750; (4) Série B^4. Campagnes, 1640–1782, including journals, correspondence between king and officers, and orders and instructions, relating to military campaigns and naval engagements. Among these papers are some in English secured from captured ships; (5) Série C^1. This series has to do with French naval officers, 1400–1750; (6) Série C^2. These papers are concerned with civil personnel at the overseas ports, 1663–1760; (7) Série C^7. Dossiers Individuels, 1689–1814, including, for example, dossiers on Montcalm (Carton 216) and Rigaud de Vaudreuil (Carton 340).

Archives Nationales

Within that great depository of official papers of the French government, the Archives Nationales, rest not only the Archives des Colonies, the Archives de la Marine, and the Archives de la Guerre (to be dealt with) but also a series of documents carrying the title Archives Nationales. Under this title the following contain series of manuscripts that throw light on the British Empire, 1748–1776: (1) Série F^{12}. Commerce et Industrie, 1700–1754. This series, pertaining to the work of the Conseil du Roi and Bureau du Commerce, embodies the chronological registers of their hearings and resolutions; (2) Série F^{15}. Hospices et Secours, 1763–1793. The documents in this series concern the aid promised to the Acadians and Canadians who went to France after the British conquest of Canada; (3) Série F^{50}. Marines et Colonies, 1658–1759. This series is concerned with such matters as the sale of lands and the appointment of guardians in the colonies; some documents also refer to the fortification of Quebec; (4) Série G^5. Administrations financières et spéciales, Amirauté et Conseil des Prises, 1675–1758. This group of papers is composed of letters patent, orders in council, reports on the capture and sale of prizes, and resolutions and judgments of the Conseil des Prises; (5) Série K. Monuments Historiques, 1540–1759. This series includes the following relevant manuscripts: (a) A document discussing the difficulty facing Canada after the British capture of Louisbourg [1758]; (b) Report on the advantageous geographical position of Saint-Malo [1758]; (c) Memorandum from the king: instructions to Vaudreuil Cavagnal, 1755; (d) Certain letters written by Vaudreuil to the ministers in the course of military operations in Canada, 1757–1759; (6) Série N. Dépot des Cartes et Plans de la Marine, 1692–1755. Maps in this series give details useful for navigation in American waters; (7) Série T. Documents Placés sous séquestre lors de la Révolution, 1718–1792. The series includes a collection of letters written by Madame Duplessis de Sainte-Hélène, a nun stationed at the Hôtel-Dieu in Québec, to Madame Hecquet, her grandmother. The letters give news of events in Canada, 1718 to 1758. The *Revue Canadienne* published them in 1875; the series has other documents of interest; (8) Série V². Secrétaires du Roi: Concerning Intendant François Bigot, 1754; (9) Série V⁷. Commissions Extraordinaires du Conseil Privé, 1698–1776. The material includes: (a) Registers of the council concerning the beaver trade in Canada, 1698–1776; (b) Judgments on those condemned following the loss of Canada; (c) Judgments in property disputes, 1758–1765; (d) Arrêts, contestations et quittances du Conseil, 1763–1776, especially as these relate to Canada.

Archives de la Guerre

The manuscript collections in Archives de la Guerre that bear upon the British Empire, 1748–1776, are as follows: (1) Archives Historiques et Archives Administratives, 1636–1759. These archives include: (a) Diplomatic correspondence of Pierre Voyer d'Argenson, Charles-Louis-Auguste Fouquet de Belle-Isle, and others, 1750–1754 (vol. 3391); (b) Extracts from the official correspondence of Antoine-Louis Rouillé, Étienne de Silhouette, and others; also reports relating to the navy and the colonies, 1749–1754 (vol. 3393); (c) Official letters relating to New World developments in 1755 (vols. 3398–3399); (d) Official letters and reports from Charles de Rohan de Soubise, Dieskau, and Anne-François Duperrier-Dumouriez, concerning the navy and the colonies; also the movement of French troops to the colonies, 1755 (vol. 3404); (e) Official correspondence of Soubise, Jean-Louis de Raymond, and other officers, including Doreil, Montreuil, and Dieskau, about the navy and the colonies, including the movement of the French fleet under Dubois de la Motte, 1755 (vol. 3405); (f) Collection of official letters of Dieskau, Saint-Julien, Montcalm, Lévis, and others about military activities in North America, as well as the fight put up by the captured *Alcide*, 1756 (vol. 3417), a volume of especial interest relating to Canada; (g) Official letters of Vaudreuil, Montcalm, Dieskau, and others about developments in America in 1757 (vol. 3457); (h) A letter written by British Admiral Warren concerning preparations for the attack on Louisbourg, 1758 (vol. 3478); (i) Collection of official correspondence of Vaudreuil, Montcalm, Lévis, and others, relating to events in Canada, including Louisbourg and the Lake George campaigns, 1758 (vols. 3498–3499); (j) Letters concerning military administration of the French colonies, 1758, (vols. 3501–3507); (k) A letter concerning the general political situation of France, 1757 (vol. 3508); (l) Reports and letters about measures for the improvement of the condition of the French infantry, 1758 (vol. 3510); (m) Official correspondence of Montcalm, Lévis, Montreuil, and others about developments in Canada, including an account of the capture of Quebec, 1759 (vol. 3540), an important volume; (n) Official correspondence of Lévis, Bourlamaque, Vaudreuil, Bigot, and others on the war in Canada, 1760 (vol. 3574), another volume of great value; (o) Documents concerning the military administration, 1760 (vol. 3577); (p) List of French prisoners of war sent from Quebec to France, 1761 (vol. 3599); (q) Materials having to do with the situation in Canada, 1761, especially with respect to the military administration (vols. 3600–3623); (r) A body of manuscripts that carries the title "Dépôt général de la Guerre" and includes a summary respecting encouragement extended to the cod fishery, 1764; also a report concerning French colonial commerce, 1764; and an account of trade in the West Indies, 1764–1765 (vol. 3674).

(2) Archives du Comité Technique du Génie, 1730–1764. These archives embodied in the Archives de la Guerre contain important documents relating to Canada and relevant to the period under examination. The manuscripts are classified by articles and files which are numbered or by register or collection, also numbered. Those that are relevant are as follows: (a) *Article 14, file 1.* Exposition of the rights of France to the eastern and southern portions of Canada and of the bad conduct of the English in pressing the Indians to take up arms against the French, 1755 (pp. 31–49); a report demonstrating the injustice of the pretensions of the English to French possessions in North America, 1755 (pp. 50–62); practical means of settling the issues between France and England over the limits of their respective colonies in America, 1755 (pp. 63–80); the importance for France and Spain to preserve Canada and Louisiana, 1755 (pp. 81–88); a description of the frontiers of Canada in the Lakes Champlain and Saint-Sacrement (Lake George) area, 1756 (pp. 89–90); account of the actual state of the colonial war with a plan of operations respecting the approaching campaign, 1759 (pp. 102–132). (b) *Article 14, file 2.* Remarks on the subject of the expansion of the territorial claims by the English, with notes on the uncivilized peoples that the English pretend have submitted to them with a description of the Indian nations that inhabit the Ohio, the Mississippi and other rivers, 1755 (pp. 165–181); a report, n.d., demonstrating the rights of France to Louisiana and

proving the bad conduct of the English who excite the natives against the French (pp. 182–187); remarks on the roadstead and bay of Chibouctou in "Acadie," 1746 (pp. 190–197). (c) *Article 15.* In this group there are three French accounts of the capture in 1756 of the British forts —Fort George, Fort Ontario and Fort Oswego—built close to the great Indian trading post Oswego but called by the French Chouaguen (pp. 2–15, and 185–201); also of especial interest are three journals and two statements relating to the siege of the fortress of Louisbourg, 1758 (pp. 72–184); likewise there is an account of the campaign at Lake George (Saint-Sacrement) during the winter of 1757 (pp. 202–212); (d) *Registre 66. Sièges et Campagnes.* Here is included a long report concerned with events at Louisbourg, 1758 (pp. 1–134); letters to Louis Franquet proposing a trip to America, 1750, together with the itinerary of the trip, 1751 (pp. 136–324). *Note.* In 1758 Franquet prepared two of the accounts referred to in *Article 15* (pp. 143–184); (e) *Recueils—Mémoires et dessins: Canada et Île Royale.* This includes a report on the need to fortify Detroit, 1752 (pp. 34–55); there is also a report on the means to increase the yield of lands in Canada, 1753 (pp. 56–91). Here are likewise plans for establishing a military hospital on the grounds of l'Hôtel-Dieu at Quebec, 1753 (pp. 92–94); an account signed by Contrecoeur of a council attended by several Indian tribes at Fort Duquesne, 1754 (pp. 95–97); an account of the siege of Fort George, 1757 (pp. 103–112); news from Île Royale, 1757 (pp. 112–118); journal of events that took place at Louisbourg in 1758 (pp. 132–225).

MINISTÈRE DES AFFAIRES ÉTRANGÈRES

In the archives of the ministry of foreign affairs are two very large collections of manuscripts concerned with French foreign relations, many of which fall within the period under examination and bear upon the British Empire, 1748–1776. They are Correspondance Politique, 1625–1783 and Mémoires et Documents, 1592–1805.

Correspondance Politique, 1625–1783

ANGLETERRE, 1625–1783

Volumes 426–429, 1749–1750. In these volumes is correspondence between Durant de Distroff, Puysieulx, Mirepoix and the royal court. The chief subjects are: British complaints about the activities of the French in Nova Scotia; the projected settlement by the English in "Acadie"; the dispute over the possession of Tobago; and the restoration to the French of Cape Breton Island. Here are also the instructions of July 13, 1749, to Mirepoix, going to London as French ambassador (vol. 426, ff. 315–339), also a list of British war ships ready to go to America, 1750 (vol. 428, f. 469).

Volumes 430–432, 1750–1751. Correspondence of Puysieulx, Rolland-Michel Barrin, the Marquis de la Galissonière, Étienne de Silhouette, Mirepoix, the Earl of Albemarle, Saint-Contest, and the court. The following manuscripts throw light on the nature of this correspondence: (1) Reports on the limits of Nova Scotia, Sept. 21, 1750 (vol. 430, ff. 169–171); (2) An account of ships captured in the late war, Nov. 17, 1750 (vol. 430, ff. 237–248); (3) A statement "État présent de la Grande-Bretagne . . . ," Jan. 2, 1751, which seeks to prove that the British have made the decision to make war on France (vol. 431, ff. 4–10); (4) British expense account for supporting the Nova Scotia establishment, June 18, 1751 (vol. 432, f. 42); (5) British expense account for maintaining troops in America, Minorca, and Gibraltar, March 5, 1751 (vol. 432, f. 368); (6) A general account of the cost of the armed service, 1751 (vol. 432, ff. 370–371).

Volume 433, 1751–1753. Correspondence between Silhouette and Albemarle, the British ambassador. The subjects treated are contained in the following documents: (1) A memorandum setting forth the British pretensions to "Acadie," Jan. 11, 1751 (vol. 433, ff. 20–39); (2) A statement concerning ship captures, April 24, 1751 (vol. 433, f. 105 and ff. 114–115); (3) Letter from the Bishop of Quebec to Rouillé, Count de Jouy, about the boundaries of "Acadie," Dec. 1751 (vol. 433, ff. 256–265); (4) A statement about the general condition of captured ships and cargoes and the indemnities demanded by the subjects of the French king by reason of these captures made by the British navy during the late war, 1752 (vol. 433, ff. 289–323).

Volumes 434–435, 1752–1753. Correspondence between Mirepoix, the Marquis de Lambertye, Saint-Contest, and the court. The subjects of this correspondence bearing upon the British Empire were: (1) The cost of the artillery and other forces maintained by Great Britain in Nova Scotia, 1752 (vol. 434, ff. 103–106); (2) State of trade between France and Great Britain, 1752 (vol. 435, ff. 144–163); (3) Ordinary charges in maintaining the British fleet in 1753 (vol. 435, f. 305); (4) The expense of the British Ordnance Bureau for the same year (vol. 435, ff. 307–308).

Volume 436, 1753. Correspondence between Mirepoix, Saint-Contest, and the court on matters contained in the following documents: (1) A report pointing out the different positions of the King of Great Britain and the King of Prussia over the question of naval prizes, March 29, 1753 (vol. 436, ff. 74–78); (2) Treatise on the legality and custom of taking prizes at sea, April 23, 1753 (vol. 436, ff. 111–138); (3) Comment on a law presented to the British Parliament for the naturalization of Jews, June 25, 1753 (vol. 436, ff. 212–217).

Volume 437, 1754. Correspondence of Mirepoix, Boutet, Saint-Contest, the Earl of Albemarle, and the court. This volume has to do with the disputes over the boundaries of "Acadie," Canada, the Ohio country and over the respective rights of France and Great Britain to the so-called "Neutral Islands" of St. Lucia, St. Vincent, Dominica, and Tobago. Also, account is taken of the apprehensions in France of the preparations of a British fleet to support the British claims.

Volume 438, 1755. Correspondence between Boutet, Rouillé, Mirepoix, and the court over the critical relations between France and Great Britain and the abandonment of all hope of conciliation. These letters stress the growth of British sea power as well as British political colonial expansion. They also indicate that Great Britain is preparing for a war in America over the issues of limits of the Ohio country, "Acadie," and Canada. Two documents in this volume are pertinent: (1) A list of British war ships placed in commission and to be armed, Feb. 28, 1755 (vol. 438, ff. 242–243); (2) A list of armed vessels in the different ports of Great Britain, April 6, 1755 (vol. 438, ff. 369–370).

Volumes 439–440, 1755–1756. Correspondence between Mirepoix and Rouillé. In this correspondence the following British names figure: The Duke of Newcastle, Sir Thomas Robinson, Lord Grantham, Lord Granville and the Earl of Holderness. The letters stress the point that Great Britain at whatever price she may pay desires war. The point is also made that the capture by Admiral Boscawen of the French war ships *Alcide* and *Lys* was the opening of hostilities, with the French limiting themselves to protesting against these hostile acts. In these volumes are to be found the following documents: (1) A report on the boundaries of "Acadie" or Nova Scotia, Canada, and the Ohio country, indicating the state of the negotiations between France and Great Britain, June 15, 1755 (vol. 439, ff. 185–188); (2) An account of the seizure of the *Alcide* by a squadron of eleven British ships commanded by Boscawen, July 20, 1755 (vol. 439, ff. 257–258); (3) A list of vessels under command of Admiral Hawke designed to cruise in the English Channel (called by the French simply la Manche), July 23, 1755 (vol. 439, f. 268); (4) A list of French vessels taken by British ships of war and brought into the harbour of Portsmouth, between Sept. 24 and Oct. 1, 1755 (vol. 439, f. 362); (5) The statement of Pedro Valmediana, translated into French from the Spanish, on the issues between France and Great Britain over their respective possessions in America, Sept. 16, 1756 (vol. 440, ff. 290–356)—a statement that supports the French territorial claims.

Volumes 441–443, 1757–1761. The correspondence of French diplomatic agents, especially that of François de Bussy, sent as a French envoy to London. William Pitt and Hans Stanley are very much in evidence in it, as the story unfolds of the British thrusts against Canada and the collapse of French resistance. Among the documents is a letter of Aug. 18, 1758 telling of the capture of Louisbourg by the British, together with the articles of its capitulation and a list of dead or wounded British officers connected with the attack on it (vol. 441, ff. 224–228). There is also a signed convention between France and Great Britain having to do with the treatment of wounded and prisoners of war, 1759 (vol. 442, ff. 34–40).

Volumes 444–446, 1761–1762. Correspondence between Bussy, Choiseul, the Earl of Egremont, and the French court concerning the terms of peace. Among the documents in this volume are the following that bear upon the British Empire: (1) A memorandum containing French proposals for a peace settlement, July 15, 1761 (vol. 444, ff. 9–22); (2) A series of demands in a paper handed to the Duke of Choiseul by Hans Stanley constituting an ultimatum by the British court, July 29, 1761 (vol. 444, ff. 50–56); (3) A French ultimatum in reply to the British ultimatum, Aug. 5, 1761 (vol. 444, ff. 77–84); (4) An account in English of exports to and imports from England and Canada, 1758–1761 (vol. 444, ff. 248–257); (5) Preliminary articles of peace signed by the British and French courts at Fontainebleau, Nov. 3, 1762 (vol. 445, ff. 105–115).

Volumes 447–448, 1762. Correspondence between Louis-Jules-Barbon Mancini-Mazarini, Duc de Nivernais, and the court over the treaty of peace with Great Britain. Among the papers are: (1) Observations of Sept. 2, 1762, respecting the preliminaries of peace (vol. 447, ff. 3–11); (2) A memorandum of Sept. 2, 1762, to serve as instructions to Nivernais, French minister plenipotentiary in London, about the peace terms (vol. 447, ff. 12–27); (3) A report setting forth the actual state of the peace negotiations between France and Great Britain (vol. 447, ff. 28–37); (4) A plan connected with the peace negotiations between France and Great Britain whereby both Spain and Portugal would also be participants, Sept. 1762 (vol. 447, ff. 108–120, 137–142, and 159–172); (5) Articles of agreement between France and Great Britain to cease hostilities, Oct. 24, 1762 (vol. 447, ff. 354–360); (6) Observations of John Russell, Duke of Bedford, and the replies of César-Gabriel de Choiseul, Duc de Praslin, on Articles 1, 4, 6, 7, 11, 14, 20, 22, 23, and 24 of proposals for a definitive treaty of peace presented by France, Sept. 28, 1763 (vol. 448, ff. 124–143); (7) Observations on proposals for a definitive treaty sent by the court of London [1762] (vol. 448, ff. 368–384).

Volumes 449–450, 1763. Here is the correspondence between Nivernais in London and the French court that complete the negotiations culminating in the Treaty of Paris of 1763. These papers are concerned with territorial limits and various regulations for avoiding all friction between Great Britain and France and concern such matters as the cod fisheries and the use of the Newfoundland shore for the drying of fish. Among the documents the following are pertinent: (1) A French statement with reference to Frenchmen held as prisoners of war in Great Britain with observations on their treatment and a proposal for their return to France (vol. 449, ff. 336–342); (2) Report upon the Acadians, joined to the despatch of Feb. 17, 1763, from London (vol. 449, ff. 343–352); (3) Report on the limits for cod fishing accorded to the French along the shores of Newfoundland as laid down by the Treaty of Utrecht of 1713 (vol. 450, f. 68); (4) Another report having to do with the establishment of the Acadians in France, March 11, 1763 (vol. 450, f. 85); (5) A list of all the Acadians domiciled in Pennsylvania, June 20, 1763 (vol. 450, ff. 416–417); (6) Census of the neutral inhabitants from Acadia detained in various parts of Maryland (list of places given, July 7, 1763) (vol. 450, ff. 440–446); (7) Return of Acadians held in Maryland, including the names of certain prisoners, July 7, 1763 (vol. 450, f. 444).

Volumes 451–454, 1763. The correspondence between the Chevalier d'Éon de Beaumont, the Comte de Guerchy, the Duc de Praslin, and the French court, largely concerned with the cod fishery, as well as other matters resulting from the Treaty of Peace. France, it was felt, should make representations to Great Britain in view of the difficulties French fishermen faced, caused by the actions of certain English ship captains respecting the places along the shore where these fishermen could operate; also as issues that should be taken up with the British government were restrictions on the use of the wood of Newfoundland, for providing facilities for the drying of the fish, and the length of time French fishermen were permitted to remain each season on the island. Two other problems were also dealt with: the British insistence on the destruction of the fortifications of Dunkirk and the matter of the Catholic religion in Canada. Among the documents are the following: (1) List of Acadian prisoners on the River St. John and at Halifax, Aug. 12, 1763 (vol. 451, ff. 58–61); (2) A comprehensive list of Acadian families in New England and New York who want to go to France, Aug. 14, 1763 (vol. 451, ff. 77–79); (3) General lists of Acadian families in 1763 that were in the Kentucky country (spelled Konchtoket), also in South Carolina, and other British colonies (vol. 451, ff. 80–81, 125–126, and 208); (4) A general enumeration of Acadian families scattered within the British North American colonies, Nov. 22, 1763 (vol. 452, f. 205); (5) Memorandum to serve as instructions to the Comte de Guerchy going to Great Britain as French ambassador, Oct. 3, 1763 (vol. 451, ff. 337–348); (6) Mémoire on the Newfoundland fisheries, Nov. 9, 1763 (vol. 452, ff. 65–67); (7) A statement joined to a letter from Abbé de la Corne, Feb. 1763, concerning the free and perpetual exercise of the Catholic religion in Canada (vol. 453, ff. 95–100); (8) Ordinance of the king of France, June 3, 1763, proclaiming the ratification of the Treaty of Peace (vol. 453, f. 201).

Volumes 455–459, 1764. Correspondence between Guerchy, the Marquis Paul de Blosset, and the French court, chiefly over the problem of the Newfoundland fishery. The Treaty of Paris guaranteed to the French fishing rights off the coast of the island between Cape Bonavista and Point Riche. But as the maps of the different geographers varied as to these points, difficulties arose immediately. It therefore seemed necessary to determine the exact location of Point Riche. Further, the English set a date for the termination of the fishing season contrary to the Treaty. France on her part demanded an exclusive right to fish in the above area while Great Britain determined that the fishery should be carried out jointly by the two nations. Another problem involved in the correspondence was the liquidation of the Canadian paper money. Great Britain requested French cooperation to deal with this question and exploratory talks had begun. The following documents illustrate the nature of the issues presented: (1) A statement that Guerchy proposed to submit to the Earl of Halifax about the cod fisheries, 1764 (vol. 455, ff. 235–242); (2) Proposed convention respecting the cod fishery on the Newfoundland coasts, 1764 (vol. 455, ff. 391–396); (3) A report, 1764, relative to the location of Point Riche as indicated by art. 13 of the Treaty of Utrecht (vol. 456, ff. 296–312 and 380–381); (4) A statement of April 10, 1764, from the Society of Jesus, so as to obtain from the British court permission to carry out the decision of the Parlement of Paris respecting the possessions of this society in those American colonies ceded to the British by the Treaty of Paris (vol. 456, ff. 255–264); (5) A list of Frenchmen who have requested a prolongation beyond a year, stipulated in the Treaty of Peace, to sell their possessions in Canada, May 1764 (vol. 457, f. 152); (6) A general state of the losses of French ship-owners by fire and the pillage of their bateaux and their fisheries accommodations left behind on the Newfoundland coasts at the end of the fishing season, June 16, 1764 (vol. 457, ff. 241–243).

Volumes 460–461, 1764. The correspondence between Ambassador Guerchy and the French court. Although these volumes are also largely concerned with the cod fishery, they bring in other points. The chief documents are as follows: (1) A tabular view of the outlay of funds in Canada between the years 1750 and 1760. Estimate made on June 29, 1764 (vol. 460, f. 281); (2) A second statement from the creditors of the Jesuits on the subject of the Canadian possessions of the latter, Dec. 23, 1764 (vol. 461, ff. 208–210); (3) An outline of the coasts of Newfoundland from Cape Bonavista to Point Riche indicating the different harbors and their capacities as such for the fisheries, 1764 (vol. 461, f. 310); (4) Tabular view of equipped ships in the different ports of France for the cod fishery off the shores of Newfoundland, 1764 (vol. 461, f. 311).

Volumes 462–465, 1765. Again correspondence between Ambassador Guerchy and the French court in connection with which both the deliberations with the British government and the despatches relate chiefly to the Newfoundland fisheries. However, Canadian paper money also figures in these deliberations. Two documents may be noted: (1) The value of Canadian paper money in possession of British subjects at the time of the signature of the Treaty of Peace, based upon their declarations made under oath before the London Mayor, Jan. 1765 (vol. 462, f. 315); (2) A discussion of proposals based upon observations and declarations made in 1764 by the French owners of ships employed in the cod fisheries on those coasts of Newfoundland reserved to France by the Treaty of Utrecht (vol. 463, ff. 101–103).

Volumes 466–467, 1765. The correspondence between Ambassador Guerchy, Guy-Jean-Baptiste Target, Clément-Charles François de l'Averdy, and the French court. Again these papers relate chiefly to the cod fisheries although some of the letters are concerned with Canadian paper money, as the following document dated 1763 indicates: The value of the Canada paper money in possession of British subjects based upon their declaration made under oath before the Mayor of London in the month of January 1763 (vol. 467, f. 66).

Volume 468, 1765. Correspondence between Blosset, Choiseul and others likewise concerned with the fisheries and paper money. Three documents in this connection should be noted: (1) The resumé of a conference on the paper money of Canada between the Marquis de Fiennes and David Hume, 1765 (vol. 468, ff. 30–34); (2) Complaints of Great Britain against French fishermen, 1765 (vol.

468, ff. 121–130); (3) A mémoire about the liquidation of the paper money of Canada, 1765 (vol. 468, ff. 243–248).

Volume 469, 1766. The correspondence between Guerchy and others, and the French court, in which is summarized various conferences and the ratification of the agreement with Great Britain respecting the liquidation of the paper money of Canada. The fisheries are also touched upon as is indicated by the following mémoire: The French reply to the memoir presented Aug. 22, 1765 by David Hume, secretary to the British ambassador and British chargé des affaires, concerning the complaints voiced against the French fishermen (vol. 469, ff. 397–402).

Volumes 470–472, 1766. Correspondence between Guerchy, Durand, Choiseul, the British Secretary of State Henry Seymour Conway, and the Duke of Richmond. This is largely concerned with the fisheries and the French possessions of St. Pierre and Miquelon off Newfoundland, although the problem of the redemption of Canadian paper money is stressed because the chief British holders of it had united in order to make good their demands, while the French inhabitants in addressing the British government complained they were in danger of losing their possessions. One document may be noted: The state of the certificates given, Aug. 7, 1766, to the holders of Canadian paper money who proved, before the Lord Mayor of London and the respective commissioners of the two courts, British ownership of these certificates the preceding July 30.

Volumes 473–476, 1767. Correspondence between Guerchy, Durand, and the French court having to do with the many changes in personnel of the British government, also the agitation taking place in the British colonies is commented upon together with the friction created by the confusion over the exact location of Point Riche and the leaving behind in Newfoundland by the French fishermen of their salt designed to preserve the cod caught in the approaching season.

Volumes 477–481, 1768. Correspondence between Durand, the Comte du Châtelet-Lomont, Batailhé de Francès, and the French court, chiefly over the British colonial crisis, with British sloops of war patrolling the American shores and the inhabitants, jealous of their liberty, exasperated at the levying of taxes. The following documents are pertinent: (1) Memorandum to serve as instructions to Châtelet-Lomont going to England as ambassador, 1768 (vol. 477, ff. 30–41); (2) A letter from Boston dated July 11, 1768, indicating the causes of the discontent in the colonies with British policy (vol. 479, ff. 330–335); (3) State of the fisheries along the coasts of New England and those on the banks of Nova Scotia, 1753 (vol. 481, f. 196); (4) The New England whale fishery, 1753 (vol. 481, ff. 197–200); (5) Articles manufactured in America, 1768 (vol. 481, ff. 201–202); (6) A list of manufactured articles that America needs, 1768 (vol. 481, f. 203).

Volumes 482–485, 1768–1769. Correspondence between Châtelet-Lomont and the French court, especially with respect to the difficulties Great Britain is experiencing with her American colonies. Account is taken of the dream that France will take the place of Great Britain in American markets. The problem of the paper money of Canada and that of the fisheries are still the uppermost issues, especially as the French fishermen are facing new difficulties by the British claims to fish in different harbours even between Newfoundland and French islands of St. Pierre and Miquelon and especially the south of Cape Bonavista. The following documents bear upon the above themes: (1) Convention for the termination of the discussions over the paper money of Canada, 1766 (vol. 482, ff. 25–31); (2) A letter of Jan. 15, 1768, signed by Jean, Baron de Kalb, giving up his position in the French government as the result of the American agitation (vol. 484, ff. 3–5). *Note.* Although de Kalb was a German, "Johann Kalb" entered the French service in 1743. He "resigned" from the French service but in reality was sent to America by Choiseul as a secret agent and in 1768–1769 was in America sounding out the feeling of Americans toward the British government. In 1775 he received permission of the French government to volunteer in the American army but did not arrive, as the result of delays, until 1777. A major general in the American army he served with distinction and died as a prisoner of war in 1780 after the Battle of Camden; (3) A report on the Newfoundland fishery for the year 1769 (vol. 484, ff. 349–359); (4) A digest of the conference between the French King's ambassador and the Earl of Hillsborough, Secretary of State for the Colonies, over the troubles during the fishing season of 1769 as indicated by a memoir presented to the British ministry (vol. 484, ff. 398–405).

Volumes 486–491, 1769–1770. Correspondence between Châtelet-Lomont, Francès, and the French court, is chiefly concerned with the problem of the Canadian paper money in possession of the British, the redemption of which continues to be delayed. Further emphasized is the desire of French cod fishermen to obtain greater freedom of action. The documents concerning these problems are as follows: (1) A table indicating the export of the merchandise of Great Britain to her colonies in North America, excluding Canada, 1769 (vol. 486, ff. 9–10); (2) A statement presented to Lord Weymouth by the holders of acknowledgements of indebtedness [reconnaissances de dette] given in place of the paper money of Canada, accompanied by an explanation pointing out the actual difference

between the acknowledgement of indebtedness and a duly executed contract (entre la reconnaissance des effets et un contrat de
rentes constituées), April 12, 1769 (vol. 486, ff. 278–282); (3) A
reply to the proposal of the British court on the subject of the conversion into contracts of the certificates furnished as a substitute for
the paper money of Canada, May 6, 1769 (vol. 487, ff. 36–44,
49–66); (4) List of British possessors of these acknowledgements
of indebtedness with the total of their exchange value, as testified
to by the committee established in London, 1769 (vol. 487, f.
138); (5) A statement regarding the redemption of the Canadian
acknowledgements of indebtedness that are owned by the British,
with the conditions under which they can be exchanged, April
3, 1770 (vol. 491, ff. 302–303).

Volumes 492–499, 1770–1772. Correspondence between Châtelet-Lomont,
Charles-Jean Garnier, Francès, and Adrien-Louis de Bonnières,
Comte de Guines. Nothing new to record. The correspondence is
mostly concerned with the fisheries and the liquidation of Canadian
paper money. Beyond these major subjects there are demands
made upon the French ambassador to redress certain specific
grievances. The following documents pertain to these problems: (1) Request made by the owners of acknowledgements of
indebtedness (reconnaissances de dette), given in exchange for
the paper money of Canada, which Henry Seymour Conway sent
to the House of Commons, May 23, 1770 (vol. 492, ff. 126–133);
(2) Inventory of the "reconnaissances du papier-monnaie du
Canada" sent to Beaujon in Paris by Francès, 1770 (vol. 493, f.
109); (3) The agreement of Admiral George Anson to the transportation, the supplying with necessities, and the settlement of
Acadians at Môle de St.-Nicolas, Aug. 15, 1771 (vol. 497, ff. 150–
157, 172–175; vol. 499, ff. 5–6, 325); (4) A report dated Jan. 25,
1772, about what took place regarding the Newfoundland fisheries during the years 1767, 1768, and 1769 (vol. 498, ff. 162–164);
(5) The address of Gilles Hocquart to the Ministry to recover his
rights to Gros-Mécatinat in Canada, 1772 (vol. 498, ff. 183–196;
vol. 499, ff. 158–159); (6) A statement of the Marquis Pierre
Rigaud de Vaudreuil to the Duc d'Aiguillon requesting compensation from the British government for the loss of his property in
Canada in 1760, contrary to the spirit of the treaty of peace, with
an enumeration of those possessions, 1772 (vol. 499, ff. 53–60,
and 175–176).

Volumes 500–506, 1772–1774. Correspondence between Guines, Garnier,
and Boynes, chiefly concerned with the complaints of the French
fishermen, the vexation created by the conduct of the British, especially in the area about Cape Bonavista. Comment is also made
on the designs of Russia, Prussia, and Austria to partition Poland,

and on the hostility shown by the American colonists toward Great Britain; there were also noted many individual requests submitted to the British ministry, through the interposition of the French ambassador, for indemnification for or return of certain possessions. The more important documents concerning the above are the following: (1) A letter from Garnier, Sept. 25, 1772, about the desire of Russia, Prussia, and Austria to partition Poland (vol. 500, ff. 141–148); (2) Mémoire about certain articles of commerce which Great Britain would trade duty free with France, 1773 (vol. 501, ff. 328–329); (3) State of the fisheries upon the coasts of Newfoundland and the Grand Banks respecting both the dried and green cod fishery in the year 1773 (vol. 503, ff. 416–422); (4) Statement about French ships employed in the cod fishery on the shores of Newfoundland, on the Grand Bank, and at St. Pierre and Miquelon, with the yield in the year 1773 (vol. 503, ff. 423–429); (5) The political situation respecting the dry cod fishery upon the coasts of Newfoundland at the end of 1773 (vol. 503, ff. 430–433); (6) Garnier's letter, June 7, 1774, to the minister, announcing that the inhabitants of the British colonies have dumped the British tea into the water (vol. 505, ff. 266–271); (7) A summary of the Quebec Act of 1774 for regulating the government of Canada with some critical observations on this law (vol. 505, f. 357).

Volumes 507–510, 1775. Letters from Garnier about the efforts to solve the problem of the Newfoundland fishery and developments in America. They make clear that the Americans are in revolt and that engagements have already taken place between the rebels and the British troops. The following documents bear upon the above: (1) State of the commerce of Great Britain and the North American colonies between 1770 and 1772 (vol. 507, ff. 126–127); (2) A report concerning the sale by Hocquart to Sieur Michel Chartier de Lotbinière of the Gros-Mécatinat concession, 1774 (vol. 507, ff. 213–214); (3) Letter written Dec. 19, 1774, informing the minister that the Anglo-American colonials have formed a confederation and have created a congress to govern themselves. The letter also contains extracts of representations made by the colonies to the government of Great Britain (vol. 507, ff. 320–331); (4) Garnier's letter to the minister, May 19, 1775, in the course of which it deals with the motion made by Charles Pratt, Lord Camden, demanding the repeal of the Quebec Act (vol. 510, ff. 112–124); (5) Guines's letter of June 26, 1775, which mentioned the fact that the American rebels have captured Fort Ticonderoga and are marching against Crown Point (vol. 510, ff. 310–314).

Volumes 511–513, 1775. Correspondence between Guines and the French court. Most of the despatches relate to the war in America between the British and colonials. In his letters the French ambassador in London informs his government of everything he can learn pertaining to the situation in America: about the capture of Ticonderoga, Colonel Preston's defeat of a group of rebels marching upon Montreal, the sending of General Howe by General Gage to seize Roxbury, the attack on Canada by Montgomery and Benedict Arnold, and the sending by the colonies of representatives to England who were not listened to. Some of the letters also comment on the friction between Spain and Portugal on the subject of their respective colonies. Among the documents are the following: (1) Letter of the American Continental Congress, Aug. 4, 1775, to Canadians inviting them to embrace the American cause (vol. 511, ff. 218–220); (2) A letter of Aug. 18, 1775, mentioning the fact that Richard Penn, deputy governor of Pennsylvania, had arrived in England with a petition from the Continental Congress (vol. 511, ff. 277–283); (3) Letter of John Hancock, President of the Congress, Philadelphia, Nov. 25, 1775, concerning the petition the Congress presented to the government of Great Britain (vol. 513, ff. 25–26); (4) Letter to the French minister from Baron de Lespérance, Dec. 5, 1775, with a description of the islands of St. Pierre and Miquelon (vol. 513, ff. 59–64); (5) A general state of the commerce of Canada in 1775 (vol. 513, f. 368).

Volumes 514–515, 1776. Correspondence between Guines, the Comte d'Alby, Garnier, and the French court with respect to the advantageous position of the American states in their struggle against Great Britain to gain their cause; the failure to regulate fisheries is also mentioned. The principal documents are the following: (1) A report regarding the Newfoundland fisheries during the 1769 season (vol. 514, ff. 182–189); (2) Reply of Gov. John Byron and Capt. Sir Hugh Palliser to the complaints about the Newfoundland fisheries embodied in the French mémoires received April 9, 1770 (vol. 514, ff. 194–200); (3) A statement presented by Pierre Roubaud dealing with his life, which was sent with a letter from Garnier dated March 8, 1776 (vol. 515, ff. 66–75); (4) Garnier's letter of March 8, 1776, mentions the proposal of Pierre Roubaud advocating a union of France and England for combating the rebellious colonials. Garnier stresses the necessity of freeing himself from this undesirable individual (vol. 515, ff. 78 and 344–347); (5) Extract from the British court *Gazette* reproducing a communique of Jan. 25, 1776, from Philadelphia and rehearsing in detail the fruitless attack of Arnold in his attempt to capture Quebec (vol. 515, ff. 105–106); (6) Garnier's letter of March 11, 1776, mentioning the death of General Montgomery and the fact that Great Britain now calls the American government the Continental Congress (vol. 515, ff. 116–120); (7) Copies of instructions given to the Newfoundland governor with reference to the right of the French to fish on the coasts of the island (vol. 515, ff. 264–269).

Volumes 516–518, 1776. Correspondence between Ambassador Garnier and the French court which makes clear the ever greater resistance of the Americans against the British and the failure of General Howe to achieve success. It stresses the fact that the latter has been obliged to abandon Boston and that the British government looks at the Howe campaign with a jaundiced eye, while pointing out the lack of success of the Americans in seeking to conquer Canada. Among the documents are the following: (1) Letter from Garnier to the minister, May 3, 1776, commenting on the conduct of Roubaud (vol. 516, ff. 8–9); (2) The same to the same, May 13, informing the French government of the possibility that Spain may invade Portugal before Great Britain could come to the aid of the latter (vol. 516, ff. 133–136); (3) The same to the same, May 31, indicating that Great Britain is about to rule on the claim of Michel Chartier de Lotbinière with respect to the loss of his Canadian property (vol. 516, ff. 247–248); (4) The same to the same, June 4, announcing the defeat of Arnold before Quebec (vol. 516, ff. 270–273); (5) A letter of Sir Guy Carleton to Lord Germain, May 14, advising him that the Americans had raised the siege of Quebec with the arrival of reinforcements from Great Britain (vol. 516, ff. 320–322); (6) Carleton's letter to Howe, Jan. 12, 1776, advising him of the defeat of General Montgomery before Quebec (vol. 516, ff. 323–325); (7) Memorandum by "Pic-de-Père" on the value of the money in use in the English continental colonies and the islands of America with respect to their circulation within the colonies themselves and in the French colonies, 1776 (vol. 517, ff. 66–92); (8) Garnier's letter to the minister, Oct. 18, 1776, with news about the war in the colonies and mentioning the reasons for the recall of Carleton (vol. 518, ff. 288–297).

Mémoires et Documents, 1592–1805

AMÉRIQUE, 1592–1785

Volume 9. Part 1, 1749–1750. Recommendations directed to the minister with respect to the administration of the colonies, together with the correspondence between France and Great Britain about the return of Cape Breton to France and proposals for the exchange of prisoners taking place in the colonies of the New World.

Volume 9. Part 2, 1750–1752. This volume concerns especially Acadia. Here is a description of the country and reports about enterprises to be launched in order to establish and preserve this place; one of the reports in it also refers to the respective claims of the French and of the English to lands in America. In this volume there is a collection of collated and legal papers concerned with French claims in North America, with the boundaries of New France, that is, Canada with Acadia. These papers were found in the secretariat of the Chateau Saint-Louis and in the office of intendant at Quebec, a search for which was made in 1750 by order of Antoine-Louis Rouillé, Comte Jouy, minister and secretary of state of the Marine (pp. 444–450).

Volume 10, Part 1, 1753–1756. This volume is also concerned with claims and counter claims to Acadia or Nova Scotia. The following documents should be noted: (1) The cost of supporting the Nova Scotia establishment, 1751–1753 (pp. 19–38); (2) Standing order for the care and the training of crews of ships sent to the American colonies, 1753 (pp. 38–63); (3) The capitulation accorded to the British troops at Fort Necessity by Louis Coulon de Villiers, 1754 (pp. 114–125); (4) Account of the capture of the ship *Alcide*, 1755 (pp. 152–155); (5) An account of what happened in Canada: the defeat of Dieskau, 1755 (pp. 180–196).

Volume 10, Part 2, 1756–1771. There are many accounts in this volume of military campaigns and of the issuing of ordinances concerned with a variety of subjects, especially with bills of exchange, the payment of debts, and the liquidation of Canadian paper money. The following documents bear upon the themes: (1) Sieur de Léry's expedition against Fort Bull, 1756 (pp. 305–308); (2) The capture of the Oswego forts, 1756 (pp. 315–331); (3) A brief description of the British possessions in North America, 1757 (pp. 332–345); (4) A joint letter from Vaudreuil and Montcalm concerning the Fort William Henry campaign, Nov. 10, 1757 (pp. 368–376); (5) Part of a letter dated July 28, 1758, written on board H.M.S. *Burford* and published in the *London Chronicle* of Aug. 24, 1758, about the Louisbourg campaign (pp. 377–384); (6) A proposal for the division of North America between the French, the British and the Spaniards, 1759 (pp. 389–393); (7) The condition of wounded French officers in connection with the battle of Quebec who were taken to the general hospital, Sept. 13, 1759 (pp. 398–403).

Volume 11, 1717–1769. Here in this volume are letters patent, decrees, and ordinances relating especially to the trade of the French colonies, the entrance and departure of merchant ships, the bonding and freight of merchandise and discipline of ship crews. The following documents may be noted: (1) The monthly charges faced by an officer who would live decently in Canada, Jan. 20, 1759 (pp. 83–84); (2) A table of expenses involved in maintaining Canada for the years 1750 to 1760 (p. 121).

Volumes 12–20, 1720–1785. These volumes are concerned among other things with the activities of the Compagnie des Indes and of the foreign trade of the French islands.

Volumes 21–23, 1686–1766. These volumes relate to the boundaries of the French colonies in America, in particular to Acadia or Nova Scotia, and to the liquidation of the colonial paper money; there is also a report on the North America fisheries (vol. 22).

Volume 24, 1518–1759. This volume concerns the long rivalry between France and England. It includes two short accounts of the discoveries of the French and the English in America; there is also a rather long report on the trade and navigation of the colonies and some extracts from reports and letters relating to the Treaty of Utrecht; finally a number of unpublished documents which discuss French claims to territory on the Ohio, the boundaries of Acadia, and the problems that both Canada and Louisiana presented to France in 1759. Among the reports may be noted that by de la Galissonière in 1751 about the French colonies in North America, with reflections on this report (pp. 180–228).

Volume 25, 1760–1763. This volume is made up also of unpublished reports and observations on them; it contains descriptions of the French and British possessions in North America, with the importance to both France and Great Britain. There is also a report having to do with the perpetual free exercise of the Roman Catholic religion in Canada with extracts from letters of Abbé de la Corne on this subject.

ANGLETERRE, 1661–1805

Volume 13, 1495–1818. This volume is devoted to the history of the Newfoundland fisheries and includes treaties concluded between France and England (as well as later Great Britain), a discussion of fishing rights and the limits imposed on each of the powers in exercising them, together with observations on the islands of St. Pierre and Miquelon.

Volume 19, 1765. In this volume is to be found a memorandum with the title, "Réflexions sur le changement qui vient d'arriver dans le ministère d'Angleterre."

Volume 41, 1755–1760. This volume contains plans and memoranda submitted to the minister relating to the problems that France and Great Britain faced with respect to their American possessions. The discussion and negotiations between the two powers had as an objective the settlement of the limits of these possessions and the preparation of a future treaty of peace that would lay down the limits of Acadia, Canada, and the Ohio country and the disposition of the islands of St. Vincent, St. Lucia, Dominica, and Tobago. Among the documents presented that should be noted is the treaty entered into on Feb. 6, 1759, between His Most Christian Majesty and His Britannic Majesty, which relates to the treatment of soldiers who were either sick, wounded, or taken prisoners of war.

Volume 42, 1761. This volume contains the observations of François de Bussy, French envoy, upon negotiations in progress in London with the British and of the plan of the latter to continue the war.

Volume 47, 1713–1805. A part of this volume is devoted to Acadia and the problems caused by the Acadian migrations. One report relates to the origin and continuance of "la nation acadienne," up to 1777. There are also letters and memoranda having to do with the demands submitted to the King of England by French Canadians for their rights and particularly for the re-establishment in Canada of the ancient French laws. Among these papers one document may be noted under title, "Origine des troubles du Canada, 1754" (pp. 64–83).

Volume 48, 1762–1810. Here is to be found outlined the preliminary articles of peace agreed upon between France and Great Britain together with royal ordinances of the king, Nov. 23, 1762, as to the terms agreed upon for the cessation of hostilities on the sea. There is also a mémoire having to do with the cod fishery on the shores of Newfoundland accorded to France by treaties.

Volume 56, 1750–1810. In this volume is the report of Pierre Roubaud under title, "Histoire du mémoire sur l'alliance de l'Angleterre et de la France, et des suites, qu'il a eues," dated London, Feb. 29, 1775 (pp. 56–93).

BIBLIOTHÈQUE NATIONALE

Beginning as the Bibliothèque du Roi in the course of the French Revolution this great library acquired its present name, the Bibliothèque Nationale, and also vast accessions of manuscripts from the sequestered libraries of the émigrés. Since then, the Bibliothèque Nationale has continued to expand and has become one of the greatest library centers in the world. Waldo G. Leland in his *Guide to Materials for American History in the Libraries and Archives of Paris* (Washington, D.C., 1932), has described the manuscript resources most pertinent for the period in the life of the British Empire under examination, with the volume number and, where given, the folio. Starting with the Manuscrits Français (Fonds Français) they are as follows:

Manuscrits Français (Fonds Français)

4586. 1776, Apr. 4, 11. Register of the destruction of Canadian paper and card money, conformably to decrees of June 29, 1765 and Jan. 17, 1776 (copy) [f. 122].

6233–6256. Colonization of French Guiana, 1763–1764 [1775], 24 vols.

6431. Papers of the Abbé Guillaume-Thomas Raynal. Memoirs relating to commerce, 1725–1771. Prices in the branches of the Compagnie des Indes: Canada, prices of beaver; West Indies, prices of raw products taken in exchange for Senegal negroes. [f. 184]. 1774. Extracts from replies by ——— Payte to queries by the Earl of Dartmouth respecting the English possessions in North America, and remarks on the Virgin Islands (English) [ff. 188–197].

7719. Extract from the register of the Cour des Aides, 1630–1779. 1757, Sept. 30. Invitation to attend a Te Deum in celebration of the victories of Montcalm in Canada [f. 531].

8290–8293. "Précis des delibérations des États [de Bretagne], 1567–1762." This précis is an analysis arranged alphabetically by subjects, of the proceedings of the États de Bretagne. The proceedings themselves, procès-verbaux, are in the Archives Départementales, Ille-et-Vilaine, at Rennes. The entries pertinent to the period 1748–1776 are:

> 1748, Oct. 3; 1750, Nov. 5; 1752, Oct. 12; 1754, Oct. 26; 1756, Dec. 12; 1758, Dec. 24. Opposition to foreign commerce in the colonies.
>
> 1759, Feb. 17. Demand that beaver trade in Canada be free.
>
> 1760, Sept. 15. Opposition to foreign commerce in the colonies.
>
> 1760, Oct. 27. Demand that the beaver trade in Canada be free; reply to argument of Compagnie des Indes.
>
> 1762, Sept. 8. Opposition to foreign commerce in the colonies.

8306–8307. "Précis par ordre de matières des mémoires, pièces et rapports de Commissions déposés au greffe des États [de Bretagne]: Under the title *Commerce,* a few documents bearing on American matters are noted as follows:

> 1760, July 16. Memoir by the Compagnie des Indes respecting exclusive trade in beaver.
>
> 1770. Memoir respecting foreign commerce in the colonies.

8968. Draft of an edict in 36 articles providing distinctive marks for free people of color and for slaves in the French colonies, by Douin, 1775, with explanatory comments [ff. 3–34].

10569. 1763, Nov. 28. Petition of the Sieur Le Loutre, missionary in Acadia, in the case brought on appeal against the seminary of the Missions Étrangères by Girard and Manach, former missionaries in Acadia [f. 159].

10716. 1760, Sept. "Mémoire sur la France et l'Angleterre," by François de Chaumont. Comparison of France and England; necessity of falling back on Louisiana if Canada should be lost [f. 27].

10764–10770. Papers of Beliardi, 1758–1770. Beliardi was an Italian who served in the French foreign service in Spain and France from 1758 to 1771. His journal of correspondence, 1758–1766, gives information on the Great War for the Empire (in vol. *10764*). His later papers (vols. *10765–10770*) deal with commercial topics and the problems of the aggressiveness of the British Empire and French relations with Spain, 1765–1770.

10991–11082. Collection relating to the Chambre des Comptes, formed by Clément de Boissy.

> *11056.* 1749. Account of receipts and expenditures for the colonies: Canada, Île Royale, Louisiana [ff. 91–97].
>
> 1603–1785. Chronological list of edicts, letters patent, arrêts, déclarations, regulations, etc. [ff. 99–117v].
>
> 1749–1777. Extracts from proceedings of the Chambre des Comptes [ff. 119–132].
>
> *11061.* 1664–1785. Chronological list of edicts, arrêts, letters patent, déclarations, etc., relating to the Compagnie des Indes [ff. 349–372].

11248. 1758, July 15, Carillon. Letter from the Chevalier de Lévis, with plans of Fort Carillon. 1758, Oct. 19, "Nouvelles du Canada du Camp de Carillon." "Relation de la victoire remportée par les troupes du Roy à Carillon le 8 juillet 1758" [ff. 247–265]. Cf *N.Y. Col. Doc.* X, 741.

11300–11301. Correspondence and original documents relating to the marine and the artillery, 1716–1778 [*11301*, ff. 4 and 11].

11334–11339. Minutes of proceedings and correspondence of the commission appointed in accordance with the arrêt of Oct. 18, 1758, to examine and verify the debts of the marine, 1758–1761.

11340–11341. "Recueil de mémoires concernant la Marine de France," 1758–1760. A prefatory note states that the memoirs in this collection have been inspired by the disorder into which the marine had fallen in 1758.

> *11340.* "Mémoire contre les Projets des Anglois sur nos Colonies

Méridionales de l'Amérique, par M. de la Galissonnière," n.d. [pp. 1–66].

> 1758, Feb. "Mémoire sur l'État présent de la Marine du Roy," by M. Le Normant [pp. 69–114].
>
> 1751. "Mémoire sur les Colonies de la France dans l'Amérique Septentrionale." Utility of the colonies: American colonies are attached to and profitable to France; necessity of fortifying Canada and Louisiana as a barrier to the English colonies, which, if not held in check, will eventually possess the continent and the islands [pp. 507–561].

11342. "Mémoire sur l'arrêt du Conseil du XV Octobre 1759 concernant le payement des lettres de change tirées des Colonies françaises de l'Amérique sur les Trésoriers desdites Colonies" [pp. 91–175].

> "Mémoire dans lequel on propose quelques moyens de rétablir le crédit des lettres de change des Colonies et de les rendre moins onéreux à l'Etat" [pp. 175–194].
>
> 1758, Aug. 12; 1759, May 16, Oct. 25. Three letters from Bigot to Berryer [pp. 199–236].

12224. "Mémoire sur la Louisiane et sur l'Amérique en général" [Post 1759]. Commerce before the war, utility of Louisiana to French manufacturers and for the maintenance of the French West Indies, cultivation of tobacco [pp. 325–342].

Here is another memoir on Louisiana. It is concerned with population, agriculture, Negroes, tobacco cultivation, cattle raising, and timber [pp. 349–362].

> "État des dépenses de la Louisiane (two copies) [pp. 365–375].
> [1756] "Mémoire sur la rivière de l'Amérique Septentrionale dite Oyo ou Ouabache par le Sr. d[e] l[a] G[range] d[e] C[hessieux], avocat au Parlement, auteur de la Conduite des François justifiée" [pp. 377–400].

13068. [c. 1761] "Précis pour le sieur, Penniseauld, cy-devant intéressé dans la traité des vivres du Canada contre M. le Procureur du Roy" [ff. 96–103v].

13359. "Introduction à la Géographie," 1773. Contains sections relating to America, New France, New England, Florida, Mexico, California, West Indies, South America, etc. [ff. 101 *et seq.*].

13373. Papers of Père Louis Bertrand Castel with letters (mostly of the year 1750) from missionaries relating to the search for a passage to China, by way of Hudson Bay [ff. 1–108].

14265–14278. General table of edicts and ordinances relating to the marine, 1661–1756.

14609. "Traité de la défense et de la conservation des colonies par M.

Dumas, Brigadier des Armées du Roy, ancien commandant des Isles de France et de Bourbon, 1775" [p. 8 *et seq.*]. References to the loss of Canada, the importance of Louisbourg, commerce of the former American colonies, etc.

14610. Same as *14609* but with the addition of an autobiography of the author, Dumas, setting forth his services in Acadia, on the Ohio, at Montreal and Quebec, 1752–1756.

16207. — [1773]. Memoir in defense of the conduct of François Bigot as intendent of Canada, with special reference to the charges on which he was tried and condemned in 1763. Presented in support of his petition for revision of his case [ff. 47–129]. [1773]. Petition of François Bigot to the King, appealing from the sentence against him of Dec. 10, 1763, and praying for a revision of his case [ff. 134–136v].

21813–22060. Archives of the Chambre Syndicale de la Librairie et Imprimerie de Paris (17th and 18th centuries). Censorship reports. See especially vol. *22014*, censorship reports 1767–1788 on works for which license or permission was requested.

Manuscrits Français, Nouvelles Acquisitions

This large collection of papers is also in the Bibliothèque Nationale. It is numbered separately. Those manuscripts that fall within the period 1748–1776 and have a bearing on the British Empire are as follows:

126. [Post 1752]. Memoir on the services and administration of the naval port and arsenal of Rochefort. By the Intendant of Rochefort (copy).

1041. 1759, Dec. "Mémoire fait dans l'intervalle entre la prise de Québec et celle de Montréal par ordre de M. le Duc de Choiseul, et dont ce ministre me dit avoir lu au feu Roy un extrait à la même époque." By [Jean Louis] Favier. Object of the memoir is to point out the consolation for the inevitable loss of her North American possessions that France may find in the increased strength and growing desire for independence of the English colonies in America [ff. 44–63].

1217. "Journal de la première campagne que j'ai faite sur le vaisseau du Roy, *Le Formidable,* commandé par M. de Macnemara et ensuite par M. le comte Du Guay." 1754, Dec. 11; 1755, Sept. 3. Transport of troops to America; capture of the *Alcide* by Boscawen, etc.

4156. "Voyage au Canada dans le nord de l'Amérique Septentrionale fait depuis l'an 1751 à 1761. Par J.C.B. Descriptions of the towns of Canada, customs of the French inhabitants and the Indians; also an account of the loss of New France.

5214. Letters, 1756, May 8, 13, 16, 23, June 1, Dunkirk [F.C.] Bart to Machault, minister of marine. News of military movements in America; declaration of war between England and France, etc. [ff. 40–45].

1766, July 9; 1767, Apr. 8, Dec. 10, New Orleans or Balize. Ulloa, Spanish governor of Louisiana, to Bory, *capitaine de vaisseau*, at Paris. Visit to the frontier of Louisiana, personal affairs, forts, relations with the English, etc. (A.L.S.) [ff. 78–83].

6464–6497. Collection of notes, extracts and transcripts made by H. Doniol for his *Histoire de la Participation de la France à l'Établissement des États-Unis d'Amérique.* Collection covers the years 1774–1785. *6464.* Transcriptions by Doniol from the Archives, Ministère des Affaires Étrangères, Correspondance Politique, Angleterre, vols. *506–513* (1774–1775). *6465. Idem,* vols. *514–16* (1776, Jan.–May). *6466. Idem,* vols. *517–19* (1776, June–Dec.). *6471.* Archives, Ministère des Affaires Étrangères, Correspondance Politique, États-Unis, vols *1–2* (1775–1777). *6481. Idem,* Supplément, vols. *1, 3;* Mémoires et Documents, États-Unis, vols. *1–4* (1765–1789). *6482.* Archives, Ministère des Affaires Étrangères, Correspondance Politique, Espagne, vols. 573–8 (1774–1775). *6483. Idem,* vols. *579–82* (1776). *6494.* Archives, Ministère des Affaires Étrangères, various series; Archives Nationales; Bibliothèque Nationale; miscellaneous. (1774–1795).

COLLECTION MARGRY

Among the so-called Nouvelles Acquisitions in the Bibliothèque Nationale is the collection of 255 volumes formed by the writer Pierre Margry (1818–1894) that are concerned with French New World expansion (vols. 9255–9510). The importance of these copies of manuscripts among other things lies in the fact that in many cases the originals have disappeared. Among the Margry transcriptions that relate to the period 1748–1776 are the following:

9273. Canada. *Collection de Mémoires et de Relations.* Published by the Quebec Literary and Historical Society (Quebec, 1840). See especially *Considerations sur l'État présent du Canada,* 1758 (f. 383).

9281. Acadia. 1603–1760. Notes, extracts, copies, and correspondence [ff. 40 to end of volume].

9283. Acadia. 1605–1752. Rough notes, extracts of memoirs, etc., chiefly from Archives des Colonies [ff. 1–396].

9286. Exploration of the West, 1663–1753. Extracts and copies of letters and memoirs relating to western posts and explorations, 1750–

1753: De Noyelle, journal of Legardeur de St. Pierre, 1750 and others [ff. 219–246, 265, 280].

9306. Canada, 1756–1757. Notes, extracts, copies of correspondence, memoirs, etc., of Bigot, Vaudreuil, Dieskau, and others taken mainly from Arch. Colonies, C¹¹A and Arch. Guerre, Corr., *3417*. Some are printed in *N.Y. Col. Docs.*

9307. Canada, 1757–1758. Chiefly copies of documents from Arch. Guerre, Corr., *3457, 3498, 3499.*

9309. Cessions of Louisiana, 1762–1804. Extracts and copies of correspondence and memoirs.

> 1769. Mar. 10, Versailles. "Idée sur l'opposition trouvée par les Espagnols à la Louisiane," by d'Estaing [f. 11].

9341. Compagnie des Indes in the eighteenth century. [1749] "Mémoire pour La France, servant à la découverte des Terres Australes," by Bénard de la Harpe [f. 370].

9400–9404. Marine of Louis XV, 1733–1774. Rough notes, extracts, etc., chiefly from Arch. Marine. Occasional references to the Mississippi, Louisiana, Louisbourg, Canada, etc.

9405. Bougainville. "Journal de l'expédition de l'Amérique commencé en l'année 1756, le 15 mars." The second part of this document deals with the campaign of Baron Dieskau of 1755 (copy, incomplete). [ff. 1–8].

"Journal des Campagnes faites en Canada pendant trois années, 1756, 1757 et 1758. . . ." By Louis Antoine, Comte de Bougainville. (Copy, ending June 22, 1758) [ff. 9–385]. See R. de Kérallain: *Les Français au Canada: la Jeunesse de Bougainville et la Guerre de Sept Ans* (1896). Note on the cost of the war in Canada, 1750–1760 [f. 385v].

9406. Bougainville. "Précis de ce qui s'est passé de plus considérable dans l'Amérique septentrionale pendant l'hiver de 1756 à 1757" [f. 34].

"Relation abrégée de la campagne du Canada jusqu'au 1ᵉʳ 7bre 1756," by Bougainville [ff. 38–40].

1756–1759. Letters from Bougainville to his brother, and to his mother, Mme. Hérault de Séchelles [ff. 42–45 *et seq.*].

"Carte des environs du fort de Carillon en Canada, à Madame la Marquise de Pompadour" [f. 50].

1757–1758. Letters from Montcalm to Mme. Hérault de Séchelles, also to the brother of Bougainville and to others [f. 53 *et seq.*].

"Relation de l'Expédition et prise du fort Guillaume Henry, le 9 aoust 1757." (Fragment) [f. 75].

"Journal de la Campagne de 1758 commencé le 23 juin," ending with "Journal de Navigation de Québec en France," Nov. 11. A note by Margry states that this is the copy of a MS loaned to him by M. de Bougainville [ff. 118–219].

"Mémoires depuis le 15 9bre 1758." The narratives by Bougainville commencing, respectively, "Je partis de Québec le 15 9bre 1758 . . ." and "Je partis de St. Malo le 22 7bre 1763 . . ." [ff. 226–233].

"Relation de la victoire remportée à Carillon par les troupes du Roy, le 8 juillet, 1758" [f. 241].

"Campagne de 1759." Narrative commencing May 23, "La crainte où l'on était . . ." [ff. 250–260].

"Relation du Siège de Québec," commencing "Depuis que les Anglais ont commencé les hostilités . . ." and ending "secours de toutes espèces dans cette colonie" [ff. 262–273].

"Relation de ce qui s'est passé à Québec en 1759" [ff. 274–279v].

"Journal fait par le Sr. Laforce, commandant les bâtiments sur le lac Ontario, du Siège de Niagara, du 6 juillet jusqu'au 14 dud" [ff. 280–283v].

1758, Dec. 29, Versailles. "Mémoire. Graces que demande M. le M'is de Montcalm comme graces à lui personnelles pour des Officiers de la Colonne ou Canadiens qui ont bien servi sous ses ordres." By Bougainville [ff. 284–284v].

1759, Sept. 2, "du Camp de Lorette." Narrative by Bougainville of the campaign of 1759, commencing "Voici mon histoire abrégé . . ." [ff. 286–291].

1759, Feb. 8. "Second Mémoire. Examen du projet de faire passer les habitans du Canada à la Louisiane" [ff. 298–302v]. Memoir proposing the transfer of the Canadians to Louisiana, and promising to develop the plan more fully in a later memoir. Memoirs exposing the advantages to France of abandoning Canada for Louisiana [ff. 305–320].

1761, July 15. Memoir on the boundaries of Louisiana in the event of the cession of Canada to England [ff. 321–321v].

1763–1764. Extracts from Arch. Affaires Étrangères: Letters of La Corn, d'Éon, de Guerchy, and Praslin; also notes on Canadian chronology [ff. 329, 336–341].

1743, May 5–Dec. 31, 1753. "Mémoire pour servir à l'histoire de ma vie," by the Marquis de Montcalm [ff. 342–353].

"Éloge historique du Marquis de Montcalm" [f. 354].

"Notice sur mon frère le Sauvage," par M. de Mun, secrétaire d'Ambassade au Brésil. Account of an Indian reputed to be the son of Bougainville [ff. 367–370].

9407. Bougainville: Copies, notes etc., from Bougainville's journals of voyages in the Pacific and around the world, 1766–1769.

9408. Bougainville: Original papers.

> 1758, Oct. 16, Carillon. "Observations Diverses sur Carillon, Fort Frédéric, et la frontière du Lac Champlain," by Desandrouins [ff. 7–9].
>
> Note on the St. John River [f. 10].
>
> 1759, Sept. 18, Duraurepay [?] to Bougainville [f. 12].
>
> [1760]"État général des officiers de trouppes de terre, de la Colonie, de la Melice, et des soldats de chaque corps qui ont été tués ou Blessés à La Bataille du 28 avril" [Ste. Foy?] [f. 19].
>
> 1761, June 27, Paris. H. Stanley to ———, transmitting reply he has received from England, that the capitulation of Canada should not be "further frustrated" [f. 20].

9410. La Pérouse and the marine, 1741–1763. Biographical notes on La Jonquière, Taffanel, and Hocquart [ff. 33–39].

> 1757, June 29, Aug. 8, 25, Sept. 17, harbours of Louisbourg or Quebec. Capt. Montalais to the minister of marine. Sickness on the vessels [ff. 145–148].
>
> 1758, June 29, on board the *Dragon.* Capt. Du Chaffault de Besné to the minister of marine. Account of the attack on Louisbourg by the English [ff. 160–163].
>
> 1758, Aug. 30, Sept. 25. Lists of vessels in Canadian waters [ff. 168–169].
>
> 1762, July 7, 9, 10, Oct. 15, 25. Letters from the Chevalier de Ternay respecting his expedition against Newfoundland [ff. 275, 284].

"Journal de ce qui s'est passé à St. Jean depuis le 8 7bre jusqu'au 15 du même mois, jour de mon départ." [By the Chevalier de Ternay] [f. 282].

9412. La Pérouse and the marine, 1761–1771. Contains a few translations of articles in English newspapers on the American colonies.

9414. La Pérouse and the marine, 1771–1786.

> 1774, Dec. 26, Amsterdam. Maillet du Clairon to the minister. Effect produced in Amsterdam by the resolutions adopted by the American colonies [f. 240].

9415. La Pérouse and the marine, 1775–1776.

> 1776, Apr. 30, Fort Royal, Martinique. D'Argout to ———. Lack of cattle caused by troubles in New England [f.179].
>
> 1776, Dec. 30, Versailles. [Minister of Marine] to the Comte Du Chaffault. Protection to American insurgent vessels must be accorded in such a way as to avoid appearance of so doing [f. 255].

9427. Marine of Louis XVI: de Ternay and La Pérouse.

> 1762. Instructions from the king, and letter from the minister of marine, Apr. 12, to de Ternay, with regard to his expedition against Newfoundland [ff. 58, 61v].

9428. Marine of Louis XVI: d'Estaing.

> 1769, May 10, Versailles. "Idée sur l'opposition trouvée par les Espagnols à La Louisiane," by d'Estaing [ff. 120–123v].

9487. Miscellany.

> [c. 1748]. Instructions to Chabert. Copy of draft in the hand of La Galissonnière [f. 90].

> 1748, Aug. 30. "Projet d'observation astronomique pour constater la position de l'entrée du golfe de St. Laurent . . . ," by M. de Chabert, ensign [f. 92].

> 1750, Dec. 12, Paris. La Galissonnière to M. de Chabert, respecting the latter's observations.

9495. 1760, Oct. 2. Representation by Solignac and Cabarrus, merchants of Louisbourg, ruined by the company of Bigot [f. 178].

End of the Margry Collection but continuation of Nouvelles Acquisitions.

11651. Narrative of the voyage of the *Étoile*, commanded by Chesnard de la Giraudais, and the *Aigle*, commanded by Duclos-Guyot, to the Falkland Islands and Straits of Magellan, 1765–1766.

20088. Marine and Colonies.

> 1757. Fragment of a relation of the sending of envoys of the Five Nations to Montreal [f. 18].

> [1759]. "Requeste des principaux habitans et négocians de Québec à Mrs. les Commandants et officiers majors de la ville de Québec." Lack of provisions, weakness of the garrison, and the necessity of a capitulation [f. 19].

> 1759, Sept. 15, Quebec. Procès-verbal of council of war [f. 20v].

> 1759, Sept. 18. Capitulation of Quebec [f. 22v].

> 1759, Sept. 21, Quebec. Bernier, commissaire des guerres, to de Ramezay, respecting lack of provisions at the General Hospital, and his conversation on the subject with the English general [f. 24].

> 1759, July 25. Second manifesto of General Wolfe; also map in colors of Fort Carillon and its environs. Order from Montcalm to Bougainville, from camp at Point Lévis [ff. 26v–28].

> 1763. Memoir of the inhabitants and merchants of Rochefort, desiring the establishment of an entrepôt and permis-

sion to trade directly with the French colonies of America and with the coast of Guinea [f. 32].

20536. 1753, Sept. 11. "Avis des députés du Commerce sur le mémoire de Mrs. les Fermiers generaux No. 3214 au sujet de l'entrée dans les pais conquis des cuirs secs provenant des colonies françaises." Memoirs and other documents relative to the fisheries, duty on fish, etc. [ff. 132, 213 *et seq.*].

20539. 1752. Memoirs and other documents dealing with trade in *eau-de-vie* to Canada, syrup from the West Indies, etc. [ff. 83, 86 *et seq.*].

20542. 1757. "Mémoire sur quelques articles relatifs au Canada et à son Commerce" [ff. 64–88].

22101. Papers of M. d'Hermand, French consul at Lisbon, Madrid and elsewhere.

1763. Memoir on trade in Newfoundland codfish carried on at Alicante [f. 281].

22192. 1755–1759, Sept. "Almanack de la Guerre, qui contient un tableau général de la Guerre depuis les premières hostilités des Anglois jusqu'à présent." Much respecting the war in America [ff. 167–200].

22220. [1762]. Lists of Canadian officials tried and convicted and their sentences [ff. 217–220].

22245. Finances, 1756–1762. "État actuel des affaires générales concernant les finances du Royaume . . . avec les affaires extraordinaires faites en France depuis et compris l'an 1756 jusqu'à la fin de l'année 1762 au sujet de la guerre" [f. 392].

22253. 1748–1762. Letters and other documents relating to commercial operations of Bigot, Gradis, Bréard, and others in Canada [ff. 155–168].

[1763]. "Conditions générales de la paix" [f. 236]. Note on the various types of Spanish vessels engaged in the American trade [f. 257].

[Post 1763]. Notes on colonial products, commerce of Canada, Canadian Indians, commerce of England, tobacco trade since 1740, etc. [ff. 371–373].

22755. 1760, Aug. 27, Gerinsdo[r]f, near Breslau. King of Prussia to M. d'Argens. France will lose Canada and Pondicherry to please the Queen of Hungary and the Czarina; contempt for Choiseul [f. 219].

22762. 1769, Mar. 10, Versailles. "Mémoire donné par M. d'Estaing dans le mois de Mars 1769 à l'instant qu'on apprit en France que les Français de la Louisiane avaient chassé les Espagnols." Example of how New Orleans should aid the separation of North America from England [ff. 75–77v].

1764, Documents relating to Martinique and St. Lucia [ff. 78, 100, 111, 147].

1763. Dec. 3, Martinique. Observations respecting commerce of the West Indies with New England, etc. [f. 105].

1764. "Essai sur la colonie de Ste. Lucie." Trade with English, salt beef and flour from Philadelphia, etc. [f. 117].

22817. 1768, Sept 21, London. Benjamin Franklin to M. Le Roy. Has introduced Abbé Taglieri to Sir John Pringle; recommends M. l'Espinasse, and sends the "Pennsylvania Farmer's Letters," which have had a "prodigious effect" in the colonies (A. L. S.) [f. 90].

23021. Papers of Du Portal, director general of fortifications in Santo Domingo, 1721–1767; correspondence with leading men in the French government relating to fortifications; engraved maps and plans of towns, harbors, forts, etc., and memoirs relating to the fortifications of Martinique.

> 1763, Oct. "Réflexions sur les moyens de deffendre les colonies de l'Amérique et principalement celle de St. Dominique." Sent by M. de Fontanelle [f. 141].

> 1764. "Mémoire sur le commerce de la colonie françoise de St. Dominique" by Foache. Foreign trade; purchase of vessels in the English colonies [f. 199].

23022. Papers of Du Portal, 1768–1770. Correspondence, drawings, etc., relating to fortifications of Santo Domingo.

> [1768]. Notes on the commerce of Môle St. Nicolas; vessels from Georgia [f. 265].

> Bill for masts [f. 272].

> 1768, Jan. 1–Mar. 31, Môle St. Nicolas. "État des differentes denrées exportées et importées tant par les Français que par les Anglais" [f. 290].

> 1769, June 20, Môle St. Nicolas. D'Anctéville to Du Portal. Introduction by the English of light-weight money made at Boston and in Rhode Island.

Collection Joly de Fleury

This collection in the Bibliothèque Nationale is made up of the papers of the family Joly de Fleury, members of which held the office of procureur général before the Parlement of Paris between 1717 and the French Revolution. These papers are in 2561 volumes. Those that have relation to the British Empire 1748–1776 are as follows:

283. "Avis et mémoires sur les affaires publiques." 1750, Sept. 10, 26. Versailles. Rouillé [Minister of Marine] to Joly de Fleury. Appointment of La Galissonnière and de Silhouette to settle with the British commissioners disputes of the two countries with respect to their American possessions. Acknowledges copies of documents relating to Acadia found in the archives of the Parlement, with list of documents [ff. 93–95].

392. "Avis et mémoires sur les affaires publiques." 1764. Proposal to the administrators of the General Hospital to furnish children for populating the colonies, with correspondence of Joly de Fleury and the Chevalier Turgot relating thereto [ff. 279–282].

393. "Avis et mémoires sur les affaires publiques." 1763–1764. Commission to the Châtelet to judge as a court of last resort the accusations brought against the Sieur Bigot with respect to abuses practised in Canada, accompanied by letters to Joly de Fleury relating to the sentence rendered in the "affaire du Canada" [ff. 70–74v].

398. "Avis et mémoires sur les affaires publiques." 1765. Draft of a *declaration* conferring upon the superior councils of Canada and Île Royale the same honors and privileges as enjoyed by the corresponding magistrates within the kingdom [ff. 333–341].

1723. "Commerce et colonies" [c. 1750]. Papers on Louisiana: On importing Negroes to and exporting tobacco from Louisiana [ff. 207–210]. [c. 1750] "Précis d'un mémoire pour l'établissement de tabac à la Louisiane" [ff. 213–215v].

2453. "Guerre d'Amérique; nouvelles à la main, 1755–1756." 1755, July 28. News of French vessels in the St. Lawrence; reasons for expecting preservation of peace [f. 3]; news of naval combat in Acadian waters, capture of Beauséjour by English [f. 5]. Sept. 21, news of the capture of Nova Scotia and New England by the French and Indians [f. 16]; Sept. 25, confirmation of news of capture of Boston [ff. 18, 23]. 1756. Translation of English declaration of war on France [f. 30]. 1756, June 9. Ordonnance du Roi portant Déclaration de Guerre contre le Roi l'Angleterre. Aug. 1, Calais. Dagieu to Joly de Fleury. Blockade of Louisbourg; defeat of Johnson [f. 38].

BIBLIOTHÈQUE DE L'ARSENAL

The Bibliothèque de l'Arsenal, another of the great public libraries of Paris, owes its name to the fact that it is located on the Rue de Sully in the surviving building of what in the early eighteenth century was the Arsenal of Paris. At first the private library of the Marquis de Paulmy and then of the Comte d'Artois, it, in the course of the French Revolution, was turned into a public library, as was the case of the Bibliothèque du Roi. It possesses some 10,000 volumes of manuscripts. See in this connection Henry Martin: *Catalogue des Manuscrits de la Bibliothèque de l'Arsenal* (8 vols., Paris, 1885–1899). We shall, however, continue to follow the Leland *Guide to Materials for American History in the Libraries and Archives of Paris*, in selecting papers from this library that bear upon the British Empire, 1748–1776. Among them are the following:

4565. "Plan de guerre contre l'Angleterre, rédigé par les ordres du feu Roi, dans les années, 1763, 1764, 1765, et 1766, par M. le comte de Broglie, et refondu et adapté aux circonstances actuelles pour être mis sous les yeux de Sa Majesté, à qui il a été envoyé le 17 décembre 1778" [269 pages].

4789. "Extrait de l'Histoire de l'Origine du Commencement et du Progrès de la Guerre en Amérique entre l'Angleterre, et ses Colonies depuis l'année 1763," to 1779 [216 pages].

5768. Papers of the Comte d'Argenson.

> 1760, June 24, Montreal. Chevalier de Lévis to d'Argenson. Siege of Quebec; arrival of the English squadron (A.L.S.) [ff. 3–4].
>
> 1762, June 19, Rochefort. This paper refers to the despatch of five vessels from Bordeaux to Louisiana, of which only one escaped capture; the inevitable loss of Louisiana to the English [f. 182].
>
> 1756, Dec. 25. *Journal Maritime de Bayonne* with news of vessels arriving from Quebec and Louisbourg [f. 235].
>
> 1755. Memoir by d'Estaing: "Examen des différentes idées que l'on avoit eues sur les occurences présentes et de celles que l'on pourrait encore y joindre." The political situation as regards Canada and Louisiana; a basis of peace without cession of Canada [ff. 272–287].
>
> 1755. Memoir by d'Estaing: "Extraits des conjectures Anglois sur leurs ministères et sur nos différents. On y a joint un exposé, distingué par province, de ce qu'ils appellent nos usurpations" [ff. 301–310].
>
> 1755, Dec. "Lettre d'un Hollandais à un Suédois" with a reply. The necessity of preventing England from becoming too powerful; English views as to Canada and Louisiana, commerce, etc. [ff. 341–364].

5769. Papers of the Comte d'Argenson.

> 1757, Jan. 22, Aug. 23. *Journal Maritime de Bayonne* with items respecting captures of vessels from Virginia and Rhode Island [ff. 2, 22].
>
> 1757–1760. Three letters from Lévis to d'Argenson giving information on the war in America [ff. 307, 357, 374].
>
> 1757–1760. Ten letters from Montreuil to d'Argenson describ-

ing the course of events in Canada. These include information on the engagements around Fort William Henry and the Battle of the Plains of Abraham [ff. 308, 310, 316 *et seq.*].

1757, Aug. 9. Articles of capitulation accorded by Montcalm to the garrison of Fort William Henry [f. 314].

1757. News from Île Royale [Cape Breton Island] [ff. 318–321v].

1757, June 26. News of effects of war in the English colonies [f. 324].

1758. Relations of the French victory at Ticonderoga in July [ff. 326–331v, 338–341].

1758, Aug. 1, Quebec. Doreil to d'Argenson. Praise of Montcalm [ff. 342–343v].

1758, Nov. 21, Montreal. Montcalm to d'Argenson (Duplicate) [ff. 354–355].

[1758]. Memorandum on Indian neutrality and English plans for attack on Canada [f. 356].

1760. Account of the victory won by the French near Quebec (that is, at Ste. Foy); also list of Canadian officers arriving in France on Nov. 27, 1760 [ff. 377–380].

6432–6465. In these thirty-three volumes is the Marquis de Paulmy collection of maps, plans, and memoirs relating to fortified places in North America. The following papers are of especial interest:

6432. 1751, Jan. "Mémoire sur les limites de la Nouvelle France par un ami de M. de la Condamine." Here the boundaries of Louisiana, Acadia, Hudson Bay, etc., are set forth (8 pp.) [No. 1].

1755. Two memoirs transmitted by Comte de Raymond: (a) "Mémoire concernant l'Isle Royale et réflexions sur cette colonie dans les circonstances présentes"; (b) "Mémoire concernant la défense de Louisbourg et des moïens à prendre pour l'assurer à la France à jamais, autant qu'il est possible" [No. 2].

1755. Two memoirs also transmitted with letters by Comte de Raymond: (a) "Mémoire par lequel il est prouvé que l'on peut assurer pour toujours la subsistance en grains des colonies de l'Isle Royale [Cape Breton Island] et Isle St. Jean [Prince Edward Island]"; (b) A similar memoir but respecting a constant supply of fresh meat [No. 3].

[Post 1763]. "Réflexions générales sur le gouvernement des îles du Vent de l'Amérique [No. 4].

6433. 1757, Aug. 3–16. "Journal de siegè du fort Georges, apellé par les Anglois William Henry, scitué au fond du lac St. Sacrement . . . Par M. Des Androuins" [No. 24].

Archives de la Bastille

The archives of the great fortress prison, the Bastille, were pillaged when this stronghold was captured by the revolutionaries in 1789. Ultimately the surviving manuscripts were transferred to the Bibliothèque de l'Arsenal. For an inventory of the archives of the Bastille see Frantz Funck-Brentano's *Catalogue des Manuscrits de la Bibliothèque de Arsenal. Tome IX Archives de la Bastille* (3 vols., Paris, 1892–1895). Those papers in this collection (all still in cartons) that throw light on the history of the British Empire, 1748–1776, are as follows:

10028. Papers of Levié, commissaire, police inspector of ports. 1755, Nov. 5; 1759, Aug. 20. Havre. Levié to [the Lieutenant of police]. Effect on the Bourse of the engagement at Fort Frederic; news from Canada.

12110–12136. Dossiers of prisoners, 1761 (*12111* includes François Bigot).

12142–12148. "Affaire du Canada," 1761–1772. These papers relate to Bigot, Péan, Cadet, and their numerous accomplices. For the most part this body of papers represents the work of the commission charged with the investigation of frauds in Canada.

12151–12166. Gives additional information on those persons involved in the "Affaire du Canada," with the nature of the punishment accorded to each of the accused.

12200. "Affaire de l'Île Royale," 1758–1764. This carton of 518 folios relates to charges of embezzlement brought against Jean de la Borde and Jacques Prévost, two prominent officials of Île Royale.

12262. "Affaire de la Louisiane," 1765–1770. This case grew out of disputes in Louisiana between Gov. Kerlérec and certain officers and officials there. A commission decided against Kerlérec in 1769 [ff. 240–250]. Included in this carton is also information compiled in 1756 among the Illinois Indians in order to learn from them the western tribes known and attached to the French, and on whom in case of need the Missouri post can rely for aid (Census) [f. 257v].

BIBLIOTHÈQUE DE LA CHAMBRE DES DÉPUTÉS

The Bibliothèque de la Chambre des Députés is located in the Palais Bourbon and contains 1546 volumes of manuscripts. For its contents in detail see Ernest Coyecque and H. Debraye: *Catalogue Général des Manuscrits des Bibliothèques Publiques de France: Chambre des Députés*

(Paris, 1907). Materials in this library bearing upon the British Empire, 1748–1776, are limited and are as follows:

1487. "Commerce général et étranger de la France dans le 4 parties du monde pendant l'année 1753" (173 pp.). A few references to the commerce of the principal towns of France with America, and a brief history of the Compagnie des Indes.

1488. Établissement de la Cie. des Indes. Son progrès, son commerce, sa régie, ses revenus particuliers, ses dépenses particulières sur les dits revenus, dettes . . . troupes . . . employés . . . ," 1754. References to the commerce of the company in America, pp. 24–26, 49–52.

BIBLIOTHÈQUE MAZARINE

The Bibliothèque Mazarine, located on Quai Conti, has been a state library since the days of the Revolution. Among the 5000 volumes of manuscripts some few papers bear upon the British Empire covering the period under examination. They are as follows:

1850. 1755. *Discussion Sommaire sur les Anciennes Limites de l'Acadie, et sur les Stipulations du Traité d'Utrecht qui y sont relatives.* [By Pidausat de Mairobert, according to Barbier] (68 pp.). [With French and German texts]. There is also "Memoire contenant les matières essentielles du commerce. . . ." The third section is devoted to complaints against the abuse by the English of the treaty of assiento and of the permission they have received to send a vessel of 500 tons to the West Indies.

3749. "Réflexions sur la guerre des Anglais, envoyées à M. de Choiseul en 1767 [pp. 1–4].

1775, July 13. "Observations sur l'armement de l'Espagne." Fortification of Pensacola by the English; revolt of the English colonies; inadvisability of Spanish aid to the insurgents [pp. 209–213].

1775, July 30. "Mémoire sur la formation et la recrutement des troupes des colonies" [pp. 214–218].

PART VIII

Spain

ARCHIVO GENERAL DE SIMANCAS AND ARCHIVO HISTÓRICO-NACIONAL, MADRID

PAPERS in Spanish depositories relating to the history of the British Empire, 1748–1776, that should be noted are at two principal places: (1) The Archivo General de Simancas, housed in a huge thirteenth-century castle situated in the village of Simancas on the main road between Valladolid and Tordesillas, and (2) The Archivo Histórico-Nacional on the second floor of the Biblioteca National in Madrid, an impressive building. A vast collection of manuscripts, the Archivo General de Indias, concerned with the internal aspects of the old Spanish Empire, is also located in Seville on the second floor of a large building, the Casa Lonja. However, the papers at Simancas and Madrid, in so far as they bear directly upon the political relations between the British Empire and the Spanish Empire for the period under review are by far the most important. In this connection two works are of great aid to the student: (1) William R. Shepherd: *Guide to the Materials for the History of the United States in Spanish Archives* (*Simancas, the Archivo Histórico-Nacional, and Seville*) (Washington, D.C., 1907), and (2) James Alexander Robertson: *List of Documents in Spanish Archives relating to the History of the United States, which have been Printed or of which Transcripts are Preserved in American Libraries* (Washington, D.C., 1910). For treaties of peace or of commerce entered into before the middle of the nineteenth century by Spain, the standard Spanish text is by Alejandro del Cantillo: *Tratados, Convenios y Declaraciones de Paz y de Commercio . . .* (Madrid, 1843).

In examining the original Spanish sources that have a direct relationship to the British Empire, 1748–1776, it is necessary to ignore many papers that relate to areas that were later to be annexed by the government of the United States. Accepting this limitation and concentrating on

events with a definite bearing upon the British Empire it should be pointed
out that documents relating to an episode are not always together: they
may be either at Simancas or in Madrid—or are missing. This is especially
true for the brief period under examination. While some of the documents
are in volumes, most of them are in bundles (*legajos*). With respect to
only one event for the period 1748–1776 are the surviving Spanish
documents quite full. These have to do with Spain's involvement, between
the years 1759 and 1764, diplomatically or as a party in the hostilities
between Great Britain and France, with the important consequences
thereof. They are as follows, with the location of the document either in
the depository at Simancas or at Madrid indicated, as well as its date:

1 7 5 9

Nov. 3, Preliminary Act at Fontainbleau for the cession of Louisiana
by France to Spain, should the latter come to the support of the former
in the course of the War being waged with Great Britain (Madrid); Nov.
13 and 23, the ratification at San Lorenzo and Versailles of the Preliminary
Act of Nov. 3 (Madrid).

1 7 6 3

Feb. 10, treaty of Spain and France with Great Britain defining the
new boundaries in North America and providing for the return of Cuba
to Spain and the cession of Florida to Great Britain (Madrid).
"Projet d'articles préliminaires arrettés entre la France et l'Angleterre"
(Simancas); Aug. 13, The Spanish ambassador at Paris, the Marquis de
Grimaldi, to the French Foreign Minister, the Duc de Choiseul (Simancas); Aug. 20 and Sept. 13, Grimaldi to the Spanish Foreign Minister, Don
Ricardo Wall (Simancas); Sept. 16, Wall to Grimaldi (Simancas); Sept.
19, Grimaldi to Wall (Simancas); Sept. 20, Choiseul to the French am-
bassador at Madrid, Pierre Paul Ossun (Simancas); Sept. 29 and Oct.
23, Wall to Grimaldi (Simancas); Nov. 3, Louis XV, King of France to
Charles III, King of Spain, (Simancas); Nov. 3, Choiseul to Ossun
(Simancas); Nov. 13, Wall to Grimaldi (Simancas); Dec. 2, Charles III
to Louis XV (Simancas); Dec. 14 and 28, Wall to the Spanish envoy at
Naples, Tanucci (Simancas).

1 7 6 4

March 19, the Prince of Masserano at Madrid to Grimaldi, with refer-
ence to the cession of Florida to Great Britain (Simancas); April 5,
Masserano to the Earl of Halifax, British Secretary of State, also about
Florida (Simancas); April 6, Masserano to Grimaldi, again about Florida
(Simancas); April 21, the Duc de Choiseul to the Spanish ambassador in

London, Joaquin Conde de Fuentes (Madrid); April 21, Louis XV to the Governor of Louisiana, M. d'Abbadie, about the transfer to Spain of Louisiana (Madrid); May 1 and June 12, Masserano to Grimaldi, concerning Florida and the evacuation of it (Simancas).

For a useful article based upon the use of the Spanish archives and concerned with the period under examination see William R. Shepherd: "The Cession of Louisiana to Spain," *Political Science Quarterly*, XIX (1904), 439–58.

PART IX

Canada

PUBLIC ARCHIVES OF CANADA, OTTAWA

THE manuscript collections of the Public Archives of Canada that relate to the British Empire, 1748–1776, are among the most important that exist when taking into account both original documents and those reproduced from collections located elsewhere, either in Great Britain, in continental Europe or in the New World. For purposes of classification these papers, both original manuscripts and those secured by transcribing or filming, or by some other process are divided by the Archives into two main groups: (1) Manuscript Groups (papers not a part of the official records of the British government in Canada since 1763), and (2) Record Groups (papers regarded as part of the official records of Canada after the Peace of Paris of 1763). In 1914 there appeared as *Publication* No. 10 of the Public Archives David W. Parker's *A Guide to the Documents in the Manuscript Room of the Public Archives of Canada.* Since then the Public Archives has had great accessions of materials. This has led to the publication in recent years by the staff of the Archives of a series of most useful pamphlets under the general heading "Preliminary Inventory." These beginning in 1952 are still in the process of preparation and publication. In them the distinction between Manuscript Groups and Record Group is maintained. We shall now consider the first of these groups.

French and British Manuscript Groups

The manuscript groups are, first of all, documents in the Public Archives that were transcribed in Paris from the Archives Nationales or from the Archives of the Ministry of Foreign Affairs, concerning French New World expansion, especially in North America, with particular reference to Canada. These documents are now listed in a series of pamphlet guides under the general title *Fonds des Manuscrits*. These guides are the following, with the number and the date of publication of each: *No. 1. Archives des Colonies* (1952); *No. 2. Archives de la Marine* (1953); *No. 3. Archives Nationales* (1953); *No. 4. Archives de la Guerre* (1953). These four guides are based upon transcripts of manuscripts in the Archives Nationales in Paris. In 1955 there appeared *No. 5. Ministère des Affaires Étrangères*, drawn from the Archives of the French Minister of Foreign Affairs. As the materials in these five inventories have already been covered in dealing with manuscripts in depositories in Paris, the student is referred to this section of the present guide.

Not only have abundant materials been drawn from depositories in France but reproductions of equally important papers have been secured in Great Britain. Among the inventories relating to the manuscript collections, two published by the Archives must be particularly mentioned: *No. 11. Colonial Office Papers Public Record Office* (1961) and *No. 21. Transcripts from Papers in the British Museum* (1955). As the pertinent papers in both the Public Record Office and the British Museum that relate to the British Empire, 1748–1776, have also been surveyed earlier in this guide, we must turn to consider other classified manuscript groups in the Public Archives of Canada, preliminary inventories of which have also appeared. The listing of the contents of these groups is here presented (without regard to date of publication of the inventory) that relate to the specific period under survey. The guides to them are as follows: *No. 18. Pre-Conquest Papers* (1964); *No. 23. Late Eighteenth Century Papers* (1957); *No. 8. Quebec Provincial and Local Records* (1961); *No. 17. Religious Archives* (1967). They will be treated in the order given above, beginning with *Pre-Conquest Papers*.

Other Manuscript Groups

PRE-CONQUEST PAPERS

Among the Pre-Conquest Papers having a bearing upon the British Empire, 1748–1776, are those grouped under the heading "Fur Trade and Indians." The following may be noted: (1) Treaty with the Indians of Nova Scotia by the government of that province on August 15, 1749; (2) The Jesuit missionary Claude Godefroy Coquart's account, April 5, 1750, addressed to Bigot, intendant of New France, of the French trading posts and the economic situation of the Indians; (3) The letter-books, 1752–1758, of Robert and John Sanders, Albany merchants, concerned in trade with inhabitants of New France; (4) An interesting "Mémoire sur la partie occidentale du Canada . . . , 1763," which deals with the area from Michilimackinac to the upper Missouri River, including the upper Mississippi, Illinois, and Wisconsin Rivers.

Under the heading "Hudson Bay" mention should be made of copies of Arthur Dobbs's papers (the originals of which are in the Public Record Office of Northern Ireland) concerned among other things with the Hudson Bay area and the quest for a Northwest Passage, but also with the desire to break the monopoly of the Hudson's Bay Company of its trade in furs with the Northern Indians.

Grouped under the heading "Religious," are to be found copies of papers secured from Rennes, France, of the famous Abbé Jean Louis Le Loutre, 1763–1772, who strove to keep the Acadians loyal to France.

Grouped under the heading "Acadia and Newfoundland" are the following papers: (1) A copy of the private letter-book, 1742–1753, of Paul Mascarene, who was at the time British governor of Annapolis Royal; (2) A copy of what is considered to be Charles Morris's survey of Nova Scotia, 1748 (?), with an account of the efforts of the French to recapture the province; (3) Copies of the papers of Thomas Pichon, who held office under the French at both Louisbourg and Fort Beauséjour and who secretly supported the British, 1750–1760; (4) Copies of correspondence and other papers, 1747–1761, of Lieut.-Gov. Charles Lawrence of Nova Scotia, including papers drawn from the Vernon-Wager manuscript collection and also the Chalmers Collection in the Library of Congress; (5) The papers, 1762–1772, of Sieur de la Rochette, commissioner in England for the reception of French Canadians and Acadians after the British conquest; (6) A statement, covering the years 1749–1756, of the British settlement and defence of Nova Scotia; (7) Copy of returns, 1751–1753, of the Île Royale (Cape Breton Island) garrison and the nature of their activities on the island.

Under the heading "Governors and Intendants, Canada" are the following papers: (1) A business letter from Jacques Pierre de Taffanel, Marquis de la Jonquière, governor of New France, to Gradis & Son, Nov. 8, 1751; (2) Letters of Pierre de Rigaud, Marquis de Vaudreuil-Cavagnial, to Duchesnay of Beauport indicating that he (Vaudreuil) had been exonerated from blame for the loss of New France, March 22, 1764; (3) Seven letters (transcripts) written by Vaudreuil to the Ministre de la Marine, about differences on Canadian affairs between Montcalm and himself, 1758–1764.

Under the heading "New France" are to be found the following pertinent collections of manuscripts: (1) Copies of the papers, 1748–1764, of Claude Pierre Pécaudy, Sieur de Contrecoeur, concerned chiefly with the Ohio Valley and the efforts of the French to control it; (2) The Robinson Collection, 1532–1899, papers collected by Peter Robinson in five volumes relating to the fur trade, missions to the Indians, the Great War for the Empire, and James Murray, as governor of Quebec; (3) The Sicotte Collection, 1716–1819, contain papers relating to New France, orders in council for the payment of royal dues from the colonies and for payment of supplies during the above war and also other papers concerning Canadians who returned to France in 1763; (4) Copies of papers relating to Kaskaskia, in the Illinois country, 1738–1831; (5) Papers copied from the Spanish Archives at Simancas, consisting chiefly of letters from the Spanish ambassador at London to the King of Spain and filed in the Archives under the heading "Inglaterra, legajos 2542–8217"; they relate chiefly to the years 1755–1763 and especially to events in the New World connected with the Great War for the Empire; in addition there are in this "New France" group papers on the Quebec Act of 1774 and the American invasion of Canada in 1775.

Also among the "Pre-Conquest" group of manuscripts and under the heading "Memoirs and Travel" should be noted the following papers: (1) Copy of the mémoires of James, Chevalier de Johnstone, a British subject who became a major in the French army, served at Louisbourg, 1751–1758, and later under Lévis and Montcalm in Canada, 1758–1760; (2) Reproduction of the journal, 1755–1760, of Maj. Charles de Plantavit, Chevalier de la Pause, covering his military service in Canada; (3) Reproduction of "Mémoires, contenant l'histoire du Canada durant la guerre et sous le Governement Anglais," written about 1760 by Louis Léonard Aumasson de Courville, who was, before its capture in 1755, the royal notary at Beauséjour; (4) The "Journalle," 1753–1799, of Boucher la Bruère, containing logs of his Atlantic voyages, records of land renting and of a flour-milling business at Quebec.

Under the heading of "French Officers" are collections of papers in the Archives that are concerned with the years 1748–1776, including those of the following officers who served in America: (1) Both originals and reproductions of the correspondence and papers of Michel Chartier, Marquis de Lotbinière, 1746–1792; (2) Papers of Antoine Gabriel François, Chevalier Benoist, including a mémoire, "Reflections sur le Canada," c. 1760; (3) Papers of Louis Franquet, Inspector-General of Fortifications in Canada, including accounts of journeys to Acadia and Île Royale in 1751 and through Canada in 1751–1752; (4) Much more important are original and reproduced papers of Louis Joseph, Marquis de Montcalm; these papers, 1743–1759, are in 9 volumes; (5) Of equal importance are original and reproduced papers, including letters from and to, François Gaston, Duc de Lévis, 1746–1778, among which are the campaign journals of Montcalm; these papers are in 14 volumes; (6) Letters received by, and other papers of, François Charles de Bourlamaque, 1756–1764, in 6 volumes; (7) Original and reproduced correspondence and other papers of Louis Antoine de Bougainville, including a journal of campaigns in North America, 1756–1763; (8) Copies of letters from Montcalm and Lévis to Monsieur La Chevardière de la Grandville, who commanded the Régiment de la Reine, 1757–1761; (9) Letter from Jean Nicolas Desandrouins, Carillon, 1756, with an account of the campaign of that year; (10) Copies of letters to and from Jean Daniel Dumas, 1760.

Under the heading "British Officers" are also collections of papers in the Archives that are concerned with the years 1748–1776. Among these are papers of the following officers who served in America: (1) A very large collection of transcripts of the papers of Jeffrey, 1st Baron Amherst (before 1761 Sir Jeffrey Amherst) and of his brother, William, Earl Amherst, including letters and despatches from many people. These valuable papers in private hands are in 78 packets and cover the years 1758–1797; (2) General James Wolfe papers, both originals and reproductions, in 10 volumes; (3) Copies of papers, 1759–1807, of George, 4th Viscount and 1st Marquis, Townshend, who was second-in-command under Wolfe in Canada and was Wolfe's successor upon his death, together with a much larger body of original papers in the Northcliffe collection to be noted; (4) Capt. Henry Pringle's letter-book, 1747–1782; especially important while Pringle was with the 27th Regiment in North America, 1757–1761; (5) Copy of the Memoirs of Baron Alexander Colville, Commander-in-Chief of the North Atlantic Squadron, 1759–1764.

The Northcliffe Collection of Manuscripts (as well as rare printed works) was purchased and presented to the Archives in 1923 by Sir Leicester Harmsworth as a memorial to a brother, Viscount Northcliffe. It consists chiefly of the two large collections of original papers. They are: (1) The General Robert Monckton papers, 1742–1782, in 90 volumes, covering Monckton's military service in Nova Scotia, 1752–1757; later during his military operations in Canada; still later in connection with the Martinique campaign and conquest of the island, 1761–1762; and, finally, as Governor of the Province of New York, 1762; (2) The Brig.-Gen. George Townshend papers (to which reference has already been made) covering the years 1759–1799, in 15 volumes, which collection, as is true of the Monckton collection, is of great importance in dealing with events of the period under review; (3) Many separate pertinent items also are in the Northcliffe Collection. Among these are the following: (a) Thomas Cole's "A Scheme to drive the French out of all the continent of America," Sept. 9, 1754; (b) *Relation de la Prise des Forts de Choueguen ou Oswego; et de ce qui s'est passé cette année en Canada* (Grenoble, 1756); (c) *An Accurate and Authentic Journal of the Siege of Quebec, 1759. By a Gentleman in an Eminent Station on the Spot* (London, 1759); (d) James Cook's "Directions for Sailing from the Island of Scaterie to Quebec . . ."; (e) Victory sermon delivered at Quebec, Sept. 27, 1759, by the Rev. Eli Dawson, chaplain of H.M.S. *Stirling Castle;* (f) Thomas Bell's "Journals," six in number covering the years 1753–1759, dealing with events on Cape Breton Island and Canada, including the Quebec expedition of 1759; (g) The order-book of General Wolfe, 1748–1759; (h) The order-book, 1758–1771, of Capt. James Smith of H.M.S. *Sea Horse;* (i) Letter written by Sieur de Ramezay, somewhat before the surrender of Quebec, describing the situation there.

Grouped under the heading "Military and Naval" the following papers in the Archives should be noted: (1) Copy of order-book relating to the French army in Canada under Montcalm and Lévis, 1756–1760, including orders for the capture of the forts at Chouaguen (Oswego) in 1756; also accounts of the capture of Fort William Henry in 1757, the Battle of Carillon in 1758, the Battle of the Plains of Abraham in 1759, and the action at Ste. Foy in 1760; (2) Papers of Maj.-Gen. Edward Braddock including his ordnance notebook (original) concerned with the Fort Duquesne expedition and also a copy of his journal of the expedition to the Ohio; (3) Commander Keppel's order-books while supporting the Braddock expedition, 1754–1755; (4) Letters of William Shirley and Charles Lawrence to the Earl of Halifax, 1754–1755, with references to the French military menace to Nova Scotia; (5) Copies of papers relating to reports on ordnance in Newfoundland and Nova Scotia, 1752 and 1754; (6) Colonel Monckton's journal concerned with the capture of Fort Beauséjour in 1755; (7) An account of the campaign against Quebec in 1759; (8) Copy of a letter in French about the effects of attacks on New France by colonial troops; (9) Reports by New England militiamen captured at Crown Point and taken to Canada for questioning [1758]; (10) Letters of William Pitt to Maj.-Gen. Abercromby, Vice-Adm. Boscawen, Gov. Charles Lawrence and Maj.-Gen. Edward Whitmore, concerning an attack on Quebec, 1758 (contemporary copies); (11) R. Townshend to Sir George Ferris, Louisbourg, Aug. 28, 1758, discussing future military plans with the capture of Louisbourg; (12) Copy of "Memoirs on the siege of Quebec and total reduction of Canada in 1759 and 1760" by John Johnson, Quarter-Master Sergeant of the 58th Regiment; (13) Incomplete "Histoire de la conquête du Canada," Quebec [1759]; (14) Copy of Sieur La Force's "Journal du Siège de Niagara," in 1759; (15) Papers, 1757–1776 (privately owned and reproduced) of George Williamson, Brigadier-General and later Major-General of the Royal Artillery and of his son, Capt. Adam Williamson, later Lieutenant-General, relating to the Louisbourg campaign of 1758, also the campaign against Montreal of 1760, that against Martinique in 1762, and the Battle of Bunker Hill in 1775; (16) Lieut. John Gowan's journal of the demolition of the Louisbourg fortifications in 1760; (17) Copy of returns of ordnance at North American garrisons, 1754; (18) Gov. Lawrence's return of troops in Nova Scotia, 1755, and Lord Loudoun's return in 1756; (19) Report on the capture of Fort Beauséjour in 1755; (20) Copy of terms of surrender, July 3, 1754, accorded by Louis Coulon de Villiers to James Mackay and George Washington and their troops, defenders of Fort Necessity; (21) Under the title "Louisbourg and Quebec" are grouped documents relating to the conquest of Canada, 1750–1760; (22) Also under "Military and Naval" are reports of British secret agents in Europe, 1755–1756, having to do with French military preparations, especially for the invasion of British-held Minorca, for a proposed invason of England, and for the sending of French reinforcements to North America;

(23) Letter from the Duke of Newcastle to Henry Bilson Legge, Chancellor of the Exchequer, Sept. 21, 1758, about military operations in the West Indies and North America; (24) Letter from Estèbe, manager in Paris for Intendant Bigot at Quebec, apparently written to Louis François Perraut (?), regarding the imminent loss of Canada, the effect of the war on France, and the problem of Canadian currency redemption, Feb. 24, 1760; (25) Fort Pitt, 1759–1760, papers, including the journal of Patterson and Hutchins of their march from Fort Pitt to Fort Presqu' Isle and back again in 1759, and Henry Gordon's description of Fort Pitt, Dec. 24, 1760; (26) Copy of the journal of Louis Guillaume de Parscau du Plessis, 1756, of a trip from France to Canada with a description of its military, economic and social conditions; (27) Copy of the journal, 1758, of David Gordon, an officer in the Highland Infantry engaged in the siege of Louisbourg; (28) Copy of extracts from the journal of Lieut. John Marr of a journey from Halifax to Lunenburg, Nova Scotia, in July 1763; (29) Copy of order-books of Commodore Augustus Keppel of the British fleet, 1754–1755, that brought the Braddock army to Virginia.

LATE-EIGHTEENTH-CENTURY PAPERS

While most of the papers in this group in the Archives are concerned with events beyond the years 1748–1776, some papers are most pertinent.

Under the heading "British Statesmen" are certain exceedingly important collections of manuscripts. Among them are the following: (1) The Dartmouth manuscripts, original papers of William Legge, 2nd Earl of Dartmouth, in 12 volumes, presented to the Archives in 1926 by the then Earl of Dartmouth. The material in each volume relates to a particular colony or area. Those volumes that bear upon North America and adjacent islands covering the years 1748–1776 are as follows: Volumes I–II, Nova Scotia, 1713–1798; Volumes V–VII, the old Province of Quebec, 1757–1792; Volume VIII, Labrador, 1772–1784; Volume IX, Newfoundland, 1759–1778; Volume XII, Island of St. John (Prince Edward Island), 1766–1776; Volume XIII, Newfoundland and Labrador, 1768, 1774. In addition to original papers there is a series of transcripts of Dartmouth Papers, the originals of which have already been noted in this guide and which are now in the Staffordshire County Record Office, Stafford, having been recently transferred there from the William Salt Library. These Dartmouth Papers, while still in the muniment room of the residence of the then Earl of Dartmouth, Patshull House, Wolverhampton, were calendared by the Historical Manuscripts Commission in its *11th Report*, Appendix 5 (1887) and also in its *14th Report*, Appendix 10 (1897); (2) Chatham Papers, transcripts of selected items from the Pitt papers in bundles in the London Public Record Office (calendared in the H.M.C. *6th Report*) that have relationship to Canada and North America; (3) Shelburne Papers (calendared in the H.M.C. *3rd, 5th and*

6th Reports). Typed copies of selected items from them, relating particularly to Canada and North America, were made while these papers were still at Lansdowne House and therefore before the bulk of these manuscripts went to the Clements Library at Ann Arbor; (4) Selected manuscripts not connected with the above series. They are: (a) "Lord Barrington's Thoughts on N. America" [May 10, 1766]. Barrington was Secretary at War; (b) Copy of letter of Solicitor General Alexander Wedderburn to Edmund Burke [1773] about the government of Quebec with report (photostat of original from the Northamptonshire Record Society); (c) Diary, 1766, of Secretary of State, Charles, 3rd Duke of Richmond, with information on Cabinet Council meetings (photostats, original privately owned).

Under the heading "American Revolution" are to be found the following papers: (1) Carleton papers, all except a few are beyond 1776 (transcribed in the Royal Institution of Great Britain); (2) "Journal of the most remarkable events which happened in Canada between the months of July, 1775 and June, 1776," anonymous writer; (3) "Letters private and official, Reports, Returns etc . . . ," of the invasion of Canada by the Americans, 1775–1776 (transcription of papers in private hands); (5) Sir John Hamilton's journal, 1775–1776, of the siege of Quebec.

Classified under the heading "Nova Scotia" are the following papers: (1) The diaries, 1766–1812, of the Connecticut-born Simeon Perkins, who settled at the fishing town of Liverpool (defective typed copy of original diaries by this prominent businessman and legislator, which have been lost); (2) Two grants to the famous Alexander McNutt and Associates of some 300,000 acres of Nova Scotia land.

Under the heading "New Brunswick" are the papers of the Loyalist lawyer Ward Chipman, of Cambridge, Massachusetts, and his son Ward Chipman, Jr., covering the years 1767–1843; the Chipmans settled in New Brunswick in 1784.

Under the heading "Prince Edward Island" is to be found the commission as governor of the island of Walter Paterson, Aug. 4, 1769.

Classified under the heading "Quebec and Lower Canada: Government" are the following papers: (1) Thirty-three proposals for governing Canada, n.d., but about 1765; (2) Paper on the debts of Canada, 1766–1767, drawn from the "registres du Conseil d'État du Roi de la France" (transcriptions); (3) Copies of acts, proclamations, legal opinions relating to the government of the Province of Quebec, 1760–1793, made by David Chisholme; (4) Reports made by Ralph Burton, military governor of Three Rivers, 1763 and by Thomas Gage, military governor of Montreal, 1763–1764, together with an extended account of the government of Three Rivers, 1760–1764.

Under the heading "Quebec and Lower Canada: Political Figures" are to be found in the Archives: (1) Transcripts of five volumes of papers of Gen. James Murray, governor of Canada. The first four shed much light on the years 1748–1776; the originals are privately owned at Bath, England. There are, in addition, transcripts of other Murray papers also privately owned, including journals and other documents relating to the capture of Quebec in 1759 and Montreal in 1760 with transcripts of correspondence by Murray or relating to him that were in the possession of John Collier, his father-in-law; (2) The letter-books of Edward William Grey, Montreal sheriff and business man, 1767–1826; (3) Letters from François Mounier to Frederick Dutens, Quebec, April 7 and Nov. 13, 1767 (in French); (4) Letter of Attorney-General Francis Masères to the Rev. Majerdie, Quebec, about the Roman Catholic religion (transcript); (5) Correspondence of Deputy Postmaster General in America Hugh Finlay with Lord Despencer, 1773–1783, about Canadian properties.

Under the heading "Quebec and Lower Canada: Merchants and Settlers" the following papers are to be found in the Archives: (1) Quartermaster George Allsopp's orderly-book, 1759, connected with Wolfe's expedition; (2) Detroit quit-rent book, 1770–1784; (3) Letters to James Morrison, Montreal merchant, 1773–1800. Under the heading "Quebec and Lower Canada: Religious and Fraternal" is the minute-book (photostat) of the Montreal Masonic lodge, 1768–1771.

QUEBEC PROVINCIAL AND LOCAL RECORDS

The manuscripts under the above heading in the Public Archives of Canada are both originals and copies of records, in French and English. They are very numerous. Only those that help to throw light on the British Empire, 1748–1776, will be considered. They are as follows:

A. Documents Généraux, 1636–1854. The following among them should be noted: (1) Correspondance Officielle, 1637–1778. Selections from the despatches and instructions of the king, ministers, governors, intendants, and principal officials of the colony (copies). The originals are in various French archives, especially the Ministries of Marine and War. The copies are not from the originals but from copies made by J. R. Brodhead for the state of New York; (2) Jugements et délibérations du Conseil Souverain, 1717–1759. Registers containing the proceedings of meetings of the Conseil Souverain which, in 1703, became the Conseil Supérieur. Transcripts from the Archives of the Province of Quebec; (3) Registre des documents déposés au Conseil Supérieur par les parties en cause, 1741–1755. In the margin of this register are indicated the dates when the documents were received. Transcripts from originals in the Archives of the Province of Quebec; (4) Ordonnances des intendants, 1705–1760. Ordinances, regulations, and other orders issued by the intendants. Copies of originals in the Archives of the Province of Quebec; (5) Registres des aveux, dénombrements et déclarations, 1723–1754, 1781. The registers contain a declaration of the rights of the seigneurs, a description of the fiefs and acts of feudal acknowledgement. Five of the eleven registers cover Jesuit lands, 1733–1754, 1781. Copies of originals in the Archives of the Province of Quebec; (6) Governor's Office, 1764–1767, 1784. Entry Book, 1764–1767. Contains copies of warrants and instructions issued by the Governor's office. Many of the documents relate to land surveys, and to the preparation of commissions and land patents.

B. Régime Militaire, 1760–1764. The manuscripts are both in French and English. The following are the most pertinent: (1) Report on the Government of Quebec and Dependencies thereof, 1762, submitted by military governor James Murray, June 5, 1762; it deals with several subjects including a project to build a citadel at Quebec, the British forces and the state of fortifications in Canada, government under French administration, church government, the Indians, revenues, population, trade and the character of the people; (2) Ordonnances et règlements concernant le district de Montréal, 1760–1764; (3) Conseil militaire de Québec, 1760–1761; (4) Conseil militaire de Montréal: jugements des causes portées en appel, 1760–1764; (5) Cour de milice de Montréal: audiences et sentences des chambres de milice, 1760–1764.

It should be noted that the Public Archives also possesses a large number of papers relating to individual seigneuries.

RELIGIOUS ARCHIVES

The Public Archives of Canada has much relevant material, both original and copied, drawn from the archives of the Catholic, Anglican, and Moravian Churches, concerned with the period 1748–1776. Besides Dominion sources, it has copies of documents of the Catholic Church from depositories in Italy and France. The most important Italian sources from which documents have been copied are the Archives of the Vatican. These documents are interesting for both the political and religious history of Canada. They include *Acta* or extracts of deliberations and decisions of the Sacred Congregation of Propaganda, 1625–1820, relating to the condition, needs, and expansion of the Roman Catholic Church in North America. The Congregation's work was based on the desires of those in authority for information which was furnished on these subjects by bishops, priests, and religious congregations in America. Also included are copies of the correspondence of the Vatican Secretary of State with the papal nuncios in France and Flanders, which throw light on the situation in New France. The letters of the French papal nuncio, 1608–1763, to be found here, are chiefly about the political and military situation of the French and English in America between 1748 and 1763. The correspondence of the papal nuncio in Flanders, 1755–1763, relates to events of the Great War for the Empire. Copies of documents from another Italian source, the Archives of the Society of Jesus in Rome, give some information on Canada to 1762. However, the greater part of these documents are before 1748.

The Canadian Archives has also reproduced records from three Parisian religious institutions: the Archdiocese of Paris, the Séminaire des Missions Étrangères and the Séminaire de Saint-Sulpice. The Archdiocese of Paris contains a register of ordinations, 1748–1889. The Public Archives has extracted information from it concerning Canadians or bearing on Canada. From the Séminaire des Missions Étrangères the Archives has transcribed twenty-five volumes of material pertinent to Canada for the period 1640–1851. This material comes from the following numbered volumes of the originals: Vols. 1–31, 33–41, 43–45, 200–218, 221–223, 225, 273, 344 and 345. The material includes correspondence with bishops, vicars apostolic and the directors of the mission seminary. Most of the pieces copied from the Séminaire de Saint-Sulpice deal with the military and ecclesiastical history of Canada. For reasons not clear, there are in this collection papers on military history, 1750–1760; these include accounts of the expeditions against Forts Renards, Chouaguen (Oswego), and William Henry and of operations on the Ohio.

In addition to the documents transcribed in Europe relating to the religious institutions of Canada, to which reference has been made, manuscripts located in Canada have been transcribed. Among the Catholic institutions in Canada from which the Archives has copied material are: the Archevêché de Québec; the Achevêché de Montréal; the Séminaire de Saint-Sulpice, Montreal; the Séminaire de Québec; the Hôpital-Général, Quebec; the Hôtel Dieu, Montreal; and the Hôtel Dieu, Quebec. Most of the records kept by these institutions are chiefly of interest either for local history or for a history of the particular religious institution. Some do have a wider importance. There are letters and orders from high church officials and reports dealing with various problems. For example, there is a copy of a report, written around 1763, deposited at the Archevêché de Québec, that is concerned with the free and perpetual exercise of the Roman Catholic religion in Canada. The records of the Hôpital-Général, Quebec, contain a list of English troops cared for between 1768 and 1769 and also a list of American troops treated in 1776. The Hôtel Dieu, Montreal, has similar records for French soldiers treated between 1755 and 1760. The Hôtel-Dieu, Quebec, has letters from Bigot, 1749–1759, Vaudreuil, 1756–1759, and Montcalm, 1756–1757.

The pertinent Anglican church records in the Canadian Archives are all copied from two sources in England: the Society for the Propagation of the Gospel in Foreign Parts and the Society for the Propagation of the Gospel in New England, generally called the New England Company. From the Society for the Propagation of the Gospel, the Archives has copied journals, 1747–1835, and selections from Series B, 1702–1799, and Series C, 1630–1860, of the Society's original letters. Letters from missionaries in Newfoundland, 1759–1785, and Nova Scotia, 1760–1786, were taken from Series B, and letters received from Newfoundland, Nova Scotia, including what is now New Brunswick, and Upper and

Lower Canada, 1756–1860, from Series C. All the calendars of letters pertaining to America in the two series were also filmed. The New England Company records, 1661–1913, on film are: The Minute-Books, 1770–1905; the Letter-Books, 1762–1772; and some pamphlets and miscellaneous documents, 1657–1913.

All the pertinent Moravian records in the Archives come from three sources: the Headquarters of the Moravian Church and the Society for the Furtherance of the Gospel, both in London, and the Moravian Archives, Bethlehem, Pennsylvania. The papers filmed in London consist of correspondence, mission diaries, accounts of voyages and other papers relating to such missions as those in Labrador and to the activities of the headquarters in London. The diaries give information on Nain, 1771–1893; Okak, 1776–1893, in Labrador; and Hutten, 1747–1753, in Germany. The papers from Bethlehem are diaries and other records relating to missions at Nain and Okak.

Record Groups

As has already been indicated, the manuscript materials in the Public Archives have been classified into two groups: The Manuscript Group and the Record Group. Among the latter collections are the following published guides that relate to Canada during the period 1748–1776: *No. 1. Executive Council, Canada, 1764–1867* (1953); *No. 4. Civil and Provincial Secretaries Offices, Canada East, 1760–1867* (1953); *No. 7. Governor General's Office* [1771–1923] (1953); *No. 8. British Military and Naval Records* [1762–1903] (1954); *No. 10. Indian Affairs* [1755–1860] (1951). They will be dealt with in the order given in so far as they shed light on the period under review.

THE EXECUTIVE COUNCIL, CANADA, 1764–1867

These are the most important political records relating to the Province of Quebec for the immediate post-conquest period. The Proclamation of 1763 and the commission and instructions given to Governor James Murray provided for a council to assist the governor in the performance of his very extensive executive and very limited legislative functions. Problems referred to the Executive Council were later classified into two series: the E Series (State Records) and L Series (Land Records). The E Series are most important containing as they do the minutes, correspondence, and audit records of the Council prior to 1776 (Minute-Books, vols. 1–6, 28, 105–115). In 1775 there begins the record of the activities of the Legislative Council (Minute-Books, 1775–1791, vols. 7–12), that was created by the Quebec Act of 1774. The correspondence of the Council, 1769–1874, in 40 vols. includes both letters received and letter-books kept in the Council office. There are also 339 volumes of audit records,

1759–1841. In addition to the above there are some petitions, 1773–1840; oaths, 1764–1862; and other papers relating to the constitutional development of Canada before the creation of a confederation but these papers are mostly after the year 1776.

The L Series contains various records dealing exclusively with activities of the Executive Council with respect to Canadian land matters. A series of volumes concern land grants made by the Council between 1764–1842; there are also six volumes concerned with "Jesuit Estates," 1743–1840, and a report on pre-conquest land grants, 1637–1759, in Quebec and Lower Canada. For other areas there are some miscellaneous records and warrant books, 1765–1845.

CIVIL AND PROVINCIAL SECRETARIES OFFICES, CANADA EAST, 1760–1867

The offices of Civil Secretary and of Provincial Secretary Canada East are closely identified with the work of the Executive Council. The office of Civil Secretary in Canada began with the formation of a civil government for the province in 1764, as the result of the conquest of Canada. Hector T. Cramahé, General Murray's secretary under the military regime, was appointed the first Civil Secretary, while Henry Ellis became in that same year Provincial Secretary (in absentia). Under the Quebec Act there was created the combined office of Provincial Secretary and Register of the Province. These two secretaries, Civil and Provincial, played a major role in the conduct of the internal affairs of the province. The Archives which received the records of these officers from the Department of State in 1906, has organized them into three divisions: Civil Secretary's Correspondence, 1760–1840; Provincial Secretary's Correspondence, 1765–1867; and Miscellaneous Records, 1763–1867.

The correspondence of the Civil Secretary is the most significant of the two groups of correspondence. The major portion of this correspondence is contained in a collection of 460 volumes known as the S series. The S series, which runs from 1760 to 1840, consists mainly of petitions, letters and reports addressed to the Governor and the Civil Secretary. The series also has many records of the Executive Council and the Provincial Secretary. A group of miscellaneous correspondence apparently accumulated by the Civil Secretary for reference purposes includes: a record of ships and cargoes arriving at Quebec, 1763; a list of bailiffs, 1768, and copies of circular letters to bailiffs and captains of militia, 1768–1778. The only pertinent materials among the Provincial Secretary's correspondence concerned with the years 1748–1776 are some letter-books, 1765–1771, which contain copies of letters written by both the Civil and Provincial secretaries.

The division of the Secretaries' records designated by the title Miscellaneous Records, 1763–1867, contains a large body of official documents of interest for the governmental affairs of Canada, 1748–1776. Among the documents included are: (1) Proclamations, 1771–1857, containing original, draft, and printed copies of proclamations issued by the Governor of Quebec, Lower Canada and Canada; (2) Ordinances, 1760–1839, among which are ordinances and regulations for the district of Montreal, 1760–1764; (3) Commissions, 1763–1833, original commissions for various offices in Quebec and Lower Canada with a few writs of summons to the Legislative Council; (4) Court records, 1765–1867, of the Court of Appeals, Court of Chancery, together with the grand jury returns, 1765; records of offences, 1765–1827; (5) Pardon records, 1766–1858; (6) School records, 1768–1856; (7) Bonds for Mediterranean Passes, 1766–1806, ship masters' bonds given upon receipt of passes to sail for Mediterranean ports; (8) Customs records, 1772–1796, returns.

GOVERNOR GENERAL'S OFFICE

Although the office of Governor General was not created until 1867 by the North American Act passed by Parliament in London, under this heading in the Public Archives there are a few papers among the records accumulated by this office that are earlier than 1776. Besides miscellaneous papers, 1774–1840, from Lower Canada, the only other material classified in this group relating to the years 1748–1776 comes from the Lieutenant-Governor's office on Prince Edward Island. This material consists of: despatches received, 1771–1873; a register of despatches received, 1771–1848, and imperial orders-in-council, 1769–1867.

BRITISH MILITARY AND NAVAL RECORDS

When the British government recalled most of the troops from Canada in 1871, provision was made to transfer to London all the records accumulated by the military since the conquest of Canada. However, through the efforts of Douglas Brymner, the first Dominion Archivist, the British government agreed to let the archives remain in Canada. Unfortunately, these records do not become extensive until after 1790. Only a few documents deal with the British Empire, 1748–1776. The correspondence of the Military Secretary contains 24 volumes on Indian Affairs, 1767–1859 (vols. 247–271). In the records of the Nova Scotia command is a royal engineer's report on Halifax fortifications, 1761 (vol. 1425). Further, among the collection of ordnance records are some reports and returns, 1757–1878; among these is a report on Quebec, 1757, made by Patrick Mackellar (vol. 89) and also a report by Thomas Sowers on the attack on Fort Frontenac in 1758 (vol. 36). The only other pertinent military records in this group are found in a miscellaneous section of the records. This section includes: Order-books, 1764–1894 (vol. 1167 ½), a collection of copies of general, militia, garrison, district, and regimental orders; warrants and establishment lists relating to the troops stationed at Louisbourg, 1757–1760 (vol. 1064A); Captain Anthony Vialar's Orderly Book, 1775–1776, which includes copies of garrison and regimental orders kept by Vialar during the siege of Quebec (vol. 1713); finally there is a group of miscellaneous papers relating to the militia of the town of Quebec, 1775–1776 (vols. 1714–1714A).

INDIAN AFFAIRS

The bulk of the papers in Record Group 10 relating to the Indians come after 1776. However, there are some documents in the Public Archives from the office of Indian Superintendent during the administration of Sir William Johnson, 1755 to 1774. These documents include Johnson's correspondence, 1756–1772, and minutes on Indian affairs, 1755–1772 (Indian Records, Series 2, vols. 4–10). These minutes of Indian affairs consist of a brief journal of Johnson's activities and complete minutes of Indian councils. Among them are the minutes of a council held with Pontiac from July 22–29, 1766, also minutes of a brief Indian Council held on May 12 of that year.

Another distinct collection of documents in this record group relates to the Six Nations for the period 1763–1810 (Indian Records, Series 2, Vol. 15). These documents discuss land problems, appointments, population, and the distribution of supplies among the Indians. Among them is a plan for the future management of Indian affairs which was written in 1764.

PROVINCIAL DEPOSITORIES

In turning now from the Public Archives of Canada at Ottawa to the provincial depositories of the area of what is the dominion of Canada it will be convenient to present, in alphabetical order, those depositories which contain collections that reflect light on the British Empire, 1748–1776.

Newfoundland

Most of the records of Newfoundland concerned with the years 1748–1776 have been drawn from depositories in London. A series of disastrous fires and neglect in other ways led to the disappearance of many of the original government papers concerned with the above years. However, papers in what had been the Colonial Secretary's Department (before political union with Canada in 1949) very fortunately were preserved in the fire-proof vault of the Court House of St. John's. Here in thirty-seven volumes are papers covering the years 1743–1840—outside of missing volume two that is concerned with the years 1752–1760. Their contents have been described by David W. Parker in his *Guide to the Materials for United States History in Canadian Archives* (Washington, D.C., 1913), pp. 284–301.

The earliest surviving volumes down to the American Declaration of Independence in the Court House, contain the following documents that help to illuminate the relations of the island with the rest of the Empire: *Vol. 1.* (1) Petition of Robert Bully of Philadelphia claiming land in St. John's under bill of sale, dated Apr. 20, 1723, Aug. 29, 1752. *Vol. 3.* (1) Proclamation by Gov. Graves requiring all masters of New England ships to "enter into obligations not to carry away any of the handicraft men, seamen or fishermen." H.M.S. *Antelope*, St. John's, Sept. 10, 1761; (2) Lord Egremont to Gov. Palliser, relating to illicit trade with the British colonies, July 9, 1763; (3) Copy of minutes of a council meeting held at St. James concerning "a clandestine trade being carried on in America," Oct. 5, 1763; (4) Palliser's "order for vessels trading to America not to carry passengers and to sail by the 5th of Nov. 1764; (5) Palliser's order to Richard Edgecombe, naval officer of Great and Little Placentia, "to be very exact in examining the clearances certificates and cockets of all New England vessels . . . upon no account to grant such certificates without being fully satisfied that the quantity of goods, especially foreign goods, have been landed," Nov. 1, 1764; (6) Order not to carry any "men passengers" to America, Nov. 1, 1764; (7) Regulations for "the fishery on the coast of Labradore, Anticosti, Madelaines and Whale Fishery," April 8, 1765; (8) Palliser to M. Gill, judge of vice-admiralty court, indicating that he was sending three New England schooners seized at St. Pierre to St. John's, July 8, 1765; (9) Palliser to Gov. Bernard, Boston, respecting illicit trade "from your province with St. Pierre," July 15, 1765; (10) Palliser to the governor of Canada, forbidding Canadians to fish or trade in Labrador, Aug. 28, 1765; (11) Decree upon Thomas Stout of the *Good Intent* for carrying passengers to New England the preceding fall, n.d.; (12) Fine on *Good Intent* compromised, the *Good Intent* carrying 60 passengers to Ireland free, Sept. 30, 1765. *Vol. 4.* (1) Palliser's order concerning the whale fishery on the coast of Labrador. Copy sent to Gov. Bernard, Boston, Aug. 1, 1766; (2) Palliser's order respecting plantation captains who refuse to show their papers, Aug. 9, 1766; (3) Palliser to Bernard, respecting whale fishery, etc., Aug. 1766; (4) Order for American vessels to leave before Oct. 31, otherwise sails and rudders to be taken away and lodged in the fort, Sept. 20, 1766; (5) Palliser's order against the firing of the woods of Labrador by vessels from the plantations, July 23, 1767; (6) Memorial from the merchant adventurers in Labrador against lawlessness of plantation crews, n.d.; (7) Palliser's answer to merchants and adventurers in Labrador, Aug. 10, 1767; (8) Byron's order for American ships to leave every year by Nov. 1, July 7,

1769; (9) Bond of £100 from Peter Curry of Philadelphia to carry passengers, July 28, 1769; (10) Byron's instructions for Fort York, Labrador, Sept. 1, 1769; (11) Bond from Isaac Phillips of Boston for £1000 indemnifying James Hay and others respecting the *Betsy*, laden with rum, which, without proper certificate, was confiscated but later released, 1770; (12) Byron's order forbidding New Englanders, etc., to establish themselves at Magdalen Islands without his permission, Aug. 12, 1771; (13) Major Gorham, lieutenant-governor of Placentia, to Byron, asking leave to go to headquarters (New York) on business. Leave granted, Oct. 10, 1770. *Vol. 5.* (1) Indenture between W. Sheppard, Boston, attorney for E. Breed of Charleston, T. Jenner, I. Miller, James Russell, administrator of estate, C. Chamber, and D. Russel on one part, and W. Corkeran of Boston transferring land, etc., in St. John's, Oct. 15, 1764; (2) Byron's orders forbidding New Englanders to settle or destroy sea-cows on Magdalen Islands without his license, Aug. 29, 1771; (3) Shuldham's order for Americans to leave before Nov. 1, June 24, 1772; (4) Shuldham's order permitting British subjects "to take salmon stations from inhabitants of Newfoundland or other his Dominions in America," [June] 24, 1772; (5) Shuldham's order enforcing customs act and navigation act, June 24, 1772; (6) Shuldham's letter requiring shipping returns, etc., to be forwarded promptly to His Majesty's Commissioners at Boston, June 25, 1772; (7) Shuldham's instructions concerning Fort York harbor; also about crimes committed by irregular crews from the colonies, Aug. 3, 1772; (8) Shuldham's order respecting sea-cow fishing at the Magdalens, April 3, 1773. *Vol. 6.* (1) Vice-Adm. Roland Duff's order respecting enticing men to America, July 12, 1775; (2) Fortification of St. John's pushed forward, 1775; (3) Gen. Gage wanting carpenters and seamen at Quebec, Sept. 11, 1775; (4) Duff to Gage, withdrawing garrison from Fort York, Labrador, for winter; commiserates his Excellency on situation he is involved in by the unhappy rebellion but hopes for a speedy restoration, Sept. 15, 1775; (5) Duff's letters to justices: "The present Exigencies on the Continent" make it necessary for Gage at Boston and Carleton at Quebec to send Capt. Campbell, R.H.E., with a party to recruit. This not to interfere with fishermen's engagements. Sept. 26, 1775; (6) Duff to Capt. Campbell: As Vice-Adm. Graves, at Boston, needs men badly for his ships he [Duff] must revoke the order to enlist for the Royal Highland Emigrants, Oct. 2, 1775; (7) Duff to Capt. Pratt: Similar letter revoking order to enlist for the Royal Fencible Americans, Oct. 2, 1775; (8) Capt. Barrett being apprehensive of attack "very early in the spring," Duff thinks affairs in America are not "so very alarming as to justify me in putting the government to any extraordinary charges . . . whilst we have so numerous a fleet in those seas," Oct. 20, 1775; (9) Gen. Howe, Halifax, to Montagu, about drafting men of the 65th into corps to serve in North America, and sending officers to England; replacing company of 65th at St. John's by company of Royal Highland Emigrants, March 19, 1776;

(11) Montagu to Howe, acknowledging instructions; no orders to victual women and children belonging to 65th or artillery, May 27, 1776.

The Newfoundland government has supplemented its original material with copies of documents transcribed from British and American depositories. The largest collection of copied material comes from the Colonial Office Papers in the British Public Record Office. The Archives has transcribed and microfilmed the entire C.O. 194 series, which contains the Colonial Office's correspondence relating to Newfoundland covering the years 1696–1798; the same is true of C.O. 195, with both Secretary of State Office and Board of Trade Office entry books relating to Newfoundland, 1623–1780, and C.O. 199, concerned largely with the fisheries but touching on other Newfoundland matters and covering the years 1715–1806. C.O. 5, a huge series, dealing with most of the colonies, 1689–1783, has also been drawn upon, as well as C.O. 43, chiefly concerned with Canada, 1763–1786.

When the author of this series was carrying on research at St. John's in the early 1950's, the volumes of transcriptions, to which reference has been made, were slumbering in the vaults of the President of the University and the original papers in the vault of the St. John's court house. Then an effort was made to concentrate at Memorial University all early materials relating to the island, as is indicated by Mr. Harvey Mitchell, Librarian and Archivist in his "Archives of Newfoundland," *American Archivist*, XXI (1958), 45–53. The reproduction of papers in London relating to Newfoundland also moves forward. It was, however, decided to create a distinct archives for the government. In 1960 a provincial archivist was appointed and the archives are now concentrated in Colonial Building, St. John's, in the custody of Mr. Allan M. Fraser, Provincial Archivist.

Nova Scotia

The Public Records of the Province of Nova Scotia, located at Halifax have been well cared for and preserved. They contain the following official papers, both originals and reproductions relative to the years 1748–1776, with the numbering of the documents retained: *No. 21.* Commission and letter-book kept at Annapolis Royal, June 1742–Nov. 1749; *Nos. 29–33.* Original despatches to the Governor of Nova Scotia from the Board of Trade, 1749–1799. Few of these come from the Board after 1768; from 1759 on their place is largely taken by despatches from the Secretary of State; *Nos. 35–48.* Transcripts or original letter-books of despatches of the governors of Nova Scotia to the Board of Trade and Secretary of State, 1749–1794; *Nos. 55–57.* Three letter-books of Sir John Wentworth as governor of New Hampshire, 1767–1770; *No. 135.* Letters, chiefly on military matters, from Governor Lawrence of Nova Scotia to the governors of other English colonies and the French governor of Île Royale or Cape Breton Island, Nov. 7, 1753–Oct. 5, 1756; *Nos. 186–203.* Minutes of the Council of Nova Scotia, 1749–1870; *Nos. 215–218.* Journals of the Council, 1758–1783, as the upper chamber of the Nova Scotia Assembly; *No. 219.* Letters of Gov. William Shirley, Sir Jeffrey Amherst, Dep. Gov. Spencer Phips, James de Lancey and Thomas Pownall on relations with France, 1749–1763; *No. 220.* Drafts of despatches (67 documents) 1752–1784, from Governor Lawrence to the Board of Trade, the Secretary of State and other officials, especially with respect to the deportation of the Acadians and the presence of New England troops in Nova Scotia; *No. 221.* Largely drafts of the governor's despatches (172 documents) to the Secretary of State, April 26, 1751–Nov. 25, 1791; *Nos. 286–298.* Volumes made up of selections from the files of the Legislative Council of Nova Scotia during the years 1760–1841; *Nos. 301–314.* Original papers selected from the files of the Assembly of Nova Scotia from 1758–1841; *No. 342.* Papers connected with Crown prosecution for such offenses as treason and sedition, 1749–1778; *No. 346.* Royal and gubernatorial proclamations issued in Nova Scotia, 1748–1807; *Nos. 348–351.* Royal instructions to governors of Nova Scotia, 1729–1846, both original and copies; *Nos. 354–356.* Imperial orders in council relating to Nova Scotia, 1752–1852; *Nos. 357–358.* Colonel John Winslow's journal during siege of Fort Beauséjour and the removal of the Acadians—copied from the original in the Massachusetts Historical Society. This has been published as volumes III and IV of the *Collections* of the Nova Scotia Historical Society; *No. 359.* Papers relating to the settlement of the old townships of Nova Scotia after the removal from them of the Acadians; *No. 409.* Papers connected with the settlements on the river St. John, 1764–1815; *No. 443.* Census returns, which have among other items, lists of rate payers of the several townships, 1770–1794; *Box No. 12* contains records of proceedings of the court of vice-admiralty in Nova Scotia for the years 1749–1759, 1761–1764, 1769–1811. David W. Parker's *Guide to the Materials for United States in Canadian Archives*, pp. 193–203.

Among the Archives' collection of private papers is a volume of the papers of Thomas Pichon. This volume comprises his journal of the siege of Fort Beauséjour and correspondence between him and British officers. Translations of these forty-seven documents have been published by John Clarence Webster in *Thomas Pichon: Spy of Beauséjour* (Sackville, N.B., 1937).

Ontario

After Canadian federation of 1867, the earlier province of Upper Canada carried the name Ontario. In its capital, Toronto, the Public Libraries have several collections of private papers which discuss military, Indian, and governmental affairs, covering the period, 1748–1776. They are as follows: (1) An account of the war with France in America between 1757 and 1759 by a "Scotch officer" of the 48th regiment; (2) Another document related to the war is a memoir on the life of the French Canadian, Captain Denys Marquis de Vitré, which denies the allegation that De Vitré piloted Wolfe up the St. Lawrence during the siege of Quebec. The memoir is based on De Vitré's own statement; (3) Information on the American Revolution is contained in the papers of Peter Russell (1733–1808) who served as a secretary to Sir Henry Clinton; these papers include two volumes on the events in 1775; among his papers are also journals which tell of life in Gibraltar, the Barbary Coast and the West Indies, 1750–1756, 1760–1761, 1775–1782; (4) The papers of William Fairfax contain some material on Indian affairs. In the Fairfax papers is a "Narrative of William Fairfax's Proceedings with the Six Nations in the Colony of Virginia," which includes Fairfax's instructions from Gov. Dinwiddie, May 1, 1753 and Fairfax's report to Dinwiddie of the meetings held with the Indians at Winchester, Va., Sept. 11–16, 1753; (5) The Samuel Peters Jarvis papers relate mostly to Indian affairs, 1763–1853. While the bulk of the material concerns the period after 1776 a number of documents are pertinent to the period preceding it. (6) Among other papers that bear upon the period under investigation are contemporary copies of documents written by James Murray, governor of Quebec, and Hugh Palliser, governor of Newfoundland. The Murray document (a contemporary copy, the original of which is in the British Museum) is his report on the state of the government of Quebec made on June 5, 1762. The Palliser document (in the Alfred Sandham collection) is a copy of the regulations for fishing off the coast of Labrador, which Palliser issued on Aug. 28, 1765. See *Guide to the Manuscript Collection in the Toronto Public Libraries* (Toronto, 1954).

Prince Edward Island

The Office of the Provincial Secretary in Charlottetown has the minutes of the Executive Council beginning in 1770; proclamations and orders of the king-in-council, 1773–1876 and commission books from 1769. The Land Office has preserved a complete set of books pertaining to land grants made from 1769. See A. G. Doughty: "The Manuscript Sources of Canadian History," *The Cambridge History of the British Empire: Volume VI. Canada and Newfoundland* (Cambridge, Eng., 1930), 831.

Province of Quebec

Depositories in the Province of Quebec hold many of the original civil and judicial records of the French and the early British regimes in Canada. The French records are the more significant group since among them are preserved all the documents which, according to the terms of the capitulation of Montreal, Sept. 8, 1760, were to remain in

Canada. These records relate to all of French Canada. The documents from the British regime are more provincial, that is, local, in character, because the documents which relate to extra-provincial affairs have been transferred to the federal government at Ottawa. In the city of Quebec, the two most important civil depositories are the Provincial Archives and the Judicial Archives.

Records preserved in the Provincial Archives include: (1) Jugements et Délibérations du Conseil Souverain, 1663–1760 (71 vols.). These are records of the sittings at Quebec of the Conseil Souverain or the Conseil Supérieur as it was entitled from 1703; (2) Registres des Insinuations du Conseil Supérieur, 1663–1758 (10 vols.). These are the official registrations by the Council of royal or other decrees, edicts, orders, etc.; (3) Ordonnances des Intendants, 1705–1760 (44 vols.). The orders issued by the Intendant throw much light on the administration of New France, 1748–1759; (4) Registres d'Intendance, 1672–1759 (2 vols.). These contain the concessions and ratifications of the intendants of land matters (en fief et en roture); (5) Acts de foi et hommage, 1667–1854 (4 vols.); (6) Registres de la Prévôté de Québec, 1666–1759 (120 vols.); (7) Records of the militia court which sat at Montreal, 1760–1764 (5 vols.), and also in Quebec; (8) A census, taken in 1765, of the districts of Montreal and Three Rivers. This has been published in *Rapport de l'Archiviste de la Province de Québec, 1936–7* (1937), 1–121.

Like the civil records, the ecclesiastical records preserved in Quebec are much more than provincial in scope. The bishop of Quebec had jurisdiction, until 1790, over the present Dominion of Canada including Newfoundland, also the whole of the Mississippi Valley and the Far West. The Archives of the Archbishopric of Quebec (Quebec became an Archbishopric in 1844) has preserved the correspondence to or from missionaries throughout the bishop's jurisdiction. In addition, the Archives has the registers of the bishops, correspondence conducted with Rome and Paris and Papal Bulls which nominated the bishops of Quebec. The Seminary of Quebec at Laval University also has many papers pertaining to the bishopric of Quebec.

The Literary and Historical Society of Quebec has donated much of its collection of original manuscripts to other institutions but it still retains some interesting documents. Among these are the following items: (1) Correspondence of a Quebec merchant named Perrault, 1755–1772, which relates to business affairs in Europe and supplies news about the Ohio (1755) and the Mississippi; (2) An account of western Canada, 1763, which describes the river systems to the southward of the Great Lakes; (3) Order-books of Murray, Carleton, and Cramahé which contain orders and march routes, 1767, also papers relating to warrants and land, 1764–1775.

In Montreal, the courthouse has judicial and notarial records, among them the records of the Prévôté of Montreal to 1764, and records of the

English courts of common pleas, quarter and petty sessions comprise the pertinent judicial records. Notice should be taken in this connection of Ordonnances et Règlements pour le gouvernement de Montréal sous l'administration militaire du Canada (1760–1764). The notarial records there cover the entire period under review, 1748–1776, and contain much information on the fur trade. This is true for the English as well as the French period, since Montreal remained the center for the fur trade after the conquest as before. The two most important types of documents to be found in the notarial records are the "congés" or permits to trade and the "engagements" or contracts between traders and voyageurs. Besides the fur trade, the notarial records yield information on the social and family history of the region. There are also in Montreal copies of the Seminary of St. Sulpice records largely relating to religious matters in Montreal, the island of which had been ceded to the Sulpicians.

The Court House at Three Rivers has judicial and notarial records similar to those at Montreal. However, these records are not as extensive as those in Montreal. Some of Three Rivers's records have also been transferred to the city of Quebec.

For the Province of Quebec see A. G. Doughty: "The Manuscript Sources of Canadian History," *The Cambridge History of the British Empire*, VI (Cambridge, 1930), 813–31; David W. Parker: *Guide to the Materials for United States History in Canadian Archives* (Washington, D.C., 1913) pp. 205–72; James Kenney: "The Public Records of the Province of Quebec, 1763–1791," in Royal Society of Canada, *Proceedings and Transactions*, 3rd ser., XXXIV (1940), Section II, 87–113; and Henry Putney Beers: *The French & British in the Old Northwest: A Bibliographical Guide to Archive and Manuscript Sources* (Detroit, 1964).

For a comprehensive guide to all of Canada see the recently published *Union List of Manuscripts in Canadian Repositories* (Ottawa, 1968).

PART X

Atlantic and
West Indies Islands

THE BAHAMAS

PROBABLY in no other British colony have neglect, the climate, and insects, as well as hostilities, taken a greater toll of the early public records than in the Bahamas, where they still remain in the custody of the various offices at Nassau. This account of manuscript sources is based on the report prepared by Dr. James M. Wright and presented to the Department of Historical Research in the Carnegie Institution of Washington and embodied by Herbert C. Bell, David W. Parker and others in their *Guide to British West Indian Archive Materials . . . for the History of the United States* (Washington, D.C., 1926), pp. 329–334. While the surviving manuscript records of the Governor's Office go back only to 1829, the manuscript minutes of the Executive or Privy Council only to 1802, and manuscript records of laws passed to 1780, there are volumes in the office of the Registrar of Records of an earlier date. Among them are the following that fall within the period 1748–1776: (1) A volume of miscellaneous deeds, 1723–1762; (2) Record book of bonds, including also appointments to military offices, instruments of pardon to slaves convicted of capital crimes, and grants of land, 1760–1772; (3) Record book of inventories of private effects, 1753–1787; (4) A volume of slave manumissions, 1740–1834; (5) A colonial secretary's book, 1733–1751; (6) A volume of records of the court of ordinary, 1772–1823.

In the committee room of the library of the House of Assembly the following two manuscript volumes of journals of the House fall within the period 1748–1776: that covering the period Feb. 4, 1760, to Aug. 8, 1766, and that covering the period Nov. 18, 1766, to Feb. 15, 1771. There is also a volume devoted to votes of the House that supposedly covers the period from Feb. 4, 1761, to May 11, 1784, but the records from the beginning of 1771 for nine years are missing. Also in the Assembly Library are printed volumes of laws of the island. Vol. I, 1729–1805, is a compilation; there is also a volume covering the years 1764–1798 but it is incomplete.

While court records in the Supreme Court archives date from 1788, there is a chest of wills (1601 in number) that cover the period 1722–1883.

With respect to Bahama parish records those of Christ Church concerned with the period 1748–1776 have in large part survived. One manuscript volume is a register of baptisms in the parish, 1733–1791; another volume is a register of marriages, 1753–1803; there are also five volumes of vestry minutes of the parish covering the period 1741–1837.

BARBADOS

It is hard today for the student of history of the British Empire to realize the importance to Great Britain of the little sugar island of Barbados in the middle of the eighteenth-century—especially before fires gutted so much of opulent and fashionable Bridgetown, the capital, in 1756 and 1760.

In 1959, the Rockefeller Foundation gave the University of the West Indies at Mona in Jamaica a grant to initiate a survey of the archives of the West Indies. The University appointed M. J. Chandler to undertake the survey in Barbados. In a two year period, he examined all classes of archives on the island and published the result of his study in *A Guide to Records in Barbados* (Oxford, 1965). This volume updates earlier surveys made by Herbert C. Bell, David W. Parker and Richard Pares by telling which records are still extant. However, since 1965, under Chandler's direction as archivist, many of the records listed in the *Guide* have been transferred to the Barbados Department of Archives established in 1964. A new bibliography, "A Guide to Source Materials for the Study of Barbados History" by Jerome Handler, will be published shortly by the Southern Illinois Press.

The Department of Archives holds the legislative and judicial records of Barbados for the period 1748–1776. The legislative records include House of Assembly minutes and the minutes of the Privy and Legislative Councils. The pertinent volumes of the House of Assembly minutes, seven in number, run from 1745 to 1778 and throw light on the Great War for the Empire, slave problems in Barbados and the economic distress caused by the American Revolution. Copies of the minutes have been made since the originals are in very poor condition. There are also eight minute-books of the Privy and Legislative Councils that cover the 1748–1776 period. Other legislative records in the archives include an incomplete set of original acts, 1717–1940. These are supplemented by contemporary copies and an official register of the acts. Mention must also be made of some duplicate despatches, 1747–1752, in the Archives. These despatches deal with fortifications, importation of negroes, population statistics and the evacuation of Tobago.

Relevant judicial records in the Department of Archives come from various courts of Common Pleas and the Court of Exchequer. Records from the courts of Common Pleas consist of precinct or record books, alphabet books and trial lists. Most of the surviving pertinent records begin either in the 1760's or 70's. Those precincts with such records are: Christ Church Precinct, St. James's Precinct, and St. Michael's Precinct. Chandler lists only Court of Exchequer deed record books and minute-books for the 1748–1776 period. The minute-books cover the period from Sept. 1750 to March 15, 1776, with a break between Sept. 1770 and March 1773.

The archives also has some documents dealing with personal matters such as deeds, wills, and powers of attorney. These have not been systematically filed. However, the deed record books are reasonably complete from 1718.

While the Department of Archives has the largest share of the Island's collection of governmental and personal records, other depositories have some interesting material. The Bridgetown City Council has preserved its own vestry minutes since August 5, 1745. This depository also contains Bridgetown "Assessment and rates, 1749–1765, 1768–1792." The Barbados Public Library holds a valuable collection of transcripts made between 1818 and 1828 by Judge Nathaniel Lucas. These consist of a series of copies of the minutes of the Barbadian Council and some miscellaneous volumes. Volumes 22 to 28 of the minutes of Council cover the 1748 to 1776 period. Richard Pares has described the eight miscellaneous volumes as giving "accounts of matters which came under Lucas's own observation, from about 1770, and elucidations of earlier documents which could not have been guessed from the documents themselves, and nobody now living could supply." The Barbados Museum and Historical Society located in St. Michael has a few eighteenth century official records and letters. The records consist of the Governor's answers to questions transmitted by the Rt. Hon. Lords Commissioners for Trade and Plantations in 1762 and correspondence with the Bahama Islands, 1755, and with Grenada, 1763. The letters discuss Barbados affairs and are addressed mainly to Joshua Sharpe, Solicitor to the Treasury, of Lincoln's Inn, and to Samuel Touchett.

Ecclesiastical records in Barbados are located, for the most part, in the churches that produced them. The records for the latter half of the eighteenth century consist almost entirely of parish registers of Anglican Churches. These registers record the births, marriages and burials which took place within a parish's jurisdiction. The churches which have eighteenth century records, either original or copies, are St. Michael's Cathedral and the following parish churches: Christ Church, St. James's,

St. John's, St. Joseph's, St. Lucy's, St. Philip's, and St. Thomas's. All the registers of these churches have been copied and deposited in the Department of Archives. The Church Book of Sharon Moravian Church is the only other pertinent ecclesiastical record. This book gives information, beginning in 1769, on the negro members of the church. The entries deal primarily with baptisms and marriages. An appendix in the book gives some information on the Moravian missionaries, their wives and children. This book has also been deposited in the Department of Archives.

BERMUDA

During the period in the early 1920's when Herbert C. Bell and David W. Parker drew up their *Guide to British West Indian Archives Materials* . . . , the surviving official records of the government of Bermuda held in the island were in the so-called Public Building in Hamilton. When the author of the series, of which this volume is the concluding number, was carrying on research in Bermuda, this material was located in a reconstructed, air-conditioned barracks outside of Hamilton. Since then there has been constructed the Bermuda Archives, adjacent to the Public Library in Hamilton. Most of the material in it relating to the period 1748–1776 is in bound volumes. There is evidence that they have been well cared for. As they are numbered it would be well to preserve this numbering. They are as follows with respect to contents:

Nos. 41–52. Commissions, 1721–1879, issued by royal warrant or by the governor's own authority to various civil officials and also naval officers;

Nos. 53–79, 62A, 79A, 392–396. Wills, 1648–1881;

Nos. 184–185. Minutes of the Council, 1722–1759;

No. 186. Minutes of the Legislative Council, 1774–1777;

Nos. 210–211. Minutes of the Council in Assembly, 1759–1765;

Nos. 222–224. Grants, 1758–1917, including crown lands and revenues arising thereupon;

Nos. 237–244. Action Books, relating to civil actions, 1700 to date;

Nos. 248–250. Vice-Admiralty papers, 1705–1765, but very incomplete; *No. 250* covers the years 1762–1765;

Nos. 316–384. Acts and Resolves, 1696 to date, including laws not confirmed by the King in Council.

The Bermuda Archives also contains parish records. Among them is that part of the personal diary of the Rev. Alexander Richardson of St. Peter's Church in St. George's Parish that covers the years 1756–1772.

JAMAICA

The public records of Jamaica are of great importance. However, it is not always easy for the student to locate the materials that may interest him or her, for the valuable aid by Herbert C. Bell and David W. Parker: *Guide to British West Indian Archives Materials, in London and on the Islands, for the History of the United States,* published by the Carnegie Institution of Washington in 1926, can no longer be relied upon. This the author of the present guide discovered in going to the island in the 1950's. Nor is the quite recent (August 1965) statement by Clinton V. Black, Government Archivist of Jamaica, in his "A List of the Records in the Jamaica Archives . . . ," *Report of the Caribbean Archives Conference held at the University of the West Indies, Mona, Jamaica, September 20–27, 1965,* pp. 371–8, any longer quite accurate respecting the location of a number of collections of documents. For example, in July 1967 many records reposing in the Colonial Secretary's Office were transferred to the Jamaica Archives. In view of the task of reorganization still proceeding at the Record Office and the Archives at Spanish Town and the Institute at Kingston it would be well for the inquiring student to consult the Archives for up-to-date information respecting the location of papers.

The island of Jamaica has had in the past four depositories with records pertinent to the period 1748–1776. These are: the Jamaica Archives, the Institute of Jamaica, the Island Record Office, and the Registrar General's Department.

The Jamaica Archives at Spanish Town contains records from the onetime Colonial Secretary's Office, the House of Assembly, various judicial and administrative departments and some local records. Manuscripts from the Colonial Secretary's Office at Kingston and now in the Archives include: (1) Copies of despatches from Jamaica to England, 1726–1898; (2) Journals of the Council, 1711–1854, sitting as a legislative body; (3) Minutes of the Council, 1661–1805, sitting in its executive capacity as advisor to the governor; (4) Proceedings of Commissioners for Forts, Fortifications and Barracks, 1769–1772. The Archives also has the manuscript copies of the journals of the House of Assembly, 1679–1810, which therefore cover the 1748–1776 period. These journals were all printed in the *Journals of the Assembly of Jamaica . . . 1663–[1826]* (15 vols., Jamaica, 1811–29).

The judicial records come from the deliberations of three courts; the Supreme Court, the Court of Chancery, and the Vice-Admiralty Court. The records of these courts are quite full. Among the Supreme Court records are: series of judgments; hurry and assignment books; pleas of the Crown; minute, order, vindication, receipt and summons books; and some judgments of the assize and circuit courts. These 800 volumes of records begin in 1680 and end in the nineteenth century. The Court of

Chancery material includes: three series of general proceedings, decrees, master's reports, petitions and recognizances, minute- and order-books, fee and file books, 900 vols., 1672–1882 (with gaps). The Vice-Admiralty Court records consist of 2,800 packets of unbound papers which deal principally with prize causes. However, there is some oyer and terminer material among these records as well as some minute-books and fee and file books. The packets extend from the mid-18th century to 1830.

The administrative records come from the Island Record Office and the Registrar General's Department. Materials taken from the Island Record Office include: (1) Accounts produce (crop accounts), 1740–1891; (2) Patents, 1661–1905; (3) Inventories, 1674–1881; (4) Letters of administration, 1710–1879; (5) Manumissions and Releases from Apprenticeship, 1740–1838; (6) Court of Ordinary—Citations, 1764–1862; (7) Court of Ordinary—Proceedings, 1754–1863; (8) Wills, 1754–1899. From the Registrar General's Department the Archives has acquired almost all of the original Church of England Parish Registers of baptisms, marriages, and burials, 1664–1880.

The Jamaica Archives besides possessing records relating to the island's general activities has local records from Kingston, St. Catherine, St. Ann and Port Royal. The records from Kingston are the most extensive. These include: vestry minutes, vestry accounts, town common council minutes, tax polls and lists of tax payers, 1744–1879. Vestry minutes make up the major portion of the records from the other three places. The dates covered by these records are: St. Catherine, 1757–1898, St. Ann, 1767–1883 and Port Royal, 1735–1886.

The Institute of Jamaica at Kingston has some official papers and records relating to various estates. Among the official papers are: (1) Letters (67 items) of Gov. Edward Trelawny, 1740–1750; (2) Papers of Gov. William Henry Lyttelton, 1764–1766. One of the latter items is a description of Jamaica, 1764, and the other, a letter to the Secretary of the Board of Trade, John Pownall, concerning the misconduct of a naval officer and the procedure for appointing deputies, 1766 (5 pp.); (3) Letters of Lieut.-Gov. Roger Hope Elletson, 1766–1768 (1 vol.); (4) Documents issued by Robert Melville as Governor of Grenada, the Grenadines, Dominica, St. Vincent and Tobago, 1764–1771, respecting the appointments of various Windward Islands officials; (5) Jamaica High Court of Vice-Admiralty, record sheets of ships captured, 1750–1806; (6) Great Britain: Lords Commissioners for Trade and Plantations, 1753, a report on "the present state of the island of Jamaica" presented to the House of Commons on Feb. 22, 1753 (49 pp.); (7) Four letters of George Brydges, 1st Baron Rodney, 1762, to William Barkham, naval officer at Antigua, concerning stores; (8) Documents relating to the Royal Dockyard at English Harbor, Antigua, 1770–1803, including pay lists for piloting, caulking, officers' expenses, and sailmaking; (9) Antigua yard cheque book, Lady Quarter to Christmas Quarter, 1775.

The Institute Reference Library also includes estates records: (1) The Dawkins Collection, 1655–c. 1780, a collection of documents dealing with the Jamaican land holdings of the Dawkins family. There are plans of estates, plats, indentures, wills, etc.; (2) Letter and account books relative to the Rio Grande Estate, owned by Sarah Smith and John Mosely, 1753–1755; (3) Papers on the Irwin and Tryall estates owned by Thomas Hall, 1758–1765; (4) Letters of Lieut.-Gov. Roger Hope Elletson concerning Hope estate matters, 1773–1780.

The Island Record Office at Spanish Town contains: (1) Laws, 1661 to the present—authenticated copies of the laws of Jamaica; (2) Deeds (Old Series), 1661 to the present, 985 libers; (3) Wills (Old Series), 1663–1871, 133 libers; (4) Powers of attorney (Old Series), 1671 to the present, 275 libers.

The Registrar General's Department has copy registers and some originals of Church of England records for baptisms, marriages and burials, 1664–1800.

THE LEEWARD ISLANDS

The principal British Leeward Islands of the West Indies whose records relating to the period 1748–1776 exist are Antigua, Montserrat, Nevis, and St. Christopher. Their manuscript holdings will be discussed in the above order. In doing so it will be well to follow E. C. Baker's A *Guide to Records in the Leeward Islands* (Oxford, 1965).

Antigua

The island of Antigua, although lacking an ample water supply, still prospered in the eighteenth century. The capital, St. John's, in the 1750's was the residence of the Governor of the Leeward Islands; a regiment of troops was also stationed on the island, which likewise had the only port in the Lesser Antilles suitable for sheltering, cleaning and refitting his Majesty's large ships. In fact the present situation of the British Leewards bears little relation to their importance in the eighteenth century.

Professor Richard Pares after visiting the island in 1930 commented that its records were as badly kept as any he had ever seen. In the twenty years that followed nothing was done to correct the situation. So, in 1954, most of the Antigua official records were transferred to the Colonial Office in London. They are now in the Ashridge Park repository of the Public Record Office. Those that have remained on the island have been described in E. C. Baker's *Guide*, reference to which has already been made. The description that follows is therefore based upon it.

The Government House and Court-House, both at St. John's, contain the largest collections of Antigua civil records. The Government House has copies of the laws of Antigua, 1668–1791, and of the laws that applied to all the Leeward Islands, 1690–1798. The Court-House has two deed record books and two court record books. The deed record books, which cover the periods 1760–1773 and 1769–1771, contain copies of agreements, appraisals of property, conveyances, manumissions, leases and powers of attorney. The court record books, 1762–1763 and 1764–1767, deal only with the proceedings of the court of common pleas. All of the pertinent records in the Court-House are in poor condition and have been microfilmed for the University of the West Indies.

The ecclesiastical records on Antigua come from the Anglican, Methodist and Moravian Churches. The Deanery, St. John's, has the most extensive collection of Anglican records. Its registers of baptisms, marriages and burials cover most of the eighteenth century. The vestry minutes from the Deanery run from 1769 to 1918. The following Anglican Churches also have registers: St. Peter's, baptism and burial registers, 1771–1835; St. George's, baptism and burial registers, 1724–1830; and St. Philip's, baptism registers, 1767–1821. Deeds, conveyances, leases and correspondence, 1769–1932, make up the Methodist records in the Manse, St. John's. The Moravians have preserved a variety of documents in Spring Gardens. Among them are: a few missionaries' memoranda, reports and correspondence, 1716–1800; deeds and plans of church sites, 1731–1958; a list of missionaries of the United Brethren stationed on Antigua, 1755–1927; registers of baptisms and deaths, 1760–1794; and lists of male and female slaves on various estates, 1771–1833. It should be noted that these early records of the Moravian Church are in the process of being transferred to the Archives of the Moravian Church located in Bethlehem, Pennsylvania.

Montserrat

The Archive Room in the Government House of Montserrat at Plymouth has ten deed record books which cover the following years: 1749–1750, 1755–1757, 1762–1770, 1762–1765, 1762–1771, 1765–1767, 1768–1770, 1770–1773, 1772–1774, 1774–1776. Likewise, Bell and Parker in their *Guide* (p. 391) refer to a volume of minutes of the Council, Oct. 5, 1759–Sept. 26, 1776, which, however, was in bad condition and could not be examined but which contained governors' commissions and instructions. The only ecclesiastical record is a Roman Catholic register of baptisms, marriages and burials, 1771–1838.

Nevis

The court-house, at Charlestown, contains the following manuscripts: Common deed record books, 1752–1801, and King's/Queen's Bench and Common Pleas court record books, 1750–1776; however, the court records for 1755 and 1768 are missing. The Anglican Church of St. John the Baptist, Figtree, has a register of baptisms, marriages and burials, 1728–1825.

St. Christopher (St. Kitts)

A very prosperous British Leeward island in the middle of the eighteenth century, St. Kitts shipped to England as much sugar as Antigua and Nevis combined, despite the fact that it has no harbour but only a shallow roadway at the capital, Basseterre.

The archives room in the government building at Basseterre has a large collection of civil records. Included among them are those that are legislative, judicial and personal in nature. The collection of legislative records with relationship to the period 1748–1776 is composed of the following: St. Christopher Council minute-books, 1748, 1755–1762, 1772–1778; Secretary's draft minute-book, 1771–1782, which includes the Assembly minutes; St. Christopher Legislative Assembly, minute-books, 1745–1753, 1756–1761, 1761–1769, 1769–1776, 1776–1778; St. Christopher and Anguilla, acts, 1755–1760, 1765–1781. It should also be noted that the Nevis Council minute-books, covering the years 1745–1748, 1761–1772, and 1772–1780, are also here. The different courts which have left pertinent records are: Court of Chancery, 1735–1757, 1769–1781; Court of Errors, minutes, 1715–1757, 1772–1819; King's Bench and Common Pleas, 1749–1779, with gaps before 1759; Court of Grand Sessions of the Peace and of Oyer and Terminer, Basseterre, minute-books, 1772–1806; Insolvent Debtors and Debtors Court, records, 1766–1768, 1769–1770, 1773–1775, and some miscellaneous court and legal records, 1740–1840. The personal records at this archives are mostly registers. They include: marriage bond books, 1771–1786; guardian bond books, 1772–1808; wills and testament bond books, 1772–1785; deed record books, 1748–1777 and Registrar in Ordinary and Provost Marshal, account books, 1753–1756, 1764–1779, 1771–1782.

All the relevant ecclesiastical records on St. Christopher come from Anglican Churches. These records consist entirely of registers of baptisms, marriages and burials. The churches which have such registers are: St. George's, Basseterre, 1747–1795; St. Thomas's (with Holy Trinity) Church, Middle Island, 1730–1826 and St. Anne's Church, Sandy Point, 1762–1826.

Anguilla and the British Virgin Islands

The Registrar's office in Anguilla has one bundle of council minutes for the period 1740–1780. The only pertinent records in the British Virgin Islands are two ordinary deed record books, 1761–1765, 1776, which are kept in the record room of the Tortola Treasury Building.

THE WINDWARD ISLANDS

The West Indies island of Dominica, earlier classified as one of the Leeward Islands, is now considered a Windward Island and is so classified. One of the so-called Neutral Islands, it was, nevertheless, colonized by the French but in 1761 was conquered by the British. In 1766 it became a free port and the following year a full-fledged royal province, with an Assembly and Council, and in 1770 William Young was made Governor-in-Chief of the island, in place of Lieutenant-Governor. A most useful guide to the state papers of Dominica and the other Windward Islands was prepared by E. C. Baker and published in Oxford in 1968 under the title *A Guide to Records in the Windward Islands*. We shall follow this guide with respect to papers bearing upon the years 1748–1776 that are still in these islands.

Three depositories at Roseau, the capital, have pertinent documents. The Archive Room in the Ministerial Building contains: (1) Privy Council Minute Books, 1775–1782; (2) Oath Books, 1774–1833; (3) Court of Ordinary, minutes, 1769–1784; (4) Court of Common Pleas, minutes, 1772–1775, executions, 1774–1790, judgments, 1775–1778; (5) Deed Record Books, 1764–1778; (6) Books of Acts, 1765–1893. The Crown Surveyor's Office has: (1) Plans copied from deed copy books of parcels of land, 1766–1829; (2) Plans of estates, 1776–1965; (3) Byre's survey of Dominica, Nov. 1776. The Cathedral of the Assumption of Our Lady of Good Haven has registers of baptisms, marriages and burials, 1730–1789. Many of the records mentioned are in poor condition. Some have been filmed.

See Baker: *A Guide to Records in the Windward Islands*, pp. 64–89.

In addition to Dominica, the islands of Grenada and also St. Lucia and St. Vincent make up the Windwards of the West Indies. Before the Great War for the Empire Grenada was a prosperous, well-settled French possession. Conquered by the British in 1762, it was ceded by France in the Treaty of Peace the following year.

The strong room of the Supreme Court Registry at St. George's contains most of the relevant records on Grenada. Among them are: (1) House of Assembly, minutes (in some instances these are described as notes), 1766–1776; (2) Drafts of messages from the Governor to the Council and Assembly, 1768–1772; (3) Original Acts, 1771–1872; (4) Deed Record Books, 2 series in English, 1763–1964, 1764–1840, and one in French, 1766–1783; (5) Certificate of mortgage entry book of the Colonial Secretary, 1774–1777; (6) Record books of the Lieut.-Governor's commissions, 1764–1856; (7) Records of various courts, Court of Common Pleas, 1765–1800; Court of Vice-Admiralty, precedent book, 1757–1820;

(8) Representation that Roman Catholics be admitted as members of council, 1772–1809; (9) Provost Marshal's record of debts, 1771–1776; (10) Roman Catholic registers of baptisms, marriages and burials on the island of Carriacou, 1762–1786, St. Jaques, Fort Royale, 1765–1785; (11) Merchant's journal, 1771–1776.

Two other depositories on the island have pertinent material. The Record Room in the Ministerial Building holds copy letter-books, outgoing, of the Administrator or Colonial Secretary of Grenada, 1764–1771. These books contain copies of letters sent locally or to London. The Public Library has one envelope of correspondence between Gen. Thomas and Gov. Dalrymple which concerns a proposed attack on Dominica in 1760. The correspondence includes a description of Dominica.

See E. C. Baker: *A Guide to Records in the Windward Islands,* pp. 4–29, and J. C. Nardin: "Les Archives Anciennes de la Grenada," *Revue Française d'Histoire d'Outre-mer,* XLIX (1962), 117–40, reprinted in French and English in *Report of the Caribbean Archives Conference Held at the University of the West Indies, Mona, Jamaica, September 20–27, 1965* (Kingston, Jamaica, n.d.), pp. 327–368.

St. Lucia, one of the so-called Neutral Islands of the West Indies, while claimed by Great Britain, was ceded to France in 1763. No other island in this area was contended for more vigorously by the two powers for over two centuries, as it passed back and forth between them until in 1814 Great Britain's right to it was acknowledged.

E. C. Baker found only a few manuscript items on St. Lucia which have a bearing on the 1748–1776 period. The Government had two sketch maps of British attacks on Morne Fortune, 1763. Mr. Leonard Devaux of Castries possessed a record of an estate sale, May 6, 1774.

See E. C. Baker: *A Guide to Records in the Windward Islands,* pp. 49–63.

St. Vincent, another of the Neutral Islands, was ceded to Great Britain in 1763 after its conquest from the French the preceding year. It was the only Windward Island heavily populated with Caribs. Surviving papers held in the Supreme Court Registrar's strong room at Kingston include: (1) Books of Acts, 1767–1772; (2) Colonial Secretary's deed record books, 1770–1776; (3) Records of births, marriages and burials on St. Vincent, 1765–1864.

See E. C. Baker: *A Guide to Records in the Windward Islands,* pp. 30–48.

TOBAGO

Allotted to Great Britain in the Treaty of Peace of 1763, Tobago, to the southward of the Windward Islands and close to South America, was but slowly settled. As another of the Neutral Islands, it was contended for between the British and the French until in 1814 it became permanently a part of the British Empire. The surviving official records falling within the period 1748–1776 and still on the island are but few. They consist of Court of Common Pleas, minutes, 1776–1778, and Marshal's Office, accounts, 1776–1784. Manuscripts in private hands at the Studley Park Estate, Tobago, include: (1) Plans and drawings, 1776, including plans of a factory, a public house and some private houses; (2) Plan of a part of Tobago, 1776, which includes the parish of St. George and parts of the parishes of St. Mary and St. Andrews; (3) List of lots in George Town, Tobago, 1776; (4) Report on economic situation in Tobago, 1776, which includes statistics on exports and describes the impact of the beginning of the American Revolution on Tobago's economy. See Enos Sewall: "List of Archives of Trinidad and Tobago," *Report of the Caribbean Archives Conference* . . . , pp. 379–407.

PART XI

The United States

WASHINGTON, D.C.

THE LIBRARY OF CONGRESS

THE Library of Congress is one of the greatest libraries in the world, dwarfing in its contents any other depository in the United States. It is therefore not possible within the necessary limits of this volume to do justice to the collections of original papers and even larger collections of reproductions (transcripts, photostats, microfilms and microprints) of original papers in Great Britain, France, Spain and elsewhere, that bear upon the British Empire, 1748–1776, and that are possessed by the Library of Congress. We shall therefore be obliged to forego any detailed comment on the contents of the collections. Happily, the student will find in the Manuscript Division of the Library the necessary aids.

Among the papers (either originals or reproductions) of colonial officials that bear upon the period under examination are those of Dennys De Berdt, Massachusetts Bay London agent, 1765–1770 (1 vol.); Sir Guy Carleton, governor of Quebec, 1774–1777 (1 vol.); Charles Garth, London agent for South Carolina and Maryland, 1766–1774 (1 box); Jared Ingersoll, Connecticut London agent and judge of the Middle District Court of Vice-Admiralty, 1740–1779 (3 boxes); Sir William Johnson, Superintendent of Indian Affairs in the Northern District, 1755–1774 (1 vol.); and Robert Monckton, British army officer and governor of the Province of New York, 1754–1763 (1 vol.).

Representing American patriot leaders are papers of Benjamin Franklin, 1726–1790 (42 vols., 6 boxes, and 5 portfolios); Thomas Jefferson, 1651–1826 (247 vols. and 10 boxes); Patrick Henry and family, 1762–1881 (1 box); James Madison, 1723–1845 (114 vols., 10 boxes, and microfilm); and George Washington, 1592–1811 (389 vols. and 44 boxes of originals; 11 vols. and 46 boxes of reproductions).

Papers of other American colonials include those of Charles Carroll, Maryland, member of the Continental Congress, and ancestors, 1684–1829

(4 vols. and 5 boxes); Silas Deane, Connecticut member of the Continental Congress and later diplomat, 1775–1784 (6 vols. and 1 box); Samuel Holten, Massachusetts member of the Continental Congress, 1744–1842 (5 containers); William Samuel Johnson, Connecticut London agent and member of the Continental Congress, 1745–1790 (1 vol.); the Pinckney family of South Carolina, 1694–1866 (5 vols. and 52 boxes); the Randolph family of Virginia, 1742–1869 (5 vols. and 52 boxes); Roger Sherman, Connecticut member of the Continental Congress, 1746–1810 (1 vol. and 2 boxes); the Shippen family of Pennsylvania, 1693–1936 (2 vols., 31 boxes, and 2 portfolios); the Rev. Ezra Stiles of Rhode Island and Connecticut, 1758–1790 (4 vols. of transcripts); and John Tyler, Virginia Revolutionary War officer and father of President Tyler, 1710–1861 (8 vols.).

Among military and naval figures are those of William Alexander, Lord Stirling, 1774–1782 (2 vols.); John Barry, Philadelphia, ship owner and later naval officer, 1770–1798 (1 box); Nathanael Greene, 1775–1783 (4 vols. and 7 boxes); and John Paul Jones, 1775–1789 (15 vols., 5 boxes, and 2 portfolios).

There are still other collections of papers of importance to the student of the history of the British Empire, 1748–1776. Among them are the so-called "Negro papers," 1734–1944 (22 boxes); "Slave papers," 1719–1860 (2 boxes and 4 portfolios); Connecticut papers, 1637–1836 (23 vols. and 3 boxes, including transcripts of colonial records); Delaware papers, 1684–1865 (4 vols., 4 boxes, and 1 pkg.); some East and West Florida papers; Georgia papers, 1732–1869 (13 vols. and 6 boxes); some early Louisiana papers; Maryland papers, 1632–1918 (including material from the Force collection); New Hampshire papers, 1629–1918 (31 vols., and 21 boxes); New York papers, 1623–1942 (67 vols. and 14 boxes); Pennsylvania papers, 1650–1925 (17 vols. and 19 boxes); Rhode Island papers, 1587–1890 (13 vols. and 4 boxes); Vermont papers, 1744–1936 (46 vols. and 5 boxes); Virginia papers, 1606–1925 (35 vols. and 32 boxes); and West Indies miscellany, 1494–1821 (28 vols., 10 boxes, and 1 portfolio).

See *Handbook of Manuscripts in the Library of Congress* (Washington, D.C., 1918); Curtis W. Garrison: *List of Manuscripts Collections in the Library of Congress to July 1931* (Washington, D.C., 1932); C. Percy Powell: *List of Manuscript Collections Received in the Library of Congress July 1931 to July 1938* (Washington, D.C., 1938); Library of Congress: *Annual Report* (1938+); *Quarterly Journal of Acquisitions* (1943+); and Philip M. Hamer, ed.: *A Guide to Archives and Manuscripts in the United States, Compiled for the National Historical Commission* (New Haven, 1961), pp. 84–121. As to the manuscript reproductions from abroad, see Grace Gardner Griffin: *A Guide to Manuscripts Relating to American History in British Depositories Reproduced for the Division of Manuscripts of the Library of Congress* (Washington, D.C., 1946) for the period down to 1943. For French and Spanish reproductions, as well as British reproductions since the appearance of the Griffin *Guide,* see again *Handbook of Manuscripts,* pp. 422–63; and also subsequent issues of the *Quarterly Journal of Acquisitions.*

It is now necessary to turn from this great national depository to those depositories in the states of the Union that throw light on the history of the British Empire for the period, 1748–1776. In doing so it will be convenient to examine them in the alphabetical order of the states. Within a state, when there may be more than one depository of manuscripts, we shall deal first of all with official collections of the state and then with other depositories proceeding alphabetically.

CALIFORNIA

San Marino

HENRY E. HUNTINGTON LIBRARY

The holdings of this library relating to the history of the British Empire, 1748–1776, are large and exceedingly important. There are collections within collections. The chief bodies of pertinent manuscripts are as follows:

(1) The Major General James Abercromby, commander of the British forces in North America, and family, papers, 1674–1787 (approx. 1,000 pieces), chiefly of interest in connection with the Fort Ticonderoga campaign of 1758, yet embodying other important papers, including a valuable lengthy analysis of the structure and functioning of the various British colonies by a relation of the general, and with the same name, James Abercromby, British agent in America and later London agent for the government of Virginia. The manuscript is entitled, "An Examination of the Acts of Parliament Relative to the Trade and the Government of our American colonies . . . 1752."

(2) The Robert Alonzo Brock collection of papers (some 2,000 pieces) covering the years 1639–1800—especially important are those concerned with Virginia lands and trade between America and Great Britain before 1800. The papers relating to trade include the following groups of manuscripts: (a) The Macajah Crew papers (150 pieces); (b) The William Cuninghame & Co. papers (100 pieces); (c) The John Cunliffe papers (58 pieces); (d) The Donald, Burton & James Brown papers (20 pieces); (e) The John Norton & Sons papers (225 pieces); (f) The Fairfax family papers (100 pieces), among which are warrants, 1749–1752, for the survey of Fairfax lands, many endorsed by Washington; (g) The Benjamin Harrison family papers (41 pieces); (h) The Lee family papers (30 pieces); (i) The Randolph family papers (27 pieces); and (j) The Charles Scott family papers (20 pieces).

(3) Canadian papers, 1642–1900 (257 pieces).

(4) The Rev. William Cooper and the Rev. Samuel Cooper sermons

in manuscript, together with papers relating to the crisis leading to the American Revolution, 1718–1798 (270 pieces).

(5) Governor Robert Dinwiddie letters, 1751–1758 (55 pieces).

(6) The Fairfax estate in Virginia papers (records of the Proprietor's Office of the Northern Neck of Virginia), 1690–1843 (350 pieces).

(7) Benjamin Franklin's holograph autobiography.

(8) The Governor Benjamin Harrison of Virginia family papers, 1701–1910 (195 pieces).

(9) The Hastings and related papers, 1100–1892 (50,000 pieces), including the papers of the British Revolutionary War general, Francis Lord Rawdon (1754–1826), who later changed his name to Rawdon-Hastings, becoming 1st Marquess of Hasting, and 2nd Earl of Moira.

(10) The Jefferson papers, 1764–1826 (800 pieces), letters, diaries, account books, surveys, architectural drawings, etc., involving Peter and Thomas Jefferson.

(11) John Campbell, 4th Earl of Loudoun, commander-in-chief of British forces in America, and family, papers, 1510–1839 (16,000 pieces), relating chiefly to Scotland and North America, especially important for the period of Loudoun's military command, 1756–1758. Among other manuscripts of special interest and pertinence in the Loudoun collection are the following: (a) Papers having to do with the Albany Congress of 1754; (b) The 1755 report of Edmond Atkin, superintendent of Indian affairs for the southern district, to the Board of Trade; (c) Thomas Pownall's proposals, about 1755, for settling a colony south of Lake Erie; (d) George Washington's report from Fort Cumberland, 1757, on the defense of the Virginia frontier; (e) Papers relating to Loudoun's council of war, July 23, 1757, to discuss the proposed attack on Louisbourg; (f) "Transactions at Fort William Henry during its siege," Aug. 1757, author unknown; (g) Articles of surrender accorded to Lieut.-Col. Monro by the Marquis de Montcalm, Aug. 9, 1757 (in French); (h) Benjamin Franklin's "List of Servants belonging to the inhabitants of Pennsylvania and taken into His Majesty's Service for whom satisfaction has not been made by the officers according to an Act of Parliament," Philadelphia, Aug. 21, 1757; (i) Four letters by Cadwallader Colden, New York, Oct. 1757, regarding Indian attacks and the need for frontier defenses, with a map; (j) Two letters from James Abercromby, May and June, 1775, about the battles of Concord and Bunker Hill.

There are also in the Loudoun collection pertinent Board of Trade commercial papers and a very large number of papers, mostly letters, from people of prominence both in England and America for the period 1748–1776, including James Abercromby, William Alexander (Lord Stirling), William Wildman Barrington, 2nd Viscount Barrington, Henry Bouquet, James Cuninghame, James de Lancey, Robert Dinwiddie, Thomas Gage, Robert Monckton, Thomas Pownall, William Shirley, and others.

(12) Robert Morris papers, 1774–1837 (320 items), including some 40 letters written by Richard Champion, Bristol merchant trading to the colonies, between the years 1774–1776.

(13) Edmond Sexton Pery, Irish leader, 1749–1798 (350 pieces).

(14) Admiral Sir George Pocock papers, 1733–1793 (1,170 pieces), including his letter-book during his naval operations off the coasts of India and Cuba, 1757–1765.

(15) The Stowe collection, 1175–1825 (525,000 pieces, 650 of which relate to America before 1800). This huge collection embodies papers of the Grenville, Temple, Nugent, and Brydges families. Among manuscripts having to do with America are West India sugar plantation papers, especially notable are those of Hope Plantation, Jamaica; papers relating to the administration of the new colonies after the Peace of Paris of 1763 as well as many papers leading up to the Peace; and those involving difficulties facing John Temple, Surveyor-General of Customs of the Northern District in America, in seeking to enforce the Trade and Navigation Acts.

(16) The Thomas Townshend (later Viscount Sydney) papers, 1765–1787 (47 pieces), covering Townshend's part in the Rockingham and Grafton ministries and his opposition to Lord North.

(17) The papers of Pierre François Rigaud, Marquis de Vaudreuil, governor-general of New France, which became embodied in the Loudoun collection when captured and turned over to Lord Loudoun in 1755. They cover the years 1740–1753 (383 pieces) and chiefly relate to developments in Louisiana while Vaudreuil was governor of that province.

(18) George Washington papers, 1749–1806 (540 pieces), especially concerned with military correspondence and land holdings.

(19) There are also miscellaneous manuscripts in the library not in the above collections, in the form of diaries, journals, letter-books, log-books, reports, etc., bearing upon the period 1748–1776. Among them are the following: (a) Lord Loudoun's notebooks and military journals, 1753–1760 (12 vols.); (b) Abijah Willard's orderly book and journal concerned with the New England expedition to Nova Scotia, 1755–1756; (c) Orderly book for the 3rd Battalion of the Pennsylvania Regiment, Hugh Mercer, colonial commander, for the campaign in 1758 against Fort Duquesne; (d) Regimental journal of the Saratoga and Lake George campaigns, kept by Obadiah Harris, May-Oct. 1758; (e) Joseph Nichols's military journal, 1758–1766, relating to the Ticonderoga campaign of the Massachusetts forces and events subsequent to it; (f) Joseph Bull's orderly book, 1759, of the 1st Battalion of the New York Regiment at Schenectady and at Forts Herkimer, Stanwix, Oswego, and Ontario; (g) Orderly book, 1759, for Samuel Grubbs's company of the Pennsylvania Provincial Forces at Carlisle and Fort Bedford; (h) Enoch Poor's journal, 1759–1760, and list of men "In the Garson. Fort Fradrick att Saint Johns"; (i) John Grant's orderly book, 1761, of Archibald McNeile's company in

the 2nd Connecticut Regiment commanded by Nathan Whiting at Crown Point; (j) "General Reports" by the Attorney and Solicitor General of Great Britain, 1763–1767, on divers subjects chiefly related to the Empire; (k) Papers laid before the Privy Council relating to the proceedings of the Assemblies of Massachusetts Bay and New York in opposition to the Stamp Act, together with all orders in council issued as a result of an examination of these proceedings; (l) James Scott's "Transactions On board the Brig[anti]ne Lydia [John Hancock, owner] myself master," in the course of seven passages between Boston and London, 1764–1766; (m) Colonial agent James Abercromby's "De Jure et Gubernatione Coloniarum, or An Inquiry into the Nature and Rights of Colonies, Ancient and Modern," c. 1775; (n) Robert Honyman's journal of a trip from Virginia to New England and return, March 1–April 28, 1775; (o) Cadwallader Colden [Jr.]'s Revolutionary War journal and other papers, 1776–1779.

See Norma B. Cuthbert: *American Manuscript Collections in the Huntington Library for the History of the Seventeenth and Eighteenth Centuries* (San Marino, Calif., 1941); Stanley M. Pargellis and Norma B. Cuthbert: "Loudoun Papers," *Huntington Library Bulletin*, No. 3 (1933), 97–107; George Sherburn, et al.: "Huntington Library Collections," *ibid.*, No. 1 (1931), 33–106; "Summary Report on the Hastings Manuscripts," *ibid.*, No. 5 (1934), 1–67; Robert C. Cleland: "The Research Facilities of the Huntington Library: Americana," *Huntington Library Quarterly*, III (1939), 135–41; the Library's *Annual Reports* (1927+), containing brief notes on acquisitions; and Philip M. Hamer: *Guide*, pp. 28–38.

CONNECTICUT

Hartford

CONNECTICUT STATE LIBRARY AND ARCHIVES

Since the State Library serves also as the State Archives of Connecticut and also contains other papers relating to Connecticut and New England, there are various materials pertaining to the pre-1776 period. On deposit are colonial legislative records from 1636, including the Connecticut Archives (legislative papers from 1636–1820, 400+ vols.); the Trumbull Collection of Connecticut Colonial Official Papers, 1631–1784, 29 vols.; and records of the colonial courts of Connecticut. Among the non-official papers are those of the following persons: Eliphalet Dyer, including a journal and some personal papers, 1763–1765; William Samuel Johnson, a letter-book and some other Johnson items, 1766–1771; Jonathan Trumbull, an account book, 1741–1771; and the Sherman W. Adams manuscript collection, relating to the French and Indian War.

See *Select List of Manuscripts in the Connecticut State Library,* Connecticut State Library, *Bulletin,* No. 9 (Hartford, Conn., 1920); Philip M. Hamer: *Guide,* pp. 56–7; and Library of Congress: *Manuscripts in Public and Private Collections* (Washington, 1924), pp. 9–10.

CONNECTICUT HISTORICAL SOCIETY

The Historical Society at Hartford contains the acts and papers of the Connecticut General Assembly, 1650–1800; the correspondence of the colony's agents in London, 1742–1759; and the correspondence with other colonies, 1753–1809. There are sermons, town and church records, and various papers relating to the French and Indian wars, 1745–1762, and to the Revolutionary War. An important part of the collections consists of papers belonging to Jonathan Trumbull, 1737–1785, including personal and business accounts, a diary, sermons, notebooks, and letters. Other papers include those of Silas Deane, 1771–1789; Thomas Fitch, 1754–1766; Nathan Hale, diary and letters to, 1773–1776; William Samuel Johnson, 1765–1790; Jonathan Law, official correspondence, 1741–1750; Israel Putnam, 1757–1773; William Williams, correspondence and miscellaneous writings, 1760–1800; Oliver Wolcott, Sr., papers, 1638–1834; and Roger Wolcott, papers, 1631–1768.

See the Connecticut Historical Society, *Annual Report* (1890+); Philip M. Hamer: *Guide,* pp. 54–6; and Library of Congress: *Manuscripts in Public and Private Collections,* pp. 6–9.

New Haven

NEW HAVEN COLONY HISTORICAL SOCIETY

Among the manuscripts of the Society are papers of both Jared Ingersoll and the Rev. Ezra Stiles. Also of some use are payrolls, muster rolls, and other papers relating to Connecticut soldiers in the Revolutionary War. See Philip M. Hamer: *Guide,* p. 60; and Library of Congress: *Manuscripts in Public and Private Collections,* p. 11.

YALE UNIVERSITY LIBRARIES

The most important body of manuscripts in the Yale Libraries concerned with the period under examination is the group comprising part of the Benjamin Franklin Collection of books, pamphlets, manuscripts, and prints assembled by William Smith Mason. Housed in the same rooms, but not at present open to use by other scholars, is the file of photocopies of all Franklin-related manuscripts that the editors of *The Papers of Benjamin Franklin* have been able to locate in libraries and other repositories or in private possession. These collected papers are being published by the Yale University Press under the joint sponsorship of the American Philosophical Society and Yale University and up to the present have been under the chief editorship of Professor Leonard W. Labaree.

Other manuscripts concerned with the period 1748–1776 in the Yale Libraries are varying numbers of those of the following individuals: Sir Joseph Banks, 1763–1819; John Bartram, 1742–1762; Sir Francis Bernard, 1758–1771; Silas Deane, 1755–1778; Jonathan Edwards, 1730–1758; Thomas Fitch, 1751–1758; Thomas Hutchinson, 1764–1765; Jared Ingersoll, 1751–1781; William Livingston of New York and New Jersey, 1742–1773; Thomas Pownall, 1758; Roger Sherman, 1766–1792; Ezra Stiles (a very large collection); Benjamin Trumbull, 1755–1820; Jonathan Trumbull, 1767–1783; Thomas Turner, English store-keeper, 1754–1761 (111 vols. of diaries); John Witherspoon, 1768, 1776; and John Joachim Zubly, 1768–1772.

See Zara Jones Powers: "American Historical Manuscripts in the [Yale] Historical Manuscript Room," *Yale University Library Gazette,* XIV (1939), 1–11; Philip M. Hamer: *Guide,* pp. 60–73; and Library of Congress: *Manuscripts in Public and Private Collections,* pp. 11–16.

Woodbury

GLEBE HOUSE, WOODBURY CENTER

Here are to be found photostatic copies of the Rev. Samuel Seabury (1729–1796) papers, 9 vols., including letters, sermons, and other papers relating to Seabury and his contemporaries. The original documents are in the Woodbury Bank Vaults. See Philip M. Hamer: *Guide,* p. 70.

DELAWARE

Dover

HALL OF RECORDS,
DELAWARE PUBLIC ARCHIVES COMMISSION

Among the papers of importance in the Hall of Records are the Governor's register, 1674–1905; the minutes of the Assembly, 1739–1810, with gaps; county and other local records, 1728–1850; records of treasurers, assessors, engineers, apprentice indentures, manumissions, and land records, 1728–1850. There are also papers of John Dickinson, George Read, and Caesar Rodney. See *Calendar of Records in the Custody of the Public Archives Commission of the State of Delaware* (Dover, Del., 1935); the Delaware Public Archives Commission: *Annual Report* (1941+); and Philip M. Hamer: *Guide*, pp. 77–8.

Wilmington

HISTORICAL SOCIETY OF DELAWARE, OLD TOWN HALL

Included among the various personal and business manuscripts are papers of Thomas Duff, a Revolutionary War officer, 1749–1807 (50 items); John Dickinson's legal notebook, 1754–1757 (2 vols.); Penn family papers, 1680–1776 (100 items); George Read and family papers, 1756–1908 (200 items); and Caesar Rodney papers, 1708–1790 (257 pieces), among them his sheriff's fee book, 1755–1757. See H. Clay Reed: "Manuscript Books in the Historical Society of Delaware," *Delaware History*, XI (1964), 65–82; and Philip M. Hamer: *Guide*, p. 79.

GEORGIA

Atlanta

DEPARTMENT OF ARCHIVES AND HISTORY

Here will be found transcripts of manuscripts secured from the British Public Record Office (39 vols.) of all materials relating to Georgia listed in the Charles M. Andrews *Guide*, I, 163–5; most of this material has been published by the State. There are, in addition, some sixteen volumes of manuscripts including papers relating to Oglethorpe and other governors covering the period from 1735 to 1783; also judicial records, some county records, and Revolutionary War records, together with other papers bearing upon the history of Georgia as a colony. See Givens Bryan: *A Report [by the Georgia Department of Archives and History] on Archival, Historical and Museum Activities in Georgia on the State and Local Level* (Atlanta, Ga., 1955); Library of Congress: *Manuscripts in Public and Private Collections*, p. 17; and Philip M. Hamer: *Guide*, p. 139.

Athens

UNIVERSITY OF GEORGIA LIBRARIES

Among the manuscript collections are transcripts of the Earl of Egmont Papers, 1732–1752 (21 vols.), including the records of the Trustees of the Colony of Georgia, the journal of William Stephens, Secretary of the Colony, and also the Georgia journal of John Wesley. There are also the Telamon Cuyler collection, 1735–1945 (15,077 items), and the Keith Read manuscript collection, 1732–1865 (3,625 items), largely concerned with the colonial period. See Philip M. Hamer: *Guide,* p. 138.

Savannah

GEORGIA HISTORICAL SOCIETY

There are a number of collections of manuscripts in the Society's library that are relevant to the period 1748–1776. Among them are the following: Brig.-Gen. and Gov. Samuel Elbert, papers, 1776–1786 (1 vol. and 2 pieces); Gen. Lachlan McIntosh, papers, 1774–1799 (1 vol. and 71 pieces); Rev. John Joachim Zubly, diary, 1770–1781 (1 vol.); and George Galphin, Indian trader at Silver Bluff, account books.

Also included among the holdings of the Society are the minutes of the Royal Governor and Council of Georgia, 1774–1775 (1 vol.); inventories of gifts given to the Indians by the colony; Savannah port records; and the records of Midway Church. Finally, there is a collection of family papers and genealogical records gathered by the Georgia Society of Colonial Dames (20 boxes).

See Lilla M. Hawes: "A Profile of the Georgia Historical Society," *Georgia Historical Quarterly,* XXXVI (1952), 132–6; and Philip M. Hamer: *Guide,* p. 142.

ILLINOIS

Urbana

ILLINOIS HISTORICAL SURVEY, UNIVERSITY OF ILLINOIS

At the University of Illinois at Urbana, rather than at the state Historical Library at Springfield, there has been concentrated by the state copies of the records of what was called the Illinois Country, an area later to become the State of Illinois. This state archival center with its copies of pre-Revolutionary War papers is called the Illinois Historical Survey.

Among the survey holdings concerned with the period 1748–1776 are the papers of George Morgan, 1766–1826 (242 items); Kaskaskia documents, 1720–1790 (microfilm copies of originals in custody of county clerk of Randolph County); Cahokia and St. Clair County papers, 1722–1809 (microfilm copies of originals in Archives Division of Illinois State Library); South Carolina colonial records, 1706–1775 (37 cartons of microfilm copies); finally, there are copies of several thousand 18th century items from archives in Great Britain, Spain, and France. See Marguerite J. Pease: *Guide to Manuscript Materials of American Origin in the Illinois Historical Survey* (1st edn., Urbana, Ill., 1951; rev. edn., 1956); also by Mrs. Pease: *Guide to Manuscript Materials Relating to Western History in Foreign Depositories Reproduced for the Illinois Historical Survey* (1st edn., Urbana, Ill., 1950; rev. edn., 1956); and Philip M. Hamer: *Guide*, p. 169.

Chicago

CHICAGO HISTORICAL SOCIETY

There are various materials in the Society's manuscript collections on the Lake Michigan Indians, 1642–1800 (1,000 pieces); documents on the French in the Mississippi Valley, 1642–1800 (2,500 items); and papers on the Revolutionary War. See G. B. Utley: "Source Material for the Study of American History in the Libraries of Chicago," Bibliographical Society of America, *Papers*, XVI (1922), 30–8; Charles B. Pike: "Chicago Historical Society," Business History Society, *Bulletin*, VIII (1934), 37–41; Philip M. Hamer: *Guide*, pp. 149–51; and Library of Congress: *Manuscripts in Public and Private Collections*, p. 18.

NEWBERRY LIBRARY

The library's most important collection of manuscripts relating to the British Empire is the Edward E. Ayer collection. It is of such direct importance to the period under examination that it would be well to present the items that are relevant as listed in a *A Checklist of Manuscripts in the Edward E. Ayer Collection* by Ruth Lapham Butler (Chicago, 1937). They are as follows:

No. 4. James Abercromby to Sir William Johnson, Dec. 27, 1757, concerning the advance of the enemy upon Schoharie (3 pp.);

No. 6. Abraham, Chief of the Mohawks, a speech to the officials of Schenectady and Albany by Little Abraham as interpreted by Samuel Kirkland, May 20, 1775 (2 pp.);

No. 7. "The Indians' answer. Present as before, Old Abraham Speaker" [1775], concerning Indian participation in the American Revolution (2 pp.);

No. 8. [An account of a visit lately made to the people called Quakers, in Philadelphia, by Papoonahoal, an Indian chief, and several other Indians, chiefly of the Minisink tribe], July 1760 (4 pp.);

No. 14. Extracts from the minutes of the Albany Committee concerning Indian disturbances in Tryon County, 1775 (7 pp.);

No. 19. Jeffrey Amherst to William Thomas, from the camp at Oswego, July 30, 1760, dealing with aid for British soldiers (2 pp.);

No. 26. John Appy to Thomas Hancock, from New York, March 2, 1760, telling of Cherokee hostilities (1 p.);

No. 27. Charles Apthorp to John Thomlinson, 1738–1739, 1751 (29 letters, originals and copies), concerning sale and shipment of merchandise;

No. 45. Bader, ———, extracts from diary, Oct. 26, 1755–Dec. 14, 1794 (12 pp.);

No. 58. Thomas Barton to Richard Peters, Redding [Reading], Pa., Feb. 6, 1756, concerning Indian atrocities at Juniata and Sherman's Creek (2 pp.);

No. 66. Anthony Benezet to Jonas Thompson, Phila., Dec. 6, 1757, concerning Friends' School, Philadelphia (3 pp.);

No. 103. Edward Braddock, orderly books, Feb. 26–June 11, 1755 and June 12–June 17, 1755, a copy from the original which is in the handwriting of George Washington (128 pp.);

No. 104. John Bradstreet, "Instructions to Capt. Howard of His Majesty's Seventeenth Regiment Foot" about taking possession of Fort Michilimackinac. From Detroit, Aug. 31, 1764 (2 pp.);

No. 105. John Brainerd, 2 letters to Eleazer Wheelock, Egg Harbour, June 23, 1757 and Princeton, April 22, 1774, concerning Indian missions and a treaty to be negotiated by Sir William Johnson;

No. 116. William Browning to Sir William Johnson, Niagara, April 30, 1764, about Pontiac's War (1 p.);

Nos. 142–143. "Journals of the Travels of Jonathan Carver in the Year 1766 and 1767" (118 pp.), photostats from original in British Museum;

No. 174. Daniel Claus to Sir William Johnson, Montreal, March 19, 1761, concerning "army affairs, Indians, and reprinting of prayerbook and catechisms in Mohawk" (4 pp.);

No. 176. Gavin Cochrane, a "Treatise on the Indians in North America written in the Year 1764" (17 pp.), copy of paper addressed to George III;

No. 178. Cadwallader Colden to Peter Collinson, N.Y., April 23, 1756, concerning "attitude of British, lack of martial spirit in the colonies, and Franklin's activities" (4 pp.);

Nos. 195–199. George Croghan, 5 letters to Thomas Gage, Sir William Johnson, Thomas Wharton, Major Funda, and David Franks, 1763–1770;

No. 204. Sir Alexander Cuming, papers concerning Georgia and the Cherokees, especially his scheme as "King of the Cherokees" for these Indians, 1755 (56 pp.);

No. 221. James Dean to Stephen Williams, Dartmouth College, Nov. 12, 1774, concerning missionary activity among Canadian Indians (2 pp.);

No. 239. John Dick to Lewis Gordon, Wyoming, Aug. 1, 1771, concerning Pennsylvania-Connecticut conflict in the Wyoming Valley (2 pp.);

No. 255. William Henry Drayton, an address to the Cherokee nation, Sept. 25, 1775 (9 pp.);

No. 277. George Etherington, 7 letters, 1763, to Charles Michel de Langlade, fils, dealing with command of the post of Mackinac, ransom of soldiers from the Indians, and supplies;

Nos. 299–300. Sieur Franquet's description of trips taken in 1752 in Canada and to the Gulf of St. Lawrence and lands adjoining, including areas in dispute between the British and France, and discussing defenses and plans for French forts (in French, 84 pp., copy);

No. 301. Levi Frisbie to Eleazar Wheelock, Ipswich, Dec. 30, 1775, on their friendship (1 p.);

No. 304. Joseph Frye, orderly book, Fort Gaspereau, later Fort Monckton, Nova Scotia, Nov. 26, 1755–March 16, 1756;

Nos. 307–309. Thomas Gage, 5 letters to William Johnson, Charles Langlade and John Penn, 1763–1771, dealing with treatment of the Indians, aggression of the settlers in western Pennsylvania, and other matters;

No. 341. George III. Instructions to Robert Monckton about Indian lands in New York, 1761 (3 pp.);

Nos. 374–375. Gideon Hawley, 2 letters, one in Dec. 1770, to Samuel Cooper telling of the longevity of the Indians; the second in Aug. 1775 to Eleazar Wheelock concerning Samuel Gilbert;

No. 403. [The Importance of attaching the Indian tribes to the English interest, 1760] (27 pp.);

No. 424. Treaty between Creeks and Great Britain, 1765, photostat from original in Archiva General de Indias, Papeles de Cuba, Seville (7 pp.);

No. 425. Treaty between Creeks and Georgia, 1768, photostat from same place as *No. 424* (1 p.);

No. 447. Thomas Jefferys, 2 letters to the Earl of Morton, Jan. 17, 1767, one concerning bankruptcy, and the other, "the identity of Mr. Green and his map";

No. 450. Guy Johnson to Sir William Johnson, N.Y., March 2, 1772, concerning Mohawk lands (2 pp.);

No. 456. Sir William Johnson to William Shirley, 1755, about superintendency of Indian affairs (1 p.);

No. 457. Sir William Johnson, 10 letters, 1755–1773, to John Penn, Thomas Gage, George Croghan, Thomas Wharton, C. Colden, and others, published in various volumes of *The Papers of Sir William Johnson;*

No. 458. Sir William Johnson, instructions for Richard Gridley, Camp at Lake George, Oct. 24, 1755, published in *ibid.,* II, 236–7;

No. 496. Laut Transcripts, 17 vols., concerned with the Hudson's Bay Company activities, various explorations and Indian relations. Among the volumes with pertinent materials are Vols. I–III: Hudson's Bay Company, minute-books, 1671–1821; Vol. V: Old stock and ledger books, 1667–1872; Vol. VI: Anthony Hendry's journal of exploratory journey, Hudson's Bay, 1754–1755, and also Matthew Cocking's journal, 1772–1773;

No. 511. William Leslye to Charles Michel de Langlade, ordering inhabitants of Michilimackinac to surrender all arms in their possession, Michilimackinac, Sept. 30, 1761 (1 p.);

No. 529. John Campbell, 4th Earl of Loudoun, 2 letters to Gov. William Denny, Jan. 1, 1756/7, Jan. 21, 1758, concerning usurpation of William Johnson's authority in Indian affairs (7 pp.);

No. 535. The Province of Massachusetts Bay to Jacob Lucke, Nov. 30, 1756;

No. 547. Donald McIntyre and others, petition to William Tryon complaining that they had been driven from their lands in Albany County, 1771 (1 p.);

No. 560. John Malcom, bill for work on sloop *Salem,* Nov. 1, 1756;

No. 565. M. Marsac, report on a trip made by order of Col. Bradstreet to the falls of St. Marie to speak to the upper nations, July 29, 1765 (3 pp.);

No. 582. William Shirley, 3 letters to William Johnson, 1755–1756, dealing with Crown Point, the garrison at Fort Hunter, the Indians, and Robert Roger's observations on the French army (7 pp.);

No. 583. Shirley to Henry Fox, New York, 1756, concerning the reduction of Canada (4 pp.);

No. 584. Gov. Francis Bernard of Massachusetts to the Council and House of Representatives regarding the defence of the settlers against Indian attacks, June 5, 1764;

No. 585. Eyre Massey, Quebec, to William Johnson, Aug. 20, 1767, suggesting Major Hughs succeed Capt. Claus (3 pp.);

No. 609. Thomas Morris to John Bradstreet, Sept. 2, 1764, concerning Detroit Indians (1 p.);

No. 615. Valentine Nevill, "The Reduction of Louisbourg. A Poem Inscribed to the Honble Edward Boscawen: Revised & Corrected. V.N. [1758]" (9 pp.);

No. 622. Gov. Benning Wentworth, 6 letters to John Thomlinson, 1742–1754, concerning New Hampshire–Massachusetts, Connecticut–New York boundary disputes and the abortive Canadian expedition (21 pp.);

No. 623. Wentworth to the Lords Commissioners of his Majesty's Treasury, Portsmouth, June 12, 1749, about funds for the Louisbourg expedition (4 pp.);

No. 629. Lieut.-Gov. Thomas Pownall of New Jersey to Sir William Johnson, Nov. 11, 1755, concerning military and Indian affairs, published in *The Papers of Sir William Johnson,* II, 289–90;

No. 632. Minutes of the New York Council, Nov. 24, 1745–July 18, 1749 (368 pp.);

No. 633. "Minutes of Council [of New York] commencing the 26th November 1750 and Ending the 19th June 1751" (39 pp.);

No. 638. Account of meeting between Gov. Clinton and Six Nations at Albany, July 1, 1751 (28 pp.), variation from version in *Documents Relating to Colonial History of New York,* VI, 717ff.;

No. 639. Lieut.-Gov. Cadwallader Colden, 3 letters to Sir William Johnson, 1763–1764, discussing Indian trade and the disposition of troops on the frontier (4 pp.);

No. 656. Samson Occom to Eleazar Wheelock, Mohegan, March 14, 1774, dealing with transfer of New England Indians to Oneida lands;

No. 695. Thomas Penn to [John Penn], London, Dec. 10, 1763, discussing Indian problems, the Pennsylvania assembly, and paper money (1 p.);

No. 696. Thomas Penn to Sir William Johnson, Sept. 7, 1764, about the Penns' policy of compensating Indians for land (2 pp.);

No. 699. Pennsylvania Commissioners to the Governor, "Report . . . concerning protection of frontier against the Indians. June 17, 1756" (2 pp.);

No. 700. Pennsylvania Commissioners to the Governor, "Report . . . concerning provisions for Col. Armstrong's battalion, Phila., Jan. 25, 1757" (2 pp.);

No. 702. Gov. Robert Hunter Morris of Pennsylvania to William Shirley, Aug. 19, 1755, explaining problem of obtaining money for the French and Indian War (3 pp.);

No. 703. Lieut.-Gov. John Penn to Sir William Johnson concerning "Indian trade and lands along the Susquehanna" (3 pp.);

No. 711. Secy. Richard Peters to Timothy Stanfield, April 15, 1757, about provisions for the Philadelphia journey of Teedyuscung and his Indians (1 p.);

No. 713. Observations of William Peters and Jacob Duché on the Quakers' role at the Easton conference between William Denny and the Indians, 1757 (6 pp.);

No. 714. "[Petition] A Messieurs St. Ange, Capitaine et Command[an]t De La partie françoise aux illinois, et Labuxiere Juge et procureur du pays, St. Louis, May 8, 1768," asking that the sale of alcohol to the Indians be prohibited (8 pp.);

No. 739. Augustine Prevost (c. 1725–1786), 2 letters to Sir William Johnson, 1772, about a new colony on the Ohio and regimental movements. Printed in *The Papers of Sir William Johnson,* VIII, 426–7, 531–3;

No. 754. "Reports for the summer of the year 1757 (to July 10th, 1758) concerning the surrender of Fort William Henry, the proposed evacuation of Fort Edward, the fall of Louisbourg, etc." (2 pp.);

No. 769. Benjamin Roberts to Sir William Johnson, London, April 27, 1770, concerning the war with France in America. Printed in *The Papers of Sir William Johnson,* VII, 606–8;

No. 774. Robert Rogers to Paul Burbeen, Feb. 15, 1761, on the settlement of the Rangers' accounts;

No. 775. "Agreement between Robert Rogers and Simon Stevens, to submit the settlement of their accounts to John Stark, Thomas Parker, Stephen Holland, Nathan Stone and Andrew McMillan, Londonderry, April 23, 1764" (2 pp.);

No. 785. Sir John St. Clair to Governor Morris, Williamsburg, Feb. 14, 1755, requesting maps of Pennsylvania, and supplies for Braddock's expedition (2 pp.);

No. 806. "A Short Discourse on the Present State of the Colonies in America with Respect to the Interest of Great Britain [1750]" (28 pp.);

No. 816. Snow Mercury: "Log of *Snow Mercury* on a voyage from New York toward Bristol. Sept. to Oct. 30, 1766; miscellaneous sailing notes and information concerning ports of call" (111 pp.);

No. 817. Snow Wennie: "Log of *Snow Wennie* on a voyage from Bristol to the West Indies and the North American colonies, from Nov. 1765 to June 1766. Captain, the Right Honorable Lord Hope; miscellaneous sailing notes and notes concerning ports of call" (148 pp.);

No. 819. "Further Report of the [South Carolina] Comm[itt]e on Acc[ount]s No. 208–220. White Outerbridge for repairs at Fort Moore; Margaret Olivier for victualling French prisoners; Commissary Pinckney's account for provisions supplied the Acadians, etc., Apr. 28, 1757" (3 pp.);

No. 831. Robert Sterling's petition for "lieutenant's portion of land [West Florida], 1776" (3 pp.);

No. 868. "Substance of an Occasional Conversation with Several Indians

after Dinner at Israel Pemberton's on the 19th of the 4 mo., 1756"
(8 pp.);

No. 877. Message to Delawares from Techtama and Homwhyowa, Cherokee chiefs, delivered to Richard Peters and Israel Pemberton in
Philadelphia, June 20, 1758 (4 pp.);

No. 886. John Thomlinson's petition to the king in council relating to
Massachusetts-New Hampshire boundary disputes and support of
Fort Dummer, Jan. 4, 1749 (7 pp.);

No. 890. Nathaniel Thwing to John Thomas, Boston, Jan. 16, 1760, on the
discharge of troops;

No. 904. George Turnbull, "Passport for M. Langlade with two *engagées*
to go to La Bay with merchandise, Michilimackinac, Aug. 6,
1770" (1 p.);

No. 905. Letter from George Turnbull, Michilimackinac, Aug. 18, 1771;

No. 952. Lieut.-Gov. Robert Dinwiddie of Virginia to Lieut.-Gov. James
Hamilton of Pennsylvania, Jan. 29, 1754, concerning Washington's
expedition to the Ohio country (3 pp.);

No. 953. Dinwiddie to Dep. Gov. R. H. Morris, Nov. 12, 1755, about arms
for the French and Indian War. Printed in Virginia Historical
Society, *Collections*, I: 63–4 and II: 264–5;

No. 975. Samuel Wharton to his partners, N.Y., March 19, 1765, discussing Indian trade (4 pp.);

No. 1006. Charles Williamson (1757–1808), papers, including information on his work as a colonizer of the "Genesee country" of
western New York, 1775–1803.

See G. B. Utley: "Source Material for the Study of American History
in the Libraries of Chicago," Bibliographical Society of America, *Papers*,
XVI (1922), 18–29; Newberry Library, *Bulletin* (1948+); Philip M.
Hamer: *Guide*, pp. 154–6; and Library of Congress: *Manuscripts in
Public and Private Collections*, pp. 18–19.

UNIVERSITY OF CHICAGO LIBRARY

The Ethno-History Collection, 1670–1840 (50,000 pp.), in the library
includes materials relating to Indian affairs in the Mississippi Valley
which are chiefly reproductions from other depositories in the United
States, Canada, and Europe. The Col. R. T. Durrett Collection, 1673–
1913 (2,800 items, mostly nineteenth century) contains diaries, Virginia
land grants, and some George Washington, John Adams, Thomas Jefferson, James Madison, and Anthony Wayne letters.

See George B. Utley: "Source Material for the Study of American
History in the Libraries of Chicago," Bibliographical Society of America,
Papers, XVI (1922), 38–43; Illinois State Library: *Illinois Libraries*, XL
(April 1958), 340–8; and Philip M. Hamer: *Guide*, pp. 158–60.

INDIANA

Bloomington

INDIANA UNIVERSITY LIBRARY

Among the manuscripts in the library falling within the period 1748–1776 are the Philip Dormer Stanhope, 4th Earl of Chesterfield, papers, 1740–1770 (330 pieces); the papers of Jonathan Williams (a relative of, and assistant to, Benjamin Franklin in France), 1766–1815 (7,182 pieces); and Horatio Walpole, 1st Baron Walpole, papers, 1715–1754 (91 items). See Doris M. Reed: "Manuscripts in the Indiana University Library," *Indiana Magazine of History*, XLIX (1953), 191–6; and Philip M. Hamer: *Guide*, pp. 171–2.

Indianapolis

INDIANA HISTORICAL SOCIETY

Here are to be found a number of papers relating to early Vincennes and to the old Northwest, 1749–1838 (500 items). See *Indiana History Bulletin* for reports of the Librarian of accessions, 1936–1947, and separate reports of the Librarian, 1948–1954, for further accessions; see also Philip M. Hamer: *Guide*, p. 176.

MARYLAND

Annapolis

HALL OF RECORDS OF MARYLAND

The official records of the Province of Maryland held in the Hall of Records contain important executive, legislative, and judicial papers for the entire colonial period, as well as the national period. In addition, these archives include the town records of Annapolis (1753+), early church records, business records, and family papers. The most important of the provincial records have been published under the editorship of William Hand Browne, *et al.* . . . , *Maryland Archives* (70 vols. +, Baltimore, 1883–1964+).

For the holdings of the Hall of Records, see *Catalogue of Archival Material* . . ., Hall of Records Commission, *Publication*, No. 2 ([Annapolis, Md., 1942]); Morris L. Radoff: "Early Annapolis Records," *Maryland Historical Magazine*, XXXV (1940), 74–8; and Philip M. Hamer: *Guide*, p. 220.

Baltimore

MARYLAND HISTORICAL SOCIETY

The Society has many collections of papers covering the colonial and Revolutionary War periods. Among the most important are the Calvert Papers, 1582–1770 (1,300 items), which relate chiefly to the American interests of the Lords Baltimore. There are also many papers concerning the Maryland-Pennsylvania boundary dispute, and at least a thousand letters embodied in the Charles Carroll of Carrollton manuscript collection covering the period 1765–1820. Finally, there are the Otho Holland Williams Papers, 1744–1794 (1,200 items), a calendar covering which was published in 1940. Williams was collector of customs at Baltimore. While most of the collection deals with the period after 1776, there are 10 items which fall within our period, including muster rolls and payrolls, a major's commission given to Williams and signed by John Hancock, and a few pertinent letters. One letter, dated October 14, 1775, gives some news of the fighting around Boston. Another letter, sent April 11, 1776 from Staten Island, gives an account of a skirmish in which Williams's company captured ten British soldiers and some weapons. This letter also describes Staten Island and New York as well fortified and relates a rumor that Parliament was sending 25,000 mercenaries to New York.

See Library of Congress: *Manuscripts in Public and Private Collections,* p. 29; Philip M. Hamer: *Guide,* pp. 223–5; and Historical Records Survey: *Calendar of the General Otho Holland Williams Papers in the Maryland Historical Society* (Baltimore, Md., 1940).

MASSACHUSETTS

Boston

ARCHIVES, STATE HOUSE

Here are housed the official records of the Province of Massachusetts Bay, as well as those of the earlier colony and later state, 1620 to date (326 vols. +). Included are records of the colonial Indian Wars and the Revolutionary War, documents of the General Court, 1629–1833, and journals of the House of Representatives, 1730 to date. There is also substantial correspondence of Thomas Hutchinson and family, 1741–1774 (1,543 items in 3 vols.) and the papers assembled by Hutchinson relating to the history of Massachusetts Bay, 1625–1771 (264 items in 3 vols.). See Philip M. Hamer: *Guide,* p. 239.

BAKER LIBRARY, HARVARD UNIVERSITY
GRADUATE SCHOOL OF BUSINESS ADMINISTRATION

The Library contains many manuscripts relating to the period 1748–1776. Among them are the following collections: (1) American farming, 1704–1925 (75 vols. and 1 box); (2) The fisheries, 1719–1765 (25 vols. and 5 boxes); (3) Mining, 1650–1918 (9 vols., 3 boxes, and 62 pieces); (4) Textile manufacturing, 1710–1938 (7,034 vols., 826 boxes, and numerous crates); (5) Tailoring and hat-making, 1736–1857 (12 vols. and 17 boxes); (6) Wood products, 1759–1907 (95 vols., 5 boxes, and 2 crates); (7) Pottery, 1747–1938 (2 vols. and 6 crates); (8) Leather manufactures, 1673–1924 (422 vols., 3 boxes, and 2 crates); (9) Coastwise shipping, 1732–1915 (105 vols. and 20 boxes); (10) Ocean shipping, 1727–1911 (337 vols. and 139 boxes); and (11) Foreign marketing, 1739–1922 (1,826 vols., 751 boxes, and 57 crates); (12) The Hancock family papers, 1712–1854, chiefly business, including John Hancock's business records, 1763–1794 (14 boxes); (13) A collection of tax and customs papers, 1658–1888 (10 vols. and 9 boxes).

See Robert W. Lovett: *List of Business Manuscripts in Baker Library* (2nd edn., Boston, 1951), and Philip M. Hamer: *Guide*, pp. 232–4.

BOSTON ATHENAEUM

Among the manuscripts is a large collection of diaries and account books, 1644–1886 (94 vols.); here also are the custom house records of both Boston and Salem, 1744–1774 (3 vols.); and ships' logs, 1762–1830 (7 vols.). See Records Survey: *Guide* for Massachusetts, pp. 16–19; Philip M. Hamer: *Guide*, pp. 234–5.

THE MASSACHUSETTS HISTORICAL SOCIETY

The Society holds a large number of family and personal collections of papers falling within the period 1748–1776. Among the more important of them are the following: (1) Adams family papers, 1639–1938 (more than 300,000 pages); (2) The Hutchinson-Oliver family papers, 1637–1859 (4 vols. and 3 boxes); (3) The Lee family of Massachusetts, 1661–1914 (86 vols. and 14 boxes); (4) The Quincy family papers, 1635–1886 (39 vols. and 27 boxes); (5) The Warren family papers, 1738–1921 (131 vols. and 4 boxes); (6) The John Winslow and family papers, 1634–1854 (6 vols. and 2 boxes); (7) The Rev. John Andrews, of Maryland and Pennsylvania, papers, 1772–1776 (1 box); (8) The Theodore Atkinson of New Hampshire papers, 1725–1766 (1 box of photostats); (9) The Gov. Jonathan Belcher papers, 1723–1755 (10 vols.); (10) The Thomas Cushing papers, 1773–1857 (1 box); (11) The John Hancock papers, 1728–1815 (1 vol. and 2 boxes); (12) The Thomas Hollis, English Whig, papers, 1759–1771 (1 vol.); (13) The Thomas Jefferson papers, 1705–1826 (77 vols. and 3 boxes); (14) The Henry Knox papers, 1770–1828 (65 vols. and 5 boxes); (15) The William Livingston of New York and New Jersey papers, 1695–1839 (6 vols. and 13 boxes); (16) Nova Scotia papers, 1687–1839, including those of Jean Paul Mascarene (1 box); (17) The James Otis papers, 1642–1823 (3 vols. and 1 box); (18) The Sir William Pepperrell papers, 1699–1779 (2 vols.); (19) Paul Revere family papers, 1746–1854 (39 vols. and 17 boxes); (20) The Jonathan Sewall, Massachusetts Bay Loyalist, papers, 1757–1789 (1 vol.); (21) The Artemas Ward papers, 1684–1775 (8 vols. and 1 box); (22) James Warren papers, 1750–1814 (4 vols.); (23) Mercy Otis Warren papers, 1703–1781 (1 vol. and 3 boxes); (24) Israel Williams, Loyalist, papers, 1730–1780 (2 vols.).

In addition, the Society possesses transcripts of important documents, among which are the instructions to the Governors of Massachusetts Bay, 1631–1775 (8 boxes).

See *Handbook of the Massachusetts Historical Society*, 1791–1948 (Boston, 1949); Stephen T. Riley: "The Manuscript Collections of the Massachusetts Historical Society: A Brief Listing," Massachusetts Historical Society, *Miscellany*, No. 5 (Boston, 1958); and Philip M. Hamer: *Guide*, pp. 240–8.

PUBLIC LIBRARY

The largest collection of manuscripts in the Library concerned with the years 1748–1776 and relating to America and Europe is the Mellen Chamberlain collection (350+ vols.). It includes twelve volumes of Massachusetts colonial and Revolutionary War papers; three devoted to New Hampshire in the 18th and 19th centuries; fifteen to men connected with the Revolution; three to signers of the Declaration of Independence; five devoted exclusively to Washington; finally, five contain letters, documents, manuscripts, and portraits relating to Benjamin Franklin, John Adams, John Hancock, Samuel Adams and Joseph Warren, and to those engaged on both sides in the battles of Lexington, Concord, and Bunker Hill. The collection also has material about both the Boston Massacre and the Boston Tea Party. Other collections in the library include John and Thomas Hancock manuscripts, 1726–1816 (2 vols.), and a considerable body of manuscripts relating to the West Indies, 1742–1851 (39 vols.). See Historical Records Survey: *Preliminary Edition of Guide to Depositories of Manuscript Collections in the United States in Massachusetts* (Boston, 1939), pp. 21–52; and Philip M. Hamer: *Guide*, pp. 235–7.

Cambridge

HOUGHTON LIBRARY OF
THE HARVARD COLLEGE LIBRARY

In this library are concentrated a number of collections of manuscripts bearing upon the political and military history of Massachusetts Bay and the British Empire, 1748–1776. Among these papers are the following: (1) Arthur Lee, London agent for Massachusetts Bay, papers, 1760–1792 (8 vols.); (2) Sir Francis Bernard, governor of Massachusetts Bay, papers, 1758–1779 (13 vols.); (3) Some papers of George Bubb Dodington, Lord Melcombe, 1749–1761 (2 boxes, including his diary); (4) Maj.-Gen. Thomas Gage, correspondence with John Bradstreet, British and colonial officer, 1759–1773 (187 pieces); (5) Letter-book of William Tryon while governor of North Carolina, 1764–1771, together with minutes of the North Carolina Council; (6) Some George Washington manuscripts, 1750–1799 (88 pieces); (7) Manuscripts relating to Canada (before and after its conquest) in the papers of Jeffrey Amherst, Guy Carleton, the Earl of Shelburne, George Lord Townshend, and James Wolfe (187 pieces); (8) Admiral Sir Charles Saunder's letter-book, 1759, as well as the *articles de capitulation* of Quebec. See W. H. Bond: "Manuscript Collections in the Houghton Library," *Autograph Collectors' Journal*, IV (1952), 32–9; and Philip M. Hamer: *Guide*, pp. 251–9.

Newton Center

ANDOVER NEWTON THEOLOGICAL
SCHOOL LIBRARY

The library has an important collection of papers pertaining specifically to the Baptists in New England. It includes a large collection of the papers of Isaac Backus, Baptist clergyman, 1746–1806. It also holds some Jonathan Edwards manuscripts. See William H. Allison: *Inventory of Unpublished Material for American Religious History . . .*, Carnegie Institution of Washington, *Publications*, No. 137 (Washington, D.C., 1910), pp. 22–5 and 34–56; and Philip M. Hamer: *Guide*, pp. 270–1.

Northampton

FORBES LIBRARY

The manuscripts of greatest interest in this library are the family papers of the Massachusetts Bay lawyer, Joseph Hawley, 1655–1788 (7 vols. and 90 pieces); here also is Seth Pomeroy's diary of the expedition against Louisbourg in 1745 and against Crown Point in 1755. See Historical Records Survey: *Guide to Depositories of Manuscript Collections . . . in Massachusetts*, pp. 88–9; and Philip M. Hamer: *Guide*, pp. 271–2.

Salem

ESSEX INSTITUTE

The papers of importance for the period 1748–1776 relate chiefly to Massachusetts Bay maritime history. These include large numbers of logs and journals of ship voyages, the very extensive customs records of Salem, Marblehead, Beverly, Newburyport, Ipswich, and Gloucester, 1738–1925, together with records of entrances and clearances of Boston and all Essex County ports, 1686–1765 (7 vols.). There are also papers of merchants, sea captains, and shipowners, and those of the Rev. Manasseh Cutler, 1763–1837 (1 envelope); the Saltonstall family, 1755–1840 (16 vols.); and the Newport merchant Aaron Lopez, 1764–1769 (1 envelope). In addition there are Salem church records, 1629–1898 (5 shelves); papers relating to the New England Society for Propagating the Gospel among the Indians; and diaries and sermons of clergymen, 1700–1926. See Howard Corning: "The Essex Institute of Salem," Business Historical Society, *Bulletin*, VII (1933), 1–5; Historical Records Survey: *Guide to Depositories of Manuscript Collections . . . in Massachusetts*, pp. 99–105; Library of Congress: *Manuscripts in Public and Private Collections*, pp. 38–40; and Philip M. Hamer: *Guide*, pp. 275–6.

Worcester

AMERICAN ANTIQUARIAN SOCIETY

There are many papers relevant to the period 1748–1776 in the library. Among those are the following: (1) John Bradstreet, military officer, correspondence with Governor William Shirley, General Gage, and Jeffrey Lord Amherst, and other papers, 1755–1773 (5 vols.); (2) Aaron Burr, letters to, 1772–1818 (1 vol.); (3) Cornelius Cuyler, fur trader and mayor of Albany, papers, 1752–1765 (1 letter-book); (4) French and

Indian War papers, relating to Louisbourg and military operations in New York (11 vols.); (5) Hancock family papers, including Thomas Hancock's correspondence, 1735–1750 (6 boxes); (6) William Henshaw, papers concerning the French and Indian War, 1758–1759 and the Revolutionary War, 1775–1777 (orderly books and 5 boxes of journals); (7) Joseph Hull, New London customs collector, records, 1733–1761; (8) Robert Rogers, colonial ranger, papers (originals and photostats); (9) The Salisbury family papers, 1674–1905 (63 vols. and 68 boxes), including those of Stephen Salisbury, Massachusetts Bay merchant and landowner; (10) The Waldo family papers, 1647–1900 (13 vols. and 2 boxes), including those of Daniel Waldo, Massachusetts Bay merchant; (11) The Ward family of Shrewsbury papers (17 vols. and 38 boxes), including those of General Artemas Ward.

See *A Guide to the Resources of the American Antiquarian Society: A National Library of American History* (Worcester, Mass., 1937); Clifford K. Shipton: "The American Antiquarian Society," *William and Mary Quarterly*, 3rd ser., II (1945), 164–72; Charles H. Lincoln: "Calendar of the Manuscripts of Sir William Johnson in the Library of the Society," American Antiquarian Society, *Proceedings*, n. ser., XVIII (1907), 367–401; also by Lincoln: "A Calendar of the Manuscripts of Col. John Bradstreet in the Library of the Society," *ibid.*, n. ser., XIX (1908), 103–81; and Philip M. Hamer: *Guide*, pp. 281–9.

MICHIGAN

Ann Arbor

WILLIAM L. CLEMENTS LIBRARY, UNIVERSITY OF MICHIGAN

The papers in the Clements Library are among the most important to be found in America relating to the British Empire, 1748–1776. Among these collections are the following: (1) Jeffrey Lord Amherst, papers, 1758–1764 (8 vols.); (2) The island of Antigua papers, 1719–1749 (19 items); (3) Landon Carter of Virginia, diary, 1766–1767 (2 vols.); (4) Gov. George Clinton of New York, papers, 1697–1759 (22 vols. numbering some 1,500 pieces); (5) Sir Henry Clinton, son of Gov. Clinton and later Commander-in-Chief of British forces in America, papers, 1750–1812 (260 vols.); (6) William Dowdeswell (1721–1775), Chancellor of the Exchequer under Rockingham, papers, 1765–1774 (1 vol.); (7) Benjamin Franklin, papers (128 items), including correspondence mostly with Joseph Galloway, 1766–1788 (21 letters); (8) Gen. Thomas Gage, Commander-in-Chief of British forces in America, papers, 1754–1783 (180 vols.); (9) Lord George Germain, Viscount Sackville, papers, 1683–1785 (22 vols.); (10) John Carteret, Earl Granville (1690–1763), proprietor of the North Carolina Granville patent, papers, 1756–1761 (1 vol.); (11) George Grenville papers, 1756–1757 (1 vol.), while Treasurer of the Navy; (12) Henry Hamilton, military papers (2 vols.), 1754–1789, military career chiefly in Canada as contained in his first journal (photostat); (13) Lieut. Jehu Hay of the British army, diary, 1763–1765, concerning Pontiac's siege of Detroit and activities in the Great Lakes country (212 pp.); (14) Henry Hulton, American customs commissioner, essays, 1773–1776 (1 vol.); (15) Gov. Thomas Hutchinson, correspondence, 1771–1780 (97 letters to or from him), also extracts from his diary, 1774–1780 (570 pp.) and two speeches, 1771 and 1773; (16) William Kennedy of Barbados, his petition and appeal to the Privy Council against the decision involving a Barbados plantation, 1752–1753 (1 vol.); (17) William Knox, a member of the Governor's Council in Georgia, London agent for Georgia and East Florida, and under secretary of state for America, papers, 1757–1809 (11 vols.); (18) Lacaita-Shelburne Papers, 1692–1885 (5 vols.), containing large numbers of letters addressed to the Earl of Shelburne, letters which were apparently at one time a part of the great Shelburne Collection to be noted; (19) Henry Laurens, papers (38 items); (20) John Lee, English lawyer involved in the Luttrell election case of 1769, papers, 1763–1817 (3 vols.); (21) Battle of Lexington, 1775, papers, including statements by 94 men (1 vol.); (22) Louisbourg siege papers, 1745–1746 (1 vol.); (23) William Henry Lyttelton, governor of South Carolina and later of Jamaica, papers, 1751–1760 (5 feet and 1,150 items); (24) Lieut. James MacDonald of the British army while at Detroit, letters, 1761–1763 (1 portfolio); (25) Frederick Mackenzie, British army officer in America, papers, 1755–1783 (3 feet of shelving); (26) Michigan correspondence by Maj. Henry Gladwin and others, 1764–1940 (1 vol.); (27) Sir William Mildmay, a British commissioner to France to settle outstanding American issues, correspondence and diplomatic papers, 1748–1756 (7 vols.); (28) Frederick Lord North papers, 1763–1783 (7 pieces, in addition to 80 letters in the Clinton papers, the Germain papers, the Knox papers, the Lee papers, the Shelburne papers, and the Townshend letter-books); (29) Nova Scotia papers, 1762–1776 (1 vol.); (30) The Rev. Jonathan Parsons of Newburyport, Massachusetts Bay, papers, 1737–1761 (1 vol.); (31) Robert Rogers, correspondence, 1761–1775 (1 vol., see also the Gage papers for other letters); (32) Thomas G. Shadwell, private secretary to the British ambassador to the court of Spain, Thomas Robinson, Baron Grantham, papers, 1773–1778 (1 vol.); (33) William Petty, Earl of Shelburne and later Marquess of Lansdowne, papers, 1663–1797 (179 vols.), an exceedingly important collection of papers, especially as so many relate to America; see also the Lacaita-Shelburne papers noted earlier, for much additional Shelburne correspondence; (34) Sir Henry Strachey, papers, 1768–1775 (2 vols.), containing reports of colonial officials; (35) Charles Townshend, letters, 1763–1776 (65 items) and also papers of his brother, Viscount George Townshend, under Wolfe in America and later Lord-Lieutenant of Ireland, letter-books, 1767–1772 (7 vols.); (36) Thomas Townshend, later Baron Sydney, a lord of the treasury, later joint paymaster of the forces, and still later in opposition to both the Grafton and North ministries, papers, 1685–1825 (4 feet of shelf space); (37) Admiral Sir Peter Warren, papers, largely concerned with the capture of Louisbourg, 1744–1752 (4 vols.); (38) George Washington, papers (147 items); (39) Alexander Wedderburn, Baron Loughborough and later Earl of Rosslyn, solicitor general, later attorney general and still later Lord Chancellor, papers, 1676–1800 (3 vols.), with most of the material relating to the period 1764–1780; (49) John Wilkes, papers, 1741–1784 (6 vols.).

See Howard H. Peckham: *Guide to the Manuscript Collections in the William L. Clements Library* (Ann Arbor, Mich., 1942); William S. Ewing: *Guide to the Manuscript Collections in the William L. Clements Library* (Ann Arbor, Mich., 1952; 2nd edn., 1953); and Philip M. Hamer: *Guide*, pp. 295–7.

With respect to the great collection of papers of the Earl of Shelburne, 1st Marquess of Lansdowne, it should be pointed out that all were calendared by the Historical Manuscripts Commission and appeared in their *Third Report*, pp. 125–47, *Fifth Report*, pp. 215–60, and *Sixth Report*, pp. 235–43, under heading "Manuscripts of the Most Honourable the Marquis of Lansdowne, at Lansdowne House." The Clements Library possesses Volumes 1–99, 101–25, 127–55, and 161–8.

Detroit

BURTON HISTORICAL COLLECTION, DETROIT PUBLIC LIBRARY

For the student interested in the British Empire, 1748–1776, the chief interest of this collection will be large numbers of papers devoted to the fur trade. Among those papers related to the Great Lakes area, including what is now the state of Michigan, are the following collections: (1) The John Porteous, Scottish fur trader, papers, 1761–1800 (8 vols. and 150 pieces); (2) The John Askin family, fur traders and merchants, papers, 1704–1891 (37 vols. and 5,000 pieces); (3) The Campau family, French officials, fur traders, merchants, etc., papers, 1715–1928 (50 vols. and 11,250 pieces); (4) The Angus and Alexander Mackintosh family, fur traders and later ship-builders, papers, 1728–1835 (6 vols., 50 pieces, and 3 reels of microfilm); (5) The Charles Christopher Trowbridge family, explorers, etc., papers, 1702–1925 (60 vols. and 9,000 pieces); (6) The John R. Williams family, fur traders, merchants, etc., 1726–1923

(48 vols. and 8,250 pieces). One very important manuscript in the Burton Collection relating to the Indian uprising under Pontiac at Detroit should be mentioned. It is Robert Navarre's "Journal ou Dictation d'une Conspiration faite par les Sauvages Contre les Anglais, et du Siège du fort de Detroix par quartre nations différentes Le 7 May, 1783" (1 ms. vol.); a copy of it is in the Clements Library.

See L. O. Woltz: "Source Material of the Detroit Public Library as Supplied by the Acquisition of the Burton Historical Collection," *Michigan History Magazine*, VI (1922), 386–99; Clarence M. Burton: "The Burton Historical Collection of the Public Library, Detroit," Bibliographical Society of America, *Papers*, XVI (1922), 10–16; Philip M. Hamer: *Guide*, pp. 300–2.

MINNESOTA

St. Paul

MINNESOTA HISTORICAL SOCIETY

The Society's manuscript holdings are mostly late eighteenth-century or later. Some papers relating to the old Northwest date from 1769; there are a few George Washington papers (31 items) between the years 1754–1796. See Grace Lee Nute and Gertrude W. Ackermann: *Guide to the Personal Papers in the Manuscript Collections of the Minnesota Historical Society* (St. Paul, Minn., 1935); Lucile M. Kane and Kathryn A. Johnson: *Manuscript Collections of the Minnesota Historical Society* (St. Paul, Minn., 1955); and Philip M. Hamer: *Guide*, pp. 320–3.

MISSISSIPPI

Jackson

MISSISSIPPI DEPARTMENT OF ARCHIVES AND HISTORY

The material held in the Archives is of importance because it embodies the records of the French, British, and Spanish administration of the region now known as the state of Mississippi during the years from 1699 to 1798. These records, in the form of transcripts drawn from other archives, are in 102 volumes. See "An Official Guide to the Historical Materials in the Mississippi Department of Archives and History," Mississippi Dept. of Archives and History, *Annual Report, 1911–1912*, Appendix (Nashville, Tenn., 1914); see also Philip M. Hamer: *Guide*, pp. 324–5.

MISSOURI

St. Louis

MISSOURI HISTORICAL SOCIETY,
JEFFERSON MEMORIAL

The chief value of the manuscripts held by the Society for the period under consideration lies in certain collections and scattered papers. Among the William K. Bixby collection are documents relating to Fort Chartres in 1739, Kaskaskia in 1753, and the Arkansas River fortifications, 1751–1755. A Julien Dubuque paper throws light on lead mines and Indian trade in 1774. For New Madrid, its archives, possessed by the Society, cover the years 1770–1805 (1,432 pieces); there also are to be found the Ste. Geneviève archives, covering the years 1769 to 1850 (2,500 pieces), and those of St. Louis for the years 1763–1818 (2,952 pieces), covering both the French and Spanish period. Finally, there are George Rogers Clark papers, 1755–1815 (550 pieces). See Library of Congress: *Manuscripts in Public and Private Collections*, pp. 451–5; Philip M. Hamer: *Guide*, pp. 331–4; and Historical Records Survey: *Guide to Depositories of Manuscript Collections in the United States: Missouri, Preliminary Edition* (St. Louis, Mo., 1940), p. 9.

NEW HAMPSHIRE

Concord

NEW HAMPSHIRE HISTORICAL SOCIETY

While most of the manuscripts in the possession of the Society are of a later period than the one under examination, the following collections are important to note: Jonathan Belcher, colonial governor, papers, 1730–1753 (3 vols.); John Wentworth, last royal governor of New Hampshire, papers, 1765–1798 (1 box); the Rev. Jeremy Belknap, papers, 1760–1790 (1 box). The Society also has many account books, diaries, logs, military records, etc., for the colonial period. It is also important to note that the Society building has been made the depository of early official records, including those of provincial New Hampshire to 1786; among them are New Hampshire deeds, town records to 1825 and court records to 1770. See Library of Congress: *Manuscripts in Public and Private Collections*, p. 55; and Philip M. Hamer: *Guide*, pp. 344–6.

Hanover

DARTMOUTH COLLEGE LIBRARY

The most important collection of manuscripts relating to the period 1748–1776 is that of the Rev. Eleazar Wheelock (1711–1779), missionary to the Indians and founder of Dartmouth College (4,000 letters and papers). See William H. Allison: *Inventory of Unpublished Materials for American Religious History in Protestant Church Archives and Other Repositories* (Washington, D.C., 1910), pp. 70–82; Library of Congress: *Manuscripts in Public and Private Collections,* p. 55; and Philip M. Hamer: *Guide,* pp. 348–9.

NEW JERSEY

Trenton

BUREAU OF ARCHIVES AND HISTORY,
STATE HOUSE ANNEX

The collections in the State Archives include among other papers bearing upon the years 1748–1776 the following: (1) Acts of the New Jersey Assembly, 1681–1802 (25 vols.); (2) Official correspondence of the Legislative Council and General Assembly concerning the affairs of the colony, 1748–1776; (3) Letters from Gov. Franklin to the legislature about the movement for independence, 1771–1775; (4) Petitions from various sources concerning local and colonial affairs especially grievances, and the movement for independence, 1751–1775; (5) A letter from George Washington discussing military tactics, 1758; (6) Papers concerning the boundary dispute between East New Jersey and West New Jersey, 1775; (7) Papers of the Committee of Safety relating to preparations for war and requests for commissions, 1775–1776; (8) Some letters of John Hancock and John Witherspoon which discuss military enlistment policies and tell of enemy movements, 1776; (9) Records of the Proprietors of East Jersey and of West Jersey, 1674–1807 (1 box and 23 items); (10) There are also other records such as those of insolvent debtors, 1747–1818 (3 vols.), and naturalization records, 1749–1810 (1 vol.). See Historical Records Survey: *Calendar of the New Jersey State Library Manuscript Collection* (Newark, N.J., 1939), pp. 5–23; Historical Records Survey: *Guide to Depositories of Manuscript Collections in the United States: New Jersey (Preliminary Edition)* (Newark, N.J., 1941), pp. 44–5; and Philip M. Hamer: *Guide,* p. 367.

Newark

NEW JERSEY HISTORICAL SOCIETY

The manuscript collections of the Society are numbered. Those that have relation to the period 1748–1776 are as follows with the number they carry:

No. 2. East Jersey manuscripts, 1672–1873, including a number of letters (c. 160 items);

No. 3. West Jersey manuscripts, 1649–1829, including a few letters (c. 62 items);

No. 4. Revolutionary era manuscripts, 1765–1790, including letters (c. 55 items);

No. 6. Provincial Congress manuscripts, 1755–1777 (c. 135 items);

No. 7. New Jersey manuscripts, 1681–1800, including letters from the following: Elias Boudinot, Abraham Clark, Gouverneur Morris, David Ogden, James Parker, John Stevens, Lord Stirling and Richard Stockton (c. 500 items);

No. 16. Lewis Morris papers, 1730–1746 (c. 100 items); early but pertinent;

No. 17. Robert Hunter Morris papers, 1734–1758 (c. 170 items);

No. 18. James Parker manuscripts, 1724–1850 (c. 500 items), many late but pertinent in dealing with confiscated estates of Loyalists;

No. 37. William Franklin papers, 1756–1813 (12 items);

No. 39. Jonathan Belcher papers, 1731–1755 (c. 100 items);

No. 46. New Jersey Assembly minutes, 1751–1752, 1776–1781, 1806–1808 (7 vols.);

No. 58. John Witherspoon papers, 1766–1784 (c. 30 items);

No. 70. James Alexander and his son, William Alexander (Lord Stirling) papers, 1711–1771 (15 vols.);

No. 237. New Jersey-New York boundary papers, 1769 (3 vols.);

No. 243. More New York and New Jersey boundary papers, 1748–1753 (2 vols.);

No. 244. Ferdinand John Paris, East Jersey Proprietors' London agent, 1744–1755 (560 items).

See Fred Shelley: *A Guide to the Manuscripts Collection of the New Jersey Historical Society* (Newark, N.J., 1957); Philip M. Hamer: *Guide*, p. 356; and Historical Records Survey: *Guide to . . . New Jersey*, pp. 24–5.

New Brunswick

RUTGERS UNIVERSITY LIBRARY

Among the most important manuscripts in the Library are the following: The Morris Family Papers, 1670–1875 (14 boxes), which include papers of Gov. Lewis Morris of New Jersey and Gov. Robert Hunter Morris of Pennsylvania; the John Romeyn Brodhead collections relating chiefly to New York, 1670–1870 (10 boxes); the George Sykes collection, 1700–1800 (20 boxes); and the Thomas Williams collection, 1767–1804 (150 items). See Herbert F. Smith: *A Guide to the Manuscript Collection of the Rutgers University Library* (New Brunswick, N.J. [1964]); Historical Records Survey: *Guide to . . . New Jersey*, pp. 27–8; and Philip M. Hamer: *Guide*, pp. 354–6.

Princeton

PRINCETON UNIVERSITY LIBRARY

There are several collections of papers of importance relating to the period under review in the library. The Andre deCoppet collection (3,700 letters and documents) contains many items relating to John Adams, Benjamin Franklin, Nathanael Greene, Alexander Hamilton, Thomas Jefferson, James Madison, Robert Morris, and George Washington. There are also a few papers relating to Benedict Arnold, George Clinton, John Hancock, Patrick Henry, Robert Howe, Henry Knox, Arthur Lee, Richard Henry Lee, Thomas Paine, Israel Putnam, Benjamin Rush, Philip Schuyler, and Jonathan Trumbull. In addition there is the Elias Boudinot collection (approx. 200 items), chiefly Boudinot's correspondence, 1772–1821; the C. P. G. Fuller collection of Aaron Burr, Jr. (1756–1836), with papers ranging from 1770 to 1836; and the Richard Stockton and family papers, from 1702 to the nineteenth century (21 boxes). Finally, there are collections of manuscripts of those closely connected with Princeton, among them papers of the following presidents: Aaron Burr (1715–1757), Jonathan Edwards (1703–1758), Samuel Davis (1723–1761), Samuel Finley (1715–1766), and John Witherspoon (1723–1794). See Alexander P. Clark: *The Manuscript Collections of the Princeton University Library: An Introductory Survey* (Princeton, N.J., 1957; rep., 1960); and Philip M. Hamer: *Guide*, pp. 358–62.

NEW YORK
Albany

THE STATE LIBRARY OF NEW YORK

The State Library is also the state's archival agency. It is rich in manuscripts relating to provincial New York and to what is now the state of Vermont (some 5,000 manuscript volumes and a million items). The English series of bound manuscript volumes (following the Dutch series) in the New York Colonial Manuscripts collection extends from 1664 to 1800 (82 vols.); there are also the Council minutes, 1668–1783

(28 vols.), land papers, 1642–1803 (63 vols.), books of letters patent, 1664–1786 (12 vols.), and books of entry of the port of New York, 1728–1766 (10 vols.). Of especial importance are the papers of Sir William Johnson, originals and transcripts, 1733–1808 (22 vols. and over 1,665 pages of transcripts), most of which have been published in the *Sir William Johnson Papers*. There are many other collections of public and private papers, including those of Nicholas Herkimer, Revolutionary War Officer, 1742–1842 (12 vols.); "Manuscripts of the Colony and State of New York in the Revolutionary War, 1775–1800" (20 vols.); the Albany Committee of Correspondence papers, 1775–1778 (2 vols.); the Harmanus Bleecker papers, 1715–1872 (2,500 items); the George Clinton papers, 1763–1844 (10 vols. and other items); the Keith family papers, 1767–1803; the Philip Schuyler papers, 1773–1812; the Christopher Champlain, merchant, papers, 1761–1797; and the Van Rensselaer–Bowie papers, 1574–1795 (copies). It should be remembered that a fire in 1911 burned many priceless manuscripts and left others charred. See Philip M. Hamer: *Guide*, pp. 373–6; Historical Records Survey: *Guide to Depositories of Manuscript Collections in New York State (exclusive of New York City)* (Albany, N.Y. 1941), pp. 1–31; Edna L. Jacobsen: "Manuscript Treasures in the New York State Library," *New York History*, XX (1939), 265–76; and Edna L. Jacobsen and Charles F. Gosnell: "History in the [New York] State Library," *New York History*, XXVII–XXIX (1946–8), *passim.*

Clinton

HAMILTON COLLEGE LIBRARY

The most important collection of manuscripts, concerned with the period 1748–1776, is that of Samuel Kirkland, Indian missionary, 1763–1807; it includes letters relating to Indian affairs from Eleazar Wheelock, Henry Knox, Timothy Pickering, Philip Schuyler, Joseph Brant, and others (25 vols. and 646 pieces). See William Nelson Fenton: "A Calendar of Manuscript Materials Relating to the History of the Six Nations or Iroquois Indians in Depositories Outside Philadelphia, 1750–1850," American Philosophical Society, *Proceedings*, XCVII (1953), 578–95; Library of Congress: *Manuscripts in Public and Private Collections*, p. 58; and Philip M. Hamer: *Guide*, p. 382.

New York City

ARCHIVES AND RECORDS CENTER

The center contains chiefly the official records of the city of New York comprising roughly those from 1675 onward, including among them the records of the city clerk. While efforts are made to gather other New York records at the William Street center, many early records are at the Hall of Records, Criminal Courts Building, Center Street. Here are the records of the Mayor's Court and of other courts such as those of the Supreme Court of Jurisdiction. See I. N. Phelps Stokes: *The Iconography of Manhattan Island* (6 vols., New York City, 1915–1929), VI, 185–223; E. B. Greene and R. B. Morris: *A Guide to the Principal Sources for Early American History . . . in the City of New York* (2nd edn., rev., 1953), pp. 208–211; Philip M. Hamer: *Guide*, pp. 413–14.

COLUMBIA UNIVERSITY LIBRARIES

While the Columbia University Libraries have many extensive manuscripts holdings relating to the nineteenth and twentieth centuries, there are also several important collections concerned with the latter part of the eighteenth century. Among these are the following: (1) The John Jay papers, 1764–1829 (2,000 items); (2) The Gouverneur Morris papers, 1768–1816 (1,371 items); (3) The Rev. Samuel Johnson, first president of King's College (Columbia University) papers, 1710–1771 (85 vols.); (4) The William Samuel Johnson papers, 1753–1813 (100 pieces); (5) The King's College and Columbia College records, 1754–1890 (42 boxes); (6) The records of cases coming before the Mayor's Court of New York City, 1681–1819 (2,000 pieces); (7) The Otis family of Massachusetts Bay papers, 1687–1863 (349 items); (8) The Philipse-Gouverneur family papers, 1654–1874 (174 pieces); (9) The Peter Van Schaack papers, 1759–1843 (6 boxes).

See Philip M. Hamer: *Guide*, pp. 403–7; E. B. Greene and R. B. Morris: *Guide*, pp. xxii–xxiii; Herbert Wallace Schneider: "A Note on the Samuel Johnson Papers," *American Historical Review*, XXXI (1925–6), 724–6; and *Manuscript Collections in the Columbia University Libraries: A Descriptive List* (New York, 1959).

FORDHAM UNIVERSITY LIBRARY

A considerable number of manuscripts are included in the Charles Allen Munn collection, mostly concerned with the second half of the 18th century and Revolutionary War. Among these are George Washington papers, 1750–1787 (3 vols. and 10 items), including three orderly books, 1775–1779, and two maps drawn by Washington, 1750 and 1787; there is also a volume of minutes and meetings of the freeholders of Westmoreland County, Va., 1775–1776. See Philip M. Hamer: *Guide*, p. 410, and E. B. Greene and R. B. Morris: *Guide*, p. xxiv.

GENERAL THEOLOGICAL SEMINARY OF THE PROTESTANT EPISCOPAL CHURCH IN THE UNITED STATES LIBRARY

Among the 4,000 or so manuscript volumes in this library are papers of two individuals pertinent to our period: (1) The Rev. Thomas Bradbury Chandler, Loyalist, diary, 1775–1785 (published in *New England Historical Register*, XXVII); and (2) The Rev. Samuel Seabury papers, 1740–1796 (250 documents, including several bound volumes). See Philip M. Hamer: *Guide*, pp. 410–11; Historical Records Survey: *Guide* for New York City, pp. 35–7; and E. B. Greene and R. B. Morris: *Guide*, p. xxiv.

MUSEUM OF THE CITY OF NEW YORK

The museum holds certain collections of manuscripts that should be mentioned. They are as follows: (1) The Samuel Jones, legal papers, 1759–1801 (100 items); (2) The Loyalist Thomas Jones papers, 1769–1792 (3 vols. and 30 pieces); (3) The Philip Livingston papers, 1744–1751 (64 pieces); and (4) The de Lancey family papers, 1686–1865 (3 vols. and 320 pieces), chiefly papers of James de Lancey, lieutenant-governor of the Province of New York. See Philip M. Hamer: *Guide*, p. 414; E. B. Greene and R. B. Morris: *Guide*, xxvi; and Historical Records Survey: *Guide* for New York City, p. 63.

NEW-YORK HISTORICAL SOCIETY LIBRARY

This library is especially rich in source materials bearing upon the period 1748–1776. Among the pertinent collections of manuscripts are the following papers: (1) Dr. Samuel Adams's journal of a voyage from Nantucket to Belle Isle, 1768; (2) The Alexander papers: Papers of James Alexander, Attorney-General of New Jersey and Surveyor-General of New York and New Jersey, and of William Alexander (Lord Stirling), Surveyor-General and Revolutionary War officer; these include extensive collections of business correspondence, accounts, bills and receipts concerning legal, shipping, and real estate transactions, with deeds, surveys, maps, and chancery papers, the majority of which relate to property in New Jersey, arranged by counties, and the rest to New York in the 18th century (69 boxes); in addition there are bound papers of Lord Stirling, 1717–1783 (5 vols.); (3) The papers of John Almon, journalist and bookseller of London, including letters and manuscript memoranda, 1770–1805 (2 vols.); (4) The papers of John Alsop and John Alsop, Jr.,

New York, letters and papers, 1730–1769 and 1775 (89 pieces); (5) The Benedict Arnold papers, especially correspondence for the years 1772–1782 (about 100 pieces); (6) The Gerardus G. Beekman, merchant, papers, New York City, including an account book, 1752–1756, and a letter-book, 1752–1770; (7) The Henry Beekman papers, New York City, 1732–1753 (107 letters); (8) The Beekman family letters, New York, 1711–1852 (1 folder); (9) Anthony Lispenard Bleecker, merchant, letter-book, 1767–1787; (10) The Bleecker family papers, New York, family letters, including letters of Barent and John R. Bleecker, 1737–1832 (1 folder); (11) The Elias Boudinot, Revolutionary War patriot of New Jersey, correspondence, 1771–1817 (50 pieces); (12) The Rev. Marston Cabot, Conn., sermons, 1730–1756 (1 vol.); (13) Papers relating to Canada: Miscellaneous papers, 1694–1814; among them: (a) Letters to the Marquis de Lotbinière from the Marquis de Vaudreuil and others, 1748–1792 (130 letters); (b) Journal kept during the building of Fort Lawrence, Chignecto, Nova Scotia, Sept. 10–Oct. 8, 1750 (in the Horatio Gates Papers); (c) Orderly book of the 3rd New York Continental Regt., Aug. 1775–March 1776, on Montgomery's Expedition, with two other journals of this expedition; (14) The George Clinton, British governor of Province of New York, manuscripts, 1744–1753 (55 pieces); (15) The George Clinton, first governor of State of New York, letters and documents, 1769–1812 (160 pieces); (16) The Clinton family, New York, family letters, 18th and early 19th centuries (2 boxes); (17) The Cadwallader Colden, lieutenant-governor of New York, letter-books, letters to Colden, and his writings on scientific and historical subjects (12 boxes), most of which have been printed or calendared in the New-York Historical Society, *Collections, 1868, 1876–1877, 1917–1923, 1934–1935*; (18) The Cadwallader Colden, Jr., of Coldenham, day book, 1767–1768; (19) The Marquis de Conti letters and papers, c. 1745–c. 1760, many addressed to the Marquis at Halifax (130 pieces); (20) James Duane, mayor of New York, papers and letters concerning his activities in public affairs, commerce, and real estate, 1767–1795 (10 boxes and 5 vols.); (21) French and Indian War papers. Among them are the following: (a) Letters relating to Louisbourg, 1744–1748 (14 letters); (b) Journals and receipt book of Captain Phineas Stevens of Massachusetts, 1746–1754; (c) Letter-book of Thomas Williams of Massachusetts on the Crown Point Expedition, 1755–1756; (d) Two account books of the commissaries appointed for the expedition against Crown Point, 1756, with accounts of provisions, camp equipment, clothing, arms, and munitions; (e) Journal of Mrs. Browne, Nov. 1754–Aug. 1757, on the Braddock expedition; (f) Diary of Carr Huse of Massachusetts, April–July 1758; (g) Diary of Samuel Man, of the British Army, stationed at Fort Frederick, 1759–1760; (h) Diary and account book of Lt. Leonard Spaulding from 1755 (stationed at Fort Edward); (i) Accounts of Francis Stephens, storekeeper and paymaster of the Ordnance Office, New

York, in account with Edward White, clerk of the store, 1757–1761, for expenses of the Ordnance Department; (j) Four account books of Cruger, Robinson, and Livingston, commissaries and paymasters of New York, 1760–1767; (k) Memorials of British officers and soldiers who served in America in the French and Indian War and in the Revolutionary War (65 pieces); (l) Miscellaneous manuscripts, 1 folder, 40 manuscripts relating to soldiers' pay, 1757, and 8 muster rolls of Orange and Ulster County, in the F. Ashton De Peyster Manuscripts; (m) Muster rolls, New York, 1755–1764, printed in The New-York Historical Society, *Collections, 1891;* (22) Horatio Gates, an extensive collection of correspondence, military papers, orderly books, bills and receipts, c. 1750–1799 (30 boxes), including his service as an officer in the British Army during the French and Indian War and his correspondence as an American general during the Revolutionary War. (Note. An announcement was made in the early 1940's that the Gates Papers were in the process of publication in The New-York Historical Society *Collections,* but as yet none of the volumes have appeared); (23) Sir Charles Hardy, governor of New York, miscellaneous papers, 1755–1757 (1 folder); (24) William Heath, Revolutionary War general, correspondence and orderly books, 1775–1783, with orders issued by him, in several orderly books, 1776–1783; (25) William Heywood, soldier and farmer, Charlestown, New Hampshire, diary, 1758–1760; (26) Rt. Rev. John Henry Hobart, Bishop of New York, correspondence, 1757–1830 (40 vols.); (27) Daniel Horsmanden, Chief Justice of the Province of New York, papers relating to the colonial history of New York, including Indian affairs, 1714–1747 (2 vols.); (28) Capt. Jonathan Houghton, Bolton, Mass., papers, including some relating to the Revolutionary War, 1739–1785; (29) Carr Huse, Newbury, Mass., diary of experiences in the French and Indian War, 1758; (30) John Jay, register of cases in New York Supreme Court, 1770–1782, kept by Jay and Robert R. Livingston (1 vol.); (31) The Rev. Samuel Johnson, Stratford, Conn., President of King's College, letters to him, 1738–1771 (1 folder); (32) Sir William Johnson, Superintendent of Indian Affairs, New York, letters, 1747–1775, also minutes of Indian conferences, 1761 and 1763 (102 pieces); (33) John Tabor Kempe, attorney general of New York, correspondence and legal papers, 1760–1780 (6 boxes, plus 9 boxes of law suits); (34) John Lacey, Revolutionary War officer, journal of a journey to the Indians in western Pennsylvania, 1773; (35) The Rev. Archibald Laidlie, papers, including diary and correspondence as pastor of the Dutch Church in New York City, 1760–1773; (36) John Lamb, Revolutionary War patriot, papers, 1765–1795 (6 boxes); (37) John Laurance, Revolutionary War officer and jurist, New York City, personal papers, 1770–1800 (1 box); (38) John Ledyard, explorer, Connecticut, 1772–1790 (26 letters and miscellaneous papers); (39) Livingston family papers, New York, with six boxes relating to the estate of Philip Livingston

(1716–1778), and three boxes of correspondence including 63 letters of Robert G. Livingston, 1736–1772, together with account books of different members of the family, 18th and early 19th centuries (10 boxes and 22 vols.); (40) Samuel Loudon, New York printer, letters and accounts, 1761–1782 (13 pieces); (41) John Henry Lydius, Albany, N.Y., 43 letters and papers, including correspondence with Col. John Stoddard, 1746–1783; (42) Alexander McDougall, agitator and Revolutionary War officer, New York, papers, 1756–1795 (7 boxes); (43) John Mc-Kesson, lawyer, New York City, papers, concerning the Committee of Safety and the New York Provincial Congress and cases in the Mayor's court, 1761–1768 (10 boxes and 11 volumes); (44) Allan McLane, Delaware Revolutionary War officer, military papers and letters, 1775–1821 (3 vols.); (45) Moot Debating Club, New York City, minutes and papers, 1768–1774 (1 package); (46) The Rev. Abel Morgan, Middletown, Monmouth Co., New Jersey, sermons, 1747–1779 (1 vol.); (47) Naval history section: (a) *Duke of Cumberland,* private ship of war, log book of two cruises against the French in the West Indies, Dec. 1758–May 1759 and Dec. 1759–July 1760 (1 vol.); (b) Narrative of British expedition against Charleston, June 1776 (1 vol.); (48) New York City, the Chamberlain's Office papers, etc., 1742–1772 (6 boxes and 5 vols.); (49) Sir William Pepperrell, 16 letters and orderly books, 1716–1757; (50) The Rev. Samuel Andrews Peters, clergyman and Loyalist, Connecticut, correspondence, 1773–1822 (8 vols., in Protestant Episcopal Church Archives on deposit in the Society Library); (51) James Pitcher, New Rochelle, New York, ledger, 1766–1782, containing accounts, household and farm information; list of inhabitants of New Rochelle, 1771, and rates of New Rochelle, 1767 (1 vol.); (52) Protestant Episcopal Church Archives, including some collections of papers already cited (58 vols.); (53) Joseph Reed, Revolutionary War general and president of the Supreme Executive Council of Pennsylvania, correspondence on military and other public affairs, 1757, 1763–1795 (12 vols.).

See *Survey of Manuscript Collections in the New-York Historical Society* (Susan E. Lyman, comp., New York, 1941); Dorothy C. Barck: "New York Historical Society," Business Historical Society, *Bulletin,* VIII (1934), 1–5; E. B. Greene and R. B. Morris: *Guide,* xxvii–xxix, *passim;* Philip M. Hamer: *Guide,* pp. 415–20; and Library of Congress: *Manuscripts in Public and Private Collections,* pp. 59–60.

NEW YORK PUBLIC LIBRARY

The manuscript collections of the library bearing upon the period 1748–1776 are very impressive. As is true of the holdings of the Library of Congress, they can only be summarized. Among the more important collections are the following: (1) The Bancroft collection of original documents and transcripts, 1585–1883 (416 vols.), which includes, among other original manuscripts, the Samuel Adams papers, 1766–1803 (13 vols. and 1,695 pieces), and the Boston Committee of Correspondence papers, 1772–1775 (16 volumes and 690 pieces); (2) The George Chalmers collection, originals and transcripts relating to a number of the colonies (25 vols.); (3) The Emmet collection (10,800 pieces), although most of the manuscripts fall beyond 1776; (4) The Thomas Jefferson papers, 1766–1826 (1 vol. expense book, 2 boxes, and 30 pieces scattered in various collections); (5) The George Washington and family papers (1 vol., 7 boxes, and 75 pieces in various collections); (6) The James Duane papers, 1750–1867 (4 vols., 75 pieces); (7) The Benjamin Franklin papers, 1713–1789 (3 vols. and 2 boxes); (8) The Robert R. Livingston papers, 1755–1794 (100 pieces); (9) The William Livingston papers, 1749–1772 (2 vols.); (10) The Samuel Meredith papers, Pennsylvania Revolutionary War Officer, 1722–1811 (65 pieces); (11) The Philip John Schuyler papers, 1756–1805 (18 vols. and 49 boxes); (12) The William Smith, New York Loyalist, papers, 1763–1783 (9 vols. and 6 boxes); (13) Pierre Van Cortlandt, lieutenant-governor of New York, and son, Philip, papers, 1667–1890 (200 pieces); (14) The William Alexander (Lord Stirling), papers, 1760–1790 (200 pieces); (15) The Horatio Gates papers, 1760–1804 (8 vols. and 3 boxes); (16) The Robert Rogers papers, 1760–1761 (2 vols.); (17) The Joseph Hawley, Massachusetts, and family papers, 1653–1789 (2 vols. and 251 pieces).

See "Manuscript Collections in the New York Public Library," New York Public Library, *Bulletin*, V (1901), 306–36; Victor Hugo Paltsits: "The Manuscript Division of the New York Public Library," *ibid.*, XIX (1915), 135–65; Historical Records Survey: *Guide* for New York City, pp. 74–92; Karl Brown: *A Guide to the Reference Collections of the New York Public Library* (New York, 1941); E. B. Greene and R. B. Morris: *Guide*, pp. xxx–xxxiii, *passim;* Philip M. Hamer: *Guide*, pp. 422–33.

NORTH CAROLINA

Raleigh

STATE DEPARTMENT OF ARCHIVES AND HISTORY

As the State's archival agency this department is the custodian of non-current official records and other papers relating chiefly to North Carolina. Among these manuscripts are legislative records, 1689–1917 (250 cu. ft.); executive records, 1663–1954 (1,500 cu. ft.); judicial records, 1690–1939 (50 cu. ft.). The executive records include papers of the following governors whose activities concern the years 1748–1776: Gabriel Johnston, 1735–1752 (22 items); Arthur Dobbs, 1754–1764 (1 box); William Tryon, 1765–1771, including Tryon's journal, 1771 (1 box and 1 microfilm reel); Josiah Martin, 1771–1775 (½ box); also papers of the President of the Council, Matthew Rowan, 1753–1754 (½ box).

Certain personal papers are of value for the period 1748–1776, such as the Alexander Brevard papers, 1757–1869 (some 300 items), the Thomas Burke papers, 1769–1782 (c. 200 items), and the Charles Earl Johnson collection, 1755–1875 (25 boxes), containing correspondence of James Iredell (1751–1799) and Samuel Johnston (1733–1816). In addition to the collections of original manuscripts, the Archives possess a large number of copies of papers drawn from such depositories as the British Public Record Office and Spanish archival depositories.

See Beth G. Crabtree: *Guide to Private Manuscript Collections in the North Carolina State Archives* (Raleigh, N.C., 1964); *Summary Guide to Research Materials in the North Carolina State Archives; Section A: Records of State Agencies* (Raleigh, N.C., 1963); *The North Carolina Historical Commission: Forty Years of Public Service, 1903–1943* (Raleigh, N.C., 1942); *Guide to the Manuscript Collections in the Archives of the North Carolina Historical Commission* (Raleigh, N.C., 1942); Daniel Leroy Corbitt: *Calendars of Manuscript Collections [of the North Carolina Historical Commission]: Volume I* (Raleigh, N.C., 1926); Library of Congress: *Manuscripts in Public and Private Collections*, pp. 62–3; and Philip M. Hamer: *Guide*, pp. 477–9. It should be noted that the name State Department of Archives and History has taken the place of the older name North Carolina Historical Commission.

Chapel Hill

UNIVERSITY OF NORTH CAROLINA LIBRARY

The library has very extensive bodies of papers. There are two main collections of manuscripts: one is the "North Carolina Collection," consisting of papers from 1570 to 1968 (over 5,000 items); the other, much more important, is the "Southern Historical Collection," 1588–1956 (over 3,000,000 pieces). While most of the material is outside the period 1748–1776, the collection does include papers of Thomas Burke, 1744–1789 (315 pieces); the James Iredell collection, 1759–1789 (23 vols.); and a considerable body of reproductions of manuscripts, including Arthur Dobbs and family papers, 1569–1845 (2 vols. and 3 microfilm reels). See Susan S. Blosser and Clyde N. Wilson, eds.: *The Southern Historical Collection: A Guide to Manuscripts* (Chapel Hill, N.C., 1970); and Philip M. Hamer: *Guide*, pp. 456–67.

Durham

DUKE UNIVERSITY LIBRARIES

The rich holdings of the Duke University Libraries pertain chiefly to the nineteenth century. However, there are papers relating to James Iredell (1751–1799), and his son, James Iredell, Jr. (125 items); Charles Cotesworth Pinckney (1746–1825) and family, 1744–1887 (1 vol. and 1,180 items); some George Washington and family papers, 1760–1859 (99 items); and Robert Carter's letter-books, 1772–1793 (18 vols. containing 3,135 letters). In addition, there are journals, diaries, etc., concerned not only with the South but other manuscripts of interest such as, rather surprisingly, Levant Company papers, 1768–1902 (3 vols. and 134 items); and, papers relating to a Jamaica plantation, 1766–1873 (9 vols. and 235 items). See Nannie M. Tilley and Noma L. Goodwin: *Guide to Manuscript Collections in the Duke University Library* (Durham, N.C., 1947); Historical Records Survey: *Guide to Depositories of Manuscript Collections in North Carolina,* North Carolina Historical Commission, *Bulletin,* No. 41, (Raleigh, N.C., 1940), pp. 10–12; and Philip M. Hamer: *Guide,* pp. 469–75.

Winston-Salem

MORAVIAN ARCHIVES

The extensive collection of manuscripts in the Archives detail the history of Moravians in North Carolina, especially at Wachovia, 1753 to date. These papers include diaries, memoirs, and letters, as well as church registers and account books (2,000 vols. and 10,000 pages of manuscripts). Historical Records Survey: *Guide to . . . North Carolina,* pp. 17–18; and Philip M. Hamer: *Guide,* p. 479.

PENNSYLVANIA

Harrisburg

WILLIAM PENN MEMORIAL MUSEUM AND ARCHIVES

Here are located the official archives of the Commonwealth of Pennsylvania. The manuscripts of chief importance held in this depository and concerned with the years 1748–1776 are the following: (1) Although the General Assembly records before 1777 are missing the Provincial Council minutes, 1682/3–1775 (20 vols.) have survived, together with the Provincial Council papers, 1682–1775 (unbound, 12 cu. ft.); (2) The Port of Philadelphia records, 1727–1838 (19 vols.+); (3) The "Register of German Passengers," with ships' lists, 1727–1807; (4) Naturalization lists, 1740–1773 (unbound, ½ cu. ft.); (5) Indian deeds, 1682–1789 (1½ cu. ft.); (6) The Commissioners for Indian Trade accounts, 1758–1766 (2 vols.); (7) The Provincial Secretary papers, 1709–1775 (1½ cu. ft.), including records of Indian trader licences issued by Richard Peters, 1743–1761, and those issued by Joseph Shippen, Jr., 1765–1771; (8) Land and survey records, 1762–1764, 1768–1769 (3 vols.); (9) The Committee of Safety minutes, June 30, 1775–July 22, 1776 (3 vols.); (10) General Loan Office Accounts, 1773–1800 (14 vols.); (11) The Baynton-Wharton-Morgan papers, 1723–1794 (51 vols.); (12) Two copies of the famous report on the American colonies by James Abercromby, 1751–1752; (13) The John Franklin papers, 1753–1828 (photostats, 250 items) pertaining to the land controversy between Connecticut and Pennsylvania settlers in the Wyoming Valley; (14) The Harris family papers, 1768–1845 (1 cu. ft.), relating to Lancaster and Centre counties; (15) The Harris-Fisher-Russell family papers, 1749–1880 (5 cu. ft.), which relate to John Harris, founder of Harrisburg, and George Fisher, founder of Middletown, and their descendants; (16) The Benjamin Lightfoot journal, 1770 (photostats, 18 sheets) pertaining to the Connecticut Wyoming settlement, Aug. 16–Sept. 15, 1770; (17) The Potts family business papers, 1705–1853 (93 items), concerned with the iron industry around Cornwall, Pennsylvania; (18) The Edward Shippen Thompson papers, 1746–1890 (4 cu. ft.), chiefly relating to Colonel James Burd and his descendants; (19) The Willing, Morris, and Swanwick Baltimore papers, 1774–1794 (½ cu. ft.), a mercantile firm of Philadelphia.

There is also an exceedingly large collection of transcripts, microfilms, photostats and photographs bearing upon Pennsylvania history. These are listed in the *Preliminary Guide to the Research Materials of the Pennsylvania Historical and Museum Commission* (Harrisburg, 1959); see also Philip M. Hamer: *Guide*, pp. 513–15.

Allentown

MUHLENBERG COLLEGE

Among the manuscript holdings of the college are the Frederick Augustus Conrad Muhlenberg journal, 1770 (1 vol.); also a collection of Pennsylvania German dialect writings (34 vols.). See Historical Records Survey: *Guide* for Pennsylvania, p. 1; and Philip M. Hamer: *Guide*, p. 508.

Bethlehem

ARCHIVES OF THE MORAVIAN CHURCH

Since Bethlehem was the headquarters of the Moravian Church in eighteenth-century America, the Archives houses much valuable material, most of which is in German. Of particular importance is the "Bethlehem Diary," 1742–1871 (44 large volumes), records kept by Bethlehem officials, including local as well as general religious and political news and missionary reports. The so-called "Unity Diary," 1747–1848, contains extracts from similar diaries of Moravian congregations throughout the world. Financial and industrial information may be obtained from the records for the period of the "Economy," 1750–1771, during which period all Bethlehem property and industries were owned by the Moravian Church.

The Indian Mission Records, 1739–1860, are extensive. They include diaries, travel journals, linguistic studies, and observations on Indians. The depository also has vital statistics for Bethlehem and other congregations, and statistics of ecclesiastical acts (confirmations, ordinations, etc.). There is also a fine collection of eighteenth-century manuscript Moravian music and a map room with approximately 800 maps and building plans. Papers of the following individuals likewise should be noted: John Ettwein, 1772–1797; John Heckwelder, 1765–1823; Augustus Gottlieb Spangenberg, 1744–1760; and David Zeisberger, 1745–1798.

See Paul A. W. Wallace: "The Moravian Records," *Indiana Magazine of History*, XLVIII (1952), 141–60; Kenneth G. Hamilton: "The Resources of the Moravian Church Archives," *Pennsylvania History*, XXVII (1960), 263–72; also by Bishop Hamilton: "The Moravian Archives at Bethlehem, Pennsylvania," *American Archivist*, XXIV (1961), 415–23; and Philip M. Hamer: *Guide*, p. 509.

Haverford

HAVERFORD COLLEGE LIBRARY

The library's Quaker Collection (50,000 items) contains considerable eighteenth-century materials, including letters of John Woolman, personal papers of other leading Friends living both in America and England, among them John and Samuel Fothergill and Anthony Benezet, together with approximately 700 manuscript journals, including those of William Hunt, Margaret Hill Morris, and William Savery. There are also documents concerned with the relations between the Quakers and the Indians, 1758–1929, a large number of family papers, as well as microfilmed copies of minutes and other records of the London Yearly Meeting, 1668–1860.

For additional information see Edwin B. Bronner: *The Quaker Collection of Haverford College Library* ([Haverford, Pa., 1963]); Thomas E. Drake: *The Quaker Collection at Haverford* (Haverford, Pa., 1956); Historical Records Survey: *Guide* for Pennsylvania, pp. 23–5; and Philip M. Hamer: *Guide,* p. 515.

Philadelphia

AMERICAN PHILOSOPHICAL SOCIETY LIBRARY

Among the manuscript collections in the library that are concerned with the period 1748–1776 are the following, arranged alphabetically: (1) Burd-Shippen papers, 1708–1792 (6 boxes and 3 vols.), relating chiefly to the French and Indian War, 1754–1763, while Col. James Burd was commander at Fort Augusta in Pennsylvania; (2) Fort Augusta account books, 1753–1765 (8 vols.); (3) Fort Pitt, cash book, 1760 (1 vol.); (4) Benjamin Franklin papers, 1642–1874 (over 16,000 pieces), a collection of great importance; (5) William Franklin, papers, 1760–1813 (1 box); (6) Haines and Twells, Philadelphia brewers, account book, 1767–1770 (1 vol.); (7) David Hall, printer and bookseller, papers, 1745–1775 (10 vols. and some 100 pieces); (8) Timothy Horsfield (1708–1773), papers, 1733–1771 (2 vols.), chiefly concerning Pennsylvania Indian affairs, particularly in 1756, with letters to or from George Croghan, Dep.-Gov. William Denny, Benjamin Franklin, Dep.-Gov. Robert Hunter Morris, Edward Shippen, Bishop Spangenberg, Teedyuscung, Conrad Weiser, and David Zeisberger; (9) Thomas Jefferson, papers, 1775–1825 (5 boxes); (10) Richard Henry Lee, correspondence (2 vols.); (11) Mason and Dixon Survey, papers of the boundary commissioners, 1760–1768 (2 vols.); (12) Muhlenberg family papers, 1769–1866, including papers of Gen. J. P. G. Muhlenberg and H. M. Muhlenberg; (13) Charles Willson Peale and family papers, 1728–1907 (3,370 pieces); (14) Thomas and Richard Penn, correspondence with James Hamilton, 1747–1771 (1 vol.); (15) William Penn and Penn family miscellaneous letters and documents, 1665–1801 (4 vols.); (16) Minutes of Pennsylvania Indian treaties and conferences, 1721–1760 (7 vols.); (17) Pennsylvania military records relating to the French and Indian War, 1756–1763 (7 vols.); (18) Richard Price, papers, 1767–1790 (90 pieces); (19) Robert Rogers, colonial ranger, papers, 1766–1767 (100 pieces); (20) Edward Shippen of Lancaster, letters and papers, 1727–1789 (3 boxes); (21) Chief Justice Frederick Smyth, papers, 1756–1816 (56 pieces), collection largely prior to the American Revolution; (22) William Strahan, printer, journals and account books, 1751–1777 (4 vols);

(23) Benjamin Vaughan, papers, 1746–1830 (1,500 pieces); (24) George Washington, papers, 1774–1781 (30 pieces).

In addition to original papers the Society has a number of important collections in the form of photostats, microfilms, etc. See Whitfield J. Bell and Murphy D. Smith: *Guide to the Archives and Manuscripts of the American Philosophical Society* (Philadelphia, 1966); *A Catalogue of Manuscripts and Printed Documents, Chiefly Americana, Selected from the Archives and Manuscript Collections of the American Philosophical Society* . . . (Philadelphia, 1937); and Philip M. Hamer: *Guide,* pp. 524–7.

FREE LIBRARY OF PHILADELPHIA

Among the manuscripts bearing upon the period 1748–1776 are the "Minutes of the Common Council of Philadelphia," 1704–1776 (6 vols.); there are also papers relating to the Pennsylvania Germans in the eighteenth century (85 pieces) and, in addition, some 1,000 decorative manuscripts in Fraktur, c. 1760–1860. See Historical Records Survey: *Guide* for Pennsylvania, p. 51; and Philip M. Hamer: *Guide,* p. 529.

HISTORICAL SOCIETY OF PENNSYLVANIA

The holdings of manuscripts that throw light on the developing British Empire are impressive. Among them are the following collections concerned with the years 1748–1776: (1) The Bartram family papers, 1738–1810 (14 vols.); (2) Colonel Elias Boudinot papers, 1716–1828 (approx. 500 items); (3) Business, professional, and personal account books, 1676–1904 (approx. 500 vols.); (4) Church and meeting house collection, 1692–1910 (approx. 100 vols.); (5) Colonial Revolutionary manuscripts, 1738–1808 (approx. 150 items); (6) The Gilbert Cope historical and genealogical collection, 1682–1924 (30,000 items), mostly Quaker materials; (7) The Cox-Parish-Wharton papers, 1600–1900 (c. 5,000 items), likewise mostly Quaker materials; (8) Custom House papers, 1704–1929 (41 boxes and 25 vols.), for the Port of Philadelphia; (9) The John Dickinson papers, 1760–1772 (8 vols.); (10) The Dreer collection, 1492–1917 (approx. 40,000 items), which includes: (a) Thomas Jefferson papers, 1774–1825 (1 vol.); (b) Benjamin Rush papers, 1739–1813 (1 vol.); and (c) George Washington papers, 1749–1839 (1 vol.); (11) The Henry Drinker papers, 1739–1869 (some 25,600 items), the papers of a Quaker merchant and his descendants; (12) The Etting Collection, 1558–

1917 (approx. 20,000 items), an especially rich collection, with respect to civic, frontier, and religious developments; (13) Forges and furnaces account books, 1726–1832 (approx. 250 vols.); (14) Benjamin Franklin papers, 1747–1794 (13 vols. containing approx. 1,000 items); (15) Edward Carey Gardiner collection, 1632–1939, papers of the Carey, Pennington, and Baird families (c. 12,000 items); (16) The Gratz collections, 1383–1921 (approx. 175,000 items), a huge body of manuscripts that includes John Dickinson correspondence, 1775–1798 (2 boxes) and Charles Thomson, 1754–1824 (4 boxes); (17) Grubb furnace and forge books, which include the Hopewell forge books, 1765–1805 (34 vols.); (18) The John Gottlieb Ernestus Heckewelder papers, 1755–1822 (150 items); (19) Indian Records collection, 1716–1856 (16 vols. and 62 pieces); (20) The Henry Laurens correspondence, 1762–1780 (approx. 1,500 items); (21) The Lightfoot papers, 1733–1816 (2,000 items); (22) In addition, the Benjamin Lightfoot journals and surveys, 1770–1772 (2 vols.); (23) The Logan Papers, 1664–1871 (approx. 12,000 items); (24) The Robert Morris business papers, 1769–1836 (approx. 250 items); (25) The Norris family papers, 1742–1860 (70 vols. and 16 boxes), including those of Isaac Norris; (26) Parker-Franklin Correspondence, 1747–1773 (approx. 150 items); (27) The Pemberton family papers, 1641–1880 (approx. 15,000 items in 70 vols.); (28) The Penn family manuscripts, 1629–1834 (approx. 25,000 items), one of the most important of the Society's collections; (29) Papers of Pennsylvania Society for Promoting the Abolition of Slavery, 1748–1916 (approx. 12,000 items); (30) The Christian Frederick Post journal, 1758 (1 vol.); (31) The Shippen family papers, 1701–1856 (approx. 10,000 items); (32) Smith family papers, 1757–1861 (approx. 300 items and 1 vol.), including papers of Provost William Smith; (33) The William Strahan, London printer, letters, 1751–1776 (40 items); (34) Tax and assessment books, Philadelphia and Montgomery counties, 1762–1855 (approx. 725 vols.); (35) The Thompson collections, 1607–1903 (125 vols. and approx. 6,350 items), papers of the Quaker Jonah Thompson and his descendants, humanitarians, merchants, ironmasters and landowners with letters from Benjamin Franklin, Robert Morris, Thomas Penn and other noted men; (36) The Charles Thomson papers, 1774–1811 (9 vols.); (37) The William Trent papers, 1775 (1 vol.); (38) General Anthony Wayne papers, 1765–1890 (approx. 6,500 items); (39) Conrad Weiser papers, 1741–1766 (approx. 250 items); (40) Wharton papers, 1679–1834 (approx. 2,000 items); (41) John Woolman papers, 1652–1830.

There are still other collections of papers which are listed as "Additional Manuscripts." Among them are the following: (42) Association, club and society records, 1764–1937 (110 vols.); (43) Board of Trade papers, 1675–1782 (146 vols. transcripts), an extraordinarily important body of manuscripts including copies of Board of Trade journals, 1675–

1782 (90 vols.); Proprietary colony records, 1697–1776 (25 vols.); and the series denominated Plantations General, 1689–1780 (28 vols.); and finally, a three-volume index; (44) Braddock's Expedition papers, 1755 (1 vol.); (45) Court records, 1676–1818 (67 vols.), which include Pennsylvania and Delaware records; (46) Pennsylvania Assembly papers, 1682–1783, most of them early (300 items); (47) Philadelphia tea shipments, 1769–1773 (1 vol.); (48) The David McNeely Stauffer collection, c. 1644–1884 (approx. 8,500 items) with many letters concerned with the years 1748–1776; (49) Tax lists, 1693–1870 (19 vols.); (50) George Croghan's journal, 1759–1763 (1 pkg.); (51) William Trent's journal at Fort Pitt, 1763 (1 vol.); (52) The Lewis Evans manuscripts, 1753 (2 vols. including one vol. of photostats); (53) George Morgan letter-book, 1767–1768; (54) Indian treaties and deeds, 1683–1756 (2 vols.), which are contemporary copies of treaties and deeds relating to Pennsylvania; (55) The Cadwalader family collection, 1630–1900 (approx. 100,000 items), including papers of Gen. John Cadwalader (1742–1786), those of Phineas Bond (1749–1815) and George Croghan papers (an exceedingly important collection, 1744–1782); (56) The Chew papers, 1739–1768 (approx. 250 items), including papers concerning the Maryland-Pennsylvania boundary dispute; (57) George Croghan papers, 1754–1808 (approx. 200 items—photostats and transcripts) in addition to papers in the Cadwalader collection; (58) Provost William Smith papers, 1690–1869 (6 vols.), separately listed from those in (32); (59) The Samuel Powel family papers, 1700–1925 (50,000 items), with papers of allied families, for Philadelphia overseas trading, 1748–1756. See *Guide to the Manuscript Collections of the Historical Society of Pennsylvania* (2nd edn., rev., Philadelphia, 1949); and Philip M. Hamer: *Guide*, pp. 530–41.

LIBRARY COMPANY OF PHILADELPHIA

The manuscripts of the Library Company are now in the physical custody of the Historical Society of Pennsylvania, while the Society's rare books have been transferred to the Library Company. Among the manuscripts with a bearing on the Empire for the years 1748–1776 that have been transferred, two collections should be mentioned: the John Dickinson papers, 1732–1808 (21 boxes), and the Benjamin Rush papers, 1762–1813 (71 vols.).

See *Descriptive Catalogue of the Du Simitière Papers in the Library Company of Philadelphia* (Philadelphia, 1940); Philip M. Hamer: *Guide*, p. 542; and Library of Congress: *Manuscripts in Public and Private Collections*, p. 68.

PRESBYTERIAN HISTORICAL SOCIETY

Here are held the principal records of the Presbyterian Church in the United States (some 400,000 manuscripts); a very considerable body of this material relates to the period 1748–1776. See Joseph B. Turner: "A Catalogue of Manuscript Records in the Possession of the Presbyterian Historical Society," *Presbyterian Historical Society Journal*, VIII (1915), 13–22; and Philip M. Hamer: *Guide*, pp. 544–5.

Pittsburgh

CARNEGIE LIBRARY OF PITTSBURGH

The most important manuscripts concerned with the years 1748–1776 are in the Isaac Craig collection. These include papers of George Croghan, 1765 (1-vol. journal), and the George Morgan papers, 1774–1778 (3 letter-books). See Historical Records Survey: *Guide* for Pennsylvania, p. 80; and Philip M. Hamer: *Guide*, p. 549.

DARLINGTON MEMORIAL LIBRARY, UNIVERSITY OF PITTSBURGH

The manuscripts in this library chiefly emphasize western Pennsylvania developments. Among those of importance are: (1) Fort Pitt manuscripts, 34 letters and papers relating to the defense and maintenance of Fort Pitt from 1758 to 1783, containing a bill to Gen. Forbes for wagons and gears, Nov. 6, 1758; (2) Pittsburgh manuscript account or waste book, including accounts of the Indian trading post at Fort Pitt under the direction of the Commissioners for Indian Affairs for Pennsylvania, June 19, 1759–June 18, 1760; with the book are 26 documents relating to the conduct of business, 1760–1765; (3) Seven documents pertaining to Braddock's expedition, 1755; (4) Minutes of the conference between Philadelphia Quakers and the Six Nations, 1756; (5) Ohio Company Papers, 1738–1801 (104 items), including papers of Thomas Cresap, George Croghan, and the journal of Christopher Gist, 1750–1751; (6) George Morgan, letterbook, 1771.

See Ruth Salisbury: "Survey of the Darlington Memorial Library," *Western Pennsylvania Historical Magazine*, XLVII (1964), pp. 19–29; Agnes Starrett: *The Darlington Memorial Library, University of Pittsburgh* (Pittsburgh, Pa., 1938); Philip M. Hamer: *Guide*, p. 549.

HISTORICAL SOCIETY OF WESTERN
PENNSYLVANIA

The holdings of chief importance for the period 1748–1776 are the following: (1) The Henry Bouquet papers, 1759–1761 (2 boxes of transcripts); (2) The George Morgan papers, 1758–1818 (1 folder); (3) A Fort Pitt daybook, 1765–1767; (4) The James Ross papers, 1700–1837 (1 box), which include letters or papers of George Washington, Robert Morris, Edmund Randolph, and the Penn family; (5) The George H. Rankin papers, including copies of documents concerning the Forbes Road. See Western Pennsylvania Historical Survey: *Inventory of Manuscript and Miscellaneous Collections of the Historical Society of Western Pennsylvania, Bibliographical Contributions*, No. 1 (Pittsburgh, Pa., 1933); and Philip M. Hamer: *Guide*, p. 550.

Swarthmore

FRIENDS HISTORICAL LIBRARY,
SWARTHMORE COLLEGE

This library is a principal depository of manuscripts relating to the Society of Friends, 1652–1956 (1,650 vols., 500 boxes, and 2,000 linear ft.); among the collections bearing upon the years 1748-1776 are the John Woolman papers, 1756–1772 (4 vols.); also the Philadelphia Yearly Meeting minutes, 1668–1954 (1,550 vols. and 8 ft.). See Historical Records Survey: *Inventory of Church Archives: Society of Friends in Pennsylvania* (1941); and Philip M. Hamer: *Guide*, pp. 552–4.

RHODE ISLAND

Providence

RHODE ISLAND STATE ARCHIVES

Here are to be found the official records of Rhode Island, 1683–1954+. Among them are the records of the General Assembly, 1683–1954+, including acts and resolves (268 vols.), and related papers such as petitions, 1725–1869 (83 vols. and 12 ft.), reports, 1728–1954 (14 vols. and 40 file drawers), and letters, 1730–1886 (65 vols. and 600 pieces). There are also the private papers of Joseph Clarke, treasurer of the colony, 1761–1777 (34 items), and of Benjamin Huntington, 1772–1790 (50 items). See Philip M. Hamer: *Guide*, pp. 565–6.

JOHN CARTER BROWN LIBRARY,
BROWN UNIVERSITY

Among the manuscripts bearing upon the years 1748–1776 in this library are those of Nicholas Brown and family, 1750–1900 (300,000 pieces). See Lawrence C. Wroth: *The First Century of the John Carter Brown Library: A History with a Guide to the Collections* (Providence, R. I., 1946); Library of Congress: *Manuscripts in Public and Private Collections*, pp. 69–70; and Philip M. Hamer: *Guide*, pp. 563–4.

RHODE ISLAND HISTORICAL SOCIETY

Among the papers held by the Society are those of Moses Brown and Obadiah Brown, account books (20 books and 3 boxes); Nicholas Cooke, Revolutionary War governor and family, 1732–1811 (2 vols.); the official records of Providence, 1639–1832 (160 vols.); and records of trade of Providence with Europe, the West Indies, and other parts of the world, 1750–1823 (20 account books and 40 vols. of correspondence). In this connection see Bradford F. Swan: "The Providence Town Papers," *Rhode Island History*, XI (July, 1952), 65–70.

Newport

NEWPORT HISTORICAL SOCIETY

The manuscripts here include the official records of the city of Newport, 1684–1775, and also church records, including those of the Society of Friends, the Congregationalists, and the Baptists; there are also many ships' logs and business records, such as those of John Bannister, 1695–1768, Aaron Lopez, 1752–1781, and William and Samuel Vernon, 1740–1782. See Philip M. Hamer: *Guide*, p. 561.

SOUTH CAROLINA

Columbia

SOUTH CAROLINA ARCHIVES DEPARTMENT

Among the holdings of the Archives concerned with the years 1748–1776 are the following: (1) The records of the Commons House of Assembly (for the colonial period) as well as those of the House of Representatives (for the national period), 1671–1889; (2) Miscellaneous papers of the governors, 1671–1958; (3) Papers of the Governor's Council, 1734–1789; (4) Quit-rent returns, 1731–1775; (5) Records of the Surveyor General's land office, 1671–1840; (6) Treasury papers, 1725–1935; (7) Records of courts of chancery, common pleas, general sessions, and probate, 1700–1785; (8) Also included are letters and documents concerning the Commissioners of Indian trade, 1749–1765 (5 vols.). There are likewise many transcripts from the British Public Record Office relating to South Carolina affairs as well as microfilms of vestry minutes and vestry records, 1725–1825. See R. H. Woody: "The Public Records of South Carolina," *American Archivist*, II (1931), 244–63; Philip M. Hamer: *Guide*, pp. 570–1; and Library of Congress: *Manuscripts in Public and Private Collections*, p. 71.

SOUTH CAROLINIANA LIBRARY, UNIVERSITY OF SOUTH CAROLINA

This library has among other papers the Gov. Patrick Noble and family papers, 1761–1878 (89 items), and those of the Kincaid-Anderson family, 1767–1926 (9 vols. and 2,575 pieces). There should be mentioned also typed copies of South Carolina county and church records, 1691–1935 (902 vols.). See Philip M. Hamer: *Guide*, pp. 571–2.

Charleston

SOUTH CAROLINA HISTORICAL SOCIETY

The most important bodies of papers in the Society library pertinent to this survey are (1) The Laurens collection, 1747–1796 (38 vols. and 670 items), including papers of Henry Laurens, and his correspondence with Washington, Franklin, and others; other collections include: (2) The Arthur Middleton papers, 1767–1782 (1 box); (3) The Christopher Gadsden papers, 1746–1801 (3 items); (4) The Pinckney family papers, 1775–1830 (4 vols. and 93 pieces), together with Mrs. Charles Pinckney's letters, 1775–1782 (17 items); (5) The Manigault family papers, 1751–1873 (5 vols. and 442 items); (6) The Theodore Gourdin family papers, 1694–1873 (1 vol. and 15 boxes); (7) Pelatiah Webster, Pennsylvania merchant, journal, 1765 (1 vol.); (8) Henry Ravenal, daybook, 1748–1771, and ledger, 1751–1783; (9) Papers of the Commissioners of Fortifications, 1751–1770 (1 vol.); (10) Records of the Court of Ordinary, 1764–1771 (1 vol.); (11) Letters to the Council of Safety, 1775 (29 items). The depository also contains numerous volumes of plantation and church records for the period 1748–1776.

See Helen C. McCormack: "A Provisional Guide to Manuscripts in the South Carolina Historical Society," *South Carolina Historical and Genealogical Magazine,* XLV(1944)–XLVIII(1947), *passim;* and Philip M. Hamer: *Guide,* pp. 568–70.

TEXAS

Dallas

SOUTHERN METHODIST UNIVERSITY LIBRARIES: METHODIST HISTORICAL LIBRARY

Two small collections held in the Methodist Historical Library are the Selina Hastings, Countess of Huntingdon, 1707–1791, correspondence (60 letters), and the John Wesley correspondence (81 letters). See Philip M. Hamer: *Guide,* p. 589.

VIRGINIA

Richmond

VIRGINIA STATE LIBRARY

This library is the state's archival agency and therefore the custodian of the official records. Among those records falling within the period 1748–1776 are the journals of the House of Burgesses, 1693–1776 (8 vols.), the journals and minute-books of the Council, 1697–1776 (19 vols.), and the great body of judicial records of a variety of kinds, 1634–1865 (3,018 vols. and 2,477,317 items), as well as a collection of "miscellaneous manuscripts," 1697–1775.

Among the personal papers are some of those of such colonial figures as Daniel Boone (1734–1820), George Rogers Clark (1752–1818), Patrick Henry (1736–1799), Thomas Jefferson (1743–1826), Henry (Light Horse Harry) Lee (1756–1818), George Mason (1725–1792), Daniel Morgan (1763–1800), Edmund Pendleton (1721–1803), and George Washington (1732–1799). There are also the letter-books of James Abercromby, 1746–1773; the William and David Allason mercantile papers, 1752–1815 (90 vols. and 3,750 items); papers of the Fairfax family, 1638–1810 (222 items); and various church records including the Anglican (Episcopalian), Baptist, Quaker, Presbyterian, Lutheran, and German Reformed, churches (250 vols.). Mention should also be made of the great collection of transcripts and microfilm of manuscripts which the Chairman of the State Library and the Librarian of the University of Virginia have drawn from Great Britain. See the State Library's *Bulletins* and *Annual Reports* for manuscript holdings; and Philip M. Hamer: *Guide,* pp. 611–14.

VIRGINIA HISTORICAL SOCIETY

Among the personal papers possessed by the Society and falling within the years 1748–1776 are those of the following: (1) President of the Council John Blair, 1751 (1 vol.); (2) Chief Justice Paul Carrington, 1755–1792 (110 items); (3) Gov. Robert Dinwiddie, 1751–1757 (20 items); (4) Francis Lightfoot Lee, 1768–1791 (40 items); (5) Richard Henry Lee, 1765–1793 (200 items); (6) William Lee, 1768–1793 (500 items); and (7) George Washington, 1754–1799 (225 items). There are also some records of the House of Burgesses, 1685–1754 (200 pp.). See *Catalogue of the Manuscripts in the Collection of the Virginia Historical Society and also Some Printed Papers* (Richmond, Va., 1901); and Philip M. Hamer: *Guide*, pp. 610–11.

Charlottesville

UNIVERSITY OF VIRGINIA LIBRARY

Among the manuscript collections in the Library that relate to the period under examination are papers of the following figures: (1) Thomas Jefferson, 1762–1826 (2,500 pieces); (2) Richard Henry Lee, 1758–1793 (450 pieces); (3) Landon Carter, 1734–1777 (190 pieces); (4) Arthur Lee, 1760–1791 (347 pieces), chiefly correspondence; (5) Francis Lightfoot Lee, 1773–1790 (25 pieces); (6) William Lee, 1773-1782 (77 pieces); and (7) The Rev. James Maury, 1743–1771 (58 pieces). There are also a number of collections of business papers such as the business letter-books of the Carters of Virginia, which cover the period, 1659–1897.

One distinguishing feature of the activities of the Library carried out in conjunction with the Virginia State Library at Richmond is the vast accumulation of microfilm and other types of reproduction of original papers having some relationship to the history of colonial Virginia, as well as other colonies, drawn from Great Britain and elsewhere. This is the so-called "Virginia Colonial Records Project." As it is a continuing project no guide can be complete. The various "Reports" in mimeograph form issued by the "Project" from time to time should be consulted. However, see Lester J. Cappon and Patricia Holbert Menk: "The Evolution of Materials for Research in Early American History in the University of Virginia Library," *William and Mary Quarterly*, 3rd ser., III (1946), 370–82; the Library's *Annual Report of the Archivist*, succeeded by the *Annual Report on Historical Collections* (1930+); Constance E. Thurlow and Francis L. Berkeley, Jr.: *A Calendar . . . on the Papers of Thomas*

Jefferson (Charlottesville, Va., 1950); Library of Congress: *Manuscripts in Public and Private Collections*, p. 75; and Philip M. Hamer: *Guide*, pp. 601–5.

Williamsburg

COLONIAL WILLIAMSBURG, INC.

Certain collections of papers possessed by Colonial Williamsburg and concerned with the years 1748–1776 should be noted. Among these are (1) The Oliver Arnold, Providence, Rhode Island, merchant, daybook, 1755–1768 (1 vol.); (2) The Dr. James Carter account book, 1752–1773 (1 vol.); The Robert Carter of Nomini Hall manuscripts, 1761–1769 (3 vols.); (4) The Robert Wormeley Carter of Sabine Hall diary, 1776; (5) The Richard Corbin and family manuscripts, 1746–1818 (3 vols. and 350 pieces); (6) The John Minson Galt and family manuscripts, 1756–1894 (10 vols. and 5,743 pieces); (7) Lieut.-Gov. Sir William Gooch papers, 1727–1751 (65 items); (8) The William Lightfoot mercantile account book, 1740–1764; (9) The John Norton and Sons, merchants, manuscripts, 1750–1795 (2,491 pieces); and especially (10) Letters of St. George Tucker (1752–1827) among the papers of the Tucker-Coleman family, 1768–1860 (24,000 pieces). There is also a large body of microfilm and typescript copies of manuscripts relating to eighteenth-century Virginia. See Lynette Adcock: *Guide to the Manuscript Collections of Colonial Williamsburg* (Williamsburg, Va., 1954); *A Brief Guide to the Record Groups in the Archives Department of Colonial Williamsburg* (Williamsburg, Va., 1951); and Philip M. Hamer: *Guide*, pp. 614–15.

WISCONSIN

Madison

STATE HISTORICAL SOCIETY OF WISCONSIN

The manuscript holdings of the Society relating to the years 1748–1776 are found chiefly in two groups: the McCormick collection and the Draper collection. Among the McCormick manuscripts are papers of James McDowell, Virginia planter, militia officer, and capitalist, 1739–1838 (6,801 items) and other materials pertaining to farming and charcoal production in the Piedmont and Virginia Valley, 1767–1910 (146 vols. and 10,964 items).

By far the most important manuscripts for our purposes, however, are in the Lyman C. Draper collection, 1755–1818 (486 vols.). It includes the following groups of manuscripts: (1) The Daniel Boone papers (32 vols.); (2) The Joseph Brant, Indian chief, papers (22 vols.); (3) The Daniel Brodhead of Pennsylvania papers (3 vols.); (4) The George Rogers Clark papers (65 vols.); (5) The James S. Goddard diary, 1766–1767 (typewritten copy); (6) The Josiah Harmer of Pennsylvania papers (2 vols. of transcripts); (7) The Charles Michel de Langlade papers, 1737–1800 (1 box); (8) The Edmund Moran of Green Bay papers, 1763-1766 (13 items).

In addition to the above-mentioned collections, there are: (9) Jesuit records, 1612–1865 (10 boxes), documents not used in Thwaites's *Jesuit Relations;* (10) Papers reproduced from Spanish archives, 1766–1805 (31 portfolios and 2 boxes), relating to Spanish control in Florida and Louisiana; (11) Papers reproduced from Canadian archives, 1680–1840 (5 boxes), concerned with exploration and Indian trade in the Old Northwest.

See Reuben Gold Thwaites: *Descriptive List of Manuscript Collections of the State Historical Society of Wisconsin* . . . (Madison, Wis., 1906); Alice E. Smith: *Guide to the Manuscripts of the Wisconsin Historical Society* (Madison, Wis., 1944); Josephine L. Harper and Sharon C. Smith: *Guide to the Manuscripts of the State Historical Society of Wisconsin: Supplement Number One* (Madison, Wis., 1957); and Philip M. Hamer: *Guide,* pp. 628–35.

Index

In order to keep the index to the present volume within manageable limits, it has been necessary to be selective. This has been especially true in dealing with such vast collections of manuscripts as those in French depositories, the contents of most of which have only a limited bearing upon the British Empire, 1748–1776. Taken together with the table of contents, the index should, nevertheless, provide adequate guidance to the contents of the volume.

* All references are not necessarily to the same vessel.

A NOTE ABOUT THE AUTHOR

LAWRENCE HENRY GIPSON is Research Professor of History, Emeritus, at Lehigh University. After receiving a bachelor of arts degree from the University of Idaho, he entered Oxford as the first Rhodes Scholar from the state of Idaho; there he gained a degree in the Oxford Honours School of Modern History. He was later a Bulkley Fellow in the graduate school at Yale, where his doctoral dissertation, *Jared Ingersoll: A Study of American Loyalism in Relation to British Colonial Government*, received the Porter Prize as the best work in literary form presented by a student in any division of the university during the preceding year; it was also awarded the Justin Winsor Prize by the American Historical Association. Since then he has written and published many works relating to colonial history, including his fifteen-volume *magnum opus*, of which this is the fifteenth and final volume. During the academic year 1951–2 he occupied the Harmsworth Chair in American History at Oxford; he also has been a member of the board of editors of the *American Historical Review*, was a founder of the Conference on Early American History, and is a past president of both the Conference on British Studies and the Pennsylvania Historical Association. He was the Honorary Consultant in American Colonial History to the Library of Congress for the period 1965 through 1967. Many prizes and honours have come to him as a result of his writing, including the Loubat, Bancroft, and Pulitzer prizes and, most recently, his election as Honorary Fellow of Lincoln College, Oxford University and Benjamin Franklin Fellow of the Royal Society of Arts.

A NOTE ON THE TYPE

THE TEXT of this book is set in Caledonia, a typeface designed by W(ILLIAM) A(DDISON) DWIGGINS for the Mergenthaler Linotype Company in 1939. Dwiggins chose to call his new type face Caledonia, the Roman name for Scotland, because it was inspired by the Scotch types cast about 1833 by Alexander Wilson & Son, Glasgow type founders. However, there is a calligraphic quality about this face that is totally lacking in the Wilson types. Dwiggins referred to an even earlier typeface for this "liveliness of action"— one cut around 1790 by William Martin for the printer William Bulmer. Caledonia has more weight than the Martin letters, and the bottom finishing strokes (serifs) of the letters are cut straight across, without brackets, to make sharp angles with the upright stems, thus giving a "modern face" appearance.

W. A. Dwiggins (1880–1956) was born in Martinsville, Ohio, and studied art in Chicago. In 1904 he moved to Hingham, Massachusetts, where he built a solid reputation as a designer of advertisements and as a calligrapher. He began an association with the Mergenthaler Linotype Company in 1929 and over the next twenty-seven years designed a number of book types for that firm. Of especial interest are the Metro series, Electra, Caledonia, Eldorado, and Falcon. In 1930, Dwiggins first became interested in marionettes, and through the years made many important contributions to the art of puppetry and the design of marionettes.

Composed, printed, and bound by
The Haddon Craftsmen, Inc., Scranton, Pa.